TEMPORARY LABOUR MIGRATION IN THE GLOBAL ERA

In the global era, controversies abound over temporary labour migration; however, it has not previously been subjected to a sustained socio-legal analysis on a comparative basis, critiquing the underpinning concepts conventionally accepted as fundamental in this area. This collection of essays aims to fill that void. Complex regulatory challenges arise from temporary labour migration. This collection examines these challenges and the extent to which temporary labour migration programmes can be ethical, equitable and efficacious and so deliver decent work for workers. Whilst the tendency for migration law to divide labour law's worker-protective mission has been observed before, the authors of the chapters comprising this collection seek not only to interrogate why and how this is so, but to go further in examining the implications and effects of a wide range of regulatory mechanisms on temporary labour migration.

Oñati International Series in Law and Society

A SERIES PUBLISHED FOR THE OÑATI INSTITUTE
FOR THE SOCIOLOGY OF LAW

Recent titles in this series

Making Human Rights Intelligible
Towards a Sociology of Human Rights
Edited by Mikael Rask Madsen and Gert Verschraegen

European Penology?
Edited by Tom Daems, Dirk van Zyl Smit and Sonja Snacken

Rights and Courts in Pursuit of Social Change
Legal Mobilisation in the Multi-Level European System
Edited by Dia Anagnostou

Women's Rights to Social Security and Social Protection
Edited by Beth Goldblatt and Lucie Lamarch

Delivering Family Justice in the 21st Century
Edited by Mavis Maclean, John Eekelaar and Benoit Bastard

Regulatory Transformations
Rethinking Economy-Society Interactions
Edited by Bettina Lange, Fiona Haines and Dania Thomas

**For the complete list of titles in this series, see
'Oñati International Series in Law and Society' link at
www.hartpub.co.uk/books/series.asp**

Temporary Labour Migration in the Global Era

The Regulatory Challenges

Edited by
Joanna Howe and Rosemary Owens

Oñati International Series in Law and Society

A SERIES PUBLISHED FOR THE
OÑATI INSTITUTE
FOR THE SOCIOLOGY OF LAW

•HART•
PUBLISHING
OXFORD AND PORTLAND, OREGON
2016

Hart Publishing
An imprint of Bloomsbury Publishing Plc

Hart Publishing Ltd
Kemp House
Chawley Park
Cumnor Hill
Oxford OX2 9PH
UK

Bloomsbury Publishing Plc
50 Bedford Square
London
WC1B 3DP
UK

www.hartpub.co.uk
www.bloomsbury.com

Published in North America (US and Canada) by
Hart Publishing
c/o International Specialized Book Services
920 NE 58th Avenue, Suite 300
Portland, OR 97213-3786
USA

www.isbs.com

First published 2016

British Library Cataloguing-in-Publication Data
A catalogue record for this book is available from the British Library.

ISBN: HB: 978-1-50990-628-4
ePDF: 978-1-50990-631-4
ePub: 978-1-50990-629-1

Library of Congress Cataloging-in-Publication Data

Names: Temporary labour migration in the global era (2015 : Oñati, Spain) Howe, Joanna, editor. | Owens, Rosemary J., editor. | Oñati International Institute for the Sociology of Law, sponsoring body.

Title: Temporary labour migration in the global era : the regulatory challenges / edited by Joanna Howe and Rosemary Owens.

Description: Oxford ; Portland, OR : Hart Publishing, An imprint of Bloomsbury Publishing Plc, 2016. | "This collection of essays had its genesis in the papers presented at a workshop on the topic "Temporary Labour Migration in the Global Era : the Regulatory Challenges", which was held at the International Institute for the Sociology of Law (IISL) in Oñati, Spain in June 2015."—ECIP galley. | Includes bibliographical references and index.

Identifiers: LCCN 2016021698 (print) | LCCN 2016022054 (ebook) | ISBN 9781509906284 (hardback : alk. paper) | ISBN 9781509906291 (Epub)

Subjects: LCSH: Foreign workers—Legal status, laws, etc.—Congresses.

Classification: LCC K1841.A46 T46 2016 (print) | LCC K1841.A46 (ebook) | DDC 344.01/544—dc23

LC record available at https://lccn.loc.gov/2016021698

Typeset by Compuscript Ltd, Shannon
Printed and bound in Great Britain by
CPI Group (UK) Ltd, Croydon CR0 4YY

Acknowledgements

This collection of essays had its genesis in the papers presented at a workshop on the topic 'Temporary Labour Migration in the Global Era: The Regulatory Challenges', which was held at the International Institute for the Sociology of Law (IISL) in Oñati, Spain in June 2015.

We wish to thank the IISL for its generous support of the workshop, which enabled the participants from nine different countries to meet together for two days of lively debate and vigorous discussion in the congenial surroundings of the historic buildings of the institute. We would like to thank Professor Dr Adam Czarnota, the Scientific Director of the institute, for his warm welcome to us and to all the staff of the institute whose work (often behind the scenes) made our stay in Oñati so productive and enjoyable. In particular, we express our deep appreciation to Malen Gordoa Mendizabal for the support she provided to participants both prior to and during the workshop. Her professionalism, her excellent organisational skills and her calm efficiency were a critical element in ensuring that our workshop was a success. Cristina Ruiz also deserves special thanks for her assistance in guiding us through the process for the submission of a proposal for publication of the papers from our workshop in the Oñati International Series in Law and Society.

The participants in our workshop enthusiastically embraced the opportunity presented by the IISL to participate in this project. We thank them especially for their willingness to make timely revisions of their papers prior both to the initial submission of the manuscript and to publication. In preparing the papers for submission and publication we also thank Kate Leeson for her careful and very professional assistance during the editing process. We were delighted when Hart Publishing agreed to publish the collection. We would like to thank, in particular, the Series Editors and those involved in the reviewing process, everyone at Hart Publishing who worked to produce this final volume and especially Emily Braggins, Assistant Editor, for guiding us through the process and Mel Hamill, Managing Editor, and Tom Adams, Production Manager, for their invaluable assistance in the editing and production of the collection.

Finally, we would like to express our heartfelt gratitude to our families without whose love and support our work would not be possible.

Joanna Howe and Rosemary Owens
University of Adelaide Law School
April 2016

Contents

Acknowledgements v
List of Contributors xi

Part I: Introduction

1. Temporary Labour Migration in the Global Era: The Regulatory Challenges 3
Joanna Howe and Rosemary Owens

Part II: Global Economic Integration and the Regulation of Temporary Labour Migration

2. Seasonal Workers and Intra-corporate Transferees in EU Law: Capital's Handmaidens? 43
Cathryn Costello and Mark Freedland

3. Temporary Labour Migration and the Trade in Services: European and Global Perspectives in an Age of Economic Integration 65
Samuel Engblom, Nicola Kountouris and Åsa Odin Ekman

4. The Distinction Between Temporary Labour Migration and Posted Work in Austria: Labour Law versus Trade Law 91
Gudrun Biffl and Isabella Skrivanek

Part III: Temporary Labour Migration in Pursuit of Economic Efficiency

5. Employer Demand for 'Skilled' Migrant Workers: Regulating Admission Under the United Kingdom's Tier 2 (General) Visa 113
Mimi Zou

6. Contesting the Demand-Driven Orthodoxy: An Assessment of the Australian Regulation of Temporary Labour Migration 131
Joanna Howe

Part IV: Temporary Labour Migration and the Production of Precarity

7. Migrant Domestic Workers in British Columbia, Canada: Unfreedom, Trafficking and Domestic Servitude 151
Judy Fudge

8. Why is Labour Protection for Temporary Migrant Workers so Fraught?: A Perspective from Australia 173
Joo-Cheong Tham, Iain Campbell and Martina Boese

Part V: Challenges in Realising Decent Work for Temporary Migrant Workers

9. Empowering Temporary Migrant Workers in Sweden: A Call for Unequal Treatment 203
Petra Herzfeld Olsson

10. Temporary Labour Migration and Modern Slavery 223
Virginia Mantouvalou

11. The Regulation of Temporary Immigration as Part of New Forms of the Supply Chain: Segmenting Labour Rights For Workers 241
Julia López López

12. Regulating Temporariness in Italian Migration Law 259
Veronica Papa

Part VI: Contesting Temporariness: Status and the Social Effects of the Legal Regulation of Temporary Labour Migration

13. The Membership of Migrant Workers and the Ethical Limits of Exclusion 277
Alexander Reilly

14. Protecting the Rights of Temporary Migrant Workers: Ideals versus Reality 299
Martin Ruhs

Part VII: The Global Challenge of Temporary Labour Migration: Regulatory Responses and Possibilities

15. Roles for Workers and Unions in Regulating Labour Recruitment in Mexico 329
Jennifer Gordon

16. Decent Labour Standards in Corporate Supply Chains: The Immokalee Workers Model 351
James J Brudney

17. Reducing Worker-Paid Migration Costs 377
Philip Martin

18. Temporary Labour Migration and Workplace Rights in Australia: Is Effective Enforcement Possible? 393
Rosemary Owens

Index 413

List of Contributors

Gudrun Biffl is Professor and Dean in the Faculty of Business and Globalisation at Danau University, Austria.

Martina Boese is Lecturer in Sociology at the School of Humanities and Social Sciences, La Trobe University, Melbourne, Australia.

James J Brudney is Professor of Law at Fordham University, New York, USA.

Iain Campbell is Senior Research Fellow at the Centre for Social Research, RMIT University, Melbourne, Australia.

Cathryn Costello is Andrew W Mellon Associate Professor in International Human Rights and Refugee Law at the University of Oxford, UK.

Åsa Odin Ekman is a Research Officer at the Swedish Confederation for Professional Employees.

Samuel Engblom is Head of Social Policy and General Counsel at the Swedish Confederation for Professional Employees.

Mark Freedland is Emeritus Professor of Employment Law at the University of Oxford, UK.

Judy Fudge is Professor of Law at the University of Kent, UK.

Jennifer Gordon is Professor of Law at Fordham University, New York, USA.

Petra Herzfeld Olsson is Associate Professor in Private Law and Senior Lecturer in International Labour Law at Uppsala University, Sweden.

Joanna Howe is Senior Lecturer at the University of Adelaide, Australia.

Nicola Kountouris is Reader in Law at UCL, London, UK.

Julia López López is Professor of Law at Pompeu Fabra University, Barcelona, Spain.

Virginia Mantouvalou is Reader in Human Rights and Labour Law at UCL, London, UK.

Philip Martin is Emeritus Professor of Law at the University of California, Davis, USA.

Rosemary Owens is Professor Emerita of Law at the University of Adelaide, Australia.

Veronica Papa is Lecturer in Labour Law at the University of Catania, Italy.

Alexander Reilly is Associate Professor in Law at the University of Adelaide, Australia.

Martin Ruhs is Associate Professor of Political Economy at the University of Oxford, UK.

Isabella Skrivanek is Lecturer in the Department for Migration and Globalization at Danau University, Austria.

Joo-Cheong Tham is Associate Professor at Melbourne Law School, University of Melbourne, Australia.

Mimi Zou is Assistant Professor at the Chinese University of Hong Kong.

Part I

Introduction

1

Temporary Labour Migration in the Global Era

The Regulatory Challenges

JOANNA HOWE AND ROSEMARY OWENS

I. INTRODUCTION

IN THE GLOBAL era, controversies abound over temporary labour migration, either undertaken through programmes designed specifically for that purpose or as an adjunct to migration for non-labour purposes. However, remarkably, there has been little scholarly attention paid to the ways in which these controversies converge around the issues of temporariness and regulation. Temporary labour migration in the global era has not previously been subjected to a sustained socio-legal analysis on a comparative basis, critiquing the underpinning concepts conventionally accepted as fundamental in this area. This collection of essays aims to fill that void.

A basic question to ask might be whether this 'new' global phenomenon is really new at all. In many ways, temporary labour migration today echoes colonial indentured labour and older forms of guest work, for example, Chinese labour in Malaya and the Dutch East Indies, and Indian 'coolies' in the West Indies.[1] As Europe industrialised, demand for labour increased exponentially, and a number of countries such as Germany, France and Switzerland designed temporary worker programmes between 1870 and 1914 to prevent workers from settling permanently. The period after the two world wars led to a new flourishing of temporary worker programmes as countries sought to rebuild.[2] For example, Britain's 'European Worker Scheme' aimed to recruit 90,000 temporary workers, largely from the ranks of refugees.[3]

[1] See, eg John Connell, 'From Blackbirds to Guestworkers in the South Pacific: Plus ça change ... ?' (2010) 20 *Economic and Labour Relations Review* 111.

[2] OECD, *International Migration Outlook: Sopemi 2011* (Paris, OECD Publishing, 2011).

[3] Stephen Castles, 'The Guest-Worker in Western Europe: An Obituary' (1986) 20 *International Migration Review* 761.

Not dissimilarly, although on a much larger scale, North America's 'Bracero Program' oversaw the annual entry of over 100,000 Mexican seasonal workers into the United States between 1942 and 1965.[4] Although decreed 'dead' over two decades ago after a faltering in the nascent new global economy led to falling demand for migrant labour,[5] temporary worker programmes are once again 'de jour' amongst policy-makers, characterised as producing a 'triple win' for all involved.[6]

Despite its long pedigree, national governments and supranational institutions continue to grapple with the complex regulatory challenges arising from temporary labour migration. The objective of this collection is to understand why this is so, and to explore the extent to which temporary labour migration programmes can be ethical, equitable and efficacious and so deliver decent work for these workers. Whilst the tendency for migration law to divide labour law's worker-protective mission has been observed before,[7] the authors of the chapters comprising this collection seek not only to interrogate why and how this is so, but to go further in examining the implications and effects of a wide range of regulatory mechanisms on temporary labour migration.

In this collection, we explore the tendency of regulation in the global era to privilege the interests of capital. To a large extent the role and purpose of temporary labour migration has become one of unlocking and maximising the entrepreneurial potential and profit-maximising capabilities of capital. This has been made possible through the process of global economic integration which has transformed temporary labour migration so that it can occur en masse, not only through targeted programmes like those with which we are historically familiar, but also, and especially, through economic zones permitting the free movement of people, and typified through the approach to regulating the global trade in services. The deference to the needs of Global Inc (to borrow a term deployed by Cathryn Costello and Mark Freedland in their chapter),[8] which is inherent in the design of most contemporary temporary labour migration programmes in receiving states, is derivative of a seemingly unquestioned economic

[4] Massimo Livi-Bacci, *A Short History of Migration* (Cambridge, Polity, 2012) 114.

[5] Castles, 'The Guest-Worker in Western Europe' (n 3).

[6] Stephen Castles and Derya Ozkul, 'Circular Migration: Triple Win, or a New Label for Temporary Migration?' in Graziano Battistella (ed), *Global and Asian Perspectives on International Migration* (New York, Springer, 2014).

[7] Cathryn Costello and Mark Freedland, 'Migrants at Work and the Division of Labour Law' in Cathryn Costello and Mark Freedland (eds), *Migrants at Work: Immigration and Vulnerability in Labour Law* (Oxford, Oxford University Press, 2014).

[8] Cathryn Costello and Mark Freedland, 'Seasonal Workers and Intra-corporate Transferees in EU Law: Capital's Handmaidens?', ch 2 in this volume.

philosophy that temporary labour migration programmes need to be less regulated by government and driven instead by the needs of business, with market responsiveness, timeliness and flexibility as the key indicators of success.

Acknowledging capital as a primary beneficiary of temporary labour migration is not to deny its transformative potential for migrant workers. Temporary labour migration is now, even more than it ever was, deeply aspirational, as migrant workers seek to take advantage of increased remuneration and job opportunities available abroad. However, the desire of many to improve their life chances through temporary labour migration has encouraged the increasing commercialisation of migration, which has opened up new global possibilities for capital, via its myriad entrepreneurial endeavours, to exploit. Contemporary labour migration, with its emblematic features of worker precarity and temporality, has proven the perfect fodder for capital's interests, and the law regulating work has struggled to respond. Whilst international law has tended to focus on the principle of equal treatment to address the problems arising from migrant workers' precarious status in the labour market, this collection raises fresh concerns about the realisation of this principle in practice. A recurring theme, borne out in several of the ensuing chapters, is not only the failure to deliver to temporary migrant workers the same wages and conditions as that of their counterparts in the local workforce, but also the use of migrant labour sometimes to the exclusion of local labour in the poorest paid and least well regulated sectors of the labour market. Viewed in this light, implicit in a number of contributions to this volume is the idea that 'dignity at work' might provide a stronger normative framework and ordering principle in regulating temporary labour migration.[9]

In developing regulatory responses to the myriad challenges arising from temporary labour migration, this collection is situated at the interface of migration law, labour law, trade law, human rights, refugee and asylum law, criminal law and national security law. Complex interactions between these disparate regulatory regimes produce both unintended consequences as well as challenges and possibilities. On one level, a regulatory response to

[9] Elsewhere Tonia Novitz and Colin Fenwick have advanced a human rights discourse to defend workers' interests as a result of globalisation: Tonia Novitz and Colin Fenwick, 'The Application of Human Rights Discourse to Labour Relations: Translation of Theory into Practice' in Tonia Novitz and Colin Fenwick (eds), *Human Rights At Work* (Oxford, Hart, 2010); see also Simon Deakin, 'Social Rights in a Globalised Economy' in Philip Alston (ed), *Labour Rights as Human Rights* (Oxford, Oxford University Press, 2005); Bob Hepple, *Labour Laws and Global Trade* (Oxford, Hart, 2005) ch 10; Judy Fudge, 'The New Discourse of Labour Rights: From Social to Fundamental Rights?' (2007) 29 *Comparative Labor Law and Policy Journal* 29.

the problems arising from excessive reliance on employer demand and the capital-driven nature of temporary labour migration programmes produces a case for tempering capital, and in particular employer requests to access temporary migrant labour, through the use of quotas, caps, occupational shortage lists and other similar but distinct regulatory mechanisms. On another level, a different set of responses reframes the regulatory responsibility in terms of national governments and supranational institutions to realise the dignity of migrant workers without constraining employer demand. Two contributors favour this macro-level approach. Martin Ruhs argues for a structural redesign of temporary migrant worker programmes so that a trade-off is allowed between some rights in return for access, and Alexander Reilly develops a normative case for giving migrant workers the possibility of transforming their temporary status into citizenship.[10] By way of contrast, a third set of responses is to develop new and innovative regulatory methods to address the challenges posed by temporary labour migration. Some of the methods explored in this collection involve regulating the supply chain for migrant labour, through developing worker-driven codes of conduct and restricting recruitment costs, as well as strategic innovations by labour inspectorates in enforcing the rights of temporary migrant workers. Such regulatory responses, although not without merit and indeed often effective in their own right, tend to operate at a more micro level.

This collection explores these themes using a socio-legal approach, conscious that the legal regulation of temporary labour migration does not evolve separately from the political, economic and social contexts in which it is embedded. Nor can temporary labour migration be understood without an interdisciplinary approach; not only are disparate law disciplines required, but also the contributions of economics, political science and sociology. Because the receiving state is predominantly responsible for regulating temporary labour migration, the essays in this collection analyse the regulatory practices of countries that host migrant workers: Australia, Austria, Canada, Italy, Spain, Sweden, the United Kingdom and the United States. It also examines how supranational organisations, such as the International Labour Organization (ILO) and the World Trade Organization (WTO), regional governance structures such as the European Union (EU), and multilateral and bilateral free trade agreements have sought to develop and disseminate new legal norms around temporary labour migration.

[10] Martin Ruhs, 'Protecting the Rights of Temporary Migrant Workers: Ideals Versus Reality', ch 14 in this volume; Alexander Reilly, 'The Membership of Migrant Workers and the Ethical Limits of Exclusion', ch 13 in this volume.

A. Defining Temporary Labour Migration

Defining 'temporary labour migration' is no straightforward matter.[11] One approach to the definition of temporary labour migration today is to limit consideration to those who migrate on a temporary basis primarily for the purpose of work.[12] These are the migrant workers who are participating generally in state-sponsored temporary labour migration programmes, such as 'skilled temporary labour', 'seasonal worker' or 'circular labour' migration schemes. While there may be particular policy and regulatory issues relevant to these groups, some other scholars have argued that such an approach elevates 'form over substance', and risks ignoring the reality of the vast numbers of people who may have migrated on a temporary basis for other purposes, but who participate in the labour market during the (temporary) period of their stay in either a transit or destination country.[13] Indeed a socio-legal approach invites an examination of the distinction between temporary labour migration conventionally understood and, for example, other migrants who also work on a temporary basis (eg students, holiday makers, trafficked workers or the providers of international services).[14] As several contributors to this volume remind us, the potential for exploitation of these workers is compounded by either their lack of a visa or their use of a visa for a non-work purpose.[15] Tham, Campbell and Boese's chapter, for example, charts the precarious labour market status of international students working in the Australian hospitality industry. Moreover, the politics of temporary labour migration in developed countries often leads to governments tacitly accepting these visa holders to meet low-skill labour shortages.[16] Excluding these workers from analysis ignores their

[11] For a summary of the quite different approaches EU Member States have adopted, see European Migration Network, *Temporary and Circular Migration: Empirical Evidence, Current Policy Practice and Future Options in EU Member States* (Brussels, European Migration Network, 2011) 12–29.

[12] See, eg Martin Ruhs, *The Price of Rights: Regulating International Labour Migration* (Princeton, NJ, Princeton University Press, 2013).

[13] See Alexander Reilly, 'Review: The Price of Rights' (2014) 35 *Adelaide Law Review* 189.

[14] These groups are often not considered in debates concerning temporary labour migration. See Joanna Howe and Alexander Reilly, 'Meeting Australia's Labour Needs: The Case for a Low Skill Work Visa' (2015) 43(2) *Federal Law Review* 259. See also the inquiry commissioned in 2015 by the Australian Senate recognising all forms of temporary migrant work entitled 'The impact of Australia's temporary work visa programs on the Australian labour market and on the temporary work visa holders', http://www.aph.gov.au/Parliamentary_Business/Committees/Senate/Education_and_Employment/temporary_work_visa.

[15] See, eg Joo-Cheong Tham, Iain Campbell and Martina Boese, 'Why is Labour Protection for Temporary Migrant Workers so Fraught? An Australian Perspective', ch 8 in this volume; Julia López López, 'The Regulation of Temporary Immigration as Part of New Forms of the Supply Chain: Segmenting Labour Rights for Workers', ch 11 in this volume; Veronica Papa, 'Regulating Temporariness in Italian Migration Law', ch 12 in this volume.

[16] For more on the politics of temporary labour migration, see Joanna Howe, 'Does Australia Need an Expert Commission to Assist with Managing its Labour Migration Program?'

contribution as workers and fails to draw attention to this growing underclass of workers invisible to the law, thus perpetuating and indeed exacerbating their exploitation. Further, because many temporary migrant workers ultimately remain long term in their destination country, with or without permission to do so, the boundary between temporariness and permanency must also be interrogated. Discourses about other groups of migrant workers, whether permanent, temporary for non-labour market purposes or undocumented, may also influence understandings of temporary migrant labour, raising in turn questions about the nature of membership, allegiance, belonging and identity in the global era—a subject that Alexander Reilly explores in his chapter on the ethical limits of exclusion.[17]

In this collection, the terminology of 'receiving country' and 'sending country' is used to connote a state's policy position with respect to temporary labour migration. The working assumption behind this is that states have a particular set of objectives to realise with respect to immigration and adopt policies accordingly, which tend to render them countries that predominantly 'receive' or 'send' migrant workers on a temporary basis. Generally, receiving countries adopt this policy as a means of addressing skills or labour shortages in the domestic economy. By way of comparison, sending countries generally rely on exporting temporary migrant labour as a means of raising national income through remittances and increasing job opportunities for their citizens. Nonetheless, at other times, in recognition of the limitations of any descriptive term, other terminology is used that is relevant to the particular context, for instance 'country of origin' and 'country of destination' reflecting a migrant worker's individual trajectory.

II. GLOBAL ECONOMIC INTEGRATION AND THE REGULATION OF TEMPORARY LABOUR MIGRATION

The dominant regulatory approach of receiving states has been to facilitate temporary labour flows according to an economic rationale. As the chapter by Biffl and Skrivanek in this collection shows, this policy choice in the structuring of the labour market also has distinct social as well as economic implications, not least for the nature and structure of unemployment, and the responses needed to address it.[18] However, the economic rationale serves

(2014) 27(3) *Australian Journal of Labour Law* 233. See also the special issue of the journal *Migration Letters* dedicated to this topic: 'Expert Commissions and Migration Policy Making' (2014) 11(1) *Migration Letters*.

[17] Reilly, 'The Membership of Migrant Workers', ch 13 in this volume.

[18] Gudrun Biffl and Isabella Skrivanek, 'The Distinction Between Temporary Labour Migration and Posted Work in Austria: Labour Law Versus Trade Law', ch 4 in this volume.

the interests of global business particularly well, because it creates a larger and more flexible labour market from which to select workers. Temporary labour migration generally means the entry into the local labour market of workers from countries with less protective or developed regulation. In competing with local workers, these migrant workers are usually willing to accept lower wages and worse conditions because their frame of reference is their country of origin.[19] Furthermore, they usually form a more compliant workforce because of their twin desire to recoup the costs of their investment in the migratory process and to send remittances home. They are especially motivated to be compliant when there is the possibility of securing permanent residency. In short, temporary labour migration increases labour supply and provides capital with a workforce that may be more motivated and certainly less likely to voice concerns to a union or other third party about their wages, conditions of employment or workplace safety.

Although it is conventionally thought that the 'migrant worker' is the subject of the law regulating temporary labour migration,[20] in this collection, a number of contributors identify a common strand in the regulatory approach of receiving countries, namely developing policies and laws around temporary labour migration with global capital as their subject. Temporary labour migration programmes have been designed according to a brief that privileges the freedom of employing organisations and their ability to access temporary migrant labour. This is not to say that these programmes do not incorporate some worker-protective elements, or that there have not been attempts to re-regulate these programmes to reduce the potential for exploitation. In the main, however, we can identify a common regulatory approach amongst receiving countries to regulate temporary labour migration from the standpoint of migration law, which tends to focus on the efficacy of the visa process and the reduction of regulatory burdens on business, rather than the traditionally worker-protective focus of the law of work. In this collection, Cathryn Costello and Mark Freedland build upon their previous work[21] by examining the distinctive role of capital in using migration in the global era as a tool to maximise profits.[22] Their chapter contrasts the EU's approach to regulating intra-corporate transferees and seasonal workers, drawing upon the evocative image of the phenomenon of temporary labour migration as 'capital's handmaiden', to shed light on the relations between labour and capital under conditions of contemporary globalisation.

[19] For more on temporary migrant workers' 'dual frame of reference', see Michael J Piore, *Birds of Passage: Migrant Labor and Industrial Societies* (Cambridge, Cambridge University Press, 1979).

[20] See, eg Costello and Freedland, 'Migrants at Work' (n 7) 4.

[21] Ibid.

[22] Costello and Freedland, 'Seasonal Workers and Intra-corporate Transferees', ch 2 in this volume.

A. Globalisation and the Changing Nature of Migration

Globalisation has provided the perfect vehicle to accelerate and facilitate temporary labour migration. Although the complex set of phenomena widely referred to as 'globalisation' defies precise definition,[23] it is commonly understood as the intensification of international economic integration.[24] Facilitated by computer and technological developments and the associated information and communications revolutions, globalisation has gained momentum by the progressive opening up of national economies (especially through trade liberalisation), the ease with which capital and corporations have adapted to (and thereby in turn promoted) a new world without borders, the increased international flows of capital, and the consequent growth of international business.

The extraordinary growth in the migratory movements of people around the world has also been a key aspect of globalisation. There is scarcely a nation-state that is not now touched by migration—either as an origin, transit or destination country for migrants. It is estimated there are more than 232 million migrants around the world.[25] Moreover, migration in the global era is an increasingly complex phenomenon, not least in the range of factors driving it. Migration is no longer (if it ever was) undertaken primarily in response to 'push' factors such as political, social, religious and cultural oppression or flight in the face of climatic, environmental or other disasters, or the 'pull' of associated or consequential family reunions.

The flows and patterns of migration are constantly changing: movements of people are occurring not only from developing to more developed economies but also between countries within those broadly framed categories, and are being driven not only by states but also by market factors. The concentration of global capital has led to demand for both highly skilled workers and for low-skilled agriculture, industrial and service workers. Temporary migrant workers feature prominently in jobs that local workers do not want and in sectors where exploitation is more likely to be prevalent

[23] See Catherine Dauvergne, *Making People Illegal: What Globalization Means for Migration and Law* (Cambridge, Cambridge University Press, 2008) 29: 'the term globalization has grown out of control. There is no longer much to be gained in pinning down a definition for this shape shifter. Rather it makes sense to use it with full consciousness of the fluidity, and its inevitable incorporation by reference of layers of meaning from the popular to the erudite.'

[24] Judy Fudge and Rosemary Owens, 'Precarious Work, Women and the New Economy: The Challenge to Legal Norms' in Judy Fudge and Rosemary Owens (eds), *Precarious Work, Women and the New Economy: The Challenge to Legal Norms* (Oxford, Hart, 2006) 4.

[25] ILO, *Labour Migration Facts and Figures*, ILO Fact Sheet (2014), http://www.ilo.org/global/about-the-ilo/media-centre/issue-briefs/WCMS_239651/lang--en/index.htm. See also ILO, *Global Estimates on Migrant Workers: Results and Methodology*, (Geneva, ILO, 2015). For an overview of labour migration in the EC/OECD countries see Maria Vincenza Desiderio, *Free Movement of Workers and Labour Market Adjustment* (Paris, OECD, 2012).

because of cost pressures in highly competitive businesses, poor workplace health and safety standards and a low level of unionisation.[26] However, the advent of highly skilled migrant worker programmes aimed at addressing a skills deficit in receiving countries where technical and vocational training often lags behind rapid changes in technology and organisation of work, means that temporary migrant labour cannot be characterised exclusively as work that is low-paid, dirty, dangerous, physically difficult, repetitious or seasonal. This is not to say, however, that temporary migrant work, even of the high-skilled variety, is not precarious. The notion of dividing temporary migrant labour according to 'skill level' is somewhat arbitrary, because it is, at least in part, a social construction, rather than an objective measure. As Rosemary Hunter has observed in the pay equity context, the traditional factors often used to identify the skill and value of work—qualifications, training, attributes, responsibility, physical work conditions, work quality, flexibility of skills, knowledge, supervision, and place and importance to the operation—can all be identified and constituted in ways that are, for instance, deeply gendered.[27] Likewise, different political, social and cultural contexts reflect and produce different deeply held assumptions and biases which affect how we identify and value skills, and which impact, in turn, upon the design of temporary worker programmes.[28]

As the boundaries around national economies have been dismantled, so too the prospects for the greater integration of labour markets have increased. Intermediary agencies, working with both state and non-state actors, have proved particularly adept at promoting temporariness as a talisman for success in the new economy and deploying migrant labour around the globe.[29] Labour migration has increased significantly in recent years, comprising an estimated 90 per cent of all migratory movements.[30] Of course many of those who migrate for other reasons are also participants in labour markets. The International Labour Organization estimated that in 2013 there were 150.3 million migrant workers.[31] Migration is thus a labour issue and

[26] These were some of the factors identified by the UN Special Rapporteur on the human rights of migrants in his report to the UN Human Rights Council, 'Labour Exploitation of Migrants', A/HRC/26/35 (April 2014), http://www.ohchr.org/Documents/Issues/SRMigrants/A.HRC.26.35.pdf. See Tham, Campbell and Boese, 'Why is Labour Protection for Temporary Migrant Workers so Fraught?: A Perspective from Australia', ch 8 in this volume.

[27] Rosemary Hunter, *The Beauty Therapist, the Mechanic, the Geoscientist and the Librarian: Addressing Undervaluation of Women's Work* (Broadway, NSW, ATN WEXDEV, 2000).

[28] Martin Ruhs and Bridget Anderson (eds), *Who Needs Migrant Workers: Labour Shortages, Immigration and Public Policy* (Oxford, Oxford University Press, 2010).

[29] On the role of such intermediaries generally, see Judy Fudge and Kendra Strauss (eds), *Temporary Work, Agencies and Unfree Labour: Insecurity in the New World of Work* (New York, Routledge, 2014).

[30] ILO, *Labour Migration Facts and Figures*.

[31] ILO, *Global Estimates on Migrant Workers* 5.

labour mobility has become a key feature of the global economy, with the World Bank estimating that remittance flows from migrant workers will reach US$479 billion in 2016.[32]

Geographers have also observed dramatic shifts in patterns of labour migration in recent decades, especially as the labour market characteristics of migrants have become more diverse than ever before. Amongst the most notable of these shifts has been a change from permanent to temporary migration.[33] For many, migration is not a one-way move away from their country of origin to a permanent home in a new destination country. In important ways, temporary migration is thus rendering more porous than ever before the borders around national labour markets.

B. Temporary Migrant Service Workers: Challenging the Labour/Trade Boundary

The single-minded pursuit of economic efficiency in regulating temporary labour migration is most apparent in the growing importance of the global trade in services. In the global era, the relationship between labour law and economic or trade law has often been portrayed as a conflictual one, and in need of reconciling for regulatory cohesion.[34] At the very least it is a complex relationship, and perhaps nowhere is this more evident than in the law relating to the temporary labour migrations that deliver the global services trade. To date less attention has been paid to the intersection of migration law and the trade/labour regulatory framework, which is the subject of the three chapters in Part II of this collection. This issue highlights the often disparate agendas of actors in sending and receiving countries—for instance, in the latter, trade unions are often seeking to protect local labour market conditions through the principle of wage parity, whilst the former countries argue in favour of more cross-country flows—and between global institutions—for example the WTO's normative concern with trade liberalisation and free movement contrasts with the ILO's rights-based agenda hinging upon equality and decent work. This tension at the multilateral and

[32] Dilip Ratha et al, *Migration and Remittances: Recent Development and Outlook*, Migration and Development Brief (Washington, DC, World Bank, 2015).

[33] For an early prediction of this trend, see Graeme Hugo, 'Migrants and Demography: Australian Trends and Issues for Policy Makers, Business and Employers' in Mary Crock and Kerry Lyon (eds), *Nation Skilling: Migration and Labour Law in Australia, Canada, New Zealand and the United Sates* (Sydney, Desert Pea Press, 2002). In 2006, it was estimated that there were three times as many temporary as permanent migrants to OECD countries: OECD, *Temporary Labour Migration: An Illusory Promise?* (Paris, OECD SOPEMI, 2008).

[34] See, eg Christine Kaufmann, *Globalisation and Labour Rights: The Conflict between Core Labour Rights and International Economic Law* (Oxford, Hart, 2007).

institutional level is reflected in regulatory debates around how to manage the global trade in services.[35]

Trade in services is usually facilitated through free trade agreements—whether at global, regional or bilateral levels—which make provision for global services to be delivered into another country, including by workers who move from their country of origin into a host country where those services are consumed.[36] Thus, article 1(2)(d) of the General Agreement on Trade in Services (GATS) (sometimes referred to as 'Mode 4'), appended to the Marrakesh Agreement establishing the WTO,[37] envisages such a migratory movement of the worker.[38] Some regional trading blocs already have considerable experience of such migratory movements. In Europe, the 'posted worker' is the epitome of the practice. In late 2015, 12 Pacific-rim countries agreed to the Trans-Pacific Partnership (TPP). While seeking to achieve greater economic integration between the signatories, a notable omission was a binding provision on labour mobility. Instead, article 12.4 of the TPP operates as a positive list, meaning that it remains in the discretion of each country to make its own commitments to any binding obligations in this area. Still more multi-state agreements are in the process of negotiation, for example the Transatlantic Trade and Investment Partnership (TTIP), and the Trade in Services Agreement (TiSA).[39]

While the negotiation processes for multi-state agreements usually extend over many years, bilateral agreements for trade in goods and services have proliferated more easily, and they often also incorporate provisions intended to facilitate the movement of natural persons between the two countries for the provision of services. The China–Australia Free Trade Agreement (ChAFTA) agreed in 2015, for example, is intended to increase greatly temporary labour flows from China to Australia and is significant for its ban on the latter using labour market testing, effectively allowing Chinese workers to replace local workers in the Australian labour market.[40]

[35] For a recent discussion of these issues, see Olivier de Schutter, *Trade in the Service of Sustainable Development: Linking Trade to Labour Rights and Environmental Standards* (Oxford, Hart, 2015).

[36] See, eg Tonia Novitz, 'Trading in Services: Commodities and Beneficiaries' in Adelle Blackett and Anne Trebilcock (eds), *Research Handbook on Transnational Labour Law* (Cheltenham, UK, Edward Elgar, 2015).

[37] General Agreement on Tariffs and Trade (GATT) [1948] ATS 23; Marrakesh Agreement Establishing the World Trade Organisation (WTO Agreement) 1869 UNTS 299; 33 ILM 1197 (1994). The GATS is Annex 1B to the Marrakesh Agreement, part of the Final Act of the Uruguay Round of Trade Negotiations1986–1994, http://www.wto.org/english/docs_e/legal_e/26-gats.pdf.

[38] Note that GATS art 1(3) may also involve the movement of persons to deliver a service.

[39] On the former, see Jeffrey S Vogt, 'The Evolution of Labour Rights and Trade—A Transatlantic Comparison and Lessons for the Transatlantic Trade and Investment Partnership' (2015) 18(4) *Journal of International Economic Law* 827.

[40] China–Australia Free Trade Agreement ch 10 Movement of Natural Persons, art 10.4, para 3.

Although to date the numbers involved in movement associated with global trade in services may be on a comparatively small scale, movement in this area is likely to increase.[41] As developed countries move more and more to becoming service economies, the issue of global trade in services is of increasing importance to them. In turn, developing countries are seeking more opportunities to participate in such trade. A resurgence in the adoption of bilateral agreements regulating the provision of services by low-skilled migrants is also evidence of this.[42] It is no surprise that increased liberalisation of world trade in services, and especially support of the growth of services exports from developing countries, remained high on the policy agenda of the WTO in the lead-up to the Doha round of negotiations in July 2015,[43] with developing countries requesting greater preferences in such arrangements, including no economic needs and labour market testing, and extending the duration of stays of their professionals. Indicative of the growing significance of trade in services, negotiations involving many WTO members, including the USA and Europe, commenced in 2013 for a new TiSA.[44]

When an international contract for the delivery of a service by a provider in one country to a consumer in another country also entails the workers of the provider moving into the other country for the period in which they will produce and deliver the service, this might ordinarily be characterised as an example of a temporary migration of the worker who will be participating in the labour market of the country in which they work. Yet this is not how such movements and the labour of these global service delivery workers tend to be conceptualised in trade agreements. The Annex of GATS on the movement of natural persons, for example, asserts: 'This agreement is not concerned with natural persons seeking access to the employment market of a Member, nor shall it apply to measures regarding citizenship, residence or employment on a permanent basis'. The GATS leaves it to members to establish their own rules regulating the movement of these workers, including issues such as the requirement of visas for the temporary entry of

[41] EU statements in 2014 suggest about 1.4 million posted workers. On growth in global services, see, eg Samuel Engblom, 'Labour Law and the Global Market for Manpower' (2012), paper on file with authors; Pasha L Hsieh, 'Liberalizing Trade in Legal Services under Asia-Pacific FTAs: The ASEAN Case' (2015) 18 *Journal of International Economic Law* 153.

[42] See Piyasini Wickramasekara, *Bi-lateral Agreements and Memoranda of Understanding on Migration of Low-skilled Workers: A Review* (Geneva, ILO, 2015).

[43] See WTO, 'WTO Members Move to Enact Bali Decision on LDC Services Waiver', media release, 5 February 2015. The Doha Agreement committed the WTO to further liberalisation of trade in services. See Doha Work Programme, Ministerial Declaration adopted on 18 December 2005 at the WTO Ministerial Conference, Hong Kong, 13–18 December 2005 esp cl 2125-27 and Annex C (Hong Kong Declaration). There has been steady progress in this area: eg in 2011, the LDC Services Waiver was adopted at the 8th Ministerial Conference allowing WTO members to deviate from MFN obligations under the services agreement. All WTO documents are available on the WTO website: www.wto.org.

[44] In April 2015, these negotiations involved 51 WTO Member States.

those who labour in the provision of services. Likewise, under the European Posted Workers Directives, as interpreted, these workers do not seek access to the local labour market of the country where they work.[45]

This conceptualisation treats the temporary movement of the worker to deliver a service as identical to delivery of goods into the destination country. In so doing, the economic and social dimensions of global trade remain separated, with the latter tending to be erased as the advantages of the former are expounded. On this view, proponents argue that there is no difference between freer trade in goods and services produced and delivered into another country by workers who remain in their home country and those delivered by service workers (including lower skilled workers) who also temporarily move into the destination country to do so. The broad economic impacts are seen as identical, as the logic of the global trade in goods is fully extended to services.[46] On this analysis, the liberalisation of world trade in services continues to have important redistributive effects and, while it is acknowledged that there are impacts on labour markets, these are depicted as being no different from those experienced in the wake of global trade in goods. Thus, in destination delivery and consumer countries, increased global competition has often meant the loss of jobs as a result of the movement of capital and 'offshoring', and a consequent de-skilling in relation to the production of particular goods or delivery of services. On the other hand, the loss of jobs in developed economies is counteracted by the gains made by those workers from developing countries, including more opportunities to contribute to service delivery. In fact, many developing countries have expressly called for greater liberalisation of service provision under Mode 4,[47] and some scholars from these countries have argued against wage parity because it effectively operates as a quota eroding 'the cost advantage of hiring foreigners'.[48]

[45] Directive 96/71/EC of the European Parliament and of the Council of 16 December 1996 concerning the posting of workers in the framework of the provision of services ('Posted Workers Directive')[1997] OJ L18/1. See also Directive 2014/67/EU of the European Parliament and of the Council of 15 May 2014 on the enforcement of Directive 96/71/EC concerning the posting of workers in the framework of the provision of services and amending Regulation (EU) No 1024/2012 on administrative cooperation through the Internal Market Information System ('Posted Workers Enforcement Directive') [2014] OJ L159/11.

[46] See, eg Alan Winters, *The Temporary Movement of Workers to Provide Services (GATS Mode 4)* (Washington, DC, World Bank, 2004); Alan Winters et al, 'Liberalising Temporary Movement of Natural Persons: An Agenda for the Development Round' (2003) 26(8) *World Economy* 1137.

[47] This is evinced by the 'plurilateral request' to the WTO submitted by Argentina, Bolivia, Brazil, Chile, Colombia, India, Pakistan, Peru, Mexico and the Philippines. For information about this plurilateral request see WTO, 'Movement of Natural Persons', https://www.wto.org/english/tratop_e/serv_e/mouvement_persons_e/mouvement_persons_e.htm.

[48] Rupa Chanda, 'Movement of Natural Persons and the GATS' (2001) 24(5) *World Economy* 631, 635. See also Sumanta Chaudhuri, Aaditya Mattoo and Richard Self, 'Moving People to Deliver Services: How Can the WTO Help?' (2004) 38(3) *Journal of World Trade* 363, 366.

It may be that in the past some of the redistributive benefits following global trade in services have been overstated, and some of the risks understated. Philip Martin thought so in 2006, and so recommended a cautious approach in assessing the economic implications of GATS Mode 4.[49] Martin pointed out that the greatest benefits accrue to developing economies when low-skilled workers are involved, but that they are often not the target of GATS and other free trade agreements, which often work best for high-skilled workers employed by multinational corporations, who can remain for quite long periods of time in the destination country. However, with high-skilled workers, there is always the risk of brain drain as their 'temporary' migration often becomes 'permanent', and Martin thought that previous experience, such as that involving Indian IT workers deployed to respond to the 'Millennium Bug' scare, may not provide an appropriate template for future movements of workers involved in global service delivery. Such arguments invite constant re-assessment, especially as, in the intervening years since Martin's evaluation, the evidence seems to indicate that there is now greater provision for low-skilled service delivery migration as part of the global trade in services with the proliferation of, for example, global construction agreements.

However, the crux of Martin's critique is the insight that the GATS Annex risked eliding the movement of the worker and their (temporary) presence in another nation-state with other forms of global service delivery by workers who remained in their country of origin and with the global trade in goods. In so doing, the human condition of these workers is erased, and these temporary migrant labourers are effectively treated as commodities.[50] The aphorism 'labour is not a commodity' encapsulates philosophical explorations into the relationship of the human person to their labour, which also seek to explain the conundrum that work cannot be separated from the human person and yet is traded in the marketplace.[51] Its deployment in political economy, and especially labour law, has a rich history.[52] In relation to temporary labour migration, generally, some have found it to be particularly potent in critiquing the dominant economic considerations put forward in this context.[53]

[49] Philip L Martin, *GATS, Migration, and Labour Standards*, Discussion Paper DP/165/2006 (Geneva, International Institute for Labour Studies, 2006).

[50] Ibid 20–21.

[51] See philosophers as diverse as John Locke, Adam Smith, Karl Marx, Karl Polyani and Hannah Arendt (to name but a few) for discussions of this idea.

[52] See Judy Fudge, 'Labour as a "Fictive Commodity": Radically Reconceptualising Labour Law' in Guy Davidov and Brian Langille (eds), *The Idea of Labour Law* (Oxford, Oxford University Press, 2011); Hugh Collins, *Employment Law* (Oxford, Oxford University Press, 2010) ch 1. See also Lucy Taksa and Dimitria Groutsis, 'Managing Diverse Commodities? From Factory Fodder to Business Asset' (2010) 20 *Economic and Labour Relations Law* 77.

[53] Stuart Rosewarne, 'Globalisation and the Commodification of Labour: Temporary Labour Migration' (2010) 20 *Economic and Labour Relations Review* 99. See also Catherine

Samuel Engblom, Nicola Kountouris and Åsa Odin Ekman's chapter extends these debates even further.[54] Not only do they challenge traditional conceptualisations of trade agreements, like the TPP, TTIP and TiSA, as being purely about economic co-operation regulating the trade in goods and services. They also argue that, given technological and other advances and the growth of global trade in services, the classifications pertaining to service delivery in these agreements are not descriptively precise enough to capture the labour intensification involved in global service delivery and, consequently, are deprived of normative force. By developing a matrix of cross-border human labour mobility processes, they provide illuminating insight into the power and potential of trade agreements to create greater economic integration without political integration. Although they argue that the current practice of wide-ranging exemptions and qualifications has meant the impact of free trade agreements on facilitating labour mobility has been minimal, they suggest that free trade agreements are unable to regulate complex human migration dynamics and, hence, are not the best vehicle for managing labour flows between countries. Instead, they argue that migration and immigration policies should be designed to promote long-term migratory patterns ensuring that workers' wages, conditions and rights are governed by their country of destination according to a principle of equal treatment and in accordance with international labour norms.

The idea of labour intensification reflects the reality that global services workers work in a particular physical, geographic location, even though in the longer term they may reside elsewhere. The social consequences for them as individuals, their families and communities (both the one in which they work, and the one in which they reside) are very real.[55] There are also substantial psychological costs associated with the 'normal' practice of temporary labour migration.[56] Thus, there are numerous individual and social issues, with potentially wide-reaching implications, turning on the denial

Dauvergne and Sarah Marsden, 'The Ideology of Temporary Labour Migration in the Post-Global Era' (2014) 18(2) *Citizenship Studies* 224, 232 relying on Hannah Arendt: 'The fact that labour is never self-contained, but is always productive of something more than itself, *and* is an aspect of being human, goes a great deal of the way to explaining why it is impossible for states to simply "import labour"'.

[54] Samuel Engblom, Nicola Kountouris and Åsa Odin Ekman, 'Temporary Labour Migration and the Trade in Services: European and Global Perspectives in an Age of Economic Integration', ch 3 in this volume.

[55] Very similar issues are evident in relation to the work migrations of 'fly-in/fly-out' or FIFO workers within (and sometimes across) national borders. For example, see a recent inquiry into this issue by the West Australian Government Education and Health Standing Committee, 'Inquiry into Mental Health Impacts of FIFO Work Arrangements' (2014), http://www.parliament.wa.gov.au/parliament/commit.nsf/(InqByName)/Inquiry+into+mental+health+impacts+of+FIFO+work+arrangements?opendocument.

[56] For an overview of research on this point, see Paul Collier, *Exodus: How Migration is Changing Our World* (Oxford, Oxford University Press, 2013) 169–76.

that global service workers are temporary migrant workers accessing the labour market in which they work. Their right to access social services while in the consumer/destination country is merely one, albeit an important one. In this collection, Gudrun Biffl and Isabella Skrivanek's chapter provides an important foray into this issue from a European perspective, by contrasting the situation of posted workers and seasonal workers.[57] They draw a key analytical distinction between the traditional reliance on seasonal workers' programmes and the growth in the number of posted workers. Temporary migrant labourers from outside Europe working on a seasonal basis are increasingly irrelevant for countries such as Austria given the expansion of the European Union and the freedom of movement of people and right to work accorded to its citizens. And as a corollary, the phenomenon of posted work is of growing importance. Biffl and Skrivanek suggest that the European social model must explicitly include all temporary migrant workers (including posted workers) or else, as a consequence of their currently differing impact on public revenues, risk the continuing erosion of redistributive principles and efforts by EU Member States.

In relation to the actual performance of their work, the essential problem in not recognising the movement and hence the human dimension of global service and posted workers temporarily based in the country into which services are delivered is a regulatory one. Under trade and regional agreements there is a strong risk that, rather than enjoying the same wages, terms and conditions as other workers alongside whom they work, these temporary migrants may be regulated by the laws of their home state. In the pre-globalised world, where the boundaries of old national economies were identical to the jurisdictional boundaries setting social laws, even the application of the rules of private international law to arrangements that might be described now as involving posted work ordinarily would not have overridden mandatory minimum work standards set by the jurisdiction in which the work was carried out.[58] However, the problem of workers effectively working side by side within the same jurisdiction but being subject to different legal arrangements has become more commonplace in the global era, making the importance of finding a solution to the intrinsic inequality and unfairness of such situations a more pressing one.[59] In the context

[57] Biffl and Skrivanek, 'The Distinction Between Temporary Labour Migration', ch 4 in this volume.

[58] See the special edition (2010) 31 *Comparative Labor Law and Policy Review*, devoted to labour issues and private international law.

[59] Agency or labour hire work is one of the ways in which this problem commonly manifests itself within labour markets. See Hugh Collins, 'Multi-segmented Workforces, Comparative Fairness, and the Capital Boundary Obstacle' in Guy Davidov and Brian Langille (eds), *Boundaries and Frontiers of Labour Law: Goals and Means in the Regulation of Work* (Oxford, Hart, 2006).

of global service agreements, the idea that these temporary migrations to deliver services involve 'workers without footprints' who do not participate in, or access, the labour market of the consuming state has been labelled a 'legal fiction'.[60]

The implications of such arrangements have perhaps been most fully played out in Europe, where the phenomenon of the 'posted worker' has been of growing practical and legal significance.[61] The 'posted worker' is conceptualised as an EU worker who is sent to another EU state by their employer who is a 'service provider' but who returns to their home state when the service is completed and does not gain access to the local labour market. The nomenclature signifies that the worker has been 'posted' in another country, implicitly for a short period of time and lacking any connection to the country in which they work. There is little precision about the length of stay of 'posted workers' who, in article 2 of the Posted Workers Directive, are defined as 'a worker who, for a limited period, carries out his work in the territory of a Member State other than the State in which he normally works'.[62]

The problems associated with posted workers, and especially the efficacy of the Posted Workers Enforcement Directive as a solution, have provoked much debate amongst scholars in Europe. The complex interactions of regulation in a changing context, including the intensification of transnational subcontracting practices, significant differences of living standards in the EU after its expansion, and the different labour standards to be found within it, are identified by some scholars as the source of the problems.[63] Given the constitutional right of freedom of movement in the EU, the transferability of lessons from the European to the global context is arguably even more complex. At the very least, however, the issue of posted work in Europe highlights the ways in which the boundaries of communities (regional or national), the differing nature of their intersections along different axes (political, social and/or economic), and the overlaying of labour markets within and across them, influences the operation and impact of regulatory regimes.[64]

[60] Lydia Hayes and Tonia Novitz, 'Workers Without Footprints: The Legal Fiction of Migrant Workers as Posted Workers' in Bernard Ryan (ed), *Labour Migration in Hard Times: Reforming Labour Market Regulation* (Liverpool, Institute for Employment Rights, 2013).

[61] See European Commission, 'Posting of Workers: EU Safeguards against Social Dumping', Memorandum, 13 May 2014; and see Biffl and Skrivanek, 'The Distinction Between Temporary Labour Migration', ch 4 in this volume.

[62] For a discussion of this and other definitional problems in terms of the employing entity and the nature of the services, see Hayes and Novitz, 'Workers Without Footprints' (n 60).

[63] Nicola Kountouris and Samuel Engblom, 'Civilising the European Posted Workers Directive' in Mark Freedland and Jeremias Prassl (eds), *Viking, Laval and Beyond* (Oxford, Hart Publishing, 2014).

[64] See Catherine Barnard, 'More Posting' (2014) 43 *International Labour Journal* 194.

III. TEMPORARY LABOUR MIGRATION IN PURSUIT OF ECONOMIC EFFICIENCY

To date, an economic perspective has been at the forefront of global policy discussions about temporary labour migration. Indeed, the very concept of temporariness, as Catherine Dauvergne and Sarah Marsden have observed, performs a significant function in attempting to transform 'people into "pure" economic inputs who will depart when their labour is no longer necessary',[65] turning on its head Max Frisch's oft-quoted aphorism about post-war Europe: 'we asked for workers, but got people'.[66] Temporary migration, it is said, results in an economic triple win: for the individual migrant, for the sending country and for the receiving country. Although that orthodoxy is increasingly contested,[67] there still remains a risk of the case in support being articulated in one-dimensional fashion, focusing on economic outcomes and ignoring other factors. The ILO suggests that, in order for the triple win to be realised in practice, there must be proper instruments of governance regulating temporary labour migration which guarantee that migrant workers receive 'a *fair share of the prosperity* which migration helps to create' (emphasis added).[68]

At the international level, temporary labour migration has been particularly embraced as part of the development agenda. Prestigious global institutions have encouraged temporary labour migration. In 2005, the World Bank estimated that moving an additional 14 million workers from low- to high-income countries would increase global income by $350 billion,[69] and the Global Commission on International Migration recommended the careful design of temporary migration programmes in order to address the economic needs of both sending and receiving countries.[70]

However, despite the conventional triple win formulation, which suggests sending countries benefit from temporary labour migration, especially

[65] Dauvergne and Marsden, 'The Ideology of Temporary Labour Migration' (n 53) 232.

[66] Max Frisch, 'Vorwort' in Alexander J Seiler, *Siamo Italiani* (Zürich, EVZ-Verlag, 1965) 7.

[67] See, eg Castles and Ozkul, 'Circular Migration' (n 6); Piyasiri Wickramasekara, *Circular Migration: A Triple Win or a Dead End*, Discussion Paper No 15 (Geneva, Global Union Research Network, 2011); Dauvergne and Marsden, 'The Ideology of Temporary Labour Migration' (n 53).

[68] ILO, *Fair Migration: Setting an ILO Agenda*, Report of the Director-General (Report I(B)) to the International Labour Conference, 103rd session, Geneva (June 2014) 4.

[69] World Bank, *Global Economic Prospects 2006: Economic Implications of Remittances and Migration* (Washington, DC, World Bank, 2005) 31.

[70] Global Commission on International Migration, *Migration in an Interconnected World: New Directions for Action* (Geneva, Global Commission on International Migration, 2005) 16.

through remittances,[71] the lens of remittance transactions is too narrow to evaluate labour migration costs. Those costs, it has been argued, must be seen in the broader context of employment and labour markets, and take into consideration issues such as the persistence of unacceptable work conditions and risks such as skill depletion.[72] Other costs—such as the social and cultural costs of separation from family and community, and the costs of reintegration of workers into their communities—have also been identified.[73]

The economic rationale for temporary labour migration has featured strongly in the discourse around the viability of these programmes in receiving countries. It is assumed that states only permit temporary labour migration if there is a net economic benefit to their own citizens. Martin Ruhs has identified economic efficiency as a functional imperative of states in designing temporary labour migration policies. In a broad sense, temporary labour migration is seen to benefit local job creation, business investment and economic growth, particularly through the introduction of new skills into the economy and by filling skill shortages, and also as a means of countering the phenomenon of an ageing population.[74]

Nonetheless, as noted above, the economic case for temporary labour migration schemes is not universally accepted.[75] There are a number of debates around particular aspects of the argument that these schemes inevitably produce economic prosperity. The extent to which temporary labour migration programmes stimulate job growth or lead to the replacement of local jobs is difficult to quantify.[76] Philip Martin identifies the displacement of local workers by temporary migrant workers as a non-linear process,[77]

[71] For example, the World Bank has commissioned a number of studies that identify the economic benefit to countries of origin of labour migration. See, eg Samuel Maimbo and Dilip Ratha (eds), *Remittances: Development Impact and Future Prospects* (Washington, DC, World Bank, 2005); Manjula Luthsia et al, *At Home and Away: Expanding Job Opportunities for Pacific Islanders Through Labour Mobility* (Washington, DC, World Bank, 2006); Pablo Fajnzylber and J Humberto Lopez, *Remittances and Development: Lessons from Latin America* (Washington, DC, World Bank, 2008); Quentin Wodon, *Migration, Remittances and Poverty: Case Studies from West Africa* (Washington, DC, World Bank, 2009).

[72] See Wickramasekara, *Circular Migration*; ILO, *Promoting Decent Work For Migrant Workers*, Discussion Paper (Geneva, ILO, 2015).

[73] See, eg Alexander Reilly, 'The Ethics of Seasonal Labour Migration' (2011) 20 *Griffith Law Review* 127, 135.

[74] Ruhs, *The Price of Rights* (n 12) 26–32.

[75] See, eg Graeme Hugo, 'Best Practice in Temporary Labour Migration for Development: A Perspective from Asia and the Pacific' (2009) 47 *International Migration* 23.

[76] For further discussion on this point, see Inter-Parliamentary Union, International Labour Organization and the Office of the United Nations High Commissioner for Human Rights, *Migration, Human Rights and Governance, Handbook for Parliamentarians No 24* (Geneva, Inter-Parliamentary Union, 2015) 22.

[77] Philip Martin, *Illegal Immigration and the Colonisation of the American Labor Market*, Paper 1 (Washington, DC, Center for Immigration Studies, 1986).

and WR Boehning explains that competition for jobs between the two groups is far more likely for certain categories of workers than for others.[78] According to demographer Graeme Hugo, employers 'will always have a "demand" for foreign workers if it results in a lowering of their costs'.[79] The simplistic notion that employers will only go to the trouble and expense of employing a migrant worker when they want to meet a skill shortage skims over a range of motives an employer may have for using a migrant worker. These could be a reluctance to invest in training for existing or prospective staff, a desire to move towards a de-unionised workforce or, for a (perhaps small) minority of employers, a belief that it is easier to avoid paying minimum wage rates and conditions for temporary migrant workers.[80]

It is clear that economic efficiency is by no means a guaranteed fruit of conventional temporary labour migration programmes. Further, the economic impact of visas that allow temporary migration for a non-work purpose but permit the visa holder to work extensively in the country of destination is often ignored. More robust assessments suggest the need for a broader consideration of the nature and distribution of any economic benefits. Thus, while temporary labour migration is often linked to the development needs of sending countries and also the economic and labour market needs of receiving countries, it also has much broader political, social, economic and cultural dimensions.

In this collection, two contributions problematise employer demand as a regulatory mechanism for determining the composition of a country's temporary labour migration intake. Joanna Howe's chapter examines the employer-driven nature of Australia's 457 visa programme and develops three concrete regulatory solutions as to how employer requests to access migrant labour could be tempered.[81] Her proposals stress the importance of regulatory design in ensuring that migrant workers are not used to replace local workers, the role of enforcement agencies, and the need for regulatory cohesion between labour law and immigration law. Her contribution, coupled with Mimi Zou's chapter on the UK approach, examine the problems arising from deference to employer needs in the design of policies and laws of receiving countries designed to facilitate the process of temporary labour migration. Zou's chapter provides a comprehensive

[78] WR Boehning, *Studies in International Labor Migration* (London, Macmillan, 1984) 86–93.

[79] Hugo, 'Best Practice in Temporary Labour Migration' (n 75) 59.

[80] See, eg Joanna Howe, 'Is the Net Cast Too Wide? An Assessment of whether the Regulatory Design of the 457 Visa Meets Australia's Skills Needs' (2013) 41 *Federal Law Review* 443.

[81] Joanna Howe, 'Contesting the Demand-Driven Orthodoxy: An Assessment of the Australian Regulation of Temporary Labour Migration', ch 6 in this volume.

examination of the regulatory mechanisms used within the UK system and, of particular relevance to the growing international interest in the role of expert commissions,[82] she identifies the essential role of the UK's Migration Advisory Committee (MAC) in contributing to migration policy.[83] Given the tendency of migration policy to be characterised by a high degree of executive discretion justified according to an imperative of providing a flexible and timely response to employer requests to access migrant labour, Zou's analysis of the MAC presents an important case study of an alternative approach to migration policy-making that is both transparent and publicly accountable.

IV. TEMPORARY LABOUR MIGRATION AND THE PRODUCTION OF PRECARITY

When state policy and regulation are focused primarily on economic issues, there is a risk that their damaging social effects, encapsulated by the precarity of temporary migrant labour, are ignored. There is a rich literature examining the precarity of temporary migrant work.[84] The potential for exploitation is increased for low-skilled migrant workers,[85] particularly those in certain industries,[86] and is often exacerbated by the presence of migration intermediaries seeking to capitalise from the commercialisation of migration.[87] Temporary labour migration worldwide has featured exploitative work conditions, substandard housing and underpayment

[82] See, eg the special issue of the journal *Migration Letters* dedicated to this topic: 'Expert Commissions and Migration Policy Making' (2014) 11(1) *Migration Letters*.

[83] Mimi Zou, 'Employer Demand for "Skilled" Migrant Workers: Regulating Admission under the United Kingdom's Tier 2 (General) Visa', ch 5 in this volume.

[84] See, eg Costello and Freedland (eds), *Migrants at Work* (n 7). See also the special edition on 'Migrant Workers' in (2009) 31 *Comparative Labor Law and Policy Journal*; the special edition on 'Vulnerabilities of Regular Labour Migration in the EU' in (2015) 31 *International Journal of Comparative Labour Law and Industrial Relations*; Laurie Berg, *Migrant Rights at Work: Law's Precariousness at the Intersection of Labour and Migration* (London, Routledge, 2015).

[85] Barbara Deegan, *Integrity/Exploitation*, Visa Subclass 457 Integrity Review Issues Paper No 3 (Canberra, Department of Immigration and Citizenship, 2008).

[86] See, eg ACL Davies, 'Migrant Workers in Agriculture' in Costello and Freedland (eds), *Migrants at Work* (n 7); Judy Fudge, 'Precarious Migrant Status and Precarious Employment: The Paradox of International Rights for Migrant Workers' (2012) 34 *Comparative Labour Law and Policy Journal* 101.

[87] See Jennifer Gordon, *Global Labor Recruitment in a Supply Chain Context*, ILO Fair Recruitment Initiative Series No 1 (Geneva, ILO, 2015); Dimitria Groutis, Di van den Broek and Will S Harvey, 'Transformations in Network Governance: The Case of Migration Intermediaries' (2015) 41 *Journal of Ethnic and Migration Studies* 1558.

of wages,[88] evincing a phenomenon that Joo-Cheong Tham, Iain Campbell and Martina Boese call 'the structural reality of non-compliance'.[89]

In this collection, two chapters identify ways in which precarity arises not only from features often inherent in the design of temporary labour migration programmes but also from the regulatory choices made in response to problems and the context in which that regulation operates. Drawing upon Australia as a case study, Tham, Campbell and Boese argue in their chapter that the structural design of temporary labour migration programmes invites and facilitates non-compliance by employers and that in certain industries, where there is greater likelihood of non-compliance, these structural features render it inevitable that most employers will employ temporary migrant workers in breach of immigration laws and policies. The sobering realisation from Tham, Campbell and Boese's chapter is that the phenomenon of temporary labour migration produces non-compliance with labour law that is not aberrational but the norm.

Judy Fudge deploys the analytical concept of 'unfree labour' to depict a broader phenomenon whereby the structural features of labour migration programmes create the conditions for exploitation to occur.[90] In her case study of domestic migrant workers, Fudge observes the practice of both the Canadian federal and British Columbia governments of regulating the problem of abuse of temporary domestic migrant workers through the lens of modern slavery. She argues that the choice to use the criminal law is 'neither natural nor inevitable' and operates to ignore the role of labour market and immigration institutions in cultivating conditions that are conducive to exploitative practices. By using the criminal law to attack the worst cases of exploitation, problems are characterised not as systemic but as individual aberrations. In this way, violations of labour standards have become normalised and accepted because only the most egregious forms of labour exploitation are targeted. While acknowledging the complexity of regulatory intersections, Fudge stresses that 'unfreedom' cannot be understood as simply a matter of legal jurisdiction without consideration of the broader social, political and economic context.[91]

[88] See, eg Mark J Miller, 'Introduction: Temporary Workers: Programs, Mechanisms, Conditions, Consequences' (1986) 20(4) *International Migration Review* 740, 747; Joanna Howe, 'The Migration Amendment (Worker Protection) Act 2008: Long Overdue Reform, But Have Migrant Workers Been Sold Short?' (2010) 24 *Australian Journal of Labour Law* 13; Reilly, 'The Ethics of Seasonal Labour Migration' (n 73).

[89] Tham, Campbell and Boese, 'Why is Labour Protection for Temporary Migrant Workers so Fraught?: A Perspective from Australia', ch 8 in this volume.

[90] Sociologists, in particular, have coined the term 'unfree labour' to denote a situation where migrant workers are constrained from freely circulating in the labour markets of receiving countries. See, eg Robert Miles, *Capitalism and Unfree Labor: Anomaly or Necessity* (New York, Tavistock, 1987); Tanya Basok, *Tortillas and Tomatoes: Transmigrant Mexican Harvesters in Canada* (Montreal, McGill-Queens University Press, 2002).

[91] Judy Fudge, 'Migrant Domestic Workers in British Columbia, Canada: Unfreedom, Trafficking and Domestic Servitude', ch 7 in this volume.

A. The Pursuit of Decent Work for Temporary Migrant Workers at the International Level

Despite its tendency to be associated with precarious work, a number of global institutions have promoted temporary migration as a means of development. The global challenge has thus been to ensure 'decent work' for all, including for temporary migrant workers.[92] As long ago as 2004, the World Commission on the Social Dimensions of Globalisation indicated that (increased) migration was one of the pathways to achieving a fairer globalisation. The proviso was that it must occur in a framework of uniform and transparent rules for cross-border migration that balanced the interests of migrants, and of countries of origin and destination.[93] Similarly, the ILO has played a major role since 2004 in championing a fair deal for migrant workers through an equality, rights-based approach.[94] The ILO's 'fair migration agenda' continues to highlight the need for decent work in countries of origin, the formulation of orderly and fair migration schemes in regional integration processes, the importance of arrangements for well-regulated and fair migration in bilateral arrangements between states, fair recruiting practices, the countering of unacceptable situations, such as trafficking in people, and the realisation of a rights-based approach, and to identify them as priorities for future action.[95]

The urgency of these issues has also garnered the attention of the world community more broadly.[96] Indeed, the international agenda for action has accepted the importance of the recognition of the human rights of all migrants and attention to the special vulnerabilities of various migrants groups, such as women and girl migrants, and young people; the need to respect and promote international labour standards and promote the rights

[92] ILO, *Decent Work*, Report of the Director-General, International Labour Conference, 87th session (June 1999).

[93] World Commission on Social Dimension of Globalisation, *A Fairer Globalization: Creating Opportunities for All* (Geneva, ILO, 1994); see also International Labour Office, *International Labour Migration: A Rights-Based Approach* (Geneva, ILO, 2010).

[94] See ILO, *International Labour Migration*. This report was largely based on ILO, 'Towards a Fair Deal for Migrant Workers in a Global Economy', Report VI, 92nd International Labour Conference, Geneva, June 2004. See also ILO, 'Resolution Concerning a Fair Deal for Migrant Workers in a Global Economy', 92nd International Labour Conference, Geneva, June 2004; Shauna Olney and Ryszard Cholewinski, 'Migrant Workers and the Right to Non-discrimination and Equality' in Costello and Freedland (eds), *Migrants at Work* (n 7).

[95] ILO, *Fair Migration* (n 68). See also ILO, *Promoting Fair Migration*, Report of the Committee of Experts on the Application of Conventions and Recommendations, General Survey concerning the migrant workers instruments, International Labour Conference, 105th session, 2016.

[96] The Global Commission on International Migration reported to the Secretary General of the UN October 2005; the Global Migration Group was formed in 2006; High Level Dialogue on International Migration and Development was held in 2006 and 2013; and the Global Forum on Migration and Development met first in 2007.

of migrants in workplaces; the importance of reducing the costs of labour migration, especially recruitment costs;[97] the elimination of the exploitation of migrants; the importance of the integration of migration into the development agenda; and the enhancement of partnerships and international co-operation.[98]

It is evident that at the level of global rhetoric there is considerable recognition of the need to consider the broader context of labour standards and labour markets in evaluating the costs of migration[99] and also acceptance of the equality of migrant workers. The principle of non-discrimination and equality for all, and for all workers including migrant workers, is a fundamental principle underpinning international law.[100] It is incorporated into relevant general human rights conventions of the United Nations, as well as the specific conventions of both the ILO and the UN relating to migrant workers.[101] Yet in the international regulatory system, deficiencies remain in seeking to address the precarious work endured by many temporary migrants.[102] As the ILO acknowledges, its conventions specifically relating to migrant workers were developed in an earlier era and different context.[103] Some migrants are excluded from the scope of these conventions, and the rights of permanent and temporary migrants are in some important respects distinguished.[104] Furthermore, these conventions have attracted few signatories.[105] While the more recent UN convention on migrant workers is generally considered an improvement in a number of respects, it too excludes

[97] See Philip Martin, 'Reducing Worker-Paid Migration Costs', ch 17 in this volume.

[98] See Declaration of the High-level Dialogue on International Migration and Development, UNGA Res 68/4 (1 October 2013) 68th session UN Doc A/RES/68/4.

[99] See ILO, *Promoting Decent Work for Migrant Workers.*

[100] See Olney and Cholewinski, 'Migrant Workers and the Right to Non-discrimination' (n 94). See also Piyasiri Wickramasekara, 'Globalisation, International Labour Migration and the Rights of Migrant Workers' (2008) 29 *Third World Quarterly* 1247.

[101] For the main specific international instruments governing migrant workers see ILO Convention Concerning Migration for Employment (Revised) 1949 (No 97); ILO Convention Concerning Migrant Workers (Supplementary Provisions) Convention 1975 (No 143); ILO Migration for Employment (Revised) Recommendation 1949 (No 86); ILO Migrant Workers Recommendation 1975 (No 151); International Convention on the Protection of all Migrant Workers and their Families UN GA Res 45/158 (18 December 1990) UN Doc A/Res/45/158. See also earlier instruments, eg ILO The Protection of Migrant Workers (Underdeveloped Countries) Recommendation 1955 No 100; ILO Plantations Convention (No 110); ILO Plantations Recommendation 1958 (No 101).

[102] See, eg Leah F Vosko, 'Out of the Shadows? The Non-Binding Multilateral Framework on Migration (2006) and Prospects for Using International Labour Regulation to Forge Global Labour Market Membership' in Davidov and Langille (eds), *The Idea of Labour Law* (n 52).

[103] See, eg ILO, *Fair Migration* (n 68).

[104] See especially Convention No 97 arts 8, 11; Convention No 143 art 11.2.

[105] Of 186 Member States of the ILO, only 49 have ratified Convention No 97 and 23 have ratified Convention No 143. This despite the fact that No 97 was designed in two separate parts which could be separately ratified, in an attempt to assuage concerns about the possibility for it to undermine temporary labour migration programmes. See especially Vosko, 'Out of the Shadows?' (n 102).

some temporary migrants from its scope, where they migrate primarily for purposes other than work, for example as students and trainees, regardless of the fact that they may nonetheless also be entitled to work during their stay in the destination country.[106] Significantly, under part V, states are able to limit the rights of some temporary migrants: frontier workers, seasonal workers, itinerant workers, project-tied workers or specified employment workers. In these ways, the international conventions specifically governing migrant workers convey the message that some temporary migrant workers are somehow less equal than others.[107] Thus, despite the acceptance of the principle of equality 'in the abstract', achieving a deep consensus on its practical attainment and implementation for temporary migrant workers remains elusive and controversial.[108]

V. CHALLENGES IN REALISING DECENT WORK FOR TEMPORARY MIGRANT WORKERS

The challenges in realising equality and attaining decent work for temporary migrant workers are explored in Part V of this collection. As well as reflecting on some of the issues relating to the precarity of temporary migrant workers that are addressed in Part IV, all of these chapters consider those issues in the context of Europe and so, in addition, highlight the complexity arising from the regulatory intersection of regional and national legal systems.

Given the significance of the European Convention on Human Rights, Virginia Mantouvalou situates her discussion of temporary labour migration in the context of debates about the rationale for considering labour rights as human rights and its implications for regulatory content.[109] Drawing upon an empirical study she conducted, she examines migrant domestic work in the United Kingdom. Significantly, most of the women she interviewed had experienced a double migration, and so in entering the United Kingdom with their employer they also brought with them in their already established work relationship the regulatory traces of another national jurisdiction.

[106] See Dauvergne, *Making People Illegal* (n 23) 19–24 on the limits of the UN convention. See also Olney and Cholewinski, 'Migrant Workers and the Right to Non-discrimination' (n 94).

[107] The ILO itself is very much alert to the criticisms. See eg ILO, *Fair Migration* (n 68). For a more optimistic view see WR Böhning, 'The Protection of Temporary Migrants by Conventions of the ILO and the UN', paper presented at International Institute for Labour Studies Workshop on Temporary Migration: Assessment and Practical Proposals for Overcoming Protection Gaps, Geneva, 18–19 September 2003.

[108] See Olney and Cholewinski, 'Migrant Workers and the Right to Non-discrimination' (n 94).

[109] Virginia Mantouvalou, 'Temporary Labour Migration and Modern Slavery', ch 10 in this volume.

Like Judy Fudge, Virginia Mantouvalou is critical of a regulatory focus on 'modern slavery'. While she accepts that it may be a necessary response to certain outcomes, she argues it is not sufficient and deflects attention from the laws, practices and regulations that produce the vulnerability of these migrant workers in the first instance.

The EU Seasonal Workers Directive provides an example of regulatory efforts at the supra-national level to enable temporary migrant workers to realise decent work.[110] Veronica Papa argues in her chapter that it is highly problematic that the directive allows seasonal workers' residency status in destination countries to be linked to their employment status.[111] Drawing upon the regulatory framework envisaged under the directive, Papa examines the situation of seasonal migrant workers in Italy and argues that their precarity in the labour market results from a public policy paradigm criminalising irregular migration, thereby obscuring the real issue of exploitation of seasonal migrant workers.

On the same theme of seasonal workers, in her chapter Julia López López examines and tries to resolve the difficult question of how to provide genuine security for these workers despite the overriding economic imperative of providing flexibility for employers.[112] She critiques the far-reaching consequences flowing from the EU's free movement of people, producing a melting pot involving substantial numbers of unemployed local workers, large outflows of Spanish workers chasing better employment prospects in other EU countries, the presence of a significant group of undocumented workers, particularly from Africa, and the continuing, and often unsated, need of Spanish agricultural employers for seasonal migrant labour. The complex interactions of these groups within the Spanish labour market remains a tremendous challenge for regulators seeking to foster compliance with labour law and migration regulations whilst addressing the challenge of labour supply.

In contrast to the difficulties of realising decent work for temporary migrant workers in the United Kingdom, Spain and Italy, Sweden's evolving model of temporary labour migration has been regarded as an 'exceptional case' by scholars and by the OECD.[113] This has been attributed to its

[110] Directive 2014/36/EU of the European Parliament and of the Council of 26 February 2014 on the conditions of entry and stay of third-country nationals for the purpose of employment as seasonal workers [2014] OJ L94/375.

[111] Papa, 'Regulating Temporariness in Italian Migration Law', ch 12 in this volume.

[112] López, 'The Regulation of Temporary Immigration', ch 11 in this volume.

[113] See, eg Martin Ruhs, 'Immigration and Labour Market Protectionism: Protecting Local Workers' Preferential Access to the Local Labour Market' in Costello and Freedland (eds), *Migrants at Work* (n 7) 76–77. See also Samuel Engblom, 'Reconciling Openness and High Labour Standards? Sweden's Attempts to Regulate Labour Migration and Trade in Services' in Costello and Freedland (eds), *Migrants at Work*; OECD, *Recruiting Immigrant Workers: Sweden* (Paris, OECD, 2011).

reliance on labour market regulation (namely that temporary migrants be employed at collectively agreed wages) to constrain employer demand for labour.[114] This is said to prevent employers relying upon these workers as a way of undercutting local job opportunities, which has been made possible in Sweden because of its strong history of collectivism and the continuing role played by unions in regulating the labour market.[115] Nonetheless, in this collection, Petra Herzfeld Olsson questions the success of Sweden's deregulated approach to temporary labour migration and its reliance on the equal treatment principle to show how the promises contained in the offer of employment made to prospective migrant workers often go unrealised and unenforced once this work is taken up.[116] In fact, Herzfeld Olsson argues that, far from being an ideal, Sweden's regulation of temporary labour migration with its reliance on the equal treatment principle ends up undermining equality for temporary migrant workers. Drawing upon a labour law approach, she proposes a new kind of employment contract for temporary migrant workers.

VI. CONTESTING TEMPORARINESS: STATUS AND THE SOCIAL EFFECTS OF THE LEGAL REGULATION OF TEMPORARY LABOUR MIGRATION

Employers' permanent demand for (and in some cases dependence upon) temporary migrant labour is often noted.[117] Yet, consistently, receiving states tend zealously to guard and constrain the conversion of temporary workers' migrant status into membership. At the same time, it would be incorrect to assert that citizenship is always the aspiration of temporary migrant workers. An increasing number of people have allegiances to many territories and places. Individuals often have multiple familial, social and cultural ties in complex networks of communities around the world. Work relations often constitute one such network. But given the large numbers involved and the fact that temporary labour migration is often a stepping stone to permanent residency, the architectural foundations of temporary labour migration programmes continue to have far-reaching implications

[114] Ruhs, 'Immigration and Labour Market Protectionism' 76–77. See also Engblom, 'Reconciling Openness and High Labour Standards?'.

[115] Engblom, 'Reconciling Openness and High Labour Standards?'.

[116] Petra Herzfeld Olsson, 'Empowering Temporary Labour Migrants in Sweden: A Call for Unequal Treatment', ch 9 in this volume.

[117] See, eg Ruhs and Anderson (eds), *Who Needs Migrant Workers?* (n 28); Andrew Geddes and Sam Scott, 'UK Food Businesses' Reliance on Low-Wage Migrant Labour: A Case of Choice or Constraint?' in Ruhs and Anderson (eds), *Who Needs Migrant Workers?*; Valeria Ottonelli and Tiziana Torres, 'Inclusivist Egalitarian Liberalism and Temporary Migration: A Dilemma' (2012) 20 *Journal of Political Philosophy* 202.

for the configuration of national populations as well as the workings of labour markets.

A key reason for temporary migrant workers' vulnerability in receiving states is their temporary status. In assessing the inadequacy of the UN Migrant Workers Convention, Catherine Dauvergne and Sarah Marsden observe that the convention may simply incorporate the logic that is inherent in the concept of temporariness.[118] In their view, while rights talk might improve some of the conditions of temporary migrant workers, it also masks the fundamental inequality at issue in temporary labour migration. Without erasing the subordination that arises from the right of the state to exclude that is implicit in 'temporariness', it is too easy (Dauvergne argues) to fall back on assertions that temporary migrant workers should have fewer rights than others. On this view, the basic inequality that needs remedying first is that which is inherent in the 'temporary' status. For many scholars, there is an ethical limit to temporary labour migration programmes and the exclusion of migrants from full membership of the community in which they work.[119] In his contribution to this collection, Alexander Reilly argues in favour of giving temporary migrant workers rights to residency, membership and ultimately citizenship of the receiving state.[120] In his view, the essence of citizenship is to focus on the real connections between persons and states that can be created through temporary migrant workers' longstanding contribution through the labour market to the host country. Along with Ruhs' contribution to this collection, Reilly's chapter builds upon existing scholarship to develop a template for temporary labour migration that seeks to realise the dignity of migrant workers without necessarily tampering with employer demand, which has traditionally been a key ordering principle of temporary labour migration programmes worldwide.

Nonetheless, receiving states' migration laws tend to prioritise national sovereignty, which the international regulatory framework has found difficult to erode. The admitted inadequacy of existing international law to respond to the issues relating to migrant workers has led more recently to the 'soft law' approach that is embodied in the Multilateral Framework on Labour Migration of 2006 developed under the auspices of the ILO.[121] Under it, the role of international labour standards is to provide a framework for 'coherent, effective and fair' national policies. The framework is

[118] Dauvergne and Marsden, 'The Ideology of Temporary Labour Migration' (n 53).

[119] See, eg Michael Walzer, *Spheres of Justice: A Defence of Pluralism and Equality* (New York, Basic Books, 1983) ch 2; Reilly, 'The Ethics of Seasonal Labour Migration' (n 73).

[120] Reilly, 'The Membership of Migrant Workers', ch 13 in this volume.

[121] ILO, *Multilateral Framework on Migration: Non-binding Principles and Guidelines for a Rights Based Approach to Labour Migration* (Geneva, ILO, 2006).

presented as a non-binding guidance, intended for adoption at national, regional and international levels, and also proffers a collection of principles and best practice examples. While in some respects reaching further than international instruments in the embrace of principles of equality, the framework ultimately falls back on the recognition of national sovereignty in the formulation of migration policy. In this sense, it stands as evidence that, as Catherine Dauvergne has argued, 'in contemporary globalizing times, migration laws and their enforcement are increasingly understood as the last bastion of sovereignty'.[122]

The prospects for this framework contributing to a successful resolution of the major issues relating to migrant workers have been questioned, perhaps unsurprisingly, by scholars such as Leah Vosko.[123] Vosko goes further to argue that there is an irreconcilable tension between the recognition of the sovereignty of nation-states to determine immigration policy and the rights and principles of international law. The multilateral framework is thus, from her perspective, merely another phase in the use of citizenship concepts to classify migrants into various tiers, each qualifying for different levels of rights, and one in which the rights of temporary migrant workers remain diminished.[124] In her view, the only real solution is to develop alternative membership norms embracing the entire global labour market. In contrast to this approach, Brian Langille has suggested, more generally, that the quest for a 'Geneva consensus' in response to global issues may be as flawed as any other version of consensus (in particular, he refers to the 'Washington consensus' regarding deregulation and the primacy of the free market). For Langille, even if 'the golden age (roughly 1978–2008) of "de-regulatory capture" is over', debate must remain around whether any single approach can advance labour rights in the new global era more effectively than a more diversified 'bottom-up' approach.[125]

[122] Dauvergne, *Making People Illegal* (n 23) 2. See also Catherine Dauvergne, 'Sovereignty, Migration and the Rule of Law in Global Times' (2004) 67 *Modern Law Review* 588.

[123] See especially Vosko, 'Out of the Shadows?' (n 102).

[124] Vosko identifies four phases of approaches to migration: the earliest phase (pre-1945), when only citizen workers were given full rights; the period pre-1990, when there was preferential treatment for citizens and permanent residents; recognition of an expanded range of categories, and treatment differentiated in relation to them, including temporary and permanent migrants were distinguished; beyond 1990, when some of these distinctions were abolished but continued to enable states to limit temporary migrants' free choice of work and other work conditions. See also Leah Vosko, *Managing the Margins: Gender, Citizenship and the International Regulation of Precarious Work* (Oxford, Oxford University Press, 2010).

[125] Brian Langille, 'Imaging Post "Geneva Consensus" Labour Law for "Post Washington Consensus" Development' (2009) 31 *Comparative Labor and Policy Law Journal* 523, 523. For a robust refutation of Langille's argument see Anne Trebilcock, 'Putting the Record Straight about International Labor Standard Setting' (2009) 31 *Comparative Labor and Policy Law Journal* 553.

VII. THE GLOBAL CHALLENGE OF TEMPORARY LABOUR MIGRATION: REGULATORY RESPONSES AND POSSIBILITIES

Despite the apparent consensus around an equality and rights-based approach, at the international level there is also a clear recognition that there remains a regulatory gap in relation to temporary migrant labour. In advocating a 'fair migration agenda', the Director-General of the ILO has indicated that it is 'essential to identify those elements that must be built into the design of the [temporary labour migration] schemes to ensure they meet basic considerations of fair treatment'.[126] The unfair and disadvantageous situation in which temporary migrant workers often find themselves remains a key challenge. In many instances, the very parameters of temporary labour migration schemes may, by definition, hinder equal treatment. The temporary nature of the schemes and specified restrictions on temporary migrants, such as in relation to either the labour market (their employer or industrial sector) or geographic mobility,[127] wages or savings, limitations on the capacity to access other schemes or family reunion, the absence of access to social protection or other non-employment related restriction have all been identified as problematic.[128] Even the concept of equality of treatment, often perceived to require a comparator, can prove particularly problematic in the face of, for example, labour market segmentation and segregation.[129] Indeed, in light of the restrictions that define the status of very many temporary migrant workers, some critics argue that in reality they are controlled through 'contracts of indenture'.[130]

Historically, the legitimacy of law and legal systems has often been portrayed as based on objectivity, as well as independence and (above all) autonomy and distinctiveness from social, economic and political systems.[131] For many lawyers, implicit in a rights-based approach is the idea

[126] ILO, *Fair Migration* (n 68) 77.

[127] The binding of temporary labour migrants to individual employers, industrial sectors or a geographic area is very common. See, eg, Israel where binding to individual employers was declared unconstitutional in 2006, only to be replaced by sectoral binding in 2011. See Hila Shamir, 'A Labor Paradigm for Human Trafficking' (2012) 60 *UCLA Law Review* 76, 121.

[128] See Martin Ruhs, *Temporary Foreign Worker Programs: Policies, Adverse Consequences and the Need to Make Them Work* Perspectives on Labour Migration 6 (Geneva, International Labour Office, 2003) 8–9. See also ILO, *The Future of ILO Activities in the Field of Migration* (Geneva, ILO, 1997) identifying many of the problems with time-bound migration and problems with recruiting agencies.

[129] See ILO, *Fair Migration* (n 68) 78. See generally Mark Freedland, 'The Segmentation of Workers' Rights and the Legal Analysis of Personal Work Relations: Defining a Problem' (2015) 36 *Comparative Labor Law and Policy Journal* 241.

[130] Rosewarne, 'Globalisation and the Commodification of Labour' (n 53).

[131] Supporters of neo-liberalism also portrayed a close, natural alliance between globalisation, de-regulation and privatisation, and the primacy of an economic perspective, and facilitated the view that labour standards were inefficient interventions distorting the natural contractual relationships of the marketplace. See Rosemary Owens, Joellen Riley and

that rights trump other interests: in a profound sense, rights are not fungible. Despite this, for others including notable economists, the regulatory challenges posed by temporary labour migration programmes can be overcome. In his chapter in this collection, Martin Ruhs calls for a reframing of the human rights–based approach to migration by developing a universal set of core rights applicable to all migrant workers, whilst explicitly permitting temporary restrictions of a few specific rights.[132] Ruhs' chapter responds to criticisms that his approach violates important international human rights principles and norms, suggesting instead that his core rights approach would have the benefit of stimulating the 'further liberalization of international labour migration', thereby increasing access to temporary labour migration to more people from countries of origin.[133] Paul Collier also believes in the transformative possibilities of temporary labour migration. He proposes a policy package for host countries that includes a ceiling for the gross level of migration; selectivity based on a number of criteria; and integration initiatives to enable migrants to be absorbed well into the economy and society of the host country.[134] It is not only the economists who regard migration as capable of being regulated and managed to improve the situation of all the individual, private/business and public/state actors involved. However, there are still a number of legal challenges involved at the interface of migration and work, especially temporary migration and work, which have seldom been examined in a sustained way.[135]

There are many possible layers of explanation for this. In part, no doubt, this is because so many regulatory arenas—including migration law, labour law, trade law, human rights, development law, refugee and asylum law, criminal law and national security law, to name but a few—are involved. Examining the intersections between multiple fields of regulation is complex, and yet essential to understanding the construction of labour markets

Jill Murray, *The Law of Work*, 2nd edn (Oxford, Oxford University Press, 2011) 46ff. Simon Deakin's work, and that of other scholars, has been particularly important in providing the empirical evidence debunking these ideas. See, eg Simon Deakin, 'The Evidence-Based Case for Labour Regulation' in Sangheon Lee and Deidre McCann (eds), *Regulating for Decent Work: New Directions in Labour Market Regulation* (Geneva, Palgrave Macmillan/ILO, 2011). See also Simon Deakin and Frank Wilkinson, *The Law of the Labour Market: Industrialization, Employment and Legal Evolution* (Oxford, Oxford University Press, 2005).

[132] Ruhs, 'Protecting the Rights of Temporary Migrant Workers', ch 14 in this volume. See also Ruhs, *The Price of* Rights (n 12) 196.

[133] Ruhs, 'Protecting the Rights of Temporary Migrant Workers', ch 14 in this volume.

[134] Collier, *Exodus* (n 56) 255–65.

[135] See Costello and Freedland (eds), *Migrants at Work* (n 7). See also the special edition on 'Migrant Workers' in (2009) 31 *Comparative Labor Law and Policy Journal*; Berg, *Migrant Rights at Work* (n 84). Although each of these contains groundbreaking recent work on the intersection of labour law and migration, none provides a sustained and singular focus on temporary labour migration.

as well as the nature of work relationships and the ways in which legal, political, social, economic and cultural contexts give them shape and meaning, and in turn are shaped by them.[136] This is no less so for those involving temporary labour migration.

Nor is this to deny contestation over the significance of, or the priorities within, these intersections. In tackling trafficking, which has become a significant source of temporary labour migration in many countries, for example, Hila Shamir has argued that utilising a human rights approach, while responding to its gendered elements, is not effective at dealing with the issues of economic exploitation.[137] A labour law approach, according to Shamir, would be a more constructive approach by attending to the structure of labour markets and facilitating a greater focus on preventing criminalisation and deportation, eliminating binding arrangements, reducing recruitment fees and the power of intermediaries, guaranteeing the right to unionise, and extending and enforcing the application of labour and employment laws to all vulnerable workers. Likewise, Costello has also argued that separating labour law from migration law is the only sure way to deal with the problem of forced labour.[138]

Further complications arise from the separate challenges and transformative possibilities opened up by globalisation in each of the regulatory fields. To take the example of labour law,[139] under pressures arising in the context of globalisation, the subjects of labour law have been redefined, not least through the production of precarious work, which has become normalised as the old industrial model of the male breadwinner has broken down irretrievably under the incessant demand for flexibility to meet the reduced production time frames of the market.[140] The challenges to the regulation of work posed through fragmentation, informalisation and commercialisation, amongst others, are also redefining the boundaries of the discipline.[141] The transformation of the firm through 'vertical disintegration',[142] the capacity

[136] See Christopher Arup et al (eds), *Labour Law and Labour Market Regulation: Essays on the Construction, Constitution, and Regulation of Labour Markets and Work Relationships* (Sydney, Federation Press, 2006).

[137] Shamir, 'A Labor Paradigm for Human Trafficking' (n 127).

[138] Cathryn Costello, 'Migrants and Forced Labour: A Labour Law Response' in Alan Bogg, Cathryn Costello, ACL Davies and Jeremias Prassl (eds), *The Autonomy of Labour Law* (Oxford, Hart Publishing, 2015).

[139] See, eg Joanne Conaghan, Richard Michael Fischl and Karl Klare (eds), *Labour Law in an Era of Globalization: Transformative Practices and Possibilities* (Oxford, Oxford University Press, 2002); John DR Craig and S Michael Lynk (eds), *Globalization and the Future of Labour Law* (Cambridge, Cambridge University Press, 2006).

[140] See, eg Fudge and Owens, *Precarious Work* (n 24); Guy Standing, *The Precariat: The New Dangerous Class* (London, Bloomsbury Academic, 2011).

[141] See Judy Fudge, Shae McCrystal and Kamala Sankaran (eds), *Challenging the Legal Boundaries of Work Regulation* (Oxford, Hart Publishing, 2012).

[142] See Hugh Collins, 'Independent Contractors and the Challenge of Vertical Disintegration to Employment Protection Laws' (1990) 10 *Oxford Journal of Legal Studies* 353.

of the corporation to operate through a network of independent but related entities, and the disaggregation of the modes of production through the formation of global supply chains have all provided further challenges to legal and regulatory systems in identifying employing businesses and responding to the demands of globalisation.[143] The reconfiguration of the divide between, and the acknowledged interdependency of, the public and private spheres, both work–family and market–state, have further produced and complicated the regulatory challenges for labour law.[144] The significance for temporary labour migration of these challenges to labour law are patent. Temporary migrant workers are amongst some of the most precarious.[145] It is in this global context, for instance, that standards for the regulation of domestic labour, which is frequently performed by temporary migrant workers and has traditionally often been excluded from labour law in many countries, were addressed with a growing sense of urgency by the ILO.[146] In virtually all sectors, the regulatory challenges associated with the precariousness of temporary migrant labour operate at every level from recruitment, often as part of complex global labour supply chains, through to the exercise of rights, including freedom of association and collective bargaining rights, and their enforcement.[147] Philip Martin's chapter in this collection provides a means to address the regulatory issues arising in the recruitment stage by minimising the costs borne by workers themselves. His chapter draws upon the situation of migrant workers from Korea, Kuwait and Spain and he proposes a cooperative framework between governments from sending and receiving countries. In Martin's view, 'worker-paid migration or recruitment costs are the new frontier in

[143] On the problems of regulating supply chains see Mark Anner, Jennifer Blair and Jeremy Blasi, 'Towards Joint Liability in Global Supply Chains: Addressing the Root Causes of Labor Violations in International Subcontracting Networks' (2013) 35 *Comparative Labor Law and Policy Journal* 1; Gordon, *Global Labour Recruitment* (n 87). On the problems of identifying the employer see Jeremias Prassl, *The Concept of the Employer* (Oxford, Oxford University Press, 2015).

[144] See eg Joanne Conaghan and Kerry Rittich (eds), *Labour Law, Work and Family* (Oxford, Oxford University Press, 2005).

[145] See eg Nicola Kountouris, 'The Legal Determinants of Precarious Work in Personal Work Relations: A European Perspective' (2012) 34 *Comparative Labor Law and Policy Journal* 21, identifying immigrant status as a key determinant of precariousness.

[146] See ILO Convention Concerning Decent Work for Domestic Workers (No 189) adopted 2011. See also Adelle Blackett, 'The Decent Work for Domestic Workers Convention and Recommendation, 2011' (2012) 106(4) *American Journal of International Law* 778.

[147] On the regulation of global supply chains and temporary migrant labour, see Gordon, *Global Labour Recruitment* (n 87); and on efforts to gain meaningful access to collective bargaining rights, see Leah F Vosko, 'Tenuously Unionised: Temporary Migrant Workers and the Limits of Formal Mechanisms Designed to Promote Collective Bargaining in British Columbia' (2014) 43 *Industrial Law Journal* 451; Leah F Vosko, 'National Sovereignty and Transnational Labour: The Case of Mexican Seasonal Agricultural Workers in British Columbia, Canada' (2013) 44 *Industrial Relations Journal* 514.

making the international labour migration system more efficient and protective of migrant workers'.[148]

Philip Martin's elucidation goes beyond labour law in finding a solution to the challenge of workers' costs in the temporary labour migration phenomenon, exemplifying how in this context the global deregulatory agenda has challenged the capacity of labour law to fulfil its 'traditional' purposes and in the process also redefined or re-ordered them.[149] Certainly in recent times the protective and redistributive roles of labour law have been augmented even more sharply by goals avowedly aimed at enhancing the capacity of labour markets to meet the demands for flexibility and productivity from the global marketplace. Modifications and adaptations of both have witnessed an emphasis, for instance, on concepts such as the development of human capabilities, maximising the opportunities to develop 'human capital' and ensuring its deployment in ways that not only fulfil individual goals but at the same time enhance the general social welfare.[150] Still others have focused on the role of labour law in correcting market failures.[151] In addition, the idea that, conceptually, labour law can be treated as an autonomous field of study is being simultaneously defended and also steadily dismantled in recognition of the increasing significance of the intersections with other areas of law and their transformative possibilities.[152]

An examination of the regulatory challenges invites not only a consideration of the complex array of purposes driving the formulation of law and policy in the global era, but also an examination of its nature and operation. Of all the disciplines, law, based as it is on assumptions related to the existence, structure and power of the nation-state, has stood to be most profoundly disrupted by globalisation.[153] Despite this and for all their inadequacies the legal systems of nation-states have also proved remarkably resilient in the face of globalisation, perhaps nowhere more so than in the area of migration. Nonetheless, as the distribution of economic and

[148] Martin, 'Reducing Worker-Paid Migration Costs', ch 17 in this volume.

[149] For a discussion of the multiple purposes of labour law and their ordering, see the essays in Davidov and Langille (eds), *Boundaries and Frontiers of Labour Law* (n 59). See also Fudge and Owens (eds), *Precarious Work* (n 24); Davidov and Langille (eds), *The Idea of Labour Law* (n 52).

[150] See, eg Amartya Sen, *Development as Freedom* (New York, Anchor, 1999); Amartya Sen, *Rationality and Freedom* (Cambridge, MA, Belknap Press, 2002). See also Brian Langille, 'Labour Law's Back Pages' in Davidov and Langille (eds), *Boundaries and Frontiers of Labour Law*.

[151] See Alan Hyde, 'What is Labour Law?' in Davidov and Langille (eds), *Boundaries and Frontiers of Labour Law* (n 59).

[152] See various contributors to Bogg et al (eds), *The Autonomy of Labour Law* (n 138), especially Jeremy Prassl and Cathryn Costello.

[153] See Rosemary Owens, 'The Future of the Law of Work: A Review Essay of Labour Law in the Era of Globalization: Transformative Practices and Possibilities' (2002) 23 *Adelaide Law Review* 245, 247; William Twinning, *Globalization and Legal Theory* (Cambridge, Cambridge University Press, 2000).

political power has been reconfigured, contest over the optimal level of regulation and its institutional locus (international, regional, nation-state, industry, trade union, non-government organisation, firm or enterprise, or individual), as well as its nature and mechanisms (whether public or private, imposed or voluntary, and hence its democratic legitimacy) has become more intense.[154]

Under the pressures and effects of globalisation, the structure of the regulatory landscape has thus been transformed.[155] Importantly, it continues to change and develop. This is so, not only within national legal and regulatory systems, but also at the global level. As the dynamics of political debates about the impacts of globalisation have changed and developed, so too have the arguments about the legitimacy and role of regulation in the new global order. However, even if it is generally conceded that the 'golden age of de-regulatory capture'[156] has begun to wane, neither the perimeter and topography of the 'new regulatory plateau' supported by international institutions such as the World Bank are yet to be clearly defined, nor their regulatory interactions with other international agencies such as the ILO clearly delineated.[157]

Scholars have devoted much time and attention to addressing the promise of regulatory theory in the global era, in spite of the many pitfalls that remain apparent. With the benefit of hindsight, it is obvious that early ideas on 'responsive regulation' in the global context were always overoptimistic. 'Responsive regulation', it was said, only required the state to intervene when the private players, who would exercise primary regulatory responsibility, failed to act effectively, thus assuming a strong sharing, if not identity, of interests and goals amongst the state, and the various players and stakeholders.[158] The development of various private transnational labour regulatory mechanisms aimed at supplementing the deficits of traditional public regulation (whether at the international level, in the home countries of multinational corporations or in developing countries) through 'self-regulation' remains under active scholarly consideration.[159]

[154] See, eg Brian Bercusson and Cynthia Estlund, *Regulating Labour in the Wake of Globalisation: New Challenges, New Institutions* (Oxford, Hart, 2008).

[155] For an overview of the changes at the global level See Owens et al, *The Law of Work* (n 131) 46–92.

[156] Langille, 'Imaging Post "Geneva Consensus" Labour Law' (n 125) 523. An important element in escaping from 'deregulatory capture' has been the evidence that regulating labour standards might in fact improve economic outcomes. See, eg Deakin, 'The Evidence-Based Case for Labour Regulation' (n 131).

[157] See Deidre McCann, 'Labour Law on the Plateau: Towards Regulatory Policy for Endogenous Norms' in Bogg et al (eds), *The Autonomy of Labour Law* (n 138).

[158] See Ian Ayres and John Braithwaite, *Responsive Regulation: Transcending the Deregulation Debate* (Oxford, Oxford University Press, 1995). See also John Braithwaite and Peter Drahos, *Global Business Regulation* (Cambridge, Cambridge University Press, 2000).

[159] See, eg, Ralf Rogowski, *Reflexive Labour Law in the World Society* (Cheltenham, UK, Edward Elgar, 2013); Kevin Kolben, 'Transnational Labour Regulation and the Limits of

Regulatory theory recognises the importance of the contributions made by a wide range of systematic attempts by both private and public actors to influence behaviour for certain goals and outcomes.[160] While it is well recognised that legal regulation plays an important role in the construction, constitution and maintenance of labour markets generally,[161] to date the insights of regulatory theory have not been applied in a systematic way to temporary labour migration. Regulatory theory also invites a greater emphasis on exploring the wide range of regulatory instruments or mechanisms that can be used to respond to work arrangements in the global era.

Three chapters in this collection explore the regulatory possibilities in responding to the precarious position of temporary migrant workers and the difficulty these workers face in accessing legal remedies. Two chapters explore the role of unions and other non-government actors in regulating the supply chain and improving the wages, working conditions and job security of temporary migrant workers. In her chapter in this collection, Jennifer Gordon draws upon the benefits accruing from union organisation of Mexican farm workers employed by US growers to illustrate how job security and improved wages and conditions can be achieved.[162] This system permits migrant workers to voice violations of their rights during the season without fear of recrimination, dismissal or not being hired the following year. In his chapter, James Brudney explores other regulatory responses to assess the precarious work status of temporary migrants.[163] Brudney refers to the success of the Coalition of Immokalee Workers (CIW) in developing bilateral agreements with major brands in the corporate food industry, a worker-driven code of conduct reinforced by effective complaint resolution and a comprehensive auditing structure which is enforced through market consequences. In terms of the latter, growers must comply with the code and pass the auditing process or they lose their ability to sell their tomatoes to buyers who have signed bilateral agreements with the CIW. What is striking about both Brudney's and Gordon's chapters is the use of a joint stakeholder method to develop a mutually agreed regulatory framework, albeit a highly resource-intensive one, to address the challenges presented by employer reliance on temporary migrant workers.

Governance' (2011) 12 *Theoretical Inquiries in Law* 403; Kevin Kolben, 'Dialogic Labor Regulation in the Global Supply Chain' (2015) 36(3) *Michigan Journal of International Law* 425.

[160] See, eg, Julia Black, 'Decentring Regulation: Understanding the Role of Regulation and Self-Regulation in a Post-regulatory World' (2001) 54 *Current Legal Problems* 103.

[161] See Arup et al (eds), *Labour Law and Labour Market Regulation* (n 136).

[162] Jennifer Gordon, 'Roles for Workers and Unions in Regulating Labour Recruitment in Mexico', ch 15 in this volume.

[163] James Brudney, 'Decent Labour Standard in Corporate Supply Chains: The Immokalee Workers Model', ch 16 in this volume.

Beyond industry or site-specific solutions, Rosemary Owens' chapter examines the possibilities and challenges arising from the use of labour inspectorates to enforce migrant workers' rights.[164] Her chapter critically examines the use of Australia's Fair Work Ombudsman (FWO) to ensure temporary migrant workers are employed in compliance with Australia's labour laws. Australia's use of a labour inspectorate is distinctive when compared with some of the other regulatory approaches in this collection where governments have preferred to use the criminal law or migration law to address issues of worker exploitation. Although Owens identifies the enforcement challenges of the FWO's work, in particular resourcing, Australia's geography, information-gathering capabilities and the difficulties involved in using different enforcement mechanisms such as litigation or enforceable undertakings, her chapter develops the possibilities of this regulatory approach which chooses to focus on varying degrees of exploitation, rather than just the most extreme cases where a trafficking situation or similar is involved.

At the global level, there have been calls for greater development of regulatory frameworks to achieve more effective international governance of both the usual types of temporary worker programmes, as well as the growing demand for trade in services. Livi-Bacci observes that, whilst there is a powerful international body (the WTO) to promote and regulate the liberalisation of trade in commerce, no such organisation exists to manage migration.[165] The creation of a Global Commission on Migration and Development by UN Secretary General Kofi Annan in 2003 has not made significant inroads into creating a regulatory framework. Its proposal of an International Global Migration Facility to co-ordinate and integrate policy planning in this area has not been realised in the ensuing decade.[166] Nor has any progress been made on the more ambitious goal identified by the Commission in 2006: 'to bring together the disparate migration-related functions of existing UN and other agencies within a single organisation and to respond to the new and complex realities of international migration'.[167] Similarly, at the scholarly level, there is debate as to how international governance of migration would best be achieved, with Jagdish Bhagwati's proposal for a World Migration Organization contested by others such as Philip Martin and Susan Martin, who identify the drawbacks of a top-down

[164] Rosemary Owens, 'Temporary Labour Migration and Workplace Rights in Australia: Is Effective Enforcement Possible?', ch 18 in this volume.

[165] Livi-Bacci, *A Short History of Migration* (n 4) 121.

[166] Global Commission on International Migration, *Migration in an Interconnected World* 77.

[167] Ibid 75.

approach to regulation of international migration.[168] The latter distinguish between the liberalisation of trade in goods, which is said to benefit all countries, and the liberalisation of trade in services where there is disagreement as to whether this inexorably and inevitably produces greater national and global economic growth for both sending and receiving countries.[169] As we noted above, while the ILO has assumed a significant role in setting an agenda for achieving decent work for migrant workers, it acknowledges that much remains to be done.

In summary, temporary labour migration in the global era continues to present a wide range of regulatory challenges at the international, regional and national levels as well as for other players such as global business, trade unions and non-government organisations. This collection of essays is offered, as we stated at the outset, as a contribution to the further development of the conversation about these issues, especially in thinking about whether temporary labour migration can be ethically, equitably and efficaciously achieved and so deliver decent work to workers.

[168] Jagdish Bhagwati, 'Borders Beyond Control' (2003) 82(1) *Foreign Affairs* 104; Philip Martin and Susan Martin, 'Global Commission on International Migration: A New Global Migration Facility' (2006) 44(1) *International Migration* 5, 11. See also Kathleen Newland, *The Governance of International Migration: Mechanisms, Processes and Institutions* (Geneva, Global Commission on International Migration, 2005) 11, 17.

[169] Martin and Martin, 'Global Commission on International Migration', ibid.

Part II

Global Economic Integration and the Regulation of Temporary Labour Migration

2

Seasonal Workers and Intra-corporate Transferees in EU Law

Capital's Handmaidens?

CATHRYN COSTELLO AND MARK FREEDLAND*

I. INTRODUCTION

THIS CHAPTER COMPARES and contrasts two recent European enactments on particular forms of temporary labour migration: seasonal work and intra-corporate transfers. Both the Seasonal Workers Directive (SWD)[1] and the ICT Directive (ICTD)[2] were adopted in 2014. They are typical of the EU's piecemeal approach to labour migration, which creates a multiplicity of distinct statuses.[3] We frame the comparison in light of our previous work examining the impact of migration law on labour law (section II). By way of general contribution to this collection's themes,

* We thank Emily Hancox and Minos Mouzourakis for most helpful research and editorial assistance.

[1] Directive 2014/36/EU of the European Parliament and of the Council of 26 February 2014 on the conditions of entry and stay of third-country nationals for the purpose of employment as seasonal workers (SWD) [2014] OJ L94/375.

[2] Directive 2014/66/EU of the European Parliament and of the Council of 15 May 2014 on the conditions of entry and residence of third-country nationals in the framework of an intra-corporate transfer (ICTD) [2014] OJ L157/1. See also Sebastian Klaus, 'Die ICT-Richtlinie: Ende einer europäischen Odyssee' (2015) *ZAR* 1.

[3] These are not the only two statuses created by EU law. For an incisive comparative overview, see Petra Herzfeld Olsson, 'The Development of an EU Policy on Workers from Third Countries: Adding New Categories to the EU Labour Market, Provided with New Combinations of Rights' in Stein Evju (ed), *Regulating Transnational Labour in Europe: The Quandaries for Multi-Level Governance* (Oslo, University of Oslo Institutt for Privatrett, 2014). See generally Cathryn Costello, 'EU Migration and Asylum Law: A Labour Law Perspective' in Alan Bogg, Cathryn Costello, Anne Davies (eds), *Edward Elgar Research Handbook on EU Labour Law* (forthcoming).

we also offer some observations on the challenges of regulating temporary labour migration under current conditions of globalisation (section III), and seek to explain some of the specificities of the EU's role in regulating immigration (section IV).

Then turning in section V to the contrast between the two directives, we aim to compare them in terms of the personal and relational dimensions of the work relations established, and in their temporal and transnational aspects. Both seasonal workers and intra-corporate transferees (ICTs) could be regarded as having a migration status that makes them vulnerable in their work relations. In addition, this vulnerability means they may accept terms and conditions that undercut domestic labour standards. Yet the two directives take starkly divergent approaches to labour rights.

Our analysis reveals striking disparities between the two directives. Most notably, the Seasonal Workers Directive contains some significant labour rights protections for seasonal workers (as Fudge and Herzfeld Olsson have demonstrated).[4] In contrast, ICTs' protections are pegged at those of local workers for remuneration, but otherwise ICTs are assimilated to the position of posted workers. We suggest that these disparities may be understood in light of the different ways in which these two kinds of workers are regarded, valued and treated by the globalised capital corporations or other institutions by which they are immediately or ultimately employed.

II. MIGRATION LAW AND LABOUR LAW

Migration law has important impacts on labour law. It creates migration *status* that in turn determines, at least in part, labour rights.[5] Migration status conveys the manner in which migration law creates personal status within the host state.[6] The move to re-introduce status over contract as a determinant of workers' rights divides the subjects of labour law, as we have observed elsewhere.[7] Labour standards may be expressly included in the very measures that regulate immigration. The SWD and ICTD are striking recent examples of this more general phenomenon.

[4] Judy Fudge and Petra Herzfeld Olsson, 'The EU Seasonal Workers Directive: When Immigration Controls Meet Labour Rights' (2014) 16(4) *European Journal of Migration and Law* 439.

[5] Bridget Anderson, 'Migration, Immigration Controls and the Fashioning of Precarious Workers' (2010) 24(2) *Work, Employment & Society* 300.

[6] For an early appreciation of this phenomenon, see Otto Kahn-Freund, 'A Note on Status and Contract in British Labour Law' (1967) 30(6) *Modern Law Review* 635.

[7] Mark Freedland and Cathryn Costello, 'Migrants at Work and the Division of Labour Law' in Cathryn Costello and Mark Freedland (eds), *Migrants at Work: Immigration and Vulnerability in Labour Law* (Oxford, Oxford University Press, 2014).

Migration law also affects the supply and demand for migrant workers. In that respect, creating an EU status for particular migrant workers is no guarantee that more workers will be granted this status. National authorities have the final say (in principle) about whether to issue such permits. Nonetheless, in the broad sense, migration law is a form of labour market *regulation*.[8] Thirdly, and relatedly, both the fact of immigration and the features of migration law have an impact on labour standards in both collective and individual labour law.

In our earlier work, in response to the question 'What does labour migration do to labour law?', we posited the following tentative replies:

1. It may affect the supply of workers.
2. It may increase segmentation of the workforce.
3. It may increase demand for migrant workers.
4. It may increase the role of intermediaries in the labour supply chain.

Much, of course, will depend on the context, and, in particular, on the migration laws in question. When we pose the question 'What does migration law do to labour law?' we arrive at several responses. What unites them is the likelihood that migration law creates vulnerability in labour relations. This is not to make any generalisations about migrants themselves, but rather to identify how migration law, as currently designed, tends to alter the work relation. In particular, we note that:

1. It increases the control of employers over the supply of labour, especially by according to them control over migration status.
2. By creating 'migration status', it introduces a personal (in the sense of status-based) rather than relation-based set of categories into labour law.
3. It may thereby also increase employers' control over local workers.
4. It increases the duties of employers to the state, in turn altering work environments by reason of requirements on employers to monitor migration status.
5. By establishing distinctions based on this migration status, it sets up tensions with non-discrimination law.
6. It may challenge collective worker-protective institutions, increasing tensions between workers, undermining solidarity and solidaristic institutions, including but not confined to trade unions.
7. It increases the temporariness and precariousness of work relations, and workers' dependency on employers.

[8] This is the central insight of Harald Bauder, *Labor Movement: How Migration Regulates Labour Markets* (Oxford, Oxford University Press, 2006).

8. It tends to force workers into particular statuses, such as that of self-employment, by placing lesser restrictions on labour migration into those statuses.
9. It imports into the conduct and regulation of employment relations its own set of offences and sanctions and its own notions of 'illegality'.
10. Depending on how they are regulated, it increases the role of intermediaries in the labour supply chain, and increases triangular labour relations.

When we look at the regulation of seasonal work in particular, we find many extreme forms of these phenomena, in particular, creating tied statuses that confine workers in the lower strata of the labour market. At first glance, ICTs may seem poles apart from seasonal workers. At one pole, we have the impoverished seasonal worker picking berries in the fields and forests (conjuring up images of extreme labour exploitation);[9] at the other, the elite management consultant or IT professional, moving within the corporate entity, from global city to global city.[10] However, we suggest that these statuses, in particular as defined in the new directives, are not so easily confined to the stereotypical case. In law, the directives do not confine the status to particular sectors, although of course migrants falling under these directives may be clustered in particular economic fields in practice.

Instead, we suggest it may be fruitful at least to begin the discussion with a legal analysis that examines the two statuses across these four dimensions: personal, relational, temporal and transnational. Concerning the first and second dimensions, these migration statuses are designed for workers who have particular roles within employing organisations, so a particular personal status and work relation; thirdly, the temporal dimension of their work relationships is defined by high degrees of employer control, as well as conditions defined by their migration status (defined by both EU and domestic rules and authorisations); fourthly, the inevitable transnational dimension of their migration profile is complex, characterised not by a singular migratory move, but multiple transnational comings and goings over time, which are also limited not only by the workers' choices, but also by migration law, employers and intermediaries.

As its title suggests, this chapter is also informed by the assumption that understanding these forms of status requires sustained attention to the role of the employing organisation. By exploring these, admittedly very different,

[9] Charles Woolfson, Petra Herzfeld Olsson and Christer Thörnqvist, 'Forced Labour and Migrant Berry Pickers in Sweden' (2012) 28 *International Journal of Comparative Labour Law and Industrial Relations* 147.

[10] Jonathan V Beaverstock, 'Transnational Elites in the City: British Highly-Skilled Inter-Company Transferees in New York City's Financial District' (2005) 31(2) *Journal of Ethnic and Migration Studies* 245.

types of temporary migration side by side we hope to shed some light on the relations between labour and capital under conditions of contemporary globalisation. Migration statuses are designed all too often to benefit employers, not workers (migrant or local). Moreover, restrictive features that are sometimes portrayed as aiming to protect local workers from competition by migrant workers are often more about constructing statuses to benefit employers.

III. TEMPORARY LABOUR MIGRATION IN A GLOBAL CONTEXT

Moving money and 'investment' across borders is relatively easy these days, perhaps selling goods and services less so, but the movement of human beings as autonomous agents is subject to increasing controls. This asymmetry is the hallmark of contemporary globalisation. Earlier eras of globalisation were characterised by relatively free movement of persons.[11] And of course, European settler colonialism gave Europeans their choice of many countries of destination, some conveniently deemed by legal fiction to be devoid of inhabitants.

While trade in goods and services is subject to a multilateral regime, only peripheral aspects of movement of persons are covered by the General Agreement on Trade in Services (GATS). Otherwise, the movement of persons is subject to no multilateral regime. Bilateral labour agreements between sending and receiving states proliferate,[12] but the differences between the multilateral regime for goods and services and the more limited regime for migration have become evident particularly following the global financial crisis of 2008.[13] While the international regime for trade has been relatively

[11] See, eg Kevin O'Rourke 'The Era of Free Movement: Lessons for Today', paper presented at Globalization, the State and Society Conference, St Louis, MO, 13–14 November 2003.

[12] See Alexander Betts and Lucie Cerna, 'High-Skilled Labour Migration' in Alexander Betts (ed), *Global Migration Governance* (Oxford, Oxford University Press, 2011) 64: 'In 2004, for example, it was estimated that there were around 176 bilateral agreements relating to labour recruitment (OECD 2004). Hatton (2007: 372) argues that the number of bilateral agreements in this area has increased significantly over time, in many cases being tailored to meet the needs of specific economic sectors in the receiving countries', citing Organisation for Economic Co-operation and Development, *Migration for Employment: Bilateral Agreements at a Crossroads* (Paris, OECD, 2004) Annex 1A; Timothy Hatton, 'Should We Have a WTO for International Migration?' (2007) 22(50) *Economic Policy* 339. See also Ryszard Cholewinski, 'Evaluating Bilateral Labour Migration Agreements in the Light of Human and Labour Rights' in Marion Panizzon, Gottfried Zürcher and Elisa Fornalé (eds), *The Palgrave Handbook of International Labour Migration: Law and Policy* (Houndmills, UK, Palgrave Macmillan, 2015).

[13] See Lucie Cerna, James Hollifeld and William Hynes, 'Trade, Migration and the Crisis of Globalization' in Panizzon et al (eds), *The Palgrave Handbook of International Labour Migration.*

successful in curbing protectionist moves, the lack of such a regime for migration has meant an increase in restrictive labour migration policies.[14] Temporary labour migration has been most affected by closure of labour markets, although high-skilled immigration has not been reduced in some countries (eg Canada and New Zealand) where it is seen as a stimulus for economic growth.[15]

If we think of globalisation as intensification of transnational activity, the hallmark of our era is that capital is highly mobile, not only financial capital, but also foreign direct investment (FDI). FDI often includes the movement of employing organisations, under a process whereby capital often protects itself in host countries through bilateral investment treaties. Given significant asymmetries between poorer countries seeking to attract FDI, and richer countries which are the bases for most global capital, a network of bilateral investment treaties (BITs) have been signed, which confer significant institutional protections on global capital. These include investor–state dispute settlement (ISDS), which gives investors the right to trigger private one-shot arbitration to challenge the practices and laws of the host state.[16] The new generation of trade and investment treaties demonstrate that capital qua 'investment' has developed a further set of institutional protections. These new agreements include the Comprehensive Economic and Trade Agreement (CETA) between the EU and Canada, the Trans-Pacific Partnership (TPP), and one still under negotiation, the Transatlantic Trade and Investment Partnership (TTIP) between the EU and US.[17] Their controversial features include, firstly, their focus on regulatory barriers to trade, meaning that they open up domestic (and EU) laws and practices to scrutiny for their impact on trade and investment. Secondly, they embody an effective merger of trade and investment law.[18] Thirdly and relatedly, these agreements aim to include protections for investors more commonly found in BITs.[19] As Cremona explains, 'The EU Member States

[14] Ibid.

[15] Ibid.

[16] José Alvarez, 'Contemporary Foreign Investment Law: An "Empire of Law" or the "Law of Empire"?' (2009) 60(4) *Alabama Law Review* 943; Marc Jacob, 'Investments, Bilateral Treaties' in Rüdiger Wolfrum (ed), *Max Planck Encyclopedia of Public International Law* (Oxford, Oxford University Press, 2014) 1061; Beth Simmons, 'Bargaining over BITs, Arbitrating Awards: The Regime for Protection and Promotion of International Investment' (2014) 66 *World Politics* 12.

[17] The Trans-Pacific Partnership (TPP) was negotiated by twelve countries: the United States, Australia, Brunei, Canada, Chile, Japan, Malaysia, Mexico, New Zealand, Peru, Singapore and Vietnam.

[18] See Sergio Puig, 'The Merging of International Trade and Investment Law' (2015) 33(1) *Berkeley Journal of International Law* 1.

[19] Markus Krajewski, 'Modalities for Investment Protection and Investor–State Dispute Settlement (ISDS) in TTIP from a Trade Union Perspective' (2014), http://ssrn.com/abstract=2519995.

have concluded over 1400 BITs and the CETA and TTIP are intended as early steps in developing an EU *acquis* in this field which would ultimately replace many of these bilateral agreements'.[20] As she notes, if the EU's aim is to promote good regulation (by encouraging deliberation on regulatory standards which have the potential to distort trade) 'then a strategy which places regulation on the defensive, and a debate couched in terms of whether there are sufficient safeguards protecting the right to regulate, is an essentially reactive stance'.[21]

These agreements do not significantly advance the agenda for more liberalised labour mobility, but rather reflect a strongly pro-trade and investor stance, which leaves workers out of the equation. To put it crudely, TTIP and similar instruments aim to protect the capacity for profit, and provide mechanisms where capital can challenge domestic laws that impact on future profits.

We suggest, tentatively, that some (albeit not all) forms of migration status serve a similar capital-led function. Suffice to state at the outset that different migrant statuses often accrue due to the transnational nature of the employing organisations' activities. Very crudely, some statuses permit workers to be moved as adjuncts to transnational service provision (as posted workers) and investment (as ICTs), and also ensure that those workers' status is kept apart from the regulatory structures of the host state. The divisive impact on the host state's labour market is key. While the worker is merely temporarily present in the host state, the practice of using temporary migrant workers is not.

Moreover, in the context of ICTs, the employing organisation has already established its transnational network, and moves its workers around it. The workers' passport is not merely that of a state, but of 'Global Inc'. Yet they may be worker-citizens of no particular country, in that their labour rights may be determined according to corporate policy, not real connection to or participation in any particular workplace or country. While posting of workers is parasitic on the employers' *temporary* service provision, ICT status depends on the employing organisation's transnational corporate reach, which may include permanent infrastructure, or may be much more ephemeral and rooted in corporate law fictions. (As will be seen, the ICTD has quite weak provisions to try to ensure the 'host entity' has genuine activity within the EU Member State.)

A further important caveat should inform our assessment of the regulation of temporary migration. Seeking to keep migration temporary by using migration law seems a regulatory strategy with a high risk of failure. Laws

20 Marise Cremona, 'Guest Editorial: Negotiating the Transatlantic Trade and Investment Partnership (TTIP)' (2015) 52(2) *Common Market Law Review* 351, 356.

21 Ibid 359.

regulating migration can have perverse effects. Empirical research has identified various substitution effects whereby migration laws lead to migrants switching categories in response to legal changes.[22] One of the strongest unanticipated effects is that regulation that seeks to keep migration temporary may contribute to its permanence. This effect arises as becoming irregular after a period of time does not always induce return, but also encourages permanent settlement in the host country, as return becomes more costly. Institutionalising temporary migration status can end up ruling out the option of coming and going to see how things work out 'back home', and makes migration permanent. This factor is a reminder that the promised 'triple win' offered by temporary labour migration programmes may lead instead to permanent undocumented migration, and a permanent population of exploitable undocumented migrants.

IV. UNDERSTANDING EU MIGRATION LAW: LIMITS AND POTENTIAL

The EU initially did not regulate migration from outside the EU into the Member States. However, the creation of a common market was one of its foundational aspects, with labour mobility as a basic feature thereof, ensuring rights of entry and residence not only for workers from other Member States holding the nationality of those states (later refashioned as EU citizens), but also for jobseekers and those engaging in any form of economic activity. Since the Treaty of Amsterdam, the EU has competence to adopt laws on migration and asylum from outside the EU, and to govern the status of so-called 'third country nationals' (or TCNs) in the EU.

The EU has now fairly comprehensively regulated asylum law, and claims that there is a 'Common European Asylum Policy'. Even in that context, though, the determination of who is a refugee and who should face deportation remains with national authorities, albeit that they now apply EU standards (and international refugee law) in so doing. Moreover, recognised refugees have a national status: they do not have intra-EU mobility rights, unlike EU citizens. In contrast, when it comes to labour migration, the EU's competence is limited in that, although it may adopt common rules, the determination of the volumes of admissions remains with the

[22] The notion of policy effectiveness is a complex one. See Mathias Czaika and Hein De Haas, 'The Effectiveness of Immigration Policies' (2013) 39(3) *Population and Development Review* 487. The various substitution effects identified by the DEMIG study carried out at the International Migration Institute at Oxford are: categorical substitution (category jumping); inter-temporal substitutions (now or never migration); spatial substitution; and reverse flow substitution. See: http://www.imi.ox.ac.uk/projects/demig.

Member States.[23] Furthermore, the principle of 'union preference' is affirmed in the legal instruments, that is, that EU citizens should have preferential access to the EU labour market.[24]

In terms of its frame of reference, the animating force of EU labour migration policy has been labour market efficiency *and* combatting 'illegal immigration', which is viewed as an exogenous phenomenon (rather than the creation of immigration laws). The ICTD speaks the language of economic efficiency—'better matching of labour supply with demand' (recital 3)—and the SWD claims 'admissions procedures capable of responding promptly to fluctuating demands for migrant labour in the labour market' (recital 3). Both measures refer to the demographic challenge facing Europe, due to its ageing population (SWD, recital 6). The SWD also emphasises the need to 'prevent overstaying' and the duties of employers under the Employer Sanctions Directive (SWD, recital 7).

Attempts to legislate for a general EU labour admissions policy and migration status valid across the EU have failed. In 2001, the Commission put forward the idea of a common framework for admitting economic migrants from third countries.[25] The proposal aimed to rationalise the conditions and procedures for entry and residence of employed and self-employed TCNs. The proposal gained support from the European Parliament, but it failed to do so in the Council.[26] Eventually, the Commission abandoned its proposal and reopened discussions with a series of communications,[27] a Green Paper on economic migration[28] and a policy plan.[29]

The only general measure on labour migration is the Single Permit Directive.[30] Its abbreviated title (Single Permit) perhaps understates its

[23] Treaty on the Functioning of the European Union art 79(5). See also ICTD art 6; SWD art 7.

[24] SWD recital 9; ICTD recital 8.

[25] European Commission, 'Proposal for a Council Directive on the Conditions of Entry and Residence of Third-Country Nationals for the Purpose of Paid Employment and Self-Employed Economic Activities' COM(2001) 386 final.

[26] Council of the European Union, 'Proposal for a Council Directive on the Conditions of Entry and Residence of Third-Country Nationals for the Purpose of Paid Employment and Self-Employed Economic Activities' ST 9862 2002 INIT.

[27] European Commission, 'Communication from the Commission to the Council, the European Parliament, the European Economic and Social Committee and the Committee of the Regions on Immigration, Integration and Employment' COM(2003) 0336 final; European Commission, 'Communication from the Commission to the Council, the European Parliament, the European Economic and Social Committee and the Committee of the Regions—A Common Agenda for Integration—Framework for the Integration of Third-Country Nationals in the European Union' COM(2005) 0389 final.

[28] European Commission, 'Green Paper on an EU Approach to Managing Economic Migration' COM(2004) 0811 final.

[29] European Commission, 'Communication from the Commission—Policy Plan on Legal Migration' COM(2005) 0669 final.

[30] Directive 2011/98/EU of the European Parliament and of the Council on 13 December 2011 on a single application procedure for a single permit for third country nationals to reside

content, as it aims to establish a single procedure, work and residence permit combined, and a common set of rights. Nonetheless, given that Member States were reluctant to commit to any form of general regulation for labour migration, it is unsurprising that the Single Permit Directive emerged as a rather limited instrument.[31] Some commentators have suggested that its equal treatment guarantee is an 'empty shell'.[32] However, whether that is so really remains up to the Court of Justice of the European Union. If traditional EU anti-discrimination precepts are brought to bear, it may have significant impact in time. In addition, as discussed further below, an expansive reading of the equal treatment guarantee may be bolstered by article 15(3) of the EU Charter of Fundamental Rights, which states that 'Nationals of third countries who are authorised to work in the territories of the Member States are entitled to working conditions equivalent to those of citizens of the Union'.

The Single Permit Directive apart, the dominant EU approach to labour migration has been piecemeal, with EU law providing a number of narrow purposive statuses, for students,[33] researchers,[34] 'highly skilled' workers under the Blue Card Directive,[35] and latterly the aforementioned seasonal workers and intra-corporate transferees. These sectoral directives have in common that they do not create a right to first entry to the EU for TCNs, but rather set out conditions under which Member States ought to afford this particular right of residence. Once that status is granted, a set of EU

and work in the territory of a Member State and on a common set of rights for third country workers legally residing in a Member State [2011] OJ L343/1.

[31] Sheena McLoughlin and Yves Pascouau, *EU Single Permit Directive: A Small Step Forward in EU Migration Policy*, EPC Policy Brief (Brussels, European Policy Centre, 2012).

[32] Ana Beduschi, 'An Empty Shell? The Protection of Social Rights of Third-Country Workers in the EU after the Single Permit Directive' (2015) 17 *European Journal of Migration and Law* 210.

[33] Council Directive 2004/114/EC of 13 December 2004 on the conditions of admission of third-country nationals for the purposes of studies, pupil exchange, unremunerated training or voluntary service (Students Directive) [2004] OJ L375/12. Note that a recast version of this directive is currently under negotiation between the Council and Parliament: European Commission, 'Proposal for a Directive of the European Parliament and of the Council on the Conditions of Entry and Residence of Third-Country Nationals for the Purposes of Research, Studies, Pupil Exchange, Remunerated and Unremunerated Training, Voluntary Service and Au Pairing (Recast)', COM(2013) 151.

[34] Council Directive 2005/71/EC of 12 October 2005 on a specific procedure for admitting third-country nationals for the purposes of scientific research (Researchers Directive) [2005] OJ L289/15. Note that a recast version of this directive is currently under negotiation between Council and Parliament. See note 33.

[35] Council Directive 2009/50 on the conditions of entry and residence of third-country nationals for the purposes of highly qualified employment (Blue Card Directive) [2009] OJ L155/17. See also Katharina Eisele, *Why Come Here if I Can go There? Assessing the 'Attractiveness' of the EU's Blue Card Directive for 'Highly Qualified' Immigrants*, Liberty and Security in Europe Paper No. 60 (Brussels, Centre for European Policy Studies, 2013).

rights follow. This approach is not self-evident. Indeed, the European Trade Union Confederation has questioned the need for the two directives under examination, suggesting that ICTs should be covered (if at all) under the EU Blue Card Directive, and that seasonal workers should be covered under the Single Permit Regime.[36] Its hostility to the proliferation of statuses is to ensure equality between local and migrant workers, in particular respect for the principle *lex loci laboris*, whereby the law of the place where work is undertaken should apply to that activity. Evidently, the EU's internal posted workers regime undermines that principle.

The Blue Card Directive on 'highly skilled' immigration lays down the conditions of entry and residence for third-country nationals (and their family members) who will be present in the territory of a Member State for more than three months for the purpose of engaging in highly qualified employment.[37] The directive creates a fast-track procedure for issuing the special residence and work permit to 'highly qualified' third-country workers who have been offered a job in the EU. Again, Member States retain control over the issuing of Blue Cards, and can also introduce their own schemes offering better conditions than the Blue Card.[38]

The two directives that are the focus of this chapter were both adopted under the EU's ordinary legislative procedure, involving the European Parliament (EP) as co-decision maker.[39] While the new increased role of the EP has been used to explain differences between previous and more recent enactments on migration, the active role of the EP is a shared feature of both directives under scrutiny here and cannot explain the differences between the seasonal workers and ICT directives.

Even if EU law creates a migration status, that status is not always valid across the EU. EU statuses differ in terms of whether they confer a *transnational* status. An odd feature of EU immigration status is that it often only allows work or residence (at least in the first instance) in one Member State, the fact that the EU is supposed to constitute an 'Area of Freedom, Security and Justice' notwithstanding. 'Mobility' rights across the EU normally only accrue on naturalisation (which confers EU citizenship), or if migrants stay

[36] 'It is not understandable why the question of ICT was not dealt with under the "EU Blue Card" initiative and that the intra-corporate transferees are excluded from the framework Directive': ETUC, 'Agenda item 9: Seasonal work and intra-corporate transfers', EC189/EN/9, ETUC Executive Committee, 13–14 October 2010, 2.

[37] Blue Card Directive art 1.

[38] Blue Card Directive arts 4(2) and 6.

[39] See, eg Christof Roos, 'EU Politics on Labour Migration: Inclusion Versus Admission' (2015) 28 *Cambridge Review of International Affairs* (forthcoming), comparing the Blue Card (2009) and Single Permit (2011); Georg Menz, 'Framing the Matter Differently: The Political Dynamics of European Union Labour Migration Policymaking' (2015) 28(4) *Cambridge Review of International Affairs* 554, comparing the Blue Card and Seasonal Workers directives.

five years and attain EU Long-Term Resident status. However, that status is subject to many conditions, and poorly implemented in practice.[40] The Blue Card Directive provides for analogous rights after a shorter time. Otherwise, mobility rights for migrant TCN workers are not usually envisaged. The EU is a single labour market for Europeans, but not non-EU migrants.[41] Indeed, intra-EU mobility was perhaps the most fraught issue in the four years of negotiations on the ICTD.[42]

A further striking feature is that EU immigration policies do not automatically pre-empt national statuses. If EU law comprehensively regulates a particular status, then Member States' competence to accord that status is limited.[43] However, they may still offer analogous status under their own domestic competence. For instance, many states continue to issue national permits to highly skilled workers, in preference to Blue Cards. The implementation studies reveal quite a complex picture with highly varied implementation.[44] EU law in this field is distinctly unfederal: in federal systems, states' migration control powers tend to be comprehensively pre-empted by federal powers. In contrast, in the EU, there is shared competence over entry and residence for some categories, and Member States retain control over naturalisation. Even where there is a status, it is usually without prejudice to Member States' rights to offer 'more favourable provisions'.[45] The mere existence of the two statuses under discussion here is thus telling. First of all, the fact of reaching agreement at EU level is itself an achievement, after long negotiation. Both measures seek in the first instance to encourage these forms of migration, and only secondly to address questions of labour rights, in the manner that reflects the highly stratified nature of the migration statuses.

[40] Council Directive 2003/109/EC of 25 November 2003 concerning the status of third-country nationals who are long-term residents (Long-Term Residents Directive) [2003] OJ L16/33; European Commission, *Report on the Application of Directive 203/109/EC Concerning the Status of Third-Country Nationals who are Long-Term Residents* (LTRD Implementation Report), COM(2011) 585.

[41] Elspeth Guild, 'The EU's Internal Market and the Fragmentary Nature of EU Labour Migration' in Costello and Freedland (eds), *Migrants at Work* (n 7).

[42] Council of the European Union, 'Proposal for a Directive of the European Parliament and of the Council on Conditions of Entry and Residence of Third-Country Nationals in the Framework of an Intra-Corporate Transfer' (8303/13). See also Alex Lazarowicz, *The Intra-Corporate Transferees Directive: Time to Break the Deadlock*, EPC Policy Brief (Brussels, European Policy Centre, 2013).

[43] Case C-542/13 *M'Bodj* [2015] OJ C65/12.

[44] European Commission, 'Communication from the Commission to the European Parliament and the Council on the Implementation of Directive 2009/50/EC on the Conditions of Entry and Residence of Third-Country Nationals for the Purpose of Highly Qualified Employment' COM(2014) 287 final. See also Lucie Cerna, 'Understanding the Diversity of EU Migration Policy in Practice: The Implementation of the Blue Card Initiative' (2013) 34(2) *Policy Studies* 180.

[45] See, eg ICTD art 4; SWD art 4.

However, EU law may not ultimately allow this stratified approach to labour rights. This is because at least some labour rights are constitutionalised in EU law, and appear in the EU Charter of Fundamental Rights. As well as containing a chapter on 'equality', not only prohibiting discrimination but positively requiring the EU to secure equality, it also contains several provisions on labour rights, including notably:

Article 15: Freedom to choose an occupation and right to engage in work

1. Everyone has the right to engage in work and to pursue a freely chosen or accepted occupation.
2. Every citizen of the Union has the freedom to seek employment, to work, to exercise the right of establishment and to provide services in any Member State.
3. *Nationals of third countries who are authorised to work in the territories of the Member States are entitled to working conditions equivalent to those of citizens of the Union* (emphasis added).

The Charter sets the conditions for legality of EU legislative measures. In other words, if a directive violates the Charter, it is amenable to annulment by the Court of Justice of the EU, or strenuous re-interpretation to avoid that fate.[46] On this basis, EU migration statuses may be open to challenge if they breach article 15(3) of the EU Charter of Fundamental Rights. Moreover, the Charter is applicable to all actions of the Member States 'implementing' EU law. This not only includes direct implementation of the directive, but also acts which cover the same material ground as EU acts, in particular if they would impede the effectiveness of EU law.

To illustrate the potential interactions, recall that many states run seasonal worker programmes for the agricultural sector, often entailing bilateral agreements with particular sending countries. Moving to an EU directive may have unintended legal consequences for these bilateral programmes. While the EU directive will not pre-empt national programmes, it *may* require that they are run in a manner compatible with EU law (if they are treated as falling within the scope of EU law). Currently, some use dubious means to ensure that workers go home at the end of the seasons. One example, which may be atypical, is nonetheless striking: a Spanish programme allegedly admits only *mothers* under 40 as seasonal agricultural workers.[47] If this programme were deemed to fall within the scope of EU

[46] For examples of this strong judicial review in action, leading to the annulment or strenuous re-interpretation of EU legislation, see Case C-236/09 *Association Belge des Consommateurs Test-Achats and Others* [2011] ECR I-00773; Case C-293/12 *Digital Rights Ireland and Seitlinger and Others (Data Protection)* [2014] OJ C175/6; Case C-540/03 *European Parliament v Council of the European Union (Family Reunification)* [2006] ECR I-05769.

[47] Susan Mannion, Peggy Petrzelka, Christy Glass and Claudia Radel, 'Keeping Them in Their Place: Migrant Women Workers in Spain's Strawberry Industry' (2011) 19(1) *International Journal of the Sociology of Agriculture and Food* 83.

law, then the EU Charter of Fundamental Rights would be applicable, as would the general principles of EU law. For now, suffice it to note that bringing matters of migration status within the scope of EU law may have some transformative legal effects, in particular if the Court of Justice is called upon to consider these questions of status inequality.[48]

V. THE TWO DIRECTIVES COMPARED

This section provides a sketch of the directives' content.

A. Personal Scope

Concerning the scope of the directives, the SWD applies to third-country nationals (TCNs) who seek admission for the 'purpose of employment as seasonal workers'. 'Seasonal workers' are defined as TCNs who stay 'legally and temporarily in the territory of a Member State to carry out an activity dependent on the passing of the seasons' under an employment contract.[49] That employment contract is with the employer in the host state.

'An activity dependent on the passing of the seasons' is defined as 'an activity that is tied to a certain time of the year by a recurring event or pattern of events linked to seasonal conditions during which required labour levels are significantly above those necessary for usually ongoing operations' (article 2(2)). When transposing the directive, Member States must list those sectors that are considered to be seasonal and, if appropriate, the list should be drawn up in consultation with the social partners.

Agency workers are *not* excluded (unlike under the ICTD). Recital 12 provides that, if national law permits, seasonal workers may continue to be agency workers, hired through agencies established on the Member States' territory and which have a 'direct contract' with the seasonal worker. Intra-corporate transfer means:

> … the temporary secondment for occupational or training purposes of a third-country national who, at the time of application for an intra-corporate transferee permit, resides outside the territory of the Member States, from an undertaking established outside the territory of a Member State, and to which the third-country national is bound by a work contract prior to and during the transfer, to an entity belonging to the undertaking or to the same group of undertakings

[48] See also Diego Acosta Arcarazo and Andrew Geddes, 'The Development, Application and Implications of an EU Rule of Law in the Area of Migration Policy' (2013) 51(2) *Journal of Common Market Studies* 179.

[49] SWD art 3(b).

> which is established in that Member State, and, where applicable, the mobility between host entities established in one or several second Member States.[50]

'Group of undertakings' is defined as 'two or more undertakings recognised as linked in national law' in various specified ways, namely majority shareholding, control, or management (article 3(l)).

The migrant must have a 'work contract' with the undertaking outside the EU, and then move to another 'entity belonging to the undertaking' or 'the same group of entities'. This loose language could facilitate transfers even to shelf companies, it would seem. The 'host entity' must be 'established' in the Member State.[51] In order to combat potential 'abuse', Member States may refuse applications where the 'host entity' has as its main purpose facilitating ICTs or does not have a genuine activity (recital 24).

The ICT Directive only covers 'managers', 'specialists' and 'trainee employees' (article 2(1)). Importantly, both the self-employed and agency workers are excluded.[52] The permit is tied: it allows the transferee only to 'exercise the specific employment activity under the permit in accordance with national law in any host entity belonging to the undertaking or group of undertakings in the first Member State' (article 17(c)).

'Manager' means a person holding a senior position, who primarily directs the management of the host entity, receiving general supervision or guidance principally from the board of directors or shareholders of the business or equivalent; that position shall include: directing the host entity or a department or subdivision of the host entity; supervising and controlling work of the other supervisory, professional or managerial employees; having the authority to recommend hiring, dismissing or other personnel action.[53]

'Specialist' means a person working within the group of undertakings possessing specialised knowledge essential to the host entity's areas of activity, techniques or management. In assessing such knowledge, account shall be taken not only of knowledge specific to the host entity, but also of whether the person has a high level of qualification including adequate professional experience referring to a type of work or activity requiring specific technical knowledge, including possible membership of an accredited profession.[54]

[50] ICTD art 3(b).

[51] This *may* require interpretation in line with freedom of establishment within the internal market context.

[52] ICTD art 2(2) states: 'This Directive shall not apply to third-country nationals who … (d) carry out activities as self-employed workers; (e) are assigned by employment agencies, temporary work agencies or any other undertakings engaging in making available labour to work under the supervision and direction of another undertaking'.

[53] ICTD art 3(e).

[54] ICTD art 3(f).

'Trainee employee' means a person with a university degree who is transferred to a host entity for career development purposes or in order to obtain training in business techniques or methods, and is paid during the transfer.[55]

These definitions are broad, and seem amenable to cover much of the workforce in some economic sectors, in particular those where specialist knowledge and a high level of qualifications are common. The definition of 'trainee' too is broad: the notion is not tied to career stage.

The migration statuses under the two directives differ sharply in another respect: ICTs have family reunification rights. In contrast, there are no family reunification rights for seasonal workers.

B. Temporal and Transnational Dimensions

There is a difference in terminology between the SWD and ICT status. The ICTD refers to 'residence', as opposed to 'stay' under the SWD. The Council insisted on amending the original reference to 'residence' in the Commission proposal, to 'stay'.

In the case of seasonal workers, Member States may issue permits ranging from five to nine months in duration within a twelve-month period.[56] Originally, the EP wanted to limit the time to six months, but some Member States insisted on an outer limit of nine months. As regards circularity, the directive obliges Member States to facilitate the re-entry of seasonal workers who have been admitted at least once every five years.[57] Facilitation measures, albeit only indicatively listed in the directive, include exemptions from the requirement to submit documentation, the issuance of several seasonal worker permits under a single decision, or accelerated admission procedures.[58] The Commission had proposed a multi-season permit, but this did not prove politically acceptable.

The Commission had aimed in its proposal to prohibit re-entry of any migrant workers who had previously overstayed. However, the final version treats any migrant worker's violation of previous permits not as a mandatory ground for rejection of further applications, but just as a permissible reason.

The ICTD equally recognises the temporary migration status of those covered by its scope: 'As intra-corporate transfers constitute temporary migration' (recital 17), the maximum duration of an intra-corporate transfer is three years for managers and specialists, and one year for trainees

[55] ICTD art 3(g).
[56] SWD art 14(1).
[57] SWD art 12(1).
[58] SWD art 12(2).

(article 12(1)). A six-month break may be required by Member States between ICT permits (article 12(2)).

The SWD explicitly states that it aims to prevent 'overstaying or temporary stay becoming permanent' and seeks to encourage circular migration, that is, ultimately returning to the home country after periods of temporary (albeit possibly prolonged) seasonal working. The SWD makes no provision for intra-EU mobility of seasonal workers. Conversely, the ICTD lays down rights to intra-EU mobility, somewhat echoing the transnational spirit of the Blue Card Directive. A distinction is drawn between short and long-term intra-EU mobility of ICTs, which is defined by a 90-day cut-off. Underlying this divide was the need to retain compatibility between the directive and the harmonised visa regime concerning authorisations for up to 90 days laid down by the EU's Schengen *acquis*.[59] Accordingly, Member States are required to issue Schengen visas to ICTs engaging in short-term mobility, while mobility exceeding 90 days is governed by authorisations under national law.

C. Labour Rights and Relations

Both forms of workers could be regarded as having a migration status that makes them vulnerable in their work relations, yet the two directives take starkly divergent approaches to their labour rights. The directives were adopted under the EU's ordinary legislative procedure, involving the European Parliament as co-decision maker. As Fudge and Herzfeld Olsson note,

> A unique aspect of the negotiations over the Seasonal Workers Directive was the extent to which the European Parliament was unified in its ambition to strengthen the rights of seasonal workers. No such similar concern was evident with respect to the groups of migrant workers that were the subjects of the other immigration directives.[60]

The result is some significant labour rights protections for seasonal workers.[61] ICTs' protections, on the other hand, are pegged at those of posted workers in the main,[62] with only remuneration to be 'not less favourable' than that for local workers in 'comparable positions'.[63] Moreover, in essence, the

[59] Regulation (EC) No 810/2009 of the European Parliament and of the Council of 13 July 2009 establishing a Community Code on Visas (Visa Code) [2009] OJ L243/1.

[60] Fudge and Herzfeld Olsson, 'The EU Seasonal Workers Directive' (n 4) 466.

[61] Ibid.

[62] ICTD art 18(1). See also Directive 96/71/EC of the European Parliament and of the Council of 16 December 1996 concerning the posting of workers in the framework of the provision of services (Posted Workers Directive) [1997] OJ L18/1.

[63] ICTD art 18(2).

ICT is a tied worker. In contrast, the SWD allows seasonal workers to be employed by different employers and to stay (up to the maximum period of nine months) to look for another employer.

The two directives embody different rules regarding TCNs' right to equal treatment. The Seasonal Workers Directive acknowledges the 'specially vulnerable nature of third-country national seasonal workers and the temporary nature of their assignment' at the outset (recital 43). Seasonal workers are thus entitled to equal treatment to local workers with regard to terms of employment, working age, working conditions such as pay and dismissal, working hours and health and safety requirements (article 23(1)(a)). They also enjoy such equal treatment concerning the right to strike and social benefits such as sickness benefits, maternity and paternity leave (article 23(1)(b)). However, family and unemployment benefits may be excluded by Member States (article 23(2)(i)). Seasonal workers are also equally treated with regard to recognition of diplomas (article 23(1)(h)), access to education and vocational training (article 23(1)(g)), including employment services offering advice on seasonal work (articles 23(1)(f), 23(2)(ii)).

At the behest of the European Parliament, the Seasonal Workers Directive also includes a provision on equal treatment to nationals concerning back payments to be made by employers (article 23(1)(c)). It provides for robust sanctions against employers (article 17). However, regarding subcontractors, the use of 'may' might undermine the effectiveness of these provisions. Third parties with a legitimate interest in ensuring compliance with the directive can lodge complaints or engage civil or administrative proceedings on behalf of the seasonal worker. It has been suggested that, all in all, these rules go 'a long way to achieving the kind of rights-based approach to migration advocated by the ILO'.[64]

The ICT Directive takes a significantly different approach to labour rights. ICTs enjoy equal treatment to posted workers with regard to the terms and conditions of employment (article 18(1)), except for remuneration. The directive provides for remuneration:

> not less favourable than the remuneration granted to nationals of the Member State where the work is carried out occupying comparable positions in accordance with applicable laws or collective agreements or practices in the Member State where the host entity is established.[65]

Equal treatment to nationals is also provided in relation to freedom of association (article 18(2)(a)), recognition of qualifications (article 18(2)(b)), social benefits (although family benefits may be excluded for transfers not

[64] Fudge and Herzfeld Olsson, 'The EU Seasonal Workers Directive' (n 4) 459.
[65] ICTD art 4(b).

exceeding nine months) (articles 18(2)(c)–(d), 18(3)), and access to goods and services (article 18(1)(e)).

D. The Posted Workers Analogy Questioned

Other contributors to this volume have addressed the troubling situation of posted workers.[66] As is now well known, the extent to which they are subject to the labour law of the host state is constrained by EU legislation[67] and case law.[68] Engblom explains the 'convulsions' caused by the *Laval* case in Sweden in light of Sweden's decision to open its labour market and rely on domestic labour laws and collective structures to ensure that demand for migrant workers was dampened, and that high labour standards for all workers in the territory were preserved.[69] *Laval* undermined that approach. Posted workers need not hold the nationality of an EU Member State. Indeed, the early posted workers cases concerned workers who *did not* have EU mobility rights themselves: the Portuguese workers in *Rush Portuguesa* did not then have EU Treaty rights, due to transitional provisions, nor did the Moroccan workers transferred from Belgium to France in *Van Der Elst*.

The workers in *Van der Elst* were of Moroccan nationality, migrants authorised to live and work in Belgium. By means of asserting its EU mobility rights as a service provider, the employer was able to bring its workforce (a team in that case of four Belgian and four Moroccan workers) with it to another Member State, thereby expanding the scope of its workers' migration status. Normally, the Moroccan workers would not have EU Treaty rights. If they had, the need to create this category of 'posted worker' would not have emerged. The case arose out of an inspection by the French Labour Inspectorate, which found the Moroccan workers did not have French permits.

The posted worker route places workers at the disposal of their employer. As independent workers, the workers in *Van der Elst* could not move to

[66] See Gudrun Biffl and Isabella Skrivanek, 'The Distinction Between Temporary Labour Migration and Posted Work in Austria: Labour Law Versus Trade Law', ch 4 in this volume.

[67] Directive 96/71/EC of the European Parliament and of the Council of 16 December 1996 concerning the posting of workers in the framework of the provision of services (Posted Workers Directive) [1997] OJ L18/1 as supplemented by Directive 2014/67/EU of the European Parliament and of the Council of 15 May 2014 on the enforcement of Directive 96/71/EC concerning the posting of workers in the framework of the provision of services [2014] OJ L 159/ 11.

[68] See especially Case C-341/05 *Laval un Partneri Ltd v Svenska Byggnadsarbetareforbundet* [2007] ECR I-11767; Case C-346/06 *Dirk Rüffert v Land Niedersachsen* [2008] ECR I-1989; Case C-319/06 *Commission v Luxembourg* [2008] ECR I-4323.

[69] Samuel Engblom, 'Reconciling Openness and High Labour Standards? Sweden's Attempts to Regulate Labour Migration and Trade in Services' in Costello and Freedland (eds), *Migrants at Work* (n 7).

France to seek or take up new employment. Their migration status in France depended on their employer. This exacerbated the workers' dependency on their employer. Moreover, the fact of posting could have also exacerbated their precarity, as they were not only temporary migrants in Belgium, but also transferred temporarily elsewhere. Thirdly, there is a posted worker protection gap: they were mainly subject to the labour law of Belgium, even though this may not be properly enforced or enforceable in France.

The point of revisiting this seminal posted worker case is to highlight its intimate linkage with temporary transnational service provision. While posted worker status apparently expands the autonomy of migrant workers, offering them added opportunities to work in other Member States without having to seek a new work permit each time, in fact it does so at the cost of additional dependency, precarity and reduction of rights. From a labour law perspective, this is troubling not only for the migrant workers but also local workers. A better approach from a labour law perspective would be not to seek to exclude the TCN migrant worker, but to include them fully, by affording all TCNs lawfully resident in an EU Member State free movement rights. At present, such mobility rights are only offered to those who attain formal EU 'Long-Term Resident' status, a status conditional on fulfilment of many conditions, and poorly implemented in practice.

The option of full inclusion in the EU labour market by granting equivalent mobility rights to nationals would, somewhat paradoxically, shore up domestic labour law and standards, thereby protecting local workers a lot more than seeking to prevent their entry. The posted worker system is lose-lose, in that the regulatory design means that posted workers are in a weaker bargaining and regulatory position, and so are more likely to undercut.

Returning to the ICT Directive, the analogy with posted workers needs to be questioned. Under the provisions of the ICTD, ICTs are to be treated equally with posted workers as regards the terms and conditions of employment other than remuneration (such as maximum work periods or safety at work). In other words, the terms and conditions of employment in the Member State to which the ICT will be transferred will be governed by the laws of his or her country of origin (the sending third country). According to the ICTD, the reason for this is that the ICTD should not give undertakings established in a sending third country any more favourable treatment than undertakings established in an EU Member State, in line with article 1(4) of the Posted Workers Directive (96/71/EC). This provision provides that '4. Undertakings established in a non-Member State must not be given more favourable treatment than undertakings established in a Member State'.

However, why use the analogy with posted workers at all? It could have been argued that posting is only relevant if the employing organisation is temporarily present in the host state providing services, and that the approach to posted workers depends on the undertakings' *right* to provide those services (in the EU context, derived from the EU Treaty's internal market freedoms). In the ICT context, this premise does not hold. So, on this basis, that commitment to 'no more favourable treatment' is inapplicable: there is no general requirement to treat undertakings alike in *different circumstances*.

Moreover, even if the commitment is applicable, it states non-EU companies should not be treated *more* favourably. However, this is precisely how global companies that can avail of the ICT route are being treated. The directive means that ICT status is regarded as a privilege for the employing organisations, irrespective of whether their employees' work rights are safeguarded according to EU standards at all. This move has also been explained as being required under GATS commitments but, as Herzfeld Olsson has demonstrated, this claim is not accurate.[70]

The workers themselves may well wish to be accorded full equal treatment with local workers, which is a stronger hallmark of the Seasonal Workers Directive. Let us recall again article 15(3) of the EU Charter: 'Nationals of third countries who are authorised to work in the territories of the Member States are entitled to working conditions equivalent to those of citizens of the Union.'

VI. CONCLUSIONS

The proliferation of migration statuses is neither obvious nor necessary in EU law. The European Trade Union Confederation urged that seasonal workers and ICTs be brought under the existing EU legal measures. The mere fact that these additional statuses exist is itself a result of catering to employer demand, rather than a move to protect workers. However, once the proposals were made, the EU political process led to a strong worker-protective content for seasonal workers. In contrast, ICTs were viewed differently, and indeed their labour rights were not a matter of concern. Rather, the posted workers anomaly has been expanded. The posted workers regime could be viewed as an unfortunate accident. It is a judicial invention that has been developed within the EU internal market to enhance freedom of transnational service provision. To extend that model to employing enterprises based outside the EU is to allow them to import third-country labour standards internally. The posted workers regime is based on the strong right to intra-EU service provision. Extending that approach to the ICT context is a remarkable enhancement of commercial freedom. The implications for workers' rights remain to be seen. But the divisive impact on European labour markets is apparent.

[70] Herzfeld Olsson, 'The Development of an EU Policy' (n 3).

3

Temporary Labour Migration and the Trade in Services

European and Global Perspectives in an Age of Economic Integration

SAMUEL ENGBLOM, NICOLA KOUNTOURIS AND ÅSA ODIN EKMAN

I. INTRODUCTION: FROM TARIFFS TO TRADE IN LABOUR-INTENSIVE SERVICES, TO GLOBAL ECONOMIC INTEGRATION

IN A RECENTLY published Current Legal Problems Lecture, Professor Tonia Novitz successfully debunked the heavily laden, if not also misguided, argument that international trade agreements are inescapably reorienting themselves towards agreements for the free movement of services, thus rendering obsolete, and possibly undesirable, a number of transnational labour law principles and regimes that were best suited to the old days of 'trade in goods'.[1] In doing so, she correctly noted that 'a neat distinction between "goods" and "services" is questionable'.[2] Similarly, in earlier jointly published work, we have sought to deconstruct the 'false dichotomy' between free movement of workers and free movement of (certain types of) services within the EU regime.[3] The critical thrust of that work addressed the emergence of the 'country of origin' principle as the

[1] Tonia Novitz, 'Evolutionary Trajectories for Transnational Labour Law: Trade in Goods to Trade in Services?' (2014) 67(1) *Current Legal Problems* 239.

[2] Ibid 244.

[3] Nicola Kountouris and Samuel Engblom, '"Protection or Protectionism": A Legal Deconstruction of the Emerging False Dilemma in European Integration' (2015) 6(1) *European Labour Law Journal* 20. In that work we noted and acknowledged that some of our analytical and normative categories draw upon Mark Freedland and Nicola Kountouris, *The Legal Regulation of Personal Work Relations* (Oxford, Oxford University Press, 2011).

key regulatory principle across free movement of goods, the free movement of services 'monolith', and some areas of 'freedom of establishment'. As a counter measure to this, we suggested that a separate and discrete area of free movement, that is to say the area of 'free movement of personal work and service providers',[4] should be regulated along the lines of the 'equal treatment principle' that currently shapes the area of 'free movement of workers'. Finally, in joint work appearing in their edited collection *Migrants at Work*,[5] Costello and Freedland have usefully identified an area of intersection, though possibly also an area of contestation, between migration law, migration practices or dynamics, and labour law, and suitably explored the impact that the former two have upon labour law, broadly understood.

This chapter seeks to deploy some of the ideas developed in these three works to explore three distinct but interlinked arguments that, in our view, support a novel approach to understanding the relationship between labour migration (temporary and not), trade (in general and in services in particular), and global economic integration. Our three arguments develop as follows. Firstly, in section II, we suggest that the various global cross-border human mobility processes currently developing under international trade agreements and mechanisms ought to be understood and analysed separately, and introduce a cross-border mobility matrix to demonstrate this. In this section, we advance the view that some labour mobility processes are better understood as labour migration processes of employees or workers, whether temporary or not in character. Other processes can be conceptualised as migration processes linked to entrepreneurial activities which can be more or less capital intensive in character. Finally, some processes can fall under mobility processes that are seemingly linked to trade in services, but with the caveat—made abundantly clear by Novitz's exegesis of the often artificial distinction between trade in goods and trade in services—that these processes can originate from different modalities and provisions of services, including modalities that are highly contingent on the supply of labour-intensive, or labour-only, services.

Secondly, in section III, we suggest that both existing and currently negotiated free trade agreements have actually developed alongside principles and subdivisions that fundamentally replicate the rather crude labour versus services distinction enshrined in existing trade agreements. At the same time they are subject to such a vast range of exemptions and qualifications that it is arguable that their impact at a macro level, in terms of their actual impact on the facilitation of human mobility processes, is likely to be minimal or non-existent.

[4] Kountouris and Engblom, 'Protection or Protectionism' 39–40.

[5] Cathryn Costello and Mark Freedland (eds), *Migrants at Work: Immigration and Vulnerability in Labour Law* (Oxford, Oxford University Press, 2014).

Finally, in section IV, we suggest that there would be ample reasons to identify within this cross-border mobility matrix an area of migration characterised by the 'provision of predominantly personal work or services', where the element of capital, in the form of tangible or intangible assets for the performance of that work or service, is only marginal or ancillary. We argue that this family of cross-border human mobility processes should become the object of separate and specific bilateral, plurilateral and multilateral negotiations with a view to regulating and promoting long-term migratory flows across countries and regions of the world on the basis of the principle of equal treatment between home workers and migrant workers (bar perhaps for particularly short postings where the integration of the migrant worker in the fabric of the host economy or society is neither necessary nor possible), and the respect for international labour standards. In a way, pushing forward the illuminating intuition developed by Costello and Freedland in their edited collection, we suggest that, just as there is a place of interaction and contestation between migration law and practices and labour law, there ought to be a similar locus of contestation between migration law, labour law and trade law, where the impact of migration law and labour *upon* trade law is fully manifested and appreciated.

The concluding paragraphs of this chapter note the changing nature of modern trade agreements, and the bearing this has on human mobility. We suggest that some of the agreements currently under negotiation are better described as agreements for regional and global economic integration, rather than traditional agreements to facilitate trade by reducing quotas and tariffs, with much greater implications for national political sovereignty. This is surely part of the explanation of the current controversies surrounding them.

II. A MATRIX OF CROSS-BORDER HUMAN LABOUR MOBILITY PROCESSES

There are several ways in which a physical person can move across borders to perform work. In this section, we develop a basic typology consisting of three main categories of mobility: labour migration of employees or workers, mobility related to entrepreneurial activities, and trade in services mobility. We develop this typology on the basis of more or less established practices emerging in existing trade and immigration agreements. It will become apparent that this basic typology can be further subdivided so as to establish a more articulate matrix based on the duration and labour intensiveness of the provision. We note that these categories, or their subcategories, do not correspond to any particular recognised legal categories. We also note that, typically, the first category—labour migration of workers—is seen as the subject of international agreements on migration, the third category is typically seen as falling within the sphere of trade agreements (and trade in services agreements in particular), and the intermediate category is equally relevant to both the domain of migration and the domain of trade (including trade and investment treaties). We feel it necessary to anticipate that, while these categories and sub-categories can be descriptively helpful, the following section III will seek to challenge their conceptual cogency and seek to reorganise them along conceptual lines that transcend the traditional subdivisions between migration, trade in services, and investment treaties.

A. Labour Migration of Employees and Workers

The most common form of labour migration is that of employees—persons moving from one country (country of origin) to another country to work as an employee for a company established in the latter country for a longer or shorter period of time. Typically, this requires a work permit which in turn is subject to conditions. In an empirical analysis of labour immigration programmes of 46 high and middle-income countries, Ruhs describes how countries try to govern labour migration through regulating openness (the number of migrants to be admitted, eg quotas, labour market tests, fees), selection (eg by skills, nationality) and rights (what rights to grant migrants after admission, eg free choice of employment, access to the welfare state, temporary or permanent residence, family reunion).[6]

As the migrating employee's employer is a company or an organisation established in the country where the work is performed (country of work), the main rule is that the labour law of the country of work applies fully to the work relationship that ensues. This follows from the mandatory nature of national labour law, making it applicable to all employees and not just citizens, as well as from private international law rules. There are nonetheless examples of countries that deny migrant employees certain rights, such as the right to form and join trade unions, or where provisions such as minimum wages are lower or non-existent for migrant workers.[7] Indeed, the reality of many migrant workers is less rosy. In a 2010 report on labour migration, the ILO pointed to poor or even dangerous working conditions, low wages that are often not paid in full, denial of the freedom of association, discrimination and xenophobia as some of the hardships facing many migrant workers. The ILO identified migration status as one of the factors affecting the working conditions of migrant workers: 'The more tenuous the

[6] Martin Ruhs, *Openness, Skills and Rights: An Empirical Analysis of Labour Immigration Programmes in 46 High- and Middle-Income Countries*, Working Paper No 88 (Oxford, Centre on Migration Policy and Society, University of Oxford, 2011) 1.

[7] This is the case in several of the Gulf States. See Ruhs, *Openness, Skills and Rights* (n 6) 11, 18.

worker's migration status, the more barriers there are to seeking redress for unfavourable treatment.'[8]

Often, labour immigration programmes grant work permits on the condition that the job in question fulfils requirements for wages and other working conditions. The conditions can be formulated in several different ways. Employers may be required to fulfil minimum standards such as paying the legal minimum wage (if such exists), to pay the 'prevailing wage', or to offer wages and other working conditions at the level of applicable collective agreements.[9]

However, labour migrants' access to social security—such as unemployment benefits, sickness benefits and pensions—is often dependent on the duration of their stay in the country of work, with temporary migrants having significantly fewer rights than those that come under labour immigration programmes aimed at permanent migration.[10] In welfare systems with employment-based benefits, the rights of temporary migrants may be restricted initially as it will take some time before they fulfil eligibility requirements. From a market for labour perspective, more interesting still is the duty of employers to pay employers' contributions. Restricted rights of migrants do not necessarily lead to restrictions on their employer's duty to pay social security contributions.

Employers established in the country of work also pay corporate taxes there, as do migrant employees who take up residence in the country of work. If the length of their stay is below a certain threshold, for example six months during one year, special rates often apply. In addition, many high-tax countries have also introduced special tax concessions for mobile high-skilled (or high-earning) workers. Some of these schemes also include reductions of social security contributions.[11]

By and large, economic analysis suggests that the presence of strong labour market institutions in host countries can have some effects both on migrant workers' mobility decisions,[12] and on the ability of national and sectoral median earnings to withstand labour supply increases.[13] However, labour market institutions are but one of several other policy and regulatory frameworks affecting mobility decisions and national labour market performances.

[8] ILO, *International Labour Migration: A Rights-Based Approach* (Geneva, International Labour Office, 2010) 77.

[9] Ruhs, *Openness, Skills and Rights* (n 6) 11.

[10] Ibid 43.

[11] OECD, *Taxation and Employment: OECD Tax Policy Studies* (Paris, OECD Publishing, 2011) 125ff.

[12] Claudia Cigagna and Giovanni Sulis, *On the Potential Interaction Between Labour Market Institutions and Immigration Policies*, Discussion Paper No 9016 (Bonn, IZA, 2015).

[13] Herbert Brücker, Elke J Jahn and Richard Upward, *Migration and Imperfect Labor Markets: Theory and Cross-Country Evidence from Denmark, Germany and the UK*, Discussion Paper No 6713 (Bonn, IZA, 2012).

B. Entrepreneur Migration

At a high level of generalisation, migration of entrepreneurs can be defined as the type of migration involving a person moving from country A (country of origin) to country B (country of work) to establish a business. The OECD's 2011 *International Migration Outlook* acknowledged that, in this context, '[a] standard practice in the entrepreneurship literature is to assimilate entrepreneurs to the self-employed, whether or not they employ other persons'.[14] International agreements can sometimes draw a distinction between 'immigrant entrepreneurs' and 'foreign investors', but even this distinction, we are told, 'is less clear-cut when the immigrant is the head of a large business'.[15] There is thus a noticeable tendency to conflate under a single and broad 'entrepreneurship' paradigm a series of phenomena that, in our view, are and should remain distinct.

Existing literature suggests that many countries operate several different schemes for migrant entrepreneurs.[16] Some countries that distinguish between migration of self-employed entrepreneurs and migration of investors emphasise the personal involvement of the former in the management of their business. The fact that entrepreneurs establish themselves in the country of work normally means that their businesses fall under the labour law, social security law and tax law of that country. They may nonetheless have limited access to social security, family allowances and benefits, and 'in most OECD countries, applicants for a permit for the exercise of an independent economic activity are required to provide proof of health insurance to guarantee that they will not be a burden on the national health system during their stay', at least initially.[17]

A key proposition of this chapter is that this level of generalisation and imprecision in the conceptualisation of categories of migrant working persons is somewhat unhelpful for the purposes of understanding labour migration processes, whether temporary or not. Arguably it should be possible to break down the broad category of entrepreneur migration into at least three subcategories, that of self-employed professional, entrepreneur and investor. In fact, some national immigration and investment programmes do so. For instance, the Canadian arrangements draw a distinction between these three main categories on the basis of the personal involvement of the migrant in the running of the business (the investor definition explicitly not requiring any such involvement) and on the basis of requirements for capital

[14] OECD, *International Migration Outlook* (Paris, OECD, 2011) 144 (footnotes omitted).

[15] OECD, *Open for Business: Migrant Entrepreneurs in OECD Countries* (Paris, OECD, 2010) 66.

[16] Ibid 63ff gives a good overview of these programmes in OECD countries.

[17] Ibid 73.

investment (the investor category necessitating a minimum investment of 400,000 CAD, the entrepreneur an investment of 300,000 CAD, and the self-employed none).[18]

C. Trade in Services Mobility

To introduce the third broad typology, we make use of the WTO's General Agreement on Trade in Services (GATS) modes, and in particular those pertaining to Modes 3 and 4. We hasten to reiterate that we feel these subdivisions are highly laden and artificial. We also note that some of the subcategories discussed therein can factually overlap with some of the categories and subcategories we have already discussed above. However, we find that relying on this established matrix can be useful, at this stage, in terms of describing some key mobility dynamics that are, in many ways, also reiterated in currently negotiated trade agreements such as TiSA.

The definition of trade in services found in article I of the GATS is commonly described as the four modes of trade in services.

— *Mode 1: Cross-border supply* is the supply of a service from the territory of one member into the territory of any other member, eg services rendered over a telephone line or the internet.
— *Mode 2: Consumption abroad* is the supply of a service in the territory of one member to the service consumer of any other member, eg tourism.
— *Mode 3: Commercial presence* is the supply of a service by a service supplier of one member, through commercial presence in the territory of any other member, eg the setting up of a branch of a company in another country.
— *Mode 4: Presence of natural persons* is the supply of a service by a service supplier of one member, through presence of natural persons of a member in the territory of any other member, eg non-nationals on consultancy or construction tasks.

'Services' here include any service in any sector except services supplied 'in the exercise of governmental authority', defined as 'any service which is supplied neither on a commercial basis nor in competition with one or more service suppliers'.[19] In the context of the present chapter, the two modes of interest are Mode 3 and Mode 4, in particular the latter, as they involve the cross-border mobility of employees and entrepreneurs.

[18] Ibid 83–88.
[19] GATS art I(3)(b)(c).

GATS Mode 3: Commercial Presence

GATS Mode 3 is the supply of a service by a service supplier of one member, through the *commercial presence* in the territory of any other member, for example through an agency, branch, subsidiary or joint venture.

GATS Mode 3 can involve cross-border labour mobility in different ways. If the company establishing itself is in fact a self-employed worker or if the establishment involves an owner of the business moving to the country of work, the situation is, in our view, essentially similar to the first two subcategories discussed above under the entrepreneur migration category: the self-employed and the entrepreneur. An interesting question, which still begs for an answer, is whether all migration of entrepreneurs between WTO members is covered by GATS Mode 3 or not.

Mode 3 can also lead to labour mobility if the company establishing itself brings one or several of its employees. If these become employed by the entity in the country of work, their movement falls within the parameters of the first broad category discussed above, that of labour migration of employees, and the labour, social security and tax law of the country of work typically applies. If they stay employed by a company in the country of origin the rules for GATS Mode 4 (presence of natural persons) as described below apply. In both cases, as the company is established in the country of work, movement of natural persons under GATS Mode 4 is more often than not linked to Mode 3.[20] This means that Mode 4 movements in the form of intra-corporate transferees, business visitors, executives, managers and specialists (see below) are dependent on foreign direct investments under Mode 3.

GATS Mode 4: Presence of Natural Persons

GATS defines Mode 4 as the supply of a service 'by a service supplier of one Member, through presence of natural persons of a Member in the territory of any other Member'. This means, most commonly, that a company in country A (the service supplier) sends one or more of its employees (natural persons) to country B to deliver a service. Another variant is that a self-employed worker from country A goes to deliver a service in country B. Both country A and country B must be WTO members and the natural persons involved must be nationals or permanent residents of a WTO member other than the country of work B. The concept resembles but is not identical to posting of workers in EU law.[21]

[20] Marion Panizzon, *Trade and Labour Migration: GATS Mode 4 and Migration Agreements*, Occasional Papers No 47 (Geneva, Friedrich Ebert Stiftung, 2010) 17.

[21] Directive 96/71/EC of the European Parliament and of the Council of 16 December 1996 concerning the posting of workers in the framework of the provision of services [1997] OJ L18/1.

GATS Mode 4 distinguishes itself from labour migration of employees by the fact that the person performing the work is employed by a service supplier in one country while carrying out work in another country. If the person instead is employed by a company in the same country where the work is performed, he or she falls in the category of labour migration of employees. The crucial point is thus the location of the employer. This view can find additional support in the Annex on Movement of Natural Persons Supplying Services under the Agreement attached to GATS, where the second paragraph states that the agreement 'shall not apply to measures affecting natural persons seeking access to the employment market of a Member'. This has been interpreted as implying that the employment of foreigners by employers established in the country of work, that is the labour migration of employees, falls outside the scope of GATS Mode 4.[22] As already explained, the location of the employer has significant consequences for the application of labour law and the duty to pay taxes and social security contributions.

Another important distinction is whether the cross-border movement is temporary or permanent. In trying to distinguish conceptually trade in services from labour migration of employees, this is not a very useful distinction, as much labour migration of employees is also temporary in nature.

From a GATS perspective, the distinction between temporary and permanent is, nonetheless, highly relevant. The second part of the aforementioned second paragraph of the Annex on Movement of Natural Persons Supplying Services under the Agreement stipulates that the agreement shall not apply to 'measures regarding citizenship, residence or employment on a permanent basis'. Neither the agreement nor the annex specifies any time frame to determine what might constitute temporary presence. Instead, the members have, in their schedules of specific commitments, indicated the permitted duration of stay for the different categories of natural persons. In practical terms, the provision means that members are free to define the mentioned aspects of their labour migration policy.

When it comes to temporary stays in their territory, however, the freedom of the members is more limited. According to paragraph four of the annex:

> ... the Agreement should not prevent a Member from applying measures to regulate the entry of natural persons into, or their temporary stay in, its territory ... provided that such measures are not applied in such a manner as to nullify or impair benefits accruing to any Member under the terms of a specific commitment.

A footnote states that 'the sole fact of requiring a visa for natural persons of certain Members and not for those of others shall not be regarded as nullifying or impairing benefits under a specific commitment'. Taken together, this means that WTO members are allowed to require that natural persons

[22] WTO Document S/C/W/301, *Presence of Natural Persons (Mode 4)*, 15 September 2009.

who enter their territory to supply a service have a work permit, but that these requirements must not be used in ways that lessen the value of their commitments.

Of the four modes of delivery, Mode 4 is the one where WTO members have opened up the least. The commitments are generally targeted at skilled workers, in particular highly educated professionals. Members' schedules also delineate access conditions by further subdivisions of Mode 4, for example independent professionals, contractual service suppliers (employees of a service supplier from country A without a commercial presence in country B delivering a service to a client in B), intra-corporate transferees (employees who are sent by their employer to work temporarily in another member where their employer has a commercial presence, but who remain employed by the company in the first state) and business visitors (employees of a service supplier in country A who enter country B to, for example, set up a commercial presence or negotiate the sale of a service).[23] In addition, there is, as mentioned above, often a linkage with Mode 3 where temporary movement of labour is conditional on foreign direct investment and the commercial presence of a foreign service supplier.

Mode 4 workers are still employed by the employer in the country of origin and are not residents of the country of work. As far as social security and taxes are concerned, they therefore normally fall under the jurisdiction of the country where the employer is established.[24] For labour law, the answer is more complicated, and takes its route through private international law.

Private international law is the set of rules that determine who has jurisdiction and which country's law should apply in cross-border situations. Within the EU, rules have been harmonised through Regulation 593/2008/EC on the law applicable to contractual obligations (Rome I). Technically, the main rule is that the parties are free to agree on the applicable law, but only as long as the employee is not deprived of protection that he or she would have had if no such agreement had been reached. In practice, the main rule is the provision in article 8.2 that the applicable law is the law of the country in which the employee 'habitually carries out his work'. The country where the work is habitually carried out shall not be deemed to have changed if the employee is temporarily employed in another country. This means that if an employee who normally works in country A is sent by his or her employer temporarily to country B to provide a service, the labour law of country A still applies. For Mode 4, these rules typically lead to the result that the labour law of the service provider's country of origin is to apply, unless the employee performs the greater part of his obligation towards the employer in the country of work. The first case must nonetheless still be considered the main rule.

23 Ibid.

24 National social security systems and tax regimes typically define their personal scope in a way that excludes persons who are resident of and employed in another country.

GATS does not contain any provisions equivalent to the European Union Directive 96/71/EC on the posting of workers, which prescribes that certain areas of the country of work labour legislation should apply to employees who are sent by their employer to provide a service in another country, regardless of Rome I rules. Instead, it is the Mode 4 workers' need for a work permit that imposes country of work labour standards on employees sent by their employers to provide services in another WTO member. As mentioned above, work permits are often conditional on the job in question fulfilling requirements regarding wages and other working conditions. It is not uncommon, however, that these requirements are less strict or waived entirely for categories of Mode 4 workers, for instance intra-corporate transferees.[25] It is important to note, however, that the fulfilment of conditions for work permits does not automatically mean that country of work labour law as such becomes applicable. Instead, it is the contract of the Mode 4 employees with their employer in the country of origin that must fulfil the requirements.

Foreign service providers that are temporary work agencies can also be affected by country of work regulation of their industry. In the EU, Directive 2008/104/EC on temporary agency work includes a principle of equal treatment which gives temporary agency workers the right to at least the basic working and employment conditions 'that would apply if they had been recruited directly by that undertaking to occupy the same job' (article 5(1)), together with rights concerning access to employment, collective facilities, vocational training and representation. These rules apply to visiting non-EU temporary work agencies as well.

A final possible route for country of work labour law to reach the working conditions of Mode 4 workers is if the foreign service provider signs a country of work collective agreement. This is not very common and preconditioned on the presence of strong trade unions and maybe even on country of work trade unions being able to take industrial action against the foreign service provider (see below).

D. A Model for Cross-Border Labour Mobility

Table 3.1 displays a basic model describing the choices a user company has to service its need for labour by means of labour sourced from abroad.

Employees are distinguished from the other labour options by the fact that they are hired directly by the user company. As shown by the table, if

[25] In a 2009 analysis of member GATS Mode 4 schedules, the WTO Secretariat writes that, out of 70 members having committed explicitly on ICT, only nine have subjected them to quotas and only a few are coupled with an economic needs test: WTO Document S/C/W/301.

a company chooses to recruit employees from abroad, they will fall in the category of labour migration of employees. If the user company instead chooses temporarily to transfer a person who is employed by another company within the same group, this could be considered an intra-corporate transfer (ICT) which falls into the trade in services category and under GATS Mode 4. If the user company instead choses a foreign temporary work agency, the category of mobility will be trade in services as long as the company providing the labour does not establish itself in the country of work. The same is true if the user company contracts a foreign labour subcontractor. Finally, self-employed persons can cross a border to perform work either through moving their business and establishing themselves in the country of work (entrepreneur migration) or maintaining their business in the country of origin and only delivering services temporarily in the country of work (trade in services).

Table 3.1: Cross-Border Labour Options

	Employees	**Temporary work agencies**	**Labour subcontracting**	**Entrepreneur/ self-employed**
Labour migration of employees	Recruitment from abroad			
Trade in services mobility (GATS Mode 4)	Intra-corporate transfers	Foreign temporary work agency	Foreign labour subcontractor	E/SE temporarily delivering services
Entrepreneur migration (incl GATS Mode 3)				E/SE establishing in country of work

Figure 3.1 seeks to describe the distinctions between the six different cross-border labour options. The distinction between labour migration of employees and trade in services under GATS Mode 4 is whether the employer is located in the country of work or in the country of origin. The distinction between trade in services under GATS Mode 4 and entrepreneur migration including GATS Mode 3 is whether the presence in the country of work is temporary or permanent. Finally, the distinction between labour migration of employees and entrepreneur migration is whether the person migrating is an employee or self-employed.

To finalise the description of the cross-border labour options, we need to indicate the applicable regulation—country of work or country of

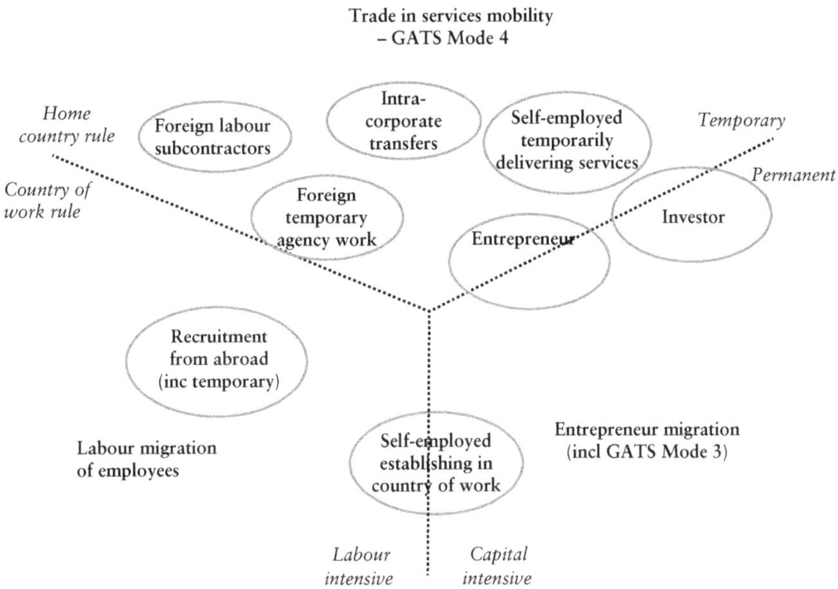

Figure 3.1: Distinctions Between the Different Cross-Border Labour Options

origin—for each option in the fields of labour law, social security and taxation.

In the case of recruitment from abroad, country of work labour law applies, and conditions for obtaining a work permit may further strengthen this, for example through requiring employers not just to comply with minimum standards but to grant wages and working conditions at the level of applicable collective agreements or corresponding to the average in the sector. If the migrant worker takes up residence in the country of work, they will belong to the country of work's social security system, both as concerns contributions and benefits. If the migrant workers' stay in the country of work is short in duration, their access to benefits may be restricted, but not necessarily the employer's duty to pay contributions, which means that it has no effect on the unit labour cost. Taxes are to be paid in the country of work, but many countries apply special (lower) rates if the duration of the stay is short or run special tax regimes for foreign experts. These affect the take-home pay of the employees rather than employers' unit labour costs, even if they could create space for slightly lower gross wages.

Intra-corporate transfers (ICT) are more complex as the employee is still employed in the country of origin, albeit in another company within the same group. The main rule is, therefore, that the employee belongs to the labour law, social security and taxation regimes of the country of origin. Conditions for work permits may, however, have the effect that the employers of intra-corporate transferees have to live up to country of work standards of wages and working conditions. ICTs are, however, sometimes exempted altogether from work permit requirements. Foreign temporary work agencies also fall predominantly under country of origin regulation. As in the case of ICTs, conditions for work permits may nonetheless have the effect that some country of work labour standards have to be considered. They may also have to follow country of work regulation on temporary work agencies. Foreign labour subcontractors follow the pattern of the former two, with country of origin regulation as the main rule, but modified through conditions for work permits. In all three cases, it is important to remember that, although there may be requirements to live up to country of work labour standards, they are still employed in the country of origin on country of origin employment contracts to which country of origin labour law applies.

Self-employed workers temporarily delivering a service do not have an employment contract, neither in the country of origin, nor the country of work. Like the other three trade in services labour options the main rules indicate that they fall under country of origin regulation in all three areas. It is hard to find information on the need for work permits. The reason is probably that most countries are reluctant to grant self-employed service providers access to their markets. In a 2009 WTO secretariat study of members' GATS Mode 4 commitments, only seven countries had included openings for independent professionals in their schedules.[26] When the category is opened up, however, work permit requirements seem to be less strict. None of the seven members that had made openings in the independent professional category had made them subject to specific quotas and only one to a labour market needs test. There are also examples of self-employed workers temporarily delivering services for a shorter period being fully exempted from work or residence permit requirements.[27] Self-employed people who establish themselves in the country of work fall under country of work legislation in all three areas (but special income tax rates may apply). If the rules are followed, migrating entrepreneurs, therefore, do not enjoy any regulatory advantage over entrepreneurs already present in that country. But again, there is a regulatory blur when it comes to distinguishing rules applicable to self-employed professionals, to small entrepreneurs and to foreign investors with a substantial amount of capital.

[26] WTO Document S/C/W/301.

[27] This is the case for example in Sweden, where self-employed people who plan to work for a shorter period than three months do not need residence permits.

Table 3.2: Applicable Regulation: Main Rules

	Labour law	Social security	Taxation
Recruitment from abroad	Country of work **work permit may require country of work standards*	Country of work **short stay may exempt from benefits*	Country of work **special income tax rates may apply if short stay or high-skilled worker*
Intra-corporate transfers	Country of origin **work permit may require country of work standards* **may be exempted from work permits*	Country of origin	Country of origin
Foreign temporary work agencies	Country of origin **work permit may require country of work standards* **country of work regulation of TWA*	Country of origin	Country of origin
Foreign labour subcontractors	Country of origin **work permit may require country of work standards*	Country of origin	Country of origin
Self-employed temporarily delivering services	Country of origin **may be exempted from work permits*	Country of origin	Country of origin
Self-employed establishing in the country of work	Country of work	Country of work **access to benefits may be restricted initially*	Country of work **special rates may apply*
Entrepreneurs	Country of work	Country of work **access to benefits may be restricted initially*	Country of work **special rates may apply*
Investors	Country of work	Ibid	Ibid

III. REGULATING THE 'SPAGHETTI BOWL' OF TRADE-RELATED TEMPORARY HUMAN MIGRATION PROCESSES

Increased trade in services tends to be viewed favourably by both politicians and economists. As the share of services increases in both high- and middle-income countries and as technological change makes earlier distinctions between traded goods (mainly manufactured goods) and non-traded goods (mainly services) to a large extent obsolete, it is natural that trade in services has become a key aspect of free trade agreements.

In the case of trade in services that includes the cross-border mobility of physical persons, however, trade negotiators have often felt the need to surround these with exemptions, restrictions and safeguards. We elaborate further on some of these rules below, but we suggest that they are a reflection of a considerable degree of national uneasiness with human mobility processes at large, including temporary processes.

A. Exemptions from GATS Principles

The basis for the GATS order is the principle of most-favoured-nation (MFN) treatment (article II). Under MFN, members are obliged to 'accord immediately and unconditionally to services and service suppliers of any other Member treatment no less favourable than that it accords to like services and service suppliers of any other country'. The MFN in the GATS is less strong than that of the General Agreement on Tariffs and Trade (GATT), as it is qualified by the possibility of derogation. MFN rules apply only if no exemption has been notified. The possibility to make exemptions is, however, limited. Importantly, it is meant in the positive, as a possibility to treat some trading partners better than others.[28] This is also the spirit of the two articles that specifically allow for economic integration through free trade areas such as the European Union (article V) and labour market integration agreements (article V bis) between a limited number of countries where at least one is a WTO member. Article V bis was inserted at a late stage in the negotiations and has been seen as an expression of the contracting parties' 'willingness to limit the possible impact on domestic immigration regimes resulting from the wide definition, in Art. I:2, of the modes of service supply, in particular mode 4'.[29] In order to prevent abuse of this possibility,

[28] Peter-Tobias Stoll and Frank Schorkopf, *WTO: World Economic Order, World Trade Law*, Max Planck Commentaries on World Trade Law (Leiden, Martinus Nijhoff, 2006) 190.

[29] Rüdiger Wolfrum, Peter-Tobias Stoll and Clemens Feinäugle, *WTO: Trade in Services*, Max Planck Commentaries on World Trade Law (Leiden, Martinus Nijhoff, 2008) 154.

the standard set for an agreement to qualify as a labour market integration agreement is high. To qualify, the agreement must establish 'full integration of the labour markets between or among the parties' and 'exempt citizens of parties to the agreement from requirements concerning residency and work permits' (article V bis). So far, only one labour market integration agreement has been notified to the WTO: the Common Nordic Labour Market covering Denmark, Iceland, Norway, Sweden and Finland.

The GATS also contains rules on market access (article XVI). GATS does not grant market access to all services as a general right. Instead, members can chose to open specific service sectors through specific commitments. Once opened up, GATS members must grant access as specified to service suppliers and services for all other members.

Under article XVII, 'each Member shall accord to services and service suppliers of any other Member, in respect to all measures affecting the supply of services, treatment no less favourable than that it accords to its own like services and service suppliers' (national treatment). There is no general guarantee of national treatment and it is not an obligation applicable to all trade in services, but only to areas where specific commitments have been made. Members are obliged to treat all foreign services or service suppliers equally, but these do not have a general right to be treated equally to domestic services or service suppliers. National treatment can be secured by treatment which is formally identical or formally different, as long as it does not distort competition.[30]

Further, articles XIX–XXI contain provisions on progressive liberalisation. These mandate new rounds of negotiations on the liberalisation of the entire sector every five years. The progressive liberalisation provisions have been described as the GATS' 'built-in agenda'.[31]

To sum up, the GATS approach is 'positive listing', in which market access is liberalised and national treatment granted only to the extent to which WTO members have entered commitments into their schedule.[32] The members enter into commitments for each of the four different modes of service, which together make up their 'schedule of commitments'. If a WTO member decides to modify their schedule, for example by retracting a commitment or re-introducing a barrier to market access, and the modification has an adverse effect on trade, it must compensate all other WTO members by offering commitments in another sector or mode of supply (article XXI).

[30] Stoll and Schorkopf, *WTO* (n 28) 191.
[31] Ibid 197.
[32] Panizzon, *Trade and Labour Migration* (n 20) 12.

B. Comprehensive Economic and Trade Agreement (CETA): White Collar and Listing of Exemptions

The negotiated but not yet adopted free trade agreement between Canada and the EU contains a chapter on the temporary entry and stay of natural persons for business purposes.[33] The scope of the chapter is limited to key personnel, contractual service suppliers, independent professionals and short-term business visitors. As we will describe below, all four are the subject of rather restrictive definitions. In addition, the parties can further limit their scope by setting up additional requirements for certain sectors or categories.

With wording taken from the GATS Annex on Movement of Natural Persons Supplying Services, article 10.2 of chapter ten on temporary entry tries to define the scope of the parties' commitments. The chapter 'shall not apply to measures affecting natural persons seeking access to the employment market of a Party, nor shall it apply to measures regarding citizenship, residence, or employment on a permanent basis' (article 10.2.2) and it should not

> prevent a Party from applying measures to regulate the entry of natural persons into, or their temporary stay in, its territory ... provided that such measures are not applied in such a manner as to nullify or impair the benefits accruing to any Party under the terms of this Chapter. (article 10.2.3)

Here, the footnote from the GATS annex that 'the sole fact of requiring a visa for natural persons of certain country and not for those of others shall not be regarded as nullifying or impairing benefits under this Chapter' has been promoted to article text (article 10.2.3). In addition, article 10.6.1, concerning obligations contained in other chapters, is a reminder that the agreement 'does not impose an obligation on a Party regarding its immigration measures, except as specifically identified in this Chapter and in Chapter Twenty-Seven (Transparency)'.

The temporary entry chapter also contains a clause on labour rights. According to article 10.2.5, 'Notwithstanding the provisions of this Chapter, all requirements of the Parties' laws regarding employment and social security measures shall continue to apply, including regulations concerning minimum wages as well as collective wage agreements'.

As indicated above, the temporary entry chapter applies to four categories: key personnel, contractual service suppliers, independent professionals and short-term business visitors. Key personnel is subdivided into business visitors for investment purposes, investors and intra-corporate transferees (further subdivided into senior personnel, specialists and graduate trainees)

[33] The consolidated CETA text following the legal review was released on 29 February 2016 http://trade.ec.europa.eu/doclib/docs/2016/february/tradoc_154329.pdf.

(article 10.1 (c)). With the exemption of graduate trainees, the definitions try to capture senior personnel in managerial positions or with special expertise and uncommon knowledge. The parties are not allowed to adopt limitations on the total number of key personnel from another party (for example, by numerical restrictions or an economic needs test), or to require work permits for business visitors for investment purposes, and must allow the employment of intra-corporate transferees.

Temporary entry of contractual service suppliers, the category that arguably could invite the kind of controversy that the posting of workers has caused in the EU, is quite strictly defined (article 10.8.7). The natural person must have a university degree or knowledge of an equivalent level, have at least three years professional experience in the sector, and have been an employee of the enterprise supplying the service for at least one year. The length of stay should be no longer than 12 months. Independent professionals (article 10.8.2) must have six years' professional experience in the sector and a university degree or equivalent. In either case, CETA only applies to service contracts that are 12 months or shorter. 'Short-term business visitors' is defined through a list of activities in an annex to the chapter (Annex 10-D). According to article 10.9.2 of the temporary entry chapter, each party should allow the entry of short-term business visitors without the requirement of a work permit or other prior approval procedures.

The EU Member States and Canada have further limited their commitments through reservations and exceptions in the annexes to the chapter. In Annex 10-B, concerning key personnel and business visitors, we find great diversity in reservations, with some countries such as Austria and the Netherlands retaining the right to apply, for example, economic needs tests for virtually all categories of short-term business visitors.

Contractual service suppliers and independent professionals have their own annex (Annex 10-E) with reservations per sector or subsector. For these categories, economic needs tests are frequent, reflecting EU Member States' labour migration regimes.

C. The Trans-Pacific Partnership

The Trans-Pacific Partnership (TPP) was agreed in early October 2015 by twelve Pacific-rim countries. It includes a chapter on temporary entry for business persons.[34] A business person is defined as a natural person who is engaged in trade in goods, the supply of services or the conduct of investment activities (article 12.1). The parties undertake to improve and speed

[34] Trans-Pacific Partnership ch 12, https://medium.com/the-trans-pacific-partnership/temporary-entry-for-business-persons-3559e41ae388.

up application procedures and to ensure that fees charged for processing applications are reasonable in that they do not unduly impair or delay trade or investments (article 12.3). Further, the parties will improve transparency regarding, for example, requirements for temporary entry and the typical timeframe within which an application is processed (article 12.6).

The TPP does not in itself contain any binding provisions on labour mobility. Under article 12.4, each party should set out in an annex the commitments it makes. The US, however, has already announced that it will not make any such commitments. As explained on the US trade representatives website, '[w]hile the other 11 parties have agreed upon country-specific reciprocal commitments on access for each other's business persons, the United States is not undertaking any commitments in this area.'[35]

From a labour perspective, an interesting clause is article 12.4.4 which gives a party a right to refuse the entry of a business person if the temporary entry of that person might affect adversely 'the settlement of any labour dispute that is in progress at the place or intended place of employment' or 'the employment of any natural person who is involved in such dispute'. A similar clause can be found in CETA, as well as in the initial offer on TTIP submitted by the EU.[36] Clearly, the provision is aimed at preventing the temporary entry of business persons to interfere with industrial action. As the European Commission explicitly makes clear in its reading guide to its TTIP offer on services and investment: 'Commitments on workers' mobility cannot be invoked to undermine people's right to strike.'[37]

D. The China-Australia Free Trade Agreement (ChAFTA)

The China-Australia Free Trade Agreement (ChAFTA), signed in 2014 and which entered into force in December 2015, includes a set of provisions aimed at facilitating, in particular, the free movement of natural persons including contractual service suppliers. These provisions, we believe, are possibly the widest contained in any of the comparable regional trade agreements discussed in the present chapter.

Article 10.4 prevents the two signatory countries from applying either caps on visas or labour market and economic needs testing to temporary workers. Annex 10-A, paras 9, 10 and 11 of ChAFTA grant entry to contractual service suppliers for four years, with the possibility of further stay,

[35] Ibid.

[36] European Union, 'Transatlantic Trade and Investment Partnership, Services and Investment Offer of the European Union' (2015), http://trade.ec.europa.eu/doclib/docs/2015/july/tradoc_153670.pdf.

[37] European Commission, 'Reading Guide: Publication of the EU Proposal on Services, Investment and E-commerce for the Transatlantic Trade and Investment Partnership' (2015) 3 fn 2, http://trade.ec.europa.eu/doclib/docs/2015/july/tradoc_153668.pdf.

and define the category quite broadly as comprising natural persons with 'trade, technical or professional skills and experience'. The category is not limited to highly skilled workers and, combined with article 10.4, para 3, Australia cannot impose labour market testing for contractual service suppliers. Annex 10-A, para 9 does, however, specify the possibility that contractual services suppliers be 'assessed as having the necessary qualifications, skills and work experience accepted as meeting Australia's standards for their nominated occupation'.

These provisions have attracted a certain degree of controversy, in Australia in particular.[38] Howe has identified the crux of the concerns surrounding them as predominantly centred on the safeguards (or absence thereof) applying to the minimum base income or salary that ought to be granted to Chinese temporary migrant service suppliers on a par with both domestic workers performing comparable services and with other foreign workers entering under the pre-existing 457 Temporary Business Sponsorship Visas,[39] who can benefit from a Temporary Skilled Migration Income Threshold.[40] These concerns, in our view, fit well within the range of legitimate domestic policy actions aimed at ensuring that the liberalisation of migration processes is governed in a way that is fair and equitable to all workers concerned and by reference to the principle of equal treatment between comparable workers providing similar work and services in a given labour market, regardless of their nationality.

E. Under Negotiation: TTIP and TiSA

To what extent cross-border mobility of natural persons will be included in the two trade agreements currently under negotiation, the Trans-Atlantic Trade and Investment Partnership (TTIP), and the Trade in Services Agreement (TiSA), is still to be confirmed. Some predictions can be made on the basis of the negotiating mandates granted to some of the parties involved, as well as leaked draft negotiating texts.

In June 2015, President Obama was granted Trade Promotion Authority (TPA), commonly referred to as 'fast-track' authority, after a long and arguably complex political process. The TPA outlines the negotiating mandate of the US not just for the now concluded TPP, but all free trade

[38] See for instance Australian Labor Party, 'Labor's China-Australia Free Trade Agreement Safeguards', fact sheet, http://www.alp.org.au/chinaftasafeguards.

[39] Joanna Howe, *The Impact of the China Australia Free Trade Agreement on Australian Job Opportunities, Wages and Conditions* (Adelaide, University of Adelaide, 2015).

[40] Which in 2015 stood at $53,900, and therefore somewhat above the $33,300 statutory minimum wage, but well below the $77,194 a year national average salary. See Australian Bureau of Statistics, '6302.0—Average Weekly Earnings, Australia, May 2015', http://www.abs.gov.au/ausstats/abs@.nsf/mf/6302.0/.

agreements under negotiation, including TTIP and TiSA, provided they are concluded within at most six years.

While temporary entry of natural persons was by no means the issue dominating the TPA debate, immigration did emerge as a contested issue at a late stage in the process. Claims were made that the TPA would enable President Obama to use the concluded trade deals as a way to 'facilitate immigration increases above current law'.[41] This was quickly debunked by the US Trade Representative.[42] The finally approved TPA confirms this, as it does not grant any authority on matters relating to either immigration or temporary entry. The outcome of the TPP negotiations clearly demonstrated the US reluctance to make further commitments regarding temporary entry as part of currently negotiated trade agreements, and the contentious nature of the issue.

It is somewhat more difficult to draw definite conclusions regarding the EU's position. While temporary entry or other cross-border mobility of natural persons have not yet reached the top of the agenda for TTIP, they have constituted a more central issue both ahead of and during the TiSA negotiations. Several low and middle income countries have for many years, and with little success, demanded greater commitments regarding Mode 4, for example by including lower-skilled workers. The publicly released EU negotiating mandates for TTIP[43] and TiSA[44] confirm a commitment to the general structure and wording of the GATS for trade in services, as well as the desire to make commitments in all four modes. However, a number of caveats apply, for TiSA in particular. In the initial offer with regards to scheduling commitments for both TiSA[45] and TTIP,[46] the EU 'reserves the right to adopt or maintain any measure with respect to the provision of services through the presence of natural persons (provision of services through mode 4)'. This suggests an overall cautiousness about making far-reaching commitments regarding Mode 4, but in the case of TTIP, the EU

[41] Jeff Sessions, 'Critical Alert: Top Five Concerns with Trade Promotion Authority', media release, 4 May 2015.

[42] Letter from Ambassador Michael Froman to Charles Grassley, Chairman, US Senate Committee on Judiciary, 22 April 2015, https://www.grassley.senate.gov/sites/default/files/judiciary/upload/Immigration,%2004-22-15,%20letter%20from%20USTR,%20immigration%20in%20trade%20agreements.pdf

[43] Council of the European Union, 'Directives for the Negotiation on the Transatlantic Trade and Investment Partnership between the European Union and the United States of America' ST 11103/13 (2014), http://data.consilium.europa.eu/doc/document/ST-11103-2013-DCL-1/en/pdf.

[44] Council of the European Union, 'Draft Directives for the negotiation of a plurilateral agreement on trade in services' 6891/13 (2015), http://data.consilium.europa.eu/doc/document/ST-6891-2013-ADD-1-DCL-1/en/pdf.

[45] European Union, 'TiSA Trade in Services Agreement European Union Schedule of Specific Commitments & List of MFN Exemptions' (2014) http://trade.ec.europa.eu/doclib/docs/2014/july/tradoc_152689.pdf.

[46] European Union, 'Transatlantic Trade and Investment Partnership',

has elsewhere been explicit about its desire to use the agreement to facilitate mobility and temporary entry for professionals.[47]

A leaked TiSA draft dating to April 2015 suggests a more restrictive EU approach in those negotiations, however.[48] The highly incomplete version of the agreement resembles the structure of the GATS, and contains two annexes of particular relevance for current purposes: the Annex on Movement of Natural Persons and the Annex on Professional Services. These provide further elaboration on the obligations of the signatories compared to the original GATS, but are replete with disagreements between the negotiating parties. The draft shows that four categories of temporary entry are being negotiated: intra-corporate transferees, business visitors, contractual services suppliers and independent professionals, the latter two being delinked from commercial presence. While the EU supports the inclusion of all four categories, it wishes to retain the possibility of subjecting the entry of the latter two categories to economic needs tests.

The rather mixed picture that emerges suggests that, while the EU is open to creating a somewhat wider framework for temporary entry, especially as compared to the US position, the Member States are, as of yet, unwilling to make ambitious absolute commitments. This general EU reluctance to make far-reaching commitments with regards to temporary entry is not reserved for trade agreements: lack of political will among the Member States has also impeded the realisation of joint policy on labour immigration, with a few exceptions. Notably for current purposes, one of these exceptions is the passing of the Directive on Intra-Corporate Transferees. This suggests a preference for regulating even temporary entry on one's own terms through legislation rather than through free trade agreements.

IV. A MORE PRINCIPLED APPROACH: EQUAL TREATMENT AND THE CONCEPT OF 'MIGRANT PERSONAL WORK AND SERVICES PROVIDERS'

As mentioned at the beginning of this chapter, trade in goods and trade in services are increasingly difficult to distinguish from each other. Even traditional manufacturing products, such as trucks, are today sold in conjunction with services.[49] We have also shown how the delivery of services

[47] European Union, 'Services in TTIP' factsheet (2015), http://trade.ec.europa.eu/doclib/docs/2015/january/tradoc_152999.2%20Services.pdf.

[48] WikiLeaks, 'Trade in Services Agreement' (2015), https://wikileaks.org/tisa/.

[49] For example, truck manufacturer Scania offers the buyers of its vehicles additional services such as maintenance, training of drivers and other services aimed at improving the customer's return on their investment in Scania's products. See: Scania, 'Services', http://www.scania.com/products-services/services/.

can involve labour mobility in a number of ways. Taken together, this should make cross-border labour mobility an important part of comprehensive trade agreements with a strong impetus for facilitating labour mobility. In the previous section, we have shown that this is not necessarily the case. Probably primarily due to US resistance, labour mobility has been left outside of TPP and has an uncertain future in the TTIP negotiations. In GATS, and most likely in TiSA, a framework for mobility is provided, but mobility is conditioned on countries making specific commitments which can be very limited in scope. The same is true for CETA which, despite limiting the scope to highly qualified and experienced professionals on contracts for less than 12 months, still allows Canada and the individual EU Member States to limit their commitments further.

The most probable explanation is that immigration is an issue that tends to be politically very sensitive, and that has not become less sensitive in recent years. National politicians are aware of the potential benefits deriving from migratory flows, in terms of addressing various types of skills shortages and demographic challenges, but are reluctant to relinquish control over who enters their territory, or at least to be perceived to do so. It must be tempting for them to seek to regulate these flows by means of arrangements that, on paper at least, only appear to be 'temporary' or seasonal. And it must be even more tempting to do so indirectly by means of trade, and trade in services, agreements, rather than directly through migration treaties. But this is also proving to be controversial, as ultimately regulating immigration through international trade agreements also involves the partial transfer of a number of key aspects of national sovereignty.

The labour law aspects of trade in services–related labour mobility stills seem to play a minor role in the policy-making process. At least from a European perspective, this is rather surprising, considering the controversy that has come to surround the posting of workers between EU Member States, with concerns of fraud and underbidding.[50] Most interesting from this perspective is CETA. The exemption of blue-collar workers is well in line with national labour immigration policies that tend to favour flows of highly skilled and educated persons and should probably not be overinterpreted as a 'Laval effect'. The insertion of a clause on labour rights in the temporary entry chapter is from this perspective more interesting.

Our prediction is that the pressure on governments from business interests to include more binding labour mobility provisions in future trade agreements will not diminish. In our view, this creates the need for a more principled approach.

As we indicated at the beginning of this chapter we suggest that there would be ample reasons to identify within our cross-border mobility matrix

[50] See, eg Mark Freedland and Jeremias Prassl (eds), *Viking, Laval, and Beyond* (Oxford, Hart Publishing, 2014).

an area of migration characterised by the 'provision of predominantly personal work or services' where the element of capital, in the form of tangible or intangible assets for the performance of that work or service, is only marginal or ancillary. We argue that this family of cross-border human mobility processes should become the object of separate and specific bilateral, plurilateral and multilateral negotiations with the view of regulating and promoting free movement across countries and regions of the world on the basis of the principle of equal treatment between home workers and migrant workers (bar perhaps for particularly short postings where the integration of the migrant worker in the fabric of the host economy or society is neither necessary nor possible), and the respect for international labour standards. In a way, we suggest a progressive assimilation of these processes to the rules currently shaping the migration of workers, and the decoupling of this broad category from the element of duration of the provision.

V. CONCLUSIONS

The analysis carried out in the previous sections reveals the regulatory trajectory of current arrangements for temporary labour migration, and the state of global economic and trade integration. It suggests that seeking to understand existing and developing trade agreements as essentially dealing with trade in goods or essentially dealing with trade in services fundamentally obscures the realities of trade agreements in general and of the human migration phenomena arising (or not arising) from them. Our view is that a better conceptualisation of these agreements (which are increasingly covering matters such as investment and investment protection, regulatory co-operation, and specific rules on dispute settlements between governments but also between corporations and governments) is to see them as agreements for global economic integration. By their nature, these new agreements affect national political sovereignty in much deeper ways than earlier 'trade in goods' agreements. This is surely part of the explanation of the controversy surrounding TTIP, TiSA and TTP negotiations.

Behind all the various 'spaghetti bowls' and regional or plurilateral attempts to rationalise them, we can see the emergence of a no doubt complex regulatory regime, but one that is fundamentally committed to economic integration in the absence of political integration, to economic governance in the absence of government. It endeavours to promote the free circulation of goods, capital and services, without recognising, let alone promoting, the essential human/labour component that is intrinsic to them. Systems of regional integration, such as the EU, which have developed more advanced, though no doubt imperfect, systems of political integration that accompany both economic *and* human integration are unsurprisingly increasingly under pressure. They are accused of taking integration way too far, by including human integration and political integration in a way that is unnecessary for, or even detrimental to, (free) market based economic integration.

We suggest that this has fundamental implications in terms of the free trade rules shaping human mobility dynamics. In particular we believe that they explain the current tendency to seek to restrict regulated immigration flows, while at the same time promoting less regulated and open forms of immigration. We also venture to suggest that these restrictions are constructed more to prevent migration than to prevent underbidding—despite the 'Laval' debate. Underbidding is of course a risk, but one that, in our view, and in this particular context, is very much used as a pretext.

Finally we feel that the, frankly unsurprising, inability of trade agreements to regulate complex human migration dynamics ought to suggest that migration and immigration rules and policies ought to be seen as the appropriate regulatory tools to engage with the, no doubt numerous and complex, challenges they pose to 21st century democratic polities. Migration and immigration policies should be designed to promote long-term migration patterns, on a 'place of work' and 'equal treatment principle' basis, and incorporate full respect of internationally recognised fundamental and labour rights standards, including the right to work for different employers. They should be kept separate from rules and arrangements for global economic integration that are primarily inspired by commodificatory rationales.

4

The Distinction Between Temporary Labour Migration and Posted Work in Austria

Labour Law versus Trade Law

GUDRUN BIFFL AND ISABELLA SKRIVANEK

I. INTRODUCTION

AUSTRIA HAS A long tradition of temporary labour migration flowing from the guest worker programmes that governed migration policy between 1962 and 1992.[1] In 1992, the temporary migration policy was abandoned in favour of an immigration policy modelled after the US system, giving family migration precedence over labour migration, while continuing to attribute an important role to migration on humanitarian grounds. This shift in policy represented a change in paradigm away from temporary migration to settler migration.[2] However, an important component of temporary labour migration was preserved, namely the seasonal worker programme.

More recently, in 1996, a new form of temporary cross-border labour mobility surfaced, flowing from increased EU integration, called posted work. It is regulated by the Posted Workers Directive of 1996 and

[1] Gudrun Biffl, 'Entwicklung der Migrationen in Österreich aus historischer Sicht' in Gudrun Biffl and Nikolaus Dimmel (eds), Migrationsmanagement: Grundzüge des Managements von Migration und Integration, vol 1 (Bad Vöslau, Omninum, 2011) 33–50.

[2] Gudrun Biffl, *Satisfying Labour Demand through Migration in Austria* (Vienna, International Organisation for Migration, 2011).

(more latterly) the Posted Workers Enforcement Directive of 2014.[3] In this chapter, we take a close look at the distinction between seasonal work and posted work as two distinct forms of temporary labour migration which are regulated by two different legal frameworks. While seasonal labour migration is regulated by labour law and is part of migration policy, the posting of workers across borders is an element of trade law, and only marginally controlled by labour law. This raises the question of the impact of these two strands of temporary migration on the labour market and on public revenue.

In what follows we provide a succinct overview firstly of seasonal migrant labour arrangements in Austria, and secondly of posted work in Austria. In the final substantive section, we identify the effect of these two different forms of temporary migrant labour on the functional mechanisms of the Austrian labour market and the employment-based social security system.

II. SEASONALITY OF WORK AND THE ROLE OF DOMESTIC AND FOREIGN LABOUR

Austria has a long history of seasonal employment dating back to the nineteenth century when citizens from the various central and eastern European regions of the Habsburg Empire came to work in what is now Austria, predominantly in construction as well as agriculture and forestry. The traditional seasonal work relations survived during the Iron Curtain era—at least as far as harvesting was concerned, particularly between Hungary and the eastern border regions of Austria (Burgenland).[4] Cross-border seasonal work was built on long-term labour relations, that is, the same persons tended to come to work for the same farmers; thus, trust was built between the two sides of the contract and also a genuine understanding of the work and the skills needed.

But agriculture and forestry are not the only economic activities that have pronounced seasonal fluctuations of employment. Construction and tourism also exhibit strong seasonal patterns. The monthly pattern differs between the various seasonal activities: tourism has two peaks over the year,

[3] Directive 96/71/EC of the European Parliament and of the Council of 16 December 1996 concerning the posting of workers in the framework of the provision of services [1997] OJ L18/1. See also Directive 2014/67/EU of the European Parliament and of the Council of 15 May 2014 on the enforcement of Directive 96/71/EC concerning the posting of workers in the framework of the provision of services and amending Regulation (EU) No 1024/2012 on administrative co-operation through the Internal Market Information System ('the IMI Regulation') [2014] OJ L159/11.

[4] Zoltan Dövényi, 'Zeitliche und räumliche Aspekte der Migrationswellen in Ungarn 1918–1995' in Gerhard Seewann (ed), *Migration und ihre Auswirkungen. Das Beispiel Ungarn 1918–1995* (Munich, South-German Historical Commission, 1997).

the winter and the summer season; construction has one peak in summer; agriculture has two peaks, one in spring and one in autumn; and forestry has one in winter. The overall outcome of the various seasonal patterns in total employment is an employment trough in January and a peak in July.

A. Pronounced Seasonal Employment Pattern in International Comparison

Seasonal work constitutes an important element of employment in Austria and accounts for a higher proportion of the workforce than in most other countries. The difference in employment between the minimum in January and the maximum in July amounted to 178,500 employees in 2013, that is, 5.1 per cent of the annual average level of employment. The seasonal variation in the numbers of foreign workers is even greater, indicating their important role in the seasonal workforce. The span between the lowest and highest employment level of foreigners over 2013, that is, between January and July, amounts to 54,300 (10.6 per cent) and is thus double the span for all employees.

Seasonal work permits (for third country citizens and citizens of EU Member States affected by transitional arrangements)[5] are issued in tourism and agriculture/forestry. Annual quotas are fixed by the Minister of Labour and Social Affairs, on the basis of an agreement between the social partners and the provinces.[6] Asylum seekers may also access these types of temporary jobs. In contrast, annual quotas are no longer set in the construction sector.

The different employment strategies in the construction industry relative to tourism and agriculture/forestry may be explained by the opposing interests of the two sides of the social partnership combined with the differing bargaining power of the workers in the respective industries. While the interests of workers are well represented in the construction sector via a high degree of unionisation and an important role of work councils at the firm level, this is not the case in the agricultural/forestry sector and in tourism, sectors that are dominated by SMEs (small and medium-sized enterprises) and a limited degree of unionisation.[7] It is in the interest of the workforce, the insiders, to protect their year-round employment and good working

[5] Citizens of the EU have a right to freedom of movement and work within the EU. However, when the EU expanded from 2004 onwards, some EU members, including Austria, imposed transitional restrictions on citizens of the newly admitted Member States, curtailing free movement of labour, to prevent immediate flooding of their labour markets.

[6] Gudrun Biffl, Lea Rennert and Petra Aigner, *Migrant Workers in Austria and Europe: Challenges for Industrial Relations, in Particular Trade Unions* (Krems an der Donau, Danube University Krems, 2011).

[7] Sabine Blaschke, 'Gewerkschaftlicher Organisationsgrad in Österreich' (1999) 28(1) Zeitschrift für Soziologie 60.

conditions; they resent being constantly put under pressure by an external seasonal workforce.[8] Accordingly, prior to the eastern enlargement of the EU, the social partners in the construction sector decided to institute an annual working hour concept (*Jahresarbeitszeitmodell*) in 1996. The model is built around variable weekly working hours over the whole year, the take-up of part of the annual vacation in December and a bonus for employers who keep their workers in employment over the Christmas holidays. The effect of this arrangement was a reduction of the seasonal variation and a stabilisation of employment over the year. In addition, the annual average number of employees in the construction sector has decreased by 17,000 workers (6.6 per cent) from 1996 to 2013. Their share decreased from 8.6 per cent of the total workforce to 7.1 per cent over the same period, partly as a result of technological change. But relative wages and working conditions were preserved.[9]

By way of contrast, the employer representatives in agriculture/forestry and tourism rejected workers' demands to implement an annual working hour arrangement. The rationale was that seasonal employment fluctuations are at no or limited cost to the employer, as long as there is abundant labour supply for these kinds of jobs in Austria or in the not too distant neighbourhood abroad. It is important to note that guaranteeing decent work for the seasonal agricultural workforce has proved difficult. As Gétaz et al show, the current work practices in industrial harvesting in many countries in Europe do not conform to the 'decent work agenda' of the ILO.[10] A report on industrial harvesting of vegetables in Marchfeld, a fertile region in the eastern provinces of Austria, corroborates the international observation that seasonal workers in Austria often experience poor working conditions (wages and working hours) and overcrowded accommodation.[11] The report suggests that these developments are new for Austria and a consequence of market liberalisation and industrialisation of agriculture, which do not halt at the borders of Austria.[12]

[8] Gudrun Biffl, 'Zuwanderung und Segmentierung des österreichischen Arbeitsmarktes: Ein Beitrag zur Insider-Outsider-Diskussion' in Karl Husa, Christof Parnreiter and Irene Stacher (eds), *Internationale Migration: Die globale Herausforderung des 21. Jahrhunderts?* (Vienna, Brandes & Apsel/Südwind, 2000) 207–27. See also Wolfgang Pollan, 'Flexible Löhne in der Bauwirtschaft' (1993) 6 Wifo-MB 335.

[9] Rechnungshof (General Accounting Office), *Bericht des Rechnungshofes über die durchschnittlichen Einkommen der gesamten Bevölkerung getrennt nach Branchen, Berufsgruppen und Funktionen für die Jahre 2010 und 2011* (Vienna, Rechnungshof, 2012). See also: Table 4.2.

[10] Raymond Gétaz, Kathi Hahn and Hannes Reiser (eds), *Bittere Ernte: Die moderne Sklaverei in der industriellen Landwirtschaft Europas* (Paris, European Civic Forum, 2004). See also ILO, 'Decent Work Agenda', http://www.ilo.org/global/about-the-ilo/decent-work-agenda/lang--en/index.htm.

[11] *Kontraste, Migration und Politik, Presse- und Informationsdienst für Sozialpolitik* (Linz, Institut für Gesellschafts- und Sozialpolitik, 2005) 20–21.

[12] Wolfgang Pirker, *Ausländische Saisonarbeitskräfte* (PhD thesis, Vienna, University of Vienna, 2010).

Tourism presents a different case altogether as it is seen as a tool for local economic development, enabling or promoting regional economic growth.[13] In Austria, employment in tourism follows a rising trend; in 2013, it accounted for 5.6 per cent of total dependent employment compared to 4.7 per cent in 1998. In addition, the spillover of tourism into other economic activities, that is the employment multiplier of tourism, is more important than in many other industries. This becomes manifest in the Austrian tourism satellite account, a standard statistical framework for the measurement of tourism activities and its interplay with other industries.[14]

B. The Legal Framework of Seasonal Migrant Labour

In Austria, the regulatory model for the recruitment of seasonal workers dates back to an amendment of the *Alien Residence Act* (Fremdengesetz 1997, FrG 1997) in 2002. The Act abolished the quota for low- and medium-skilled labour migration and only highly skilled workers could continue to enter for work (‘*Schlüsselkräfte*’). Labour demand for lower skills was to be satisfied by domestic labour and family migration, complemented by seasonal workers. The Federal Ministry for Labour and Social Affairs could admit such temporary seasonal workers by decree. This provision was later modified and transferred from the Alien Residence Act to the Foreign Employment Act 2011 (article 5(1)).

The seasonal work permit is limited to six months but can be extended by a further six months. After twelve months, the seasonal worker cannot receive a further permit for two months. For a work permit to be granted, labour market testing is required, that is, potential employers have to prove that they are unable to fill the seasonal posts using domestic labour. So-called ‘core seasonal workers’ are exempt from labour market testing.[15] Core seasonal workers are seasonal workers who worked for at least four months in the last five years. They need confirmation of their core seasonal worker status from the Public Employment Service.[16] This group of workers

[13] Anne-Mette Hjalager and Steen Andersen, ‘Tourism Employment: Contingent Work or Professional Career?’ (2001) 23(2) Employee Relations 115; Lee Jolliffe and Regena Farnsworth, ‘Seasonality in Tourism Employment: Human Resource Challenges’ (2003) 15(6) International Journal of Contemporary Hospitality Management 312; OECD, ‘LEED Programme (Local Economic and Employment Development)’, http://www.oecd.org/employment/leed/.

[14] Peter Laimer and Egon Smeral, *Ein Tourismus-Satellitenkonto für Österreich: Methodik, Ergebnisse und Prognosen für die Jahre 2000 bis 2013* (Vienna, Statistics Austria and WIFO, 2012).

[15] Regulated in Foreign Employment Act 2011 art 5, which came into effect on 1 May 2011.

[16] Arbeitsmarktservice Österreich, ‘Beschäftigungsbewilligung für Saisonarbeitskräfte (Kontingentbewilligung) [Employment Permit for Seasonal Workers (Contingent Approval)]’, http://www.ams.at/service-unternehmen/auslaenderinnen/zugangsberechtigungen/beschaeftigungsbewilligung-saisonarbeitskraefte-kontingentbewilligung.

may be employed without going through the quota proceedings but they still need a seasonal work permit. The introduction of the 'core seasonal worker' status in 2011 was an acknowledgement of the interests of the two parties, the employers and workers, in regular seasonal employment where the employer and the worker know and trust each other. Foreign workers who had worked in the previous three years under the quota for seasonal workers in agriculture/forestry and who were subject to the transitional arrangements regarding free mobility could be granted a work permit in forestry/agriculture for up to nine months.[17] In 2015, transitional arrangements continue to apply for workers from Croatia, potentially until 2020. In addition to a quota of seasonal workers, a quota for harvesting was introduced, where harvesters may work for up to six weeks in Austria ('*Erntehelfer*').

While the law on temporary foreign employment is quite general and does not limit temporary work permits to seasonal work, the reality is that temporary work permits are only issued for work in tourism and agriculture/forestry—with the exception of a small quota for the EURO 2008 football event and the world ski championship in Austria in 2012/13.

C. Labour Market Impact of Seasonal Work

Various factors influence seasonal employment, apart from seasonal weather conditions, in particular the economic situation, technological developments and institutional regulations. Regulations may be prompted by labour market and migration policy or else by institutional changes like European enlargement and concomitant free labour movement. While the former changes the regulatory framework within which market forces may come to play, the latter widens the space for market forces, thereby affecting the supply of labour in the various occupations at the going wage rates. This is to say that there is, in principle, in the medium and long run a certain substitutability between labour and capital. In other words, investment in certain production techniques may allow continued employment the year round, thereby reducing the need for additional seasonal labour. This strategy will be favoured in occupations that experience labour scarcities at the going wage rate and working conditions, either as a result of market forces (faster growth in labour demand than in labour supply), or because of disproportionate rises in wage costs due to an egalitarian wage policy as in Sweden.[18] Sweden provides a good example of the preference for investment in production techniques in the housing sector, which allows for year-round employment rather than employing seasonal foreign workers in the summer.

[17] Foreign Employment Act 2011 art 32a.

[18] Thorsten Schulten, *Solidarische Lohnpolitik in Europa, Ansätze und Perspektiven einer Europäisierung gewerkschaftlicher Lohnpolitik*, Discussion Paper No 92 (Düsseldorf, Institute of Economic and Social Research (WSI), 2001).

Given the fairly small numbers of seasonal workers relative to total employment, the overall effect of seasonal work permits on wages and unemployment is quite small. However, in the industries affected, the impact is not negligible. About two thirds of seasonal foreign workers are in agriculture and forestry and one third in tourism. Accordingly, seasonal foreign workers make up a high proportion of foreign wage and salary earners in agriculture and forestry, namely some 80 per cent in 2013. In tourism the share is much lower; only 6 per cent of all foreign workers in tourism work on the basis of a seasonal work permit.

While the numbers of seasonal workers are quite small on an annual average, the numbers of permits issued in the course of a year are quite high, as large numbers of individuals enter possibly several times a year to take up seasonal jobs.

Figure 4.1 provides an overview of the composition of the seasonal work permits issued per year by sector—tourism, agriculture/forestry and harvesting—between 1997 and 2013. The rising numbers of seasonal permits, excluding harvesting, from 26,000 in 1997 to a high of 50,300 in 2008 indicate that seasonal work was an important way to enter the Austrian labour market for citizens of the accession countries, the new EU Member States to the east of Austria. The economic decline in 2009

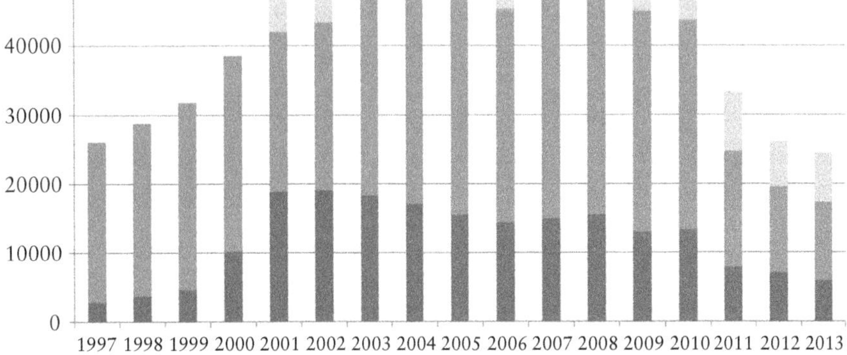

Figure 4.1: Seasonal Work Permits Issued in Tourism, Agriculture/Forestry and Harvesting, Sum over the Year: 1997–2013[19]

[19] Source: Austrian Public Employment Service/Labour Market Research and Statistics, author's calculations.

following the global financial crisis reduced their numbers, and the end of transitional regulations governing the entry of workers from some new EU Member States in 2011 added to the decline. Therefore, in 2013, only 17,300 permits were issued to third-country citizens and the remaining two EU Member States with transitional regulations, Bulgaria and Romania.

Seasonal employment was an important instrument to pave the way into the Austrian labour market for citizens of EU Member States with transitional regulations; in accordance with the EU principle of community preference, they were prioritised in the issue of seasonal work permits.[20]

D. The Labour Market Impact of Seasonal Work in the Industries Concerned

Today, agriculture and tourism rely on foreign labour more than any other industry and their dependence upon foreign labour has increased over time (see Table 4.1). In 2013, 48 per cent of the wage and salary earners in agriculture were foreigners and 43 per cent in tourism compared to 16 per cent in total employment. Also construction industries have an above average share of foreign workers: 23.2 per cent in 2013. As mentioned above, the strategies adopted to cope with seasonal employment fluctuations differed between construction on the one hand and tourism and agriculture on the other. While the former introduced an annual flexible working hour model and abandoned seasonal migrant work, the latter took full advantage of the abundant external labour supply and adopted a seasonal migrant work model.

Table 4.1: Number and Share of Foreign Workers by Industry, Yearly Averages for 1998, 2004, 2007, 2013[21]

Sector	Agriculture, forestry		Tourism		Construction		All	
Year	*Number*	*Share*	*Number*	*Share*	*Number*	*Share*	*Number*	*Share*
1998	5,412	20.5	38,306	26.5	46,991	17.7	298,582	9.7
2004	7,789	28.1	49,969	31.4	43,874	18.5	362,299	11.3
2007	8,941	30.5	57,836	34.2	47,424	19.1	412,578	12.3
2013	10,405	47.8	83,669	42.6	57,591	23.2	556,752	16.0

The seasonal migrant work strategy resulted in rising seasonal employment fluctuations in agriculture/forestry and tourism. Employment in agriculture exhibits the highest fluctuations, followed by tourism. These fluctuations are not fully mirrored in the seasonal unemployment pattern, as seasonal

[20] Foreign Employment Act art 32a.
[21] Source: BALIweb, author's calculations.

workers who are working on the basis of a seasonal work permit may not access unemployment benefits. Thus, the practice of raising labour supply via seasonal work permits depresses the unemployment rate because seasonal unemployment is exported. However, this situation may change with free mobility of labour as citizens of EU Member States may access these types of jobs and continue to reside in Austria, thereby raising the domestic labour supply over the full year.

The impact on wages and unemployment remains an open question, depending on institutional regulations, for example the reduction of seasonal work permits for third-country citizens, and technological change. What we see today is a rise in unemployment, particularly of unskilled labourers, in the wake of the end of the transitional regulations in 2011. As to wages, wages in agriculture/forestry and tourism are at the bottom end of the wage scale. It can be taken from Table 4.2 that 50 per cent of the 47,000 wage and salary earners in agriculture/forestry earned less than 4,000 euros per annum, only a quarter earned more than 12,000 euros, and a quarter earned no more than 1,050 euros. It can be assumed that the latter group is mainly composed of harvesters. Their monthly gross wage is set at about 1,000 euros in the respective collective agreements.[22] Incomes are generally higher in tourism than in agriculture, but relatively low compared to construction, the other important seasonal employment industry. In 2010, one quarter of the 294,800 wage and salary earners in tourism earned less than 3,000 euros, half of them less than 10,000 and only one quarter about 18,000 euros or more. In comparison, of the 283,700 wage and salary earners in construction, the lowest quarter of income earners earned not much less than the top quarter in tourism.

Seasonal Work Permits in Agriculture and Forestry

The employment of seasonal workers was of great relevance for the agricultural sector before the eastern enlargement of the EU and during the operation of the transitional regulations. Between 2000 and 2010, more than 60 per cent of foreign workers in agriculture and forestry had a temporary work permit (excluding harvesters). In May 2011, the transitional arrangements for workers from the central and eastern European Union Member States came to an end. As a consequence, the number of foreigners with temporary work permits dropped substantially. Quotas for seasonal workers were adjusted downwards and the number of seasonal work permits fell accordingly.[23]

[22] See Collective Agreement for Workers at Farms in Lower Austria, cited in Pirker, Ausländische Saisonarbeitskräfte 297.

[23] Julia Bock-Schappelwein and Peter Huber, 'Differenzierung der Nachfrage nach ausländischen Arbeitskräften' in Gudrun Biffl, Julia Bock-Schappelwein and Peter Huber (eds), *Zur Niederlassung von Ausländern und Ausländerinnen in Österreich* (Vienna, Bundesministerium für Inneres, 2011).

Table 4.2: Annual Gross Income of Wage and Salary Earners in Austria by Industry Sectors, 2010

	Industry sectors	Wage and salary earners				
		Number of persons	25%	50%	75%	Arithmetic mean
			earn less than ... euros			
A	**Agriculture, forestry, fishing**	**46,652**	**1,045**	**3,973**	**12,035**	**9,068**
B	Mining and quarrying	6,793	24,165	33,566	48,099	40,814
C	Manufacturing	620,771	21,133	31,500	43,487	35,334
D	Energy	29,065	32,904	49,613	69,082	53,407
E	Water supply, sewerage, waste management and remediation	17,124	17,617	27,291	36,327	29,176
F	**Construction**	**283,651**	**16,660**	**26,385**	**34,377**	**27,847**
G	Wholesale and retail trade; repair of motor vehicles and motorcycles	591,430	10,782	20,395	31,467	25,040
H	Transportation and storage	210,644	16,710	28,861	38,677	30,823
I	**Tourism**	**294,771**	**2,971**	**9,693**	**17,678**	**11,704**
J	Information and communication activities	89,607	19,100	38,271	56,882	42,612
K	Financial and insurance activities	131,470	22,881	40,015	61,754	48,350
L	Real estate activities	44,771	7,129	21,047	36,590	27,177
M	Professional, scientific, technical, administration services	174,307	9,155	24,827	41,487	33,233
N	Support service activities	239,700	5,116	14,417	23,718	16,934
O	Public administration and defence; compulsory social security	573,123	23,400	34,871	48,889	37,327
P	Education	100,503	3,884	17,699	33,903	24,859
Q	Human health and social work activities	259,420	9,595	19,786	30,354	22,347

(continued)

Table 4.2: *(Continued)*

	Industry sectors	Wage and salary earners				
		Number of persons	25%	50%	75%	Arithmetic mean
			earn less than ... euros			
R	Arts, entertainment and recreation	50,996	4,200	15,450	30,700	23,059
S	Other services	97,321	8,330	17,483	30,091	22,611
T	Activities of households as employers; Undifferentiated goods- and services-producing activities of households for own use	1,505	2,825	8,025	17,390	11,879
U	Activities of exterritorial organisations and bodies	76	19,748	36,093	52,148	37,877
	Unknown	36,665	291	1,101	4,296	9,094
	Total	3,900,365	11,213	24,516	37,974	28,715

With the end of the transitional arrangements for the central and eastern European Union Member States, temporary permits for seasonal workers lost relevance as a side entrance to the Austrian labour market. In 2013, the share of seasonal work permit holders among foreign workers in agriculture was below 50 per cent. It remains an open question whether the former permit holders are now working in the same jobs but with comprehensive social security coverage or if they have taken up better paid and more stable jobs in other industrial sectors. In 2013, 38 per cent of the seasonal work permits in agriculture (excluding harvesting) were issued to Romanians, 18 per cent to Bosnians and 15 per cent to Ukrainians. A further 4–9 per cent of permits were issued to citizens of the Republic of Kosovo, Croats and Serbs. Permits for harvesting went first and foremost to Romanians (85 per cent). Bulgarians, Bosnians, Serbs and Croats had shares between 3 and 5 per cent. This pattern shows that seasonal work is a small temporary 'entrance gate' to the Austrian labour market for migrants from the former guest worker regions in Yugoslavia. While Croats continue to be subject to EU labour market transitional arrangements, Ukrainians are 'newcomers' to this job segment. While only 100 seasonal work permits were issued to Ukrainians in 1997, their numbers rose to 1400 in 2004 and further to 1800 in 2013, after a transitory slowdown in the wake of the eastern enlargement of the EU in 2007, when EU-2 citizens (ie those from Bulgaria and Romania) enjoyed preferential treatment.

Seasonal Work Permits in Tourism

Tourism is the single most important employment sector for migrant workers: in July 2013, 15 per cent of foreign wage and salary earners worked in tourism, a further 13 per cent in trade and repair works, and 11 per cent in construction. Only 3 per cent of all foreign workers were employed in agriculture.

Only a small proportion of migrant workers are employed on the basis of a seasonal permit: in 2007, 7.7 per cent, following a declining trend as citizens of the new EU Member States received the right to free mobility and, therefore, no longer needed preferential treatment via seasonal work permits. With the end of transitional arrangements for the EU-8 in 2011, the yearly seasonal quotas for tourism were adjusted downwards and the number of permit holders dropped.[24] Seasonal permit workers in tourism today tend to originate from Bosnia-Herzegovina (38 per cent of all seasonal work permits in 2013), Croatia (30 per cent) and Serbia (13 per cent).

E. Prospects for Seasonal Work

The introduction of the seasonal worker model for tourism and agriculture/forestry in 2002 was a compromise between the two coalition partners in government: the conservative People's Party (ÖVP) and the right-wing Freedom Party (FPÖ). The objective of the Freedom Party was 'zero immigration' while the employer-driven People's Party called for foreign workers. The reorientation of migration policy towards temporary migration rather than settlement was, in the eye of the governing Freedom Party, an end to the 'wrong immigration policy path' of the former Social Democratic government, which had opened the 'doors to Austria' in the late 1980s.[25] Even though the Freedom Party opposed immigration, it acknowledged the need for seasonal work, particularly in tourism. But immigration had to be regulated to minimise competition with domestic labour—a conviction the Social Democrats shared with the Freedom Party. Accordingly, labour market testing had to apply. The People's Party was also in favour and stated that it was 'correct' not to grant the right of settlement and family reunion to seasonal workers. The Social Democratic opposition criticised the model as a return to the former guest worker model, by allowing seasonal work for up to 12 months within 14 months. However, when they returned to

[24] The eight countries that joined the EU on 1 May 2004 are: Czech Republic, Estonia, Hungary, Latvia, Lithuania, Poland, Slovakia and Slovenia. EU-8 nationals had restricted access to work, ie labour market testing was imposed between 2004 and 2011, effectively excluding unskilled labourers from accessing regular all year round work in Austria.

[25] Isabella Skrivanek, *Die österreichische AusländerInnenbeschäftigungspolitik 1987–2006: Inhalte und Veränderungen* (Masters thesis, Vienna, University of Vienna, 2008) 111f.

power in 2007, they did not make any major changes to the seasonal worker model. Instead, they used this model to promote the access of citizens of the new EU Member States to the labour market, particularly for unskilled and semi-skilled workers.

In a situation like today with high and rising unemployment, where there is not enough demand for labour to keep everybody employed even in the seasonal peak, a model favouring year-round employment like the one in the construction sector tends to exacerbate the unemployment problem of peripheral workers. Free mobility of labour increases the labour supply and with it also unemployment unless the migrant workers have scarce skills and are able to enter jobs where their skills are desperately needed. The question that remains to be answered is whether it is preferable, from a labour market policy perspective, to promote seasonal employment, thereby ensuring work contact for a larger number of workers, or to give preference to durable year-round jobs for a smaller number of workers. In either case, the unemployment rate could be the same but the long-term implications would be different: in the first case, the incidence of unemployment is high and the duration of the unemployment spell short (seasonal unemployment); in the second case, the incidence of unemployment is low but the duration of the unemployment spell is long, thereby contributing to long-term and, thus, structural unemployment. The second policy option would require greater reliance on active labour market policy, in particular more education and training measures, to raise the employability of the unemployed and reduce long-term unemployment.

III. POSTED WORK AND LABOUR MARKET IMPACT

A relatively new phenomenon on the Austrian labour market is posted work, that is, cross-border services provided by persons who are employed in one country but carry out work in another. The ILO includes this group of persons amongst migrants who are covered by the Migration for Employment Convention (Revised) 1949 (No 97) and the Migrant Workers (Supplementary Provisions) Convention 1975 (No 143);[26] this means, amongst other things, that under these conventions posted workers have the right to equal treatment.

[26] ILO Convention No 97 focuses on the right to equal treatment, and ILO Convention No 143 undertakes to respect the human rights of all migrant workers (art 1), and encourages regulations to reduce migration in abusive conditions and to promote equality and integration. Only 49 countries, mostly emigration countries, have ratified ILO Convention No 97; while even fewer, 23 countries, have ratified ILO Convention No 143. The scope of most other ILO conventions is, however, broad enough to cover migrant workers: see, eg Freedom of Association and Protection of the Right to Organise Convention 1948 (No 87), and the Equality of Treatment (Social Security) Convention 1962 (No 118).

The distinction between temporary migration and posted work is somewhat blurred, as can be exemplified by temporary work in harvesting. In the case of migrant workers from non-EU countries who are employed directly by the local farmer, national immigration regulations apply, while in the case of services provision by a posted worker from a foreign company, General Agreement on Trade in Services (GATS) rules apply. The posting of workers within the EU (ie from one EU country to another EU country) is governed by the relevant European directives, which broadly incorporate the same trade law approach.[27]

Opening up to freer trade and confronting national labour institutions and legislation with the logic of trade through the promotion of services mobility (GATS Mode 4) means ensuring unimpeded competition between the EU Member States.[28] In theory, under the assumption of perfect competition and constant returns to scale, such a course should lead to economic benefits and higher living standards for all. In practice, the outcome for most countries may not be so simple, and the economic and social effects are a matter of controversy.

A. Posted Work in Austria

Given the complexity of employment relationships involved in services mobility involving cross-border movement of persons, it is hard to establish the exact numbers of foreign persons and working hours involved. However, Austria, a country with comparatively good data on migration and cross-border service provision, has a reasonable basis for assessing the effect of services mobility on the labour market.

Posted Workers from Third Countries and EU Member States with Transitional Regulations

Given its long border with the new EU Member States in the east, Austria imposed transitional agreements on the EU-10 Member States of 2004[29] and the EU-2 Member States of 2007 (Romania and Bulgaria), involving regulations on labour migration (labour market testing)—thereby curtailing free mobility of labour—and on cross-border posting of workers (for certain occupations and industries)—thereby curtailing free mobility of services. The Austrian Labour Market Service has been monitoring the inflow of

[27] See above n 3.

[28] For a discussion of GATS Mode 4 see Samuel Engblom, Nicola Kountouris and Åsa Odin Ekman, 'Temporary Labour Migration and the Trade in Services: European and Global Perspectives in an Age of Economic Integration', ch 3 in this volume.

[29] The countries concerned were Estonia, Latvia, Lithuania, Slovakia, Czech Republic, Poland, Hungary, Slovenia, Cyprus and Malta. Transitional regulations were imposed on all except Malta and Cyprus.

third-country posted workers and those from EU Member States under transitional regulations since 1997. It differentiates between liberalised services, which may enter freely—in this case the service provision is only registered (*Entsendebestätigung*)—and controlled services for which certain restrictions prevail (*Entsendebewilligung*). The controlled services are gardening, certain services in the stone, metal and construction industries, security and cleaning services, home care services and social work. Posting workers in those services require an authorisation, which in effect has to state that the national interests are not jeopardised by the specific service provision. This regulation is analogous to labour market testing of migrants.

In view of restrictions on cross-border service provision in certain occupations, many people from the new EU Member States have set up businesses as independent contractors, largely self-employed homecare service providers and, to a lesser extent, providers of certain building services. In addition, the number of posted workers from the EU-12[30] increased after enlargement, both in the liberalised and the sheltered occupations. The numbers of registered and authorised posted workers of third-country citizens (ie those from outside the EU) reached a high of 7,500 in 2005, some two per cent of all foreign workers, and declined thereafter, in particular after the end of the transitional regulations, to 5,300 in 2012. The most important third-country sources of posted workers in 2012 were Bosnia-Herzegovina, Croatia and Serbia, followed by Russia and India. The major industries in which posted workers provide their services are business-oriented services, the building industry, manufacturing and arts, sports and entertainment.

Posted EU Workers in the Light of Free Services Mobility

While the total number of posted workers from third countries and EU-12 Member States during transitional regulations is comparatively small, this is not the case for posted workers who enjoy free mobility within the EU. Article 12 of Regulation 883/2004/EC provides the legal basis for posting workers across EU Member States. Its aim is to facilitate the freedom to provide services for the benefit of employers who post workers to Member States other than those in which they are established, as well as the freedom of workers to move to other Member States, for example transport workers. Specific regulations pertain to the posting of workers to another Member State for a temporary period and where a person is working in two or more Member States, and certain categories of workers such as civil servants. The rules for determining which Member State's legislation is to apply are set out in articles 11–16 of Regulation 883/2004/EC and the related implementing provisions are set out in articles 14–21 of Regulation 987/2009/EC.

According to Eurostat/OECD data on posted workers, the total number of posted workers in Austria from another EU Member State or European

[30] The countries that joined the EU in 2004 and 2007.

Economic Area (EEA)/European Free Trade Association (EFTA) country rose from 37,400 in 2008 to 76,300 in 2011, that is, it more than doubled over a span of three years. The proportion of posted workers relative to the total salaried Austrian workforce amounted to 1.4 per cent in 2011, relative to the foreign work force at 16 per cent. This is a somewhat higher share than on average in the EU, where 1.5 million posted workers were registered in 2011, which is less than 1 per cent of the total workforce. The major source countries of posted workers in Austria are Germany, providing 51 per cent of all posted workers in 2011, followed by Slovenia, Hungary, Poland and Slovakia.

Austria is also a sending country of posted workers. The number of Austrians who are posted to another EU/EEA country is also on the rise, from 16,200 in 2008 to 28,800 in 2011. This means that somewhat less than one per cent of the Austrian workforce were posted abroad to provide a service. The major destination countries are the major trading partners of Austria, namely Germany, Italy and the Netherlands. In 2011, the number of Austrian posted workers to another EU/EEA state was about a third of the number of workers posted to Austria.

B. Prospects for Posted Work in the EU/EEA

The development of posted work is quite dynamic in the EU/EEA. The numbers of posted workers rose from a total of 1.29 million in 2008 to 1.5 million in 2011, that is, by some 220,000 or 17 per cent. The most important destination countries of posted workers are Germany and France; those two countries alone receive almost 40 per cent of all posted workers in the EU. The major source countries of posted workers differ in magnitude between the two countries: while 40 per cent of all posted workers in Germany come from Poland, followed by other EU-12 Member States, the source countries in France are far more widespread and largely neighbouring countries, such as Spain, UK, Germany, Luxembourg and Belgium. Of the EU-12 countries, Poland posts the most workers to France (16 per cent of all posted workers to France).

Poland appears to be specialising in posting workers. But on average new EU Member States[31] tend to be source countries rather than recipient countries of posted workers and old EU Member States[32] receiving countries. About 80 per cent of the posted workers are posted in one other EU/EEA state, 15 per cent are posted in two or more countries and a fairly

[31] Those countries that joined the European Union in 2004 and later.

[32] Those countries that joined the European Union before 2004, ie Germany, Italy, Luxembourg, Belgium, France, the Netherlands, United Kingdom, Ireland, Denmark, Greece, Spain, Portugal, Austria, Finland and Sweden.

small proportion (1.3 per cent) are engaged in international transport. International transport is a very specific sector where obtaining relevant information is not easy and securing proper working conditions remains a challenge.[33]

Given the increasing role of services in employment creation, the numbers of posted workers relative to migrant workers may increase quickly.[34] In view of strict wage regulations and control of working conditions in the case of migrants and the limited controls and controllability of wages and working conditions of posted workers, the posting of workers may actually take precedence over other forms of temporary immigration for companies seeking to satisfy their labour demands in a flexible way.

The use of posted workers represents yet another facet of the diversification of forms of employment, with core workers (insiders) being increasingly complemented by temporary workers (outsiders), who are either employed in leasing firms registered in Austria and working for various companies in Austria or in an enterprise registered in a foreign country but carrying out a specific task/service in Austria.

EU policy is set to promote free movement of goods and services,[35] including short-term labour migration regulated by the Services Directive.[36] Therefore, we may see a further rise in posted workers in the future.

IV. WHAT MAKES POSTING WORKERS SO DIFFERENT FROM TEMPORARY LABOUR MIGRATION?

While we do not question the economic benefits of free trade in commodities as one of the four 'fundamental freedoms'[37] of the European Union, the impact of posted work—as distinct from immigration—on labour markets

[33] For experiences with parcel services, see Harald Voitl, 'Transnationalität als Herausforderung und Chance: am Beispiel der globalen Branche der Paketdienstleister' in Gudrun Biffl and Lydia Rössl (eds), *Migration and Integration: Dialog zwischen Politik, Wissenschaft und Praxis* (Bad Vöslau, Omninum, 2011).

[34] Gudrun Biffl, 'Workers' Rights and Economic Freedoms' in Markus Marterbauer and Christine Mayerhuber (eds), *Entwürfe für die Zukunft von Wirtschafts- und Sozialpolitik* (Vienna, Lexis Nexis Orac Publ, 2010); Gudrun Biffl, 'Towards a Common Migration Policy: Potential Impact on the EU Economy' (2006) 1 Journal of Labour Market Research 1.

[35] Editorial, 'Mobility of Services and Posting of Workers in the Enlarged Europe: Challenges for Labour Market Regulation' (2006) 12(2) *Transfer* 137, 138.

[36] Directive 2006/123/EC of the European Parliament and of the Council of 12 December 2006 on services in the internal market [2006] OJ L376/36 (henceforth 'Services Directive'); see also Charles Woolfson and Jeff Sommers, 'Labour Mobility in Construction: European Implications of the Laval un Partneri Dispute with Swedish Labour' (2006) 12(1) European Journal of Industrial Relations 49.

[37] The four fundamental freedoms, freedom of movement of goods, services, persons and capital between the Member States, are the pillars of the single market established in the European Economic Community Treaty of Rome in 1957.

and the welfare system is less clear. Some commentators argue that the economic advantages of GATS Mode 4 services mobility are more straightforward and less costly than permanent immigration and similar to the trade in goods.[38] In the former, services come into the country; in the latter, goods. According to the World Trade Organization (WTO), the main advantage is derived from the temporary character of posted work, thus, avoiding additional costs in terms of infrastructure and social and cultural integration associated with permanent immigration.[39] This judgement is based on the assumption that posted workers, as a special case of temporary migrants, will return to their country of origin. Assuming this will happen, the question remains to what extent the preference of institutions like the WTO for services mobility is the result of an underestimation or neglect of the social costs of trade, in particular the impact on working conditions given widely differing wage and employment conditions across EU Member States. In addition, the use of service providers rather than local or immigrant labour may impact on the education and career choices of local youth, raising issues of long-term competitiveness.

The major question remains, however, to what extent the imports of services via Mode 4 and immigration differ in their economic and labour market impact. In the case of immigration, it can be said that the pressure on wages and employment opportunities increases with the elasticity of substitution of migrant versus resident labour. Thus, in occupations and industries in which migrant labour is complementary to resident labour, residents profit from migrant labour in terms of job opportunities and relative wages. In contrast, where migrant labour and resident labour are substitutes, the wages and employment of residents are adversely affected. Apart from these structural and distributive effects, migration contributes to economic growth.

The major distinguishing factor between the impact on the labour market of immigration and trade is that the latter acts directly on labour demand, in particular on the industrial composition, while migration affects the size and composition of labour supply and, thus, the productive potential. While migration tends to raise the labour supply at the lower and upper end of the skill spectrum, where transferability of skills is relatively high, services mobility Mode 4 has the potential to cut into the medium skill segment. This is what we tend to see in the majority of cross-border service provision

[38] Allan Winters, Terrie Louise Walmsley, Zhen Kun Wang and Roman Grynberg, 'Negotiating the Liberalization of the Temporary Movement of Natural Persons' (2003) 26(8) The World Economy 1137.

[39] WTO, *World Trade Report: The Liberalization of Services Trade through the Movement of Natural Persons* (Geneva, WTO, 2004).

in Austria. Moreover, migration and services mobility are inevitably linked with higher relative wages in the industries/occupations of the destination countries, as Samuelson and Andersen and Sorensen point out.[40]

But what really distinguishes migration from services mobility, apart from skill composition, is the differing impact on public revenues as a result of different taxation regimes. While migrants pay social security contributions which are levied on labour (employer and employee contributions) and income tax, posted workers are employed in their country of origin, thus, not paying into the social security funds of the service receiving country. Public revenues from posted workers accrue only from taxation of the imported service (value added tax). Currently, the revenues from taxation of imported services accrue to the source country of the posted worker.

A further important factor to be taken into account is that the different bases of the two taxes, the value added tax which focuses on the final product and the tax of the factor of production, labour, may have a different effect on the productive potential of the economy and the funding of the welfare state—apart from a different impact on tax revenues due to a differing potential for tax evasions. While the value added tax system is fairly harmonised across the EU, this is not the case for labour taxation (income tax and social security contributions), explaining part of the differences in wages between EU Member States. In the case of Austria, labour taxation is the major source of funding of the social security system (health, unemployment, retirement). By encouraging the movement of posted workers in place of migrant workers, employment growth may be negatively affected, thereby jeopardising the quality of social services provision. Accordingly, a rising number of posted workers at the cost of employment growth in Austria may raise concerns about the sustainability of the funding system of social services and promote a shift away from employment-based taxes to services taxation.

V. CONCLUSIONS

Over the last two decades the seasonal migrant worker scheme in Austria has shown a high degree of flexibility and adaptability to changing institutional, economic and political environments. The regulations try to find

[40] Paul Samuelson, 'Where Ricardo and Mill Rebut and Confirm Arguments of Mainstream Economists Supporting Globalisation' (2004) 18(3) Journal of Economic Perspectives 135; Torben Andersen and Allan Sorensen, 'Product Market Integration, Wages and Inequality', Discussion Paper No 4963 (London, Centre for Economic Policy Research, 2005).

a balance between often opposing interests, be it on political party policy lines, a social partnership perspective or differing power constellations of labour and capital. While conservative right-wing forces hoped to stem the tide of immigration to Austria by allowing temporary seasonal workers to enter without the right to settle, the preferential treatment given to citizens of EU Member States, who would eventually have the right to free mobility of labour and settlement, facilitated immigration rather than prohibiting it.

Posted work, on the other hand, may be seen as another facet of the diversification of employment forms at the margins of the labour market where core workers (insiders) are increasingly complemented by various forms of temporary labour (outsiders). Both involve challenges for industrial relations. Workers in the construction sector have defended their good working conditions and wages by voting for flexible working hours rather than temporary seasonal workers. However, the same was not possible in tourism and agriculture/forestry, industries with rather weak degrees of labour organisation. The ample supply of labour at the going wage rate together with workers' weak collective voice in these two industries tipped the scale in favour of seasonal work permits.

A challenging feature of posted work as compared to temporary migrant labour is the different impact on public revenues of the destination country and, as a result, on the funding of the welfare system. This is a contentious issue in countries where social security contributions are the major source of funding. In addition, value added tax revenues go to the source country of posted workers which is another drain on public revenues of the host country. So far, the proportion of posted workers is relatively small. However, a rapid growth in this source of labour could cause social discontent in those EU Member States with relatively better pay, conditions of work and welfare benefits. An increased use of posted workers may become instrumental in promoting the harmonisation of labour taxation in Europe and thereby socio-economic integration. The challenge in that context will be the establishment of a European social model which puts people first and which is a compromise between hard core neo-liberal promoters of the 'minimal state' on the one hand and the defenders of a social democratic powerful state on the other.

Part III

Temporary Labour Migration in Pursuit of Economic Efficiency

5

Employer Demand for 'Skilled' Migrant Workers

Regulating Admission Under the United Kingdom's Tier 2 (General) Visa

MIMI ZOU

I. INTRODUCTION

TEMPORARY MIGRANT WORKER programmes (TMWPs) have expanded across diverse sectors and skills in a number of industrialised market economies. There has been a growing emphasis on 'slotting' migrants under these schemes into segments of the economy 'where deficiencies in domestic training institutions, rapidly and newly emerging sectors, and employer preferences for flexibility imply shortages'.[1] The admission framework is one of the most contested regulatory components of TMWPs. Employers desire a laissez faire model where they have the freedom to decide who and how many migrants to admit. At the same time, policy makers recognise the need to safeguard resident workers' privileged access to the labour market. The conditions of entry also affect the rights of the migrants, which typically entail restrictions on their choice of employment in the host state.

'Shortages' and 'skills'—which premise the 'need' for migrant labour—are highly problematic concepts to define and operationalise in the regulatory design of TMWPs. The admission model underpinning many contemporary TMWPs could be characterised as an employer-driven 'demand' approach, where the employer seeks the state's permission to recruit and 'sponsor'

[1] Georg Menz and Alexander Caviedes, 'Introduction: Patterns, Trends, and (Ir)Regularities in the Politics and Economics of Labour Migration in Europe' in George Menz and Alexander Caviedes (eds), *Labour Migration in Europe* (Basingstoke, Palgrave Macmillan, 2010) 19.

migrants to fill particular job vacancies.[2] In comparison, a 'supply' approach usually entails admitting migrants where they have met certain human capital criteria such as education and qualifications, without a job offer as a condition for entry.[3]

As Ruhs argues, 'the level of labour immigration that is in the interest of individual employers is unlikely to coincide with that in the best interest of the economy as whole'.[4] Even if employers are required to show that no suitably skilled resident worker is available for a particular position, the existence of unfilled vacancies does not per se 'indicate labour shortage that would justify the admission of migrant workers'.[5] In dealing with the different interests of labour market actors, governments have commonly touted the need for 'objective' and 'evidence-based' means of evaluating a 'genuine' labour market need for migrant labour.[6]

This chapter probes into the fundamental regulatory challenges arising from the employer-driven admission model underpinning the United Kingdom's Tier 2 (General) visa. I analyse how these challenges are manifested in the espoused policy rationale of addressing 'skill shortages' under this scheme, which is the primary route for non-European Economic Area (EEA) migrants to be employed in the UK. It has generally been subject to much less policy and scholarly attention in comparison to the regulatory issues around EEA labour migration. Among the socio-legal scholarship examining contemporary TMWPs, there have been very few in-depth case studies of skilled schemes and of the particular issues of 'skill' and 'skills need'.

Section II provides an overview of the scheme's evolution from the work permits system to its current form under the points-based system (PBS). In section III, I analyse the admission regime in detail using a typology of numerical, demand and supply-related conditions of entry. Drawing on this analysis, the final discussion in section IV problematises the raison d'être of TMWPs in light of the dominant regulatory role played by employers in driving the admission process and sponsorship arrangement. Despite attempts to introduce 'evidence-based' assessments of 'skill shortages' under the Tier 2 (General) visa scheme, namely through an independent advisory body, there remains considerable room for employers to assert their 'need' for particular types of 'skilled' migrant labour.

[2] Philip Martin and Martin Ruhs, 'Independent Commissions and Labour Migration: The British MAC' (2014) 11 *Migration Letters* 23.

[3] Giovanni Facchini and Elisabetta Lodigiani, 'Attracting Skilled Immigrants: An Overview of Recent Policy Developments in Advanced Countries' (2014) 229 *National Institute Economic Review* 3.

[4] Martin Ruhs, 'The Potential of Temporary Migration Programmes in Future International Migration Policy' (2006) 145 *International Labour Review* 7, 14–15.

[5] Martin Ruhs, *The Price of Rights: Regulating International Labour Migration* (Princeton, NJ, Princeton University Press, 2013) 180.

[6] Jonathan Chaloff, 'Structuring Evidence-Based Regulation of Labour Migration', paper presented at Expert Commissions and Migration Policy Making Conference, Davis, CA, 18 April 2013.

II. BACKGROUND TO THE TIER 2 (GENERAL) VISA SCHEME

A. The Work Permit System

For much of the twentieth century, the UK has been a 'reluctant immigration state' with one of the strictest immigration regimes among industrialised countries.[7] In the mid–late 1990s, Tony Blair's Labour government significantly liberalised labour migration policies for both EEA and non-EEA nationals. The annual number of applications under the work permits system for non-EEA nationals rose from 38,617 to 155,216 between 1995 and 2002.[8]

Reforms to the work permit system were aimed at making it more flexible, efficient and responsive to employer demand in the public and private sectors. They included attenuating the required qualifications and experience levels; relaxing labour market testing requirements; introducing multiple-entry work permits; increasing the maximum duration of a work permit from four to five years; eliminating the need for an additional work permit to engage in supplementary employment; and providing a path for foreign students to switch to work permits without leaving the UK.[9] After an internal review, the unit responsible for issuing work permits, Work Permits (UK), introduced a simpler system for processing applications and the turnaround time became 'a matter of days rather than weeks'.[10]

This liberalisation policy was driven by the belief that labour migration brought significant economic benefits.[11] The government's pre-budget review in 1999 highlighted the need for the UK to:

> attract the most skilled and most enterprising people from abroad to add to the skill pool of resident workers ... address skills gaps, both where there are transient shortages in particular areas, for example, among IT workers, or where skills shortages persist.[12]

In a 2000 White Paper on migration, the increase in the number of skilled migrants under the system was presented as 'the badge of success'.[13]

Under the work permits system, Clarke and Salt found that the largest national group was Indians with 18,999 visa grants (21 per cent of the total)

[7] Chris Wright, 'Policy Legacies, Visa Reform and the Resilience of Immigration Politics' (2012) 35 *West European Politics* 726, 728.

[8] James Clarke and John Salt, 'Work Permits and Foreign Labour in the UK: A Statistical Review' (2003) 111 *Labour Market Trends* 563, 565.

[9] Will Somerville, *Immigration Under New Labour* (Bristol, Policy Press, 2007) 30–31.

[10] Clarke and Salt, 'Work Permits' (n 8) 565.

[11] Martin Ruhs, 'Economic Research and Labour Immigration Policy' (2008) 24 *Oxford Review of Economic Policy* 403, 404.

[12] Cited in Nicolas Rollason, 'International Mobility of Highly Skilled Workers: The UK Perspective' in OECD, *International Mobility of the Highly Skilled* (Paris, OECD, 2002) 333.

[13] Don Flynn, 'British Immigration Policy, New Labour, and the Rights of Migrants: A Critical Assessment', Signs of the Times Seminar, London, 25 November 2002.

in 2002, which rose from only 1,007 (8 per cent) in 1995.[14] There were also notable large increases for Filipinos, South Africans and Malaysians between 1997 and 2002. Combining the data for nationalities and occupations, Clarke and Salt further found that many of the migrants from the Philippines, Zimbabwe and Nigeria were health associate professionals, those from India were engineers and computer specialists, and those from Japan and the US filled managerial and administrative positions. Specifically, Filipinos accounted for a third of health associate professionals, and Indians 70 per cent of engineers and technologists and 78 per cent of computer analysts or programmers on work permits. Around 21 per cent of grants to Chinese nationals were for catering occupations.[15]

At the same time, a Highly Skilled Migrants Programme (HSMP) was launched in 2002. The HSMP was aimed at boosting the UK's skilled labour supply. Without requiring a job offer, migrants who met the admission criteria (which included qualifications, work experience, past earnings, achievement in their chosen field and HSMP priority occupations) could enter the UK to look for work or be self-employed. The initial period of leave granted was one year, which could be extended for a further three years after which they could apply for settlement.[16] In addition, there was considerable expansion of low-skilled TMWPs such as the quota-based Sector-Based Scheme and the seasonal agricultural workers scheme. Finally, the core aspect of this liberalisation policy was the lifting of full restrictions on labour market access for the new 'Accession 8' EEA nationals (from Central and Eastern Europe) at the time of European Union enlargement in 2004.[17]

At the time, there was a certain consensus among stakeholders around the opening up of legal channels for labour migration.[18] The relaxation of the work permits system largely slipped under the public radar compared to the highly visible policy campaign to 'act tough' on asylum seekers. As Wright observes, during the period of 2000 to 2004, labour immigration controls in the UK were liberalised to a greater degree than in any other reluctant immigration state.[19] However, this liberalisation was short-lived, as public backlash saw the return of a restrictionist agenda under the third term of the Blair-Gordon Labour government.

[14] Clarke and Salt, 'Work Permits' (n 8) 572.

[15] Ibid.

[16] Ibid 572–73.

[17] The eight countries that joined the EU on 1 May 2004 were: Czech Republic, Estonia, Hungary, Latvia, Lithuania, Poland, Slovakia and Slovenia. Many A8 nationals had restrictions on their rights to work, claim benefits, and access social housing during their accession period. These restrictions ended on 1 May 2011.

[18] Camilla Devitt, *Labour Migration Governance in Contemporary Europe: The UK Case*, FIERI Working Papers (Torino, FIERI, 2012) 7.

[19] Wright, 'Policy Legacies' (n 7) 733.

B. The Points-Based System

From 2008 onwards, a new points-based system (PBS) to regulate non-EEA migration was introduced.[20] A primary goal was to tighten the selection of migrants employed in the UK to increase the skills requirement for applicants.[21] The PBS consolidated over 80 former visa routes for non-EEA migrants into a five-tiered structure: exceptionally skilled or 'high-value' individuals (Tier 1), skilled workers with a job offer (Tier 2), a limited number of temporary low-skilled workers (Tier 3), which has been suspended on the premise that such labour could be sourced from EEA nationals, students (Tier 4), and youth mobility visas (Tier 5).

The work permits scheme was replaced with the Tier 2 (General) visa. There are also three other categories under Tier 2: intra-company transferees (ICT), ministers of religion and sports people. In 2009, the number of migrants admitted under the Tier 2 scheme (across all categories) was 33,685 (including 24,460 main applicants and 9,220 dependants).[22] Among this group of Tier 2, the general category consisted only of 8,970 main applicants, with 14,200 visas granted under the intra-company transfer route.[23]

An independent advisory body was set up with the introduction of the PBS: the Migration Advisory Committee (MAC). Comprising of a small appointed group of labour market experts, the MAC's key function is to provide the UK government with 'independent and evidence-based advice' on how immigration selection under the PBS could best address domestic labour needs.[24] The MAC's role has primarily been concerned with the admission criteria for Tier 2: the identification of 'skilled' jobs and the compilation and updating of the Shortage Occupation List (SOL). The MAC has also responded to government requests for reviews of various labour migration issues.

Upon the election of David Cameron's coalition government in 2010, the PBS became more restrictive as the government sought to reduce non-EEA net immigration from 'hundreds of thousands a year, to just tens of thousands'.[25] Since 6 April 2011, the Tier 2 (General) visa has been subject to an annual limit of 20,700 places for out-of-country new applicants

[20] Home Office, *A Points-Based System: Making Migration Work for Britain* (London, Home Office, 2006).

[21] Philip Martin, 'A Need for Migrant Labour? UK–US Comparisons' in Martin Ruhs and Bridget Anderson (eds), *Who Needs Migrant Workers: Labour Shortages, Immigration, and Public Policy* (Oxford, Oxford University Press, 2010).

[22] Home Office, *Control of Immigration Statistics: United Kingdom 2009* (London, Home Office, 2010) 21.

[23] Home Office, *Immigration Statistics: October to December 2012* (London, Home Office, 2013) table ad.03.w.

[24] MAC, *Skilled Shortage Sensible: The Recommended Shortage Occupation Lists for the UK and Scotland* (London, MAC, 2008).

[25] David Cameron, 'Immigration Speech', Ipswich, 25 March 2013.

seeking entry clearance. In 2012, only 9,421 out-of-country Tier 2 (General) visas were issued.[26] At the same time, two main categories under Tier 1 were closed: the 'general' route that allowed highly skilled migrants to enter the UK without a job or sponsor, and the post-study work route for foreign students to remain in the UK after graduation to search for work.

In the year ending September 2014, 13,646 Certificates of Sponsorship (CoS) were issued under the Tier 2 (General) route for out-of-country applicants. Another 32,575 CoS were issued for the Tier 2 visa ICT route.[27] The number of Tier 2 applications was 52,214 during this period, mostly for the information and communication sector (43 per cent), professional, scientific and technical activities (19 per cent), financial and insurance activities (12 per cent), human health and social work activities (6 per cent), and manufacturing (4 per cent).[28] Recent data combining a breakdown of sectors with nationalities is not available, although the MAC noted that the information and communication sector, by a large margin, has been the largest user of Tier 2 (especially the ICT route), particularly in recruiting Indian nationals.[29]

III. THE ADMISSION OF MIGRANTS: A TYPOLOGY

In 2015, the breakdown in the Tier 2 (General) visa points allocation under the PBS consists of: 30 points for having a sponsor and a valid CoS, 20 points for meeting an appropriate salary and allowances threshold, 10 points for English language proficiency, and 10 points for maintenance funds.[30] If the sponsored job is on the SOL or has a gross annual salary package of £155,300 or more, the visa applicant will receive 30 points for the assignment of a CoS. Otherwise, the job offered to the applicant must pass a resident labour market test (RLMT). In this section, I map this admission regime onto a typology of controls as identified by Ruhs: quotas, and demand-side and supply-side restrictions.[31]

A. Caps and Quotas

Determining how many migrants to admit is often a core aspect of labour migration policy, especially when headlines constantly draw attention

[26] Home Office, *Immigration Statistics* table wk.01.

[27] MAC, *Partial Review of the SOL for the UK and for Scotland* (London, MAC, 2015) 1.

[28] Home Office, *Immigration Statistics, July–September 2014* (London, MAC, 2014).

[29] MAC, *Analysis of the Points-Based System: Tier 2 and Dependants* (London, MAC, 2009) 8.

[30] UK Immigration Rules, para 245HB; UK Visas & Immigration, *Tier 2 of the Points Based System—Policy Guidance (Version 11/15)* (London, UK Visas & Immigration, 2015).

[31] Ruhs, *The Price of Rights* (n 5).

to the 'numbers' in this politically sensitive arena. Yet 'numbers' can be manipulated considerably in the compilation and usage of immigration statistics. For policy makers, quotas, caps and targets are the most direct instruments to restrict the scale and size of the intake under migration programmes. There may be 'hard' caps that cannot be exceeded when the quota is reached for the year. Alternatively, 'soft' targets may be implemented as a guideline rather than fixing a numerical ceiling.

Caps and targets can apply to migrants across the skills spectrum, sectors and occupations, geographical regions and/or in some cases countries of origin. Permanent migration programmes in traditional settlement countries commonly feature an overall planning target that is adjusted from year to year.[32] In contrast, the more flexible mechanism of TMWPs is less likely to have a set quota, as employers' demand for migrant workers is the primary determinant of the number of temporary work permits and visas issued.

Prior to 2011, the work permits system/Tier 2 (General) visa had no such limit, since the scheme was perceived as an 'automatic stabiliser' in adjusting to cyclical changes in labour demand.[33] Since 2011, an annual 'hard' cap of 20,700 has been introduced for applicants from outside the UK or those switching into this category as a dependent of a Tier 4 student visa holder. These applications are subject to a so-called 'restricted' CoS.[34] The annual cap is divided into monthly allocations of restricted CoS. Since its introduction, the monthly quota has only been reached in 2015.[35] Employers have generally criticised the cap for hindering their flexibility in 'accessing the migrant labour they value most highly',[36] as well as affecting business competitiveness and stunting economic recovery.[37]

B. Demand-Side Restrictions

A Job Offer as a Precondition for Entry

Under the Tier 2 (General) visa scheme, a job offer is the basis of a mandated employer sponsorship of the migrant's visa. Thus, a migrant's legal authorisation to enter and work in the UK is predicated on a contract of employment with an eligible sponsor at the time the visa is applied for. Advocates

[32] OECD, 'Managing Migration—Are Quotas and Numerical Limits the Solution?' in OECD, *International Migration Outlook* (Paris, OECD, 2006).

[33] MAC, *Analysis of the Points-Based System* 1 (n 29).

[34] Melanie Gower, *April 2011 Changes to Tier 1 and Tier 2 of the Points-Based System and Indefinite Leave* (House of Commons Standard Note, SN/HA/5922 2011) 1.

[35] Dominic Casciani, 'Skilled Workers Immigration Cap Hit', *BBC News*, 11 June 2015.

[36] Alasdair Murray, *Britain's Points Based Migration System* (London, CentreForum, 2011) 8.

[37] London Chamber of Commerce and Industry, *Migration Reform: Caps Don't Fit* (London, LCCI, 2011); Asa Bennett, 'David Cameron's Attack on Immigration is "Anti-Growth" and "Complete Nonsense", Say Business Groups', *Huffington Post UK*, 23 July 2013.

of an employer-driven admission model premised on a job offer argue that it facilitates greater labour market efficiency than supply-led schemes, since migrants' skills more directly match the specific demand of employers.[38] They claim that this model is more responsive to cyclical fluctuations, as a slowdown in employer demand for labour would (notionally) reduce immigration intakes without requiring any time-consuming and cumbersome policy changes.[39] Employer sponsorship arrangements are also perceived to offer advantages for employers seeking workers in targeted areas of the labour market, such as in remote locations or sectors/occupations with acute shortages.

There is a further claim that an employer-led, demand-based admission model is more likely to obtain better labour market outcomes for migrants since they are more likely to work in a job relevant to their skills, qualifications, and experience.[40] Employer selection from the onset is said to prevent the risk of an initial period of unemployment that a migrant may face under a supply-led scheme, particularly where there is a failure to recognise the migrant's skills and credentials.[41]

Underpinning some of the above claims is an 'employer-knows-best' approach to identifying and addressing labour and skill shortages. However, employer-driven admission procedures do not necessarily mean that migrants' skills are better matched with labour market needs, which should be distinguished from the employer's specific needs. A migrant worker can still be overqualified or underqualified for the job that forms the basis of her sponsorship. Under a system of employer sponsorship, the labour market outcomes for migrants can critically depend on the employer's goodwill and the worker's relative bargaining power.

Labour Market Testing: Trust the Employer?

The requirement of a job offer is usually accompanied by labour market testing to assess whether employers' requests for migrant labour represent genuine shortages that cannot be filled in the domestic labour market. Labour market testing seeks to ensure that employers can bring in migrants only after making reasonable attempts to recruit qualified residents. The policy intent is to protect and privilege the employment opportunities of the resident workforce. Forms of labour market tests can be broadly categorised

[38] Demetrios G Papademetriou, Will Somerville and Hiroyuki Tanaka, *Hybrid Immigration-Selection Systems: The Next Generation of Economic Migration Schemes* (Washington, DC, Migration Policy Institute, 2008).

[39] OECD, *International Migration Outlook: SOPEMI 2011* (Paris, OECD, 2011) 107.

[40] OECD, *International Migration Outlook: SOPEMI 2010* (Paris, OECD, 2009) 104.

[41] Demetrios G Papademetriou and Madeleine Sumption, *Rethinking Points Systems and Employer-Selected Immigration* (Washington, DC, Migration Policy Institute, 2011) 4.

into self-attestation by the employer and a stronger certification test by a government agency or institution.

The self-attestation approach is largely based on employer say so in declaring that they have been unsuccessful in searching for suitably qualified resident workers. Checks on employers' recruitment efforts do not feature heavily under this 'trust the employer' approach. In comparison, certification generally requires stricter evidential requirements to obtain confirmation or verification from a particular body (such as a public employment agency) that the requirements of the labour market test have been met before any applications are submitted. The effectiveness of certification depends on the design and enforcement of pre-admission checks.[42] These forms of labour market testing may apply to all sectors and occupations covered by a TMWP, or in some cases, certain sectors or occupations may be exempted, such as those where there is a known shortage of resident workers.[43]

Under the Tier 2 (General) visa, the RLMT requires employers to advertise the job vacancy in specified forms of media for at least 28 calendar days in accordance with the methods specified in the Tier 2 sponsor guidelines.[44] The sponsor must specify in the advertisement the job title, job description, location, salary, requisite qualifications, skills, experience, and closing date for applications.[45] The CoS must be assigned within six months from when the vacancy is first advertised (or twelve months for PhD-level occupations).[46]

There is still a substantial degree of 'trust the employer' in this approach since the employer essentially tests the market themselves. There is a risk that the RLMT may simply be a tick-box exercise without sufficient pre-admission checks. The benefits of the RLMT have been described by the Confederation of British Industry as allowing 'firms to test the market themselves and ensur[ing] employers can hire with flexibility and speed'.[47]

'Shortage' Occupations and Sectors

A common alternative to labour market testing is the creation and periodic review of a specified list of shortage occupations at national and/or regional/sector levels. This list may be drawn up by the labour and/or immigration department, or by independent expert panels or a group of stakeholders such as employers, industry groups, trade unions and local authorities.

[42] MAC, *Analysis of the Points-Based System* (n 29) 79.
[43] Ruhs, *The Price of Rights* (n 5).
[44] UK Visas & Immigration, *Tier 2 and 5 of the Points Based System Guidance for Sponsors* (London, UK Visas & Immigration, 2015) paras 28.16–28.42.
[45] Ibid para 28.18.
[46] Ibid para 29.2.
[47] Murray, *Britain's Points Based Migration System* (n 36) 41.

Employers can bring in migrants to fill vacancies for occupations on this list, usually without needing to undertake a labour market test. A shortage occupation list, as a method of admission under TMWPs, raises challenging questions about how to determine the nature and duration of particular shortages in the labour market accurately and objectively.

The SOL under the Tier 2 (General) visa scheme is regularly reviewed by the MAC, which makes robust and detailed expert analysis of skill shortages in and across sectors by examining top-down indicators and bottom-up evidence from stakeholders. The government has largely drawn on the MAC's recommendations to update the SOL. In this respect, the MAC is a vital institution in the architecture of the Tier 2 (General) visa scheme, enabling it to fulfil its key rationale of meeting genuine skill shortages. On the whole, the SOL appears to be used for occupations that tend to have a lower salary than those on the RLMT route and predominantly within certain industries such as skilled trades (including chefs and cooks), textiles, printing, and caring and personal services.[48]

In 2011–2012, the SOL route accounted for 15 per cent of the out-of-country CoS granted for Tier 2 (General) visas.[49] In 2014, it accounted for 10 per cent of the out-of-country CoS granted.[50] The number of (British and migrant) workers in the UK employed in SOL occupations has fallen from over a million in 2008 to only 180,000 in 2012–2013.[51] This raises the question of its practical value given the availability and greater accessibility of the RLMT route for employers to recruit migrant workers. The MAC investigated the government's requests for consultation on closing the RLMT route[52] and on combining the two routes,[53] but concluded that RLMT remained a necessary avenue for employers to address local shortages.

The MAC was further asked in 2012 to advise on the proposed inclusion of a 'sunset clause' in SOL that would automatically remove occupations from the list after two years. With an emphasis that the SOL would only provide temporary relief to labour shortages, the government's rationale for the proposal was 'to discourage complacency and over-reliance on migrant labour among employers'; 'motivate employers to train and up-skill resident workers'; and 'alert education providers and governing bodies to the efficacy of their attempts to address skill shortages'.[54] The MAC recommended the

[48] MAC, *Limits on Migration: Limits on Tier 1 and Tier 2 for 2011/12 and Supporting Policies* (London, MAC, 2010) 90–91.

[49] MAC, *2012 Review of NQF* (London, MAC, 2010) 19.

[50] MAC, *Partial Review of the SOL* (n 27) 1.

[51] MAC, *Full Review of the Recommended Shortage Occupation Lists for the UK and Scotland, a Sunset Clause and the Creative Occupations* (London, MAC, 2013) 5.

[52] MAC, *Analysis of the Points-Based System* (n 29).

[53] MAC, *Limits on Migration* (n 42).

[54] MAC, *Full Review of the Recommended Shortage Occupation Lists* (n 51).

retention of frequent reviews of the SOL rather than introducing a sunset clause. It reasoned that the clause would not take sufficient consideration of individual sectors' economic conditions or the time required to train domestic workers. It also considered that a sunset clause was a 'disproportionate response' since immigration inflows under SOL were so small compared to other routes of entry.[55]

Nevertheless, a shortage list, even one that is regularly updated like the SOL, is inherently limited in its ability to capture every industry, sector, and regional and local variation. Moreover, the possible inclusion of certain lower-skilled occupations on these lists raises the question of whether employers are facing labour shortages rather than specific skill shortages. Yet shortage lists can serve an important political function by communicating to the public that such schemes are highly selective and focused on the specific skills that are most needed in the resident labour market.[56] Compared to labour market testing, the very specificity of a shortage list can lead to substantial contestation between stakeholders over the nature and extent of particular shortages, as employers, business and industry groups, professional bodies, and trade unions seek to influence the compilation and review of such lists.

The Malleability of 'Skills'

The Tier 2 (General) visa is restricted to the sponsorship and nomination of migrants in skilled occupations. However, the indicators or criteria for identifying 'skills' are highly contested. The formal frameworks for ascertaining the requisite level of skills for eligible occupations have largely been academic and vocational qualifications. The threshold in July 2015 is National Qualifications Framework (NQF) Level 6, which is described with reference to qualifications equivalent to bachelor's degrees with honours, graduate diplomas and certificates.

If the skills frameworks under TMWPs are too rigidly defined and applied in a tick-box manner, this may create problems for certain occupations and sectors that have a stronger focus on 'soft' skills. An example is the care sector, where the formal qualifications of carers (including those with many years of experience) can often be lower than the requisite formal skills threshold but entail a high level of interpersonal skills that are difficult to measure. Care work was excluded from the MAC's first list of 'skilled' occupations for the Tier 2 (General) visa in 2008. Subsequently, in 2009, the MAC added the position of senior skilled care workers if certain criteria were met, including the possession of NVQ2+ qualifications, minimum

[55] Ibid 1.
[56] Chaloff, 'Structuring Evidence-Based Regulation' (n 6) 8.

experience and pay, and supervisory responsibility in the post to which they are recruited.[57]

Yet the problems associated with defining 'skills' can mean that 'skill shortages' can become so far-reaching as to include the shortage of any job that requires some degree of 'skill'.[58] Although the skills threshold under the Tier 2 (General) visa has increased since 2009, certain occupations such as senior care workers, butchers and meat cutters, and chefs have remained on the SOL. The MAC has found that some occupations with acute shortages, as a whole, did not meet its 'skill' criteria but recommended their inclusion on the SOL subject to minimum pay and relevant experience thresholds.[59] It should be noted that many of these occupations (except for the highly qualified) were taken off the list in 2011 as the limits on admission under the Tier 2 (General) visas have become more restrictive.

Chefs and cooks working in ethnic cuisine restaurants, an occupation that has featured in the gazetted list of eligible occupations and SOL, is an example of employer demand for particular groups of 'skilled' migrants. This demand may be related to these migrants' authentic culinary skills, knowledge (including the customs and language of the workplace), and experience of a particular culture or tradition that may not be easily transferrable to resident workers—a reason cited in a MAC review for why some ethnic restaurants and food businesses continue to rely on migrant labour even in recessions.[60] However, this demand may in practice stem from reasons other than the migrant's 'cultural capital',[61] including a willingness to work unsocial hours and for lower wages compared to resident workers.[62]

Ruhs and Anderson argue that a flexible approach to defining and assessing skills and skill requirements in the admissions criteria for TMWPs could go beyond formal credentials and account for the shifting nature of job skill demands in an economy with a large, growing services sector and rapid technological change.[63] At the same time, it should be emphasised that employers play a critical role in shaping the demand for particular types of 'skills'. There have also been arguments that employers are better judges of the 'soft' skills and capabilities that they find valuable, such as an ability to

[57] MAC, *Skilled Shortage Sensible* (n 24) 177.

[58] Ken Mayhew, 'Migrant Workers: Who Needs Them? A Commentary' in Ruhs and Anderson (eds), *Who Needs Migrant Workers?* 54.

[59] MAC, *SOL Review 2009* (London, MAC, 2009) 160.

[60] Ibid.

[61] Martin Ruhs and Bridget Anderson, 'Migrant Workers: Who Needs Them? A Framework for the Analysis of Staff Shortages, Immigration, and Public Policy' in Ruhs and Anderson (eds), *Who Needs Migrant Workers?* (n 21) 33.

[62] MAC, *SOL Review 2009* (n 59) 155, 159.

[63] Ruhs and Anderson, 'Migrant Workers' (n 61).

work in teams, problem-solving capabilities, and customer service skills.[64] Yet these 'soft' skills may actually be referring to certain traits, attitudes, and qualities of a more acquiescent workforce that employers can more easily control.

Wages Requirement

The Tier 2 (General) visa imposes restrictions on the minimum wage thresholds at which the migrants are to be employed. Such restrictions may serve as a de facto limit on admission under employer-driven TMWPs if employers find it more expensive to source labour from overseas than to hire or to up-skill resident workers. Ruhs distinguishes three types of wage restrictions based on the degree of policy openness. The most open policy would simply require the employer to comply with the legal minimum wage. A more restrictive 'intermediate' approach would entail paying migrants at least the average or prevailing wage in the relevant occupation and/or sector. Finally, the most restrictive policy would require employers to meet prevailing industrial standards as determined by collective agreements, which is most common in strong co-ordinated market economies and welfare states.[65]

The wage and salary requirements under the Tier 2 (General) visa fall into the intermediate category. It adopts a two-tier approach based on a general minimum salary threshold—only jobs above £20,800 can be sponsored, as well as a market rate or an appropriate rate of pay specific to the occupation in question.[66] The 'appropriate' annual salary rates for certain occupations are set out in a sector-based code of practice issued and revised by UK Visas & Immigration, generally following the recommendations of the MAC.[67] The occupational salary rates under this code are divided into 'new entrant' and 'experienced worker' categories, based on the Office of National Statistics' Annual Survey of Hours and Earnings.

Employers' demand for migrants to fill domestic shortages can depend on the prevailing level of wages and employment conditions, which may not attract a sufficient supply of resident workers. Thus, 'shortages' can be created in a way that gives credence to employers' demand for migrants who may be willing to accept the lower wages and conditions offered. Despite the attempt under the Tier 2 (General) visa scheme to specify an 'appropriate'

64 Elizabeth Collett and Fabian Zuleeg, *Soft, Scarce, and Super Skills: Sourcing the Next Generation of Migrant Workers in Europe* (Washington, DC, Migration Policy Institute, 2008).

65 Ruhs, *The Price of Rights* (n 5).

66 UK Visas & Immigration, *Tier 2 and 5 of the Points Based System* (n 44) paras 79–86.

67 UK Visas & Immigration, *Codes of Practice for Skilled Workers Standard Occupational Classification (SOC) Codes and Minimum Appropriate Salary Rates*, version 04/15 (London, UK Visas & Immigration, 2015).

rate based on the sector/occupation, the rates of pay can vary widely across workplaces and geographical locations within the same sectors and occupations. Furthermore, this variance of pay may be more pronounced under decentralised systems of wage determination (at the enterprise level), which have been promoted in the UK over the past two decades.

C. Supply-Side Restrictions

Personal Attributes and Grounds

Some labour migration programmes have explicit restrictions or preferences based on the personal characteristics of migrants such as their nationality or country of origin, age, gender, or marital status. The Tier 2 (General) visa does not have conditions of entry that overtly admit workers based on these grounds and attributes. However, given its employer-driven nature, employers may have considerable latitude in selecting migrants with certain desirable traits. For instance, employers may prefer younger visa holders without dependants, since this group is likely to be more 'flexible' and willing to work longer and unsociable hours.[68] The employer can further save on the time and costs associated with potential spousal and dependant visa applications and travel arrangements.

Nationality and country of origin can also influence employers' selection of migrant workers. As Ruhs and Anderson observe, national stereotyping in recruitment is often not 'reducible to simple individual prejudices, but is related to how employers respond to, and perpetuate, wider structural imbalances and inequalities in local and global markets'.[69] Migrants' frame of reference for what constitutes an 'acceptable' level of wages and working conditions in the host state could be contingent on the standards back in their home countries.

Language Skills Requirements

Migrants are required to have a certain level of English language skills. Under the Tier 2 (General) visa scheme, the language requirement is a 'basic conversation' level, equivalent to B1 on the Common European Framework of Reference for Languages. The migrant is required to be a national of a majority English-speaking country; or to pass an approved English language test; or to hold a degree that was taught in English and is equivalent to a UK bachelor's degree.[70]

[68] Bridget Anderson, 'Migration, Immigration Controls and the Fashioning of Precarious Workers' (2010) 24 *Work, Employment and Society* 300.

[69] Ruhs and Anderson, 'Migrant Workers' (n 61) 28.

[70] UK Visas & Immigration, *Tier 2 of the Points Based System* (n 30) para 133.

There have been claims that employers are best able to judge the required language standards of sponsored workers, which depend on the nature of the nominated occupation.[71] Employers have contended that for some job specifications, such as those in the creative arts and ethnic catering businesses, language proficiency may not actually be necessary to core tasks of the job.[72] Another objection to the English language proficiency requirement came from the trade union Unite, which argued before the Home Affairs Committee that it introduced 'bias in favour of migrants from English-speaking countries and against those from the developing world'.[73]

Self-Sufficiency

Requirements of 'self-sufficiency' on the part of migrants and their families usually reflect the policy consideration of minimising migrants' access to the host state's public funds and social welfare. Tier 2 (General) visa applicants must meet and demonstrate sufficient personal savings of at least £945 at the time of writing (November 2015) or the eligible sponsoring employer must undertake to maintain and accommodate them during the first month of their employment.[74] Requirements of self-sufficiency may pose certain challenges for visa applicants from developing countries, because of insufficient savings and/or poor documentation.[75] The disparity in incomes and savings between the host states and some home states can make it extremely difficult for even those in skilled, professional jobs to meet this criterion prior to their visa application. Some migrants may have to rely more on their sponsoring employers to provide the necessary assurance of maintenance to meet such requirements.

IV. MEETING 'SKILL SHORTAGES'?

The espoused objective of the Tier 2 (General) visa scheme is to respond to resident labour market needs where genuine skill shortages exist. As I have argued, employers play a key role in this regulatory framework in asserting the 'need' for migrant workers. Other research has shown that, for a variety of reasons, employers can develop a preference for recruiting specific types of migrant workers instead of local workers. As Ruhs and Anderson put it, 'what employers want' is influenced by what they 'think they can get' from

71 House of Commons Home Affairs Committee, *Managing Migration: The Points-Based System* (London, Stationery Office, 2009) 41–44.

72 Ibid 42.

73 Ibid.

74 UK Visas & Immigration, *Tier 2 of the Points Based System* paras (n 30) 165, 168.

75 House of Commons Home Affairs Committee, *Managing Migration* 39–40.

different groups of workers.[76] The demand and supply for migrant labour are interrelated and mutually conditioning. The 'needs' of employers can often become a proxy for general labour market needs under an employer-driven admission regime.

There may be short-term, cyclical shortages based on fluctuations in the demand for skilled labour. Shortages can also be of a medium to long-term structural nature, arising from the rapid growth of certain sectors and the lack of sufficiently skilled and trained resident workers. A specific type of structural shortage pertains to public or public-funded jobs, such as those in health and caring work, where constraints on public spending can create a mismatch between supply and demand by generating a prevailing level of wages that is too low for resident workers.[77]

The contested nature of 'skill shortages' has led to the establishment of independent advisory bodies such as the MAC to assist governments to formulate policies and identify shortages through expert research and analysis with input from various stakeholders. Rather than merely rely on employer attestation that 'shortages' exist, this approach can consider broader labour market and economic factors as well as the interests of diverse labour market actors. Notwithstanding the use of expert knowledge and evidence through the MAC, the concept of 'skills' is itself notoriously difficult to define. Employers' conceptualisation of 'skills' may be much broader than formal qualifications and experience, encompassing 'soft skills' and other desirable personal attributes of workers.

Furthermore, the notion of a 'shortage' may reflect employers' demand for migrants who are willing to tolerate prevailing wages and working conditions in certain occupations that cannot attract a sufficient supply of resident workers.[78] Even where the wages in the 'skill shortage' occupation and/or sector are much higher than the labour market average, employers' use of migrant labour may help to moderate wage demands by resident workers. Cangiano and Walsh's survey of 557 home care providers in the UK found that employers' demand for migrant care workers was largely based on the recruitment difficulties arising from low wages and working conditions, and that 'UK workers demanded higher wages'.[79]

An important question is whether TMWPs, framed as meeting skill shortages on a temporary basis, are being used to counteract the decline in training of the resident workforce. Under the Tier 2 (General) visa scheme,

[76] Ruhs and Anderson, 'Migrant Workers' (61) 16.
[77] Ibid 44.
[78] Ibid.
[79] Alessio Cangiano and Kieran Walsh, 'From Recruitment Processes and Immigration Regulations: The Disjointed Pathways to Employing Migrant Carers in Ageing Societies' (2014) 28 *Work, Employment and Society* 372.

the MAC's approach to formulating the SOL and other related policies has taken into account the 'sensibility' of employing migrant labour, including its impact on employers' incentives to invest in training and up-skilling UK workers.[80] The increasingly restrictive immigration policy in the UK from 2009 onwards prompted the formalisation of a more co-ordinated government policy on immigration, education and training, and skills development. To a large extent, this was 'a reaction to the limits to be imposed on immigration and a concern with ensuring that employers would be able to source skills'.[81]

The 'system effects' from labour market structures, institutions and regulatory frameworks can dissuade employers from alternatives other than recruiting migrants to respond to actual and perceived skill shortages.[82] This can lead to a long-term reliance on temporary migrant labour. For instance, the deregulatory and decentralised labour market policies in the UK since the 1980s saw the government's retreat from national training policy co-ordination and the decline of trade union influence in negotiations over workplace training. Employer preferences for certain skills profiles of migrants are shaped by the exigencies of production strategies as well as education and training schemes associated with the particular liberal market economies of the UK. As Menz has argued, employers actively seek migrant labour that can accommodate existing firm strategies as well as skills requirements that local educational and training facilities have not produced.[83]

There can also be broader 'system effects' from other realms of social and economic policies that affect employers' responses to labour shortages in private and public sectors. As highlighted earlier, an example is the heavy reliance on migrant labour in the care work and assistance sector in the UK.[84] Improving the wages, working conditions, career prospects and social status of jobs in this sector would arguably attract more resident workers. However, this could require governments to increase expenditure on publicly provided care. In the current context of cutbacks in public spending, regulatory requirements on staffing levels, and organisational reforms to increase efficiency and flexibility in this sector,[85] the ensuing 'system effects' are likely to intensify employers' reliance on temporary migrant labour and their claims of skill shortages.

[80] MAC, *Full Review of the Recommended Shortage Occupation Lists* (n 50) 39.

[81] Devitt, *Labour Migration Governance* (n 18) 29.

[82] Ruhs and Anderson, 'Migrant Workers' (n 61) 42–44.

[83] Georg Menz, 'Employers, Trade Unions, Varieties of Capitalism, and Labour Migration Policies' in Menz and Caviedes (eds), *Labour Migration in Europe* (n 1).

[84] Cangiano and Walsh, 'From Recruitment Processes' (n 79).

[85] Ruhs and Anderson, 'Migrant Workers' (n 61) 44.

V. CONCLUSION

The UK's Tier 2 (General) visa scheme reflects an employer-led, demand-based model of regulating admission. Under this model, employers' specific 'need' for migrant workers tends to be the key driver of decisions regarding whom to admit, how many to admit, and the conditions of their entry. As the Tier 2 (General) visa scheme shows, there is considerable deference to employers' self-attestation and assurance that admission criteria have actually been fulfilled, such as whether or not the sponsored migrant actually possesses the skills and qualifications for the job.

In recent years, policy makers have sought to put a 'brake' on the number of migrants admitted under the scheme. Furthermore, the MAC has played a vital role in seeking to balance the interests of different labour market actors when advising policy makers on the highly contested notions of 'skills' and 'shortages'. As this chapter has highlighted, assessing claims of 'skill and labour shortages', which underpin the primary rationale of the Tier 2 (General) visa, can be notoriously difficult. An independent expert institution cannot be the ultimate panacea to resolve the tensions between the conflicting goals inherent in TMWPs. The broader 'system effect' of such schemes suggests that employers' demand for temporary migrant labour may have become a permanent feature in specific sectors and occupations of the economy. These key insights from this case study in the UK will hopefully contribute to the ongoing research and policy debates on regulating the admission of skilled temporary migrants in a number of advanced industrialised economies, particularly in assessing the 'need' for these workers.

6

Contesting the Demand-Driven Orthodoxy

An Assessment of the Australian Regulation of Temporary Labour Migration

JOANNA HOWE

I. INTRODUCTION

REGULATING THE TEMPORARY movement of workers across borders is no simple endeavour. Most destination countries regulate entry of temporary migrant workers via a demand-driven mechanism tempered by government controls. No destination country uses a demand-driven model that gives employers unfettered access to temporary migrant labour. Even the United States' H-1B programme is capped, requires employers to complete an application to access temporary migrant labour and incorporates regulation (albeit weakly enforced according to Ruhs)[1] to ensure that the 'prevailing local wage' is paid. Some schemes, like the United Kingdom's Tier 2 pathway which uses caps, and Australia's 457 visa which does not, only offer a very limited form of scrutiny of employer attestation that a skill shortage exists, as this occurs after an offer of employment is made to a temporary migrant worker (or in most cases, not at all).[2] Other

[1] Martin Ruhs, 'Immigration and Labour Market Protectionism: Protecting Local Workers' Preferential Access to the Local Labour Market' in Cathryn Costello and Mark Freedland (eds), *Migrants at Work: Immigration and Vulnerability in Labour Law* (Oxford, Oxford University Press, 2014) 70.

[2] Martin Ruhs points out that in the UK an employer's attestation that a skill shortage exists is rarely checked and that there is no published data on how many employers have faced punitive measures or had their applications rejected for making a false or fraudulent attestation: Ruhs, 'Immigration and Labour Market Protectionism' 70. A similar point can be made about Australia's model of employer-conducted labour market testing. See Joanna Howe, 'Is the Net Cast Too Wide? An Assessment of Whether the Regulatory Design of the 457 Visa Meets Australia's Skill Needs' (2013) 41 *Federal Law Review* 443.

countries, like Germany and Ireland, use a certification model where an individual employer's request to access temporary migrant labour must be verified by a government agency.[3] Sweden, which has been labelled an exceptional case because of its reliance on labour market regulation to constrain employer demand for labour (namely requiring that temporary migrants are employed at collectively agreed wages), evinces a demand-driven approach underscored by a regulatory requirement for employers to test the local labour market.[4]

With destination countries increasingly favouring demand-driven temporary labour migration programmes, this chapter begins by using Australia's 457 visa as a case study to interrogate the reasons for the existence of this regulatory consensus and to unpack the economic orthodoxy supporting a demand-driven approach.[5] This is followed by a consideration of how well Australia's employer-led attestation model survives under labour law's gaze, influenced by Freedland and Kountouris's normative conception of its 'worker-protective' mission.[6] Drawing on comparative practice, in the following section I consider whether stronger regulation of employer demand is needed to enforce fundamental worker-protective norms and to ensure that temporary labour migration programmes achieve the national interest. I argue there needs to be greater regulation of employer attestation that a skill shortage exists through a structural redesign of the 457 visa, increasing the enforcement capacity of the regulator and ensuring regulatory cohesion between immigration law and labour law.

II. THE DEMAND-DRIVEN ORTHODOXY

Australia's 457 visa is predicated fundamentally on employer demand for temporary migrant labour. Shortly after its inception in 1996, Crock observed that the most striking aspect of the programme was 'the emphasis that is placed on the needs and wishes of employers'.[7] The Australian orthodoxy at the time, which has remained virtually unchallenged in the ensuing

[3] Ruhs, 'Immigration and Labour Market Protectionism', ibid 74.

[4] Ruhs, 'Immigration and Labour Market Protectionism', ibid 76–77. See also Samuel Engblom, 'Reconciling Openness and High Labour Standards? Sweden's Attempts to Regulate Labour Migration and Trade in Services' in Costello and Freedland (eds), *Migrants at Work*.

[5] The 457 visa was introduced by the Howard coalition government on 1 August 1996, through the insertion of a new pt 457 in sch 2 of the Migration Regulations (Amendment) 1996 No 76.

[6] Mark Freedland and Nicola Kountouris, *The Legal Construction of Personal Work Relations* (Oxford, Oxford University Press, 2011) 372.

[7] Mary Crock, 'Immigration and Labour Law: Targeting the Nation's Skills Needs' in Andrew Frazer, Ron McCallum and Paul Ronfeldt (eds), *Individual Contracts and Workplace Relations*, Working Paper No 50 (Sydney, Australian Centre for Industrial Relations Research and Training, 1997) 141.

two decades, is that a demand-driven approach is the most efficacious way to meet skill shortages in the domestic labour market at short notice. In this section, I unpack this orthodoxy.

Australia's 457 visa is uncapped so employers determine how many temporary migrant workers enter Australia. Employers initiate the migration process through making a request to the Department of Immigration to sponsor a temporary migrant worker.[8] Only temporary migrant workers with a job offer from an Australian employer are eligible for a 457 visa. A few regulatory constraints moderate employer demand. For a start, a temporary migrant worker's occupation must be skilled and present on an occupational shortage list, and the migrant worker's salary must exceed the threshold set by the government. In addition, for some occupations, an employer must test the labour market, although this requirement is not onerous, with one job advertisement, even if it is placed on social media, satisfying departmental requirements.[9] This combination of a limited form of government regulation and employer demand is consistent with its purpose. The 457 visa's objective is 'to enable employers to address labour shortages by bringing in genuinely skilled workers where they cannot find an appropriately skilled Australian'.[10]

The 457 visa has surpassed expectations of how interested employers would be in it as a way of recruiting staff. Conceived in the Roach Report,[11] it was primarily about 'intra-company transfers', 'not meant to apply to the traditional skilled trades or to professions like nursing and teaching' and was never intended to become 'an instrument for overcoming long term labour market deficiencies'.[12] It was seen as a means of giving Australian employers access to highly skilled workers in a competitive global market.[13] The programme could be underpinned by employer demand because employers

[8] The federal government department responsible for the 457 visa is the Department of Immigration and Border Protection (DIBP). Prior to this change in 2014, it was called the Department of Immigration and Citizenship (DIAC). At the time of the 457 visa's introduction, it was called the Department of Immigration and Multicultural Affairs (DIMA). Hereafter, DIBP will be referred to as the 'Department of Immigration'.

[9] Department of Immigration and Border Protection, *Labour Market Testing in the Subclass 457 Visa Programme: Frequently Asked Questions* (Canberra, Department of Immigration and Border Protection, 2013).

[10] Department of Immigration and Border Protection, *Booklet 9—Temporary Work (Skilled) (Subclass 457) Visa* (Canberra, Department of Immigration and Border Protection, 2014). This objective is set in policy, not legislation. The legislative and regulatory framework for the 457 visa does not include an objects clause, despite calls by some scholars that it include this. See Joo-Cheong Tham, 'Submission to the Senate Legal and Constitutional Affairs Committee Inquiry into the Migration Amendment (Temporary Sponsored Visas) Bill 2013', 21 June 2013.

[11] Committee of Inquiry into the Temporary Entry of Business People and Highly Skilled Specialists, *Business Temporary Entry: Future Directions* (Canberra, Australian Government Publishing Service, 1995) 84.

[12] Ibid 4.

[13] See, eg Lucie Cerna, *Selecting the Best and the Brightest* (Oxford, Migration Observatory, 2011).

would have to make themselves attractive in order to recruit internationally, otherwise migrant workers would go elsewhere. In this way, employer demand would interact with migrant worker supply in the market, and the right wages and conditions would be offered for the worker. In the years since its inception, the 457 visa programme can no longer be accurately described as only allowing the importation of highly skilled workers. But if the 457 visa has outgrown its origins, what of the demand-driven principle underpinning it? In order to consider whether this principle is still a useful regulatory tool for determining the composition of Australia's temporary migrant workforce, we first need to interrogate its raison d'être.

A primary rationale for this demand-driven model is that temporary migrant workers can be efficiently deployed to meet domestic skill shortages. For employers, this means that, once a skill shortage has been identified, an appropriately skilled and experienced temporary migrant worker can be recruited. The timely remedying of an employer's skill shortage means that an employer's business operations are not stymied, thereby expanding domestic employment and output. This also promotes greater business confidence and investment in the domestic economy. The argument is often made that, during phases of economic growth, the Australian economy is ill-equipped to train local workers to meet the demands of employers. The mining industry is a good example. In this context, it is argued that skill shortages can be fatal to projects, as they can increase the construction phase of projects, resulting in increased costs and faltering investor confidence.[14] Confirmation of this can be found in Bahn's study of the Western Australian resources sector. She suggests that without recourse to the 457 visa, employers are forced to 'restrict firm growth and only take on work that current staff could handle'.[15] Bahn found that employers turned to 457 visa holders as 'a buffer' during the construction phase of resource projects because of an absence of domestic workers with specialised skills but that this reliance on temporary migrant labour was reduced once the undersupply of skilled workers was ameliorated. Similarly, the Department of Immigration found that the trifecta of a faltering global economy, a contraction in the resources sector and increased net interstate migration to Western Australia increased the availability of domestic skilled labour, which corresponded with resource firms reducing their demand for workers on 457 visas. Although this research supports the theory that a demand-driven approach is responsive to changes in the economy and the labour market, Bahn acknowledges the limitations of her study, namely its narrow frame of reference because of her reliance on highly skilled workers, its

[14] See, eg Business Council of Australia, *Pipeline or Pipe Dream? Securing Australia's Investment Future* (Melbourne, Business Council of Australia, 2012).

[15] Susanne Bahn, 'Workers on 457 Visas: Evidence from the West Australian Resources Sector' (2013) 39 *Australian Bulletin of Labour* 34, 35.

small sample size and its focus on one sector.[16] Whether a demand-driven approach is as effective in low-wage sectors employing large numbers of 457 visa holders with less specialised skills is less certain. I will revisit this question later in this chapter.[17]

Another basis for the demand-driven principle is that migrant workers achieve stronger labour market outcomes than other types of migrants who enter Australia without pre-arranged employment. The 457 visa is designed to ensure temporary migrant workers are employed straight away and no time is 'wasted' in unemployment searching for a job. Cully's study of the labour market absorption effect of employer-sponsored migrant workers finds these workers are more likely to be employed in skilled jobs and earn more than migrant workers entering Australia through a pathway other than the 457 visa.[18] Cully concludes that his study 'provides support for the shift more than a decade ago towards embracing demand-driven migration' but its utility in proving this point is limited by its narrow focus on labour market outcomes for temporary migrant workers.[19] This ignores the impact that their employment has on the labour market outcomes, both in the short term and long term, of local workers, and also whether temporary migrant workers are being employed in positions commensurate to their skill level.[20] By way of example, an investigation by the Australian Workforce and Productivity Agency found that migrant workers trained as accountants were often employed in entry level and administrative accounting positions, which of course has implications for the employment opportunities of local workers and the positive economic impact these migrant workers are able to bring about.[21]

A demand-driven approach to determining the composition of Australia's temporary migrant workforce is supported by an analysis of its macro-economic impact. The Productivity Commission has found that employer-sponsored migrants under the skilled category increased domestic real incomes. The commission found that, whilst migrants themselves were the main benefactors from immigration, the impact on industries employing

[16] Ibid 54.

[17] See, eg Martina Boese, Iain Campbell, Winsome Roberts and Joo-Cheong Tham, 'Temporary Migrant Nurses in Australia: Sites and Sources of Precariousness' (2013) 24 *Economic and Labour Relations Review* 316.

[18] Mark Cully, *Skilled Migration Selection Policies: Recent Australian Reforms* (Canberra, Department of Immigration and Citizenship, 2012).

[19] Ibid 1.

[20] For the importance of the latter, see OECD, *International Migration Outlook: Sopemi 2011* (Paris, OECD Publishing, 2014).

[21] Australian Workforce and Productivity Agency, *Demand and Supply of Accountants: March 2014* (Canberra, Australian Workforce and Productivity Agency, 2014). The Australian Workforce and Productivity Agency has since been disbanded with some of its operations subsumed into the Department of Industry. For more, see Joanna Howe, 'Does Australia Need an Expert Commission to Assist with Managing its Labour Migration Program?' (2014) 27 *Australian Journal of Labour Law* 233.

skilled immigrants is also substantial, with higher returns to capital and slower real wage growth as a consequence.[22] The latter is a cause for concern for local workers who prefer higher real wages growth and may become less interested in a particular occupation if temporary migrants constitute a substantial proportion of the workforce. Some scholars have observed that this can lead to 'path dependencies'[23] or 'structural embeddedness'[24] as employers' temporary demand for migrant labour becomes permanent.[25] These scholars suggest that a temporary skill shortage can become an ongoing one as local workers become less attracted to a job characterised by a high proportion of temporary migrant workers as this produces slower real wages growth and poorer working conditions.

An important qualification on the demand-driven principle underpinning the 457 visa is the relationship between employer demand for temporary migrant labour and investment in training. One of the rationales for *temporary* workers under the 457 visa programme was that, whilst a temporary migrant worker could fill a short-term need, training local workers would ultimately lead to an Australian worker performing that job in the long term. In the initial years of the 457 visa programme, sponsorship applications were sent to the Department of Employment, Training and Youth Affairs where an officer would have five days to assess an employer's reputation and training records.[26] Only employers with a demonstrable training record would be approved for sponsorship. Over time this has been diluted so that employers are required either to make an annual contribution to an industry training fund or to spend at least one per cent of their annual payroll on training their Australian employees.[27] This use of training benchmarks has been criticised as it has failed to prevent an employer's reliance on a 457 visa worker to remedy a skill shortage from producing long-term dependence on temporary migrant labour.[28]

[22] Productivity Commission, *Economic Impacts of Migration and Population Growth* (Melbourne, Productivity Commission, 2006) 153.

[23] Martin Ruhs and Bridget Anderson, 'Migrant Workers: Who Needs Them? A Framework for the Analysis of Staff Shortages, Immigration and Public Policy' in Martin Ruhs and Bridget Anderson (eds), *Who Needs Migrant Workers: Labour Shortages, Immigration and Public Policy* (Oxford, Oxford University Press, 2010) 39.

[24] Cornelius, cited in Ruhs and Anderson, ibid 39.

[25] See also Cathryn Costello, 'Migrants and Forced Labour: A Labour Law Response' in Alan Bogg, Cathryn Costello, Anne Davies and Jeremias Prassl (eds), *The Autonomy of Labour Law* (London, Bloomsbury, 2015) 211.

[26] Bob Birrell, 'A Note on the New Rules Governing the Temporary Entry of Business People and Highly Skilled Specialists' 4(4) (1996) *People and Place* 76, 77.

[27] Migration Regulations 1994 (Cth) reg 2.59.

[28] See, eg John Azarias, Jenny Lambert, Peter McDonald and Katie Malyon, *Robust New Foundations: A Streamlined Transparent and Responsive System for the 457 Programme. An Independent Review into Integrity in the Subclass 457 Programme* (Canberra, Department of Immigration and Border Protection, 2014) 11.

In essence, the economic orthodoxy underpinning Australia's 457 visa programme is that the demand-driven approach benefits migrants, employers and the economy as a whole. In this way, it is seen to achieve both economic efficiency and redistributive goals. Nonetheless, as I have briefly flagged above, and will examine more closely below, this economic orthodoxy is worthy of challenge. Not only does a demand-driven approach insufficiently realise labour law's worker-protective mission, but a demand-driven approach also fails to meet its objective of efficiently identifying and meeting skill shortages.

III. CHALLENGING THE ORTHODOXY

In this section I demonstrate that there are major concerns over the extent of supervision of employer demand in determining the composition of Australia's temporary migration intake. Further, I argue that, contrary to the orthodoxy, the Australian government has the capacity (and indeed the obligation) to ensure employer requests for 457 visas achieve stronger scrutiny and accountability in this area. In this section, I outline a number of critiques of Australia's demand-driven temporary migration programme.

Wright and Constantin observe that Australia's 457 visa programme uses employer demand as a proxy for skill shortages.[29] A skill shortage is not merely demonstrated through failed recruitment efforts but by wage increases failing to stimulate an increase in labour supply. Australia's demand-driven model makes employers the arbiter of whether an occupation is experiencing a shortage: there is no rigorous external assessment of the accuracy of an employer's attestation that a skill shortage exists. Employers are required to attest to the existence of a skill shortage and satisfy a weak evidentiary burden of failed recruitment efforts. The problem with using employer demand to determine which skills are in short supply is that it can lead to the artificial creation of skill shortages. This can occur because, when an employer is unable to recruit a local worker to fill a job vacancy, it can apply to the Department of Immigration to sponsor a 457 visa worker. The department concludes that a skill shortage exists because no local workers are available or willing to perform the job. Over time, the presence of 457 visa holders in particular occupations leads to employers becoming reliant on migrant workers to perform certain jobs and the short-term skill shortage becomes a permanent one.

[29] Chris Wright and Andreea Constantin, 'An Analysis of Employers' Use of Temporary Skilled Visas in Australia', Submission to the Senate Education and Employment References Committee Inquiry into the Impact of Australia's Temporary Work Visa Programs on the Australian Labour Market and on the Temporary Work Visa Holders, 1 May 2015.

A number of scholars have observed the ability of temporary migrant worker programmes to produce permanent skill shortages because of the impact that increasing labour supply has on wages and conditions for a particular job.[30] Costello says that 'temporary status creates permanent demand' because temporary migrant workers are more willing to accept lower wages and conditions as their right to remain in the country of destination is contingent upon their being employed, whereas local workers have no such inducement.[31] Ruhs argues there is a risk that, if not managed properly, demand-driven labour immigration programs like the 457 visa can potentially create labour market distortions, by inducing employers to develop structural preferences for migrant labour in ways that erode local job opportunities.[32] He proposes that policies be designed with reference to a broader range of policy principles other than simply 'employer interests'.[33]

The 457 visa's demand-driven nature appears to rest on an assumption that the short-term interests of employers are consistent with, and reflect, the long-term interests of the Australian economy. This is not necessarily so. Whilst it may be in employers' interests to have more of a given skill available at all times and it benefits employers to create artificial skill shortages through embedding lower wages and conditions that can only be met by temporary labour migration, this does not account for the economic and social costs of oversupply of specific skills within the Australian economy. One adverse social consequence of oversupply is the resulting tension between local workers and temporary migrant workers, with the latter unfairly cast as 'stealing' local jobs. The economic consequences of oversupply can include reduced living standards for local workers as it reduces their job opportunities and puts downward pressure on wages and conditions for certain jobs. It can also reduce investment in training for local workers or reduce the incentive for employers to innovate or adopt other meaningful measures to address a skill shortage.[34]

A related problem is that using a demand-driven model to determine skill shortages may reflect employers' preference for behavioural traits associated with migrant workers rather than actual skill shortages. A study of employers' motivations for accessing 457 visa workers found that these were varied and were not always contingent upon whether a particular occupation

[30] See, eg Andrew Geddes and Sam Scott, 'UK Food Businesses' Reliance on Low-Wage Migrant Labour: A Case of Choice or Constraint?' in Ruhs and Anderson (eds), *Who Needs Migrant Workers* (n 23); Valeria Ottonelli and Tiziana Torres, 'Inclusivist Egalitarian Liberalism and Temporary Migration: A Dilemma' (2012) 20 *Journal of Political Philosophy* 202.

[31] Costello, 'Migrants and Forced Labour' (n 25) 210.

[32] Martin Ruhs, *The Price of Rights: Regulating International Labor Migration* (Princeton, NJ: Princeton University Press, 2013) 179–83.

[33] Ibid.

[34] See, eg Francis Green, Stephen Machin and David Wilkinson, 'The Meaning and Determinants of Skills Shortages' (1998) 60 *Oxford Bulletin of Economics and Statistics* 165.

was in shortage.[35] This study found that a significant minority of employers sought to acquire 457 visa holders with certain behavioural traits, reflecting an 'embedded preference' for temporary migrant workers as a way of gaining a competitive advantage.[36] This is supported by scholarship which suggests employers prefer migrant workers because their labour costs less and is easier to dispose of,[37] and they are more likely to be 'compliant, easy to discipline and cooperative'.[38] In effect, this means Australia's 457 visa programme allows 'selection of those prepared to do the work on the employers' terms',[39] as there is little scrutiny of employer attestation that a skill shortage exists. In practice, a demand-driven temporary migration program is highly susceptible to abuse because employers may use it not only to meet genuine skill shortages but as a way of getting around recruitment difficulties because the employer is offering inadequate wages and conditions to attract local workers or to recruit for behaviour traits which they perceive as being less present in local workers. In this way, Australia's demand-driven model masks the myriad motivations employers have for accessing temporary migrant labour and is an imprecise mechanism for determining whether a shortage actually exists. As Hugo puts it, 'employers will always have a "demand" for foreign workers if it results in a lowering of their costs'.[40]

From a labour law perspective, a demand-driven approach entrenches the precarity of temporary migrant workers as the latter's right to remain in the country of destination is contingent upon the employer's continuing demand for their labour. In the case of the 457 visa programme, a visa holder has 90 days to secure a new sponsorship arrangement before they are required to return to their country of origin.[41] Thus, withdrawal of support from the employer-sponsor may mean cancellation of the visa, rendering a migrant worker's position even more fragile and volatile. This threat, actual or perceived, may induce a temporary migrant worker to accept any degree of substandard working conditions.[42] In 2015, a situation involving

[35] Wright and Constantin, 'An Analysis of Employers' Use' (n 29).

[36] Ibid.

[37] Michael J Piore, *Birds of Passage: Migrant Labor and Industrial Societies* (Cambridge, Cambridge University Press, 1979).

[38] Ruhs and Anderson, 'Migrant Workers' (n 23) 20.

[39] Elaine Moriarty, James Wickham, Torben Krings, Justyna Salamonska and Alicja Bobek, 'Taking on Almost Everyone?' Migrant and Employer Recruitment Strategies in a Booming Labour Market' 23 (2012) *International Journal of Human Resource Management* 1871, 1872.

[40] Graeme Hugo, 'Best Practice in Temporary Labour Migration for Development: A Perspective from Asia and the Pacific' (2009) 47(5) *International Migration* 23, 59.

[41] Visa condition 8107.

[42] See, eg *Jones v Hanssen Pty Ltd* [2008] FMCA 291; BC200801596 at [8]–[9]. This case was later appealed and the Federal Court reduced the penalty imposed on the employer because the federal magistrate placed too much emphasis on the vulnerable position of the 457 visa holders, rather than articulating the actual detriment suffered by them: *Hanssen Pty Ltd v Jones* (2009) 179 IR 57; [2009] FCA 192; BC200901181.

an Indian chef who was forced to work twelve hours per day, seven days per week, and was virtually unpaid led the court to question the integrity of the 457 visa programme as a mechanism for meeting skill shortages. Judge Driver stated, 'the starting proposition that the respondents were unable to find an Indian chef in Australia is risible'.[43] Although this case is at the extreme end of exploitation of the 457 visa programme, the demand-driven nature of the programme renders a temporary migrant worker more vulnerable because of the binary role of employer and sponsor. Costello characterises this as an additional layer of dependence, created by the tie of migration status to employment,[44] which intensifies the inherently unequal nature of employment relationships.

Another structural feature of the demand-driven nature of the 457 visa programme which tends to entrench the precarity of visa holders is that, in most cases, employer sponsorship is a precondition for obtaining permanent residency.[45] The Deegan Report identified that the promise of permanent residency can be an incentive for migrant workers to accept poorer wages and conditions.[46] Its response was to propose that in determining eligibility for permanent residency more weight should be given to the length of time a visa holder has worked for any Australian employer rather than the willingness of one employer sponsor.[47]

Another difficulty with using employer demand to determine skill shortages is that migration intermediaries, who profit from facilitating temporary labour migration flows, have a vested interest in inflating employer demand. At the inception of the 457 visa programme in 1996, this was less of an issue but increasingly migration is being commercialised, with migration intermediaries in the form of migration agents and labour hire companies seeking to profit from accelerating temporary labour migration. Traditionally, temporary labour migration is conceived of as a triple win, with benefits ensuing to migrant workers and their countries of origin and destination.[48] Absent from this analysis is the benefit to migration intermediaries seeking to profit from temporary migration. Migration intermediaries have two

[43] *RAM v D&D Indian Fine Foods Pty Ltd & Anor* [2015] FCCA 389, para 187.

[44] Costello, 'Migrants and Forced Labour' (n 25) 210.

[45] Although these visa holders can apply for permanent residency under the points-based system, the primary route is the Employer Nomination Scheme and the Regional Sponsored Migration Scheme, both of which are contingent upon employer sponsorship.

[46] Visa Subclass 457 Integrity Review, *Final Report* (Canberra, Commonwealth of Australia, 2008) 32 ('*Deegan Report*') 51. For more on the ERG Review and the Deegan Review, see Joanna Howe, 'The Migration Amendment (Worker Protection) Act 2008: Long Overdue Reform, But Have Migrant Workers Been Sold Short?' (2010) 24 *Australian Journal of Labour Law* 13.

[47] *Deegan Report* 51.

[48] Stephen Castles and Derya Ozkul, 'Circular Migration: Triple Win, or a New Label for Temporary Migration?' in Graziano Battistella (ed), *Global and Asian Perspectives on International Migration* (Dordrecht, Springer, 2014).

primary functions: first, to match employers with prospective temporary migrant workers and second, to determine the terms and conditions of the employment contract. For employers, this outsources the challenges associated with recruitment and the ongoing regulatory burden of complying with employment laws and migration laws as a third party is responsible for wage payments, superannuation and taxation. For migrant workers, this means they are able to find employment in a destination country and receive assistance with housing, transport and visa issues. Migration intermediaries profit from both employers and migrant workers by charging a fee for these services. It is, therefore, in their interest to inflate employer demand by encouraging employers to use temporary migrant labour rather than local workers as this increases their potential for profits. The increasing role of migration intermediaries brings into question the utility of using employer demand to determine skill shortages.

Additionally, the presence of migration intermediaries in shaping employer demand for temporary migrant labour is concerning because of its potential to erode labour standards. The pre-existing vulnerability of labour hire workers is compounded by temporary labour migration as workers' temporariness and migrant status renders them highly susceptible to exploitation.[49] The Deegan Review recognised that 'reliance upon migration and recruitment agents both in Australia and offshore' was a source of vulnerability for migrant workers.[50] Numerous examples have emerged of labour hire companies seeking to sell temporary migrant labour to employers resulting in the underpayment of wages,[51] overcrowded housing,[52] and the misclassification of workers to avoid minimum wages and conditions.[53] The precarious position of temporary migrants was also highlighted in a recent study of temporary migrant workers in the Australian horticulture industry.[54] This found that these workers were frequently exploited by

[49] For literature on the regulatory challenges associated with global labour recruitment, see Jennifer Gordon, *Joint Liability Approaches to Regulating Recruitment*, Fordham Law Legal Studies Research Paper No. 2518519 (New York, Fordham University, 2014).

[50] *Deegan Report* (n 46) 63.

[51] Fair Work Ombudsman, 'Labour Hire Operators Face Court for Allegedly Underpaying Foreign Worker $8000', media release, 20 April 2012; See, eg *Fair Work Ombudsman v Crystal Carwash Café Pty Ltd (No 2)* [2014] FCA 827; *Fair Work Ombudsman v Glad Group* [2012] FMCA 731.

[52] See, eg the ABC *Four Corners* investigation into the use of labour hire companies in the horticulture industry: ABC, *Four Corners*, 'Slaving Away', 4 May 2015. For a transcript of the story, see http://www.abc.net.au/4corners/stories/2015/05/04/4227055.htm.

[53] Eg, a Victorian labour hire company was banned from sponsoring workers under the 457 visa programme because it was employing workers on a casual basis rather than paying them their proper entitlements: Minister for Immigration and Citizenship, Chris Bowen, 'Victorian Company First to be Banned Under 457 Visa Programme', media release, 17 February 2012.

[54] Diane van den Broek, Dimitria Groutsis, Malcolm Rimmer and Elsa Underhill, 'Entrepreneurial Middle Men on the Harvest Trail: Ethics, Society and Migrant Work', paper presented at The Political Economy of Work and Labor Markets: Workplace Regimes in Comparative Perspective, Society for the Advancement of Socio-Economics Conference, Chicago, 12 July 2014.

labour hire contractors, hostel operators and other intermediaries seeking to 'sell' migrant labour to employers. This study found that the increasing 'commercialisation of migration' has opened up possibilities for entrepreneurship but that this has ethical implications as entrepreneurs do not necessarily have social ethics or the same impetus to act ethically as employers. The study concluded that the presence of migration intermediaries has resulted in a race to the bottom for horticulture wages in Australia. Whilst this study largely relied on seasonal workers and not 457 visa holders, it does illustrate what can happen in a demand-driven system.[55] If employers' demand for labour is the main criterion, entrepreneurs will seek to meet this demand in order to make a profit. This can lead to the creation of migrant labour supply chains where it is the migrant worker who loses out: the employer gets access to cheap labour and the supply chain operator makes a profit.

IV. FUTURE DIRECTIONS FOR REFORM OF THE 457 VISA PROGRAMME

Having explored the practical failings of the current method of using employer demand to determine shortages, in this section I examine the Australian regulatory framework for the 457 visa programme and consider to what extent it may dictate greater scrutiny of employer requests to access temporary migrant labour. In developing this argument, I build on the recommendation of a number of significant reviews of the 457 visa programme, which have called for greater limits on employer demand.[56] I explain that the basis of such limits is to ensure that it is not just employers and supply chain operators who benefit from temporary labour migration but also local workers and migrant workers, and to ensure the 457 visa programme serves the national interest. The limitations I envisage fall into three categories: first, the regulatory design of the 457 visa; secondly, the enforcement capacity of the labour inspectorate, and thirdly, the need for regulatory cohesion between immigration law and labour law. It is only by developing an understanding of these categories that a complete and satisfying explanation for the necessity and scope of limitations on employer demand emerges. In developing these limits, I consider a number of other jurisdictions where limits are being applied.

In terms of regulatory design, the demand-driven principle underpinning the 457 visa should be limited by independent authentication of employer

[55] Compare the Swedish situation where intermediaries are paid large amounts of money to facilitate temporary migration flows: Engblom, 'Reconciling Openness and High Labour Standards?' (n 4) 354.

[56] See, eg Wright and Constantin, 'An Analysis of Employers' Use' (n 29); Azarias et al, *Robust New Foundations* (n 28); Australian Senate, Constitutional and Legal Affairs Committee Inquiry into the Subclass 457 Visa, Majority Report (2013).

attestation that a skill shortage exists. Lists of occupational shortages should be independently developed. This is despite the drawbacks of independent labour market testing, namely that it is hard for government agencies to identify and quantify skill shortages as 'occupation is not an innate characteristic',[57] particularly in a geographically dispersed country like Australia,[58] and there can be a time lag between identification and when an occupation is made eligible for temporary labour migration.[59] To date, the Australian approach has been to require that 457 visa holders be paid above a minimum threshold for temporary migrant workers and 'market salary rates'.[60] The rationale for the former is to prevent the use of 457 visa holders for low-skilled or semi-skilled work, whilst for the latter, market salary rates are intended to operate as a market-based price signal that effectively renders a migrant worker more expensive to hire than a local worker in the same occupation, as an employer using the former needs to cover additional costs associated with nomination and sponsorship under the 457 visa scheme. Nonetheless, this has proven to be fairly problematic as the difficulty lies in identifying the market rate for a particular locality. This cannot be easily ascertained and necessitates a consideration of a wide range of enterprise agreements and common law contracts for equivalent workers in the region.[61]

It is a delicate balancing exercise to determine how to moderate employer demand. The 457 visa programme certainly relies too heavily on employer assertions that a skill shortage exists without the necessary checks and balances. Broadly speaking, the 'right' policy mix probably includes an independently and credibly compiled occupational shortage list, a requirement that 457 visa holders are paid more than (or at least at the upper end of) market salary rates or that wages and conditions are co-determined with the relevant union before a temporary migrant worker can be engaged. This would limit the incentive for employers to pursue 457 visa holders for a reason other than a genuine skill shortage as it would be more costly to do so.

Whilst it is vital that the structural design of the 457 visa programme deters the artificial creation of skill shortages, equally critical is a strong enforcement agency to ensure temporary migrant workers are being employed according to the wages and conditions stated on the sponsorship agreement and in compliance with local labour laws. Although Sweden does not have a labour market inspectorate, the high rate of unionism

[57] Anna Platonova and Giuliana Urso (eds), *Labour Shortages and Migration Policy* (Geneva, International Organization for Migration, 2012) 15.

[58] *Deegan Report* (n 46) 39.

[59] See, eg Howe, 'Is the Net Cast Too Wide?' (n 2).

[60] 457 visa holders' salaries must be above the Temporary Skilled Migration Income Threshold (TSMIT). The TSMIT was set at $53,900 on 1 July 2013.

[61] Joo-Cheong Tham and Iain Campbell, *Temporary Migrant Labour in Australia: The 457 Visa Scheme and Challenges for Labour Regulation*, Working Paper No 50 (Melbourne, Centre for Employment and Labour Relations Law, University of Melbourne, 2011) 26.

provides some regulation of the labour market. Even so cases have emerged in Sweden of exploitative work arrangements involving temporary migrant workers.[62] In 2012, the Swedish government introduced regulatory reforms in some low-skilled sectors in an effort to address this.[63] Australia does have the benefit of an established labour inspectorate in the Fair Work Ombudsman (FWO), which is an independent statutory authority created under the Fair Work Act 2009 (Cth). The FWO has identified migrant workers as particularly vulnerable to exploitation. More than one tenth of all complaints received by the FWO were from visa holders and the FWO has recovered more than $1.1 million on behalf of temporary migrant workers in 2013–2014.[64] The FWO currently has an Overseas Workers' Team and a Regional Services Team, both of which have investigatory and educative functions. For example, in January 2015, the FWO issued a warning to growers, accommodation providers and labour hire contractors that unlawful treatment of vulnerable backpackers and seasonal workers would not be tolerated, and that those participating in illegal practices could be held liable as accessories.[65] At the same time, the FWO's Regional Services Team was educating stakeholders and reviewing compliance across Australia within the fruit and vegetable growing supply chains as part of its Harvest Trail initiative.[66] The FWO also has an important role in pursuing prosecutions of employers involved in exploiting temporary migrant workers.[67] Whilst these and other enforcement initiatives of the FWO are important, the regulatory capacity of the FWO is necessarily bounded by the huge challenge presented by Australia's geography and the significant number of 457 visa holders. It seems unlikely that the FWO's resourcing is sufficient. FWO has 300 inspectors divided into teams: compliance, early intervention, alternative dispute resolution and campaigns.[68] Its inspectorate is required to serve up to 11.6 million workers,[69] a significant portion of which are temporary migrants with work rights in the domestic economy.[70]

[62] Engblom, 'Reconciling Openness and High Labour Standards?' (n 4) 356.

[63] Ibid.

[64] Natalie James, *Fair Work Ombudsman Annual Report 2013–2014* (Melbourne, FWO, 2014).

[65] Fair Work Ombudsman, 'Harvest Trail Campaign', http://www.fairwork.gov.au/how-we-will-help/helping-the-community/campaigns/national-campaigns/harvest-trail-campaign; see also Michaelia Cash, Assistant Minister for Immigration and Border Protection, 'Allegations of Worker Exploitation', media release, 5 May 2015.

[66] Ibid.

[67] See, eg FWO, *Litigation Policy*, 4th edn (Canberra, Commonwealth of Australia, 2013).

[68] Department of Immigration and Border Protection, *Annual Report 2013–2014* (Canberra, DIBP, 2014) 71–72.

[69] Australian Bureau of Statistics, *Australian Labour Market Statistics, Cat. No. 6105* (Canberra, ABS, 2014).

[70] Eg in 2013–2014 visas were issued for 260,303 international students, 258,248 working holiday makers and 126,350 subclass 457 visa holders: DIAC, *Annual Report 2012–2013* (Canberra, DIAC, 2013) 2.

A final issue to address is the need for regulatory cohesion between labour law and immigration law. There are a number of facets to this. Firstly, migrant workers need to be protected if they breach immigration law by performing a different job or being in receipt of lower wages and conditions than those specified in the sponsorship agreement. Under Australian immigration law, a person may be fined, detained or deported if they are performing work that breaches the visa's conditions.[71] This means that, if an employer pays a 457 visa holder lower wages than the Temporary Skilled Migration Income Threshold or the market salary rate as determined in the sponsorship agreement, this can have dire consequences for the temporary migrant worker. For the worker, this potentially means deportation whilst for the employer this may involve civil or criminal penalties (although these have rarely been applied) and the trouble of finding a replacement worker. In this situation, the intersection between labour law and immigration law leads to the unintended consequence of increasing the precarity of the migrant worker without properly functioning as an incentive for employers to follow Australian labour law and the terms of the sponsorship agreement.[72] This has the binary effect of inhibiting migrant workers from reporting their situation to the authorities whilst 'unscrupulous employers will calculate the savings from long-term exploitation of ... workers against the risk of detection and penalty'.[73]

A second reform necessary to ensure regulatory cohesion is that 457 visa holders should be allowed to exercise their legal rights under the Fair Work Act 2009 (Cth) before being forced to return to their country of origin because they no longer have an employer-sponsor. For example, an important legal right which Australian labour law accords to employees is the ability to challenge their dismissal via an independent adjudicative mechanism. Unfair dismissal law allows an employee to bring a claim within fourteen days to the Fair Work Commission that the dismissal was 'harsh, unjust or unreasonable'.[74] Under immigration law, visa condition 8107 only provides 457 visa holders with 90 days to secure a new employer-sponsor before the visa expires. Whilst half of unfair dismissal applications are resolved in 51 days, a substantial minority takes significantly longer, with a further 40 per cent of applications taking up to 146 days to

[71] Migration Act 1958 (Cth) s 235.

[72] For anecdotal evidence of this, see the stories of 457 visa holders reported on the ABC's Radio National programme: Claudia Taranto, 'Workers Without Borders: The Rise of Temporary Migrant Labour', 18 May 2015, http://www.abc.net.au/radionational/programs/earshot/the-rise-of-temporary-migrant-labour/6472368.

[73] Stephen Clibborn, 'Why Undocumented Immigrant Workers Should Have Workplace Rights' (2015) 26(3) *Economic and Labour Relations Review* 465.

[74] For more on Australian unfair dismissal law, see Joanna Howe, 'Poles Apart? The Contestation between the Ideas of No Fault Dismissal and Unfair Dismissal for Protecting Job Security' (2013) 42(2) *Industrial Law Journal* 122.

reach resolution.[75] The remaining 10 per cent take even longer than this.[76] A failure to provide 457 visa holders with an extension of time on their visa to exhaust their legal claims (whether it be unfair dismissal, discrimination or adverse action) further entrenches the precarity of temporary migrant workers. Visa condition 8107 acts as a barrier to these workers exercising their legal rights because of the prohibitive combination of the unlikelihood of their legal claims being resolved in 90 days and the time and resources required to find a new employer-sponsor. This means that 457 visa holders do not properly have a right to redress for unfair dismissal, thus, enhancing their susceptibility to arbitrary dismissal at the hands of their employer. Their job insecurity is worsened by the insecurity of their migration status, as arbitrary dismissal not only means they are out of a job but also that they risk deportation if they cannot secure new employment within the 90-day time limit. This greatly increases the power imbalance between 457 visa holders and their employers. Of course, it is possible that, if visa condition 8107 was amended, it may result in some temporary migrant workers launching frivolous legal claims in order to extend their visa term and to provide them with more time to find a new employer-sponsor. However, this is fairly unlikely given the financial and other resources required to pursue legal claims, which most 457 visa holders will not have at their disposal. Further, the possibility of pursuing vexatious claims is a charge that can be levelled at local workers too and Australian legislators have still deemed it necessary to provide legal protection of job security.

A third area requiring reform in order to achieve regulatory cohesion between immigration law and labour law is to prevent information being channelled from the labour inspectorate to immigration authorities. In 2013, the FWO's powers were strengthened to give it a specific role in the enforcement of migrant workers' right. This has meant that the FWO performs a dual regulatory role as its inspectors pursue breaches of the Fair Work Act 2009 (Cth) and non-compliance with 457 visa conditions. This means that the FWO may pass information on to the Department of Immigration when it uncovers exploitative work arrangements involving temporary migrant workers such as underpayment of wages. As has been identified above, this can adversely impact the migration status of temporary migrant workers. The relationship between the FWO and the Department of Immigration acts as a disincentive to migrant workers informing the FWO about exploitative work arrangements as it may have consequences for their visa. Clibborn

[75] FWC, *Annual Report 2013–2014* (Canberra, FWC, 2014).
[76] Ibid.

suggests that the FWO and the department should 'formally and publicly establish independence from each other' and 'cease information sharing'.[77] For example, a recent investigation by FWO inspectors and officials from the Department of Immigration into visa fraud and worker exploitation led to the detention of 38 illegal workers, six of whom had been working in breach of their visa conditions.[78] This punitive action against temporary migrant workers found in exploitative work arrangements strongly deters them from informing authorities about their situation and inhibits their ability to trust that information they provide to the FWO will not be passed on to the Department of Immigration. It is often asserted that temporary migrant workers should not accept work, wages or conditions that do not match their sponsorship agreement but this often obscures the reality of their situation: they need work to support themselves as they are not eligible for social security and they are often in debt, having paid large amounts of money to procure a visa to enter Australia in the first place. They also may be unfamiliar with their legal rights under the sponsorship agreement or Australian labour law. Given this, it seems rather disingenuous and counterproductive to penalise them for acquiescing to exploitative work arrangements.

V. CONCLUSION

In this chapter I have considered whether it is time for a shift away from the demand-driven orthodoxy underpinning the 457 visa programme. I have argued that such a shift should be informed by comparative practice in which limits are drawn on employer requests to access temporary migrant labour. There needs to be greater regulation of employer attestation that a skill shortage exists through a structural redesign of the 457 visa, increasing the enforcement capacity of the regulator and ensuring regulatory cohesion between immigration law and labour law. This is not to diminish the importance of employer demand as one aspect of the regulatory framework for determining the composition of Australia's temporary migrant worker programme. However, the Australian government has both the capacity and obligation to ensure that employer requests for 457 visas are met with stronger scrutiny and accountability.

[77] Clibborn, 'Why Undocumented Immigrant Workers' (n 73) 7. See also Rosemary Owens, 'Temporary Labour Migration and Workplace Rights in Australia: Is Effective Enforcement Possible?', ch 18 in this volume.

[78] Michaelia Cash, 'Illegal Workers Targeted Nationally', media release, 28 May 2015.

Part IV

Temporary Labour Migration and the Production of Precarity

7

Migrant Domestic Workers in British Columbia, Canada

Unfreedom, Trafficking and Domestic Servitude

JUDY FUDGE

I. INTRODUCTION

'SLAVERY IS A weed that grows in any soil' is the epigraph with which Benjamin Perrin begins his influential 2010 book, *Invisible Chains: Canada's Underground World of Human Trafficking*.[1] Taken from Edmund Burke's 1775 speech on conciliation with America, it conveys the idea that slavery is not a social and legal institution that requires actual cultivation. *Invisible Chains* encapsulates the prevailing conservative approach to the problem of 'modern slavery' and trafficking, which regards the criminal law as a punitive and redemptive force to be brought to bear against evil perpetrators who exploit vulnerable victims. This approach has dominated the political landscape in Canada since 2006, when a minority Conservative government first took power federally. Perrin helped to shape the federal government's human trafficking policy, first in his capacity as a Senior Advisor to the federal Minister of Citizenship and Immigration, and then as a Special Advisor Legal Affairs and Policy in the Office of the Prime Minister, where he was lead policy advisor on all matters related to Public Safety Canada and Citizenship and Immigration Canada. This approach also influenced the British Columbia (BC) government, which in 2007 was the first government in Canada to set up an office dedicated to combatting trafficking in persons. Although initially both levels of government focused

[1] Benjamin Perrin, *Invisible Chains: Canada's Underground World of Human Trafficking* (Toronto, Viking, 2010).

almost exclusively on trafficking for the purposes of sexual exploitation, they later also became concerned with labour trafficking. In 2011, the deployment of anti-trafficking laws became British Columbia's preferred method for addressing problems relating to the exploitation of migrant domestic workers. That year the provincial government prosecuted two employers under the trafficking provisions in the Immigration and Refugees Protection Act (IRPA) for trafficking for the purposes of domestic servitude. Since then, both the Conservative federal and the BC provincial governments, as well as civil society advocates, have characterised the abuse of migrant domestic workers as a form of trafficking and modern day slavery.[2]

How did the exploitation and mistreatment of migrant domestic workers in Canada come to be seen as a problem of labour trafficking, modern slavery and domestic servitude? The answer to this question is not obvious. The deployment of criminal law to resolve the problem of the long-documented abuse of migrant domestic workers in Canada is neither natural nor inevitable, but is instead a result of a series of social and political choices. Advocates, public officials, the media and politicians often invoke the criminal law for its symbolic power because it has become the pre-eminent way of expressing social opprobrium. But the criminal law is also replete with specific legal technicalities (such as burdens of proof), technologies and personnel (police and crown prosecutors), and goals (punishment not compensation) that portray both a social problem and its solution in a specific way. There are other ways of understanding the problem of the exploitation of migrant domestic workers; the failure of states to enforce labour rights or to regulate recruitment agencies in combination with restrictive immigration controls can be seen as producing fertile soil for abusive employment practices. I will attempt to show how the 'modern slavery' frame of criminal law and trafficking focuses on 'individualised instances of domination' and thus operates to occlude analyses that attempt to account for how states are involved in structuring labour markets for migrant workers that encourage exploitative practices by employers.[3]

To do so, I will use the example of how domestic servitude and labour trafficking became the predominant legal categories for characterising migrant domestic workers' abuse in British Columbia to illustrate both the complex nature of labour unfreedom and the social foundations of legal characterisation. I begin by offering a socio-legal account of the legal characterisation of domestic workers' unfreedom that emphasises the generative nature of

[2] The Conservative federal government was defeated in the 2015 federal election, and, as yet, it is too soon to tell what the Liberal government's approach to migrant workers and labour exploitation will be. Although the British Columbia government is Liberal, in BC Liberals are much closer to the federal Conservative party than they are to the federal Liberal party.

[3] Genevieve LeBaron, 'Unfree Labor Beyond Binaries: Insecurity, Social Hierarchy, and Labor Market Restructuring' (2015) 17 *International Journal of Feminist Politics* 1, 2.

legal characterisation and explains how legal jurisdictions that pertain to the same social activity gain different impetus depending upon the social and political context in which they operate. In the third part, I recount how the abuse of migrant domestic workers in British Columbia came to be seen as a problem of domestic servitude to be addressed through laws prohibiting trafficking in human beings. I also show how in British Columbia the power of criminal law jurisdiction was enhanced at the expense of labour law jurisdiction and how federally the immigration jurisdiction drew closer to migrant controls and farther away from migrants' rights. To conclude, I reflect on the significance of the choice of legal jurisdiction to characterise the problem of the exploitation of migrant workers.

II. LEGAL CONSTRUCTION, JURISDICTION AND MIGRANT DOMESTIC WORKERS' UNFREEDOM

The example of migrant domestic workers illuminates the different dimensions of unfreedom that are involved in a labour regime.[4] The host state's imposition of restrictive immigration conditions on migrant domestic workers renders them unfree at the moment of contract, and creates conditions that lead to extreme exploitation by employers. For example, most migrant worker visa programmes tie a worker's visa to ongoing employment with a specific employer, impose restrictions on where migrant workers may reside (often within the employer's home), by what means (if any) they may obtain permanent residence or citizenship, and under what conditions (if any) they can be joined by dependents. In some cases, migrants' passports are confiscated on arrival. Many programmes also set out conditions of termination of the contract of employment that are different for domestic migrant workers than for other types of workers and which result in deportation if they leave their employer, for instance, or if they become pregnant.

The reasons for the particular constitution of the unfreedom of this group of migrant workers relate, at least in part, to the political economy of waged domestic labour in a globalised market.[5] The increase in women's labour force participation, falling fertility rates, increasing life expectancy, changes in family structure, a shortage of public care, and the increasing marketisation of care create demand for migrant domestic workers.[6] On

[4] Abigail B Bakan and Daiva Stasiulis, 'The Political Economy of Migrant Live-in Caregivers: A Case of Unfree Labour' in Patti Tamara Lenard and Christine Straehle (eds), *Legislated Inequality: Temporary Labour Migration in Canada* (Montreal, McGill-Queens University Press, 2012).

[5] Ibid 5–6.

[6] Judy Fudge, 'Global Care Chains, Employment Agencies and the Conundrum of Jurisdiction: Decent Work for Domestic Workers in Canada' (2011) 23 *Canadian Journal of Women and the Law* 235.

the supply side, economic trends such as growing inequalities between high- and low-income countries and insecurity, vulnerability and instability due to economic crises combine with the gendered nature of reproductive labour to increase the numbers of women who migrate in order to obtain paid work.[7] In a number of developing countries, remittances are crucial for the survival of households, communities and states.[8] Exporting workers is one key means by which governments cope with unemployment and foreign debt.[9]

Through the intersection of categories of social difference such as race, class, gender, citizenship and sexuality, precarious migrant status is assigned to migrant domestic workers in ways that structure their unfreedom and privilege the social reproduction of some groups over others.[10] This unfreedom is an attribute of the work relation and of related multi-level structures that arise from, and shape, the operation of social and economic power and the institutionalisation of labour markets. Unlike the case in many sectors, the employer of a domestic worker is an individual or household, not a firm, although agencies play an important role in both placing migrants and providing domestic and care services.

The second dimension of the unfreedom of domestic migrant workers is where they work—and often live. The household is understood in 'advanced' capitalist economies as a separate domain from the workplace. A defining characteristic of the work performed by migrant domestic workers is that it takes place within the home, the private domain of the family, where women's unpaid work is invisible and not economically valued. The private nature of their workplace limits employment-related legal protections to which domestic workers are entitled, or, if they apply, it makes them difficult to enforce.

The final, important aspect of the unfreedom of migrant domestic workers is that it is temporally and spatially varied and specific. In the UK, domestic labour has historical roots in the concept of menial service, which fell somewhere between contractual freedom and paternalism.[11] Contemporary discourses of servitude and slavery have roots in both this tradition and in abolitionist movements that sought to outlaw the trade in African slaves whilst simultaneously embedding relations of unfree labour that were of a different type and order than chattel slavery. In the United States,

[7] Lourdes Beneria, 'The Crisis of Care, International Migration, and Public Policy' (2008) 14 *Feminist Economics* 1.

[8] Saskia Sassen, 'Global Cities and Survival Circuits' in Barbara Ehrenreich and Arlie Russell Hochschild (eds), *Global Woman: Nannies, Maids and Sex Workers in the New Economy* (New York, Henry Holt, 2002) 39.

[9] Robyn Magalit Rodriguez, *Migrants for Export: How the Philippines State Brokers Labor to the World* (Minneapolis, MN, University of Minnesota Press, 2010).

[10] Bakan and Stasiulis, 'The Political Economy' (n 4).

[11] Ibid.

domestic work has strong ties with chattel slavery, and how 'home' slaves, once 'freed', were transformed into domestic servants.[12] Canada's links to the Caribbean through common membership in the Commonwealth help to explain the emergence of a small immigration programme to admit domestic workers from Caribbean states, while its explicitly racist policy (until 1962) of restricting West Indian immigration to Canada accounts for the more onerous conditions that were imposed on domestic workers from the Caribbean than domestic workers from Europe.[13] Thus, there are structural and systemic processes that operate at multiple scales and produce different regimes of unfree labour at specific times and places. Notions of race and 'foreignness' also play an important role in shaping the different legal institutions and labour relations that give rise to various forms of unfree labour.[14]

Cathryn Costello notes that unfree labour is not a legal concept and that it should not be equated with the legal concept of forced labour.[15] She regards its utility in its capacity to demonstrate the complex political economy of labour relations, which can be used to inform our understanding of how the legal categories of forced labour, servitude and slavery apply to different kinds of employment relation. She is primarily concerned with the integrity of the legal concepts and their application to complex fact situations. By contrast, what I am interested in is the interaction between social and legal characterisations of unfreedom in order to understand the social foundations of legal technicalities and their associated legal domains. I am concerned with how legal concepts take their meaning in specific social contexts.

How migrant workers' unfreedom is characterised for the purposes of providing mechanisms of legal redress raises important questions of legal epistemology and methodology as well as the relationship between legal and other social systems.[16] Legal characterisation is often seen as the process by which different regulatory paradigms are assigned to resolve a social problem. Regulatory paradigms or contexts involve assumptions about the nature and causes of the problem, the goals of regulation, and the strategies

[12] Evelyn Nakano Glenn, *Forced to Care: Coercion and Caregiving in America* (Cambridge, MA, Harvard, 2010).

[13] Daiva Stasiulis and Abigail B Bakan, *Negotiating Citizenship: Migrant Women in Canada and the Global System* (Toronto, University of Toronto Press, 2005).

[14] Nandita Sharma, *Home Economics: Nationalism and the Making of 'Migrant Workers' in Canada* (Toronto, University of Toronto Press, 2006); Julia O'Connell Davidson, *Modern Slavery: The Margins of Freedom* (Baskingstoke, Palgrave Macmillan, 2015).

[15] Cathryn Costello, 'Migrants and Forced Labour: A Labour Law Response' in Alan Bogg, Cathryn Costello, Anne Davies and Jeremias Prassl (eds), *The Autonomy of Labour Law* (Oxford, Hart, 2015) 198.

[16] Judy Fudge and Kendra Strauss, 'Migrants, Unfree Labour, and the Legal Construction of Domestic Servitude: Migrant Domestic Workers in the UK' in Cathryn Costello and Mark Freedland (eds), *Migrants at Work* (Oxford, Oxford University Press, 2015).

or techniques of regulation, which include burden of proof, remedy and redress, and form and process of adjudication.[17]

Legal scholars acknowledge that the process of legal characterisation is 'not a neutral one' since 'legal categories are not immutable abstractions into which sets of facts can be squeezed regardless of whether or not they fit'.[18] Typically, there is a range of possible legal categories inhabiting different regulatory contexts or paradigms. In Canada, there are at least four different regulatory contexts or domains (crime, labour, human rights and immigration) operating at the international, national and subnational levels, each of which involves a wide range of institutions, discourses and practices that govern migrant domestic workers.[19]

The process of legal characterisation operates at two levels: the meso level of the institutional/discursive construction of regulatory contexts and the micro level of deciding whether a particular instance falls with a specific regulatory context. At the meso level, legal characterisation involves legal construction, which is the active assignment of legal consequences to legal character.[20] This process forges the link between legal character and incidents, thereby creating a microsystem with a particular political and forensic dynamic that derives from the regulatory context. Each regulatory context also has its own complex internal structure and dynamic made up of different layers and scales of legal principle, doctrine and institutions. Different layers of regulation—from international law and constitutional norms, through specific statutes, to the contract of employment—are integrated into each other. These regulatory layers not only interact with each other as normative legal constructs; they also interact with the patterns and constructions with which those involved in the making of work relations place or seek to place their own dealings or arrangements. In this way, the process of legal construction has real ideological and material effects on how social actors organise their relations and activities.

Marianna Valverde's concept of jurisdiction is useful for elaborating the internal construction of a regulatory context. While jurisdiction is typically identified with the 'where' (territory) and the 'who' (authority) of governance, Valverde explains that 'jurisdiction also differentiates and organizes the "what" of governance—and most importantly because of its relative invisibility, the "how" of governance'.[21] The objects of governance—what

[17] Hila Shamir, 'A Labor Paradigm for Human Trafficking' (2012) 72 *UCLA Law Review* 76.

[18] Andrea Bianchi, 'Terrorism and Armed Conflict: Insights from a Law and Literature Perspective' (2011) 24 *Leiden Journal of International Law* 1, 3.

[19] Fudge, 'Global Care Chains' (n 6).

[20] Mark Freedland and Nicola Kountouris, *The Legal Construction of Personal Work Relations* (Oxford, Oxford University Press, 2011).

[21] Marianna Valverde, 'Jurisdiction and Scale: Legal "Technicalities" as Resources for Theory' (2009) 18 *Social & Legal Studies* 140, 145.

is to be regulated—for example, whether the exploitation of domestic workers is a matter of criminal or labour law or whether the treatment of migrant workers falls within immigration or criminal law, are associated with governance technologies (how the object should be governed), which, in turn, can be understood in terms of institutional capacities and rationalities as well as social and political norms and practices. Jurisdiction sets the outer boundaries of the process of legal characterisation, and it is an outcome of social and political contestation. It functions to allocate social relations and social activities into different legal domains or regulatory contexts.

Jurisdiction also has an external dimension. Chantal Thomas describes how several jurisdictions or regulatory contexts operate to construct a complex web of legal governance at the international level for migrant workers. These different regulatory domains or jurisdictions are dynamic, plural, overlapping and permeable, involving a number of institutions, actors and discourses that operate across a range of scales, with different degrees of attachment or embeddedness. While there are legal techniques for resolving apparent conflicts about the appropriate or correct normative characterisation, it does not follow that this legal pluralism operates as a harmonious legal order since the different jurisdictions reflect contested and complicated histories involving the interaction of political economy and historical contingency.[22]

For migrant domestic workers, the important issue is not so much which jurisdiction prevails, but, rather, how the different jurisdictions fit together to govern the social processes that produce the different dimensions of unfreedom. It is helpful to think of the legal governance of migrant domestic workers as composed of regulatory domains or spheres of jurisdictions that can attract or repel each other. The internal structure of each sphere or domain is internally complex, composed of a specific regulatory paradigm, with its own social assumptions, goals and technologies. The domains operate simultaneously along and across different scales and institutions and they have varying degrees of influence on one another. Externally, the borders between the spheres or domains may overlap or bleed into each other; two or more jurisdictions can share discourses, doctrines and institutions. The relationship between the different spheres is crucial in understanding the normative or legal characterisation of domestic workers' unfreedom. Moreover, jurisdictions interact in a social and political environment, which can function as a conductor that amplifies the force of a particular jurisdiction or an insulator that weakens the influence of one jurisdiction when compared with another. For example, governments that embrace a 'law and order' agenda and that tend to demonise migrant workers as a threat to

[22] Chantal Thomas, 'Convergence and Divergences in International Legal Norms on Migrant Workers' (2011) 32 *Comparative Labor Law and Policy Journal* 405, 408.

their own citizens imbue the criminal law jurisdiction with a great deal more force than that of labour law when it comes to addressing the exploitation of migrant domestic workers. As the following case study will show, the problem with the modern slavery approach to coercive forms of labour control is that it tends to overbear other jurisdictions such as labour law that can be used to remedy the problem of exploitation.

III. TRAFFICKING, MODERN SLAVERY AND DOMESTIC SERVITUDE IN BRITISH COLUMBIA

A. The Construction of Migrant Domestic Workers through Immigration and Labour Laws

Under the Canadian Constitution, the federal government has primary jurisdiction over immigration, whereas the provincial and territorial governments have authority over employment and labour law in their territory. Joining up these two levels of government for the purpose of regulating the terms and conditions of work of migrant domestic workers has been an enduring challenge.[23]

The Live-In Caregiver Program (LCP), which was established in 1992 and operated until October 2014, illustrates how immigration and employment law combined to create a labour market that cultivated abusive practices by employers. A special stream of the general Temporary Foreign Workers Program (TFWP), the LCP was designed to fill a specific labour shortage—the lack of people willing to reside in private households and provide care to members of those households. Like the other streams of the TFWP, it was employer driven, and it tied the migrant worker's entitlement to work in Canada to an ongoing employment relationship with a specific employer.[24] However, what distinguished the LCP from other streams of the TFWP is that it required the migrant worker to live in the household of the person for whom the worker cared. Thus, the LCP constructed a double unfreedom: not only was the caregiver's immigration status tied to a specific employment relationship with a particular employer so that she was not free to circulate in the labour market, the caregiver was also not free to choose her residence. The quid pro quo was that the LCP provided a unique pathway to permanent residency for workers who were designated low skilled. On completion of 24 months of authorised full-time live-in employment within four years of their arrival date, caregivers were entitled

[23] Fudge, 'Global Care Chains' (n 6).

[24] Judy Fudge and Fiona MacPhail, 'The Temporary Foreign Worker Program in Canada' (2009) 31 *Comparative Labor Law and Policy Journal* 101.

to apply for a change of status to permanent residency without having to leave Canada and without an employer's nomination. They were also eligible to sponsor close family members as permanent residents.

In order to hire a caregiver under the LCP, prospective employers had to obtain a labour market opinion from the relevant federal ministry. To do so, they had to detail their recruitment efforts and meet minimum advertising requirements. They also had to sign an employment contract setting out the terms and conditions of the migrant worker's employment. However, this contract is not enforceable in statutory employment tribunals. Nor was there a broad compliance mechanism or even a voluntary reporting initiative associated with the LCP.

Despite the LCP's popularity among Canadian families and migrant domestic workers, the programme has received a great deal of criticism.[25] Some of this criticism also pertains to the TFWP in general—for example, the link between the migrant workers' visa and an employment relationship with a specified employer, and the failure of the federal and provincial governments to monitor the programme in order to ensure that employers are abiding by the terms of the labour market opinion and employment contracts. Illegal recruitment fees, unpaid wages, and unpaid and excessive overtime were recurring complaints.[26] But the live-in requirement, which was specific to the LCP, was seen as making migrant caregivers especially vulnerable to exploitation.

In recognition of the specific vulnerability of domestic workers, most of whom are migrants and thus required to live in their employer's residence, anyone who employs a domestic worker in British Columbia is required to register under the Employment Standards Act (ESA) and to provide the domestic worker with a written contract that outlines her duties, hours of work, wages, and charges for room and board. However, the registry has not served an enforcement function. Moreover, since 2001, the province has moved almost exclusively to a complaint-based method of enforcing the ESA. Given live-in caregivers' threefold dependence on their employers—for a job, for a place to live and for migrant status—it is not likely that they will complain about violations of their labour standards.

British Columbia also prohibits employment agencies from charging fees to workers in order to place them in employment and requires the agencies to be licensed. Agencies are, however, permitted to charge people seeking employment for other services, such as resume writing and immigration services, which causes grave problems for characterising the nature of any fee

[25] Abigail B Bakan and Daiva Stasiulis (eds), *Not One of the Family: Foreign Domestic Workers in Canada* (Toronto, University of Toronto Press, 1997).

[26] Fudge, 'Global Care Chains' (n 6).

imposed by an agency for services rendered to a domestic worker. The ESA also provides a very light touch licensing system for employment agencies.[27] Despite incontrovertible evidence that recruiters have charged domestic workers illegal fees in order to place them in employment and engaged in fraudulent activities, the province has not introduced regulation nor devoted resources to address the problem.[28]

B. Criminal Law and Immigration Law: Trafficking

Canada introduced an anti-trafficking provision into the new Immigration and Refugee Protection Act 2001 (IRPA), which came into effect in 2002. Focused on organising entry to Canada, the IRPA trafficking offence does not explicitly require the exploitation of an individual, only that entry was 'facilitated through abduction, fraud, deception, or use or threat of coercion' (s 118). Exploitation is treated as an aggravating factor when it comes to sentencing (s 121). Thus, the IRPA trafficking provision is limited to foreign nationals who have been brought into Canada by unauthorised means. Where individuals are brought into Canada using authorised means, such as the TFWP, and then later exploited, the IRPA offence simply has no purchase.

By contrast, the offence in the Criminal Code, which only came into effect in 2005, does not require movement, either nationally or internationally, but instead focuses on the presence of exploitation, which is defined very narrowly. The prosecutor must establish that the accused's 'conduct could reasonably be expected to cause the other person to believe that their safety or the safety of a person known to them would be threatened if they failed to provide, or offer to provide, the labour or service' (s 279.04). In Canada, anti-trafficking campaigns by law enforcement officials and civil society groups initially tended to concentrate on sexual exploitation and prostitution. Advocates of a more robust approach to labour trafficking complain that definitional hurdles have been compounded by evidentiary burdens to make it difficult to deploy the Criminal Code trafficking offence to deal with problems of labour abuse.[29]

[27] Employment Standards Act 1996 (BC) c 113, ss 1(1), 12; Employment Standards Regulation BC 396/95, s 4.

[28] Judy Fudge and Daniel Parrot, 'Placing Filipino Caregivers in Canadian Homes: Regulating Transnational Employment Agencies in British Columbia' in Judy Fudge and Kendra Straus (eds), *Temporary Work, Agencies and Unfree Labour: Insecurity in the New World of Work* (New York, Routledge, 2013).

[29] Julie Kaye and Bethany Hastie, 'The Canadian Criminal Code Offence of Trafficking in Persons: Challenges from the Field and within the Law' (2015) 3 Social Inclusion 88; Anette Sikka, *Labour Trafficking in Canada: Indicators, Stakeholders, and Investigative Methods Law* (Ottawa, Enforcement and Policing Branch Public Safety Canada, 2013).

C. Labour Trafficking and Domestic Servitude

A decisive turn towards using trafficking to prosecute employers accused of engaging in 'domestic servitude' occurred in British Columbia in 2011 when crown prosecutors launched two cases under the IRPA. The choice of pursuing the trafficking charge under the IRPA instead of the Criminal Code was obvious since the former does not require proof of exploitation. The central question in each case was whether the accused had organised the unauthorised entry for the domestic worker through the use of fraud, deception or coercion.

The political and geographic context helps to explain both the timing and locale of the complaints. Trafficking for domestic servitude only achieved legal and political prominence with the publication in 2010 of Perrin's widely publicised book *Invisible Chains*. British Columbia was particularly receptive to extending the notion of trafficking to tackle unauthorised migration. In 2007, the province established the Office to Combat Trafficking in People (OCTIP), the first body of its kind in Canada. The focus on trafficking involving unauthorised entry to Canada reflected the original impetus for the OCTIP, which was the landing of four boatloads of unauthorised Chinese migrants on the shores of British Columbia in 1999.[30]

The two British Columbia cases of trafficking for domestic servitude received a great deal of publicity. Despite the fact that the decisions, which were rendered in 2013, came to opposite conclusions, they both illustrate the profound problem with using a penal provision in the immigration legislation to tackle labour exploitation and the extent to which convictions hinge on controversial assessments of credibility. Notably, neither case involved migrant workers who were admitted through the LCP.

R v Orr involved a complex tangle of civil and criminal litigation, which was still not resolved by July 2015. Leticia Sarmiento, a national of the Philippines, began to work for Mr Orr and his wife, Ms Huen, in Hong Kong in 2007. When the family decided to return to Canada, where Orr was a citizen, Sarmiento was invited to come to Canada and work for them. Orr told her that she would work eight hours a day, be paid according to Canadian law, and that he would help her obtain permanent residence status after two years. Sarmiento entered Canada under a Temporary Resident Visa, and she did not need a work permit because, under the IRPA, a caregiver can work in Canada for a maximum of six months while accompanying their employer. However, Sarmiento's 2009 request for an extension of her visa, which Orr prepared for her, was denied and she was required to leave Canada immediately. Orr continued to employ Sarmiento for another year.

[30] Perrin, *Invisible Chains* (n 1).

In June 2010, Sarmiento quarrelled with Ms Huen, and called the police, who came to the Orr home and ultimately removed Sarmiento from the home.

The jury found that Orr continued to employ Sarmiento despite his knowledge that she was unauthorised and that he had deceived her as to her terms and conditions of employment, and thus that he was guilty of violating the trafficking provision in the IRPA. At the sentencing hearing, the Crown sought a sentence of between five and six years, arguing that Sarmiento 'was kept in a situation of isolation and control amounting to modern day slavery'.[31] With a maximum of life sentence for the offence and no minimum, the sentencing judge has a great deal of discretion in designing the appropriate sentence. The judge concluded that the Crown failed 'to prove that Sarmiento was subject to humiliating and degrading treatment'.[32] However, he noted that Orr knew that Sarmiento 'was not authorised to be or to work in Canada', and that he 'did profit from his employment due to the low wage paid', which was below the statutory minimum rate.[33] Remarking that the 'lack of significant aggravating factors puts this offence at the lower end of the continuum', the judge sentenced Orr to 18 months in prison.[34]

Before Orr was convicted, Sarmiento, with the support of the West Coast Domestic Workers Association (WCDWA), an advocacy group for migrant domestic workers, brought a claim to the Employment Standards Branch seeking to recover unpaid wages. Under the Employment Standards Act, she was eligible to claim the difference between what she was paid and the minimum wage rate, overtime pay, payment for statutory holidays and vacation pay for six months. On the basis of submissions by the WCDWA, on 23 November 2012, the Director's delegate determined that Orr was liable to pay Sarmiento $30,662.90 for unpaid wages, as well as $3,500 in penalties for seven violations of the ESA.

Orr appealed, and the Employment Standards Tribunal released its decision on 19 June 2013, precisely one week before the jury convicted him of human trafficking for domestic servitude.[35] In granting the appeal, the tribunal chastised the delegate for failing to hold an oral hearing, accepting 'lawyer-scripted statements' written by the WCDWA as Sarmiento's evidence, and unfairly requiring Orr's evidence to be given on oath while not imposing the same condition on Sarmiento.[36] Thus, he ordered a new oral hearing and cancelled the determination. Sarmiento and the Director of the Employment Standards Branch sought reconsideration of the tribunal's

[31] *R v Orr*, 2013 BCSC 1883, para 33.
[32] Ibid para 44.
[33] Ibid para 77.
[34] Ibid para 79.
[35] Appeal decision, BC EST#DO49/13.
[36] Ibid para 26.

decision before a three-member panel of another tribunal, which released its decision precisely one week after the judge handed down Orr's 18-month sentence for trafficking for domestic servitude.[37] Accepting the previous tribunal's concern with the nature of Sarmiento's evidence and the requirement that Orr, and not Sarmiento, provide sworn statements, the panel ruled that the applications warranted reconsideration. There is no public record of any subsequent decision regarding Sarmiento's claim for unpaid wages.

Orr also filed an appeal against his conviction under the IRPA for trafficking for domestic servitude, arguing, among other things, that the trial judge was wrong to allow the testimony of an expert witness and that it was unreasonable for the jury to convict him. The Court of Appeal released its decision on 3 March 2015, and ordered a new trial.[38] The three-member panel held that the trial judge erred in admitting opinion evidence of an expert, which was critical because defence counsel intended to use the complainant's delay in reporting her circumstances to authorities to challenge her credibility at trial. Five years after Sarmiento first contacted the police neither her civil complaint nor the criminal charges were resolved.

In the second case, *R v Ladha*, which was decided on 22 November 2013, the accused was acquitted. The Royal Canadian Mounted Police (RCMP) laid human trafficking charges following a lengthy investigation by the Federal Border Integrity Program in British Columbia.[39] Like *Orr*, *Ladha* turned around issues of credibility. MH complained that Mrs Ladha had tricked her into coming to Canada from Tanzania when she offered her a job in a hair salon. According to MH, when she arrived in Canada, Ladha put her to work cleaning a huge home, and serving the Ladha family for 16 to 18 hours a day. By contrast, the accused alleged that she had befriended MH who worked as a domestic worker for her family in Tanzania and who later worked as a cleaner at her hair salon there. She claimed she brought MH to Canada on a six-month visitor's visa, which she later extended, and she attempted to get a work visa for her. When she was unable to obtain a work permit for MH, Ladha planned to take her back to Tanzania. Weeks before her planned departure for Tanzania, MH left Ladha's house and contacted the police to report that she had been trafficked. The judge concluded that the Crown had not proved beyond reasonable doubt the charge that Ladha had trafficked MH for the purposes of domestic servitude, remarking that he was 'left with the conviction that the allegations made by MH are improbable'.[40]

The legal technicalities of the combined criminal/immigration jurisdiction of the trafficking offence under the IRPA that make convictions so difficult

[37] Reconsideration application, BC EST#RD082/13.
[38] *R v Orr* [2015] BCCA 88.
[39] *R v Ladha* [2013] BCSC 2437.
[40] Ibid para 100.

are evident when these IRPA domestic servitude cases are contrasted with a decision of the British Columbia Human Rights Tribunal that was released on 1 April 2015.[41] This case involved a complaint of discrimination by a Filipino national who was brought to Canada by her employers, who were Hong Kong nationals, to work for them as a domestic worker. PN had worked for the respondents (FR, the husband, and MR, the wife) for a year in Hong Kong before travelling with them on a three-month visitor visa. Before travelling to Canada, FR had PN sign an agreement that set out the terms of her employment and her undertaking to repay the visa fee and airfare in addition to a month's salary should she decide not to go to Canada to work for them. Once in Canada, PN resided with FR, MR and their two children in a hotel suite while they were purchasing and readying a home. PN complained that she worked long hours, had only one day off a week, received less than $500 pay for her work while in Canada, and that FR had sexually assaulted her, and MR had treated her in a humiliating manner. Six weeks after she arrived in Canada, PN walked away from the hotel. When she initially called the police, they told her that the jurisdiction for resolving her problem was Hong Kong. PN eventually ended up at a women's shelter for trafficked women, where she lived for a year and a half and received assistance with filing a human rights complaint.

Adopting an analysis of discrimination that looked at the effect of multiple protected grounds' intersection, the Human Rights Tribunal concluded that PN had many characteristics protected by the Human Rights Code: 'she is a young mother from the Philippines and these protected characteristics are age, sex, family status, colour, ancestry and place of origin'.[42] The tribunal also found that PN was subject to two forms of adverse impact or discrimination: sexual assault, which amounted to a prohibited form of sexual harassment under the Human Rights Code, and exploitation. Not only did PN's employers not adhere to the requirements set out in the LCP, which served as a benchmark of decent standards; she 'was a virtual slave'.[43] Finally, the tribunal found that there was a nexus between the prohibited grounds and the adverse treatment: PN was sexually assaulted because she was a woman and the threats that worked to keep her quiet were due to her family status. It awarded PN back pay calculated at the British Columbia minimum wage rate for the hours she worked for FR and MR in Canada, which amounted to $5,866.89, but refused to award her compensation for the loss of prospective wages since she was not entitled to work in Canada. However, the tribunal granted her $50,000.00 as damages for injury to dignity, feelings and self-respect. But, given the fact that FR resides in Hong Kong, enforcing

[41] *PN v FR and Another (No 2)* [2015] BCHRT 60.
[42] Ibid para 92.
[43] Ibid para 101.

the award will be difficult. Moreover, at the time that the tribunal released its decision, PN still did not have status to work in Canada.

The legal technicalities of the criminal/immigration law jurisdiction of trafficking under the IRPA and the human rights jurisdiction of discrimination are profoundly different. Convictions for trafficking under the IRPA require proof beyond reasonable doubt and, thus, the elements of deception, fraud and coercion are difficult to establish. Moreover, the focus under the IRPA is on whether or not entry was unauthorised. None of these elements must be established in a human rights complaint, where the issue is discrimination on a prohibited ground, and the goal is to compensate the victim, and not to punish the perpetrator. Under human rights law, the complainant only has to establish a prima facie case of discrimination on the basis of a prohibited ground for the burden to shift to the respondent to disprove the discrimination or to justify it. However, despite the legal and evidentiary hurdles, one of the benefits of pursuing the trafficking offences is that victims are eligible for a temporary resident permit, which entitles them to remain in Canada for an additional six months, and in some circumstances for up to three years.

The results of these cases of domestic servitude raise some bigger questions. How has the approach to labour trafficking and domestic servitude evolved both in Brisitsh Columbia and federally? How does trafficking for the purpose of domestic servitude link up with growing resistance to temporary foreign workers in Canada? I will address these questions in turn.

D. Combatting Domestic Servitude in British Columbia: When Jurisdictions Collide

In March 2013, the British Columbia Ministry of Justice released BC's Action Plan to Combat Human Trafficking, 2013–2016, which began with the declaration that 'human trafficking is a form of modern-day slavery and a serious human rights violation'.[44] This document marked a widening of focus by the OCTIP from trafficking for sexual exploitation to include trafficking for labour exploitation. Moreover, it specifically emphasised domestic servitude, noting that two cases of trafficking for purposes of domestic servitude, the *Orr* and *Ladha* cases, were before the courts. Live-in caregivers, domestic workers and nannies, along with other temporary foreign workers such as seasonal workers, were identified as a priority focus area. The government pledged to support British Columbia-focused research on the vulnerabilities of temporary foreign workers, and it partnered with

[44] British Columbia, Ministry of Justice, *BC's Action Plan to Combat Human Trafficking, 2013–2016* (Victoria, BC, Ministry of Justice, 2014) iii.

the WCDWA, a non-profit organisation with a long history of advocating on behalf of migrant domestic workers admitted to Canada, and the International Centre for Criminal Law Reform and Criminal Justice Policy (ICCLR), a joint initiative of the federal and British Columbia governments, two British Columbia universities and the International Society for the Reform of Criminal Law.

The ensuing research illustrates how different legal jurisdictions frame the problem of domestic servitude and the difficulty of combining them in order to have a coherent multifaceted approach. The WCDWA organised focus groups and engaged in in-depth interviews involving 61 migrant workers in British Columbia, of which 19 had entered Canada via the LCP. Its 2014 report, *Labour Trafficking & Migrant Workers in British Columbia*, found that the link between the worker's migration status and ongoing employer support in the immigration programme combined with the lack of enforcement of labour standards to create a situation which enabled traffickers to intimidate migrant workers. It concluded that a 'broader understanding of force, coercion and fear' than physical coercion 'is necessary in dealing with labour trafficking cases'.[45] In order to reduce labour trafficking, it advocated abolishing the live-in requirement of the LCP, giving live-in caregivers permanent residence upon arrival in Canada, increasing spot checks in homes where caregivers are employed in order to ensure that employers are adhering to their contracts and to labour standards, and replacing the current for-profit recruitment system with a non-profit hiring hall model for hiring and recruiting migrant workers that would be run by a multi-sectoral agency composed of unions, workers' organisations and migrant workers' advocacy groups.

By contrast, the report by the ICCLR, which was released at the same time as the WCDWA report, was lodged firmly within a criminal law frame. Written by the expert witness whose testimony in the *Orr* case was ruled inadmissible by the British Columbia Court of Appeal, the report emphasised the personal characteristics of 'victims of domestic servitude' that made them vulnerable to exploitation, and not the broader structural and institutional factors that made it possible to exploit them. Relying on the RCMP's threat assessment of human trafficking, the report identified recruiters, placement agencies and labour leasing agencies, which often charged large fees to migrant workers, as key actors. Specific features of domestic work, the location within a private residence and the informal nature of the employment contracts, were also seen as conducive to exploitation. Although the report referred to the UN and ILO's indicators of forced labour in general and domestic servitude in particular, as well as the ILO's Convention on

[45] West Coast Domestic Workers Association, *Labour Trafficking & Migrant Workers in British Columbia* (Vancouver, WCDWA, 2014) 24.

Domestic Work, there was no discussion of the LCP or any of the voluminous Canadian literature on the problems with enforcing labour standards for workers admitted under it.[46]

A Labour Trafficking Roundtable in March 2014, which was hosted by all of the key players in British Columbia,[47] identified a number of structural issues, such as immigration controls and the lack of enforcement of employment standards and labour relations in British Columbia, as contributing to the problem of domestic servitude. Suspicion by Canadian officials as to the credibility of victims (characterised as 'queue jumpers' or 'bogus refugees') as well as cultural challenges ('exploitation and normalcy might mean very different things to each individual worker compared to the dominant Western cultural understanding of labour standards and human rights') were also seen as creating barriers for victims to come forward.[48] The roundtable recommended funding to train the police and community groups, transferrable or open work permits that allow trafficked individuals to change employers, enforcement of labour laws and a central registry for domestic workers.

Notably, the British Columbia government failed to adopt any of the recommendations designed to improve the enforcement of labour standards. The British Columbia Ministry of Labour did not step up its proactive enforcement of labour standards and it has not made use of the legal requirement for employers of domestic workers to register their workers as an enforcement tool. It has also refused to introduce legislation targeting recruitment agencies that place migrant workers with British Columbia employers, preferring to see the problem as one emanating from 'foreign' brokers rather than a home-grown problem.[49] This approach stands in marked contrast to the approach in Manitoba, Saskatchewan, Nova Scotia and Ontario, which have, to varying degrees, tightened the regulation of employment agencies to put an end to the practice of imposing placement fees on migrant workers and deceptive recruitment practices.[50] Criminal enforcement of immigration controls has been the British Columbia government's preferred strategy for dealing with the abuse of migrant domestic workers.

[46] Yvon Dandurand, *Human Trafficking for Domestic Servitude: Patterns of Deception and Coercion and their Impact on Victims. Research Note for the Office to Combat Trafficking in Persons* (Vancouver, BC, OCTIP, 2014).

[47] The OCTIP, the British Columbia Ministry of Justice, the WCDWA and the ICCLR hosted the event and the panellists included the prosecutors in the *Orr* and *Ladha* cases, the executive director of the WCDWA who was involved in the *Orr* case, and Dandurand. OCTIP, Labour Trafficking Roundtable Summary (Vancouver, BC, OCTIP, 2014) 4–5.

[48] Ibid 6.

[49] Fudge and Parrot, 'Placing Filipino Caregivers' (n 28).

[50] Fay Faraday, *Profiting from the Precarious: How Recruitment Practices Exploit Migrant Workers* (Toronto, Metcalfe Foundation, 2014).

E. Forced Labour and Immigration Controls

At the same time as the criminal jurisdiction has engulfed the labour law approach to labour trafficking and domestic servitude in British Columbia, the former Conservative federal government's 'new-found interest in addressing labour exploitation and labour trafficking', especially with respect to temporary migrant workers, coincided with bad press that employers were exploiting migrant workers admitted under the TFWP.[51] This concern with the exploitation of migrant workers was followed by a series of scandals that employers were using 'foreign' workers to replace Canadians.[52] Although the government expressly linked measures that were designed to prevent employers from abusing the TFWP to the fight against forced labour, by focusing on the abusive practices of employers rather than the combined contribution of precarious migrant status and poorly enforced labour standards, it created a context in which it was able to restrict the admission of live-in caregivers.

In its first National Action Plan to Combat Human Trafficking, the federal government harnessed its fight against labour trafficking to its policy of tightening immigration controls to ensure that employers did not violate the TFWP.[53] The plan emphasised the changes that the federal government made to the TFWP. While most of the changes targeted employers who did not adhere to the terms set out in the employment authorisation or who violated provincial employment or recruitment laws, some were directed specifically at the LCP. Starting on 1 April 2010, prospective employers were required to demonstrate that they had sufficient income to pay a live-in caregiver and were providing a private, furnished room with a lock. The latter requirement was designed to protect domestic workers' privacy and personal integrity. The federal government made it easier for live-in caregivers to obtain permanent residence by reducing the work period requirement and extending the eligibility period. The LCP was also brought in line with the other low-skilled streams of the TFWP by requiring employers both to cover all recruitment and travel costs and to sign an enhanced mandatory employment contract. However, the largest complaint—the requirement that caregivers live in the employer's residence—remained.

Labour exploitation of migrant workers admitted under the TFWP was a specific focus of attention at a November 2013 National Forum and Workshop on Trafficking in Persons, which was sponsored by the Canadian

[51] Sikka, Labour Trafficking in Canada (n 29) 31.

[52] Judy Fudge, 'Justice For Whom? Migrant Workers in Canada' in Janine Brodie (ed), *Inequalities and Social Justice in Contemporary Canada* (Toronto, University of Toronto Press, forthcoming).

[53] Canada, *National Action Plan to Combat Human Trafficking*, Cat No PS4-175/2012E-PDF (Ottawa, 2012).

Council for Refugees, a national non-profit umbrella organisation committed to the rights and protection of refugees and other vulnerable migrants.[54] The forum's conclusions emphasised that the nature of the migrant workers' visa, which tied the worker's migrant status to a specific employer, combined with the lack of enforcement of migrant workers' employment rights to provide a fertile ground for labour exploitation. In order to combat labour trafficking, the council recommended that the migrant workers' visa not be tied to a single employer, that employers should be subject to mandatory monitoring, and that low-skilled migrant workers should be given the same access to permanent resident status as high-skilled.

The federal government was able simply to sidestep this criticism by using another legal domain to frame the problem of trafficking. By articulating the issue of labour trafficking in the context of criminal law and national immigration policies, the government was able to formulate the fight against it by curbing immigration rather than loosening immigration controls that made migrant workers highly dependent upon specific employers or improving the enforcement of labour standards. The federal government did, however, make one important concession to migrants' rights advocates. Repeating complaints by caregivers that the live-in requirement felt like 'modern-day slavery to them', the Immigration Minister announced that he would be dropping the mandatory live-in requirement.[55] At the same time, the government also eliminated the LCP as a special category of temporary foreign work, which included the entitlement to permanent residence for themselves and immediate family members upon meeting the LCP requirements. Under the new caregiver programmes, eligibility for permanent resident status now includes the ability to become economically established in Canada, and is subject to numerical caps. Caregivers will still be allowed to include their immediate family members in applications for permanent resident status, but they will be evaluated under the same criteria as any other application under the TFWP—that is, according to the points-based system.[56] Thus, it is likely that the numbers of caregivers who achieve permanent residence will decline, and that they will have a more difficult time sponsoring family members. It is also unlikely that many childcare workers admitted through the new scheme will be able to reside outside their employers' homes. Not only are the wages of childcare providers very low, employers who are employing a temporary foreign worker to care for their children want someone who

[54] Canadian Council for Refugees, *National Forum and Workshop on Trafficking in Persons: Forum and Workshop Report* (Montreal, CCR, 2013).

[55] CIC News, 'Major Reforms to Caregiver Program Announced By Canadian Government', CIC News, November 2014.

[56] Canada Economic and Social Development, *Overhauling the Temporary Foreign Worker Program: Putting Canadians First* (Ottawa, Employment and Social Development Canada, 2014).

is readily available.[57] Although employers cannot require a caregiver to live in their home, an employer and foreign caregiver can decide that a live-in arrangement is the most suitable.

IV. CONCLUSION

The former Conservative federal government responded to the complaints that migrant domestic workers in Canada were subject to conditions of 'modern slavery' by liberating them from one form of unfreedom—the requirement that they live in their employer's home. Yet, at the same time it both failed to loosen the tie between their migrant status and employment relationship and made their transition to permanent residence more precarious. It has also refused to ratify the ILO's 2011 Domestic Workers Convention, and it has failed to put pressure on the provinces and territories to bring their labour laws pertaining to domestic workers into line with the international standard. The British Columbia government continues to rely on individual complaints as the method of enforcing its labour standards, and it has abandoned the registry for domestic workers as an enforcement tool and stonewalled requests that it follow the lead of its sister provinces which have implemented effective licensing regimes that have driven out unscrupulous recruiters. Both the federal and British Columbia governments have ignored the role of labour market and immigration institutions in cultivating conditions that are conducive to exploitative practices, and instead have focused on using the criminal law to weed out bad actors.

British Columbia's attempt to deal with domestic servitude raises the question of whether it is possible to combine a range of different legal jurisdictions in order to combat the problem of labour exploitation or whether one jurisdiction tends to overwhelm the others. The case study suggests that an answer that relies solely on legal definitions of different forms of labour unfreedom will not suffice. The broader social, political and economic context is critical to understanding how different legal jurisdictions or domains gain or lose force in relation to one another. Despite the best efforts of migrant rights advocates, the federal government did not use the trafficking framework to dismantle the immigration controls that make migrant workers vulnerable to labour exploitation; instead, trafficking became part of the justification for more tightly controlling national borders through the use of increased police and criminal powers.

[57] Geraldine Pratt and Philippine Women Centre, *From Migrant to Immigrant: Domestic Workers Settle in Vancouver, Canada, RIIM Working Paper Series 03-18* (Vancouver, Research on Immigration and Integration in the Metropolis, 2003) 24.

Nor has a focus on labour trafficking shifted the federal and British Columbia governments from the criminal law to consider labour law as a way of rooting out the causes of labour exploitation. In fact, it has tended to reify the distinction between labour exploitation and simply violating labour standards. Commenting on the relative dearth of possible, let alone confirmed, cases of labour trafficking, one researcher noted that 'the investigation of labour trafficking involves extremely complex analyses, involving immigration policies, temporary worker programmes, employment standards deviations and criminal charges under both the Criminal Code and the Immigration and Refugee Protection Act'.[58] This complexity leads law enforcement officials to question where 'employment standards violations end and issues of criminal enforcement and human trafficking begin'.[59] Thus, the challenge becomes distinguishing 'between labour infractions and forced labour, and between smuggled individuals, and trafficked individuals'.[60] In a political climate where regulating labour markets is seen as bad for business and enforcing labour standards is regarded as a form of red tape, violations of labour standards become normalised and egregious forms of labour exploitation become the exclusive focus of official concern. In a political economy in which policing borders and combating crime are key government priorities, criminal law and border control approaches to trafficking are amplified at the expense of labour law or migrant rights.

[58] Sikka, Labour Trafficking in Canada (n 29) 5.
[59] Ibid 29.
[60] OCTIP, Labour Trafficking Roundtable Summary (n 47) 5.

8

Why is Labour Protection for Temporary Migrant Workers so Fraught?

A Perspective from Australia

JOO-CHEONG THAM, IAIN CAMPBELL AND MARTINA BOESE*

I. THE BROKEN PROMISE OF PROTECTION FOR TEMPORARY MIGRANT WORKERS

THE TWENTY-FIRST CENTURY has witnessed a global resurgence of interest in temporary labour migration schemes as a policy measure.[1] Even nations that were traditionally countries of permanent settlement like Australia have experienced a sharp growth in temporary migrant workers.[2]

This development is surrounded by fierce controversy. At one level, there is strong debate concerning the effects of temporary labour migration—whether it secures, as its advocates claim, a triple 'win' for migrants (wages and enhancement of skills), their countries (remittances) and host countries (addressing labour shortages) or, on the other hand, whether it paves the way for the exploitation of migrant workers, stunted development of their countries and displacement of local workers in host countries. At another level, there are highly contested questions concerning the rights of temporary migrant workers: To what extent should such

* Research for this chapter was funded by an Australian Research Council grant for the project 'Precariousness in Law and Labour Markets: The Case of Temporary Migrant Workers'. Special thanks to Jason Goliszek for his excellent research assistance.

[1] See Global Commission on International Migration, *Migration in an Interconnected World: New Directions for Action* (Geneva, GCIM, 2005).

[2] Graeme Hugo, 'Globalization and Changes in Australian International Migration' (2006) 23(2) *Journal of Population Research* 107.

workers have rights equal to those enjoyed by the permanent residents and citizens of their host country?[3] When is it justifiable to 'trade off' the rights of these workers for greater openness of their host countries' labour markets?[4] What entitlement, if any, should these workers have to permanent residence in their host countries?[5]

There is, however, a clear point of consensus in this complex and evolving debate: temporary migrant workers should effectively enjoy whatever legal protection is provided in relation to their working conditions.[6] The International Labour Organization's (ILO) Multilateral Framework on Labour Migration, for one, states that the rights of migrant workers 'should be protected by the effective application and enforcement of national laws and regulations'.[7]

It is not difficult to see why there is such strong consensus on this principle. There is a cluster of compelling justifications relating to the legitimacy of the host state: the legitimacy of law as a (key) instrument of the state; the rule of law as a liberal principle; and, in democratic societies, the rule of law as a democratic principle. There is also a cluster of policy rationales for this principle that relate to temporary labour migration: preventing exploitation of migrant workers; protecting the employment opportunities and working conditions of local workers; ensuring that the intake of migrant workers properly addresses labour shortages and that a 'level playing field' exists amongst employers. What is least controversial may, however, be the most intractable.

Non-compliance with labour protection appears to be widespread in relation to temporary migrant work. As the ILO states:

> For many, migrating for work may be a rewarding and positive experience, but for an unacceptably large proportion of migrants, working conditions are abusive and exploitative, and may be characterized by forced labour, low wages, poor

[3] See Judy Fudge, 'Precarious Migrant Status and Precarious Employment: The Paradox of International Rights for Migrant Workers' (2012) 34 *Comparative Labour Law and Policy Journal* 95; Joo-Cheong Tham and Iain Campbell, *Temporary Migrant Labour in Australia: The 457 Visa Scheme and Challenges for Labour Regulation*, Working Paper No 50 (Melbourne, Centre for Employment and Labour Relations Law, 2011) 26–34.

[4] Martin Ruhs and Phillip Martin, 'Numbers v Rights: Trade-Offs and Guest Worker Programs' (2008) 42(1) *International Migration Review* 249; Martin Ruhs, *The Price of Rights: Regulating International Labor Migration* (Princeton, NJ, Princetown University Press, 2013) ch 7.

[5] Joseph H Carens, 'Live-in Domestics, Seasonal Workers, and Others Hard to Locate on the Map of Democracy' (2008) 16(4) *Journal of Political Philosophy* 419.

[6] 'Labour protection', or 'protective regulation', can be found in various areas of law including labour laws, immigration laws, anti-discrimination laws, occupational health and safety laws, and social security laws.

[7] International Labour Organization, *Multilateral Framework on Labour Migration: Non-binding Principles and Guidelines for a Rights-Based Approach to Labour Migration* (Geneva, ILO, 2006) 19.

> working environment, a virtual absence of social protection, the denial of freedom of association and union rights, discrimination and xenophobia, as well as social exclusion, all of which rob workers of the potential benefits of working in another country.[8]

Why is this the case? Why is labour protection for temporary migrant workers so fraught?

This chapter provides an Australian perspective on these questions, with a focus on two key groups of Australian temporary migrant workers: workers on the Temporary Work (Skilled) (Subclass 457) visas (457 visa workers) and international student workers. Our principal argument is that that the problem of non-compliance with protective regulation relating to these temporary migrant workers results from the interaction of their vulnerability—including their precarious migrant status—with employer practices in poorly regulated industries.

The chapter begins by outlining the contemporary features of temporary labour migration and its regulation in Australia, focusing on two major groups: 457 visa workers and international student workers. We then present evidence of non-compliance with protective regulation in relation to both groups of workers. This is followed by an analysis of underlying causes of such non-compliance: the vulnerability of these workers and its interaction with dominant employer practices in poorly regulated industries. We conclude by criticising the view that non-compliance with labour protection is an aberration, and argue that the risk of non-compliance experienced by temporary migrant workers is structural and that this risk needs to be addressed through an integrated suite of immigration and labour law strategies.

II. TEMPORARY LABOUR MIGRATION AND ITS REGULATION IN AUSTRALIA: THE CASE OF 457 VISA WORKERS AND INTERNATIONAL STUDENT WORKERS

A. Threshold Definitions

We define a 'temporary migrant worker' as a worker who has a limited right of residence in their host country and who works for pay during the period

[8] International Labour Organization, *Towards a Fair Deal for Migrant Workers in the Global Economy* (Geneva, ILO, 2004) 41. For the Canadian and UK experience, see respectively Fay Faraday, *Made in Canada: How the Law Constructs Migrant Workers' Insecurity* (Toronto, Metcalf Foundation, 2012) 5–6; Catherine Barnard, 'Enforcement of Employment Rights by Migrant Workers in the UK: The Case of EU-8 Migrants' in Cathryn Costello and Mark Freedland (eds), *Migrants at Work: Immigration and Vulnerability in Labour Law* (Oxford, Oxford University Press, 2014).

of residence. We define 'temporary migrant work' as the work performed by these workers, and define 'temporary labour migration programmes' as government schemes that permit temporary migrant work.[9]

This cluster of definitions is anchored upon the work performed by those with a particular migrant status—the activity that should be the principal focus of studies on temporary labour migration. In this respect, it is consistent with the definition adopted by the United Nations Convention on the Protection of the Rights of All Migrant Workers and Members of their Families, which defines a 'migrant worker' as 'a person who is to be engaged, is engaged or has been engaged in a remunerated activity in a State of which he or she is not a national'.[10]

These definitions have two important implications. First, they do not turn on the intentions for migration. As such, these definitions contrast with the definitions adopted in the relevant ILO conventions, which refer to a 'migrant for employment', defined as 'a person who *migrates from one country to another with a view to being employed* otherwise than on his own account and includes any person regularly admitted as a migrant for employment'.[11] (emphasis added) Such an emphasis on original intentions is too rigid, and does not allow for the changes in intentions and plans that frequently accompany any migration experience.

Second, our definition of 'temporary labour migration programmes' is not restricted to schemes that have the primary purpose of facilitating temporary migrant work (dedicated temporary labour migration programmes). It extends to other schemes which have a range of purposes and allow temporary migrants to participate in the labour market of the host country (de facto temporary labour migration programmes).

These definitions, in particular their use of the descriptor 'temporary', should, however, be carefully understood. Temporary migrant workers are only 'temporary' in the sense that they have a limited right of residence. They are not necessarily 'temporary' in terms of the length of their residence in Australia—many of them have lived in this country for years. Neither are temporary migrant workers, according to these definitions, necessarily 'temporary' in terms of their intention to continue residing in Australia—many aspire to secure permanent residence in this country through what has been called 'two-step' or 'staggered' migration.[12]

[9] Martina Boese, Iain Campbell, Winsome Roberts and Joo-Cheong Tham, 'Temporary Migrant Nurses in Australia: Sites and Sources of Precariousness' (2013) 24 *Economic and Labour Relations Review* 316, 317.

[10] International Convention on the Protection of the Rights of All Migrant Workers and Members of their Families (adopted 18 December 1990, entered into force 1 July 2003) art 2(1).

[11] ILO Migration for Employment Convention (Revised) 1949 (No 97) (entered into force 22 January 1952) art 11. See also ILO Migrant Workers (Supplementary Provisions) Convention 1975 (No 143) (entered into force 9 December 1978) art 11(1).

[12] Robert Gregory, *The Two-Step Australian Immigration Policy and its Impact on Immigrant Employment Outcomes*, Discussion Paper no 8061 (Bonn, IZA, 2014); Shanthi Robertson and Anjena Runganaikaloo, 'Lives in Limbo: Migration Experiences in Australia's Education–Migration Nexus' (2014) 14(2) *Ethnicities* 208.

Furthermore, reliance by employers on such workers is not necessarily 'temporary'—many key sectors like hospitality and agriculture have come to rely heavily on temporary migrant workers. These enduring aspects of temporary migrant work in Australia make it apt to speak of the 'permanence of temporary migration'.[13]

B. Temporary Labour Migration Programmes, Temporary Migrant Workers and Temporary Migrant Work in Australia

The principal dedicated temporary labour migration programme in Australia is the 457 visa scheme (officially entitled the Temporary Work (Skilled) visa (subclass 457)). This scheme provides for employer-sponsored visas in a range of occupations for up to four years per visa (which can be renewed).[14] The other—much smaller—dedicated temporary labour migration programme is the Seasonal Worker Program (subclass 416). This scheme allows employers, mainly in the horticulture industry, to sponsor workers from nine Pacific Island countries and Timor-Leste.[15]

Alongside these two dedicated temporary labour migration programmes is a proliferation of de facto temporary labour migration programmes. There is the range of visas provided under the international student programme (subclasses 570–75).[16] Related to this programme is the temporary graduate visa (subclass 485), which enables international students who have recently graduated from an Australian education institution to work in Australia. This programme has two streams: the graduate work

[13] See Peter Mares, 'The Permanent Shift to Temporary Migration', *Inside Story*, 17 June 2009, http://inside.org.au/the-permanent-shift to temporary-migration/; Jenna Hennebry, *Permanently Temporary? Agricultural Migrant Workers and Their Integration in Canada* (Montreal, IRPP, 2012).

[14] Migration Regulations 1994 (Cth) sch 2, subclass 457. For analysis of the regulatory framework of the 457 visa scheme, see Joanna Howe, 'The Migration Amendment (Worker Protection) Act 2008: Long Overdue Reform, But Have Migrant Workers been Sold Short?' (2010) 24(2) *Australian Journal of Labour Law* 13; Iain Campbell and Joo-Cheong Tham, 'Labour Market Deregulation and Temporary Migrant Labour Schemes: An Analysis of the 457 Visa Program' (2013) 26 *Australian Journal of Labour Law* 239; Joanna Howe, 'Is the Net Cast Too Wide? An Assessment of Whether the Regulatory Design of the 457 Visa Meets Australia's Skill Needs' (2013) 41(3) *Federal Law Review* 443; Joanna Howe, 'Accountability and Transparency under the Subclass 457 Visa Program: Is there Cause for Concern' (2014) 21 *Australian Journal of Administrative Law* 139; Joanna Howe, 'Enterprise Migration Agreements under the Subclass 457 Visa: Much Ado about Nothing?' (2014) 27 *Australian Journal of Labour Law* 86; Laurie Berg, *Migrant Rights at Work: Law's Precariousness at the Intersection of Immigration and Labour* (London, Routledge, 2015) 107–45.

[15] Migration Regulations 1994 (Cth) sch 2, subclass 416. See Alexander Reilly, 'The Ethics of Seasonal Labour Migration' (2011) 20 *Griffith Law Review* 127.

[16] Migration Regulations 1994 (Cth) sch 2, subclasses 570–75. For discussion of the regulatory framework for international students, see Alexander Reilly, 'Protecting Vulnerable Migrant Workers: The Case of International Students' (2012) 25 *Australian Journal of Labour Law* 181; Berg, *Migrant Rights at Work* (n 14) 95–101.

stream and the post-study work stream. Under the graduate work stream, those graduates with skills and qualifications that relate to an occupation on the Skills Occupation List are eligible for an 18-month visa. Under the post-study work stream, international students who graduate with a higher education degree from an Australian education provider, regardless of their field of study, are eligible for a visa of up to four years (depending on their qualification).[17]

There are two other significant de facto temporary labour migration programmes in Australia. First is the working holiday programme, which encompasses subclass 417 (Working Holiday) and subclass 462 (Work and Holiday) visas. This programme allows people aged between 18 and 30 from a range of countries with which Australia has a relevant bilateral arrangement to have a working holiday in Australia.[18] Second is the Special Category Visa (subclass 444), which is granted upon entry to New Zealand citizens (regardless of the purpose of their visit to Australia) and allows them to live and work in Australia without restriction.[19]

With the exception of the Work and Holiday (462) visa, these programmes are uncapped, and the numbers achieving visa grants have increased rapidly over the past decade. Table 8.1 provides the stock figures for visa holders under the various programmes as at 31 December 2014.[20] In total, they numbered nearly 1.3 million visa holders with work rights, at a time when around 11.6 million people were employed in the Australian workforce.[21]

[17] Migration Regulations 1994 (Cth) sch 2, subclass 485. For a recent discussion of the experiences of temporary graduate visa holders, see Shanthi Robertson, 'Time and Temporary Migration: The Case of Temporary Graduate Workers and Working Holiday Makers in Australia' (2014) 40(12) *Journal of Ethnic and Migration Studies* 1915.

[18] Migration Regulations 1994 (Cth) sch 2, subclasses 417 and 462.

[19] Ibid sch 2, subclass 444. New Zealand citizens in Australia constitute a distinctive group amongst temporary migrants. Subclass 444 is a '[t]emporary visa permitting the holder to remain in Australia while the holder is a New Zealand citizen' (ibid sch 2, cl 444.511). Hence, holders of the 444 visa have an unrestricted ability to stay in Australia and in that sense are not 'temporary' migrants. Yet, they are said to hold a 'temporary visa' (see definition of 'temporary visa' in *Migration Act 1958* (Cth) s 30(2)) and, in key respects, do not enjoy the rights and entitlements of Australian permanent residents. See discussion in Peter Mares, *Temporary Migration and its Implications for Australia*, Papers on Parliament No 57 (Canberra, Parliament of Australia, 2012).

[20] All except the figures pertaining to the Seasonal Worker Program 3 are sourced from Department of Immigration and Border Protection, *Temporary Entrants and New Zealand Citizens in Australia—As at 30 June 2014* (Canberra, Department of Immigration and Border Protection, 2014).

[21] Australian Bureau of Statistics, *Labour Force, Australia—April 2015*, Cat No 6202 (Canberra, ABS, 2015) 7.

Table 8.1: Visa-holders under Temporary Labour Migration Programmes in Australia (Number of Persons)

Dedicated temporary labour migration programmes	**Stock figures (31 December 2014)**
457 visa scheme	167,910
Seasonal Worker Program	2014[22]
De facto temporary labour migration programmes	
International student programme	303,170
Temporary graduate visa scheme	19,510
Working holiday programme	160,940
New Zealand citizens	623,440
Total	**1,276,984**

Stock figures of visa holders under the temporary labour migration programmes do not equate to the actual number of temporary migrant workers. They count the number of visa holders with work rights—potential temporary migrant workers—but not all of these migrants exercise their work rights at the one time. We can presume that all migrants in the Seasonal Worker Program are employed, and the same is true for primary 457 visa holders. But some secondary 457 visa holders (dependents of primary 457 visa holders), international students, temporary graduates, working holiday makers and New Zealand citizens do not exercise their work rights at all during their period of temporary residency, and others may be employed only for part of their period of temporary residency. On the other hand, the above-mentioned list does not include the estimated 100,000 migrants working without legal permission who do fit the definition of temporary migrant workers.[23]

How many temporary migrant workers are in Australia then? Unfortunately, no precise answer can be given to this question. Though the trend is steadily upward, the number is likely to fluctuate, depending on factors such as the season, the phases of the education system, labour market conditions and the vagaries of policy decisions on possible paths to permanent

[22] The figure for the Seasonal Worker Program for the 2013–2014 financial year is found in Department of Employment, *Seasonal Worker Program Report: July to September 2014* (Canberra, Department of Employment, 2015) 7.

[23] Stephen Howells, *Report of the 2010 Review of the Migration Amendment (Employer Sanctions) Act 2007* (Canberra, Commonwealth of Australia, 2010) 12; see also Stephen Clibborn, 'Why Undocumented Immigrant Workers should have Workplace Rights' (2015) 26(3) *Economic and Labour Relations Review* 465.

residence. Nevertheless, the impact on the labour market is likely to be substantial.[24]

Some employment information is available for the dedicated schemes.[25] There is, however, a stark absence of labour market information on visa holders under the de facto temporary labour migration schemes. This gap highlights the 'invisibility' of de facto temporary labour migration schemes in policy discourse on temporary labour migration, reflecting a narrow view of temporary labour migration schemes that is confined to dedicated schemes. The case of international student workers illustrates this point. A review of media releases from the Commonwealth ministers responsible for higher education from 2010 to the present did not find a single media release which dealt with work performed by international students. This is despite the ubiquity of international student workers in Australian capital cities; the high proportion of international students engaged in paid employment (estimated to be more than half);[26] and the significance of international student workers to the Australian labour market. A 2011 estimate suggested that these workers constitute between one and two per cent of the total Australian workforce.[27]

C. Labour Protection of Temporary Migrant Work

The key sources of labour protection for local workers are also available to temporary migrant workers. The principal statute is the Fair Work Act 2009 (Cth), which establishes a national system of labour law.[28] The Fair Work Act provides labour protection in various ways, including by providing a 'guaranteed safety net of fair, relevant and enforceable minimum terms and conditions' (s 3(b)) through the National Employment Standards which deal with 10 matters (s 61); modern awards which provide for minimum terms and conditions in particular industries or occupations (part 2-3); and national minimum wages (part 2-6), set at $17.29 per hour in the 2015–16 financial year.[29] The Fair Work Act also establishes the Fair

[24] For an early discussion of impact, see Graham Hugo, 'Temporary Migration and the Labour Market in Australia (2006) 37(2) *Australian Geographer* 211.

[25] Department of Immigration and Border Protection, *Subclass 457 Quarterly Report—Quarter Ending at 31 March 2015* (Canberra, Department of Immigration and Border Protection, 2015).

[26] Australian Education International, *2006 International Student Survey: Report of the Consolidated Results from the Four Education Sectors in Australia* (Canberra, Commonwealth of Australia, 2007); Simon Marginson, Christopher Nyland, Erlenawati Sawir and Helen Forbes-Mewett, *International Student Security* (Cambridge, Cambridge University Press, 2010) 134.

[27] Reilly, 'Protecting Vulnerable Migrant Workers' (n 16) 185.

[28] Fair Work Act 2009 (Cth) ss 13–14.

[29] *Annual Wage Review 2014–2015* [2015] FWCFB 3500.

Work Ombudsman, the national enforcement agency for the Act,[30] while maintaining elements of the historic reliance on trade unions as enforcement actors[31] and providing for an individual complaints process.[32]

Another source of labour protection for workers in Australia (including temporary migrant workers) are anti-discrimination laws. Such laws are significant given discrimination in the workplace is often identified as a source of ill-treatment experienced by migrant workers.[33] Such discrimination against migrant workers can occur for various reasons (migrant status, nationality, skin colour, ethnicity, religious beliefs, level of English proficiency). Some of this discrimination will be illegal due to the statutory prohibitions against racial discrimination—these prohibitions generally make illegal discrimination based on colour, ethnicity and nationality in relation to employment.[34] Discrimination based on the level of English proficiency is not, however, prohibited, and discrimination based on religious beliefs is not uniformly prohibited in Australia, with such prohibition existing only at the Commonwealth level and in New South Wales.

It is unclear whether discrimination based on migrant status is illegal, and this poses complicated and unresolved issues concerning the scope of statutory prohibitions against racial discrimination. In most jurisdictions, these prohibitions do not explicitly cover migrant status. It is possible, however, that 'race'—which is inclusively defined in many instances[35]—may extend to migrant status. It is also possible that migrant status may still

[30] Pt 5-2. For research on the Fair Work Ombudsman, see Glenda Maconachie and Miles Goodwin, 'Does Institutional Location Protect from Political Influence? The Case of a Minimum Labour Standards Enforcement Agency in Australia' (2011) 46(1) *Australian Journal of Political Science* 105; Tess Hardy and John Howe, 'Too Soft or Too Severe? Enforceable Undertakings and the Regulatory Dilemma facing the Fair Work Ombudsman' (2013) 41 *Federal Law Review* 1; Tess Hardy, John Howe and Sean Cooney, 'Less Energetic But More Enlightened? Exploring the Fair Work Ombudsman's Use of Litigation in Regulatory Enforcement' (2013) 35 *Sydney Law Review* 565; John Howe, Tess Hardy and Sean Cooney, 'Mandate, Discretion and Professionalisation in an Employment Standards Enforcement Agency: An Antipodean Experience' (2013) 35 *Law & Policy* 81.

[31] Tess Hardy and John Howe, 'Partners in Enforcement? The New Balance Between Government and Trade Union Enforcement of Employment Standards in Australia' (2009) 22 *Australian Journal of Labour Law* 306.

[32] Fair Work Act 2009 (Cth) s 539.

[33] ILO, *Towards a Fair Deal* 46–48; Bridget Anderson and Martin Ruhs, 'Migrant Workers: Who Needs Them? A Framework for the Analysis of Staff Shortages, Immigration, and Public Policy' in Martin Ruhs and Bridget Anderson (eds), *Who Needs Migrant Workers? Labour Shortages, Immigration and Public Policy* (Oxford, Oxford University Press, 2010) 27–28.

[34] Racial Discrimination Act 1975 (Cth) s 15; Anti-Discrimination Act 1977 (NSW) s 8; Anti-Discrimination Act 1991 (Qld) ss 13–15A; Equal Opportunity Act 1984 (SA) ss 30–34; Anti-Discrimination Act 1998 (Tas) s 22(1)(a); Equal Opportunity Act 2010 (Vic) ss 16–29; Equal Opportunity Act 1984 (WA) s 4; Discrimination Act 1991 (ACT) ss 10–17; Anti-Discrimination Act (NT) s 31; Fair Work Act 2009 (Cth) s 351.

[35] Anti-Discrimination Act 1977 (NSW) s 4; Anti-Discrimination Act 1991 (Qld) dictionary; Anti-Discrimination Act 1998 (Tas) s 3; Equal Opportunity Act 2010 (Vic) s 4; Equal Opportunity Act 1984 (WA) s 4; Discrimination Act 1991 (ACT) dictionary; Anti-Discrimination Act (NT) s 4.

be covered through nationality and/or national origin. The foregoing reasons are arguably why the Australian Human Rights Commission interprets the prohibition in the Commonwealth Racial Discrimination Act against discrimination on the basis of 'race, colour, descent or national or ethnic origin'[36] to include 'immigrant status'.[37]

This broad interpretation of the Racial Discrimination Act, as well as the explicit prohibitions against discrimination based on immigrant status in Tasmania and the Northern Territory,[38] raise a further question: does immigrant status extend to *temporary* migrant status given that an immigrant is usually understood as a person who migrates to live permanently in the host country?[39]

A further source of labour protection for temporary migrant workers under *dedicated* temporary labour migration programmes in Australia is immigration law: the Migration Act 1958 (Cth) and the Migration Regulations 1994 (Cth). Workers under the 457 visa scheme are required to be paid no less than the Temporary Skilled Migration Income Threshold stipulated by the Immigration Minister (presently AUD$53,900 per annum)[40] as a condition of approval of the nomination of the worker.[41] The terms and conditions of employment of the 457 visa worker are required to be 'no less favourable than the terms and conditions of employment that the person provides, or would provide, to an Australian citizen or an Australian permanent resident to perform equivalent work in the person's workplace at the same location'. The 'no less favourable' requirement is both a condition of approval of the worker's nomination[42] and also a sponsorship obligation.[43] The responsibility for administering these provisions lies primarily with the Immigration Department; whilst the Fair Work Ombudsman possesses inspection—but not enforcement—powers in relation to sponsorship obligations.[44]

III. EMPLOYER NON-COMPLIANCE AND TEMPORARY MIGRANT WORKERS IN AUSTRALIA

When it comes to labour protection (regulation protecting working conditions), non-compliance refers to employer practices in breach of

36 Racial Discrimination Act 1975 (Cth) s 9(1).

37 Australian Human Rights Commission, *Racial Discrimination: Know Your Rights* (Sydney, AHRC, 2012) 2.

38 Anti-Discrimination Act 1998 (Tas) s 3(e); Anti-Discrimination Act (NT) s 4(a).

39 Oxford University Press, *Oxford Dictionaries* (2015), www.oxforddictionaries.com/us/definition/american_english/immigrant.

40 Migration Regulations 1994 (Cth), Specification of Income Threshold and Annual Earnings 2015, IMMI 15/050.

41 Migration Regulations 1994 (Cth) reg 2.72(10)(cc).

42 Ibid reg 2.72(10)(c).

43 Ibid reg 2.79.

44 Migration Act 1958 (Cth) s 140V.

the standards laid down by such regulation.[45] It may involve technical breaches, but it is usually identified with the imposition, by the employer, of poor quality wages and working conditions. Non-compliance can involve practices in breach of the Fair Work Act such as underpayment of wages (eg below national minimum wage) and non-payment of wages (eg non-payment for probationary periods). It can also involve employer breaches of anti-discrimination law and, in the case of temporary migrant workers, breaches of protective regulation found in immigration law.

Employer non-compliance with labour protection is not uncommon in Australia. Indeed, a major review of data collected by the workplace enforcement agencies has concluded that 'achieving widespread employer compliance with minimum employment standards in Australia is a major and ongoing challenge in Australia',[46] and this viewpoint has been endorsed by the current Fair Work Ombudsman, Natalie James.[47] In a similar vein, earlier studies suggest that employer non-compliance with minimum employment standards 'has been both significant and sustained', and that it is likely to have increased in the wake of labour market deregulation and the decline of trade union strength.[48]

The problem of non-compliance appears to be particularly acute in relation to temporary migrant workers, which is highlighted by ongoing controversies surrounding the exploitation of these workers.[49] In 2012, the Fair Work Ombudsman established an Overseas Worker Team as a response to the growing number of complaints from temporary migrant workers.[50] In 2013–14, complaints from these workers accounted for more than 10 per cent of all complaints received by the ombudsman, an increase

[45] There are other types of non-compliance with labour laws including by workers and trade unions.

[46] John Howe, Tess Hardy and Sean Cooney, *The Transformation of Enforcement of Minimum Employment Standards in Australia: A Review of the FWO's Activities from 2006–2012* (Melbourne, Centre for Employment and Labour Relations Law, Melbourne Law School, 2013) 10.

[47] Natalie James, *FWO's Response to the University of Melbourne's Research Report 'The Transformation of Enforcement of Minimum Employment Standards in Australia: A Review of the FWO's Activities from 2006–2012'* (Canberra, FWO, 2014) 2.

[48] Glenda Maconachie and Miles Goodwin, 'Employer Evasion of Workers' Entitlements 1986–1995: Why, What and Whose?' (2010) 52(4) *Journal of Industrial Relations* 419, 420. See also Glenda Maconachie and Miles Goodwin, 'Recouping Wage Underpayment: Increasingly Less Likely' (2006) 41(3) *Australian Journal of Social Issues* 327.

[49] See, eg Abby Dinham, 'Dodgy Employers Investigated over "Exploitation" of 457 Visa Holders', *SBS*, 8 October 2014, www.sbs.com.au/news/article/2014/10/07/dodgy-employers-investigated-over-exploitation-457-visa-holders; Caro Meldrum-Hanna and Ali Russell, 'Slaving Away', *Four Corners*, 4 May 2015, http://www.abc.net.au/4corners/stories/2015/05/04/4227055.htm; Adele Ferguson and Klaus Toft, '7-Eleven: The Price of Convenience', *Four Corners*, 31 August 2015, http://www.abc.net.au/4corners/stories/2015/08/30/4301164.htm.

[50] Interview with Carey Trundle, Director, Overseas Worker Team, Fair Work Ombudsman, 25 February 2015.

of 25 per cent from 2012–13.[51] As an indication of the seriousness of the breaches involved, one third of the ombudsman's current legal actions involve migrant workers.[52] In the following sections, we set out evidence of non-compliance in relation to workers covered by Australia's principal dedicated temporary labour migration programme (the 457 visa programme), and by one of Australia's key de facto temporary labour migration programmes (the international student programme).

A. 457 Visa Workers

The evidence concerning the extent of employer non-compliance in relation to primary visa holders under the 457 visa scheme is conflicting. One body of evidence suggests that non-compliance is *not* widespread. A Department of Immigration online survey of almost 4,000 457 visa workers in 2012 found that:

— Five per cent of the workers surveyed felt their employers were not meeting their sponsorship obligations; and
— Seven per cent of these workers indicated that their conditions were not equivalent to those of their Australian co-workers.[53]

Similarly, the 2014 Integrity Review, after assessing the data on cases monitored by the Immigration Department, observed that, '[w]ith the exception of 2011 (when it was lower), the overall level of serious non-compliance averaged a little over one per cent of all active cases'.[54]

On the other hand, figures from the Fair Work Ombudsman suggest a more significant problem of non-compliance. In 2013–14, the Ombudsman assessed 1,029 entities employing 1,902 primary visa holders under the 457 visa scheme. More than 20 per cent (243) of these entities were referred to the Immigration Department due to concerns that 338 employees were either not being paid their nominated salary and/or not working in their nominated occupation.[55] A similar story emerges from the audit by the Ombudsman of 560 primary visa holders on the 457 visa scheme, with

[51] Fair Work Ombudsman, *Annual Report: 2013–2014* (Canberra, FWO, 2014) 30.

[52] Nick Toscano, 'Many Migrants Exploited at Work, Audit Reveals', *The Age*, 30 May 2015, 7.

[53] Department of Immigration and Border Protection, *Filling the Gaps: Findings from the 2012 Survey of Subclass 457 Employers & Employees* (Canberra, Department of Immigration and Border Protection, 2014) 4.

[54] John Azarias, Jenny Lambert, Peter McDonald and Katie Malyon, *Robust New Foundations: A Streamlined, Transparent and Responsive System for the 457 Program: An Independent Review into Integrity in the Subclass 457 Program* (Canberra, Department of Immigration and Border Protection, 2014) 85.

[55] Fair Work Ombudsman, *Annual Report: 2013–2014* 30.

20 per cent of these workers suspected of not being paid their nominated salary and/or not working in their nominated occupation.[56]

The evidence from monitoring by the Fair Work Ombudsman is consistent with reports from investigative journalists and trade unions. In its submission to a 2015 Senate Inquiry into temporary work visas, the Australian Council of Trade Unions (ACTU) compiled a list of cases involving non-compliance in relation to 457 visa workers, arguing that these cases point to a pattern of abuse.[57]

It should be remembered that not all discrimination against 457 visa workers is illegal, and whether it is depends very much on the reason for the discrimination. That noted, the 2012 Immigration Department survey indicates that overt discrimination in the workplace against 457 visa workers only affects a minority of these workers. Whilst 16 per cent of the survey's respondents stated that they had been discriminated against based on skin colour, ethnic origin and/or religious beliefs in the past 12 months, only 0.5 per cent indicated that such discrimination occurred *in the workplace*.[58] Of the 5 per cent of respondents who felt that their sponsors were not meeting their obligations, less than 0.5 per cent thought this was due to discrimination against them on the basis of being a migrant.[59]

It should be emphasised that, even if non-compliance affects a minority of 457 visa workers, this nevertheless points to serious consequences for workers. The ACTU submission to the Senate inquiry into temporary work visas includes frightening accounts of gross underpayment and non-payment (including non-payment for six weeks), employer provision of sub-standard accommodation (eg almost 30 workers living in a five-bedroom house) and extreme overwork (eg 6–7 days a week, up to 10–12 hours a day).[60] There are some horrific instances of exploitation of 457 visa workers, some of which have been the subject of legal proceedings. One illustration of this is the case of *Ram v D&D Indian Fine Foods Pty Ltd*,[61] which concerned events that took place between 4 August 2007 and 4 December 2008. In this case, Federal Circuit Court Judge Driver said the following:

> I find that Mr Ram, a man who was functionally illiterate, spoke virtually no English and had no contacts in the Australian community, was brought from India to work 12 hours per day, seven days per week in the respondents' restaurant. Over 16 months, Mr Ram was not paid, beyond the small foreign exchange transfers sent to his wife, and received no leave. The respondents built a facade upon

[56] Toscano, 'Many Migrants Exploited at Work' (n 52).

[57] Australian Council of Trade Unions, *Submission to the Senate Inquiry into the Temporary Work Visa Program* (1 May 2015) 62–68, app 4.

[58] Department of Immigration and Border Protection, *Filling the Gaps* (n 53) 31.

[59] Ibid.

[60] ACTU, *Submission to the Senate Inquiry* 62–68, app 4.

[61] *Ram v D&D Indian Fine Foods Pty Ltd* [2015] FCCA 389 (Federal Circuit Court, 27 March 2015, Driver J).

sham documents, to deceive the Department of Immigration and the ATO and attempted to deceive this Court, in an effort to create the illusion that there was an employment arrangement in accordance with Australian law.[62]

B. International Student Workers

The 'invisibility' of international student work in terms of policy discourse explains why there is less systematic evidence on the problem of non-compliance as it relates to international student workers. The available evidence is, however, disturbing. It points to extensive non-compliance with labour protection in relation to international student work, to an extent that is clearly greater than that for 457 visa workers. For international students, securing 'safe and fair' employment is a pressing challenge.[63]

A 2005 study based on 200 interviews by Marginson et al found that 58 per cent of interviewees who reported an hourly rate were paid under the minimum wage, earning between $7 and $15 per hour.[64] The authors argue that all students, when employed, can experience 'ultra-exploitation and other problems at work', but international students seem to experience worse treatment.[65] An ethnographic study conducted by Baas in 2005 cited extensive breaches of the law, which were regarded as normal by many of the Indian international students involved in the study.[66] Similarly, recent reports of the experiences of international students in the cleaning industry point to phenomena such as poor working conditions, sham contracting and cash-in-hand arrangements that involve underpayments and undercutting of collective agreements.[67]

The submission of the Victorian Human Rights and Equal Opportunity Commission to the Victorian Government Taskforce on Overseas Student Experience, which documented the racism and exploitation suffered by international student workers in Victoria, as reflected from the complaints it received, indicates that discrimination in breach of laws is another area of non-compliance.[68] Studies suggest that international students do face discrimination in the labour market with some elements of this reported

[62] Ibid para 76.

[63] Australian Human Rights Commission, *Principles to Promote and Protect the Human Rights of International Students* (Sydney, AHRC, 2012) 5.

[64] Marginson et al, *International Student Security* (n 26) 136.

[65] Ibid 16.

[66] Michiel Baas, *Imagined Mobility: Migration and Transnationalism among Indian Students in Australia* (London, Anthem Press, 2012) ch 5.

[67] Victorian TAFE International and United Voice, *Taken to the Cleaners: Experiences of International Students Working in the Australian Retail Cleaning Industry* (Melbourne, United Voice, 2012); United Voice, *A Dirty Business: The Exploitation of International Students in Melbourne's Office Cleaning Industry* (Melbourne, United Voice, 2013).

[68] Victorian Human Rights and Equal Opportunity Commission, *Submission to Victorian Overseas Student Taskforce* (2008).

discrimination likely to be illegal (based on skin colour, religious beliefs, ethnicity), while other elements are not necessarily so (perceived lack of English proficiency, lack of permanent residence). They further indicate that such discrimination tends to occur at the point of entry to the workplace—securing a job—rather than through inferior working conditions within the workplace. In the Marginson et al study, a small number of respondents said that they experienced overt discrimination within the labour market, with most references to discrimination relating to the inability to find decent work.[69] That discrimination against international students tends to occur in relation to securing a job does not mean that it is not a source of vulnerability. On the contrary, such discrimination can produce vulnerability by channelling international student workers into precarious jobs, including those with illegal working conditions, through their resignation to inferior working conditions.

IV. THE UNDERLYING CAUSES OF NON-COMPLIANCE IN RELATION TO TEMPORARY MIGRANT WORK IN AUSTRALIA

What explains the non-compliance with labour protection in relation to 457 visa workers and international student workers? A useful starting point, often stressed in the literature, concerns the vulnerability of particular groups of workers. Particular groups of workers are more vulnerable to employer non-compliance with labour protection. They include young workers, female workers[70] and those engaged in precarious work (eg low-wage work).[71] Migrant workers—including temporary migrant workers—count amongst such 'at-risk' workers.

Vulnerability to employer non-compliance can derive from several different sources. It is associated most closely in the literature on vulnerable workers with personal attributes and circumstances such as age, skill level and social support.[72] More recently, a vigorous literature has sprung up to stress the special impact of immigration regulations on the vulnerability of different groups of temporary migrant workers, thereby contributing to their concentration in precarious work.[73] This centres on the shortfall of rights

[69] Marginson et al, *International Student Security* (n 26) 138–42.

[70] Maconachie and Goodwin, 'Employer Evasion' (n 48).

[71] See David Weil, 'Enforcing Labour Standards in Fissured Workplaces: The US Experience' (2011) 22 *Economic and Labour Relations Review* 33, 34–35.

[72] Anna Pollert and Andy Charlwood, 'The Vulnerable Worker in Britain and Problems at Work' (2009) 22(3) *Work, Employment and Society* 343.

[73] Luin Goldring, Carolina Berinstein and Judith K Bernhard, 'Institutionalizing Precarious Migratory Status in Canada' (2009) 13 *Citizenship Studies* 239; Bridget Anderson, 'Migration, Immigration Controls and the Fashioning of Precarious Workers' (2010) 24(2) *Work, Employment and Society* 300; Fudge, 'Precarious Migrant Status' (n 3). For the fullest application of the argument to Australia, particularly in connection with 457 visa workers, see Berg, *Migrant Rights at Work* (n 14).

and entitlements experienced by temporary migrant workers compared to those enjoyed by citizens (or permanent residents). Goldring, Berinstein and Bernhard have characterised this shortfall as 'precarious migrant status' and suggested that it includes dimensions such as:

— limited work authorisation
— limited right of residence
— dependence on a third party for the right of residence, and
— limited access to public goods.[74]

The two sources of vulnerability are not completely distinct. They can interact and indeed overlap, as can be seen with factors such as financial pressure, which is a characteristic of most workers under capitalist employment relations, but is often exacerbated for temporary migrant workers, who may incur high levels of debt as a result of their migration pathway, are distant from family support, and are generally excluded from access to social security and other forms of social support in the host country. Similarly, a lack of familiarity with employment regulations can be linked with youth and inexperience but also with recent arrival from a country with distinct customs, traditions and forms of labour protection.[75]

A. Vulnerability of 457 Visa Workers

The extent of vulnerability experienced by 457 visa workers is contested. On the one hand, 457 visa workers may be regarded as being insulated against vulnerability because they are highly skilled workers in demand from employers. This, however, is often an appearance rather than the reality. Though many primary visa holders are indeed classified as 'skilled', this is not necessarily true of secondary visa holders who are working in Australia. Moreover, even for primary visa holders the definition of skilled occupations is broad, and can allow room for the employment of less skilled workers.[76] Similarly, the requirement of labour market testing is subject to broad-ranging exceptions relating to skills and occupations and obligations under international trade agreements.[77]

[74] See Goldring et al, 'Institutionalizing Precarious Migratory Status'.

[75] Malcolm Sargeant and Eric Tucker, 'Layers of Vulnerability in Occupational Health and Safety for Migrant Workers: Case Studies from Canada and the United Kingdom' (2010) 7(2) *Policy and Practice in Occupational Health and Safety* 51; Sylvia Yuan, Trudie Cain and Paul Spoonley, *Temporary Migrants as Vulnerable Workers: A Literature Review* (Wellington, Ministry of Business, Innovation and Employment, 2014).

[76] The list of eligible occupations is provided by the Consolidated Sponsored Occupations List, https://www.border.gov.au/Trav/Work/Work/Skills-assessment-and-assessing-authorities/skilled-occupations-lists/CSOL.

[77] Migration Act 1958 (Cth) ss 140GBA, 140GBC.

On the other hand, many 457 visa workers are subject to definite sources of vulnerability associated with both their personal characteristics and circumstances and their precarious migrant status. For example, one important aspect of vulnerability is a lack of understanding of workplace entitlements.[78] This lack of understanding may result from the fact that some 457 visa workers are new entrants to the Australian labour market and, therefore, are only just beginning to gain knowledge of the laws that apply to their work—a point that applies especially to 457 visa workers who have just migrated to Australia. It may also result from a lack of proficiency in the English language. It is also likely to result from the lack of proper information concerning their workplace entitlements.

457 visa workers may share with local workers sources of vulnerability such as lack of understanding of workplace entitlements and lack of access to information concerning such entitlements, but this combines with sources that are distinctive to temporary migrant workers. As Piore has argued, many temporary migrant workers operate with a 'dual frame of reference' that assesses the wages and conditions they experience in the receiving country with reference to those in their country of origin.[79] Given global disparities in wealth, many 457 visa workers are migrating from countries that have a large 'wage gap' with Australia. This may lead to a willingness to accept conditions that are in breach of Australian laws in the belief that these conditions are superior to those that would be experienced in their country of origin, a willingness that might be openly exploited by some employers.[80] Another circumstance that might compound this source of vulnerability is the extent to which 457 visa workers are 'remittance workers' who transfer a considerable portion of their wages to their country of origin.[81]

With respect to precarious migrant status, the main factor determining the 'structural vulnerability'[82] of 457 visa workers to non-compliance is the high level of dependence on the sponsoring employer built into the design of the scheme. This dependence stems from various circumstances, the most important of which is dependence on a third party for the right of residence. As the Deegan Review states:

> Despite the views of some employers and employer organisations, Subclass 457 visa holders are different from other employees in Australian workplaces. They

[78] As the 2014 Integrity Review of the 457 visa programme states, '457 visa holders who have a good understanding of their workplace rights are less susceptible to exploitation': Azarias et al, *Robust New Foundations* (n 54) 75.

[79] Michael Piore, *Birds of Passage: Migrant Labour and Industrial Societies* (Cambridge, Cambridge University Press, 1979).

[80] Anderson and Ruhs, 'Migrant Workers' (n 33) 29.

[81] Yuan et al, *Temporary Migrants as Vulnerable Workers* (n 75) 38.

[82] Mary Crock, Sean Howe and Ron McCallum, 'Conflicted Priorities? Enforcing Fairness for Temporary Migrant Workers in Australia' in Costello and Freedland (eds), *Migrants at Work* (n 8) 437–38.

> are the only group of employees whose ability to remain in Australia is largely dependent upon their employment and to a large extent, their employer. It is for these reasons that visa holders are vulnerable and are open to exploitation.[83]

In this context, the ability of the sponsoring employer to terminate the employment of the 457 visa worker can amount to a power to remove the worker from Australia. Not surprisingly, the Deegan Review found that there is a perception amongst 457 workers that the sponsoring employer can cancel their visas, despite this power formally residing with the Immigration Department.[84]

Dependence is also conditioned by the long-term aims of workers, who often wish to stay and work in Australia beyond the term of their current visas. As these aims need to be realised in an increasingly employer-driven migration programme that requires employer sponsorship for the main temporary and permanent labour migration visas, this can result in further dependence on the sponsoring employer. This is clearly the case with 457 visa workers seeking another 457 visa. Most of the 457 visa workers seeking a pathway to permanent residence[85] rely on the Employer Nomination Scheme or the Regional Sponsored Migration Scheme, both of which depend on the sponsorship of an employer.[86] This formal dependence sits alongside a general perception that employer sponsorship is necessary for a successful permanent residence application. Both can result in a willingness to work in breach of workplace laws. As the Deegan Review notes:

> where a visa holder has permanent residency as a goal that person may endure, without complaint, substandard living conditions, illegal or unfair deductions from wages, and other forms of exploitation in order not to jeopardise the goal of permanent residency.[87]

Cutting across the various sources of dependence is the shadow of irregular status stemming from another aspect of precarious migrant status: limited work authorisation. It is a cruel irony that if a 457 visa worker is engaged by an employer in violation of protective laws, this can, in fact, strengthen the hand of the employer. For instance, 457 visa workers who work in a job classification different (most likely lower) from that stated in their visas would be in breach of Visa Condition 8107. Not only would the visa be

[83] Visa Subclass 457 Integrity Review, *Final Report* (Canberra, Commonwealth of Australia, 2008) 69 ('Deegan Review').

[84] Visa Subclass 457 Integrity Review, *Issues Paper #3: Integrity/Exploitation* (Canberra, Commonwealth of Australia, 2008) 27.

[85] Visa Subclass 457 External Reference Group, *Final Report to the Minister for Immigration and Citizenship* (Canberra, Commonwealth of Australia, 2008) 23; Department of Immigration and Border Protection, *Filling the Gaps* (n 53) 39–40.

[86] See Deegan Review (n 83) 50.

[87] Ibid 49.

liable to cancellation in this scenario,[88] but the worker would also be committing a criminal offence.[89]

More than this, visa breaches (eg working in a job classification different from that stated in the visa) can profoundly impact upon the enforceability of labour laws. The limited Australian case law adopts a 'non-protection' approach,[90] with authorities disturbingly finding that breaches of a visa have the consequence of voiding any contract of employment, thereby resulting in the non-application of labour laws.[91]

These sources of vulnerability highlight the constrained ability of many 457 visa workers to enforce their rights. 457 visa workers also face other barriers in enforcing their legal rights. Under the Fair Work Act, complaints through legal proceedings remain a key avenue for enforcing rights, alongside the enforcement activities of the Fair Work Ombudsman and trade unions. But legal proceedings imply procedural hurdles and legal costs that are generally 'loaded against the worker who must carry the claim against the employer'.[92]

A different kind of constraint operates in relation to breaches of labour protection under the Migration Act and the Migration Regulations. As explained earlier, employers of 457 visa workers are subject to various sponsorship obligations including the requirement to provide them 'no less favourable' working conditions. Breaches of these obligations cannot, however, be enforced by the 457 visa workers or their representatives (eg trade union officials), as the power to enforce resides solely with the Immigration Minister and the Immigration Department.[93] While having a formal right to enforce through a complaint-based system is problematic, having no right to enforce is even more so.

B. Vulnerability of International Student Workers

International students can be seen as a particularly vulnerable group in the labour market, as a result of personal characteristics such as youth, limited employment experience and low English-language proficiency, as well

[88] Migration Act 1958 (Cth) s 116.

[89] Ibid s 235.

[90] Elaine Dewhurst, 'The Right of Irregular Immigrants to Back Pay: The Spectrum of Protection in International, Regional and National Legal Systems' in Costello and Freedland (eds), *Migrants at Work* (n 8) 217–19.

[91] See discussion in Graeme Orr, 'Unauthorised Workers: Labouring Beneath the Law' in Christopher Arup et al, *Labour Law and Labour Market Regulation* (Sydney, Federation Press, 2006); Reilly, 'Protecting Vulnerable Migrant Workers' (n 16).

[92] Chris Arup and Carolyn Sutherland, 'The Recovery of Wages: Legal Services and Access to Justice' (2009) 35 *Monash University Law* Review 96, 105.

[93] Migration Regulations 1994 (Cth) regs 140K–140RB.

as aspects of precarious migrant status such as insecure financial position, insecure residence status and the impact of restrictions on work entitlements.[94] Some attributes are shared with local workers, especially local students, but others appear distinctive to their position as international students.[95]

International students are usually new entrants to the Australian labour market. This circumstance is often compounded by the relative youth of international students—a fact that can be a source of vulnerability due to limited labour market experience and the perception of some employers that young workers are more amenable to poor working conditions.

As with 457 visa workers, there can be a lack of understanding of their workplace rights due to lack of access to adequate information concerning these rights and to poor levels of English proficiency. Like 457 visa workers, international student workers can also experience vulnerability due to their precarious migrant status. Limited access to public goods, particularly the lack of access to student allowances (Austudy payments) and the requirement to pay (substantial) international student fees, can exacerbate the financial pressure faced by these workers.

In addition, international students—except for those on the Postgraduate Research (Subclass 574) visa who have unlimited work rights—are subject to Visa Condition 8105, which stipulates that 'the holder must not engage in work in Australia for more than 40 hours a fortnight during any fortnight when the holder's course of study or training is in session'.[96] In some cases, breach of this restriction can enable employers to leverage working conditions in breach of labour laws. As the Knight Review report states:

> There is anecdotal evidence, particularly from trade unions, that the most unscrupulous employers exploit international students once they agree to an initial breach of their work rights. Such employers then demand all sorts of things from their international student employees—work at reduced wages, breaches of occupational health and safety conditions, even sexual favours. In effect, the international students are blackmailed by the threat of the employer reporting the student for their initial breach. Under the current rules a reported breach of work rights can lead to a mandatory cancellation of the student visa.[97]

The precariousness resulting from breaches of the working hours visa condition also contributes to vulnerability in relation to the enforcement of workplace rights of international student workers. Like 457 visa workers, international student workers confront case law which holds that visa breaches translate into the non-enforceability of labour protection;

[94] Reilly, 'Protecting Vulnerable Migrant Workers' (n 16) 186–95; Berg, *Migrant Rights at Work* (n 14) 97–101.

[95] Reilly, 'Protecting Vulnerable Migrant Workers' (n 16).

[96] Migration Regulations 1994 (Cth) sch 8, Visa Condition 8105.

[97] Michael Knight, *Strategic Review of the Student Visa Program 2011* (Canberra, Commonwealth of Australia, 2011) 85.

international student workers may also fear that complaints concerning these rights might result in the Immigration Department being notified of their visa breaches, thereby jeopardising their ability to stay in Australia.[98] These sources of vulnerability combine with the difficulties that all workers generally experience in bringing legal proceedings to produce formidable hurdles to international student workers enforcing their workplace rights.

A simple comparison of international students and 457 visa workers suggests that the former are less vulnerable than the latter. In particular, international students do not seem to be as susceptible to the impact of precarious migrant status. Though some suffer an impact, vulnerability due to precarious migrant status does not generally apply to *all* international student workers; not all international student workers experience financial pressures due to limited access to public goods, and clearly not all international student workers experience vulnerability upon breaching the working hours restrictions in their visas, restrictions that still permit substantial part-time work. Moreover, since 2013, the harshness of these restrictions has been ameliorated as mandatory cancellation of visas has been replaced with discretionary cancellation.[99]

Moreover, unlike employer-sponsored migrant workers like the 457 visa workers, international student workers are not dependent upon employment and their employers for continued residence in Australia. They also experience less precariousness arising from a desire to obtain permanent residence than 457 visa workers: for international student workers who aspire to permanent residency, their employer when they are students is unlikely to be the employer sponsoring their permanent residence applications. Further, the wage gap between the country of origin and Australia is less salient, because international student workers are—overwhelmingly—coming to Australia with the primary motivation to study rather than to engage in paid work. Correspondingly, it will be rare for international student workers to be 'remittance' workers; indeed, the flow of money would typically be in the opposite direction, with families in the country of origin providing money to fund the education of international student workers.

The argument that international students are less vulnerable than 457 visa workers may appear paradoxical in the light of the evidence that wages and working conditions are poorer and that employer non-compliance is more widespread for international students (as starkly illustrated by the systemic under-payment of international student workers by 7-Eleven franchisees).[100] The answer to this apparent paradox can be found by looking more closely at the industries in which international students and 457 visa workers are employed.

[98] Andrew Stewart and Rosemary Owens, *The Nature, Prevalence and Regulation of Unpaid Work Experience, Internship and Trial Periods in Australia* (Canberra, FWO, 2013) 181.

[99] Migration Legislation Amendment Regulation 2013 (No 1) repealing reg 2.43(2)(b).

[100] Ferguson and Toft, '7-Eleven' (n 49).

V. EMPLOYER PRACTICES IN POORLY REGULATED INDUSTRIES

The vulnerability of temporary migrant workers is an attribute of their workplace relationships—particularly with their employers. Given this, analysis of employer non-compliance in the case of 457 visa holders and international students needs to reach beyond factors of vulnerability located at the level of the workers, whether this is framed in terms of personal characteristics, such as lack of knowledge of employment standards, or in terms of precarious migrant status. Such factors define the *risk* that workers will experience precarious working conditions based on employer non-compliance. Whether that risk is realised, however, depends on employer labour-use practices. It is, therefore, necessary to look directly at employers and the broad range of factors that shape their labour-use practices.[101]

Employer practices are sometimes considered just at an enterprise or workplace level, in effect at an individual level. Thus, ministerial accounts of the exploitation of 457 visa workers often lay the blame on 'unscrupulous employers'[102] and 'rogue employers'[103] 'who do not operate within the law'.[104] These are employers that deviate from the norm in a situation where 'most employers do the right thing'.[105] These accounts are correct to place the actions of employers at the centre of non-compliance: it is the duty of employers to ensure compliance with laws that protect working conditions. It is not up to the workers to ensure that the practices of their employers are legally compliant. Rather it is the duty of employers to take affirmative steps to ascertain their obligations to their employees and to fulfil these obligations. As Judge Riley of the Federal Circuit Court stated, 'it is incumbent upon employers to make all necessary enquiries to ascertain their employees' proper entitlements and pay their employees at the proper rates'.[106] These governmental accounts are also right to state that

[101] Jill Rubery and Frank Wilkinson (eds), *Employer Strategy and the Labour Market* (Oxford, Oxford University Press, 1994); Ruhs and Anderson (eds), *Who Needs Migrant Workers?* (n 33).

[102] Christopher Evans, Minister for Tertiary Education, Skills, Jobs and Workplace Relations, 'Australian Jobs and Foreign Workers must be Protected', media release, 16 February 2011.

[103] Brendan O'Connor, Minister for Immigration and Citizenship, and Bill Shorten, Minister for Employment and Workplace Relations, 'Fair Work Inspectors to Monitor Rogue 457 Employers', media release, 18 March 2013.

[104] Peter Dutton, Minister for Immigration and Border Protection, and Michaelia Cash, Assistant Minister for Immigration and Border Protection, 'Illegal Workers Targeted Nationally', media release, 28 May 2015.

[105] Chris Bowen, Minister for Immigration and Citizenship, 'First Ever Termination of a Labour Agreement', media release, 15 February 2012. See also Michaelia Cash, Assistant Minister for Immigration and Border Protection, 'Work Visa Scams: Don't Pay the Price', media release, 1 October 2014, which states that 'Minister Cash said although the overwhelming majority of people do the right thing, it is a small minority who don't abide by their obligations or attempt to defraud our migration programs'.

[106] *Fair Work Ombudsman v Hongyun Chinese Restaurant Pty Ltd (In Liquidation) & Ors* [2013] FCCA 52, para 35 (24 April 2013).

employers have not just a legal duty, but also a moral duty to treat workers with respect and dignity and to promote fairness in the workplace and the labour market.

These accounts, however, neglect the fact that employer non-compliance is not just the product of individual attitudes or moral dispositions; instead it is heavily influenced by structural or contextual conditions. One crucial structural factor is what can be loosely described as the industry setting. It is increasingly recognised in the literature that employer labour-use practices are nestled in industry settings. Thus, employer non-compliance is concentrated in what could be called 'hazardous' industries, while other industries enjoy high levels of employer compliance.[107] The list of industries currently subject to national campaigns from the Fair Work Ombudsman indicate which industries are experiencing pressing issues of non-compliance. They include:

— hospitality industry;
— children's services;
— agricultural industry with a focus on the 'Harvest Trail';
— building and construction industry;
— cleaning industry;
— textile, clothing and footwear industry.[108]

Why are industry settings important as a structural factor? They express relations of inter-employer competition (and learning), which link together employers in particular industries. They often express common technical or technological imperatives or common features to do with work organisation, job and task descriptions, relative importance of labour costs, and size. In addition, employers are often connected at the industry level in employer associations and in dealings with trade unions, and, even if they stand outside formal industrial relations, they may orient their employment practices in terms of what they identify as custom and practice in the local industry.

One aspect of industry settings, which is particularly important in Australia, is that it positions employers similarly in terms of labour market regulation. The main vehicle of protective regulation in Australia has been through detailed awards, generally structured at an industry level, and the differences amongst such awards have created a complex patchwork of rights and entitlements. The process of labour market deregulation since the early 1990s, driven by dominant philosophies of neo-liberalism, has not simplified the industry pattern of protective regulation. On the contrary, labour market deregulation has itself proceeded according to distinct

[107] Maconachie and Goodwin, 'Employer Evasion' (n 48); Weil, 'Enforcing Labour Standards' (n 71) 35–36.

[108] See Fair Work Australia, 'National Campaigns', www.fairwork.gov.au/how-we-will-help/helping-the-community/campaigns/national-campaigns.

industry patterns and continues to produce distinct results.[109] As a result, some industries are characterised by effective protective regulation, producing high minimum labour standards, and opportunities for employee voice through union membership and enterprise bargaining. Other industries appear more poorly regulated in the sense that award reliance is high and minimum labour standards are low, often marked by low wages and extensive opportunities for use of casual employment and other forms of precarious employment and subcontracting.[110]

The divergence between well-regulated and poorly regulated industries provides a platform for industry or sectoral patterns of employer non-compliance.[111] Not only are standards lower in the poorly regulated industries, they also tend to be those industries with high levels of employer non-compliance. The absence of trade unions deprives workers of the main collective mechanism for enforcing workplace rights, leaving workers either to acquiesce when suspecting breaches of their rights or, in rarer instances, to rely upon individual enforcement strategies which suffer from formidable barriers and questionable effectiveness. Another factor is the dominance of casual work and other forms of precarious employment, which conceal and indeed often legitimise poor treatment of workers.[112] Generally understood by both employer and employee as payment by the hour without the accrual of any rights and entitlements, casual work readily spills over into informal or illegal work, which is off the books and remunerated according to what the employer rather than labour law deems fair and appropriate.

Employer non-compliance in 'hazardous' industries can affect many, though by no means all, workers in such industries. It particularly affects vulnerable workers, including the two groups of temporary migrant workers analysed in this chapter. As noted above, employer non-compliance affects a significant minority of 457 visa holders. These workers share a common vulnerability as a result of their precarious migrant status, which produces substantial dependence on the employer. The extent to which this vulnerability leads to poor quality or precarious work, founded on employer non-compliance, depends heavily on factors associated with the industries in which they are employed.

457 visa holders are spread through a number of industries. In the latest statistics (31 March 2015), the top five industry divisions employing these visa holders were: (1) accommodation and food services; (2) construction;

[109] Mark Bray and Elsa Underhill, 'Industry Differences in the Neoliberal Transformation of Australian Industrial Relations' (2009) 40(5) *Industrial Relations Journal* 372.

[110] Ibid. See also Campbell and Tham, 'Labour Market Deregulation' (n 14).

[111] David Weil, 'Rethinking the Regulation of Vulnerable Work in the USA: A Sector-Based Approach' (2009) 51(3) *Journal of Industrial Relations* 411; Maconachie and Goodwin, 'Employer Evasion' (n 48) 429–35.

[112] Maconachie and Goodwin, 'Employer Evasion' (n 48) 423–24.

(3) other services; (4) health care and social assistance; and (5) information media and telecommunications.[113]

Existing studies, both quantitative and qualitative, indicate that the work experiences of 457 visa holders vary dramatically according to the industry in which they are employed.[114] For example, the general field of health care and social assistance seems to produce relatively few concerns. We conducted an extensive case study in this sector in 2012, which involved in-depth interviews with 26 registered nurses on 457 visas, predominantly in public hospitals. The study found that these nurses were well integrated within the health care workforce in terms of formal wages and conditions, with little evidence of employer non-compliance with minimum employment standards (even though there was precariousness in other aspects of their migration pathways). This situation could be attributed above all to features of the industry such as good labour regulation, based on high levels of union membership amongst nurses, with union density exceeding 90 per cent, and effective bargaining with large employers, many in the public sector, who were committed to decent wages and working conditions.[115] Though key informants spoke of problems in the past, especially in association with the registered individual contracts allowed during the Howard government (1996–2007), and problems continued to be evident in parts of the aged care sector, in general the situation was relatively good.[116] Other industries such as mining may also offer good employment conditions with little employer recourse to non-compliance.[117]

On the other hand, there are several industries in which non-compliance is clearly more of a problem for 457 workers. It is noteworthy that the three main industry divisions in which 457 visa holders are employed are also 'hazardous' industries known for high levels of non-compliance for all workers. As a result, 457 visa holders have been caught up in practices prevalent within these industries. The 2014 Integrity Review found that the level

[113] Department of Immigration and Border Protection, *Subclass 457 Quarterly Report*. The occupational distribution tells a similar story; thus, the top five nominated occupations of these visa holders were: (1) cook; 2) café or restaurant manager; (3) marketing specialist; (4) chef; (5) developer programmer (ibid 15).

[114] Department of Immigration and Border Protection, *Filling the Gaps* (n 53). A qualitative study of Indian 457 visa holders contrasts experiences in the IT sector, where working conditions were generally good, with the experiences of unionised blue-collar workers and with the highly precarious work of those in the hospitality sector, 'who had little union representation and faced a combination of factors that aggravated their situation of precariousness': Selvaraj Velayutham 'Precarious Experiences of Indians in Australia on 457 Temporary Work Visas' (2013) 24(3) *Economic and Labour Relations Review* 359.

[115] Boese et al, 'Temporary Migrant Nurses' (n 9) 333.

[116] Ibid; Nick Blake, 'Nursing Migration: Issues of Equity and Balance' (2010) 18(2) *People and Place* 19.

[117] Susanne Bahn, 'Workers on 457 Visas: Evidence from the Western Australian Resources Sector' (2013) 39(2) *Australian Bulletin of Labour* 50.

of non-compliance with sponsorship obligations is significantly higher in construction, hospitality and retail.[118] The review said that the hospitality, restaurant and tourism industries 'are industries in which the level of sanctioning is high and in which there is scope for nefarious practices'.[119] The 2012 survey of employers sponsoring 457 visa holders revealed a similar industry pattern, with employers in accommodation and food services, and to a lesser extent construction and manufacturing, citing access to behavioural traits such as 'increased loyalty', 'hard work' and 'better attitude' as benefits of using the programme,[120] traits that can often be a proxy for a 'greater willingness to do the job *on the employer's terms*'.[121] (emphasis added)

As noted above, employer non-compliance is widespread in connection with international students. International students are more concentrated than 457 visa holders and the industries in which they are concentrated, such as accommodation and food services, cleaning and retail, are precisely those that are identified as poorly regulated and 'hazardous' industries. As a result, the risks associated with their vulnerability tend to be readily translated into precarious working conditions.

Unfortunately, detailed studies of work and working conditions for international students are lacking in Australia. However, evidence for their concentration in a small range of industries, starting with cafes, restaurants and retail outlets, is straightforward.[122] This industry distribution maps well with compelling evidence of poor wages and working conditions, including those that are associated with employer non-compliance. Specific industry studies are few, though a union, United Voice, has produced some stimulating studies in the cleaning industry.[123] Our own case study of cafes, restaurants and takeaway food services in the Melbourne CBD included in-depth interviews with 21 international students, which revealed poor working conditions and extensive non-compliance. Most jobs held by the 21 interviewees were classified as casual, almost half could be described as informal jobs (without a tax file number, with cash-in-hand payments), and all but one of the interviewees had experience of some sort of underpayment or non-payment of wages. Many of the international students that we interviewed complained of discrimination in recruitment practices, which in effect pushed them into poor quality or precarious jobs in a narrow range

[118] Azarias et al, *Robust New Foundations* (n 54) 87.

[119] Ibid 43.

[120] Chris Wright and Andreea Constantin, *An Analysis of Employers' Use of Temporary Skilled Visas in Australia*, Working Paper (Sydney, University of Sydney, 2015).

[121] Anderson and Ruhs, 'Migrant Workers' (n 33) 30.

[122] Marginson et al, *International Student Security* (n 26).

[123] Victorian TAFE International and United Voice, *Taken to the Cleaners*; United Voice, *A Dirty Business*.

of industries. These findings are consistent with those in a 2015 report by the Fair Work Ombudsman on restaurants, cafes and catering which found 58 per cent of the 1,066 audited businesses failed to meet all their workplace obligations, with most breaches relating to wage entitlements.[124]

To sum up, for both 457 visa holders and international students, experiences of employer non-compliance seem to be based on an interaction of factors of vulnerability with employer practices in poorly regulated industries.

VI. CONCLUDING THOUGHTS

The analysis in this chapter, using the Australian examples of 457 visa holders and international students, suggests that the problem of non-compliance with protective regulation relating to temporary migrant workers results from the interaction of their vulnerability—including their precarious migrant status—with employer practices of poorly regulated industries. We reject the common explanations of employer non-compliance that are exclusively focused at the level of the individual, either the vulnerable individual migrant worker or the individual employer, who is seen as a 'rogue' employer who has stepped outside the mainstream moral consensus. These explanations are too narrow and cast non-compliance as aberrant. Instead, we argue that employer non-compliance must be seen as shaped by structural preconditions and causes (see Table 8.2).

Table 8.2: Non-compliance as Aberration Versus Non-compliance as Structural

Non-compliance as aberration	Non-compliance as structural
Causes arise from outside the law Engaged by employers that are not part of the mainstream	Causes shaped by the law Attends many employment relationships to a greater or lesser degree
State of exception in labour markets where legality is the norm	Subversion of labour protection is the norm in key parts of the labour market

Key implications follow from viewing non-compliance as structural in relation to temporary migrant workers. The first is a rejection of an inevitability thesis that would condemn temporary migrant work to the realm of illegal working conditions. If non-compliance arises from particular immigration

[124] See Fair Work Ombudsman, *National Hospitality Industry Campaign: Restaurants, Cafes and Catering (Wave 2)* (Canberra, FWO, 2015) 4.

and labour market structures, these structures are amenable to change—the choices made by the receiving state, its political community and employers shape these structures. Second, given that the structural risk of non-compliance in relation to temporary migrant workers stems from the interaction of their vulnerability, particularly their precarious migrant status, and employer practices in poorly regulated labour markets, it follows that such risk needs to be addressed through an integrated suite of immigration and labour law strategies and that immigration law strategies by themselves are unlikely to provide effective countervailing measures.

Part V

Challenges in Realising Decent Work for Temporary Migrant Workers

9

Empowering Temporary Migrant Workers in Sweden

A Call for Unequal Treatment

PETRA HERZFELD OLSSON

I. INTRODUCTION

THE REASONS WHY an individual decides to move temporarily to work in another country are complex. Macro- and micro-level factors interact in different ways and pure neo-classical economic theoretical explanations based only on transaction costs and economic disparities as pull and push factors are inadequate.[1] Differentials in wages and employment conditions function as a necessary though not sufficient condition for international migration to occur.[2] On a micro-level, the decision to migrate to work abroad can be part of a household's strategy to 'diversify its labour portfolio and reduce risks to income as long as conditions in the various labour markets are weakly or negatively correlated'.[3] Thus, the decision to leave one country for another includes a number of considerations, of which the expected economic gain is one.

In this chapter I will discuss the foreseeability of the income that will be earned when choosing Sweden as the destination country. I will discuss two crucial aspects: first, ensuring that the working conditions offered before arrival can be enforced when the work is conducted and secondly, the

[1] Stephen Castles, Hein de Haas and Mark J Miller, *Age of Migration: International Population Movements in the Modern World*, 5th edn (Basingstoke, UK, Palgrave Macmillan, 2014) 25ff; Douglas S Massey, Joaquin Arango, Graeme Hugo, Ali Kouaouci, Adela Pellegrino and J Edward Taylor, *Worlds in Motion: Understanding International Migration at the end of the Millennium* (Oxford, Clarendon Press, 2008) 8ff, 15f.

[2] Massey et al, *Worlds in Motion* 279.

[3] Ibid 278.

importance of effective employment protection. The level of employment protection can be decisive both for the probability that the migrant worker will enforce the rights they are entitled to and to ensure that the employment will last as long as expected.[4] When discussing this issue, the combined effect of migration law and labour law must be taken into account. If migrant workers risk losing their employment when they try to enforce the employment conditions they are entitled to, the price of enforcement will be extremely high if the work and residence permit is connected to that particular employment.[5] In such a case, the migrant worker will be doubly punished as both the employment and the right to stay in the country will be lost. If the law provides for effective employment protection, the risks connected to such enforcement will be reduced and will thereby counteract abuse of working conditions.

This question is particularly important in a system like the Swedish one, a purely employer-driven labour migration regime where no labour market tests are conducted, no points system or quotas are applied and no particular skills are required. When migrant workers lose their original job, the probability of finding a new job during the short period available is very low for workers in sectors where there is no labour shortage and unemployment is high.

The importance of ensuring that the working conditions offered before arrival can be enforced when the work is conducted is not only relevant in a Swedish context. A number of EU directives and ILO Convention No 189 on Decent Work for Domestic Workers prescribe that a valid work contract or a binding job offer must be attached to an application for a work permit or have been received prior to crossing the border to take up domestic work.[6] There seems to be some level of consensus regarding the importance of being aware of the working conditions applicable to the forthcoming work. Another question is whether it is reasonable to expect strong employment protection leading to guaranteed work for a specific period of time. The EU Seasonal Workers Directive deals with that point in a thought-provoking way.[7]

[4] Bridget Anderson, 'Migration, Immigration Control and the Fashioning of Precarious Workers' (2010) 24(2) *Work, Employment and Society* 300, 313.

[5] Ibid; Judy Fudge, 'Precarious Migrant Status and Precarious Employment: The Paradox of International Rights for Migrant Workers' (2012) 34(95) *Comparative Labour law and Policy Journal* 122; Mark Freedland and Cathryn Costello, 'Introduction' in Cathryn Costello and Mark Freedland (eds), *Migrants at Work: Immigration and Vulnerability in Labour Law* (Oxford, Oxford University Press, 2014).

[6] For example Directive 2014/36/EU on the conditions of entry and stay of third-country nationals for the purpose of employment as seasonal workers [2014] OJ L94/375 (Seasonal Workers Directive) arts 5, 6; ILO Convention No 189 (2011) on Decent Work for Domestic Workers art 8.1.

[7] Seasonal Workers Directive art 17.2.

In this chapter, first I explain why I have chosen a legalistic approach. Secondly, I describe the basic features of the Swedish law on labour migration followed by some facts and figures: how many migrant workers enter the Swedish labour market each year and which sectors do they work in? In order to explain why it is important to try to find more effective ways to protect migrant workers in Sweden, I briefly describe the level of abuse and sort of abuses that take place. This is followed by an examination of the interaction between the administrative labour migration process and contract law in establishing an employment contract. I then explain the shortcomings of permanent employment contracts in protecting workers. In the following section, I raise the question whether the EU Seasonal Workers Directive can provide any inspiration. Finally, I suggest a new kind of employment contract for temporary migrant workers.

II. WHY A LEGALISTIC APPROACH?

It is clear that working conditions are more likely to be abused in an environment where there is no effective enforcement mechanism. In Sweden, trade unions carry the main responsibility for enforcing employment conditions and wages. Temporary migrant workers are seldom unionised and often not covered by collective agreements.[8] Migrant workers are, therefore, in most cases left alone with the responsibility to safeguard the enforcement of their working conditions. It is obvious that making the individual employee responsible for the enforcement of employment conditions is problematic. Institutional support is normally required.[9] The likeliness that migrant workers will enforce the rights they are entitled to also depends on a number of other factors. Often migrant workers are not even aware of their rights.[10] The risk of losing one's residence and work permit, including the expected income if one complains, is also crucial.[11] The importance of protecting the employment contract itself has so far gained little attention in this regard. Focusing on formal protection in law can seem meaningless if there are no effective means available to enforce the rights. But a first step

[8] Samuel Engblom, 'Reconciling Openness and High Labour Standards? Sweden's Attempts to Regulate Labour Migration and Trade in Services' in Costello and Freedland (eds), *Migrants at Work* 355.

[9] Jonas Malmberg, *The Impact of the ECJ Judgments on Viking, Laval, Rüffert and Luxembourg on the Practice of Collective Bargaining and the Effectiveness of Social Action*, EMPL Study (Brussels, European Parliament, 2010) 15.

[10] Shauna Olney and Ryszard Cholewinski, 'Migrant Workers and the Rights to Non-discrimination and Equality' in Costello and Freedland (eds), *Migrants at Work* 277.

[11] Joanna Howe and Rosemary Owens, 'Temporary Labour Migration in a Globalised World: The Regulatory Challenges', ch 1 in this volume; Anderson, 'Migration, Immigration Control' (n 4) 309f.

must be to ensure that the law establishes the necessary formal foundation; otherwise, the enforcement mechanisms are of no help. Demanding strong legal protection beyond the requirements of equal treatment, which I ultimately will do, might seem surprising and even counterproductive.[12] That of course depends on one's goal, as I will discuss.

III. THE SWEDISH REGULATION OF LABOUR MIGRATION

The Swedish labour migration scheme is purely employer demand–driven. Individual employers decide whether they need to recruit workers from third countries (from outside EU/EEA countries, Switzerland and the Nordic countries). In order to be granted a work permit, the migrant worker, therefore, needs to receive an offer of employment from the employer. No labour market tests are done, no skill preferences based in law or quotas apply, and the system is open to all sectors of the labour market.[13] The only requirement that on paper could look similar to such requirements is the demand that employers respect the principle of European Union preference. In reality, that only means that the vacancy must have been published on the websites of the Swedish Public Employment Service and the European Employment Services for at least ten days.[14] The implementation of the new EU directive on conditions of entry and residence of third-country nationals for the purposes of highly qualified employment and seasonal employment has and will (the Seasonal Workers Directive has not been implemented yet) to a certain extent modify this uniform approach.[15]

The government that introduced this labour migration policy in 2008 was of the opinion that the individual employer is best placed to know what skills are required in the business and what recruitment needs exist. The ambition was to make it easier for employers to recruit labour from third countries.[16] Previously, the system was based on labour market tests conducted by the Swedish Public Employment Service.[17] In order to ensure that

[12] Martin Ruhs, *The Price of Rights: Regulating International Labor Migration* (Oxford, Oxford University Press, 2013) 196ff.

[13] Some groups like artists do not need a work permit, however, and persons applying for a job in certain sectors facing labour shortages can enter Sweden to meet with a particular employer without yet having received a job offer.

[14] Government Bill 2013/14:227 p 8.

[15] Seasonal Workers Directive; Directive 2009/50/EC on the conditions of entry and residence of third-country nationals for the purpose of highly qualified employment [2009] OJ L155/17; Catharina Calleman, 'The Most Open System among OECD Countries: Swedish Regulation of Labour Migration' (2015) 5(1) *Nordic Journal of Migration Research* 28, 34.

[16] Government Bill 2007/08:147 pp 1, 26.

[17] See, eg Engblom, 'Reconciling Openness' (n 8) 351.

migrant workers would not replace national workers after the reform, the terms of employment must be similar to those offered to Swedish workers.[18] The offer of employment, therefore, must specify wages, insurance and other terms of employment and these must not be worse than those provided for in the relevant collective agreements or provided for by customs in the occupation or industry.[19] The relevant trade union must be given an opportunity to verify whether the terms are in accordance with the collective agreements.[20] In this context, it is worth remembering that collective agreements still play a significant role in setting wages and other working conditions in Sweden. In 2014, 90 per cent of the labour market was covered by collective agreements and in 2015, 69 per cent of workers were organised in trade unions.[21]

The offer of employment is a document administered by the Swedish Migration Agency, the authority that makes decisions on work and residence permits. This document must clarify whether the employer is covered by a collective agreement and in that case it must identify the trade union party. The document must also specify the wages, the working time, the applicable insurance, the kind of employment and the period of employment.[22] The combined effect of the specified wages and the working time is also important to fulfill the last requirement for being granted a work permit. Migrant workers must be able to support themselves, meaning that their total income must be more than the level for upholding social assistance (13,000 SEK per month, around 1,200 Euro).[23]

All work permits are temporary. They are granted for the duration of the employment offered but for no longer than two years. Work permits may be extended an unlimited number of times but the total period may only exceed four years in exceptional cases.[24] After having worked legally in Sweden for four years within a seven-year period, the migrant worker may be granted a permanent residence permit.[25] The work permit is tied to a specific employer and to a specific type of work (occupation) for the first two years but after two years it is only tied to a specific type of work.[26]

18 Government Bill 2007/08:147, pp 27ff.

19 Foreign Act 2005:716 s 6.2.

20 Foreign Ordinance 2006:97 s 5.7.

21 Mediation Office, *Avtalsrörelsen och lönebildningen* (Stockholm, Mediation Office, 2015) 46, 46.

22 The document can be found at: http://www.migrationsverket.se/download/18.5e83388f141c129ba6312eab/anst_erbj_232011_sv.pdf.

23 Foreign Act s 6.2; Migrationsverket, 'Work Permit Requirements', http://www.migrationsverket.se/English/Private-individuals/Working-in-Sweden/Employed/Work-permit-requirements.html.

24 Foreign Act s 6.2a.

25 Ibid s 5.5.

26 Ibid s 6.2a.

If the migrant worker wants to change employer or type of work, they must apply for a new work permit. That can be done from within Sweden as long as the previous residence permit is still valid.[27] The work permit and/or residence permit may be revoked if the employment has ceased and shall be revoked if the working conditions applied do not fulfil the requirements in the law, meaning for example that they are worse than those provided for in the relevant collective agreement or the employment has not begun four months after arrival.[28] In order to ensure that the migrant worker is not too dependent on the employer, they can stay in Sweden for three to four months to search for a new job if they lose the job that the work permit is connected to.[29] If they need a new or prolonged work permit, they can apply for it from within Sweden.[30]

IV. SOME FACTS AND FIGURES

The numbers of migrant workers admitted to Sweden for work during the years 2000 to 2014 have been quite stable (see Table 9.1). A more detailed analysis leads to somewhat different conclusions. The figures are a bit misleading, for example because migrant workers from the ten new EU Member States (mainly Eastern European) that entered the EU in 2004 have not needed a work permit to work in Sweden since 2004. During 2014, more than 30,000 posted workers from EU Member States were reported at the Swedish Work Environment Authority.[31] Before 2004, posted workers coming from the new EU Member States needed a work permit to work in Sweden.

The decrease in permits between 2004 and 2005 is related to a temporary interruption in issuing seasonal work permits. The idea was that migrant workers from the new EU Member States would replace other seasonal migrants. To a certain extent that happened. But since 2008 when seasonal workers from outside the EU were welcome again on the same basis as other migrant workers, they have been quite successful in finding employment. The largest group granted work permits in Sweden 2014 was migrant workers in the agricultural and fisheries sector, typically seasonal workers and mainly berry pickers (2885). I will discuss other explanations for the fluctuations in section V.

[27] Government Bill 2007/08:146 p 33; *Foreign Ordinance* s 5.3.

[28] Foreign Act ss 7:3, 7:7e.

[29] Ibid ss 7:3, 7:7e.

[30] Foreign Ordinance s 5:3; Swedish Migration Agency website, http://www.migrationsverket.se/.

[31] Arbetsmiljöverket, *Register för företag som utstationerar arbetstagare till Sverige* (Report from the Swedish Work Environment Authority on registered postings) (Stockholm: Swedish Work Environment Authority, 2015) 5.

Table 9.1: Temporary Permits, 2000–2014 Labour Market[32]

Origin	2000	2004	2005	2008	2009	2010	2011	2012	2013	2014
USA	2475	606	629	720	567	567	738	799	808	848
India	567	901	760	2,393	2,156	2,027	2,492	2,948	3,251	3,443
Thailand	881	75	323	3,985	6,230	3,592	2,895	5,834	6,438	3,033
China	394	318	479	1,976	1,603	1,812	1,458	1,317	1,273	1,337
Syria	72	38	32	58	199	435	645	534	727	780
Poland	1917	1402	—	—	—	—	—	—	—	—
Ukraine	1,874	679	547	1,263	1,496	823	826	757	630	670
Total	**15,759**	**8,529**	**5,985**	**14,513**	**17,954**	**16,373**	**17,877**	**19,986**	**19,292**	**15,872**

[32] Source: Swedish Migration Agency. These numbers also capture those who come to Sweden for work but are exempted from the obligation to apply for a work permit, like artists, sports people, au pairs, etc.

The second largest group of migrant workers being issued work permits in 2014 was computing professionals (2,525) and the third largest group IT architects, system analysts and test managers (903), followed by housekeeping and restaurant service workers (666), architects, engineers and related professionals (424), restaurant workers (364), cleaners (208), business professionals (199), personal care workers (189), and cooks and cold-buffet managers (188).[33] These figures reveal a quite clear picture, namely that migrant workers coming to Sweden can be divided into three groups: highly qualified workers, seasonal workers in the agricultural sector and workers in the low-skilled services sector.[34]

The national origins of the migrant workers vary a lot. India (3,443) and Thailand (3,033) were the major sending countries in 2014, followed by China (1,337), Syria (780), Turkey (513), Ukraine (670) and the USA (845). Different national groups dominate different sectors. Indians mainly work in the highly skilled sector, Thais in the agricultural sector, and Chinese workers are divided between the highly skilled sector and the low-skilled service sector. Syrians and Turks work in the low-skilled service sector. Ukrainians work in the agricultural sector and the migrant workers from the US in the highly qualified sector.[35]

Beside the substantial number of seasonal migrant workers who were admitted again through the reform, the major visible effect of the new labour migration regime introduced in 2008 is that a new group has entered the Swedish labour market: migrant workers in the low-skilled service sector.[36]

One reasonable explanation for the relatively low increase in labour migration in general after 2008 is the low activity of recruitment agencies in this field. There are few external actors helping to match migrant workers with Swedish employers.[37] One exception is temporary work agencies in Bangkok that post berry pickers to Swedish forests.[38] Many of the highly qualified workers are intra-corporate transferees working for multinational companies that have their own systems for allocating the right

[33] Swedish Migration Agency, 'Work Permits Granted 2014', http://www.migrationsverket.se/download/18.39a9cd9514a346077211b06/1422893141261/Beviljade+arbetstillst%C3%A5nd+2014+-+Work+permits+granted+2014.pdf.

[34] Henrik Emilsson, 'Who Gets in and Why? The Swedish Experiences with Demand-Driven Migration—Some Preliminary Results' (2014) 3 *Nordic Journal of Migration Research* 134, 138.

[35] Swedish Migration Agency, 'Work Permits Granted 2014' (n 33).

[36] OECD, *Recruiting Immigrant Workers: Sweden 2011* (Paris, OECD Publishing, 2011) 106, 132.

[37] Emilsson, Who Gets in and Why?' (n 34) 138.

[38] See, eg Charlotta Hedberg, 'Thailändska bärplockare—hushållsstrategier på en global arbetsmarknad' in Catharina Calleman and Petra Herzfeld Olsson, *Arbetskraft från hela världen—hur blev det med 2008 års reform* (Stockholm, DELMI, 2015).

workers to the right place.[39] Factors hindering labour migration include time-consuming professional validation procedures, which are necessary for many occupations in the health sector where clear shortages exist, and the related and separate Swedish language demands.[40]

V. ABUSES AND RESPONSES

The Swedish Migration Agency reported recently that the labour migration regime is extensively abused.[41] The agency's primary concern seems to be bogus employment. The work permit system is used by migrants who do not fulfil the criteria for asylum but are still eager to escape their home countries. In these cases, the migrants have not succeeded in finding a proper job in Sweden before they enter the country. In some of those cases, the migrant workers even pay their own wages. The 'employer' can be a relative who wants to help but cannot afford to pay the required wages or someone who wants to take economic advantage of the situation through selling work permits.[42] Other kinds of problems have also been reported. Reports from the Hotel and Restaurant Trade Union, which has been investigating the true working conditions of a number of migrant workers within its sector, explain that almost none of the employers checked applied the terms of employment required by the Foreign Act.[43] Recurring reports on abuses within the berry picking industry have been published.[44] Problems have also been reported from the highly skilled sector.[45] They are, however,

[39] Emilsson, 'Who Gets in and Why?' 139; Charlotta Hedberg, Brita Hermelin and Kristina Westermark, 'Transnational Spaces "From Above"—The Role of Institutions in Promoting Highly Skilled Labour Migrations from India to Sweden' (2014) 105(5) *Tijdschrift voor Economische en Sociale Geografie* 511; Pieter Bevelander, Henrik Emilsson, Karin Magnusson and Sayaka Osanami Törngren (eds), *Världens öppnaste land: arbetskraftsinvandring efter reformen 2008*, Fores Studie 2014:1 (Falun, Fores, 2015).

[40] Emilsson, 'Who Gets in and Why?' (n 34) 138.

[41] Swedish Migration Agency, *Yttrande rörande förslaget om åtgärder mot missbruk av reglerna för arbetskraftsinvandring* (Statement of opinion from the Migration Agency on a new proposal from the government regarding labour migration), Ds 2013:57 (Stockholm, Swedish Migration Agency, 2013) 1.

[42] Veronica Nordlund and Lisa Pelling, *Ny väg in: Intervjustudie* (Stockholm, Global Utmaning, 2012).

[43] Jeanette Gustavsson et al, 'Migrationsprojektet', http://hrftest.s3-eu-west-1.amazonaws.com/2015/02/rapport_migrationsprojektet_slutrapport_mars_2011.pdf; Hotell och restaurangfacket, *Till vilket pris som helst?* (Stockholm, Hotell och restaurangfacket, 2012).

[44] Charles Woolfson, Petra Herzfeld Olsson and Christer Thörnqvist, 'Forced Labour and Migrant Berry Pickers in Sweden' (2012) 28(2) *International Journal of Comparative Labour Law and Industrial Relations* 148.

[45] Peter Larsson, Sveriges Ingenjörer and Inlägg Anställningsavtal, 'Därför bryter vi samarbetet med Migrationsverket', *Svenska Dagbladet*, 1 June 2011; see also Karin Magnusson and Sayaka Osanami Törmgren, 'Migration och integration av högkvalificerade arbetskraftsinvandrare' in Bevelander et al (eds), *Världens öppnaste land* 130ff.

quite rare. Highly skilled workers seldom face the same kinds of abuses as more vulnerable workers.[46] Research indicates that the wage level among migrant workers within a number of occupations is considerably lower than the average wage level in the relevant sector. This is particularly clear in the low-skilled service sector but also among some highly qualified occupations like IT specialists.[47] Recently, one of the major Swedish morning newspapers published a series of articles under the headline 'The Invisible'. The articles described the working conditions of a number of Mongolian cleaners who were cleaning two of the most profitable supermarkets in the Stockholm area. The cleaning was outsourced to another company whose business model seemed to be to employ migrants in different types of precarious statuses. Their wages were about one third of the wage stipulated in the relevant collective agreement.[48]

The government and the Swedish Migration Agency have responded to these reports. Since 2011, the Swedish Migration Agency has introduced targeted controls of employers in the sectors that are most prone to abuse: berry picking, cleaning, hotels and restaurants, construction, retail, farming and forestry, auto repair, service and temporary agency work. The number of approved work permits within those sectors has decreased since the introduction of these controls.[49]

In 2014 the government introduced new regulations aiming to detect and hinder abuse of the system. The Migration Agency was given the right to control migrant workers' employment conditions in retrospect. At the request of the Migration Agency, employers are now required to provide written information on the conditions applying to the position. Inaccurate information may lead to a fine or imprisonment. If the controls clarify that the employment has not commenced within four months or if the working conditions do not meet the requirements of section 6.2 of the Foreign Act, meaning at least in line with the relevant collective agreement or custom, the work permit shall be revoked unless the migrant worker has found alternative employment within four months.[50] An established failure of an employer to apply the required level of working conditions will, accordingly, mainly affect the migrant worker, who risks losing their residence permit if they do not find alternative work. The new provisions have been criticised

[46] Joseph H Carens, *The Ethics of Immigration* (Oxford, Oxford University Press, 2013) 122–23; Catherine Dauvergne and Sarah Marsden, 'Beyond Numbers Versus Rights: Shifting the Parameters of Debate on Temporary Labour Migration' (2014) 15 *International Migration & Integration* 525, 526.

[47] Henrik Emilsson,' Sverige och arbetskraftsinvandringen' in Bevelander et al (eds), *Världens öppnaste land* 63.

[48] Dagens Nyheter, 'Städar sju dagar i veckan—får ut 7000 kronor i månaden', *Fokus De osynliga*, 28 May 2015.

[49] Calleman, 'The Most Open System' 31 (n 15).

[50] Foreign Act s 7.7e; Government Bill 2013/14:227.

for being imbalanced and for not addressing the problems of non-binding offers of employment or the lack of sanctions directed towards employers who fail to abide by the rules.[51]

On 2 July 2015, the government appointed a new inquiry to suggest measures that could counteract abuse of migrant workers. The inquiry will present its finding in September 2016.[52]

VI. THE OFFER OF EMPLOYMENT AND THE EMPLOYMENT CONTRACT

At first sight, it can seem quite easy for migrant workers to predict the applicable working conditions and calculate their expected income when choosing Sweden as a destination country. In order to get a work permit, the migrant worker needs to fill in a form supplied by the Migration Agency called 'Offer of Employment', which must specify the wages, the working time and the period of employment, and attach it to the application. As I have explained, the Foreign Act prescribes that in order to be granted a work permit the migrant worker must be offered a job where the wages, insurance and other working conditions are at least in line with the relevant collective agreement or when no such collective agreement exists, relevant custom in the sector.[53]

In recent years, a number of abuses related to migrant workers have been reported, as indicated above. Migrant workers have faced employment conditions that are different to those prescribed in the Offer of Employment form. The abuse has partly been explained by the fact that the offer of employment is not considered to be binding in the sense that it is up to the migrant worker to accept it and, thereby, establish an employment contract. According to Swedish law, an employment contract is concluded when the parties declare a common will to establish such a contract. It can be oral as well as written and no formalities have to be applied. General principles of contract law govern the process.[54] An offer of employment binds the employer in the law of contract and it is up to the employee to accept the offer and, thereby, establish an enforceable employment contract.[55] The Offer of Employment form that is part of the work and residence permit

[51] Calleman, 'The Most Open System' 34 (n15); Engblom, 'Reconciling Openness' (n 8) 355f.

[52] Kommittédirektiv 2015:75 'Åtgärder för att stärka invandrares ställning på arbetsmarknaden' (Instructions to a government-appointed inquiry to propose measures to strengthen the position of migrants in the labour market).

[53] Foreign Act s 6.2.

[54] Kent Källström and Jonas Malmberg, *Anställningsförhållandet* (Uppsala, Iustus, 2013) 109f.

[55] Law of Contract 1915:218 ss 1–7.

process is not considered to be such a binding offer.[56] That offer of employment is part of the migration law process, an administrative law procedure separate from the law of contract. This means that the employer can give the migrant worker another real offer of employment with a different content within the contract law procedure and that offer will accordingly then establish the basis for the employment contract.

If an undisputable employment contract has been concluded with a different content than that prescribed in the offer of employment form that employment contract will apply. But often it is not undisputable—the employment conditions that have been agreed upon might be unclear. In those cases, the Offer of Employment form can be used as evidence when a court seeks to establish the true content of the employment contract.[57] However, if the employer can prove that other conditions have been agreed upon, those will apply.[58]

The weakness of the applicable system is to a certain extent explained by the way the Swedish labour market is regulated. There is no legislated minimum wage in Sweden. The wage is set in collective or individual agreements. There is no process of extending the application of the collective agreements to a whole sector or branch. The collective agreement binds only the parties and their members, meaning that trade union members cannot conclude a valid individual contract that deviates from the collective agreement their trade union has concluded with the employer. About 90 per cent of the Swedish labour market is covered by collective agreements. But temporary migrant workers are seldom members of Swedish trade unions and often employed in companies not covered by collective agreements.[59] If the migrant worker is not unionised, or unionised but not covered by a collective agreement, they are free to conclude any individual employment contract in accordance with the law. Hence, in such cases the parties can agree on wages far below the level in collective agreements applicable to other companies in the sector. In very special cases, an agreed wage has been adjusted through section 36 of the law of contract as being unreasonable.[60]

If the terms agreed upon in the employment contract are worse than those required in the Foreign Act (meaning worse than those provided for in a relevant collective agreement) the work permit can be revoked. The migrant

[56] Calleman, 'The Most Open System' (n 15) 31; Charles Woolfson, J Fudge and Christer Thörnqvist, 'Migrant Precarity and Future Challenges to Labour Standards in Sweden' (2014) 35(4) *Economic and Industrial Democracy* 695, 702.

[57] Labour Court AD 2007 no 1.

[58] Labour Court AD 2012 no 34; Labour Court AD 2015 no 19.

[59] Engblom, 'Reconciling Openness' (n 8) 355; Olle Frödin and Anders Kjellberg, 'Arbetskraftsmigration i restaurang och städbranscherna' in Catharina Calleman and Petra Herzfeld Olsson (eds), *Arbetskraft från hela världen: Hur blev det med 2008 års reform?* (Stockholm, DELMI, 2008).

[60] Tore Sigeman and Erik Sjödin, *Arbetsrätten* (Mölnlycke, Nordstedts juridik, 2013) 171.

worker cannot deduce their labour rights from the Foreign Act, however. The migrant worker, like any employee, must base their demands on the terms of the employment contract and applicable labour laws.

A number of stakeholders have argued for the introduction of a truly binding offer of employment in the migration process.[61] One crucial question is of course what that would imply. Should this binding offer of employment establish an ordinary employment contract? Some of the trade unions seem to argue for something different. The white-collar confederation TCO, for example, argues for a provision guaranteeing that migrant workers must be guaranteed at least the wages and other employment conditions that are prescribed in the offer of employment, or an alternative solution implying that damages shall be paid if the wages, insurance and other conditions do not correspond to those in the offer of employment. The starting point in the latter case would be that the migrant worker should be put in the same position as if the conditions in the offer of employment had been applied.[62]

Many discussions of labour migration include a call for equal treatment between migrant workers and nationals.[63] However, when discussing the employment contract, its conclusion and effects, it is not obvious that an ordinary employment contract is the best tool to prevent abuse of the labour migration system—a different, unequal treatment of migrant workers might be preferable. An ordinary employment contract is enforceable but can always be renegotiated if the parties so agree. On the other hand, it seems reasonable that migrant workers should be able to foresee the applicable working conditions when they decide to move to Sweden for work.

It is also quite logical that a system like the Swedish labour migration system, which is based on the condition that migrant workers will only be admitted to the Swedish labour market if they are going to work under the same working conditions as Swedish workers, should be constructed in a way that ensures that this condition can be upheld in practice.

Technically, this goal can be solved in different ways. The TCO seems to suggest that a special legal provision should prohibit the parties to the employment contract from agreeing on wages and working conditions below the level that is communicated to the Swedish Migration Agency when the

[61] Swedish Trade Union Confederation, *Fusk och utnyttjande—om avregleringen av arbetskraftsinvandringen* (Stockholm, LO, 2013); Swedish Confederation of Professional Employees, *Arbetskraftsinvandring—Bättre kontroll för bibehållen öppenhet* (Stockholm, TCO, 2013); 'Pelling Sju förslag för att stärka de osynligas rättigheter', *DN Debatt*, 2 June 2015; Social Democratic parliamentarians' proposals to Parliament, 2012.

[62] Swedish Confederation of Professional Employees, *Arbetskraftsinvandring—Bättre kontroll för bibehållen öppenhet* (Stockholm, TCO, 2013).

[63] See, eg Howe and Owens, 'Temporary Labour Migration in a Globalised World' (n 11); ILO, *Multilateral Framework on Migration: Non-binding Principles and Guidelines for a Rights-Based Approach to Labour Migration* (Geneva, ILO, 2006); Olney and Cholewinski, 'Migrant Workers' (n 10) 259, 281.

application for a work permit is made. This is a clear deviation from the ordinary starting points that are applicable to the employment contract. The idea seems to be that the ordinary means to compensate for the subordination of individual workers are not functioning for migrant workers. The trade unions have thereby admitted that they cannot take responsibility for strengthening migrant workers' bargaining power due to the inherent differences between migrant workers and Swedish workers and, therefore, the legislature must step in and compensate for their incapacity.

Another way of solving this dilemma is to ensure that the employer cannot unilaterally change the wages and working conditions agreed upon. That seems to be the government's preferred solution. The inquiry appointed in July 2015 has been instructed to consider whether to recommend attaching an employment contract to the application for a work permit and whether restrictions on employers worsening the working conditions after the work permit has been approved can be an effective tool in counteracting abuse.[64]

Another factor that has not been touched upon in the Swedish debate is the role the level of employment protection plays in creating opportunities for abuse. That aspect is, however, crucial for ensuring that the working conditions that are agreed upon are those that will be applied. In the following section, I will, therefore, add this aspect to the discussion and explain why it has to be taken into consideration when looking for a solution preventing exploitation of migrant workers and abuse of the Swedish labour migration regime.

VII. EMPLOYMENT PROTECTION

In Swedish law, there are only two types of employment contracts: permanent and fixed-term contracts.[65] Both types of contract can be terminated if the employee has grossly neglected their obligations towards the employer. In that case, the contract is terminated immediately.[66] A fixed-term contract cannot be unilaterally terminated in advance for any other reasons—it is terminated when it expires if it is not prolonged.[67] There are four types of fixed-term contracts: a general fixed-term contract, a temporary substitute contract, seasonal employment, and contracts for employees who have attained the age of 67. If a general fixed-term contract or a substitute contract last for more than two years in a five-year period, they automatically turn into a permanent contract.[68]

[64] Directive 2015:75 (n 52) p 7f.
[65] Employment Protection Act 1982:80 ss 4, 5.
[66] Ibid s 18.
[67] Ibid s 5.
[68] Ibid.

A permanent employment contract can be terminated by the employer if they have objective reasons.[69] There are two types of reasons that are considered to be objective: the reasons can either be related to the company (shortage of work) or to the individual employee (personal reasons). Personal reasons might include the employee acting disloyally towards the employer or in other ways not fulfilling their obligations in the employment contract. It is quite difficult for an employer to prove that the misconduct is so grave that it justifies dismissal. If the reasons are related to the operation of the business, the situation is very different. Shortage of work can occur through a reorganisation of the plant, if the demand for its products has decreased or if a part of the business is sold. Any reason that is not related to the individual employee is in principle considered to fulfil the requirements for shortage of work. The employer has very wide discretion in deciding whether a shortage of work situation has occurred. The Labour Court seldom questions that assessment. A shortage of work situation also occurs if the employer can no longer pay the wages the parties have agreed on in the employment contract. In that case, the employment contract can be terminated and a new one entered into with new conditions if the parties so wish.[70]

In order to avoid arbitrary shortage of work decisions, the employer cannot freely pick and choose the employees who will be made redundant. The employer must apply the seniority principle, meaning that the last employed in the sector affected by the redundancy will be the first to go.[71] The only way to deviate from this rule is through a collective agreement. A period of notice has to be applied. That period is one month if the employment has lasted for a shorter period than two years.[72]

A surprisingly high number of offers of employment state that the migrant worker will be employed on a permanent contract. About half of the work permits issued within the restaurant and cleaning sectors in Stockholm in 2013 were based on permanent contracts.[73] It is unclear why this is the case as the work permit can only last for two years. In reality, a permanent contract does not even provide migrant workers with the normal protection provided to Swedish workers on permanent contracts as the protection afforded depends on whether the migrant workers have valid work permits. In order to get an extension of a work permit, the employer has to send in a new offer of employment to the Swedish Migration Agency. It is difficult

[69] Ibid s 7.

[70] Jonas Malmberg, *Anställningsavtalet* (Uppsala, Iustus, 1997) 324ff; Labour Court AD 2012 no 67; Labour Court AD 1978 no 68.

[71] Employment Protection Act s 22.

[72] Ibid s 11.

[73] Frödin and Kjellberg, 'Arbetskraftsmigration i restaurang och städbranscherna'; Catharina Calleman, 'Arbetskraftsinvandring för arbete i privata hushåll' in Catharina Calleman et al *Rena hem på smutsiga villkor—hushållstjänster, migration och globalisering* (Göteborg, Makadam förlag, 2013).

to detect an obligation for the employer to do that from the permanent employment contract. If the employer does not do that, the migrant worker can lose their work permit and, in that case, the employer does not have to fulfil the obligations arising from the employment contract.[74] In that case, the employer will commit a criminal offence if they continue to employ the migrant worker.[75] A number of employers have been convicted for employing migrant workers without the correct work permit. They are fined and obliged to pay an additional fee if the employment has lasted for more than three months.[76]

VIII. THE COMBINED EFFECTS OF LABOUR LAW, MIGRATION LAW AND SOCIAL LAW

It is clear from the above that a permanent employment contract offers limited protection for the migrant worker. If the employer cannot or does not want to pay the wages agreed upon in the employment contract, it is easy to terminate the contract and only be liable for one month's wages. This is a scenario that can take place independently if the employer is prevented from renegotiating the wages and working conditions. This is the way Swedish labour law works. These starting points are applicable to all workers in the Swedish labour market. The question arises whether it would be reasonable to argue that migrant workers should be treated differently from other workers.

Migrant workers take a risk when they decide to move to Sweden to take up employment. There are a number of differences between the situations of migrant workers and Swedish workers. The migrant worker depends on a particular employer for their right to stay in Sweden (except for the three to four months' extra stay) and for their maintenance. If the employer wants to terminate the employment contract due to a shortage of work and re-employ the migrant worker at a lower cost, the Swedish system offers the migrant worker limited alternative income possibilities. In order to get unemployment benefits, a worker must either have been registered at an unemployment benefit scheme for 12 months or in order to get the basic minimum level have been working to a certain extent for at least 6 months.[77] In order to be guaranteed social assistance one has to reside in a particular municipality. One can only be registered as a resident if one is planning to stay there for at least a year.[78]

[74] Labour Court AD 1979 no 90.

[75] Foreign Act s 20:5.

[76] See, eg, Swedish court cases from the first and second instances: Linköpings TR Dom, 11 March 2013, Mål no B 151-13 and Svea Hovrätt Dom, 26 August 2014, Mål no B 2002-14.

[77] Unemployment Insurance Act (1997:238) ss 6, 7, 12.

[78] Social Services Act (2010:110) ch 2a; Socialstyrelsen, *Rätten till socialt bistånd för medborgare inom EU/EES-området: En vägledning* (Stockholm, Socialstyrelsen, 2014).

In a welfare society, the starting point is that the state will provide additional protection when individuals cannot support themselves. The inherent risk of loss of employment that the market entails is modified by an active redistribution policy and social rights. The welfare state to a varied degree liberates the worker from dependence on their employer. The level of independence provided depends on the strength of the social rights.[79] The migrant worker with a permanent contract is, however, provided with a very limited independence during their first year in Sweden. Besides, the migrant worker only has three to four months to find a new job if the first job is lost, otherwise the work and residence permit will be revoked, a period that migrant workers find very short.[80] The combined effect of employment law, migration law and social law, contrary to the ambitions of the welfare state, make migrant workers quite dependent on their first employer.

It can of course be argued that, in a regulated migration regime like Sweden's, it is always up to the state to decide on what premises a foreigner shall be given the right to cross the Swedish border and to stay in Sweden. In the demand-driven Swedish labour migration system, this right is to a great extent related to a particular job. If that job is lost the right to stay is also lost. On the other hand, we must consider what level of risk migrant workers should reasonably be expected to take when deciding to leave their country to perform a specific job in Sweden. We should also ask what incentives migrant workers have to enforce the working conditions the work permit is based on if enforcing those conditions can lead to a loss of employment.

One question, therefore, is whether it would be reasonable to adapt the labour law in order to fulfil the aim of decommodifying migrant workers and, thereby, ensuring that they can safely enforce the rights that Swedish law anticipates they will be provided with and also fulfil their ambitions for the trip, usually to earn a particular amount of money.

IX. ALTERNATIVE SOLUTIONS: ARTICLE 17 OF THE SEASONAL WORKERS DIRECTIVE

The vulnerability that is created by the interaction of employer-driven labour migration systems and temporary work permits is well established.[81] An attempt to strengthen the position of migrant workers can be detected in the EU Seasonal Workers Directive. During the negotiations, many parties recognised the particular vulnerability of seasonal workers and that

79 Gøsta Esping-Andersen, *The Three Worlds of Welfare Capitalism* (Cambridge, Polity Press, 1990) 3, 18f, 22.

80 Magnusson and Osanami Törmgren, 'Migration och integration av högkvalificerade arbetskraftsinvandrare' (n 45) 121.

81 See, eg Fudge, 'Precarious Migrant Status' (n 5); Anderson, 'Migration, Immigration Control' (n 4); Freedland and Costello (eds), *Migrants at Work* (n 5).

awareness is also to a certain degree reflected in the adopted text.[82] The directive has to be implemented into Swedish law by 30 September 2016.

In this context, I will focus on one paragraph in the directive's article 17 on sanctions against employers. According to article 17.2, the Member States shall ensure that, if the authorisation for the purpose of seasonal work is withdrawn pursuant to specified factors, the employer shall be liable to pay compensation to the seasonal worker in accordance with procedures under national law. Any liability shall cover any outstanding obligations which the employer would have to respect if the authorisation for the purpose of seasonal work had not been withdrawn. This far-reaching liability shall be applicable if the work permit is withdrawn because the employer has acted reprehensibly in the following particular ways:

- The employer has been sanctioned in accordance with national law for undeclared work and/or illegal employment.
- The employer's business is being or has been wound up under national insolvency laws or no economic activity is taking place.
- The employer has been sanctioned because it has not fulfilled its obligations under the directive (articles 17, 9.2.c).
- The employer has failed to meet its legal obligations regarding social security, taxation, labour rights, working conditions or terms of employment, as provided for in applicable law and/or collective agreements.
- The employer has not fulfilled its obligation under the work contract.
- Within the 12 months immediately preceding the date of the application, the employer has abolished a full-time position in order to create the vacancy that the employer is trying to fill by use of this directive.

One of the situations that has been identified as troublesome in Swedish law does not seem to be covered by the provisions in article 17. If the employer dismisses the migrant worker due to a shortage of work in accordance with Swedish labour law, this provision will not help the migrant. However, if the migrant worker is re-employed under conditions that violate section 6.2 of the Foreign Act (goes below the level prescribed in the comparable collective agreement), the work permit can be withdrawn and, in that case, should the employer be held accountable according to article 17 in the directive and liable to pay outstanding obligations? The liability in article 17 is only applicable if the worker's work permit is withdrawn. No liability would, in a Swedish context, take effect during the three to four month transition period when the migrant worker has a right to stay to try to find another job in Sweden.

[82] Judy Fudge and Petra Herzfeld Olsson, 'The EU Seasonal Workers Directive: When Immigration Controls Meet Labour Rights' (2014) 16 *European Journal of International Law* 439.

The main purpose of article 17 is to ensure that the seasonal migrant worker does not bear the cost when their work permit is withdrawn because the employer has violated the law or in other ways acted improperly. Even if the migrant worker loses the right to stay and work, the economic injury must be limited.

When implemented, this directive will only provide for compensation for migrant workers in Sweden in a very few cases and for a limited group: seasonal migrant workers. The intention behind this provision, namely that migrant workers should not bear the burden when they lose their work permits due to the behaviour of their employers, could however be transferred to the broader context that is the focus of this chapter. That an employer can legally demand that the migrant worker accept other terms and conditions of the employment contract than those on which the work permit is based cannot be considered to be in alignment with the thinking behind article 17 of the Seasonal Workers Directive.

X. A PARTICULAR EMPLOYMENT CONTRACT

It is clear, if we borrow the terminology developed by Freedland and Kountouris, that Swedish law must be amended in order to share the risks between migrant workers and employers.[83] Introducing a special employment contract for migrant workers could be one alternative solution. That employment contract could during the first one or two years have the same legal effect as a fixed-term employment contract. That means that it cannot be terminated in advance unless one of the parties has grossly neglected their obligations in the contract. During this period the migrant worker cannot risk losing their job when enforcing the terms of the employment contract. I have previously explained how easy it is to dismiss a worker due to shortage of work according to Swedish law. Employers have sometimes used that argument in order to circumvent employment protections. Complaining about that in court is, however, a time-consuming, expensive and unpredictable exercise. If migrant workers are guaranteed employment for a specific period of time, this issue cannot even be disputed.

XI. CONCLUSIONS

One starting point for the Swedish labour migration regime is that the wage and working conditions of migrant workers should be similar to Swedish

[83] The concept of risk mutualisation is developed in a labour law context in Mark Freedland and Nicola Kountouris, *The Legal Construction of Personal Work Relations* (Oxford, Oxford University Press, 2011) 439f.

workers. The combined effect of Swedish migration, labour and social law cannot guarantee that this starting point is upheld. The vulnerability that is inherent in temporary migration schemes where the migrant worker's stay on the territory depends on a particular employer must be taken into consideration. I suggest that a first step must be to ensure that work permits are based on employment contracts that migrant workers can enforce. However, they will only be enforced if the risk connected to that enforcement is not too high. I, therefore, accordingly suggest that there must be a guarantee that enforcement cannot lead to a termination of the employment contract. It is also reasonable to claim that a temporary migrant worker must be able to foresee what income they will earn from the move to an employer demand–driven system like the Swedish one. If an employer decides to recruit a worker from a third country, it is reasonable to require that the employer should safeguard this income during the period of employment covered by the work permit. Therefore, I suggest that the employment contract the migrant worker should be provided with should carry with it the legal effect of a fixed-term employment contract, meaning that the employer can only terminate the contract unilaterally if the employee has grossly neglected their obligations towards the employer. If the employer terminates the contract for other reasons, it would be liable to pay damages that would put the migrant worker in the same position as if the contract had not been terminated. Such a construction of the employment contract would establish the necessary legal basis for ensuring that the starting points of the Swedish labour migration regime can be upheld and that the division of risks between the migrant worker and the employer is balanced.

The vulnerability created by temporary migration schemes can prevent migrant workers from enforcing their rights. Exceptional measures have to be taken in order to balance that vulnerability. Unequal treatment compared to domestic workers might be required. Temporary migrant workers must be empowered by the law in order to reduce the risks they face when trying to enforce their rights. In the Swedish context, establishing a new kind of employment contract for migrant workers with a fixed-term contract's legal effects can be the tool to achieve this goal. So, I argue for unequal treatment in order to promote equality.

10

Temporary Labour Migration and Modern Slavery

VIRGINIA MANTOUVALOU*

I. INTRODUCTION

TEMPORARY LABOUR MIGRATION is a complex phenomenon that requires a variety of regulatory responses, as Howe and Owens explained in the introductory chapter. In this chapter, I focus on modern slavery legislation as a response to challenges set by temporary labour migration. When classifying a labour relation as slavery or servitude, the emphasis is on the most restrictive labour migration regimes, on sectors that are particularly precarious, and on the worst forms of exploitation of migrant workers under such regimes.

Section II of the chapter examines temporary labour migration regimes and some possible implications for the human rights of workers. Section III explores how human rights law has addressed issues affecting migrant workers with a precarious immigration status through the prohibition of slavery, servitude, and forced and compulsory labour in the context of the European Convention on Human Rights (ECHR). It also assesses the UK Overseas Domestic Worker (ODW) visa, which is a very restrictive temporary labour migration regime that has been central in discussions of modern slavery legislation in the UK. Section IV examines the UK response to the ECHR case law, and more specifically, the UK Modern Slavery Act 2015, which left the ODW visa unchanged at large, despite its serious problems that may lead to a violation of the ECHR.[1] In the case of the ODW visa, the

* I am grateful to Hugh Collins, Joanna Howe and Rosemary Owens for comments on a draft. Many thanks are also due to all Onati workshop participants and particularly to Judy Fudge.

[1] Virginia Mantouvalou, '"Am I Free Now?" Overseas Domestic Workers in Slavery' (2015) 42 *Journal of Law and Society* 329.

employer does not own the employee (contrary to chattel slavery). However, the employer 'owns' the employee's right to work, which creates unprecedented power of control, as I explain on the basis of an empirical project that I conducted. Section V turns to some effects of classifying a temporary work visa as slavery and servitude, and suggests that an exclusive focus on criminalisation firstly is not a necessary implication of human rights law, and secondly, is insufficient as a regulatory response to the plight of temporary migrant workers who are exploited or abused. The final section concludes that temporary labour migration regimes in precarious sectors may be acceptable only when there is an unconditional right to change employer.

II. TEMPORARY LABOUR MIGRATION AND HUMAN RIGHTS

Temporary labour migration regimes are schemes that are restrictive in terms of the length of time that the migrant worker can stay in the receiving country. Other restrictions, in addition to time, include binding the worker to a particular work sector or a particular employer. Such regimes are used in many legal orders. Research has highlighted challenges in regulation and negative consequences of the schemes, many of which restrict the human rights of migrant workers.[2] For example, some of the regimes do not permit workers to be accompanied by a family member, which has repercussions for the private and family life of the migrant worker. In Singapore, unskilled migrant workers do not have the right to cohabit with or get married to a Singaporean national or a permanent resident, and female temporary migrant workers have a duty to have a pregnancy test every six months, with a threat of deportation if they are pregnant.[3]

A further significant restriction in many temporary labour migration regimes involves the sponsorship system. Migrant workers must be sponsored by an employer, and their visa sometimes ties them to this employer, in the sense that it is unlawful for them to change employer. Immigration regimes have generally been criticised in literature that has shown that it is not only undocumented workers that are vulnerable to exploitation, but also workers under restrictive visas.[4] When the worker is tied to the employer,

[2] Martin Ruhs, *Temporary Labour Migration Programmes: Policies, Adverse Consequences and the Need to Make them Work* (Geneva, International Labour Office, 2003); Rosie Cox, 'Gendered Work and Migration Regimes' in Liam Leonard and Ragnhild Aslaug Sollund (eds), *Transnational Migration, Gender and Rights* (Bingley, Emerald, 2012) 33.

[3] Ruhs, *Temporary Labour Migration Programmes* 9.

[4] Bridget Anderson, 'Migration, Immigration Controls, and the Fashioning of Precarious Workers' (2010) 24 *Work, Employment and Society* 300.

the employer can exercise great control over them. Immigration regimes can, therefore, create what has sometimes been described as precarious work.[5] Restrictions imposed on workers under temporary labour migration regimes exemplify how employers are given means to control workers through immigration law in ways that may affect their fundamental human rights. Are these restrictions just?

Some theoretical scholarship has debated the question whether such regimes should be permitted as a matter of justice. The theoretical debate can help us put the temporary labour migration and slavery conundrum in a broader context. Joseph Carens has argued, for instance, that, even if it is justified to have a worker tied to an employer, this should be for a very limited period of time (suggesting a maximum of three months), but even then there should be an 'escape clause for abusive behaviour by the employer'.[6] This means that workers who are abused should have a right to change employer at any time. Carens argues that limiting low-skilled workers to a particular sector would also be problematic and suggests that

> the state's use of restrictions on the economic activities a temporary worker can undertake involves a deliberate element of exploitation or a deliberate element of unfairness, because it forces temporary workers to perform tasks for wages that are lower than they could command if they were free to compete on the entire labour market.[7]

The rights of temporary migrant workers are contested.[8] David Miller has drawn a distinction between human rights and citizenship rights in the present context.[9] He suggests that human rights are those that everyone has, irrespective of immigration status, simply by virtue of being human. These must be respected universally and unconditionally. Citizenship rights, on the other hand, are rights of members of particular societies by virtue of this membership, and they can be claimed against other members of this society; citizenship rights also come with citizenship duties.

Miller says that migrants should enjoy human rights. However, he says that there is no human right to be paid for work that someone has performed, according to his or her contract, but that there is a right to be paid a living wage on the basis of a human right to subsistence. On temporary

[5] Judy Fudge and Rosemary Owens (eds), *Precarious Work, Women and the New Economy: The Challenge to Legal Norms* (Oxford, Hart Publishing, 2006).

[6] Joseph Carens, 'Live-in Domestics, Seasonal Workers, and Others Hard to Locate on the Map of Democracy' (2008) 16 *Journal of Political Philosophy* 419, 431.

[7] Ibid 432.

[8] See also Alexander Reilly, 'The Membership of Migrant Workers and the Ethical Limits of Exclusion', ch 13 in this volume; Martin Ruhs, 'Protecting the Rights of Temporary Migrant Workers: Ideals Versus Reality', ch 14 in this volume.

[9] David Miller, 'Irregular Migrants: An Alternative Perspective' (2008) 22 *Ethics and International Affairs* 193, 194–95.

migrants more particularly, Miller says that their human rights must be protected. He continues:

> But beyond that, their position is better understood in contractual terms: what rights they get should depend on what agreements they have made (or are in place) before they enter. They may be able to benefit from reciprocal agreements between states, such as those that now exist within the EU, in which case they are certainly entitled to whatever such agreements stipulate. Otherwise, it is their responsibility to ensure that the work contracts they sign are adequate to provide for their needs.[10]

In response to Miller's critique, Carens argued that citizenship rights should be divided into three subcategories: rights to fair working conditions, rights to participation in social programmes that are tied to workforce participation, and, rights to participation in other social programmes.[11] He finds no justification for treating temporary migrant workers differently to citizens in the case of most of these programmes, and only suggests that a few of the redistributive social programmes may justifiably be restricted for a period of time for temporary migrant workers.

This theoretical debate highlights the complexities of the problem of migrant workers' entitlements. There are two points that need to be further considered on the basis of the above exchange.

A. Labour Rights as Human Rights

A first question that emerges from Miller is which workers' rights are human rights. If we classify some workers' rights as human rights, all workers, irrespective of immigration status, should enjoy them. Undocumented workers too have human rights.[12] In this context, it can be said that Miller adopts a narrow definition of workers' rights as human rights,[13] which we can question. The underlying moral justification of human rights can help us identify which workers' rights should be classified as human rights. Miller suggests that the right to be remunerated according to what has been agreed in an employment contract is not a human right. Is this correct? Can someone

[10] Ibid 196.

[11] Joseph Carens, *The Ethics of Immigration* (Oxford, Oxford University Press, 2013) 114.

[12] *Juridical Condition and Rights of the Undocumented Migrants*, Advisory Opinion OC-18/03, 17 September 2003, Inter-AmCtHR (Ser A) No 18 (2003). For a note, see Sarah H Cleveland, 'Legal Status and Rights of Undocumented Workers' (2005) 99 *American Journal of International Law* 460.

[13] See Hugh Collins, 'Theories of Rights as Justifications for Labour Law' in Guy Davidov and Brian Langille (eds), *The Idea of Labour Law* (Oxford, Oxford University Press, 2011) 137; Virginia Mantouvalou, 'Are Labour Rights Human Rights?' (2012) 3 *European Labour Law Journal* 151.

have a human right to what has been agreed by contract? The answer to this question depends on the justification of human rights. I have previously argued that workers who are not paid in accordance with their employment contract are possibly being exploited.[14] If one justification of human rights is the protection of individuals from exploitation by employers, migrant workers may be entitled to be paid in accordance with their contractual terms. A further question to address is what is meant by workers' exploitation. For present purposes, the definition of exploitation that I am using has three elements: (a) vulnerability of the worker, which has been created or exacerbated by law, (b) abuse of this vulnerability, and (c) an aim to make a profit.[15] A broader conception of workers' rights as human rights that regards the prohibition of exploitation as a justification of certain human rights could require the employer to pay the worker in accordance with the contractual agreement.[16] There is no reason to believe that the prohibition of exploitation should apply to citizens only, and not to everyone.

If we turn to international human rights law for guidance on which workers' rights are universal human rights, the UN Convention on the Rights of Migrant Workers and Members of their Families recognises a range of rights of seasonal workers.[17] In 1949, the ILO adopted the Migration for Employment Convention (Revised) 1949 (No 97), to which it later added the Migrant Workers (Supplementary Provisions) Convention 1975 (No 143). These two conventions are applicable to everyone who is a 'migrant for employment'.[18] That term is defined to mean a person who 'migrates from one country to another with a view to being employed otherwise than on his own account'. It follows that the conventions do not contain a blanket exclusion of temporary migrant workers from their scope.[19]

The Universal Declaration of Human Rights (UDHR) contains several labour rights that everyone has, without distinguishing between

[14] Virginia Mantouvalou, 'The Right to Non-Exploitative Work' in Virginia Mantouvalou (ed), *The Right to Work: Legal and Philosophical Perspectives* (Oxford, Hart Publishing, 2015) 39.

[15] Ibid 48 ff.

[16] Ibid.

[17] UN Convention on the Rights of Migrant Workers and Members of their Families, adopted by General Assembly Resolution 45/158 of 18 December 1990, article 59.

[18] See art 11 in each case. Note that Convention No 143 contains a significant caveat. The definition covers only Pt II of the Convention, which concerns rights of equal treatment.

[19] For discussion and analysis of the protection of migrant workers in international labour law, see Leah Vosko, 'Out of the Shadows? The Non-Binding Multilateral Framework on Migration (2006) and Prospects for Using International Labour Regulation to Forge Global Labour Market Membership' in Langille and Davidov (eds), *The Idea of Labour Law* (n 13) 365; Shauna Olney and Ryszard Cholewinski, 'Migrant Workers and the Right to Non-Discrimination and Equality' in Cathryn Costello and Mark Freedland (eds), *Migrants at Work* (Oxford, Oxford University Press, 2014) 259; Bernard Ryan and Virginia Mantouvalou, 'The Social and Labour Rights of Migrants in International Law' in Ruth Rubio-Marín (ed), *Human Rights and Immigration* (Oxford, Oxford University Press, 2014) 177.

non-nationals and nationals. It provides that everyone has a right to work, to free choice of employment, to just and favourable conditions of work, and to protection against unemployment;[20] everyone has a right to equal pay for work of equal value;[21] everyone has a right to just remuneration that guarantees a right to dignity for the worker and his or her family, which may be supplemented by welfare support;[22] and everyone has a right to be a trade union member.[23] It also provides for a right to holidays with pay. In relation to this latter right, it has been argued that a right to holidays with pay is not a basic human right.[24] However, it is important to appreciate that

> the full right recognised is a right to 'rest, leisure, and reasonable limitation of working hours and periodic holidays with pay'. Denial of this right would indeed be a serious affront to human dignity; it was, for example, one of the most oppressive features of unregulated nineteenth-century capitalism.[25]

The question of which labour rights are human rights, in other words, brings to the surface issues of human rights theory on the justification of workers' rights, as well as human rights practice and the content of legal documents. There is scope for analysis and cross-fertilisation between theory and practice.[26] On the basis of both theory and practice, it can fairly be argued that Miller adopts an unduly narrow conception of labour rights as human rights.

B. Consent

A second, related point stemming from Miller's analysis involves the weight to be given to consent of the workers to working conditions that, in his view, are not classified as human rights. First, we should appreciate that some temporary migrant workers (and some migrant workers more generally) escape living and working conditions in their home country that are such that make it very questionable how free they have been in agreeing to migrate and work in the conditions that they do. A subcategory of migrant workers are considered today to be in fact victims of trafficking which means that they may have been forced to migrate by being deceived or otherwise coerced.

[20] See UDHR art 23(1). See also the analysis in Hugh Collins, 'Is There a Human Right to Work?' in Virginia Mantouvalou (ed), *The Right to Work: Legal and Philosophical Perspectives* (Oxford, Hart Publishing, 2015) 17.

[21] UDHR art 23(2).

[22] UDHR art 23(3).

[23] UDHR art 23(4).

[24] Maurice Cranston, *What are Human Rights?* (London, Bodley Head, 1973) 66–67.

[25] Jack Donnelly, *Universal Human Rights*, 2nd edn (Ithaca, NY, Cornell University Press, 2003) 28.

[26] On the role of human rights practice in developing human rights theory, see Allen Buchanan, *The Heart of Human Rights* (Oxford, Oxford University Press, 2013).

The law on human trafficking makes the worker's consent irrelevant for this reason.[27] Some temporary labour migration regimes may be particularly open to abuse by those who want to traffic migrant workers. These issues will be explored in the section that follows on modern slavery.

III. MODERN SLAVERY

One of the most famous temporary labour migration systems, for its negative effects on workers' rights, is the *kafala* system in Gulf countries. There are different variations of *kafala* in different Gulf countries. In Qatar, for example, the *kafala* system means that the worker is linked to the sponsoring employer, and cannot work for anyone else or indeed leave the country unless the employer agrees to it. This has been heavily criticised by labour and human rights organisations.[28] The UN Special Rapporteur on the Human Rights of Migrants said:

> The *kafala* system enables unscrupulous employers to exploit employees. Frequent cases of abuse against migrants include the confiscation of passports, refusal to give 'no objection' certificates (allowing migrants to change employer) or exit permits and refusal to pay migrants' plane tickets to return home.[29]

In 2010, the UN High Commissioner for Human Rights urged the Gulf states 'to replace the *kafala* system with updated labour laws that can better balance rights and duties'.[30] A similar regime to the *kafala* has also existed in the UK since 2012. The UK ODW visa does not permit domestic workers to change employer, contrary to the regime that existed before 2012. This change occurred against the background of the so-called points-based system. Under this system, the policy is not to grant visas to low-skilled migrants, which includes domestic workers, who are typically viewed as low-skilled workers.[31] Under the new regime, when migrant domestic

[27] See, eg art 4(b) of the 2005 Council of Europe Convention on Action Against Trafficking in Human Beings.

[28] For criticisms of the *kafala* system in Qatar see, eg ILO Governing Body 320th Session, Geneva, 13–27 March 2014, Report of the Director General. On Saudi Arabia, see ILO Observation (CEACR), adopted 2009, published 99th ILC session (2010), Forced Labour Convention No 29; see also Human Rights Watch, *'I Already Bought You'—Abuse and Exploitation of Female Migrant Domestic Workers in the United Arab Emirates* (New York, Human Rights Watch, 2014).

[29] Report of the Special Rapporteur on the human rights of migrants, François Crépeau, on his mission to Qatar, 3 to 10 November 2013, para 25.

[30] Navanethem Pillay, 'Human Rights and the Gulf Region', address by UN High Commissioner for Human Rights, Jeddah, Saudi Arabia, 19 April 2010.

[31] Bridget Anderson, *Us and Them* (Oxford, Oxford University Press, 2013) 175. See further discussion of the system in Martin Ruhs, *The Price of Rights: Regulating International Labor Migration* (Princeton, NJ, Princeton University Press, 2013) 92.

workers arrive lawfully in the country accompanying an employer, their visa status ties them to this employer.[32] Their residency status is lawful only for as long as the employer with whom they entered employs them, up to a maximum of six months. The six-month period is not renewable. I will return to this later on in this chapter.

Both the *kafala* system and the UK ODW visa system have been criticised for leading to situations of slavery.[33] In relation to my previous discussion of human rights of temporary migrant workers, few would disagree about the nature of the prohibition of slavery, servitude, and forced and compulsory labour as a labour right, which is also a human right. The tendency to examine migrant workers' rights in the context of slavery has partly been triggered by judicial decisions of human rights monitoring bodies that examined the concepts of slavery, servitude, and forced and compulsory labour in order to consider whether the living and working conditions of migrant workers could fall in this category. These bodies have addressed restrictions of the freedom of migrant workers through the lens of the prohibition of slavery, servitude, and forced and compulsory labour, and have revived scholarly interest that has explored the relevance of the prohibition to the modern employment relation. The European Court of Human Rights (ECtHR) has played an important role in this context. The ECHR prohibits slavery, servitude, and forced and compulsory labour (article 4). For many years, the ECtHR rejected applications by individuals who claimed that they were victims of a violation of article 4. This changed in 2005 when the ECtHR started exploring the prohibition in a series of cases that involved migrant workers.

In the case law of the Court, immigration status has played an important role in the determination of whether someone's working conditions violate the prohibition of slavery, servitude, and forced and compulsory labour. The case *Siliadin v France*[34] was not about a temporary migrant worker but a migrant domestic worker who was undocumented, and a minor at the time that she was exploited by her employers. The Court explained that the applicant's situation could not be classified as slavery because there was

[32] See Immigration Rules, 159A–159H, https://www.gov.uk/guidance/immigration-rules/immigration-rules-part-5-working-in-the-uk.

[33] On the *kafala* system, see, eg UN Human Rights Council, *Report of the Special Rapporteur on Contemporary Forms of Slavery, Including its Causes and Consequences*, 18 June 2010, paras 47–48. On the UK system, see Bridget Anderson, *Britain's Secret Slaves: Migrant Domestic Workers in the UK* (London, Anti-Slavery International, 1993); Daphne Demetriou, '"Tied Visas" and Inadequate Labour Protections: A Formula for Abuse and Exploitation of Migrant Domestic Workers Under a Tied Visa in the United Kingdom' (2015) *Anti-Trafficking Review* 69; Mantouvalou, 'Am I Free Now?' (n 1).

[34] *Siliadin v France* App No 73316/01, 26 July 2005. See Virginia Mantouvalou, 'Servitude and Forced Labour in the 21st Century: The Human Rights of Domestic Workers' (2006) 35 *Industrial Law Journal* 395.

no legal right of ownership over her in French law, but that it constituted 'servitude', which also fell within the scope of article 4 of the ECHR. The Court defined 'servitude' as 'an obligation to provide one's services that is imposed by the use of coercion, and is to be linked with the concept of "slavery"'.[35] Factors that contributed to the classification of Siliadin's situation as servitude included her living and working conditions, her fear that was nurtured by her employers, and the facts that her passport had been confiscated and that she was not allowed to leave the household. The legal implication of this classification as a result of *Siliadin* was that France had a positive obligation under the ECHR to criminalise this type of exploitative relationship.

Subsequent case law dealt with a temporary labour migration regime. *Rantsev* involved a young woman from Russia who was brought to Cyprus under an 'artiste visa'. An 'artiste' was defined in the legislation as 'any alien who wishes to enter Cyprus in order to work in a cabaret, musical-dancing place or other night entertainment place and has attained the age of 18 years'.[36] These permits are valid for a period of three months that can be extended for another three months. The establishment owner applies for the visa on behalf of the artiste in question. Under this scheme, Ms Rantseva received a temporary work and residence permit. Having worked at a cabaret for a few days, she escaped, only to be captured soon after and taken to the police. Since her immigration status was not irregular, the police returned her to her employer. Later that night she was found dead on the street below the flat where she was staying. The Court did not distinguish between slavery and servitude here (contrary to *Siliadin*), but said that human trafficking is covered by article 4. In this case, a particular concern was the fact that the cabaret managers made an application for an entry permit for the artiste in a way that rendered the migrant dependent on the employer or agent.

The Court accepted that the artiste visa scheme made individuals vulnerable to traffickers.[37] In addition, it found that the obligation of the employers to inform the authorities if an artiste leaves her employment is a legitimate means to the end of monitoring compliance with immigration law. However, it is only the authorities that should take steps in the event of non-compliance. Monitoring compliance cannot be the duty of the manager. This is why the Court was particularly troubled by the practice of asking cabaret owners and managers to lodge a bank guarantee to be used to cover artistes whom they employed. *Rantsev* shows, then, that a visa regime that is very restrictive and creates strong ties between the worker and the employer,

[35] *Siliadin*, para 124.
[36] *Rantsev v Cyprus and Russia* App No 25965/04, 7 January 2010, para 113.
[37] *Rantsev*, paras 89, 91, 94, 100.

creating the opportunity to exercise great control over her, may breach the Convention.

Two points need to be highlighted here. First, in the rulings of the ECtHR, migration status (either a restrictive visa or the status of someone as an undocumented worker) has emerged as a factor that creates vulnerability to coercion, and to restrictions of freedom that have been classified as slavery or servitude. Second, a further significant feature of this case law is that it comes from work sectors that are precarious, namely domestic work and sex work.

Against this background, it is no coincidence that the UK ODW visa has also been heavily criticised and was described as a visa that can lead to 'modern slavery' in the context of the drafting of the UK Modern Slavery Act 2015. To assess the effects of this visa on migrant domestic workers but also question some of the statements in the earlier section that discussed the consent of workers to their terms of employment, I will use evidence from an empirical research project in which I interviewed 24 migrant domestic workers under the ODW visa and the diplomatic visa, which also ties workers to the employer.[38] The project revealed that the visa regime creates a group of workers who are particularly prone to exploitation and to situations that can be classified as slavery.

Almost all of my interviewees were already migrant workers before they arrived in the UK. Originally, they came from countries in Southeast Asia (such as the Philippines or Indonesia), South Asia (India) or North Africa, and they migrated to work for employers in the Middle East or North Africa. They arrived in the UK from these countries where they were already tied to their employer through the *kafala* system. Some of the interviewees who were migrant workers before arriving in the UK explained that they did not want to come to the UK, but that the employers required them to do so. One of the workers said: 'I did not want to come here. Because her son [for whom they wanted me to work in the UK] is too … I don't like him … his attitude. They forced me to come here.'

In this particular example, the interviewee suggested that the employers abused the overseas domestic worker visa regime, which requires that a worker be already employed for at least 12 months prior to applying for an ODW visa. The employers transferred the worker to another employer (their son in this case) who had not employed the worker before. Similarly, another worker said that the employer brought her to work for his sister who was ill and needed a carer, again breaching the 12-month safeguard. This was contrary to the worker's own wishes, but she reported that she was required to do it because that woman's domestic worker could not

[38] For further discussion of the findings of the interviews see Mantouvalou, 'Am I Free Now?' (n 1).

accompany her for the reason that she had not been working for her for one year (as the ODW visa requires). Other workers said that the employers used to lock them in their flat or in their hotel room while they were in the UK.

The position of these workers can be such that they may agree to contractual terms that they do not fully understand or that they do not understand at all, in circumstances where they have no other options. From my empirical project, it was evident that some of these workers escaped appalling living conditions in their home country, which brought into question whether they had any real choice as to whether to migrate or not and what weight to give to their 'consent' to their employment conditions.[39] For instance, one of the workers whom I interviewed responded to my question about whom she supports in her home country as follows:

> I support my mom. My dad has passed away. My mom pays for medicine because she has problems with her legs. She always has to take this medicine and drink a special kind of milk. We also don't have our own house; we come from another city. We have suffered from the tsunami ... I think about my mom being alone there without family ... My dad died when my mom was pregnant with my brother. Other members of our family have passed away. We don't have any family ... My brother was sick and my mom didn't tell me. She borrowed money from the neighbours. That's why I was working here. I just finished paying the money back for when my brother was in the hospital.

Some of the safeguards that are supposed to be in place to protect workers under the ODW visa are that written terms and conditions need to be agreed between the employer and the worker before entry in the UK. That information is then given to the workers by UK authorities before they arrive so that they are made aware of their rights and how to seek help while in the country.[40] However, it is important to realise that these domestic workers are sometimes asked to sign agreements that they do not understand, which are drafted in a language that they cannot read. In the interviews that I conducted, the few workers who did sign a contract explained that they did not understand it or that the terms of their work did not comply with it in reality. One interviewee said, for example: 'Yes, I saw a paper. But I don't know how to read. So, they gave me a paper and said "sign here".'

On the basis of the above, it is very questionable whether the agreement of the temporary migrant workers to their working conditions should carry much weight in considering the fairness of the particular temporary migration regime. In fact, given the situation of low-skilled migrant workers who

[39] See generally Jeremy Waldron, 'Homelessness and the Issue of Freedom', in Jeremy Waldron, *Liberal Rights: Collected Papers 1981–1991* (Cambridge, Cambridge University Press, 1993) 309.

[40] Home Office, *Statement of Intent: Changes to Tier 1, Tier 2 and Tier 5 of the Points Based System; Overseas Domestic Workers; and Visitors* (London, UK Home Office, 2012).

are employed in precarious sectors, there is a need for further safeguards to protect migrant workers under a temporary work visa.

In addition to the issue of consent, the interviews revealed that migrant domestic workers who are tied to their employer are seriously exploited and sometimes sexually or physically abused. The fact that their visa ties them to their employer means that, if they escape, they become undocumented and are trapped in ongoing cycles of exploitation, an issue that I will discuss further in the section that follows.

IV. THE UK MODERN SLAVERY ACT 2015

Partly in order to address the issues highlighted in the case law of the ECtHR, the UK adopted legislation to address 'modern slavery'. The explanatory notes of the UK Modern Slavery Act 2015 state that

> ... modern slavery is a brutal form of organized crime in which people are treated as commodities and exploited for criminal gain ... Modern slavery, in particular human trafficking, is an international problem and victims may have entered the United Kingdom legally, on forged documentation or clandestinely, or they may be British citizens living in the United Kingdom. Modern slavery takes a number of forms, including sexual exploitation, forced labour and domestic servitude, and victims come from all walks of life.[41]

In response to that, the Modern Slavery Act codifies and consolidates existing offences and increases sentences for most serious offenders. The offences in the Act appear under two headings: first, slavery, servitude, and forced and compulsory labour; second, human trafficking (ss 1–2). Section 1 says:

> A person commits an offence if—(a) the person holds another person in slavery or servitude and the circumstances are such that the person knows or ought to know that the other person is held in slavery or servitude, or (b) the person requires another person to perform forced or compulsory labour and the circumstances are such that the person knows or ought to know that the other person is being required to perform forced or compulsory labour.

In determining whether the offence has been committed, the Act also says that regard must be had to all circumstances, including personal circumstances, that make someone vulnerable, as well as the type of work that the person is required to do, particularly exploitative work.[42] It also explains that the person's consent is irrelevant.

The provision on human trafficking in the Modern Slavery Act provides as follows: 'A person commits an offence if the person arranges or facilitates

[41] Explanatory Notes, para 4.
[42] Section 3 of the Act defines exploitation.

the travel of another person ("V") with a view to V being exploited' (s 2). Consent is again made irrelevant. The greatest difficulty with the above offences involves enforcement, so the Act introduces certain provisions aiming to address this. It introduces Slavery and Trafficking Prevention and Risk Orders, sets up the institution of an Anti-Slavery Commissioner, and contains certain provisions on protection of victims. It also includes a section on businesses and transparency in global supply chains.

The Act explains that the section on slavery, servitude, and forced and compulsory labour must be construed in accordance with case law of the ECtHR under article 4 of the ECHR, which was discussed earlier. This is, in any case, an obligation under the UK Human Rights Act 1998, which incorporates the rights of the Convention in English law.

The Modern Slavery Act was described by the Home Secretary, Theresa May, as a 'historic milestone' that 'sends the strongest possible signal to criminals that if you are involved in this vile trade you will be arrested, you will be prosecuted and you will be locked up. And it says to victims, you are not alone—we are here to help you.'[43] But this celebratory tone has not been shared by everyone. Cathryn Costello, for instance, observed that the Act 'exemplifies the tendency to obscure labour law concerns ... The criminal law approach focuses on the outcome (the forced labour itself), rather than understanding the laws, practices, and regulatory gaps that set up the vulnerability to forced labour.'[44]

A further source of scepticism is that the UK ODW visa remained unchanged under the Modern Slavery Act 2015, even though it became a crucial political issue and severe criticisms were expressed at various stages of the parliamentary debates during the drafting of the Act.[45] Can it be said that the ODW visa can lead to slavery or servitude in line with the ECHR case law described above and in breach of the Modern Slavery Act? In a manner similar to the Cypriot artiste visa, the UK ODW visa and diplomatic visa do not create a legal right of ownership of the employers over the workers. However, many of the domestic workers I interviewed in my project reported having been treated like objects and having faced serious coercion. One of the interviewees who did not know that her visa was not renewable

[43] Karen Bradley and Theresa May, 'Historic Law to End Modern Slavery Passed', Home Office, 26 March 2015, https://www.gov.uk/government/news/historic-law-to-end-modern-slavery-passed.

[44] Cathryn Costello, 'Migrants and Forced Labour: A Labour Law Response' in Alan Bogg, Cathryn Costello, Anne Davies and Jeremias Prassl (eds), *The Autonomy of Labour Law* (Oxford, Hart Publishing, 2015) 191.

[45] See Joint Committee on the Draft Modern Slavery Bill, *Report—Draft Modern Slavery Bill* (London, Stationery Office, 2014) 100; House of Commons Public Bill Committee on the Modern Slavery Bill (14 October 2014); Hansard HL col 1853 ff (10 December 2014); Hansard HL col 1689 ff (25 February 2015); Hansard HC col 645 ff (17 March 2015); Hansard HL col 1426 ff (25 March 2015).

and asked her employer to have it renewed was told: 'Who are you? You are just a worker. Don't complain about the visa, otherwise I'll send you back to Indonesia and you will never come to London or Dubai again.'

The domestic workers interviewed used words that conveyed that they felt objectified. They often said that the employers 'brought them' to the country, sometimes against their will, and did not let them leave the household unaccompanied. One of the workers explained that she had previously worked for other employers who had 'transferred' her to the employer with whom she entered the UK. At the airport, upon arrival, the workers suggested that they felt that the employer was in charge of the situation. This sense of objectification may be reinforced by the fact that the visa on the workers' passport mentions the name of the employer. The workers themselves seem to have accepted their objectification, having realised that they have no reasonable alternative exactly because of their great economic need. Even though the employers do not own the employees, they own the employees' right to work, which provides great power of control, akin to chattel slavery.

The UK ODW visa may give rise to a violation of both positive and negative state obligations under the ECHR.[46] Positive obligations under article 4 were first discussed in *Siliadin*[47] and further developed in *Rantsev*. These may, for example, arise when state authorities are

> ... aware, or ought to have been aware, of circumstances giving rise to a credible suspicion that an identified individual had been, or was at real and immediate risk of being, trafficked or exploited ... In the case of an answer in the affirmative, there will be a violation of Article 4 of the Convention where the authorities fail to take appropriate measures within the scope of their powers to remove the individual from that situation or risk.[48]

The reality that some of the interviewees have been recognised as victims of human trafficking reinforces the belief that these visas can raise issues under the convention.

In addition, the restrictions of the visa regime itself can give rise to a violation of the negative obligations under the convention. Here I will focus on state obligations to refrain from action that puts individuals at risk of a violation of human rights. Such a violation would occur, for instance, if a state that imprisons individuals (positive action) does not take further action to ensure that prison conditions are decent and that prisoners are not at risk of abuse. In the case of the visa, the violation of negative obligations arises

[46] On positive obligations, see Dean Spielmann, 'The European Convention on Human Rights, the European Court of Human Rights' in Dawn Oliver and Jörg Fedtke (eds), *Human Rights and the Private Sphere* (London, Routledge, 2007) 427.

[47] See Holly Cullen, '*Siliadin v France*: Positive Obligations under Article 4 of the European Convention on Human Rights' (2006) 6 *Human Rights Law Review* 585.

[48] *Rantsev* (n 36) para 286.

because the visa restrictions lead workers to be undocumented, and hence further prone to exploitation, exactly because of their undocumented status. Many of the workers interviewed reported being exploited by employers after they became undocumented and said that their undocumented status made them more vulnerable to exploitation. Moreover, there is little that they can do to hold the new employers to account, not only because they are very fearful, as emerged from this study, but also because of their undocumented status.[49]

Despite the fact that the ODW visa can be classified as a visa that may lead to situations of slavery, the House of Commons rejected an amendment to the Modern Slavery Bill proposed in the House of Lords which would have protected migrant domestic workers admitted to the UK under the ODW visa. Baroness Butler-Sloss called the proposed amendment 'almost blackmail'[50] because of the perceived risk that the Bill would be entirely blocked as a result of the disagreement between the two Houses on the issue of the amendment to the ODW visa. Lord Hylton proposed Amendment 72 which provided a number of legal protections, including a right to change employer and to renew the visa for consecutive periods of twelve months. The amendment was rejected by the House of Commons, however, which replaced it with a clause that gives domestic workers that have been formally identified as victims of trafficking or servitude a possibility of being granted a six-month visa as a domestic worker with no recourse to public funds.[51] Given the fear that these workers experience and the fact that almost none of them wish to go to the authorities while their immigration status is not secure, it is unlikely that the new provision will help address their plight.[52]

V. VICTIMS OR WORKERS?

Scholars have criticised some of ECHR article 4 decisions for their focus on slavery, instead of a broader conception of workers' rights as human rights.

[49] See *Hounga v Allen and Another* [2014] UKSC 47 on appeal from [2012] EWCA Civ 609. For analysis, see Alan Bogg and Sarah Green, 'Rights Are Not Just for the Virtuous: What *Hounga* Means for the Illegality Defence in the Discrimination Torts' (2015) 44 *Industrial Law Journal* 101.

[50] Hansard HL col 1436 (25 March 2015).

[51] Modern Slavery Act 2015 s 53. The government also set up an independent review of the ODW visa by barrister James Ewins.

[52] See also Immigration Law Practitioners' Association, 'Briefing for Ping Pong, Modern Slavery Bill, House of Commons', 17 March 2015, http://www.ilpa.org.uk/resources.php/30797/ilpa-briefing-for-ping-pong-modern-slavery-bill-house-of-commons-16-march-2015; Immigration Law Practitioners' Association, 'Briefing for Modern Slavery Bill Ping Pong, House of Lords Overseas Domestic Workers', 23 March 2015, http://www.ilpa.org.uk/resources.php/30835/ilpa-briefing-for-modern-slavery-bill-ping-pong-house-of-lords-overseas-domestic-workers-25-march-20.

It has been suggested that an implication of these decisions is that states need to criminalise the employers' conduct. This is partly correct, but this requirement to criminalise misplaces the focus from more general issues of workers' rights.[53] If the sole means to address the exploitation of vulnerable migrant workers under a temporary visa is the criminalisation of the employer's conduct, the response will be unduly narrow. Criminalising the employer may be important symbolically. However, enforcing criminal law in situations such as that of migrant domestic workers is challenging. Most of the workers are fearful of the authorities, as my interviewees stressed, because the conditions of their visa mean that they will be undocumented if they are no longer employed, and that they will be deported. The Modern Slavery Act does little to empower domestic and other migrant workers. It recognises some limited rights to 'victims' of slavery, but says nothing of workers' rights more broadly. It overlooks the fact that many of these workers are vulnerable to situations of slavery exactly because of the law: because they are trapped in a restrictive migration regime, are employed in a precarious sector, and are also excluded from other labour protective legislation. Domestic workers are already in a situation of 'legislative precariousness',[54] which means that they are excluded from labour protective legislation. Examining their condition solely through the lens of slavery, without further extending the protection of their labour rights, such as a minimum wage or working hours, is insufficient.

However, on the basis of the ECHR and human rights law more generally, the consequences of classifying an exploitative employment relationship as slavery or servitude are not limited to criminalisation. The ECtHR has said that 'the duty to penalise and prosecute trafficking is only one aspect of member states' general undertaking to combat trafficking. The extent of the positive obligations arising under Article 4 must be considered within this broader context'.[55] Following *Rantsev,* there should be a requirement that the current very restrictive visa regime be abolished.

A temporary labour visa does not have to lead to situations of slavery, of course, if the right conditions are set. What are the safeguards that need to be in place in order to protect these workers from severe exploitation? Domestic workers must have a right to change employers and remain in the UK. This right should not be conditional on exploitation or abuse, contrary to what Carens has argued. Making the right to change employer conditional on abuse or exploitation would probably make it ineffective, because

[53] Janie A Chuang, 'Exploitation Creep and the Unmaking of Human Trafficking Law' (2014) 108 *American Journal of International Law* 609; Hila Shamir, 'A Labor Paradigm for Human Trafficking' (2012) 60 *UCLA Law Review* 76.

[54] Virginia Mantouvalou, 'Human Rights for Precarious Workers: The Legislative Precariousness of Domestic Workers' (2012) 34 *Comparative Labor Law and Policy Journal* 133.

[55] *Rantsev* (n 36), para 285.

it would be very difficult to prove the abuse, particularly for workers employed in the household of the employer. In order for domestic workers to be able to find new employment as domestic workers, they need to have a right to stay for long periods if employed, as they did before 2012. The ratification of ILO Convention No 189 on Domestic Workers (2011), which contains many labour rights, is also very important, both symbolically and practically.[56] In addition, it should be appreciated that a change in the law that would no longer tie the worker to a particular employer would not be sufficient without further safeguards in place; employers may be prepared to break the law, as some already do. One additional safeguard may be the provision and renewal of a special ID card or visa, which the employee would collect personally from the authorities, unaccompanied by their employers.[57] A personal interview in this process can help review living and working conditions. Additionally, the requirement that the employers open a bank account in the sole name of the domestic worker and make payments in that bank account (rather than in cash) can also help guarantee that the worker is paid, and that the payment is in accordance with the law.[58] Other safeguards should include information and a contract in a language that the domestic worker can understand.

Protections such as the above can protect temporary migrant workers from the worst forms of labour exploitation that may nowadays be classified as slavery. In addition to this, however, it is necessary to examine the labour rights of temporary migrant workers more broadly.

VI. CONCLUSION

This chapter examined temporary labour migration and modern slavery. It first placed temporary labour migration in a broader context of the discussion of labour rights as human rights. It then turned to the prohibition of slavery, servitude, and forced and compulsory labour in human rights law, in order to examine how this has dealt with migrant workers in a

[56] On the ILO Convention on Domestic Workers, see Einat Albin and Virginia Mantouvalou, 'The ILO Convention on Domestic Workers: From the Shadows to the Light' (2012) 41 *Industrial Law Journal* 67; Adelle Blackett, 'The Decent Work for Domestic Workers Convention and Recommendation 2011' (2012) 106 *American Journal of International Law* 778; Sandra Fredman, 'Home from Home: Migrant Domestic Workers and the International Labour Organisation Convention on Domestic Workers' in Cathryn Costello and Mark Freedland (eds), *Migrants at Work* (Oxford, Oxford University Press, 2014) 399; Martin Oelz, 'The ILO's Domestic Workers Convention and Recommendation: A Window of Opportunity for Social Justice' (2014) 153 *International Labour Review* 143.

[57] Organisation for Security and Co-operation in Europe, *How to Prevent Human Trafficking for Domestic Servitude in Diplomatic Households and Protect Private Domestic Workers* (Vienna, OSCE, 2014) 37.

[58] Austria has such a system. See OSCE, ibid 36.

precarious position. The UK Modern Slavery Act was also examined. The Act left unprotected one of the most vulnerable groups of workers, migrant domestic workers under a temporary visa, even though their situation can be classified as slavery, servitude, or forced and compulsory labour. The employers of these domestic workers own not the employees themselves, but the employees' right to work. This gives the employers unprecedented power to control these precarious workers. I have argued that criminalisation of slavery, servitude, and forced and compulsory labour may be a necessary consequence when classifying an employment relation as such. It is important symbolically, and may also be important practically, if properly enforced. However, it is not sufficient. Slavery legislation as a response to the plight of temporary migrant workers treats them as victims, rather than workers who have labour rights that must be protected. The legislation is extremely difficult to enforce when the worker is tied to an employer, because of the fear of deportation. This is why temporary labour migration regimes in precarious sectors can only be acceptable if the worker can freely change employer.[59]

[59] See also James Ewins, *Independent Review of the Overseas Domestic Worker Visa* (London, UK Government, 2015). This report was commissioned by the government in the context of the Modern Slavery Act. It recommends a universal right to change employer for UK overseas domestic workers.

11

The Regulation of Temporary Immigration as Part of New Forms of the Supply Chain

Segmenting Labour Rights for Workers

JULIA LÓPEZ LÓPEZ

I. INTRODUCTION

THE REGULATION OF immigration—itself a complex phenomenon that is strongly shaped by global capitalism and transnational corporations—is one of the most fundamental challenges to face societies in recent decades. Poverty and wars have increased the movement of people from their countries of origin, as they try to improve their living conditions. Regulating the vast worldwide pattern of movement of human beings is a challenge that presents us with multiple dimensions (ethics, human rights, social and labour rights) and choices that have implications for the way we organise our societies in the future. Multiple actors and institutions participate in shaping immigration policies, a significant component of which is constituted by labour law. In labour law's increasingly global scenario, a central challenge is to limit the power of corporations[1]—for example by guaranteeing certain minimum labour standards for all[2]—and if this objective is to be met the input of all these actors is necessary.

[1] See Richard M Locke, *The Promise and Limits of Private Power: Promoting Labor Standards in a Global Economy* (Cambridge, Cambridge University Press, 2013). See also Jeffrey Neilson, Bill Oritchard and Henry Wai-cung Yeuug, 'Global Value Chains and Global Production Networks in the Changing International Political Economy: An Introduction' (2014) 21 *International Review of Political Economy* 1.

[2] See Daniel Berliner, Anne Regan Greenleaf, Milli Lake, Margaret Levi and Jennifer Noveck, *Labor Standards in International Supply Chains: Aligning Rights and Incentives* (Cheltenham, UK, Edward Elgar, 2015).

I argue that the temporary migration effect forms part of the economically driven 'supply chain'. Temporary migrant workers move from their countries of origin at the periphery of the modern organisation of production systems, to countries more central to it in recurring but bounded periods of time, perpetuating their status as migrants. Seasonal migrants whose temporary status is strongly shaped by this transnational logic are part of the global 'commodity chain'.[3]

The crucial issue is not only where the worker is located geographically at any one point in time, but also from an economic standpoint the insertion of these workers into the production system and the way in which local providers sell the resulting products of their labour to large corporations. In Spain, these large corporations are predominantly food companies. Similar examples are to be found elsewhere. In the US, for instance, the Temporary Agricultural Worker Program H-24 farmers complain that they have to pay for workers' housing, transportation, visas and other fees which—they assert—make the programme uncompetitive, given the alternative option of employing undocumented farm workers who lack such minimal forms of support. Farm owners also claim that the time it takes to process requests for temporary migrant status has created a serious 'undersupply' of workers during the harvest season.[4]

The temporary status of such migrant workers has important consequences for social rights. Both the growing segmentation of labour status and the flexibility that employers have pursued are reflected in the regulation and labour conditions of migrant workers. The frontier between informality and formality constitutes a challenge for regulatory systems. In the case of temporary migrant workers, the price paid for regulations that eliminate workers' prior irregular status is the reduction of their fundamental rights. Temporary migrant workers are formally recognised, but they lack many fundamental rights previously understood to be linked to formal recognition as a legal immigrant. This points to the importance of reconstructing the overall legal order shaping workers' rights both nationally and internationally in order to forge a complete strategy to guarantee human rights for all, including migrant workers.

The instruments regulating migrant labour are very complex and multilayered, and include international, European Union and national regulations, incorporating not only hard law but also soft law and hybrid arrangements.

[3] The term 'commodity chain' is from Gary Gereffi and Miguel Korzeniewicz, *Commodity Chains and Global Capitalism* (West Port, CT, Praeger, 1994).

[4] Jeff Dayton-Johnson, Antje Pfeiffer, Kirsten Schuettler and Johanna Schuwinn, 'Migration and Employment' in OECD, *Promoting Pro-Poor Growth: Employment* (Paris, OECD, 2009) 161.

The evolution of the regulatory role of the ILO and its standards provides an illustration of this. As well as the conventional role of the ILO's labour standard setting instruments of conventions and recommendations, the ILO has adopted a broad co-ordinated approach to regulation as reflected in its strategic agendas. The ILO has also worked with other international agencies to embed labour standards in a broad range of other soft regulatory instruments. For example, the Fundamental Principles and Rights at Work identified in the ILO's 1998 Declaration of the same name,[5] have been incorporated into the United Nations' 'Global Compact'.[6] This soft regulatory mechanism is aimed at, amongst other things, improving labour conditions for all and especially those workers employed by corporations operating in a transnational context.

The ILO's Declaration on Fundamental Principles and Rights at Work (1998) and the Declaration on Social Justice for a Fair Globalisation adopted by the International Labour Conference of the ILO in 2008 and its follow-up agenda establish some of the primary points of reference for the framing of migration policy at the international level.[7] The declarations have set a common floor of rights for all actors and institutions integrating justice as part of a global strategy to guarantee fair standards and labour rights for all. The United Nations' Global Compact aims to implicate corporations in the call to recognise fundamental rights for all. This soft law initiative complements the ILO conventions and is intended to be integrated in this broader framework as part of the multi-level global effort to guarantee workers' rights. The Decent Work Agenda is another important part of the ILO's constellation of strategies, presenting labour rights as human rights in the current geography of labour law.[8] From this standpoint, the treatment of migrant workers is relevant not only for the debate on employment policies, but also for defining freedoms and rights, and for tying these concepts to the many levels of labour law.[9]

At the international level, the ILO has played a major role since 2004 in championing a fair deal for migrant workers through an equality and

[5] ILO Declaration on Fundamental Principles and Rights at Work (1998), http://www.ilo.org/declaration/thedeclaration/textdeclaration/lang--en/index.htm.

[6] For information on the Global Compact see www.unglobalcompact.org.

[7] See also ILO, 'Fair Migration: Setting an ILO Agenda', Report of the Director-General (Report I(B)) to the International Labour Conference, 103rd session, Geneva, June 2014. Information about the Declaration on Social Justice for a fair Globalization and its follow-up can be found at http://www.ilo.org/global/about-the-ilo/mission-and-objectives/WCMS_099766/lang--en/index.htm.

[8] See ILO, 'Decent Work Agenda', http://www.ilo.org/global/about-the-ilo/decent-work-agenda/lang--en/index.htm.

[9] See Federico Fabbrini, 'The Constitutionalization of International Law: A Comparative Federal Perspective' (2013/14) 6(2) *European Journal of Legal Studies* 7.

rights-based approach.[10] The ILO reaffirmed this approach at the 2014 International Labour Conference, contributing to a strengthened multilateral labour rights agenda on migration.[11] The ILO Conventions No 97 and No 143 on migration should be interpreted within this frame of reference. Yet, as has been pointed out for some time, the situation of migrants poses major difficulties which are not easily addressed by the regulation of temporary migrants.[12] These problems include the dependence of labour markets on the presence of migrants—employers assume they will be available when markets need them—and the dependence of migrants' families and communities on remittances sent home by migrant workers.

II. EUROPEAN UNION REGULATION OF MIGRATION: A CONTRADICTORY AND UNBALANCED FRAMEWORK FOR MIGRANT WORKERS' FUNDAMENTAL RIGHTS

In recent decades, the European Union has been facing a humanitarian crisis especially in the southern rim member countries—Spain, Italy and Greece—because of the massive and tragic arrival on Europe's southern coast through irregular means of people displaced by wars, poverty and environmental disasters. The Member States are not able to resolve this challenge alone because national instruments are insufficient. This situation highlights the reality that migration is not only an employment issue and underscores the significance of conditions in countries of origin.

In the European Union, the regulation of temporary migration has been developed on the basis of the principles of subsidiarity and proportionality which underpin the relations between the European Union and its Member States: article 5 of the Treaty on European Union defines the division of competences between the Union and Member States.[13] This determines to what extent the EU can exercise the competences conferred upon it by the treaty. By virtue of the principle of proportionality, the means implemented by the EU in order to meet the objectives set by the treaty cannot go beyond what is necessary.

[10] See International Labour Office, *International Labour Migration: A Rights-Based Approach* (Geneva, ILO, 2010). This report was largely based on ILO, 'Towards a Fair Deal for Migrant Workers in a Global Economy', Report VI, 92nd International Labour Conference, June 2004. See also ILO, 'Resolution Concerning a Fair Deal for Migrant Workers in a Global Economy', 92nd International Labour Conference (June 2004).

[11] See ILO, 'Fair Migration' (n 7).

[12] See Philip Martin, 'Managing Labor Migration: Temporary Workers Programmes for the 21st Century', paper presented at International Symposium on International Migration and Development, Population Division, Department of Economic and Social Affairs, UN Secretariat, Turin, Italy, 28–30 June 2006 (UN/POP/MIG/SYMP/2006/07).

[13] See consolidated versions of the Treaty on European Union and the Treaty on the Functioning of the European Union [2012] OJ C 326/13.

At a general level, in the European Union, the principles for regulating freedom of movement are clear: the first one is the freedom of movement for European citizens as part of the constitutional foundation of the EU model embodied by the treaty and its norms. This recognises the right of citizens and their family members to move and reside freely within the territories of all Member States. The second principle is to control the entry of non-nationals into the European Union. Unsuccessful policies on protection and asylum and the mass influx of displaced persons—such as Directive 2013/32/EU[14] and Council Directive 2001/55/EC[15]—reveal that a fundamental goal for the European Union is to guarantee another (albeit implicit) approach, namely the marketisation of migration policies in order to supply markets with a flexible labour force. These predominant principles put in place a contradictory framework for migration which combines on the one hand hard and soft law on migration and asylum as well as the rights of reunification of families with, on the other hand, security and terrorism strategies. This contradictory framework has created separate worlds for immigrants and citizens, and inside the definition of migrant, it has forged a status distinction between long-term residents and short-term residents including seasonal workers.

The European Union's hard law regulation guarantees freedom of movement for European Union citizens, a provision that has encouraged a new form of mobility.[16] The freedom of movement for citizens is reinforced by norms on co-ordination of social security systems, based on fundamental principles: the principle of equal treatment, the principle of cross-country aggregation of periods of social security enrolment, the non-overlapping of benefits, and the co-ordination of instruments in social security systems.[17] This regulation on combining social security coverage in different Member States applies to all nationals of an EU country who are or who have been covered by the social security legislation of any one of those countries, as well as to members of their family and their survivors. It also applies to third-country nationals living legally in the EU whose situation connects them to several Member States.

[14] Directive of the European Parliament and of the Council of 26 June 2013 on common procedures for granting and withdrawing international protection [2013] OJ L180/60.

[15] Council Directive of 20 July 2001 on minimum standards for giving temporary protection in the event of a mass influx of displaced persons and on measures promoting a balance of efforts between Member States in receiving such persons and bearing the consequences thereof [2001] OJ L212/12.

[16] See Treaty on the Functioning of Europe art 45 on freedom of movement of workers. See also Torben Krings, Elaine Moriarty, James Wickham, Alicia Bobek and Justyna Salamonska, *New Mobilities in Europe: Polish Migration to Ireland Post-2004* (Manchester, Manchester University Press, 2013).

[17] Regulation (EC) No 883/2004 of the European Parliament and of the Council of 29 April 2004 on co-ordination of social security systems [2004] OJ L166/1.

For third-country citizens, the European Union has developed the necessary legal basis for measures covering various areas of immigration policy. The European Commission has adopted a community approach because the decision to admit third-country nationals into the territory of any one Member State inevitably affects the other Member States, and yet each Member State determines the number of third-country nationals that it will admit.[18]

The European Union, despite directives on reunification of families, treats the regulation of migrants in a contradictory manner, often shaped by employment policy or security issues. Contradictions in the European Union approach to migration emerge when we examine the complete set of migration regulations and related European Union norms. In the case of seasonal workers and temporary migrants, the differences between their treatment and that of European Union citizens and residents emerge very clearly—condemning temporary migrant workers to a very precarious status.

Reflecting this problem, the European Trade Union Confederation (ETUC) is critical of the European Union's handling of migrants, arguing that its policy is oriented towards guaranteeing a workforce for the labour market.[19] The European trade unions have pointed to international instruments such as the Declaration of Philadelphia, which articulates the view that labour is not a commodity,[20] and the resolution concerning a fair deal for migrant workers in a global economy adopted by the ILO in 2004.[21] This resolution calls for a rights-based approach to labour migration, insisting that migrant workers are entitled to fundamental rights. The ETUC defends the principles of equality and non-discrimination, along with practical measures such as training. It articulates these goals from the perspective offered by the capability approach within the more holistic frame of the fight against xenophobia.[22]

III. FLEXIBILITY AND MARKETISATION: TRENDS IN EUROPEAN UNION MIGRATION POLICIES AND THEIR IMPACT ON SEASONAL MIGRANT WORKERS IN SPAIN

To understand the approach towards temporary migrants in the European Union, it is necessary to mention two major documents underpinning

[18] Regulation No 1030/2002 of the Council of 13 June 2002, laying down a uniform format for residence permits for third country nationals [2002] OJ L157/1.

[19] European Trade Union Confederation, 'The ETUC Asks to Stop the Intra Corporate Transfer Directive: Posting of Workers from Third-Countries is Unacceptable Without a Full Equal Treatment Provisions in Favour of Migrants', media release, 6 February 2014.

[20] See Declaration of the Aims and Purposes of the International Labour Organization (Declaration of Philadelphia 1944), annex to the ILO Constitution.

[21] See n 10 above.

[22] ETUC Strategy and Action Plan 2011–2015.

policy: the Green Paper on an EU approach to managing economic migration[23] and the Green Paper on modernising labour law.[24]

On 10 January 2005, the European Commission launched the Green Paper on managing economic migration which set down the main principles for regulating immigration. Despite the EU Commission's acceptance of the competence of Member States to determine the number of third-country nationals that they can admit, the Commission proposed a common approach to national migration policies. This Green Paper serves as a primary reference point to understand the European Union's migration policies and to identify their significance for employment policy, the segmentation of workers' (and migrants') status and the diversification of rights. The main foundation of EU migration policy is the community preference principle. It establishes that when a Member State considers requests for admission to its territories for the purpose of employment, migrants can only be hired when vacancies in a Member State cannot be filled by workers belonging to any of the following groups: nationals, the nationals of other EU Member States, and non-EU nationals who are already residents of the EU on a permanent basis, thus forming part of the Member State's regular labour market. This principle creates a different status for migrants depending on whether or not they have documentation to support their entry to the Member State and the length of their stay. This differentiation reflects a strategy to guarantee a workforce for the labour market, while at the same time trying to ensure that it is only what is truly necessary for the labour market. The directives on the right to family reunification and the status of long-term residents have to be read in this context.[25]

Beyond this combined soft and hard law regulation of migration, a crucial point of reference is an element of policy that has brought about the segmentation of migrant statuses. This is the policy on temporary contracts. The Green Paper on modernising labour law set out a model of regulation of industrial relations for Member States. This model included the individualisation of labour law, the temporary contract as a foundation of the system, the promotion of self-employment, the flexibility of labour conditions and the flexible termination of contracts. The soft law orientation provided by the Green Paper has been used to change hard law within Member States. The European Union Strategies of Employment 2020 and the Open Method of Co-ordination have provided a model for domestic

[23] European Commission, 'Green Paper on an EU Approach to Managing Economic Migration' COM(2004) 811.

[24] European Commission, 'Green Paper on Modernising Labour Law to Meet the Challenges of the 21st Century' COM(2006) 708.

[25] See Council Directive 2003/86/EC of 22 September 2003 on the right to family reunification [2003] OJ L251/12; Council Directive 2003/109/EC of 25 November 2003 concerning the status of third-country nationals who are long-term residents [2004] OJ L16/44.

national regulation of temporary contracts and precariousness—elements that generate contradictions with the hard European labour law which prohibited chains of temporary contracts.[26]

In the framework described, the European Union Strategies of Employment 2020 created a model of flexisecurity based on the fusion of mechanisms of flexibility and security as part of the general policies on employment, reacting against elevated levels of unemployment in the European Union. Flexisecurity is defined as a high level of flexibility, both internal and external, involving a liberalisation of the termination of contracts, balancing the *flexibility* of transitioning between jobs with the *security* provided by employment training and substantial unemployment benefits in the hope of increasing employability. This strategy was expected to be applied by the Member States.

The flexisecurity model was successfully applied in Austria. However, it did not have the same results in other countries, such as Spain, where the level of unemployment is very high and where the implementation of this approach lacked the security element, resulting in a model of flexiprecarity.[27] Temporary migrant work has to be read in this context.

The European Union has also regulated temporary work under two main principles: the first is the prohibition of discrimination between temporary and non-temporary workers; and the second is the prohibition of chains of temporary contracts which create a vicious circle of precarity.[28] Temporary migrants are considered under the regulatory approach of the European Union as short-term residents. They are condemned to be migrants on an interminable basis because the definition of this category of temporary workers is that they are residents of their countries of origin and they have to return there after each period of work. In this sense, these workers suffer a double segmentation of status because they are both migrants and temporary workers. They are not European citizens and they are not long-term residents, nor will they be in the future. On the other hand, they have no permanent contract and they have even more precarious conditions in labour and pensions than the local temporary workers. A multiple segmentation of status and a crossroad of temporary contracts creates a permanent limbo for these workers both in terms of their labour rights and their social security benefits.

[26] Council Directive 1999/70/EC of 28 June 1999 concerning the framework agreement on fixed-term work concluded by ETUC, UNICE and CEEP [1999] OJ L175/43.

[27] See Julia Lopez, Alexandre de le Court and Sergio Canalda, 'Breaking the Equilibrium between Flexibility and Security: Flexiprecarity as the Spanish Version of the Model' (2014) 5 *European Labour Law Journal* 18.

[28] Council Directive 99/70/EC of 28 of June 1999, concerning the framework agreement on fixed-term work conclude by ETUC, UNICE and CEEP [1999] OJ L175/43.

The European Union's system of regulating temporary migration thus offers a mix of very contradictory policies, some of which approach migration from a human rights perspective, and some of which treat the migrant as a commodity. The document that should be the basis for this policy, the Charter of Fundamental Rights of the European Union,[29] has been marginalised by Member States in the application of the European Union system. The charter recognises workers' individual and collective rights and welfare state benefits which are applied to temporary migration in, among other cases, Spain.

IV. THE REGULATION OF TEMPORARY SEASONAL MIGRATION IN SPAIN: THE IMPLEMENTATION OF THE FLEXIPRECARITY MODEL

The European Union has pressured Spain to enact important changes in labour market regulation, supposedly implementing the flexisecurity model, but the result has been a case of flexi*precarity* characterised by an increase in both internal and external flexibility without guarantees of mechanisms of security in employability, for example through training. Moreover, the security offered by unemployment benefits has been reduced. The flexibility provided by new forms of temporary contracts and other measures facilitating the termination of labour contracts has not been matched by improvements in security. This backdrop helps to contextualise the regulation of seasonal migrants in the Spanish labour market. The treatment of these temporary migrants and their role in the system have formed part of broader dynamics with very severe consequences for labour rights in recent decades.

Temporary migrant workers in Spain are concentrated in the agricultural sector. Within the Spanish economy as a whole, unemployment is, along with Greece, the highest in the European Union. Regional unemployment rates varied widely across the 272 regions of the EU in 2014, with the lowest rates recorded in the regions of Praha in the Czech Republic and Oberbayern in Germany (both 2.5%) followed by Tübingen, Oberpfalz, Niederbayern and Unterfranken (all below 3.0%) in Germany, while the highest rates were registered in the Spanish regions of Andalucía (34.8%), the Canarias (32.4%), Ceuta (31.9%), Extremadura (29.8%) and Castilla-la Mancha (29.0%).[30] All these regions have temporary migration, but it is also important to point out that the crisis has inverted the orientation

[29] [2000] OJ C364/1.

[30] Eurostat Statistics Explained, 'Unemployment Statistics at Regional Level', April 2015, http://ec.europa.eu/eurostat/statistics-explained/index.php/Unemployment_statistics_at_regional_level.

of migration in Spain. The country is now experiencing a net outflow of migration. The extraordinarily high rate of unemployment has created an outflow of highly educated young Spaniards to different countries of the European Union. The balance of the geography of migration has changed, as Figure 11.1 shows.

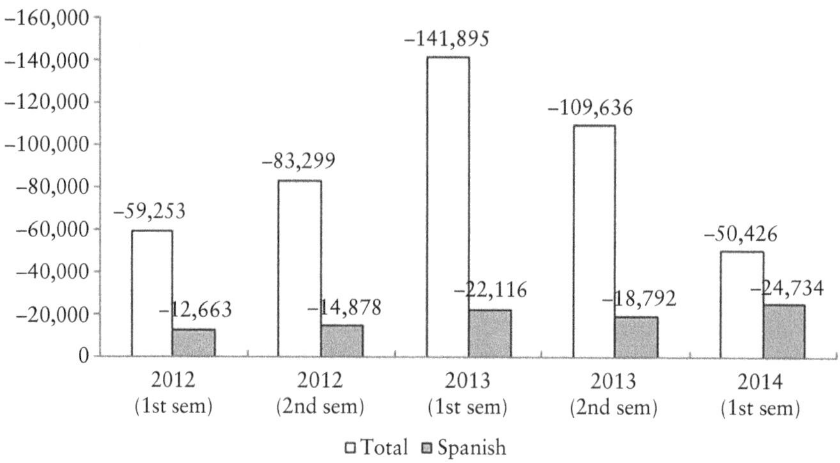

Figure 11.1: Net Migration, 2012–2014[31]

Beyond the unemployment rate, the Spanish labour market has other problems: it is fragmented and the regulation of labour status and workers' rights is segmented, as a comparative analysis with other national cases shows.[32] In Spain, the evolution of the legal concept of worker and employee has generated a broad spectrum of statuses and has created a segmentation of social rights which goes further than the concept of segmentation of labour markets as such, challenging the identity of labour law. Who are the subjects of fundamental labour rights that labour law guarantees for all? One inevitably confronts this question in analysing the situation in Spain. The integration of migrants within the concept of the worker has to deal with the complex regulation of labour markets configured by differential status linked to the type of work contract and, in the case of migrants, country of origin, especially for non-resident workers. Another important element of the model of regulation of seasonal workers in Spain concerns the multi-level

[31] Source: own elaboration of data from Spanish Ministry of Labour and Employment, 2014.

[32] See Julia Lopez, 'Segmentation and the Debate on Labor Law' (2015) 36 *Comparative Labor Law and Policy Journal* 177.

nature of public administration in the process of admission of migrants. The Comunidades Autonomas decide with the central state the number of immigrants who are to be admitted.

Within Spanish regions tensions have emerged over the overlapping of new migration with high unemployment. Andalucía and Cataluña are the regions which have received the most seasonal migrant workers in the agricultural sector and they have high levels of unemployment. The crisis has had an important impact on the map of migration. Spain dramatically reduced the number of visas issued to seasonal workers after 2009.[33] Local workers have occupied the jobs that were traditionally held by third-country citizens. The economic crisis has generated several types of change, including increasing informality in the sector, with informal workers from Africa competing with local workers, and with a decline in salaries and labour conditions. Tensions are increasing in regions such as Andalucía because the lower number of seasonal migrant workers has been replaced by more informal workers competing with local workers with low salaries and labour conditions.

The difficult question to resolve is how it is possible to create a sustainable system of regulation for migrant workers which recognises their labour rights as part of the larger subject matter of human rights. The framework underpinning the Spanish regulatory system for seasonal migration involves integrating all the elements of multi-level instruments. Among the components of this complex process of integration, the ILO conventions play an important role along with soft law instruments such as the Fair Globalisation Strategy and the Global Compact, which commit signatories to the project of construction of human rights. Within Spain, article 10.2 of the Constitution establishes the applicability of all rights included within the UN Declaration of Human Rights. Moreover, Spain has ratified ILO Convention No 97 on migration and is obliged to respect its content. Spain has also ratified a very large number of ILO conventions,[34] including the eight fundamental ones. Thus, international legal standards are incorporated within the Spanish system.

The complex practice of migration can only be adequately regulated through collaboration between receiving countries and countries of origin. Agreements pursuant to this principle have integrated the realities and specificities of the regions hoping to reduce the traffic of human beings. Spain has signed different Co-operation Framework Agreements on

[33] See European Migration Network, *Temporary and Circular Migration: Empirical Evidence, Current Policy Practice and Future Options in Spain* (Brussels, European Migration Network, 2010).

[34] Spain has ratified 133 ILO conventions, 87 of which are currently in force.

immigration[35] with countries of origin and agreements to control the migratory flux into Spain.[36]

As noted above, another crucial principle is that of subsidiarity and proportionality. Spain is part of the European Union and thus EU norms apply. A crucial factor for Spain is the implementation of Directive 2014/36/EU on the conditions of entry and stay of third-country nationals for the purpose of employment as seasonal workers.[37] The directive sets the floor of regulation for Member States and leaves them to develop their own policy. The directive opens the possibility for seasonal workers who are already in an EU Member State to extend their work contract or change their employer at least once, provided they fulfil the entry conditions and there are no applicable grounds for refusal. This creates a continuity in the status of migrant workers through a chain of contracts with the same or different employers.

Within the maximum period of stay, Member States may allow more than one extension of the contract with the same employer as well as the conclusion of contracts with more than one different employer. With this norm, the European Union promotes *circular migration*, involving the re-entry of third-country nationals who return every year to the EU to do seasonal work.

The legal treatment of seasonal migrant workers is internally contradictory: the directive recognises that seasonal workers are entitled to equal treatment with nationals of the host Member State at least with regard to terms of employment, including the minimum working age, working conditions, including pay and dismissal, working hours, leave and holidays, and health and safety requirements in the workplace. Equal treatment with nationals also applies to certain branches of social security (benefits linked to sickness, invalidity and old age). But because of the temporary nature of the stay of seasonal workers, Member States are *not* obliged to apply equal treatment on unemployment and family benefits and can limit equal treatment on tax benefits and on education and vocational training. Seasonal workers also have the right to join a trade union and are entitled to access social security, pensions, training, advice on seasonal work offered by employment offices, and other public services, except for public housing.

[35] Spain has signed Co-operation Framework Agreements with: Guinea Bissau (Official Bulletin of 3 June 2009); Niger (Official Bulletin of 3 July 2008); Mali (Official Bulletin of 4 June 2008); Cabo Verde (Official Bulletin of 14 February 2008); Guinea (Official Bulletin of 30 January 2007); and Gambia (Official Bulletin of 9 October 2006).

[36] Spain has signed agreements with: Ukraine (Official Bulletin of 10 August 2011); Mauritania (Official Bulletin of 30 October 2007); Dominican Republic (Official Bulletin of 5 February 2002); Morocco (Official Bulletin of 20 September 2001); Ecuador (Official Bulletin of 10 July 2001); and Colombia (Official Bulletin of 4 July 2001).

[37] Directive 2014/36/EU of the European Parliament and of the Council of 26 February 2014 on the conditions of entry and stay of third-country nationals for the purpose of employment as seasonal workers [2014] OJ L94/375.

The assumption that temporary contracts limit rights, with the excuse of the economic crisis, has permitted the conversion of these workers into a cheap labour force. These workers in effect form part of the global supply chain along with local and long-term migrant workers, but they do not have the same rights as those other workers. Spanish regulation weakens the social rights of this group.

These principles have to compete with the EU's flexisecurity model, which aims to guarantee an equilibrium between markets and rights. This equilibrium is not present in the directive because no training or unemployment benefits are provided for seasonal workers. Thus, the legal treatment of seasonal migrant workers in effect breaches the main principle of EU regulation which is equality and non-discrimination.

What are the concrete implications of this overall set of factors for the regulation of migrant seasonal workers in Spain? The relevant Spanish regulation is contained in the Law 'Orgánica' on rights and freedoms of foreigners and their social rights in Spain (last version LO 10/2011 and Regulation 16/2012), Regulation 557/2011 of 20 April 2011 (last version Regulation 844/2013) and Order ESS/25005/2014 on contracts for migrants in their own country. The main feature of these norms is informed by the principle of commodification of labour: the temporary seasonal workers visa requires such workers to have a labour contract. They are only authorised to stay in the country for the period of the labour contract. The workers can be hired for a specific service, for professional training, or temporary labour contracts for artists or professional athletes, with a limited duration of 12 months stay.

The limit for labour contracts is 9 months in a period of 12 months. Temporary migrants are not eligible for unemployment benefits. This clearly runs counter to the flexisecurity model as these workers experience flexible work without the mechanism of security. They have a special agreement for social security protection which creates a different status than local temporary workers. As noted above, temporary migrants do not have unemployment benefits. The employer has to pay the travel expenses and housing for seasonal migrant workers. Housing must be of a standard that respects the dignity of the worker and meets basic conditions of health and safety. It is the obligation of the employer to guarantee the return of the seasonal worker to their country of origin when the labour contract expires. This is a very important point because it guarantees that if the worker does not return to their country of origin their status will be unauthorised.

The process of hiring seasonal workers in their countries starts with an application to the Employment Public Service and the Employment Service of the Comunidades Autonomas. National residents have preference for any job vacancies. If there are insufficient national residents interested in being hired, the administration sends the hiring task to the Employers Association. The Employers Association then requests the administration to issue labour contracts for temporary migrant workers. The request for temporary residency and labour contracts for seasonal migrants is made by employers to the administration. The period of residency is to be the duration of the labour contract, which is a maximum of 9 months. It is possible to extend this period in extraordinary circumstances, but if the extension is longer than 12 months the employer has to prove that this extension is necessary to finish the job.

The regulation of seasonal and temporary migrant work creates a very precarious status for these workers. The temporary contract and the promise to return to their country of origin leaves these workers without a future in which to improve their labour and social conditions. The shortfall that these persons have in social protection is not justified because of their status as temporary workers. From the perspective of the principles articulated in EU regulations—namely integration, collaboration, subsidiarity and proportionality as well as equal treatment and non-discrimination—the fundamental rights of these immigrants are not guaranteed. The result is also negative from the perspective of the flexisecurity model, implemented in the European Union through soft law regulation, because the mechanism of security is not applied to these immigrants. In this case, the discriminatory model is actually promoted by the European Union and spread by the subsidiarity principle.

The lack of unemployment protection and family pensions is not justified taking account the period of the contracts: 9 months in a period of 12 months is a long expanse of time for a temporary contract, with the possibility left open in the directive and in the Spanish regulations to extend this initial period to 12 months or exceptionally beyond that time frame. The fact that the employer has to guarantee the return of the immigrant to their country of origin when the labour contract ends, even though the immigrant can return every season to work in Spain, underscores the point that the regulation treats temporary migrants as a commodity in the production system.

Nonetheless, it is important to acknowledge that the regulation of temporary migration has improved the transition between informal and formal work. This is a great achievement but at the same time this process has increased the segmentation of labour rights, creating a corpus of regulation specific to seasonal migrant workers but with important consequences for all workers. The spill-over generated by this added segmentation of regulations has negative consequences for the hiring process of all workers and also for labour conditions—especially in regions such as Andalucía and Cataluña with very high unemployment rates.

Current labour law regulation in Spain, especially the Legal Market Reform of 2012,[38] has weakened the role of collective rights—the crucial

[38] Legal Market Reform 3/2012 of 6 July 2012, Official State Journal, 7 July 2012.

mechanism that labour law provides to counteract the private power of corporations. The individualisation of labour conditions, the promotion of company-level collective bargaining reducing the sectoral level of negotiation, and the lack of co-ordination of units all combine to worsen living and working conditions for all. This general deterioration of course includes temporary migrants—who are especially affected—and increases inequality in society.

The 2012 reform has increased internal flexibility through mechanisms that augment the unilateral power of the employer, thus tending to de-contractualise labour law. The reform has reduced the role of collective bargaining. Under the flexisecurity model, the reform has facilitated the termination of labour contracts, again augmenting unilateral employer power. Yet Spanish training measures fail to provide security. The clearest example is the training contract for young people. This has generated a de facto increase in age discrimination both in working conditions and social security protection (especially pensions). Unemployment benefits are decreasing because of the reduction of beneficiaries and payment amounts.

The individualisation of labour conditions, the expansion of temporary contracts and the diminishing power of unions due to the reform have worsened the segmentation of labour statuses. For temporary workers, the 2012 attempt to weaken the role of sectoral bargaining in the industrial relations system leaves them with diminished protection. This has increased the polarisation of labour conditions between fixed-term workers and temporary ones.

The 2012 Labour Market Reform in Spain adopted a model of collective bargaining that restricts the application of expired collective agreements during negotiations of new ones (called a period of 'ultra-activity') by introducing a maximum period of one year after which an expired collective agreement ceases to apply. This reduces the possibility of extending agreements, thus diminishing their role as a source of regulation.

The reaction of courts applying the reform has been diverse. The Tribunal Supremo (Supreme Court), in a judgment of 22 December 2014, qualified the effects of the end of the application of expired collective agreements by ruling that before the agreement expires its conditions are incorporated into the workers' individual contracts.[39] Therefore, those conditions continue to apply as individual contractual conditions after the period of 'ultra-activity', even if the collective agreement has ceased to be applicable.

On the other hand, the important case law Judgment no 8/2015 of 22 January 2015 of the Constitutional Court declares Law 3/2012

[39] Case-law of the Supreme Court no 264/2014 of 22 December 2014.

reforming Spanish labour law to be in conformity with the Constitution. The constitutional challenge was directed, among other things, against the infringement of the constitutional fundamental right of trade unions to collective bargaining and the constitutional right to collective bargaining, involving the autonomy of workers and employers in concluding collective agreements. These issues were raised because the 2012 reform allows unilateral modification by the employer of work conditions contained in collective agreements, obligatory arbitration in case of disagreement about the temporary suspension of the application of a collective agreement in the company and provides a preference for the application of company-level agreements in certain matters. Departing from its traditional approach of assessing whether the essential content of constitutional and fundamental rights has been affected, the Court justified the restriction of those rights by referring to the intended objective of employment creation expressed in the preamble of the law. It held that the regulation is not irrational with regards to those objectives (without assessing whether those measures effectively contribute towards those objectives) and that the restrictions are accompanied by appropriate procedural or material limits (economic, production or technological causes for unilateral modification and suspension, and conciliation and mediation procedures before obligatory arbitration). The judgment of the Constitutional Court was accompanied by an important dissenting opinion which heavily criticised both the material content of the judgment as well as its constitutional methodological approach.

This legal reform has created a map of precarious regulation for all workers but especially temporary migrant workers. This constellation of changes adverse to workers' interests and rights was the consequence of the implementation of European Union policies and austerity programmes. The austerity plan involved cutting the budget for unemployment benefits and the welfare state, creating a scenario in which local workers and workers in irregular situations compete with temporary migrants to obtain jobs. The policy design was premised on the goal of providing a large pool of cheap labour for export-oriented activity but clearly not on guaranteeing labour rights for migrant workers under the standards of the Decent Work Agenda of the ILO.

V. POLICIES OF DE-COMMODIFICATION OF TEMPORARY IMMIGRATION: A MULTI-LEVEL APPROACH

In the face of the current tendency towards the commodification of labour law—focusing increasingly on market-based logics instead of rights—it is important to forge countervailing responses to market abuses and to guarantee fundamental rights for all workers, including temporary migrant workers. This objective would be served by integrating the instruments of the multi-level legal system—which emphasise human rights—within the legal handling of seasonal migrant workers in Spain. The overall set of hard and soft law instruments of relevance is quite large—including ILO conventions, the Decent Work Agenda, hard European Union law such as regulations and directives, including those concerning equality and discrimination, the norm on temporary contracts prohibiting the abuses of chains of contracts, and the Charter of Fundamental Rights. These legal instruments should be applied in the way article 10.2 of the Spanish Constitution sets down.[40] The main strategy to de-commodify migration is to approach regulation as a way to guarantee fundamental rights and not as a way to promote the functionality of markets.

In this vein, the Charter of Fundamental Rights offers seasonal migrant workers a floor which should be respected under the solidarity principle. The charter consolidates an interpretation of solidarity as being embodied in collective labour law, incorporating freedom of association, participation, collective bargaining and the right to strike in the definition. Solidarity also is reflected in welfare state protection, as recognised in the Decent Work Agenda which understands that decent work implies an extension of social security protection. The concept of solidarity also includes protection against unfair dismissal. Decent work implies equality and non-discrimination, participation, and welfare state protections. These global soft law instruments offer a foundation for the protection of labour rights. The test which is implicitly set up by this international soft law is not incorporated into the regulation of temporary migration in Spain. Principles such as integration, collaboration, subsidiarity, and equality and non-discrimination should be observed in the construction of seasonal migrants' rights—but that is not the case in Spain. By way of contrast, Sweden regulates temporary migrant workers in a way that permits them, after a period of time with temporary residence, to apply for permanent residency. Comparative labour law models, such as this one, can help.[41]

The lack of commitment of all actors including governments, unions, NGO actors and consumers to guaranteeing minimal standards[42] is a major failure of migration policies. Under the principles set down in the Decent Work Agenda, which include equality and non-discrimination, the elimination of child labour, participation and the extension of social security benefits, the policies on temporary migrant workers set down by the European Union and Spain are unsuccessful.

[40] See Ruth Dukes, *The Labour Constitution: The Enduring Idea of Labour Law* (Oxford, Oxford University Press, 2014).

[41] See generally Matt Finkin and Guy Mundlak (eds), *Comparative Labour Law* (London, Edward Elgar, 2015).

[42] Berliner et al, *Labor Standards in International Supply Chains* (n 2).

The tension between markets and rights as the basis for formulating migration policy emerges clearly in the case of social rights and their encounter with economic pressures. Seasonal workers are one of the cases that challenge the frontier between informal and formal work as part of the identity of labour law. The movement of workers from their countries of origin to work for local suppliers of global corporations questions the classic definition of the supply chain which implies that workers participate in the production process without migrating. This approach is supported because the migrants are, in our case study in Spain, being denied some fundamental rights integrated in the European Union's framework and in national legal systems. Migration status is created in Spain as a separate group of norms that ignores the overall framework of the legal system composed by international, European Union, Spanish constitutional and other norms.

The Decent Work Agenda as a minimal floor creates a standard of minimal protection, but European Union and Spanish regulation does not respect this floor. Immigration should occupy a primary place in the political agenda and not only in the newspapers, with their constant reminders of the fight of human beings to cross the borders between states to find a better life for themselves and their families.

12

Regulating Temporariness in Italian Migration Law

VERONICA PAPA

I. INTRODUCTION

THIS CHAPTER EXAMINES economic migration, and more specifically the role of labour law in regulating labour migration in Italy. Before analysing the Italian legal framework surrounding migration, however, it is worthwhile making some preliminary remarks about the semantic and methodological premises underlying it.

First, immigration is a pluralistic notion. When used as a singular noun, immigration (especially in the context of economic migration) might be assumed to be a simple and unitary phenomenon. On the contrary, it is a very complex issue, both because of the existence of various levels of regulation and on account of the multifaceted nature of migratory flows.

It is also important to note that, while the right to enter and stay in Italian territory is governed by national legislation, other aspects of migration are regulated at a sub-national or regional level.[1] On this point, the Italian Constitutional Court has stated on more than one occasion that the discipline of immigration is not restricted to entry and stay in the state, but extends into other aspects of this phenomenon—such as social assistance, education, health and housing—in which there are overlapping national and regional legislative competences.[2] In fact, in recent years one of the most significant aspects of migration policies has been the increasingly prominent role of the regions in developing policies for the integration of migrants.

[1] According to art 117 of the Italian Constitution, 'the State has exclusive legislative powers' in the matters of 'immigration' (lett b) and of 'right of asylum and legal status of non-EU citizens' (lett a).

[2] See, eg Constitutional Court 7 July 2010, no 269; Constitutional Court 18 October 2010, no 299; Constitutional Court 21 February 2011, no 61.

Seen from another perspective, however, given that migration law constitutes a typical area of interaction between different levels of governance, it cannot be approached without considering the supranational level of regulation on this subject. Within the context of European integration, immigration is an area of common policy as set out in article 79 of the Treaty on the Functioning of the European Union (TFEU).[3] Hence, even though EU legislation still covers only limited, and mostly sectoral, areas that are probably meant to remain weakly regulated—due to overlapping national vetoes—the existence of a supranational (European) legislative competence in relation to the immigration of third-country nationals cannot be ignored.

In addition, the geographic and temporal proximity of the dramatic drownings of shipwrecked migrants attempting to cross the Mediterranean Sea makes it all the more difficult to focus merely on labour migration. Moreover, within the context of mass exoduses, the notion of labour migration is becoming increasingly hybridised with those of refugees or asylum seekers (often escaping contemporaneously from poverty, conflicts and persecution). Recognising the growing awareness of the multidimensionality and transversal nature of migration, this chapter will provide an overview of the Italian legal framework for labour migration.

At this point, it should also be stated that Italian migration law does not expressly provide for a framework with which to manage temporary or circular migration. The notion of temporary labour migration, which is subject to intense scrutiny by many national parliaments, cannot simply be transposed into the Italian legislative context. In this context, the notion of temporary migration needs to be examined from two perspectives. On the one hand, the temporary nature of the period of access to the labour market of host countries—typically regulated by temporary migration programmes—can be compared to the temporariness of the residence permit system elaborated by the Italian legislature and its functional correlation to the demands of the national labour market. On the other hand, another regulatory aspect of Italian law, which in some respects is comparable to the notion of temporary labour migration, is the seasonal workers residence permit.

This chapter will focus principally on the most critical points of Italian law regarding seasonal labour migration. However, as many of these points also relate to the regulation of labour migration generally, as opposed to the specific domain of seasonal work, part of this chapter will also be devoted to analysing the general failure of the inspirational vision underlying the Consolidated Law on Immigration.

[3] Consolidated Version of the Treaty on the Functioning of the European Union [2012] OJ C326. TFEU art 79 states: 'The Union shall develop a common immigration policy aimed at ensuring, at all stages, the efficient management of migration flows, fair treatment of third-country nationals residing legally in Member States, and the prevention of, and enhanced measures to combat, illegal immigration and trafficking in human beings'.

II. LABOUR MIGRATION IN ITALIAN LAW: AN OVERVIEW

As indicated above, many of the failings of the legislation on the migration of third-country nationals are not limited to seasonal work migration, but apply equally to the overall legal framework for labour migration. The core contents of the legal framework of labour migration are set forth in the Consolidated Law on Immigration.[4]

Italian law requires that employment contracts for migrant workers respect the principles of equality and non-discrimination. The principle of equal treatment for migrants at work is derived from numerous regulatory sources. First of all, article 10 of the Constitution, which provides that the legal status of foreigners shall be regulated by law in conformity with international law and treaties, refers to the international laws on migrants' equality.[5] Secondly, article 15.3 of the Charter of Fundamental Rights of the European Union states that 'nationals of third countries who are authorised to work in the territories of the Member States are entitled to working conditions equivalent to those of citizens of the Union'. Accordingly, article 2 para 3 of the Consolidated Law on Immigration guarantees migrants who are legally resident in the state territory 'equal treatment and full equality of rights equivalent to Italian workers'. So, while Italian legislation allows specific (and not equality-oriented) regulations in relation to access to the labour market for third-country nationals, a robust multilevel legislative framework ensures non-discrimination towards legally resident migrants.

Despite this formal declaration of equal treatment and rights, in practice, the relevance of these provisions remains rather limited. Given that, under the current system of admission to Italian territory, the right to equal working conditions is enforceable only with regard to regular migrants, and considering that the condition of being a regular migrant depends on the pre-existence of an employment contract, the whole area seems to be a vicious circle, which amplifies the risks of exploitation, generating and perpetuating the irregular status of many migrants. This may in part explain why studies of economic migration[6]—a theme often neglected by labour

[4] Consolidated Law on Immigration, Legislative Decree no 286/1998 (Consolidated Act of Provisions concerning immigration and the condition of third country nationals), which has been subject to several reforms in recent years.

[5] In particular, to art 8 of the ILO Convention No 143 (1975) Concerning Migrations in Abusive Conditions and the Promotion of Equality of Opportunity and Treatment of Migrant Workers. According to this provision, 'on condition that he has resided legally in the territory for the purpose of employment, the migrant worker ... shall enjoy equality of treatment with nationals in respect in particular of guarantees of security of employment, the provision of alternative employment, relief work and retraining'.

[6] Laura Calafà, 'Stranieri tra politiche e diritti dopo Lisbona: la stagione degli ossimori?' (2011) 3 *Lavoro e diritto* 527; William Chiaromonte, *Lavoro e diritti sociali degli stranieri: Il governo delle migrazioni economiche in Italia e in Europa* (Padova, Giappichelli, 2013).

law scholars—focus on migrants' access to the national labour market rather than on employment contracts for non-EU citizens. For the same reason, this analysis will focus mainly on the admission system for labour migration, which is indeed the area in which most legal disputes concerning the legal status of foreign migrant workers arise.[7]

A. The 'Impossibility' of Labour Migration: Conditions of Access to Work for Third-Country Nationals

In addition to questions about the effectiveness of the legal framework of protection of migrant workers,[8] the operational dysfunctions of the Consolidated Law on Immigration are mainly connected to the regulation of admission to the national labour market.

Before discussing seasonal employment for migrants, the analysis will focus on the (general) legal mechanism of access to the labour market, for two reasons. First, as anticipated above, most of the inconsistencies of Italian migration law relate not only to the specific question of seasonal work, but also, more generally, to the regulatory paradigm on which the law is based. Secondly, even if the notion of temporary/circular migration is not used by Italian legislation, and even if this topic is almost neglected by Italian labour law scholars, the entire admission system—especially subsequent to the amendments introduced by the so-called Bossi-Fini law[9]—appears to be constructed around a concept of 'temporariness'.

Temporary labour migration can be approximately defined—based on the various semantic interpretations proposed by different legislative texts—as migration 'with the intention that afterwards there will be a return to the country of origin'.[10] This concept of temporary stay seems to underpin current Italian migration law. In fact, considering the system of admission

[7] That does not mean that the issues related to residence contracts for dependent employment are irrelevant here. As Calafà noted, this contract can be positively defined as an 'impossible employment contract', with regard to the qualities of its 'counterparts, its contents, the context surrounding it, for the objectives that it should be pursuing, but mostly, because of the impossibility of classifying it under the traditional labour law canons'. Laura Calafà, *Migrazione economica e contratto di lavoro degli stranieri* (Bologna, Il Mulino, 2013) 120.

[8] On the ineffectiveness of the formal equality conditions see, among others, Emanuele Galossi, Salvo Leonardi and Francesca Carrera, *Combating Discrimination against Migrant Workers: Making Industrial Relations Work for Decent Work. Briefing on the Situation in Italy* (Paris, IRES, 2013).

[9] Law no 189/2002—commonly known as 'Bossi-Fini' after the names of the two Italian politicians who proposed it—introduced multiple modifications to the previous legislative framework on immigration and right to asylum.

[10] European Migration Network, *EMN Asylum and Migration Glossary 3.0* (Brussels, European Migration Network, 2014) 281.

to state territory and employment, it can be inferred that there is a legislative bias towards temporariness.

In this sense, the notion of temporary migration can be easily compared to the Italian approach to migration as a whole. The inclusion criteria adopted by Italian legislators are to a certain extent comparable to the German concept of guest worker (*gastarbeiter*).[11] Briefly, a 'guest worker' can be loosely considered as a 'transitory guest', whose presence in the state territory is inextricably linked to the demand for labour, and who must be repatriated to their country of origin upon termination of the employment relationship. This is very similar to the notions applied in Italian migration law. In fact, this assumption clearly underlies the legislative intent to cover national labour shortages, as the legislative provisions make the issue of a residence permit strictly conditional upon the existence of a valid employment contract.

The same legislative bias towards temporariness is also quite apparent in the (exclusionary) model of integration chosen by the Italian legislature in the preferential regulation of seasonal workers permits and the various forms of restriction of access to social rights for migrant workers (with specific regard to the exclusion of migrants from non-contributory welfare benefits).[12] The current legal framework of economic migration is, therefore, tied to two key principles: (i) the stipulation of annual maximum entry quotas based on nationality;[13] and (ii) the establishment of a binding nexus making the issue of a residence permit conditional upon the existence of a pre-existing employment contract.

Moreover, the effects of the restrictive prerequisites for legal residency in Italian territory are made harsher by misinterpretation of labour market necessities[14] and unreasonable bureaucratic delays in determining residence applications. This ultimately provides a strong incentive for irregular labour migration.

[11] See Armando Tursi, *La riforma della normativa in materia di immigrazione del 2002: una ricognizione critica, tra politica e tecnica legislativa*, Working Paper No 14 (Catania, Centre for the Study of European Labour Law'Massimo D'Antona', 2004).

[12] For a comprehensive approach to this topic, see Chiaromonte, *Lavoro e diritti sociali degli stranieri* (n 6).

[13] The entry quotas are contained in a decree adopted by the Presidency of the Council of Ministers on an annual basis. The decree sets maximum quotas for different types of workers—seasonal, non-seasonal and self-employed—by nationality.

[14] Alberto Guariso, 'Le incrollabili ipocrisie in tema di lavoro immigrato' (2006) 1 *Rivista Critica di Diritto del lavoro* 35. On the constant mismatch between the 'legal hurdles of access to work for migrants ... and the structural demand for migrant workers' as a general feature of the Italian labour migration system, see William Chiaromonte, 'A New EU Legal Regime on Labour Migration? The Italian Implementation of Directives 2011/98, 2009/50 and 2014/36' in R Blanpain, F Hendrickx and P Herzfeld Olsson (eds), *National Effects of the Implementation of Three EU Directives on Labour Migration from Third Countries* (forthcoming).

In fact, on the one hand, the entry quotas established annually by the Italian government often remain below the actual market demand for migrant labour;[15] on the other, the procedure for legally hiring non-EU citizens is particularly long and burdensome (from a purely formalistic perspective, without even taking into account the additional inconveniences and delays that may arise in practice). Under this procedure, an employer needs to apply for a work permit for a migrant, which will only be granted if the application falls within the quota set by the government. Accordingly, an employer submits a proposal for a 'residence contract', and at the same time guarantees to provide suitable accommodation, as well as pay the costs of the return journey for the migrant worker upon termination of the contract (see article 22 of the Consolidated Law on Immigration). Under this regulatory framework, aspiring migrant workers can only legally gain access to Italy if they can show proof of an employment contract with an employer based in Italy.

The inadequacy of this entry mechanism is obvious, as highlighted below. On the one hand, the entire procedure is based on the false assumption that employers are willing to bear all the costs and the bureaucratic burdens arising from this legal mechanism, which in most cases means employing workers that they probably do not even know. According to this procedure, non-EU citizens should still be in their country of origin at the time of the application for 'residence permits' (at this stage, the migrants are in theory still applying for their entry visas). On the other hand, the fallacy of this premise is particularly clear as regards recruitment of unskilled labour. In such cases, as is well-known, from the employer's perspective the individual skills of the particular worker are mainly irrelevant while, on the contrary, other aspects such as the quick or immediate availability of labour are a priority. Hence, it is highly unlikely that employers would be prepared to wait for several months for the unskilled workers to become available for employment; conversely—as very often happens in practice—they can 'informally' hire migrant workers (whether undocumented or with inadequate visas, such as a visa for tourist purposes), and eventually regularise their status at a later date, for example, by taking advantage of the enactment of periodic migration amnesties[16] or waiting for the annual Flows Decree and then applying for a work permit for migrant workers who are actually already employed in Italy. In such cases, once an employer has obtained the

[15] See Amnesty International, *Exploited Labour: Migrant Workers in Italy's Agricultural Sector*, (London, Amnesty International, 2012); European Migration Network-Italy, *Quarto Rapporto EMN Italia: Canali Migratori, Visti e flussi irregolari* (Rome, IDOS, 2012).

[16] In this context, the recurrent use of *ex post facto* regularisation programmes has been read as a functional equivalent of active labour migration policies. See Ester Salis, *Labour Migration Governance in Contemporary Europe: The Case of Italy*, Working Paper (Torino, FIERI, 2012) 30.

work permits (known as a '*nulla-osta*'), the migrant workers need to return to their country of origin to collect their entry visas and then come back to Italy (this time, having in their possession a regular entry visa).

The outcome of this procedure is a glaring example of the failure of the Italian labour market paradigm, since this interferes with market freedom in two ways: (a) by preventing employers from recruiting workers without incurring legislative and administrative burdens (consequently increasing transactional costs); and (b) by generating a competitive disadvantage vis-à-vis Italy's 'competitors' (other countries) who are not burdened by such formalistic constraints when recruiting foreign migrant workers.

As many authors have pointed out, this is one of the weakest points of the entire Italian labour migration system.[17] Paradoxically, the provisions aimed at combating and eliminating illegal immigration have in practice actually created the preconditions for undocumented (and therefore more vulnerable) labour, through the establishment of a mostly impracticable regular migration channel. Ultimately, this keeps migrants in the shadows of the legal labour market.

B. Defining Seasonality? Temporary Migration under the Consolidated Law on Immigration

As anticipated above, the notion of temporary labour migration cannot be automatically transposed into the Italian legal framework for labour migration. In fact, there is no express definition of the concept under the Italian system.

Yet even if the notion of temporary migration is still not legally defined as such, it is nonetheless possible to enumerate several cases in which permits are granted for temporary access at national borders (for instance, for students, researchers, self-employed people and seasonal workers). The most important of these short-term mobility permits, for the purpose of this chapter, is framed by articles 24 and 25 of the Consolidated Law on Immigration in relation to seasonal employment, which establishes a system that can be equated to the concept of temporary labour migration.

According to article 24, a seasonal work permit is valid for a minimum period of 20 days and a maximum of 9 months, depending on the duration of the seasonal work offered. It is possible to change employers during

[17] Compare: Silvana Sciarra and William Chiaromonte, 'Migration Status in Labour and Social Security Law: Between Inclusion and Exclusion in Italy' in Cathryn Costello and Mark Freedland (eds), *Migrants at Work: Immigration and Vulnerability in Labour Law* (Oxford, Oxford University Press, 2014) 122; Monica McBritton, 'Lavoro degli immigrati e lavoro sommerso: l'inadeguatezza della normativa' (2014) 3 *Questione giustizia* 171.

the permitted period of residence in Italy. The procedure for obtaining a residence permit for seasonal work is similar to the one analysed above, regarding residence permits for employment contracts for a fixed-term or indefinite period: even seasonal workers are only granted access to the state territory if they are within the quotas set by the Flows Decree. Moreover, even for seasonal employment, an employer who is willing to hire a non-EU citizen needs to make an application to the local administrative immigration authorities for a residence contract and undertake to comply with all the obligations imposed by article 22 of the Consolidated Law on Immigration (regarding accommodation and repatriation costs for the migrant worker). Once the employer has obtained a work permit, the migrant can apply for an entry visa, which—following his or her legal entry into Italian territory and the conclusion of a residence contract—can be converted into a residence permit.

While establishing a procedural framework for the grant of seasonal work permits, the Consolidated Law on Immigration fails to provide a legal definition of seasonal work, which impacts on the overall rationality of the regulation. Under Italian law, seasonal employment contracts are a subspecies of the more comprehensive legal notion of fixed-term contracts.[18] The distinction between the latter and the seasonal work contract is relevant not only from a theoretical perspective, but also for a number of regulatory reasons (not least on account of the separate entry quota systems for seasonal and non-seasonal employment, and also given the partially differentiated regulation of the right of entry and residence under the seasonal permits system).[19]

The only distinctive parameter indicating the seasonal nature of the activity, as set forth in the annual Flows Decree, is the reference to the sectors in which it is possible to avail oneself of seasonal migrant workers, namely, agriculture and tourism.[20] Yet the effect of this indication, determining which sectors are available for seasonal employment, seems to be undermined by its apparently non-restrictive nature. In fact, further analysis of this provision of the Flows Decree reveals that entry quotas concern '*in particular* the needs of the agricultural and the tourist sectors', (emphasis added) which would seem to suggest that this formulation is in fact more open-ended.

[18] In fact, the legal basis for the definition of seasonal work is contained in the Presidential Decree of 7 October 1963 no 1525 (Presidential Decree that specifies seasonal activities for the purposes of the discipline of the fixed term contract).

[19] The entry quotas for seasonal work are normally set by a separate Flows Decree. For 2015, the entry quotas are set out by the Decree of the President of the Council of Ministers of 2 April 2015, Temporary planning of entry flows for non-EU workers for seasonal employment in state territory.

[20] For 2015, see article 1 of the Flows Decree, ibid.

The ambivalent character of this provision, and hence of the national legislation, could in part be resolved by the supranational regulatory instrument for seasonal employment that will enter into force in 2016 at the European level. Accordingly, the Seasonal Workers Directive provides that 'the Member States shall, where appropriate in consultation with the social partners, list those sectors of employment which include activities that are dependent on the passing of the seasons'.[21] Further definitions of 'seasonality' are contained in the directive. Article 3(c) defines an activity that depends on the passing of seasons as 'an activity that is tied to a certain time of the year by a recurring event or pattern of events linked to seasonal conditions during which required labour levels are significantly above those necessary for usually ongoing operations'. Moreover, according to recital 13 of the directive, 'activities dependent on the passing of the seasons are typically to be found in sectors such as agriculture and horticulture, in particular during the planting or harvesting period, or tourism, in particular during the holiday period'. The transposition of these provisions might encourage Italian legislators to formulate a legal definition of seasonal work under labour migration law, thereby restricting it to a (closed) list of activities.

C. Between Temporariness and Circularity: The Residence Permit for Seasonal Workers under Italian Migration Law

The reasons for having a specific permit for seasonal workers relate to: (a) the need to introduce a faster procedure for issuing work permits (within 20 days[22] after the application being lodged by the employer), and (b) the simplification of some procedural steps, with the introduction, in limited cases, of tacit approval provisions. Under the tacit approval procedure, if the administrative authorities fail to issue a refusal within 20 days from the day on which the application was filed, the latter is considered accepted, but this only applies to workers already authorised in the previous year to carry out seasonal work for the same employer and who will be repatriated on expiry of the permit. Other specific features of the residence permit system for seasonal employment include a right of precedence for the return

[21] Directive 2014/36 of 26 February 2014 on the conditions of entry and stay of third-country nationals for the purpose of employment as seasonal workers [2014] OJ L94/375 (Seasonal Workers Directive) art 2. For a comprehensive analysis of the Seasonal Workers Directive, see Judy Fudge and Petra Herzfeld Olsson, 'The EU Seasonal Workers Directive: When Immigration Controls Meet Labour Rights' (2014) 16(4) *European Journal of Migration and the Law* 439.

[22] As opposed to the maximum period of 60 days contemplated for the issue of work permits for fixed-term or open-ended employment contracts.

to Italy of third-country nationals who worked in seasonal employment in Italy during the previous year and, in such cases, the possibility of converting a seasonal employment residence permit into one for employed work, either for a fixed-term or indefinite period, subject to quotas in the Flows Decree.[23] Finally, an employer may apply for multi-seasonal residence permits, valid for a maximum of three years, for seasonal workers who have worked for them for two consecutive seasons.[24]

Hence, the Italian regulation of seasonal work through residence permits can arguably be defined as a hybridisation of temporary and circular migration models.[25] In fact, on the one hand, the legislative framework for seasonal workers permits shares a common characteristic with temporary migration through the provision of short-term residence permits, which are renewable subject to certain conditions; and, on the other, some of its characteristics are similar to those of circular migration, given that the above-mentioned permits have an 'element of circularity in them, as they allow for repeated back-and-forth mobility over a period of time'.[26]

D. Protecting Seasonal Migrant Workers from Economic and Social Exploitation between National and Supranational Law

As has already been observed, vulnerability is one of the distinguishing features of the status of migrants.[27] This is particularly true with regard to the status of temporary (in Italy, seasonal) migrants. In fact, seasonal migrant worker status has come to serve as an umbrella term that masks various forms of precarity: atypical working contracts, employment in small businesses and in sectors dominated by the shadow economy, and informal labour (which is common in agriculture, the principal sector of seasonal migrant work).

In addition, seasonal migration is often demand-driven, in other words, governed by the needs of the labour market in certain areas and at

[23] Consolidated Law on Immigration art 24 para 4. See also Council of State, s IV, 3 May 2010, no 2498.

[24] Consolidated Law on Immigration art 5 para 3.

[25] See European Migration Network, *Asylum and Migration Glossary 3.0, A Tool for Better Comparability* (Brussels, European Migration Network, 2014).

[26] See European Migration Network, *Temporary and Circular Migration: Empirical Evidence, Current Policy Practice and Future Options in EU Member States* (Brussels, European Migration Network, 2011) 41. On some experiences of circular migration, see Camilla Devitt, 'Circular Economic Migration between Italy and Morocco' in Anna Triandafyllidou (ed), *Circular Migration Between Europe and Its Neighbourhood: Choice Or Necessity?* (Oxford, Oxford University Press, 2013).

[27] See also Costello and Freedland (eds), *Migrants at Work* (n 17).

specific times of the year.[28] In this context, the current Italian regulatory framework—in particular the regulation of admissions and access to the labour market—actually contributes to the employer-driven nature of seasonal migration, given the wording of its legislative provisions, which are couched in such a way that 'the worker's legal status becomes … dependent on the employer'.[29]

If, in general, the legal connection between the residence permit and the employment contract potentially makes foreign workers susceptible to blackmail in the workplace,[30] this risk is further aggravated by the short-term, temporary nature of seasonal migration. In these cases, in fact, the intrinsic temporariness of migration makes the relationship between the non-EU citizen and the host state all the more precarious, as it impacts negatively on the possibility of such migrants achieving a degree of social integration (considered to be a necessary prerequisite for developing awareness of migrants' rights).

As empirical research has shown, the shortcomings of the seasonal permit system (insufficient regular migration channels, time-consuming and bureaucratic procedures, and the lack of availability of permanent regularisation mechanisms) ultimately create the conditions for it to be routinely abused.[31] Due to the legislative symbiosis between legal residence and employment contracts (as discussed above), the work permits system is heavily dependent on recruitment agencies and intermediaries, which in turn makes the system susceptible to the infiltration of illegal intermediaries. From this perspective, the widespread counterfeiting of work permits in practice confirms the inadequacy of the system of access to the national labour market created by Italian legislators. Apart from the existence of illegal forms of intermediation, this kind of work permits system makes the migration process more costly, and creates the additional risk within this hiring mechanism that

[28] Sheena McLoughlin and Rainer Münz, *Temporary and Circular Migration: Opportunities and Challenges*, Working Paper (Brussels, European Policy Centre, 2011) 35. See also Joanna Howe, 'Contesting the Demand-Driven Orthodoxy: An Assessment of the Australian Regulation of Temporary Labour Migration', ch 6 in this volume.

[29] Sciarra and Chiaromonte, 'Migration Status in Labour and Social Security Law' 125 (n 17).

[30] Galossi, Leonardi and Carrera, *Combating Discrimination against Migrant Workers* 5 (n 8).

[31] The ineffectiveness of the seasonal permits system in several areas of Southern Italy was analysed in a study published by the International Organization for Migration. See International Organization for Migration, *Stagione amara: Rapporto sul sistema di ingresso per lavoro stagionale e sulle condizioni dei migranti impiegati in agricoltura in Campania, Puglia e Sicilia* (Geneva, International Organization for Migration, 2010). According to research conducted by Amnesty International, the seasonal permits system is often used as a smuggling and trafficking mechanism, whereby migrants wishing to migrate to Italy can obtain an authorisation to work through friends already in Italy, or buy a permit through trafficking organisations. See Amnesty International, *Exploited Labour* (n 15).

employers 'almost invariably transfer the risks and costs associated with migration back onto the workers themselves'.[32]

Considering that the institutionalisation of the symbiosis between legal residence in the host state and a pre-existing employment contract creates one of the main sources of vulnerability of migrants' legal status, then it is all the more regrettable that this link has more recently been instituted at supranational level too, through the adoption of the Seasonal Workers Directive.[33] In addition to formulating common admission rules,[34] the directive lays down certain provisions that could contribute to improving the working conditions of seasonal migrant workers. Among them, mention should be made of the introduction of compulsory requirements for a 'valid work contract' in article 6. In fact, according to article 6.1, a work contract (or the binding job offer) must include specific details of the job, notably: (i) place and type of the work; (ii) duration of employment; (iii) remuneration; (iv) working hours; (v) the amount of any paid leave; and any 'other relevant working conditions'.[35] In accordance with article 6.2, these working conditions have to 'comply with applicable law, collective agreements and/or practice'. In any case, even if these provisions could have positive ramifications on the legal status and working conditions of seasonal migrant workers, for example, by giving them 'a way to prove the conditions of employment in the event of a dispute', the wording of the directive does not hint at what effects might flow from these documents (in particular, with regard to their enforceability).[36]

Another aspect of the directive that could to a certain extent have positive effects on the Italian legal framework is the facilitation of complaints (article 25). Accordingly, Member States shall ensure that 'effective mechanisms' are in place with which to lodge complaints against employers directly or 'through third parties which have, in accordance with the criteria

[32] See Cathryn Costello, 'Migrants and Forced Labour: A Labour Law Response' in Alan Bogg, Cathryn Costello, Anne Davies and Jeremias Prassl (eds), *The Autonomy of Labour Law* (Oxford, Oxford University Press, 2015) 208. The proliferation of work permit counterfeiting systems confirms the assumption that one of the most vulnerable moments on the way towards labour migration occurs even before the migrant has left his or her country of origin. See Jennifer Gordon, 'Roles for Workers and Unions in Regulating Labour Recruitment in Mexico', ch 15 in this volume.

[33] According to Seasonal Workers Directive art 6 (Criteria and requirements for admission as a seasonal worker for stays exceeding 90 days), in fact, 'applications for admission to a Member State ... shall be accompanied by: ... a valid work contract or ... a binding job offer to work as a seasonal worker in the Member State concerned with an employer established in that Member State'.

[34] Seasonal Workers Directive art 6.

[35] Other conditions imposed by art 6 include the requirement that the application to enter as a seasonal worker is accompanied by proof of having, or having applied for, medical insurance (art 6.1.b); proof of adequate accommodation (art 6.1.c); and proof of adequate financial means without needing to rely on the social security system of the host state (art 6.3).

[36] Fudge and Herzfeld Olsson, 'The EU Seasonal Workers Directive' (n 21) 452.

laid down by their national law, a legitimate interest in ensuring compliance with this Directive, or through a competent authority of the Member State'. In this regard, the directive provides that Member States shall ensure that such legitimate third parties are able to 'engage either on behalf of or in support of a seasonal worker, with his or her approval, in any administrative or civil proceedings'. However, the formulation of this article is ambivalent. On the one hand, the facilitation of complaints provision, especially with regard to the participation of 'third parties' or 'competent authorities' authorised to lodge complaints 'on behalf or in support of a seasonal worker', might effectively improve the enforcement of the directive, by allowing recognised NGOs and associations that protect migrants' rights to provide support and legal assistance to file complaints. On the other, the lack of any provision regarding forms of collective complaints is a glaring omission, given that third parties have been expressly granted a legitimate interest in enforcing the directive. This would, therefore, appear to restrict the applicability of article 25 (facilitation of complaints) to the actual violation of individual migrants' rights, rather than providing a right to file collective complaints—necessary for the enforcement of protection mechanisms against collective violations of migrants' rights and/or structural forms of discrimination. Such a right is currently included in the Consolidated Law on Immigration article 44.10, whereby, whenever collective discrimination arises—even in cases in which it is not possible directly and immediately to identify actual victims of the discrimination—local representatives of trade unions may file a complaint. However, the field of application of the right to file collective complaints under Italian migration law is restricted to employers' acts that constitute discrimination on grounds of racial or ethnic origin, or for reasons related to religion, language, nationality and geographic origin. Another weak point of article 25 of the EU directive is that the mechanism for facilitating complaints remains entirely at the discretion of each Member State.

The remaining parts of the Seasonal Workers Directive will have little impact on the Italian legal framework, as the latter already includes provisions that comply with the major obligations stipulated by the directive: the availability of accommodation, facilitation of re-entry and the right to equal treatment. The Consolidated Law on Immigration already guarantees regular migrants 'equal treatment and full equality of rights equivalent to Italian workers'(article 2.2), so the right to equal treatment (article 23) will not have substantial effects on the Italian legal framework. The right to equal treatment imposed by the directive can be restricted as regards family benefits, unemployment benefits, education and tax benefits, which is similar to the limitation of social security benefits already provided by the Italian legislature (under article 22.11 of the Consolidated Law on Immigration). Therefore, even on this point, the directive will not have a positive impact on the conditions of migrant workers under the Italian legal framework.

III. SEASONAL MIGRANTS IN ITALIAN MIGRATION LAW: BETWEEN SECURITISATION POLICIES AND EXPLOITATION

> Considering the specially vulnerable situation of third-country national seasonal workers and the temporary nature of their assignment, there is a need to provide effective protection of the rights of third-country national seasonal workers ... to check regularly for compliance and to fully guarantee respect for the principle of equal treatment with workers who are nationals of the host Member State.[37]

> The typical day of a migrant employed as a seasonal worker starts at about 4.30 in the morning when they go to the recruitment spots. Squares, junctions and roads are the places in which the supply and demand of underground labour meet ... Those who are not chosen go back 'home', to wait for another 'opportunity'.[38]

The two quotations above address two of the most crucial issues of the Italian legal framework on seasonal migration: (i) the need to guarantee to seasonal workers 'effective' protection measures, given their high degree of vulnerability; and (ii) the lack of regular migration channels, with its manifest consequences on the working and living conditions of irregular migrants (who are relegated to the margins of the labour market) and to the increasing importance of (mostly illegal) labour supply chains. Both of these issues can be concisely summarised under the label of 'lack of effectiveness' of the Italian system of seasonal migration.

Although it is not possible to address the issue of the questionable 'ethics' of seasonal migration[39] within the limited scope of this chapter, and without making assumptions about the desirability of temporary labour migration or circular labour migration programmes themselves, nonetheless the legal regulation of seasonal migration and the legal status of migrants cannot be addressed without taking into consideration the effectiveness of the legal framework aimed at protecting them.

In this respect, the inconsistencies of the Italian seasonal migration system will not be resolved by implementing the Seasonal Workers Directive either, as the directive assumes the same admission model (ie there must be a pre-existing valid employment contract) that has already proved to be a failure in the Italian context. Further still, the directive lacks clarity on the role of intermediaries. On the other hand, the limited scope of the protective legislation offered to non-EU workers (both at national and supranational level), who have yet to arrive in the receiving territory (or, under the directive,

[37] Seasonal Workers Directive recital 43.

[38] Médecins Sans Frontières, *A Season in Hell: MSF Report on the Conditions of Migrants Employed in the Agricultural Sector in Southern Italy* (Paris, MSF, 2008) 3.

[39] This expression is borrowed from Alexander Reilly, 'The Ethics of Seasonal Labour Migration' (2011) 20 *Griffith Law Review* 127.

the EU), seems to ignore the reality of the high number of irregular migrants already employed under precarious working conditions in the main sectors that employ seasonal migrants.

Another major feature of the Italian approach to migration is its legislative obsession with securitisation policies,[40] relegating the role of labour law to a secondary position in the regulation of migration issues. In recent years, this approach has been exalted through the adoption of 'security packages' and the criminalisation of illegal entry and residence.[41] In this respect, the ILO Committee of Experts expressed concern that the criminalisation of irregular migration in the Security Package would 'further marginalise and stigmatise migrant workers in an irregular situation, and increase their vulnerability to exploitation and violation of their basic human rights'.[42]

On the securitisation side of labour migration law, legislators have trumped up increasingly severe sanctions against employers and incorporated the crime of 'illegal intermediation and labour exploitation' into the Italian Criminal Code (a phenomenon often known by the evocative Italian term *caporalato*).[43] Considering the almost omnipresent symbiosis between irregular migrant status and unlawful intermediation in practice, resulting almost inevitably in exploitation, it can be concluded that the Italian legal framework for the protection of migrant workers is largely ineffective if not farcical. One must seriously doubt whether there is any concrete possibility of implementing this provision, considering, in particular, that the criminalisation of irregular migration will prevent irregular migrants from filing complaints against the abuses of their so-called 'caporali'.[44]

To conclude, the Italian approach to temporary labour migration appears to be mostly ineffective and heavily biased towards public safety policy implementation. In this regard, even if the criminalisation of the various forms of illegal intermediation could prevent exploitative conduct, the

[40] The same accusation can be levelled at the EU approach to labour migration.

[41] Consolidated Law on Immigration art 10 bis.

[42] International Labour Conference, *Report of the Committee of Experts on the Application of Conventions and Recommendations, Direct Request Concerning Forced Labour Convention, 1930 (No 29)* (Geneva, ILO, 2010) 727. Also note that in 2014, the Italian Parliament delegated the government—according to art 2.3 para b, Law no 67/2014—to issue a legislative decree, including, among other measures, the decriminalisation of the crime of illegal entry and stay and its transformation into an administrative offence. The legislative decree has not yet been approved by the government.

[43] Art 603 bis of the Criminal Code, introduced by art 12, Law No 148, 14 September 2011, on 'Other urgent measures for financial stabilisation and development'.

[44] In the same direction, in 2012, the legislature introduced a residence permit that can be granted for humanitarian reasons to migrant workers who are victims of 'particularly exploitative working conditions'. In order to receive the permit, they must report their employers to the public authorities and co-operate in the subsequent criminal proceedings against them. Legislative Decree No 109 of 16 July 2012 (the so-called 'Rosarno Law').

ex post facto punitive system does not seem consistent with the aim of *preventing* any harm to the dignity of non-EU workers. So, in this sense, the regulatory approach adopted should focus more on the introduction of measures aimed at avoiding, *ex ante*, the exploitation of seasonal migrants. To do so, it would need to shift from the public safety paradigm of labour migration towards a more human rights–oriented approach.

Part VI

Contesting Temporariness: Status and the Social Effects of the Legal Regulation of Temporary Labour Migration

13

The Membership of Migrant Workers and the Ethical Limits of Exclusion

ALEXANDER REILLY

> The primary good that we distribute to one another is membership in some human community. And what we do with regard to membership structures all our other distributive choices.[1]

I. INTRODUCTION

THIS CHAPTER EXPLORES the relationship between temporary workers and membership. I analyse shifts in the role and significance of citizenship as the primary mechanism for defining membership in political communities.[2] I argue that a transformation of the two dimensions of citizenship, as a status and a source of rights, means that living and working in a state is now a primary basis for a claim to full membership in the state.[3]

Establishing a connection between citizenship and work is not just of theoretical interest. Temporariness is itself a diminution of rights and political

[1] Michael Walzer, *Spheres of Justice: A Defense of Pluralism and Equality* (New York, Basic Books, 1983) 31.

[2] In this chapter, citizenship is the formal legal status representing full membership in a state. What constitutes full membership may vary from state to state, but must include at least security of residence in the state and the right to participate fully in the civil and political life of the state. The social rights attached to citizenship may vary from state to state. Membership is a non-legal term that reflects the underlying relationship between people and states. Full membership is equivalent to citizenship. However, a person can still be a member without the full conferral of citizenship. Membership is a consideration for every resident, temporary or permanent, in a state. It is not associated with any particular rights, but membership rights increase over time as the relationship between a state and its residents deepens. Full membership is realised when migrants become permanent residents, at which point the rights attached to citizenship and membership are coextensive.

[3] I take these dimensions of citizenship from Christian Joppke, *Citizenship and Immigration* (Cambridge, Polity Press, 2010). See also Linda Bosniak, *The Citizen and the Alien: Dilemmas of Contemporary Membership* (Princeton, NJ, Princeton University Press, 2008).

power, and thus a source of vulnerability in the workplace. The relationship between work and membership has been a dominant theme in discussions of the ethics of labour migration schemes.[4] This chapter contributes to this literature by identifying the many ways that work is related to claims for membership, by outlining the ethical limits of temporary work that can occur outside the rubric of membership, and squarely confronting the practical implications of a demand that states confer membership on migrant workers. If states are required to offer membership to workers based on their residence and work, they may tighten entry requirements in the short term, placing new restrictions on the global movement of people. I argue, however, that in the long term granting membership rights to migrant workers leads to a more satisfactory transnational movement of people. If states are able to benefit from the labour of migrant workers without offering permanent residence and a pathway to citizenship, they can retain their privilege in the long term, maintaining and entrenching inequality between nations and people.[5]

Scholars have established a clear relationship between the temporary status of migrant workers and their vulnerability in the workplace.[6] However, scholars differ on the best way to address this vulnerability. There are three legal frameworks for addressing migrant worker rights in the workplace: citizenship, human rights and labour rights.[7] Each framework has its particular advantages. Citizenship focuses on the rights associated with membership which are backed by stronger enforceability mechanisms because of migrants' security of residence. Human rights are important for requiring universal minimum standards of treatment for workers, and labour rights attend to vulnerabilities that are associated with differences in power and class between employers and employees.[8] The three frameworks for regulation are complementary, filling the 'blind spots' of the other frameworks.[9]

[4] See, eg Judy Fudge, 'Making Claims for Migrant Workers: Human Rights and Citizenship' (2014) 18 *Citizenship Studies* 29; Martin Ruhs, *The Price of Rights: Regulating International Labor Migration* (Princeton, NJ, Princeton University Press, 2013); Joseph Carens, 'An Overview of the Ethics of Immigration' (2014) 17(5) *Critical Review of International and Political Philosophy* 538; Walzer, *Spheres of Justice* (n 1).

[5] For a stinging critique of citizenship as an inherited entitlement, see Ayelet Shachar, 'The Worth of Citizenship in an Unequal World' (2007) 8 *Theoretical Inquiries in Law* 367.

[6] See, eg Judy Fudge, 'Precarious Migrant Status and Precarious Employment: The Paradox of International Rights for Migrant Workers' (2013) 34 *Comparative Labour Law and Policy Journal* 95; Leah Vosko (ed), *Precarious Employment: Understanding Labour Market Insecurity in Canada* (Montreal, McGill-Queens University Press, 2006); Ian Campbell and Joo-Cheong Tham, 'Labour Market Deregulation and Temporary Migrant Labour Schemes: An Analysis of the 475 Visa Program' (2013) 26(3) *Australian Journal of Labour Law* 239.

[7] See generally Guy Mundlak, 'Industrial Citizenship, Social Citizenship, Corporate Citizenship: I Just Want My Wages' (2007) 8 *Theoretical Inquiries in Law* 719.

[8] Ibid 726–30.

[9] Ibid 730.

Some scholars are concerned that the focus on membership can require too high a standard of protection for workers, leading high-income states to restrict opportunities for migrant workers. Martin Ruhs put this position powerfully in his 2013 book, *The Price of Rights*.[10] Although Ruhs' main focus is on international human rights, his position has particular implications for the case put in this chapter for granting membership rights to migrant workers. I will address Ruhs' arguments in section V.

Other scholars argue that the vulnerability of migrant workers is adequately addressed through the application of international human rights standards and robust domestic labour laws.[11] Judy Fudge looks for a convergence between human rights and a cosmopolitan citizenship. She argues that it is possible to assert a membership status less than national citizenship that provides robust protections for migrant workers. Fudge argues that one can have a degree of unfreedom in relation to citizenship status, while retaining freedom in the labour market.[12] For Fudge, it is possible to disaggregate different components of citizenship. Drawing on the work of JL Cohen,[13] Fudge argues that it is possible to distinguish between the democratic components of membership, such as equality and freedom, which are due to all residents, from the juridical component of citizenship that determines a person's status in the political community and the right to participate fully in its processes of government, which can be denied to non-citizen workers.

Although citizenship rights may be disaggregated in this way, I do not believe that political rights alone are able to address the core vulnerability of migrant workers, which derives from their insecure residence. If a person's residence is insecure, the rights pinned to this residence are also insecure. The fact of temporariness itself means the same substantive right has a diminished value for the migrant worker.

I am, therefore, persuaded by scholars who argue that the vulnerability of migrant workers is inherent in their migration status and that the only way to remove the vulnerability is for states to address the membership of migrant workers as a condition of their working and living in the state. Michael Walzer articulated this strongly in his discussion of membership in *Spheres of Justice* in 1983, provocatively equating migrant workers to 'live-in servants' of the state.[14] More recently, Dauvergne and Marsden have extended Hannah Arendt's analysis of the exclusion of refugees and stateless people from rights protection due to the lack of state membership granted

[10] Ruhs, *The Price of Rights* (n 4).

[11] Ruhs, *The Price of Rights* (n 4); Anna Stilz, 'Guestworkers and Second-Class Citizenship' (2010) 29 *Policy and Society* 295; Fudge, 'Making Claims' (n 4).

[12] Fudge, 'Making Claims' (n 4) 38.

[13] Jean L Cohen, 'Changing Paradigms of Citizenship and the Exclusiveness of the Demos' (1999) 14(3) *International Sociology* 245.

[14] Walzer, *Spheres of Justice* (n 1) ch 2.

to migrant workers. The migrant worker is accepted into the state, not as an equal, but as a labour input in the economy.[15]

If unfreedom is implied in the very terms of employment of the migrant worker, what is required to address this unfreedom? From one perspective the inherent vulnerability of temporary workers casts doubt over the ethics of temporary labour migration at all.[16] In this chapter, I make a different claim: that temporary labour schemes remain ethical as long as states attend to the membership claims of migrant workers in a timely fashion. If states are not prepared to recognise residence and work as establishing an entitlement to membership, then temporary labour schemes should be strictly time limited. Time limiting labour migration schemes does not address their intrinsically exploitative character. However, I accept that, consistent with liberal values, the human agency and freedom of temporary migrant workers requires that they be free to enter a less than equal employment relationship, at least for a time. But if labour is not simply a 'commodity',[17] the longer a worker's association with the state, the greater the worker's entitlement to membership in the state, and the greater their claim to equal status and rights vis-à-vis citizens of the state. This is both an empirical and a normative claim. It is empirical because it reflects state practice. It is normative because it is an argument for what ought to be the basis of citizenship.

II. TRANSFORMATION OF CITIZENSHIP

The idea of citizenship went through dramatic changes in the twentieth century as the world opened up to migration and adopted a universal conception of rights. Up to the middle of the twentieth century, the main purpose of citizenship was to define membership in political communities, to protect members from the danger of 'enemies' or 'strangers'[18] and to bind citizens to a single sovereign, thereby relieving them of the ubiquitous possibility of violence towards each other.[19] In this guise, citizenship was a status signifying the boundary of inclusiveness in the community, and indicating a political unity.

[15] Catherine Dauvergne and Sarah Marsden, 'The Ideology of Temporary Labour Migration in the Post-global Era' (2014) 18 *Citizenship Studies* 224, 235.

[16] See Walzer, *Spheres of Justice* (n 1) 31.

[17] For a discussion of the increasing commodification of labour, see Stuart Rosewarne, 'Globalisation and the Commodification of Labour: Temporary Labour Migration' (2010) 20(2) *Economic and Labour Relations Review* 99.

[18] Carl Schmitt, *The Concept of the Political*, trans George Schwab (Chicago, Chicago University Press, 1996) 27.

[19] Thomas Hobbes, *Leviathan*, ed JCA Gaskin (Oxford, Oxford University Press, [1651] 1998).

The increasing movement between states in the twentieth century has complicated the role of citizenship in defining the nation.[20] As the political community became increasingly heterogeneous, membership could no longer be simply assigned as a product of birth or ancestry. Citizenship has necessarily focused on the real connections between persons and states. Residence and other factors have grown in importance as indicators of membership. As early as 1953, the International Court of Justice indicated that a range of factors were relevant to establishing a person's membership in a state, and consequent right to protection of the state, including a person's 'habitual residence', 'centre of interests', 'family ties', and 'participation in public life'.[21] The converse is also true: where there are real connections these form the basis for claims to a right of naturalisation.[22]

Furthermore, citizenship has come to embody not only a status but also an entitlement to rights.[23] TH Marshall argued for a modern conception of citizenship based on equality under a common law rather than on feudal notions of kinship or common descent.[24] Citizenship brought together people of different classes, wealth and education, and conferred equal rights upon them.[25] Although citizenship works against inequality, it does not eliminate it. The very need for rights to be articulated as the core of citizenship suggests that differences in class, wealth and opportunity are endemic.

The transformation of citizenship has been so dramatic that it has been possible to consider citizenship as a 'post-national' status. Core economic, political and social rights are being granted to non-citizens, thus reducing the importance of citizenship as a status.[26] In such analyses, aliens are considered to have a de facto citizenship status in the state. International conventions on the rights of migrant workers aspire to a post-national citizenship by placing obligations on states to provide a wide range of rights to migrant workers, while placing no obligation on states to grant long-term migrant workers permanent residence and citizenship.[27]

The end game of post-national citizenship is the collapse of citizenship altogether. For Aihwa Ong, allegiance to a state is but one of many

[20] Joppke, *Citizenship and Immigration* (n 3) 5.

[21] *Liechtenstein v Guatemala*, International Court of Justice, summary of judgment, 6 June 1955, 33, http://www.icj-cij.org/docket/files/18/2676.pdf.

[22] Joppke, *Citizenship and Immigration* (n 3) 45.

[23] Ibid.

[24] TH Marshall, *Citizenship and Social Class: And Other Essays* (Cambridge, Cambridge University Press, 1950).

[25] Joppke, *Citizenship and Immigration* (n 3) 10.

[26] Yasemin Soysal, *Limits of Citizenship: Migrants and Postnational Membership in Europe* (Chicago, University of Chicago Press, 1995); Bosniak, *The Citizen and the Alien* (n 3); Veit Bader, 'Citizenship and Exclusion: Radical Democracy, Community and Justice. Or What is Wrong with Communitarianism?' (1995) 23(2) *Political Theory* 211, 212.

[27] See, eg Joanna Howe and Rosemary Owens, 'Temporary Labour Migration in a Globalised World: The Regulatory Challenges', ch 1 in this volume.

allegiances people hold, and not necessarily the most important one. As rights and protections long associated with citizenship are becoming disarticulated from the state, they are re-articulated with elements such as 'market-based interests, transnational agencies, mobile elites, and marginalized populations'.[28] The end game is a world without borders.[29]

However, the phenomenon of a post-national world is not yet upon us. At most, we are in a phase of trans-nationality,[30] with frequent movement across state borders, but in which citizenship continues to plays a role in setting the criteria for inclusion and exclusion. The attribution of membership is constitutive of the state[31] and, as the power of states wanes in the face of globalisation, it remains a continuing bastion of sovereign power.[32]

Although there is great force in a focus on the human rights of migrant workers, having membership in a particular state still plays a fundamental role in the wellbeing and security of people.[33] Furthermore, if we take membership seriously, attention can turn to how a fair allocation of resources can be achieved among nation-states, rather than waiting for their demise. As Rainer Baubock puts it, '[i]nstead of portraying migrants as harbingers of the end of the nation-state, we should rather think how to transform nation-states so that increasingly mobile populations can still share in political authority, a bounded territory and a common historical horizon'.[34]

The continued strength of state sovereignty means that the international human rights regime is necessarily limited. The Universal Declaration of Human Rights sets out a comprehensive list of human rights that transcend state boundaries, but at the same time upholds the 'sovereignty of individual states'.[35] The limits of international law protection of workers is a product of the dual function of citizenship. As a determinant of membership, citizenship has an exclusionary function, while among members, citizenship ensures an equality of rights which is a function of inclusion.[36] When we

[28] Aihwa Ong, '(Re)Articulations of Citizenship' (2005) 38 *Political Science and Politics* 697, 697.

[29] Joseph Carens, 'Aliens and Citizens: The Case for Open Borders' (2002) 49(2) *Review of Politics* 251.

[30] Peggy Levitt, 'Transnational Migrants: When "Home" Means More Than One Country', Migration Information Source, 1 October 2004; Daniel Conway and Pauline Leonard, *Migration, Space and Transnational Identities: The British in South Africa* (London, Pan MacMillan, 2014).

[31] Walzer, *Spheres of Justice* (n 1).

[32] Catherine Dauvergne, *Making People Illegal: What Globalization Means for Migration and Law* (Cambridge, Cambridge University Press, 1999).

[33] Audrey Macklin, 'Who is the Citizen's Other?' (2007) 8 *Theoretical Inquiries in Law* 333, 336.

[34] Rainer Baubock, 'International Migration and Liberal Democracies: The Challenge of Integration' (2001) 35(4) *Patterns of Prejudice* 33.

[35] Seyla Benhabib, 'Borders, Boundaries and Citizenship' (2005) 38(4) *Political Science and Politics* 673, 674.

[36] Bosniak, *The Citizen and the Alien* Introduction (n 3).

turn our attention to the exclusive function of citizenship, it becomes apparent that the alien cannot possibly hope to achieve equal rights to citizens. The very point of excluding others is to maintain certain privileges and advantages of membership.[37] Citizenship rights, then, constitute a different category of rights from international human rights. They derive from the relationship people have with states. They are not based in universal notions of human dignity, but on entitlements inherent in membership of a state.[38] Having no control over the exclusive function of conferring membership, the best international law can do to protect migrant workers is to replicate the rights conferred on citizens within the state.

The efforts of the international community to require states to provide a range of civil, political, economic and social rights to migrant workers have been only partially successful. The 1990 International Convention on the Protection of the Rights of All Migrant Workers and Members of their Families has the least ratifications of any major international human rights treaty.[39] This reflects the function of migrant work in the global economy. The temporariness of migrant workers is ideologically retained, and their rights ideologically constrained, to advance the cause of wealth creation in receiving states.[40]

To achieve true equality for migrant workers, analysis must focus on the role of citizenship to provide equal rights to migrant workers. However, the state is conflicted. It needs the outsider's help to sustain its wealth and privilege, but does not want to share that wealth through granting membership. Thus, the exclusionary function of citizenship has moved from the border, and now occurs within the state. Instead of refusing entry, states admit outsiders with reduced rights vis-à-vis members. As a result, within the state we find multiple forms of membership, including citizens, permanent residents, a range of temporary workers with differing rights to work and visitors.[41] This creates a problem for the second, liberal role of citizenship of creating an entitlement to equal rights for members of the political community.[42]

Despite the desire of wealthy states to retain and build their economic privilege, the recognition of the residence and work of migrants as a pathway to membership is well advanced. Permanent residency is offered to many migrant workers who successfully integrate into the community. Two-step migration, where naturalisation follows a period of residence in the state, is

[37] Walzer, *Spheres of Justice* (n 1).

[38] Mundlak, 'Industrial Citizenship' (n 7); Ruhs, *The Price of Rights* (n 4) 24.

[39] Ruhs, *The Price of Rights* (n 4) 16; International Convention on the Protection of the Rights of All Migrant Workers and Members of their Families (adopted 18 December 1990, entered into force 1 July 2003).

[40] Dauvergne and Marsden, 'The Ideology of Temporary Labour Migration' (n 15).

[41] Robin Cohen, *The New Helots: Migrants in the International Division of Labour* (Aldershot, Avebury, 2003).

[42] Bosniak, *The Citizen and the Alien* (n 3).

used both by states and workers to determine whether to offer and whether to commit to full membership.[43] Even since 2001, when there has been a new emphasis on loyalty to the nation in the face of fears of international terrorism, nations have not returned to a more limited ethnically focused membership based on ancestry and birth. Instead there has been a growth in the use of citizenship tests which focus on the values required of citizens.[44]

The transformation of citizenship is not yet complete. Barbieri argues that the final stage is to remove control of citizenship from nation-states. Although states might be left to choose who to invite into their political communities, and might have a wide discretion to determine the extent of basic rights and freedoms within the community, the right to citizenship itself should be determined 'according to criteria that goes beyond the interests of individual states'.[45] This is because citizenship is transnational, and the granting of political membership is so fundamental to a person's dignity and basic rights that it needs to be attributed according to external criteria.[46] It is the plight of the migrant worker, above all others, that requires this transformation in the attribution of citizenship.

III. RETHINKING CITIZENSHIP AND WORK

In this section I argue for a new association between work and citizenship. The basis for a connection between work and citizenship draws on both liberal and national arguments. It is influenced by both cosmopolitan and communitarian ideas. Whereas these ideas are often considered to be in opposition,[47] I argue that they are capable of providing alternative, and reinforcing, justifications for the relationship between citizenship and work. The foundation of membership is the real connections people develop with places.[48] Because these connections develop over time, membership is not an all or nothing status, but a set of rights and responsibilities that increase as a person's connection to a territory deepens.[49]

[43] In the Australian context, see, eg Lesley-Anne Hawthorne, 'Australia' in Christian Joppke and F Leslie Seidel (eds), *Immigrant Integration in Federal Countries* (Montreal, McGill-Queens University Press, 2012).

[44] Joppke, *Citizenship and Immigration* (n 3) 64.

[45] William Barbieri, *Ethics of Citizenship: Immigration and Group Rights in Germany* (Durham, NC, Duke University Press, 1998) 127.

[46] Ibid 128–29.

[47] Benhabib, 'Borders, Boundaries and Citizenship' (n 35) 674.

[48] Stephen Castles and Alastair Davidson, *Citizenship and Migration: Globalization and the Politics of Belonging* (New York, Routledge, 2000), 24.

[49] For an example of this approach to territorial membership, see Joseph Carens, 'On Belonging: What We Owe People Who Stay' Summer 2005 *Boston Review*; Carens, 'An Overview of the Ethics' (n 4).

Work is universal, liberal, tangible and democratic. It provides a contrasting basis for attribution of membership to birth and ancestry which are intrinsically illiberal and undemocratic. However, the case I am making here is for the *expansion* of citizenship, not for a replacement of birth and ancestry as fundamental indicators of membership. Birth right and ancestry continue to provide a stable foundation for membership in a world of increased movement of people. Indeed, they make temporary movement of people possible. Having a home liberates people to explore the world. Furthermore, if contribution through labour were the primary basis for membership, membership would become narrowly available to the fittest, strongest and most deserving because of their contribution.

A. Territorial Presence and Membership

The most substantial connection to place, and thus the starting point for any claim to citizenship, is territorial presence.[50] It is the foundation of *jus soli* (birth right citizenship) and *jus sanguinis* (ancestral citizenship). The connection between people and place is ancient in origin. It is the foundation of a range of legal claims—from Indigenous land rights[51] to claims to adverse possession in property law.[52] Place provides us with a sense of our origin, and also provides an end point for a journey, thereby securing us against perpetual movement.[53] We give meaning to place. Those meanings tie us to place and give us a sense of belonging.[54] The concept of private property loosened connections, transforming property into an abstract relationship.[55] Nonetheless, possession and presence retain a powerful claim of right in property law. The foundation of a right to land remains the control one exercises over the land through occupation and use.[56] Connections to territory work in the same way. Presence in a territory creates a connection

[50] Linda Bosniak goes so far as to contemplate the possibility that mere presence in a territory should be the basis for citizenship. See Linda Bosniak, 'Ethical Territoriality and the Rights of Immigrants' (2007) 8 *Theoretical Inquiries in Law* 389, 407.

[51] See, eg *Mabo v Queensland (No 2)* (1992) 175 *CLR* 1; Henry Reynolds, *The Law of the Land* (Ringwood, Vic, Penguin, 1996); Deborah Bird Rose, *Nourishing Terrains: Australian Aboriginal Views of Landscape and Wilderness* (Canberra, Australian Heritage Commission, 1996).

[52] Kevin Gray and Susan Gray, 'The Idea of Property' in S Bright and J Dewar (eds), *Land Law: Themes and Perspectives* (Oxford, Oxford University Press, 1998).

[53] Alexander Reilly, 'Cartography, Property and the Aesthetics of Place' (2004) 34 *Studies in Law, Politics and Society* 221, 224.

[54] Edward Casey, *Getting Back into Place: Toward a New Understanding of the Place World* (Bloomington, IN, Indiana University Press, 1993) ix.

[55] Alain Pottage, 'The Measure of Land' (1994) 57 *Modern Law Review* 361.

[56] Kevin Gray and Susan Gray, *Elements of Property Law* (Oxford, Oxford University Press, 2000) 228.

to territory which grows stronger and more complex over time. With that growing connection, the entitlement to remain on the territory increases.

B. Contribution and Membership

In an analysis of American citizenship, Judith Shklar suggests that citizenship has always come with an obligation to 'earn'.[57] The model citizen is the person who earns income, pays their taxes and maintains their household. For Shklar, the construction of the independent citizen-earner links to an argument that the government has an obligation to create employment and provide the opportunity for citizens to earn a living wage.[58] Similarly, Frank Munger asserts that 'social rights—and, therefore, full citizenship—follow from fulfilment of the obligation to work. Full social citizenship is a benefit derived from fulfilment of a social contract and not from legal status as a citizen.'[59]

There is an intuitive logic to the proposition that a contribution to the state leads to claims to membership. It is why we contemplate the membership rights of migrant workers but not visitors to the state, even when their length of residence in the state is the same. It is why there was a special pathway to permanence in the Canadian Care Worker programme, and why two-step migration processes are common in many states.

The idea of the attainment of rights through work was the basis of Locke's theory of private property—by working the land, people develop an entitlement to the land.[60] This relationship between toil and entitlement has the same logic when applied to an entitlement to live and reside in the territory of one's work.[61] The claim of migrant workers is particularly strong as their work is *necessary* work. They have been accepted into the state to do the work that local workers are not trained to do, or are not prepared to do. In this sense, the entry of migrant workers might be compared with the right of strangers to move into countries 'not sufficiently inhabited' which was the fundamental justification for colonial expansion in the eighteenth century.[62]

[57] Judith Shklar, *American Citizenship: The Quest for Inclusion* (Cambridge, MA, Harvard University Press, 1991) 64–67.

[58] Ibid 64.

[59] Frank Munger, 'Poverty, Welfare and the Affirmative State' (2003) 37 *Law and Society Review* 659, 674.

[60] John Locke, *Second Treatise on Government* (New York, Barnes and Noble, 1966) ch 5, s 32.

[61] There is a clear irony in drawing on the work of Locke here, as his theory of private property provided the justification for the colonisation of territories where the original peoples did not engage in European styles of agriculture, whereas the association of work and membership in the political community represents a challenge to the privilege of these same colonising powers and settler societies.

[62] Emer de Vattel, *Law of Nations* (London, GG and J Robinson, 1797) bk I, pp 100–101; *Mabo v Queensland (No 2)* (n 51) 33.

The invitation to work in the state is an important part of the migrant worker's entitlement. It is an indication that their work is considered a valuable contribution, and in this way it might be distinguished from the work of unauthorised workers. This means a distinction can be drawn between the membership entitlements of legal and illegal workers on the basis of their contribution to the state through work. It does not deny the possibility of illegal workers gaining an entitlement to membership through work, but it may suggest that membership rights will take longer to attain based on the criteria for membership.

C. Integration and Membership

Over time, workers develop increasingly strong social and economic ties to the state in which they work. Work is a source of identity, and helps individuals find their place in the broader community.[63] Their identity becomes increasingly connected to the people they meet and the places they occupy.[64] At some point, Carens argues, 'a threshold is passed. [Migrants] … simply are members of the community with a strong moral claim to have that membership officially recognised by the state'.[65] Although work is not essential for the development of the ties to people and place that found a claim to membership in this way, work itself is a means of integrating into a new society.[66]

Work can be a way to form significant social networks.[67] Working together promotes a sense of 'interdependence and common fate'.[68] The workplace is a 'deliberative forum' for issues inside and outside the workplace. In the workplace, people are not bound to their sectarian allegiances, but can build new community relationships that cross ethnic and cultural lines.[69]

It needs to be recognised that for some vulnerable migrant workers, particularly from language backgrounds different from their employers and fellow workers, work can be a barrier to integration. Low-paid work for long hours in remote locations on limited pay can leave migrants with no

[63] Vicki Schulz, 'Life's Work' (2000) 100 *Columbia Law Review* 1881, 1889–90; Jennifer Gordon and RA Lenhardt, 'Rethinking Work and Citizenship' (2008) 55 *UCLA Law Review* 1161, 1194.

[64] Hiroshi Motomura, *Americans in Waiting: The Lost Story of Immigration and Citizenship in the United States* (New York, Oxford University Press, 2006) 11.

[65] Carens, 'An Overview of the Ethics' (n 4) 543.

[66] Joseph Carens, 'The Rights of Irregular Migrants' (2008) 22(2) *Ethics and International Affairs* 163.

[67] Gordon and Lenhardt, 'Rethinking Work and Citizenship' (n 63) 1191–92.

[68] Cynthia Estlund, 'Working Together: The Workplace, Civil Society and the Law' (2000) 89 *Georgia Law Journal* 1, 30.

[69] Ibid 53.

capacity or time to pursue interests and connections outside the workplace. It is important that for workers in this situation lack of integration is not a ground for denying citizenship. Instead, it points to a need for stronger labour law regimes to protect workers from the possibility of such isolation.

D. Human Dignity and Membership

Immanuel Kant recognised that human beings have 'intrinsic worth', and argued that this was an underlying moral principle in the organisation of human affairs.[70] It required that humans be treated always as an end and never as a means. This perspective is necessary to counter the pressure to align temporary migration programmes more and more closely to the labour market. Temporary workers are not only an 'input' in the labour market equation,[71] or 'factors of production'.[72] The principle of human dignity reminds us that while 'labour remains theoretical ... people are not'.[73]

For Michael Walzer, the implication of Kant's exhortation is clear. The only purpose for denying membership is to deprive individuals of the security and sense of worth that comes with membership. For Walzer, guest worker programmes deny membership precisely to place such workers in an inferior position, willing to do difficult work for inadequate pay that they would refuse to do if they had political agency.[74]

Linda Bosniak agrees, proposing that: 'to the extent we allow for a class of persons to subsist among us in a less-than-fully-incorporated status, we will have entrenched and institutionalized caste-based distinctions'.[75] Identification with a political community provides a sense of self in the world and is indispensable to being fully human. Or as Hannah Arendt states, 'The chief difference between slave labour and modern free labour is not that the labourer possesses personal freedom, but that he is admitted to the political realm and fully emancipated as a citizen'.[76]

However, the freedom of individuals to choose their path in life is also central to their human dignity. It might be argued to be patronising to remove the choice to enter a less than perfect employment relationship for

[70] Immanuel Kant, *Groundwork of the Metaphysics of Morals* (1785); Immanuel Kant, 'Lecture on Ethics' (1779) as discussed in James Rachels, *The Elements of Moral Philosophy* (New York, Random House, 1986) 114–17.

[71] Dauvergne and Marsden, 'The Ideology of Temporary Labour Migration' (n 15) 235.

[72] Rosewarne, 'Globalisation and the Commodification of Labour' (n 17) 103.

[73] Dauvergne and Marsden, 'The Ideology of Temporary Labour Migration' (n 15) 234.

[74] Walzer, *Spheres of Justice* (n 1) 59.

[75] Bosniak, 'Ethical Territoriality' (n 50) 407.

[76] Hannah Arendt, *The Human Condition* (Chicago, University of Chicago Press, 1998) 217.

some other gain. As Anna Stilz puts it, ought not a 'fully cognizant adult with the capacity to consent, with a right to abode elsewhere and with transferable skills in the labour market be able to waive a claim to membership for a beneficial employment opportunity?'[77]

Martin Ruhs argues that there must be 'at least some minimal degree of choice in … people's decisions to move abroad for employment purposes'.[78] It is necessary, therefore, to consider agency and the overall interests of migrants when thinking about whether 'trade-offs should be tolerated'.[79] Stuart Rosewarne warns that the agency of temporary migrant workers is highly constrained as a result of the global commodification of labour. The migrant worker is in a more subordinate position than the 'classic wage worker', and the agency of workers must be considered in the context of the significant degree of 'unfreedom' in the employment relationship.[80]

I agree with Ruhs and Stilz that, from the perspective of human dignity, the agency of migrant workers must be considered. It is not in conformity with a robust sense of human dignity that workers are assumed to be unequal, vulnerable and incapable of entering a fair contract of work in a receiving state without full membership. However, human dignity also requires that, from the moment workers reside and work in a state, any inequality in their status and rights is a factor that works against a diagnosis of dignity. Any inequality can only be tolerated in the short term to secure the dignity of the worker in the medium and long terms.

E. Equality and Membership

Equality is closely linked to human dignity. Inequality based on arbitrary characteristics is an affront to dignity. But equality is also a liberal notion. For Seyla Benhabib, equal participation of people residing in a state is central to the democratic legitimacy of states: 'all those whose interests are affected by collective decisions in which they have a stake—as workers, parents, residents—also have a say in these decisions'.[81] From the perspective of the migrant worker it is a claim of right; a claim to receive the same recognition in terms of personal remuneration, and also a claim to equal participation in the society in which the work is performed.

The argument for equality based on democratic legitimacy does not necessarily require equality from the moment migrant workers arrive in a state.

[77] Stilz, 'Guestworkers and Second-Class Citizenship' (n 11) 298.
[78] Ruhs, *The Price of Rights* (n 4) 7.
[79] Ibid.
[80] Rosewarne, 'Globalisation and the Commodification of Labour' (n 17) 105.
[81] Benhabib, 'Borders, Boundaries and Citizenship' (n 35) 676.

Their stake in the state increases over time, until a point is reached when migrant workers belong to the 'community of meaning' that constitutes the state.[82]

From a communitarian perspective, society needs to be based on a principle of equality among members. 'We ought not to subjugate aliens, not because we owe them anything, but to preserve our society as a community of equals'.[83] Out of a concern for this broader notion of equality, Walzer argues that states must take the decision to admit aliens very seriously. Equal citizenship plays a primary regulative role in Walzer's concept of justice.[84] The admission of an alien carries with it the obligation to treat the alien equally in all respects. '[M]embers must be prepared to accept, as their own equals in a world of shared obligations, the men and women they admit'.[85]

The concern here is about how the twin characteristics of being temporary and being alien leave migrant workers open to a structural or inherent inequality and vulnerability to exploitation. If this structural vulnerability exists, temporary workers cannot be considered to have effective agency. Their apparent choice to enter the labour market of another country for economic gain is tainted by the migrant worker's unequal bargaining position.[86]

Against these arguments of equality, Martin Ruhs and others argue that it is ethical for migrants to trade some rights to gain access to work opportunities in a state, and thus to be unequal in some respects.[87] Ruhs takes a pragmatic approach to rights, rejecting a strict universalism as unworkable in a world that is itself based on deep inequalities between nations. For Ruhs, it makes no sense to deny migrants an opportunity to improve their circumstances through access to better labour markets with superior pay and conditions to those they can access at home. Furthermore, migrants have the capacity to choose the trade-offs involved in migration for employment.[88] The basis of economic migration is utility maximisation.

[82] Gordon and Lenhardt, 'Rethinking Work and Citizenship' (n 63) 1187–88.

[83] Owen Fiss, *A Community of Equals: The Constitutional Protection of New Americans* (Boston, MA, Beacon Press, 1999) 17.

[84] David Miller, 'Introduction' in Michael Walzer and David Miller (eds), *Pluralism, Justice, and Equality* (Oxford, Oxford University Press, 1995) 3.

[85] Walzer, *Spheres of Justice* (n 1) 52.

[86] Compare Martin Ruhs, 'Designing Viable and Ethical Labour Immigration Policies' in *International Organization of Migration, World Migration 2005* (Geneva, International Organization of Migration, 2005); Ruhs, *The Price of Rights* (n 4). For Ruhs, the agency of the migrant worker is an important factor in determining whether temporary labour migration is ethical.

[87] See Howard Chang, 'Liberal Ideals and Political Feasibility: Guest-Worker Programs as Second-Best Policies' (2002) 27(3) *North Carolina Journal of International Law and Commercial Regulation* 465; Daniel A Bell, *Beyond Liberal Democracy: Political Thinking for an East Asian Context* (Princeton, NJ, Princeton University Press, 2006); Robert Mayer, 'Guestworkers and Exploitation' (2005) 67 *Review of Politics* 311.

[88] Ruhs, *The Price of Rights* (n 4) 131–34.

Migrants and states both focus on what they can offer and receive in a rational exchange.[89]

Allowing for the agency of migrant workers in their relationship with states and employers, Ruhs is able to adopt a consequentialist framework to analyse the extent to which migrant workers can trade their rights for other benefits. He poses the question to what extent, if at all, the outcomes for collectives (such as economic efficiency or distribution) and the economic welfare of individuals should be given priority over individual rights.[90]

Under classical liberal theory, the individual can maintain their freedom in the face of a relationship in which they are potentially exploited, if they are free to leave.[91] However, in relation to transnational movement of migrant workers this freedom is constrained in several ways. Fundamentally, the freedom is constrained by the disparity in wealth between the states migrants enter and the states to which they must return. This disparity provides a strong incentive for migrant workers to stay despite their lack of freedom. Furthermore, migrant workers are constrained by the investment they have made to come to the state in search of work.[92]

A 'rational exchange' assumes an equality of bargaining power. Migrant workers can only contemplate giving up rights if they have the social power to do so.[93] As Dauvergne and Marsden state, 'It is perilously easy to assert that temporary migrant workers should have fewer rights than permanent workers or than citizens. Indeed, temporary migrant worker programmes begin from this supposition.'[94] For this reason, states ought not to rely on the migrant worker's choice to be exploited. Taking work seriously as a basis for membership means that the traditional exchange of labour for reward has to be conceived more broadly. Migrant workers exchange their economic contribution, their compliance with the law and their participation in cultural norms of the state for membership in the state.[95]

Although the willingness of the states of origin of migrant workers and the workers themselves to enter unequal employment relations has clear implications for the human dignity of migrant workers, for Ruhs, Stilz and Fudge, sufficient equality can be preserved by providing the migrant with core basic civil and political rights that cannot be traded. For Stilz, non-tradeable rights include 'rights to a fair trial, free speech, and integrity

[89] Brigit Anderson, Us and Them? The Dangerous Politics of Immigration Control (Oxford, Oxford University Press, 2013) 48.
[90] Ruhs, *The Price of Rights* (n 4) 157.
[91] Barbieri, *Ethics of Citizenship* (n 45) 96.
[92] Alexander Reilly, 'Ethics of Seasonal Labour Migration' (2011) 20 *Griffith Law Review* 127, 143.
[93] Dauvergne and Marsden, 'The Ideology of Temporary Labour Migration' (n 15) 236.
[94] Ibid 237.
[95] Joppke, *Citizenship and Immigration* (n 3) 59.

of the body'.[96] Fudge distinguishes between political rights, which must be available equally to all resident workers, and judicial rights, which relate to citizenship status and are available only to citizens.[97]

Ruhs discusses 'core' civil and political rights as being available to all residents regardless of citizenship.[98] The rights that are tradeable include the right to choose employment, the right to family reunion and the right to permanent residence. Ruhs acknowledges that policies restricting rights are 'second-best policies', but argues that from a broader perspective they are ethically justifiable.[99]

The deprivation of all these rights comes at a particular cost to the migrant worker. Temporary migrants are not part of a free labour market—it is highly regulated. The regulation is needed to protect workers. However, the regulation cannot provide equal protection.[100] States are not able to control the conditions of work of migrant workers. Whatever may be the strength of labour market protection of migrant workers in theory, it cannot be enforced perfectly in practice. The functionalist approach to allowing a trade-off of rights for benefits is problematic in this regard. The trading of some rights such as freedom of choice in employment, and a right to residency, is responsible for an increase in the vulnerability of workers, and workplace regulation is not able to redress this vulnerability.

IV. THE MEMBERSHIP ENTITLEMENTS OF MIGRANT WORKERS

If the association between work and membership is strong, what does it require? In this section, I argue that it requires an increase in membership rights over time. Basic civil and political rights, as recognised in the Universal Declaration of Human Rights and the International Covenant on Civil and Political Rights, necessarily follow migrant workers wherever they travel and regardless of their length of time in a state. So, for example, workers should immediately have access to equal pay and conditions of work as local workers. There are other rights that accrue over time, and the longer a migrant lives and works in a territory, the stronger the claim to these rights becomes.

Approaching the issue of migrant workers' relationship to receiving states from the perspective of membership requires a nuanced approach to the accrual of rights. Membership in the state is an issue immediately, and rights

[96] Stilz, 'Guestworkers and Second-Class Citizenship' (n 11) 297.
[97] Fudge, 'Making Claims' (n 4).
[98] Ruhs, *The Price of Rights* (n 4) 185.
[99] Ibid 155.
[100] Walzer, *Spheres of Justice* (n 1) 57.

expand incrementally as residence and work increase. This means the rights to freedom of employment, family reunion, access to social welfare and residence must all be separately considered against the membership requirements of migrant workers.

It may be legitimate to restrict the family rights of migrant workers and their freedom of employment as a condition of entry to a state. However, they become important issues for the dignity and equality of the worker as soon as they enter and work in the state. Rights to family reunion and unrestricted employment should accrue more quickly than a right to permanent residence because they are important for the welfare of the workers in a foreign location. Without access to their most important social ties, and source of emotional and physical support, migrant workers might be tempted to maximise their time at work, having no family or other social responsibilities to provide meaning outside work. The fact that their social responsibilities are located in another country means that their only contribution to family is financial. This may create an incentive to work long hours in order to maximise this financial contribution, and in order to be reunited with family as quickly as possible. The social isolation of migrant workers from their families makes them likely to be 'target' earners, who are not sensitive to the value of their labour.[101] 'If wages go down, they simply work more to achieve their financial goals'.[102]

Restrictions on the right to access alternative employment is a source of vulnerability for migrant workers, and thus should be strictly time limited. As with family reunion, making employment a condition of maintaining a visa means that workers may feel tied to their employer, creating a structural inequality in the relationship which may lead to the possibility of exploitation.

Finally, migrant workers should be offered permanent residence and a pathway to full membership in a timely fashion.[103] Permanent residence is the final right of significance. The state ought to offer the opportunity for full membership through the conferral of citizenship at some time after workers have become permanent residents. However, given that not all states recognise dual citizenship, it is a legitimate choice for migrants to choose to remain a full member of one community while working in another.

[101] Harald Bauder, *Labor Movement: How Migration Regulates Labor Markets* (Oxford, Oxford University Press, 2006) 19–21.

[102] Reilly, 'Ethics of Seasonal Labour Migration' (n 92) 133.

[103] Martin Ruhs recommends a maximum of four years (*The Price of Rights* (n 4) 176–77). There is no magic to this number. It accords to the electoral cycle in many countries. Four years is a sufficient period of time for migrant workers to have formed deep relationships with the place in which they work and, if they have not, there is a serious question about whether they are in a healthy employment relationship. The maximum time period could also be measured in terms of the sacrifice migrant workers have made, the level of commitment to the receiving state that is represented by the time period, the proportion of the life cycle that it represents, or the proportion of a migrant's active working life.

The distinction between permanent residents and citizens varies across states, although most states confer the full range of civil and political rights on citizens, except the right to vote. Also the residence of citizens is generally more secure than permanent residents, not being conditional on good character and behaviour. In a review of citizenship in the UK, Lord Goldsmith recommended abolishing permanent residency. 'Permanent residency blurs the distinction between citizens and non-citizens. We should expect people who are settled in the UK for the long-term to become citizens.'[104] For Goldsmith, the point of abolishing permanent residence is to draw a bright line between citizens and non-citizens. Temporary residents then have a choice to upgrade their status to that of citizens, or be exposed to a lack of rights as aliens. Goldsmith's recommendation is a move away from a graded system of membership. There comes a point at which both states and migrants must commit to a new relationship of rights and responsibilities embodied in the concept of citizenship.

Taking an instrumental approach to the analysis of migrant rights, Ruhs is able to countenance the possibility that different migrants will have different rights. Ruhs notes that states confer more rights on high-skilled workers than on low-skilled workers, including better pathways to permanency and more flexible rights to employment in the host state. Ruhs accepts that this is a rational and justifiable distinction from a pragmatic standpoint, and accepts it as a necessary compromise in relation to workers' rights.[105]

The implication of my position is that this flexibility is not open to the state. A distinction can be drawn between high- and low-skill migrants in the decision to permit entry. In other words, it is legitimate for states to make more pathways to entry available for high-skilled migrants. However, once states accept migrant workers, no matter their skills and background, it is difficult to justify a distinction between high- and low-skill workers.[106] Low-skill workers should have the same opportunity for reunification with family, and the same claim to freedom of employment and permanent residence.[107] These rights are required to maintain the dignity of all migrant workers, regardless of their education and skills. In contrast to Ruhs' position, the claim to membership of low-skill workers may in fact be greater from a liberal rights perspective in order to maintain their dignity, ensure their equality, and to protect them from precarious employment and exploitation.

[104] Lord Goldsmith, *Citizenship: Our Common Bond* (London, Ministry of Justice, 2008) 6.

[105] Ruhs, *The Price of Rights* (n 4) ch 3.

[106] Dauvergne and Marsden also make this point in 'The Ideology of Temporary Labour Migration' (n 15) 240.

[107] For an example of a migration system that does not distinguish between high- and low-skilled workers, see the Swedish temporary labour migration policy discussed in Ruhs, *The Price of Rights* (n 4) 101.

V. IMPLICATIONS OF RECOGNISING RESIDENCE AND WORK AS A PRIMARY BASIS FOR MEMBERSHIP

The reason a consequentialist approach to the ethics of labour migration is so appealing is because labour migration provides an economic benefit to all parties—sending and receiving states, migrant workers and employers. There can be little doubt that this is the case. Receiving countries and sending countries actively pursue labour migration opportunities for their nationals in high-income countries, and the World Bank and other organisations actively promote labour migration as a means of improving the income of people from poor nations, and to reduce inequality between states.[108] Paradoxically, some low-income states have rejected requirements for wage parity as undermining their competitive advantage in cheap labour.[109]

At the time he was writing, Walzer was able to draw only on isolated examples of migrant worker schemes, in particular the guest workers schemes in Germany and the United States in the 1960s. Since then, labour migration has increased dramatically and has become an important contributor of wealth and economic opportunity not only for migrant workers, but also for their states of origin, which benefit economically from remittances from workers who are able to earn significantly higher wages in receiving states. In the twenty-first century, labour migration is understood not only in terms of individual justice for migrant workers, but as an issue of global justice, with labour migration being a positive source of employment for workers and wealth creation for developing states, leading more rapidly to an equalisation of wealth between states. Abundant, cheap labour is an economic resource for low-income states in the global economy. The World Bank estimated that remittances in the developed world would reach $440 million in 2015.[110]

There is no question that recognising membership rights of migrant workers will come at the cost of free movement of labour and have an economic impact. But it is important not to overstate this. Where there are genuine labour shortages, states can still bring in migrant labour. States have a choice of short-term migrant labour while they improve training of locals in the industry, or if the shortage is longer term, receiving permanent migrants who can assist in resolving the labour problem. Of course, as permanent migrants with a right to freedom of employment, the workers may move out of the industry, thus requiring other solutions such as a focus on training.[111]

[108] See, eg World Bank, *Global Economic Prospects 2006: Economic Implications of Remittances and Migration* (New York, World Bank, 2006); International Organization for Migration, *Labour Migration and Human Development: 2012 Annual Report* (Geneva, International Organization for Migration, 2012). See discussion in Ruhs, *The Price of Rights* (n 4) 126.

[109] Ruhs, *The Price of Rights* (n 4) 8.

[110] World Bank, 'Remittances Growth to Slow Sharply in 2015, as Europe and Russia Stay Weak; Pick Up Expected Next Year', media release, 13 April 2015.

[111] Ruhs, *The Price of Rights* (n 4) 27.

The economic 'win-win-win' that temporary migration achieves is highly appealing. However, it may be that the economic case is overstated. States need migrants. As low-income countries develop increasingly large middle classes, with increasing demands for material goods and services, more and more labour from traditional sending countries will be needed at home, and wages will increase.[112] This phenomenon is well advanced in China.[113] Therefore, the requirement to offer membership may not be a significant disincentive for states to receive migrant workers in the future. In fact, offering permanent residence may be necessary to provide an advantage in the competition for migrant workers.[114]

Ruhs hypothesises and demonstrates empirically that there is a relationship between openness to migrants and the level of rights they are afforded in the state. When the right is to equal membership, there is a considerable tightening of access to the state.[115] He concludes that '[t]he most likely clean-hands alternative to guest worker programmes for low- and medium-skilled workers is exclusion'.[116]

However, Ruhs' analysis is only able to consider state behaviour under an environment where there are no restrictions on the state's power to deny membership to migrant workers. It is uncertain how a requirement to grant membership rights would affect state behaviour. Ultimately, high-income states want migrant workers. If the workers need to be granted membership for their entry, states may be forced to modernise their approach to citizenship or miss out on the benefit of migrant labour.

The other possibility is not so benign. If states restrict access, this may lead to an increase in illegal migration. People are prepared to migrate for better economic opportunities and, in the absence of legal opportunities to do so, will migrate to work without the permission of receiving states. This in turn will create a class of even more vulnerable migrants in the labour market. I have argued elsewhere that this possibility cannot act as a justification for tolerating exploitative employment relationships within the law.[117] The answer lies in other policy alternatives, and may ultimately lead us to a radical rethinking of the role of state borders.[118]

[112] See, eg OECD, International Migration Outlook 2012 (Paris, OECD, 2012) 201.

[113] Fei Guo, Zhiming Cheng, Graeme Hugo and Wenshu Gao, 'Wages and Employment Status of China's Migrant Workers' in Mark Wang, Pookong Kee and Jia Gao (eds), *Transforming Chinese Cities* (London, Routledge, 2014).

[114] Ruhs, *The Price of Rights* (n 4) 105–6. This is already done in many states for skilled migrants.

[115] Ibid 6.

[116] Ibid 172.

[117] Reilly, 'Ethics of Seasonal Labour Migration' (n 92) 136.

[118] Carens, 'Aliens and Citizens' (n 29).

Requiring states to offer permanent residence in the short term may be a better path to more open societies in the future. Although temporary labour programmes are seen as the transition to more open migration, they might in fact have the opposite effect of allowing states to deny membership while getting the benefit of cheap migrant labour. The danger of allowing workers to move freely between states, but with reduced rights and no claim to membership, is that there is a permanent underclass of workers satisfying the economic needs of wealthy states.

VI. CONCLUSION

Attending to the membership claims of migrant workers clarifies the ethical boundaries of temporary labour migration programmes. Inequality between nations is an ethical consideration for all nations, but it ought not to be achieved at the expense of the equality and human dignity of migrant workers. Requiring attention to membership rights prevents labour migration being a primary means for addressing inequalities between states. Workers should be allowed to migrate to work, but only under conditions that ensure their human dignity, provide for their substantive equality and recognise their labour, not as an input in the economy, but as part of an ongoing relationship with states that leads to recognition of workers as members.

14

Protecting the Rights of Temporary Migrant Workers

Ideals versus Reality

MARTIN RUHS

I. INTRODUCTION

THIS CHAPTER DISCUSSES some of the key critiques of my book *The Price of Rights: Regulating International Labor Migration*.[1] The book was motivated by the large gap between the rights of migrant workers stipulated in international human rights law and the rights that migrants working in high-income countries experience in practice. In the book, I analyse how and why high-income countries restrict the rights of migrant workers as part of their labour immigration policies and discuss the implications for policy debates about regulating labour migration and protecting migrants. My core argument is that there are trade-offs in the policies of high-income countries between openness to admitting migrant workers and some of the rights granted to migrants after admission. Insisting on greater equality of rights for migrant workers can come at the price of more restrictive admission policies, especially for lower-skilled workers. I advocate the liberalisation of international labour migration through temporary migration programmes that protect a universal set of core rights and account for the interests of nation-states by restricting a few specific rights that create net costs for receiving countries.

I wrote *The Price of Rights* (henceforth, *PoR*) with the hope of engaging academic researchers as well as a policy audience with an interest in

[1] Martin Ruhs, *The Price of Rights: Regulating International Labor Migration* (Princeton, NJ, Princeton University Press, 2013).

international labour migration and the rights of migrant workers. My aim was to generate analysis and debate about the interrelationships between migrant rights, labour migration and development; and, more specifically, about the tension that can arise between promoting 'more migration' and 'more rights' for migrant workers—a critically important but greatly under-researched issue in analyses and policy debates of international labour migration. As I explained in the conclusion of *PoR*, the book is meant as a contribution to analysis and debate. It 'cannot and should not settle the positive and normative questions raised'.[2]

As of September 2015 (ie two years since publication), *PoR* has received 24 reviews by academics from a range of disciplines (including economics, politics, law, sociology, development and geography) as well as policy experts and 'practitioners'.[3] It is clear that the analysis and policy recommendations of the book have divided opinion and generated considerable debate. For example (perhaps not entirely surprisingly), in the 'international policy world', the book has been enthusiastically and publicly endorsed by officials at the World Bank and the International Organization for Migration, and severely criticised by officials at the International Labour Organization and Office of the High Commissioner for Human Rights.

The first part of this chapter summarises the key findings and arguments of *PoR*. Readers who have read my book can skip this part completely. In the second part, I discuss and respond to some of the most common comments and critiques. In doing so, I hope to encourage further debate and highlight a range of issues for future research. I conclude with a proposal for a new 'global migrant rights database' which could lead to a step-change in the analysis and protection of migrants' rights around the world.

II. THE PRICE OF RIGHTS: SUMMARY OF KEY ARGUMENTS AND ANALYSIS

This overview focuses on six key elements and findings of the theoretical and empirical analysis in *PoR*.

A. Migrant Rights as Instruments of Labour Immigration Policy

A key argument and starting point of *PoR* is that we need to expand current debates and analyses of migrant rights by complementing conversations about the human rights of migrants with a systematic, dispassionate

[2] Ruhs, *The Price of Rights* (n 1) 199.

[3] Links to all the reviews are available here: http://priceofrights.com/thebook.php.

analysis of the interests and roles of nation-states in granting and restricting the rights of migrant workers. This is because the rights of migrant workers not only have intrinsic value, as underscored by human rights approaches, but also play an important instrumental role in shaping the effects of international labour migration for receiving countries, migrants and their countries of origin.

For example, whether or not migrants enjoy the right to free choice of employment and other employment-related rights in the receiving country's labour market is likely to affect their productivity and earnings, remittances and competition with local workers. The fiscal effects of immigration critically depend on whether and how migrants' social rights (including access to public services and welfare benefits) are restricted. Migrants' incentives and behaviour in and beyond the labour market—for instance, the extent to which they acquire language and other skills relevant to employment and life in the host country—will be influenced by whether or not they have—or are on a path to acquiring—the rights to permanent residence and citizenship.

Because rights shape the effects of labour immigration, migrant rights are in practice a core component of nation-states' labour immigration policies. At its core, the design of labour immigration policy requires simultaneous policy decisions on how to regulate the number of migrants to be admitted (eg through quotas or points-based systems); how to select migrants (eg by skill and/or nationality); and what rights to grant migrants after admission (eg temporary or permanent residence, access to welfare benefits, and limited or unlimited rights to employment). When receiving countries decide on these three issues, the impacts on the 'national interest' (however defined) of the existing residents in the host countries are likely to be of great significance. Policy decisions on the number, selection and rights of migrant workers can also be influenced by their consequences for the interests of migrants and their countries of origin, whose actions and policies can play an important role in supporting, sustaining or undermining particular labour immigration policy decisions in migrant-receiving countries.

B. 'Openness versus Rights' and Other Key Features of Labour Immigration Policies in High-Income Countries

To study how high- and middle-income countries regulate labour immigration and the rights of migrant workers in practice, I created and analysed two separate indices that measure: (i) the openness of 104 labour immigration programmes in 46 high- and middle-income countries to admitting migrant workers; and (ii) the legal rights (civil and political, economic, social, residency and family reunion rights) granted to migrant workers admitted under these programmes. Appendix A briefly describes the methodology for constructing these indices.

The key features of labour immigration policies discussed below refer to policies as they existed in 2009.

Temporary Migration Programmes Predominate

The great majority of labour immigration programmes in high- and middle-income countries (just under 90 per cent in my study) are temporary migration programmes (TMPs), that is, programmes that grant temporary residence status on arrival (although some of them allow a transfer to permanent residence status after some time). The existing permanent immigration programmes (ie programmes that grant permanent residence on arrival) target higher-skilled workers. Nevertheless, as shown in Figure 14.1, even among programmes that target very high-skilled workers only, two-thirds are associated with temporary rather than permanent residence status on arrival.

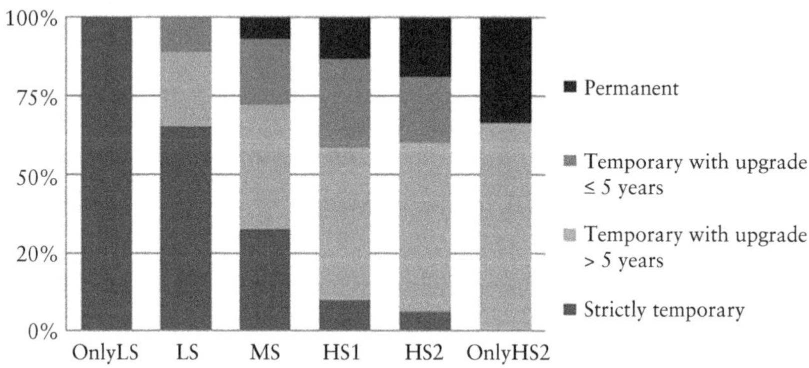

Figure 14.1: Temporary and Permanent Labour Immigration Programmes by Targeted Skills, 2009[4]

[4] See Ruhs, *The Price of Rights* (n 1). Notes—only LS: programmes that target low-skilled workers only; LS: programmes that target low-skilled workers (less than high-school and no vocational skills) and possibly others; MS: programmes that target medium-skilled workers (with high school, vocational training or trades qualification) and possibly others; HS1: programmes that target high-skilled workers (with first degree from university or equivalent) and possibly others; HS2: programmes that target high or very high-skilled workers (with second or third degrees from university or equivalent) and possibly others; only HS2: programmes that target very high-skilled workers only.

Greater Openness to Skilled Labour Immigration

Programmes that target higher-skilled migrant workers place fewer restrictions on admission than programmes targeting lower-skilled migrants. Exceptions include the US, Sweden and the Gulf States.

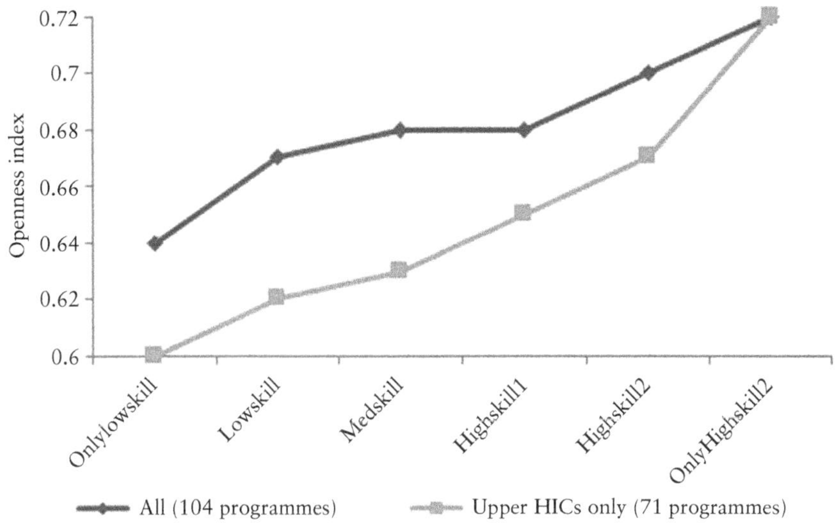

Figure 14.2: Aggregate Openness Index by Targeted Skill Level, 2009[5]

More Rights for Migrants Under Skilled Labour Immigration Programmes

There is a positive relationship between some of the rights granted to migrant workers and the skill level targeted by the immigration programme, that is, programmes that target higher-skilled migrants impose fewer restrictions on some rights than programmes targeting lower-skilled migrants. This holds for many but not all rights. As shown in Figure 14.3, political rights and economic rights are less sensitive to targeted skills than social rights, residence rights and family rights.

[5] See Ruhs, *The Price of Rights* (n 1). Notes: Upper HICs: upper high-income countries. An increasing openness score indicates greater openness toward (ie fewer restrictions on) the admission of migrant workers.

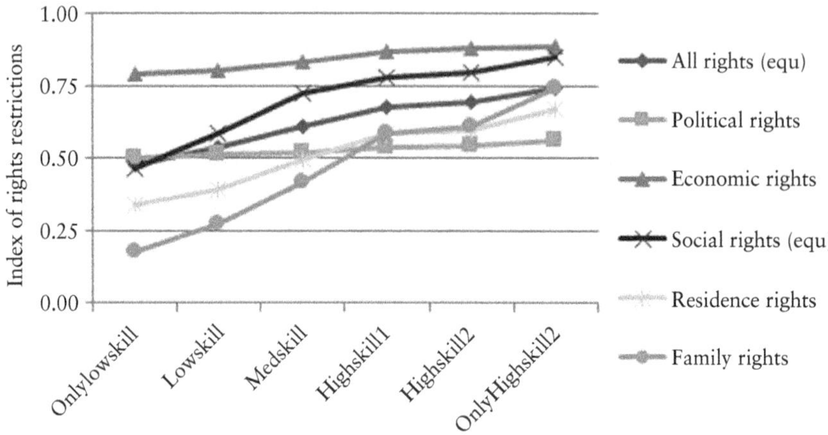

Figure 14.3: Migrant Rights and Targeted Skills, All Programmes, 2009[6]

Trade-Offs Between Openness and Some Rights

As shown in Table 14.1, in upper-high-income countries there is also evidence that labour immigration programmes can be characterised by trade-offs between openness and some migrant rights, that is, programmes that are more open to admitting migrant workers are also more restrictive with regard to specific rights. It is crucial to emphasise that the trade-off between openness and rights affects only a few specific rights rather than all rights, and that they most commonly include selected social and economic rights as well as rights relating to residency and family reunion. My empirical analysis suggests that trade-offs between openness and migrant rights can be found in policies that target a range of skills, but are generally not present in labour immigration programmes specifically designed for admitting the most highly skilled workers, for whom there is intense international competition.

[6] See Ruhs, *The Price of Rights* (n 1). Note: 0 = most restrictive; 1 = least restrictive (no restrictions).

Table 14.1: Correlations Between Openness and Rights (Aggregate and Sub-indices), Labour Immigration Programmes in Upper-High-Income Countries, 2009[7]

	Openness					
Targeted skill level	Only LS	LS	MS	HS1	HS2	Only HS2
Observations	11	30	28	40	41	10
Aggregate rights			-0.341 (0.08)	-0.402 (0.01)	-0.349 (0.02)	
Political rights						
Economic rights			-0.372 (0.05)	-0.311 (0.05)		
Social rights			-0.32 (0.09)	-0.33 (0.03)	-0.339 (0.03)	
Residence rights			-0.327 (0.09)	-0.36 (0.02)	-0.3 (0.06)	
Family rights				-0.33 (0.04)	-0.31 (0.04)	

C. Consistency with 'Rational' Policy Making Based on the 'National Interest'

These key features of labour immigration policies in high-income countries are, I argue, consistent with a 'rational' national policy-making process based on the costs and benefits of immigration for receiving countries. In *PoR*, I suggest that the regulation of labour immigration can be described as a matter of 'choice under constraints'. Nation-states decide how to regulate the number, selection and rights of migrant workers admitted in order to achieve a common set of potential objectives—economic efficiency, distribution, social cohesion and national identity, and national security and public order—given a common set of potential constraints and institutional factors that limit and mediate the ways in which the pursuit of policy objectives

[7] See Ruhs, *The Price of Rights* (n 1) 85. Notes: p-values in parentheses; correlations with $p > 0.10$ are not shown; $N = 71$ programmes; LS: programmes that target low-skilled workers (less than high-school and no vocational skills) and possibly others; MS: programmes that target medium-skilled workers (with high school, vocational training or trades qualification) and possibly others; HS1: programmes that target high-skilled workers (with first degree from university or equivalent) and possibly others; HS2: programmes that target high or very high-skilled workers (with second or third degrees from university or equivalent) and possibly others. Please note: many programmes cover more than one skill group.

translates into actual policies. These constraints and institutional factors stem from nation-states' incomplete capacity to control immigration; domestic liberal institutions and international rights regimes; and the prevailing national political system, production regime (including labour market policies) and welfare system. Taken together, these constraints and institutions define as well as circumscribe the policy space for the regulation of labour immigration in particular countries. The relative significance assigned to each of the policy objectives, the ways in which competing goals are managed, and the strength and impacts of the constraints and institutional factors are all highly specific to country and time. Variation in objectives and constraints leads to different 'national policy spaces' and labour immigration policy regimes that vary both across countries and over time.

This basic model of immigration policy making suggests relationships between openness, skills and rights that are consistent with the key features of high-income countries' labour immigration policies in practice. First, high-income countries can be expected to be more open to high- than low-skilled immigration. This is partly because, compared to low-skilled migrants, higher-skilled migrants can be expected to generate greater complementarities with the skills and capital of existing residents in high-income countries, greater long-term growth effects and greater net fiscal benefits. Secondly, we can expect labour immigration programmes that target higher-skilled migrant workers to grant migrants more rights than those targeting lower-skilled workers. This expectation is partly motivated by the fact that the provision of some rights (eg social rights) creates costs and benefits that can be expected to vary with the skill level and earnings of the rights holder. For instance, granting low-skilled migrants full access to the welfare state can be expected to create greater net costs (or smaller net benefits) for the host country than affording these same rights to high-skilled migrants in high-paid jobs. The third expectation is that there can be a trade-off (a negative relationship) between openness and some of the rights of some migrant workers admitted to high-income countries, that is, greater openness to admitting migrant workers will be associated with relatively fewer rights for migrants and vice versa. The basis for this expectation is closely related to the first two: if certain rights for some migrants create net costs for the receiving country (eg full access to the welfare state for low-skilled migrant workers), policy openness to admitting such migrants can be expected to depend critically on the extent to which some of these costly rights can be restricted.

Of course, mere consistency between a theoretical model and empirical findings does not necessarily mean that the model explains reality in practice. Given what we know about the messiness and numerous potential determinants of national policy-making processes in practice, can it really be reasonable to explain policies with reference to a 'rational' national policy maker in the ways assumed by my model? Do nation-states really restrict the rights of migrants in an instrumental way, that is, based on an assessment of costs and benefits for the host country? In *PoR*, I use a series of mini case studies of policy making in a range of different high-income countries to show that policy decisions about the scale, selection and rights of migrant workers are frequently, and arguably *mostly*, taken based on an assessment about the consequences for the national interest. In other words, while it might be true that not every aspect of the policy-making process is rational and consistent, there is a relatively high degree of 'agency' of the state in many countries when it comes to the design of national labour immigration policies. As I discuss in detail in *PoR*, exceptional cases can be explained without undermining the model. But of course there are always some differences across countries with implications for the applicability of the model that I have proposed.

D. Migrants and Their Countries of Origin: Trading Rights for Access

Migrant workers and their countries of origin are acutely aware of and engage with the trade-off between openness and rights in practice. Every day, migrant workers are making choices about whether to stay at home, or move and work abroad under restricted rights. Large numbers are currently choosing the latter, that is, they are tolerating restrictions of some of their rights in exchange for the opportunity to migrate and work abroad. To be sure, this choice is sometimes misinformed and, in many ways, constrained by larger structural factors, including global economic inequalities and nation-states that restrict access to their territories through immigration control measures. Nevertheless, there is at least some minimal degree of choice in most people's decisions to move abroad for employment purposes. This points to the significance of considering the agency, 'voice' and overall interests of migrants when explaining existing migration flows and policies, and when thinking normatively about whether particular trade-offs should be tolerated. Given that the human development of people is multidimensional and includes more considerations than just access to legal rights, it is not surprising to see migrant workers making 'sacrifices' in some dimensions of development (eg limited access to some legal rights) in exchange for advancing others (eg opportunities to access employment at higher wages and raise the household incomes of their families).

Many low-income countries sending migrant workers abroad make a similar choice. To the extent that they can influence the labour immigration policies of high-income countries, most low-income countries are pursuing emigration policies that are, often explicitly, based on the dual objectives of sending more workers abroad and better protecting them while there. Most low-income countries are acutely aware of the trade-off between access to labour markets in high-income countries and some migrant rights. For example, the policies of Asian countries sending migrants to the

Gulf States, and Latin American countries sending low-skilled workers to the United States and Canada, clearly show that few of these countries are willing to insist on full and equal rights for fear of reduced access to the labour markets of these higher-income countries.[8] Again, this is not surprising given that labour emigration can generate large income gains for migrants and their families as well as benefiting the wider development of migrants' home countries. The World Bank and other development organisations are actively promoting more international labour migration as one of the most effective ways of raising the incomes of workers in low-income countries.

E. The Ethical Case for Expanded Temporary Migration Programmes (TMPs) that Restrict Migrant Rights

As my intention is to contribute to national and international policy debates, I argue for a pragmatic approach that is both realistic, by taking account of existing realities in labour immigration policy making, and idealistic, by giving more weight to the interests of migrants and countries of origin than most high-income countries currently do when designing labour immigration policies. Based on this approach, I contend that there is a strong normative case for tolerating the selective, evidence-based, temporary restriction of a few specific rights under new and expanded TMPs that help liberalise international labour migration, especially of lower-skilled workers whose international movement is currently most restricted and who would, therefore, reap large human development gains from employment abroad. Any rights restrictions should, in my view, be limited to the right to free choice of employment, equal access to means-tested public benefits, the right to family reunion, and the right to permanent residence and citizenship. Rights restrictions need to be evidence-based in the sense that there must be a clear case that they create specific costs that the receiving country wishes to avoid or minimise to enable greater openness to admitting migrant workers. In other words, restricting these rights would lead high-income countries to be more open to labour immigration than would be the case if the rights could not be restricted. I also hold that any rights restrictions should be time-limited (eg limited to about four years). After this period, migrants should be granted access to permanent residence (and thus eventually citizenship) or required to leave. Finally, these rights restrictions are only acceptable, in my view, if they are accompanied by a number of supporting policies including the transparency of policies along with the effective protection of opportunities for migrant workers to exit TMPs whenever they wish and choose to do so.

[8] Witness, for instance, the muted reaction of the Nepalese government to the deaths of their citizens in Qatar. With the current arrangement suiting both nations' economic interests, the two governments even held a joint press conference to say migrant rights were 'fully respected'.

F. Global Governance: The Case for a 'Core-Rights' Approach

The Price of Rights highlights the danger of a blind spot in human rights-based approaches to migration. Such arguments are often focused on protecting and promoting the rights of *existing* migrants without considering the consequences for nation-states' policies for admitting new migrant workers, that is, without considering the interests of the large number of *potential future migrants* who are still in their countries of origin and seeking to access the labour markets of higher-income countries. The trade-off between openness and some specific migrant rights in high-income countries' labour immigration policies means that insisting on equality of rights for migrant workers can come at the price of more restrictive admission policies and, therefore, discourage the further liberalisation of international labour migration. Put differently, human rights–based approaches to migration that demand all the rights stipulated in the existing international labour standards run the danger of doing good in one area (ie promoting the rights of existing migrants) while doing harm in another (ie decreasing opportunities for workers to migrate and legally work in higher-income countries). Most UN agencies and other organisations advocating a human rights–based approach based on the International Convention on the Protection of the Rights of All Migrant Workers and Members of Their Families (CMW) have been reluctant to acknowledge, let alone engage with, this dilemma.[9]

PoR concludes that there is a strong case for advocating a rights-based approach to international labour migration that is premised on the protection of a universal set of 'core rights' and accounts for the interests of nation-states by explicitly tolerating temporary restrictions of a few specific rights that can be shown to create net costs for receiving countries. Restricting these rights should encourage the further liberalisation of international labour migration. Exactly which rights would be on this list of 'core rights' is up for debate, but it is a debate that should, in my view, be at the centre of discussions on the global governance of migration. A 'core' list would include fewer rights than the 1990 convention, but more countries would be likely to accept it. Most significantly, that would include those countries that admit large numbers of migrant workers and currently have minimal incentive to improve conditions. Thus, given the mass numbers involved, overall protection for migrant workers would be increased. It might be a counter-intuitive conclusion, but it is one grounded in reality: when it comes to protecting migrant rights, it turns out less is more.

[9] International Convention on the Protection of the Rights of All Migrant Workers and Members of Their Families (adopted by General Assembly resolution 45/158 of 18 December 1990, entered into force 1 July 2003).

III. A RESPONSE TO REVIEWS

In the remainder of this chapter, I briefly respond to some of the most common critiques of *PoR*. I have grouped the comments under six headings relating to:

1. gaps and 'exceptional cases' in my policy analysis;
2. the scope and limits of my quantitative analysis of admission policies and migrant rights;
3. the (ir)rationality of the policy-making process;
4. the feasibility of TMPs, especially the enforcement of employment rights and return;
5. the ethics of my approach and of TMPs more generally;
6. my argument for a core-rights approach and the implications for human rights.

A. Policy Analysis: Gaps and 'Exceptional' Cases

Irregular Migration

Alba asks why the empirical analysis in the book focuses on legal labour migration and excludes illegal migration to high-income countries.[10] Illegality in migration and employment of migrants is obviously an important issue in some countries but it is important to remember that the vast majority of international labour migration occurs through legal channels that are regulated by nation-states. Given that my analysis already included over 104 labour immigration programmes in over 46 countries, I excluded policies towards illegal migration partly on pragmatic grounds. I agree that it would be desirable to analyse illegal migration and the rights of illegally resident migrants. There are obvious methodological challenges but one could try to measure, first, the policies put in place to prevent and reduce illegal immigration and, second, the legal rights granted to migrant workers without legal residence status. In the context of my book, the interesting question would be whether there is evidence of a systematic trade-off between national policies to prevent/reduce illegal immigration on the one hand, and the legal rights granted to migrants who are illegally resident on the other.

Free Movement in the European Union

A number of reviewers suggested that 'free movement' migration within the EU shows that the trade-off between openness and rights in labour

[10] Francisco Alba, 'Martin Ruhs' *The Price of Rights*: Flexible Accommodation vs. All-Encompassing Norms?' (2015) 3(2) *Migration Studies* 295.

migration can be overcome. These reviewers thus queried why I excluded free movement migration from my analysis.[11]

As I explain in the book, there are two main reasons why I excluded migrants moving under free movement agreements from the analysis in *PoR*. First, although significant in some countries, free movement agreements account for a minority of international labour migrants. Second, most free movement agreements cannot be considered labour immigration policies as they are typically part of larger regional harmonisation and integration policies that involve a wide range of policies and objectives (eg free trade and investment policies).

It is true, however, that free movement within the EU constitutes an important and interesting special case because it does not currently involve a trade-off between openness and rights: EU *workers* have both the right to migrate and work in any EU Member State and the right to equal access to that country's welfare state. In the context of the issues discussed in my book, it is interesting to ask whether this 'EU exceptionalism', that is, the combination of open borders and equal access to welfare states for EU workers, is sustainable.

Before EU enlargement in 2004, the principle of free movement for EU workers was remarkably stable and relatively unchallenged by individual EU Member States. This may be partially explained by the fact that levels of GDP per capita of the EU Member States were relatively similar (with some notable exceptions including, for example, Portugal and Spain). As a consequence, intra-EU migration remained relatively low and, in most EU countries, was not particularly controversial in public policy debates. The 'politics of free movement' began to change after the EU enlargements of 2004 and 2007 when ten lower-income countries in Eastern Europe joined the EU. Britain, which has seen very large inflows of Eastern European workers since 2004, has been one of the strongest advocates for reforming the rules for the free movement of workers within the EU, but other countries including Germany, the Netherlands and Denmark have called for policy changes as well.

The recent debates about free movement in the EU are directly based on the tension between 'unrestricted access to labour markets' (ie 'openness') and 'equal access to the welfare state' (ie social rights). As far as I am aware, Britain is the only EU country whose government has openly suggested (at least in domestic policy debates) introducing restrictions on both EU immigration and EU workers' access to benefits. Other EU countries have proposed policies that would protect the unrestricted movement of workers across EU countries but introduce greater restrictions on EU migrants'

[11] Don Flynn, 'The Migrant Rights Conundrum: What Are We Campaigning For?', *Migrant Rights Network Blog*, 4 November 2013; K Seegobin, 'Review: The Price of Rights' (2014) 14(2) *Studies in Ethnicity and Nationalism* 383; Alba, 'Martin Ruhs' (n 1) *The Price of Rights*'.

access to the welfare systems of Member States. Arguably, the political sustainability of free movement of workers within the EU will depend, at least in part, on whether and how the rules of free movement will change to take account of the tension between 'access' and 'rights'.[12]

Sweden

In 2008, Sweden introduced a new labour immigration programme that admits both high- and lower-skilled migrant workers and grants them the same rights. Alberti and Benton argue that the case of Sweden shows that it is possible for high-income countries to implement labour immigration policies that do not treat high- and low-skilled migrants differently, and that do not involve a trade-off between openness and rights.[13]

In *PoR*, I argue that Sweden's 'exceptionalism' can be explained by the relative recency of the policy (at the time of writing my book, ie 2012) and its experimental nature. I speculated that Sweden would come under pressure to start making a distinction in its policy approach to high- and low-skilled migrants and that the tensions between openness and rights would eventually come to the fore.

So, what has happened to Sweden's labour immigration policies over the past few years? While the core features of the labour immigration policies introduced in Sweden in 2008 are still in place, some policy changes have been made. Engblom discusses a number of new regulations that the Swedish Migration Board has implemented in recent years, partly in response to concerns about the effects of rapidly increasing low-skilled immigration in certain low-waged occupations such as cherry picking.[14] These policy changes, most of which were aimed at ensuring the effective enforcement of minimum standards and conditions in occupations with a small or no union presence, led to a considerable decline in work permits issued for these jobs.

There has also been increasing debate about the link between Sweden's policies for admitting migrant workers and shortages in the Swedish labour market, especially in lower-skilled occupations. Some analysts and commentators have argued that a considerable share of lower-skilled migrants

[12] For a more detailed discussion, see Martin Ruhs, *Is Unrestricted Immigration Compatible with Inclusive Welfare States? The (Un)sustainability of EU Exceptionalism*, COMPAS Working Paper (Oxford, COMPAS, 2015).

[13] Gabriella Alberti, 'Book Review: The Price of Rights' (2014) 52(2) *British Journal of Industrial Relations* 387; M Benton, 'Review: The Price of Rights' (2014) 26 *European Journal of Development Research* 933.

[14] Samuel Engblom, 'Reconciling Openness and High Labour Standards? Sweden's Attempts to Regulate Labour Migration and Trade in Services' in Cathryn Costello and Mark Freedland (eds), *Migrants at Work: Immigration and Vulnerability in Labour Law* (Oxford, Oxford University Press, 2014).

are employed in occupations that are not suffering from labour shortages[15] (a very slippery concept, as discussed in the collection edited by Ruhs and Anderson).[16] It remains to be seen whether and how these findings and arguments lead to policy change over the coming years.

B. Policy Analysis: Focus and Methods

Interaction with Other Immigration Policies

Reilly and Sherrell make an important point about the limitation of focusing on labour immigration policy, defined in *PoR* as policies for the admission of migrants for the primary purpose of employment.[17] Clearly (and as I explain in chapter 4 of *PoR*), many migrants not admitted for the primary purpose of employment may nevertheless take up work in the host country and eventually become classified as migrant workers (eg recognised refugees, dependents, students working part time, working holiday makers, etc). Reilly and Sherrell rightly argue that there could be important interrelationships between policies for admitting migrant workers, students, dependents, working holiday makers and so on. One could argue, for example, that a relatively restrictive labour immigration programme for low-skilled migrants may be explained, at least in part, by a working holiday maker programme that admits large numbers of people. While it is not immediately obvious how these interrelationships between different types of immigration policies would affect the tensions between openness and rights in labour migration, I agree that the analysis of these interrelationships constitutes an important area for future research.

Limits of Quantitative Methods and the Case for Mixed Methods

Alberti and Palander query the usefulness and limits of quantitative indicators and indices to measure and analyse immigration policies.[18] While I am convinced about the need and usefulness of more and better quantitative

[15] See, eg Henrik Emilsson, 'Who Gets In and Why? The Swedish Experience with Demand-Driven Labour Migration—Some Preliminary Results' (2014) 4(3) *Nordic Journal of Migration Research* 134.

[16] Martin Ruhs and Bridget Anderson (eds), *Who Needs Migrant Workers? Labour Shortages, Immigration and Public Policy* (Oxford, Oxford University Press, 2010).

[17] Alexander Reilly, 'Review: The Price of Rights' (2014) 35 *Adelaide Law Review* 189; Henry Sherrell, 'Book Review: Martin Ruhs' "The Price of Rights"', *Value for Money* blog, 12 January 2014.

[18] Alberti, 'Book Review: The Price of Rights'; Jaana Palander, 'Review: The Price of Rights' (2014) 4(3) *Nordic Journal of Migration Research* 157.

policy indicators,[19] I agree that there will always be strong limitations and caveats that need to be kept in mind. Can a policy really be quantified and measured by an index? Can the presence and scope of rights be reduced to a number? Most importantly, can we really compare and integrate measures of different types of rights that, some contend, are incommensurable? These are all legitimate questions. They do not invalidate the usefulness of the exercise, however; what they do suggest is that any results need to be carefully discussed and interpreted in light of the underlying assumptions and limitations. The obvious implication is that it is important to be as open and transparent as possible about the methodology along with its limitations, and carefully explain all the assumptions and decisions made at various stages of the analysis.

There is, in my view, a very strong case for a mixed method approach to analysing immigration policies. More quantitative approaches can be helpful in suggesting systematic patterns and potential relationships, but qualitative and in-depth analyses of policy processes need to remain central to research in this area. I agree with Reilly who argues for more in-depth research that drills down into the characteristics and interrelationships between policies toward various categories of migrants in different countries.[20]

The aim of the brief 'case studies' in *PoR* was not to provide a comprehensive and in-depth analysis of the determinants of different countries' policies, which would have been impossible within the scope and structure of the book. Instead, I was trying to provide some evidence to support my general claim that, when high-income countries decide on how to design their labour immigration policies (including what rights to grant to migrant workers), they consider the likely consequences, that is, the costs and benefits for their national interests (however defined). The case studies show that restrictions of migrants' rights are an important instrument of high-income countries' labour immigration policies in practice. At the same time, when low-income countries consider whether and how to help protect the rights of their nationals working abroad, they consider the costs and benefits of doing so including the impact on the scale of labour emigration and remittances.

C. The (Ir)rationality of the Policy-Making Process

The empirical findings of *PoR* may be compatible with a range of different explanations and conceptualisations of policy-making processes.

[19] For an excellent review of the small but rapidly growing body of research on measuring immigration and citizenship policies, see Marc Helbling, Liv Bjerre, Friederike Römer and Malisa Zobel, 'How to Measure Immigration Policies' (2013) 1(2) *Migration and Citizenship* 4.

[20] Reilly, 'Review: The Price of Rights' (n 17).

The research literature on the determinants and processes of migration policies (and public policies more generally) has identified a range of potential factors including interests, institutions and ideas.[21] A key question relates to the degree of 'agency' of the nation-state, that is, the extent to which nation-states can be analysed as unitary and independent actors that are able to formulate and pursue 'national' policy objectives.

As I discussed above, my theoretical approach in *PoR* conceptualised the design of labour immigration policy in high-income countries as a process of 'choice under constraints'. I thus assume a considerable degree of 'agency' of the nation-state. A number of reviewers including Flynn and Gzesh argue that my approach to conceptualising the migration policy-making process is too 'state-centric' and assumes too much 'rationality'.[22]

Having observed and at times been involved in migration policy making in different countries for almost 20 years, I am of course aware that migration policies are not always the outcome of rational processes. In the UK, for example, the Home Office and the Business Department have on various occasions openly disagreed on the direction of future immigration policy, which means that policy outputs can sometimes be explained, at least in part, by the power struggles between these two (and sometimes also other) government departments. I also agree that interest groups, especially employers, can be important influencers of migration policies.

Nevertheless, and as I discuss in *PoR*, I do think that nation-states have significantly more 'agency' in migration policy making than implied by some of the research literature on the determinants of migration policies. For example, employers are clearly important but they do not always 'get what they want'. The aim of chapter 5 of *PoR* is to explore the determinants and some of the processes of policy making in different countries. The case studies in this chapter are brief and clearly exploratory—but they do, in my view, show that policy decisions on how to regulate the admission and rights of migrant workers in high-income countries are firmly based on assessments of the consequences of admitting migrants and granting or restricting rights for the national interests of migrant-receiving countries. With few exceptions, high-income countries are more open and grant more rights to high- than low-skilled migrant workers because they consider these policies to be in their best national interests. Given the disagreements about the multifaceted consequences of immigration for the receiving country,

[21] See, eg Gary Freeman, 'Modes of Immigration Politics in Liberal Democratic States' (1995) 19(3) *International Migration Review* 881; Kitty Calavita, *Inside the State* (New York, Routledge, 1992); Alex Balch, 'Labour and Epistemic Communities: The Case of "Managed Migration" in the UK' (2009) 11(4) *British Journal of Politics and International Relations* 613.

[22] Flynn, 'The Migrant Rights Conundrum' (n 11); Susan Gzesh, 'Book Review of The Price of Rights: Regulating International Labor Migration' (2014) 2(1) *Journal of Migration and Human Security* 15.

it is no surprise that the impact assessments of specific admission policies and rights restrictions are commonly contested as well as continuously evolving in different countries. While the degree to which policy decisions are informed by evidence about real effects versus perceptions of likely effects varies across countries, it is clear that assessments of the impact on the national interest are a core factor explaining the policy choices observed in high-income countries in practice.

D. Feasibility of Enforcement: Employment Rights and Return under TMPs

A number of reviewers have questioned the feasibility of implementing and enforcing the rules of the improved and expanded temporary migration programmes that I propose in *PoR*. In particular, Gzesh asks if it will be possible to protect the employment rights of migrants admitted under TMPs effectively.[23] Benton is sceptical about whether it will be possible to encourage or facilitate the return of migrants whose temporary work permits have expired and who have not been granted a permanent residence permit.[24]

There is a large research literature on the 'failure' of past guest worker programmes which have commonly been associated with (at least) three adverse and, arguably, unintended consequences: (1) the exploitation of migrant workers; (2) the growing reliance and eventual structural dependence of certain industries on the continued employment of migrant labour; and (3) the non-return and eventual settlement of many supposedly 'temporary' migrant workers. In light of this past experience, it is not surprising that proposals for 'new and improved' TMPs are viewed with scepticism.

In *PoR*, I propose a series of policies that are aimed at 'learning from past policy mistakes' in order to increase the likelihood that the new programmes will achieve their stated policy objectives (including the effective protection of the rights of migrants in the labour market). A large number of researchers of past guest worker policies around the world have concluded that all TMPs are 'bound to fail'. I do not share this assessment. While I recognise the many challenges that the implementation of TMPs raises, I think the potential benefits of such programmes for all sides (receiving countries, migrants and their countries of origin) should encourage us to experiment with new programmes that try to avoid past policy mistakes. The first step should be to conduct pilot programmes that test the new policies. The new programmes for low-skilled workers in NZ and Australia are examples of how initial pilots can provide opportunities to fine-tune and eventually expand new TMPs.

[23] Gzesh, 'Book Review of The Price of Rights' (n 22).
[24] Benton, 'Review: The Price of Rights' (n 13).

E. Ethics

Why Four Years?

In my discussion of new and improved TMPs, I suggest that temporary work permits should be limited to a maximum of four years. After this period receiving countries need either to offer migrants permanent residence or to ask them to leave. I do not support long-term or permanent exclusion of migrant workers from equal access to citizenship rights.

Mares, Gzesh and Reilly ask why I am suggesting four years rather than, say, two, five or ten years?[25] As Joseph Carens points out, philosophical reflection cannot provide a clear answer to the question of how long migrants' rights can justifiably be restricted.[26] As I explained in *PoR*, it is hard to justify the difference between three, four and five years, so I agree that four years is, to a degree, an arbitrary number. But anything less than three years seems too short to ensure that the policy generates the intended benefits (especially for migrants), while restrictions that last longer than five years seem to come close to long-term or permanent exclusion from equal citizenship rights—which I reject.

Reilly raises another question about the four-year period that I propose: 'Could there be a distinction between high- and low-skilled workers in relation to this length of time, based on their contribution to the receiving state, their vulnerability to exploitation or their level of integration?'[27] I agree that this is an important question. My initial response is that it is certainly possible and may well be desirable to make such a distinction and grant migrants access to permanent residence after three, four or five years based on certain clear criteria.[28]

Reinforcing the Status Quo?

A number of reviewers suggested that my emphasis on trade-offs and core rights 'essentially reinforces the "status quo"'.[29] Provencher suggests that

[25] Peter Mares, 'The Ethical Case for Guest Workers', *Inside Story*, 21 October 2013; Gzesh, 'Book Review of The Price of Rights' (n 22); Reilly, 'Review: The Price of Rights' (n 17).

[26] Joseph Carens, 'Live-in Domestics, Seasonal Workers, and Others Hard to Locate on the Map of Democracy' (2008) 16(4) *Journal of Political Philosophy* 371.

[27] Reilly, 'Review: The Price of Rights' (n 17) 192.

[28] The relatively short period (two years) after which Canada's Live-in Caregiver programme enabled migrants to transfer to permanent residence was partly justified by the difficult work involved, ie live-in caregivers 'earn' the right to expedited access to permanent residence.

[29] Flynn, 'The Migrant Rights Conundrum' (n 11). See also Wayne Palmer, 'Review of *The Price of Rights*' (2014) 23(1) *Asia Pacific Migration Journal* 127; Michelle Leighton, 'Review: The Price of Rights: Regulating International Labor Migration' (2015) 154(2) *International Labour Review* 277.

my policy recommendations are 'not progressive enough'[30] and Benton warns that 'we need equally to resist the force of the economist's trump: the trade-off'.[31] Leighton argues that the analysis in PoR 'offers a policy description that appears to perpetuate, rather than reduce, inequitable treatment and discrimination in the labour force'.[32] Pecoud eloquently summarises this line of critique: 'In the eternal opposition between idealists and realists, Martin Ruhs thus lies clearly in the second camp, with the risk of engaging in a brilliant plea for the status quo'.[33]

It is true that my normative approach is 'realistic' in the sense that I start with certain 'givens' including the existence of the nation-state and the need for national policy makers to give at least some preference to the interests of citizens (or residents) over those of non-citizens or people living in other countries. By analysing the instrumental role of rights and the effects of rights on the national interests of nation-states, the book provides some 'realism' to academic analysis and normative debates about international labour migration and the rights of migrants.

As Carens suggested, and as I discuss in detail in chapter 7 of *PoR*, there is a fundamental difference between 'realistic' and 'idealistic' approaches to the ethics of immigration.[34] The realistic approach is firmly based on existing realities, and stresses the importance of avoiding overly large discrepancies between the *ought* and the *can*. In contrast, the idealistic approach is less constrained by considerations of practicality and focuses only on what *ought to be*, regardless of whether or not the implied policies are currently feasible. Carens makes the important point that 'the assumptions we adopt should depend in part on the purposes of our inquiry'.[35] If the objective of the ethical discourse is to yield practical policy implications—as it is in my normative analysis in *PoR*—there is a strong argument to be made for adopting a combination of both approaches.

I would describe my approach as a combination of idealistic and realistic elements. My recommendations are 'idealistic' in the sense that they put much more weight in the design of labour immigration policies on the interests of migrants and their sending countries than is currently the case in most high-income countries. The approach is 'realistic' in the sense that

[30] Martin Provencher, 'Les Droits des travailleurs migrants temporaires: Entre droits fondamentaux et droits sociaux', Article général, Centre d'Etudes et de Recherches Internationales, Université de Montréal, 10 April 2014.

[31] Benton, 'Review: The Price of Rights' (n 13) 935.

[32] Leighton, 'Review: The Price of Rights' (n 29) 278.

[33] Antoine Pecoud, 'Review: The Price of Rights' (2014) 64(3) *Critique Internationale* 161, 164.

[34] Joseph Carens, 'Realistic and Idealistic Approaches to the Ethics of Migration' (1996) 30(1) *International Migration Review* 156.

[35] Ibid 169.

it accepts that high-income countries are unlikely to adopt policies that are perceived to create considerable net costs for their 'national interests'.

A key question for anybody struggling with these issues is what we accept as 'given' and unchangeable in the short- to medium-term future. An important related question is how short-term realism affects the likelihood of the implementation of more idealistic approaches in the long run. These are clearly hard and contested questions that we can and should debate.

I agree that some of the rights restrictions that I 'accept' in my policy recommendations for new and better temporary migration programmes are already in place in many high-income countries. *PoR* provides a detailed analysis of which specific rights restrictions I would find acceptable on a temporary basis and why. But I reject the notion that 'nothing would change' if my proposed new policies were implemented. One key change would be that the policies I propose would, I argue, lead to a liberalisation of international labour migration through more and expanded legal channels for labour migration to high-income countries, especially for lower-skilled workers whose international movement is currently most restricted. It is hard to think of any policies that would improve the human development of workers and their families in low-income countries more than giving them the opportunity to access and work in high-income countries.

F. Global Governance

Human Rights: Straw Man?

While the analysis and core arguments in *PoR* can be made without reference to 'human rights', the book does start and end with a discussion of the human rights of migrants. I argue that, for the purpose of informing policy debates and policy making, the International Convention on the Protection of the Rights of All Migrant Workers and Members of Their Families (CMW) is too demanding and should be complemented (but not replaced) by a list of core rights that includes fewer rights than the CMW but has a higher chance of acceptance by high-income countries with large numbers of migrants.

The discussion of the human rights of migrants in *PoR* has attracted considerable criticism from some (but not all) international organisations and legal scholars. The most common critique is that, by arguing that the CMW cannot accommodate some of the rights restrictions and trade-offs I propose, I essentially set up a 'straw man' because, they argue, the CMW does allow for a wide range of temporary rights restrictions. As Mayer argues, 'when concluding that this analysis calls for "a reframing of the human rights-based approach to migration as currently advocated by most UN agencies" (p16), Ruhs may to some extent appear to rebut a straw-man's argument'.[36]

As a political economist, I have always been very interested in rights in general and human rights in particular, but I do not claim to have particular legal expertise on this topic. I feel I learnt a lot about human rights while doing the research for *PoR*, but I still remain surprised and somewhat confused by the wide range of interpretations of the CMW in analysis and debates about international labour migration. One the one hand, the CMW is frequently used to criticise restrictions of migrant rights (including the types of temporary restrictions that I propose in *PoR*). At the same time, I have been told that the CMW is in fact highly flexible and can accommodate a wide range of restrictions. It sometimes seems as if the CMW is *both* very demanding and at the same time infinitely flexible and accommodating of national interests of nation-states. I understand that there are debates about the meaning and implementation of the 'proportionality principle'. For example, in her review of *PoR*, Gzesh argues that situations when non-fundamental human rights can be abrogated are 'restricted to serious temporary emergencies of national security' and cannot be justified based on the trade-offs and factors discussed in *PoR*.[37] Other scholars have provided me with a different and broader interpretation of the proportionality principle. I remember a presentation I gave at the Office of the High Commissioner for Human Rights in 2010 where I asked whether the CMW was, in principle, compatible with the types of temporary migration programmes that we currently see in liberal democracies. I did not get an answer. Perhaps this ambiguity is intended and not surprising to legal scholars but I do think it would be helpful to the debate if some of these points could be discussed more explicitly.

Strategies for Migrant Rights Activists

Alba argues that my efforts to convince migrant rights advocates to adopt a core-rights approach are unlikely to succeed and, in any case, undesirable:

> To uphold and advance this legal international regime is one of the major aims of migrants' rights advocates. Thus, Ruhs' final quest, to transform the supporters of the CMW into advocates of a limited set of 'core rights' for migrant workers, and to lead efforts to promote research and debate on 'the existence and dynamics of trade-offs between specific rights and admission policies' (p199), seems futile. Any such trade-offs would detract from the integrity of that legal regime's architecture.[38]

[36] Benoit Mayer, 'Review: The Price of Rights' (2014) 14(4) *Human Rights Law Review* 779, 783.

[37] Gzesh, 'Book Review of The Price of Rights' (n 22) 18.

[38] Alba, 'Martin Ruhs' *The Price of Rights*' (n 10) 298.

'Futile' seems a strong word given the wide range of interests and different approaches adopted by different migrant rights activists and organisations. There may well be good reasons for rejecting my analysis and policy proposals but arguing that they detract from the integrity of international legal regimes for the rights of migrant workers is, in my view, not enough.

IV. CONCLUSION: THE CASE FOR A GLOBAL MIGRANT RIGHTS DATABASE

I conclude with a suggestion for future research. Rather than presenting a list of issues and research questions, I focus on one particular innovation that could lead to a step-change in the analysis and protection of migrants' rights around world: the creation of a global migrant rights database.

It is in my view absolutely essential for both research and policy debates on international migration that we improve the measurement of migrant rights. Future research should extend my approach of measuring specific rights to more countries, study rights over time, and analyse rights both de jure and in practice. Future analysis also needs to include the rights of, and the immigration policies for admitting, other types of migrants such as family migrants, students, asylum seekers and refugees, irregular migrants and so on. Various research projects are under way that measure immigration policies for admitting different types of migrants,[39] but I am not aware of any ongoing work on creating a systematic global migrant rights database.

How could it be done? The indicators could be conceptualised and designed by a group of experts including migrant rights specialists and measurement experts. The analysis could then be implemented by a group of country experts. If the information were collected every year, it would be possible to build up a longitudinal database of indicators of rights protections/restrictions across countries and different groups of migrants and over time.

In addition to facilitating comprehensive monitoring, this database would allow analysis of the patterns, determinants and effects of restrictions of migrant rights. A range of questions could be analysed, for example:

- Patterns, variations and trends: how do rights restrictions vary across different rights, groups of migrants and countries? Which rights are most commonly restricted? How do rights restrictions evolve over time?
- Determinants: What are the drivers of restrictions of the rights of migrants? How are rights restrictions related to labour markets, welfare

[39] See, eg, Helbling et al, 'How to Measure Immigration Policies' (n 19).

states and admission policies? What are the characteristics and drivers of different 'varieties' of immigration policies (including restrictions of migrant rights)?

— Impacts: What are the effects of restricting the rights of migrants on the migrants themselves, migrant-receiving countries and migrant-sending countries?

Crucially, the indicators would need to be presented in a way that makes them transparent and accessible to anybody for use and analysis. For example, the different migrant rights indicators could be presented on a dedicated website where people can download and interact with the data to create their own indices based on their own preferred indicators.[40]

In addition to providing the basis for new research, the migrant rights database would generate significant benefits for policy debates. It would enable policy makers to assess their policies towards migrants critically in light of international experiences and assess the effectiveness of different policy interventions. A global migrant rights index would also empower stakeholders and advocacy groups to campaign on migration and migrant rights issues more effectively based on a rigorous and widely respected evidence base.

So why does it not yet exist? A key challenge is that, to be useful, a global migrant rights database needs to be created in a rigorous and credible way, which means it will require significant resources. We are essentially talking about trying to provide a 'global public good'.

In theory, standard-setting organisations such as the Office of the High Commissioner for Human Rights and the International Labour Organization should have a great interest in promoting the development of such a database. In practice, the work of the UN and other international organisations is often constrained by the interests of their Member States.

Immigration and the rights of migrants are among the most salient and controversial public policy issues in many countries. Consequently, the development of any index that could be used to rank countries according to their policies towards migration and migrants is likely to be opposed by Member States who are concerned that their position in the final ranking may not look 'favourable' from a domestic political perspective (some governments will not want to be seen to be 'too open and generous' towards migrants, while others may not want to be seen as much more restrictive than comparable countries).

But things might be changing. In late 2012, I proposed the creation of a global migrant rights database at a migration workshop organised by

[40] See, eg, the interactive presentation of the UNDP's Human Development Indicators, http://hdr.undp.org/en/data.

KNOMAD, a new research programme on migration and development overseen by the World Bank. In early 2013, KNOMAD decided to go ahead with (a version of) this project.[41] It remains to be seen how rigorous and credible KNOMAD's new database will be, or indeed how much the project will prioritise a discussion of potential indicators of rights over actual measurement. Nevertheless, the fact that a major international organisation has committed to thinking about systematically measuring and analysing migrant rights around the world is definitely an encouraging step forward.

APPENDIX A: SUMMARY OF THE METHODOLOGY FOR CONSTRUCTING INDICATORS OF 'OPENNESS' AND 'MIGRANT RIGHTS' IN *THE PRICE OF RIGHTS*[42]

Labour immigration programmes

The analysis in *PoR* focuses on labour immigration programmes, defined as policies for regulating the number, skills and rights of migrants who are admitted for the primary purpose of work. For countries in the European Union, I focus on policies for admitting non-EEA[43] workers only.

Unit of analysis

Most countries operate different labour immigration policies for admitting migrants for employment in low-, medium- and high-skilled jobs. Policies for different skill groups of workers are typically associated with different degrees of policy openness and rights for migrants. This is why I use labour immigration programmes rather than countries as a whole as my unit of analysis.

Targeted skill level

Each of the programmes included in my analysis was assigned one or more 'targeted skill level'. The targeted skill level of a labour immigration programme reflects the skills required in the (specific or range of) jobs that

[41] See KNOMAD, 'Migrant Rights and Social Aspects of Migration', http://www.knomad.org/thematic-working-groups/migrant-rights-and-social-aspects-of-migration.

[42] For a more detailed discussion, see Ruhs, *The Price of Rights* (n 1) ch 4.

[43] The European Economic Area (EEA) includes all countries of the EU, plus Norway, Liechtenstein and Iceland.

migrants are admitted to fill. I distinguish between programs that target: low-skilled workers (LS) with less than high-school and no vocational skills; medium-skilled workers (MS) with high school, vocational training or trades qualifications; high-skilled workers (HS1) with first degrees from university or equivalent; and very high-skilled workers (HS2) with second or third degrees from university or equivalent. Many programs cover more than one skill group. Given that there is no universal definition of skill, the classification inevitably requires a degree of judgement.

Policy openness indicators

I have defined openness as 'policy openness' measured by the scale and strength of policy restrictions on the admission and employment of migrant workers. My policy openness index includes three types of restrictions: (i) quotas; (ii) criteria that employers in the host country need to meet to employ migrant workers legally ('demand restrictions'); and (iii) criteria that potential migrant workers need to meet to be admitted to the host country ('supply restrictions'). The openness index comprises a total of twelve indicators: existence, types and strength of quotas; demand restrictions including the requirement of a job offer; strength of labour market tests; restrictions on wages and conditions; occupational/sectoral restrictions; economic fees for employing migrants; the degree of trade union involvement; supply restrictions including nationality and age restrictions; gender and marital status restrictions; specific skills requirements; language requirements; and self-sufficiency requirements.

Migrant rights indicators

My indicators of migrant rights include a mix of different types of rights including: five civil and political rights (vote, stand for election, associate, keep identity documents, protection of criminal courts); five economic rights (free choice of employment, equal pay, equal conditions other than pay, join trade unions, redress in case of contract violation); five social rights (access to unemployment benefits, public pension schemes, public education and training, social housing, public health services); five 'residency rights' (time limit on residence, security of residence dependent on employment and criminal convictions, direct access to citizenship, redress in case of withdrawal of residence permit); and three rights related to family reunion (family reunion, spouse's right to work, redress).

Focus on policies and rights 'de jure'

In my analysis, the term 'migrant rights' refers to the legal rights (defined here as the rights granted by national laws and policies) granted to migrant workers on admission under a particular labour immigration programme. So my indicators measure rights in laws and regulations rather than in practice.

Part VII

The Global Challenge of Temporary Labour Migration: Regulatory Responses and Possibilities

15

Roles for Workers and Unions in Regulating Labour Recruitment in Mexico

JENNIFER GORDON*

I. INTRODUCTION

ONE OF THE most exploitative phases of transnational labour migration—recruitment for work abroad—takes place before a migrant has even left her home country. During the recruitment process, it is routine for recruiters and their agents to make false promises about the jobs on offer, charge would-be migrants fees that exceed their annual income, and offer loans at usurious rates, demanding property deeds as collateral.[1] These practices, and others that are even more disturbing, reflect the fact that recruitment is a functionally unregulated field. Origin

* This chapter was made possible through generous support from the Solidarity Center and is part of its Transformation of Work research series, which is funded by the Office of Democracy and Governance, Bureau for Democracy, Conflict, and Humanitarian Assistance, US Agency for International Development, under the terms of Award No AID-OAA-L-11-00001. The opinions expressed herein are those of the author and do not necessarily reflect the views of the US Agency for International Development. Alex Cárdenas provided essential research assistance. My greatest appreciation goes to the advocates, organisers and guest workers who have shared their time and insight with me over the course of this project.

[1] The problems of labour recruitment have been well documented. In the Mexico–US context, see Alejandra Constanza, Ancheita Pagaza and Gisele Lisa Bonnici, *Quo Vadis? Recruitment and Contracting of Migrant Workers and Their Access to Social Security: The Dynamics of Temporary Migrant Labour Systems in North and Central America* (Mexico City, INEDIM, 2013) 40; Centro de los Derechos del Migrante, *Recruitment Revealed: Fundamental Flaws in the H-2 Temporary Worker Program and Recommendations for Change* (Mexico City, Centro de los Derechos del Migrante, 2013); Ashwini Sukthankar, *Visas, Inc: Corporate Control and Policy Incoherence in the US Temporary Labor System* (New York, Global Workers Justice Alliance, 2012) 40–45; International Labour Recruitment Working Group, *The American Dream Up for Sale: A Blueprint for Ending International Labor Recruitment Abuse* (Washington, DC, International Labour Recruitment Working Group, 2013); Mary Bauer and Meredith Stewart, *Close to Slavery: Guestworker Programs in the United States* (Montgomery, AL, Southern Poverty Law Center, 2013).

countries are deeply conflicted about any enforcement that might limit their citizens' access to employment abroad,[2] and destination nations too often regard what happens to migrants on other shores as none of their concern. Recruitment is also a heavily subcontracted industry, which allows the principal actors to avoid what liability exists by pointing to entities further down the chain. Frequently, then, the only real law recruitment firms face is that of supply and demand. In a context where the number of would-be migrant workers far exceeds the availability of employment, opportunities for abuse abound.

Fortunately, this is a moment of active experimentation around the world with new standards and strategies to curb recruitment violations. I argue that this developing field would benefit from additional attention to three features: a primary (or at least equal) focus on the ultimate employer as the target of enforcement, the creation of meaningful economic incentives for employer and recruiter compliance, and more active roles for workers in the fight against recruitment abuses. In a paper published by the International Labour Organization in 2015, I address the first two issues.[3] I contend that a key goal of efforts to regulate recruitment should be to reshape the incentives of the entities at the top of the product or service supply chain, so that in turn they become the forces driving compliance by the recruiters below. Likewise, recruiters at the top of labour supply chains must be made liable for the false promises and unauthorised charges of their sub-agents and brokers.

In this chapter, I address the final issue of migrant worker agency and participation, examining roles for guest workers themselves as organisers, monitors and policy setters in supply chain initiatives and other efforts to address recruitment violations. I begin with an argument for the importance of such initiatives. I then set out and analyse case studies of three very different efforts to engage migrants in this way, all with a base in Mexico and all involving workers who travel to the United States to do seasonal low-wage work using 'H-2' visas.[4] The chapter concludes with an analysis of recurring challenges and lessons for the future.

[2] See Nicole Constable, *Maid to Order in Hong Kong: Stories of Migrant Workers*, 2nd edn (Ithaca, NY, Cornell University Press, 2007) 40; Judy Fudge, 'Global Care Chains, Employment Agencies and the Conundrum of Jurisdiction: Decent Work for Domestic Workers in Canada' (2011) 23 *Canadian Journal of Women in Law* 234, 244–46.

[3] Jennifer Gordon, *Global Labor Recruitment in a Supply Chain Context*, ILO Fair Recruitment Initiative Series No 1 (Geneva, ILO, 2015).

[4] I discuss two of these initiatives—FLOC and EFI-CIERTO—in Gordon, *Global Labour Recruitment*, with an emphasis on how they use supply chain strategies.

II. RECRUITMENT REGULATION IN MEXICO AND THE UNITED STATES

For many decades, Mexico regulated labour recruitment solely through Article 28 of its Federal Labour Law. Article 28 mandates that all employers of Mexican guest workers sign a written contract with those workers, specifying the nature of the job and establishing wages and working conditions. Employers must commit to paying for the worker's return trip and specify housing and medical care arrangements.[5] This law was rarely if ever enforced.[6]

A 2012 reform of the Mexican Federal Labour Law, and corresponding regulations promulgated in 2014, improved the law governing recruitment. Recruitment agencies now must register with the Secretary of Labour and Social Welfare and certify the promises made in the contract between the employer and the worker. Both the law and the regulations prohibit recruiters from charging migrants a fee or making false/misleading statements. Finally, agencies may not discriminate against workers for any reason, including advocating for their own or others' rights.[7] These laws are quite strong, but their enforcement remains lax.

While the United States extensively (if often ineffectually) regulates the terms of *employment* for H-2 visa holders, US officials have generally emphasised that the terms of *recruitment* should be addressed by origin country governments.[8] Nonetheless, the US Department of Labour prohibits employers from accepting or requesting money from migrants for recruitment costs,[9] and requires employers contractually to forbid their labour recruiters from seeking or accepting payments from prospective employees.[10] These provisions appear to be rarely enforced.[11] The Department of Homeland Security likewise should not grant a petition for H-2 visas if it is made aware that the employer or its recruiter collects a fee from a worker to access H-2 employment.[12]

[5] Ley Federal del Trabajo (Federal Labour Law) 1970 (Mex) art 28; ProDESC, *Article 28 of Mexico's Federal Labor Law: Legal Analysis* (memo, no date) (on file with author).

[6] Jorge Fernandez Souza, Magistrate Judge, Professor of Law and former Dean, Universidad Autónoma Metropolitana, México, Remarks at the Binational Labour Justice Convening, Mexico City, 6 October 2007.

[7] Decreto por el que se reforman, adicionan y derogan diversas disposiciones del Reglamento de Agencias de Colocación de Trabajadores (Decree Amending, Supplementing and Repealing Various Provisions of the Regulation of Worker Placement Agencies), Ley Federal de Trabajo (Federal Labour Law) art 28-B, 21 May 2014.

[8] See Eleanor G Carr, 'Search for a Round Peg: Seeking a Remedy for Recruitment Abuses in the US Guest Worker Program' (2010) 43 *Columbia Journal of Law and Social Problems* 399, 410–11.

[9] H-2A: 20 CFR § 655.135(j); H-2B: 20 CFR 503.16(o).

[10] 20 CFR § 655.135(k).

[11] See Carr, 'Search for a Round Peg' fn 64. See also 'Letter from Low Wage Worker Legal Network et al. to Elaine L. Chao, U.S. Sec'y of Labor', 7 July 2008.

[12] See, eg 8 CFR § 214.2(h)(5)(xi)(A); 8 CFR § 214.2(h)(6)(i)(B).

III. THE IMPORTANCE OF MIGRANT PARTICIPATION IN EFFORTS TO REGULATE RECRUITMENT

Within the past decade, advocates from the US and (to a lesser extent) Mexico, as well as some US trade unions, have begun highlighting and attempting to combat the flaws in the existing regulation of recruitment in both countries.[13] Traditionally, migrants' participation in such efforts has been limited to receiving know-your-rights education before departure and bringing claims after their rights have been violated. In addition, migrant workers who have been severely abused are sometimes asked to give testimony in support of policy changes.[14]

In this chapter, I argue that migrants have the knowledge and ability to contribute much more than they currently do to the improvement of conditions on the ground. Potential roles for workers include as policy designers, recommending standards and procedures based on their intimate knowledge of how the recruitment system works; monitors and enforcers, deputised to observe recruiter behaviour and provided with multiple routes to report non-compliance; peer educators, providing information pre- and post-departure not only about formal rights but about real conditions and sources of support on the ground; and as participants in unions and in NGO campaigns to change the behaviour of governments, employers and recruiters.

Broader and more active migrant participation in efforts to address recruitment abuses is essential for a number of reasons:

— **Democracy and self-representation:** As the central participants in global labour migration, migrants should have the opportunity to represent themselves in shaping efforts to address those problems. This is particularly important since migrants may have different perspectives than advocates on some issues.

— **Quality of initiatives developed:** Migrants have the most detailed and accurate knowledge of the problems they face during recruitment and employment, and also experience first-hand the obstacles to enforcing

[13] In the US, the Centro de los Derechos del Migrante (CDM), Global Workers Justice Alliance (Global Workers), National Guestworkers Alliance and Southern Poverty Law Center have been in the forefront in this regard. Other key actors include the global union federation Education International on behalf of teachers, the Alliance for Ethical International Recruitment Practices on behalf of migrant nurses, and a number of other unions and non-profit organisations. The International Labor Recruitment Working Group was founded in 2011 by these labour groups and several key anti-trafficking organisations to co-ordinate recruitment-related advocacy in the US and international fora. In Mexico, key actors have included ProDESC, CDM, Global Workers, the Jornaleros-SAFE project and Mexican think tank INEDIM.

[14] In addition to the three case studies profiled in this chapter, US exceptions to this assertion include the National Guestworkers Alliance (NGA), headquartered in New Orleans, and the

existing policies. They are therefore in a unique position to offer observations about failures in the migration process and to propose concrete, context-specific and reality-based reforms.

— **Effective monitoring and enforcement:** Migrants are present during all recruitment and employment transactions in both origin and destination countries, and thus are uniquely positioned to monitor recruiters' and employers' compliance with laws and private agreements—so long as they are aware of what their rights are, can easily access reporting mechanisms that trigger enforcement and have effective protection from retaliation.

— **Building a path to rights and representation:** For guest workers to overcome the many obstacles to their participation in organising and advocacy efforts, and for those efforts to succeed, the migrants must be able to rely on anti-retaliation mechanisms and ongoing institutional support.

Organisations working from a physical base in origin countries—ideally groups native to those countries, but also including destination-country actors with origin-country offices and activities—are in a position to support these processes in ways that organisations solely based at the destination cannot. Recruitment can only be monitored where it takes place. When migrants are back home between seasons, they have the privacy and time to meet and talk openly with advocates and organisers, unlike in the destination country given the surveillance and fear of retaliation they experience on the job. Also, migrants are citizens in their origin countries as they are not abroad, and thus are in a better position to demand action from their governments.

The following section profiles three efforts with a presence in Mexico that have taken diverging routes to the same goal: reaching labour migrants while they are at home, in order to engage them actively in efforts to advance and protect their own rights during recruitment and while employed abroad.

Centro de los Derechos del Migrante (CDM), a US non-profit based in Mexico. I discuss NGA's work briefly in the first case study and in the final section, but do not describe it more fully here because it does not have staff that work in Mexico. CDM is largely dedicated to rights education, the facilitation of legal representation for transnational migrants, and policy advocacy on their behalf. While worker activism is not CDM's primary focus, it has developed migrant worker committees whose members carry out outreach and peer education and participate in the organisation's advocacy efforts, and in at least one case CDM has supported migrant worker organising in the United States. See CDM, 'Program Areas', http://www.cdmigrante.org/cdms-work/program-areas/.

IV. CASE STUDIES

A. ProDESC and the Coalición de Trabajadoras y Trabajadores Temporales de Sinaloa, Mexico[15]

The Proyecto de Derechos Económicos, Sociales, y Culturales (Economic, Social and Cultural Rights Project, or 'ProDESC' for its initials in Spanish) is a Mexican human rights organisation founded in 2005 that works with migrants, miners, indigenous communities and communal landowners in Mexico to defend and advance their rights.[16] In the migration context, it has emphasised the need for improvements in Mexican policy and enforcement practices, as well as for transnational collaborations between advocates. ProDESC uses what it terms an 'integrated' approach to its advocacy, combining community education and organising with human rights litigation and policy interventions. It seeks to bridge the gap between the lawyer-led approach of many high-profile international human rights organisations and the purely local emphasis of many bottom-up community organisations.

ProDESC began working on recruitment issues in 2008, counselling workers who had experienced fraud in Mexico. Its engagement with these issues entered a new stage in 2011, when—in collaboration with the National Guestworkers Alliance (NGA), based in New Orleans, Louisiana—it began a joint effort to build bi-national support for migrants from Sinaloa on Mexico's west coast who worked seasonally in the Louisiana seafood industry.[17] Outreach by ProDESC and NGA started with active NGA members, H-2B guest workers who had returned from Louisiana to Sinaloa for the off season. ProDESC organisers built on the contacts from there, with a particular focus on the town of Topolobampo, which has a concentration of migrants to the Louisiana seafood industry. The process of gathering information and building trust took two years of house visits and small gatherings, followed by a series of larger public meetings.

Migrants raised fraud, illegal fees and the unpredictability of rehire as critical problems with the recruitment process. They also highlighted the informal structure of recruitment in the Louisiana seafood industry, where many companies appoint as recruiter a migrant worker in whom the employer has confidence. Employers do not ordinarily pay the chosen worker for playing this role, but she receives significant benefits, often including the opportunity to select the highest-paying assignments and the best living arrangements for herself and her relatives. Even more important is the power

[15] This case study is based on a series of interviews with Alejandra Ancheita, Atzín Gordillo Acevedo and Dante López at ProDESC, and with Olivia Guzmán and Joba Reyes of the Sinaloa Coalition of Temporary Workers on 12 March 2014.

[16] For a description of ProDESC's campaigns, see http://www.prodesc.org.mx/en/.

[17] Interview with Alejandra Ancheita, ProDESC, 20 November 2014.

that the worker/recruiter exercises in Mexico. She can give preference to friends and family in the recruitment process, while demanding money and favours from others in exchange for putting their names on the recruitment list. This arrangement creates great anxiety for migrants, whose access to work each season depends on staying on the worker/recruiter's good side year-round.

In June of 2013, a group of migrants in Sinaloa reported to ProDESC that they had been defrauded by the agent of a recruitment agency in another state, Monterrey. The agent had called a public meeting in a Sinaloa village, offering jobs in the US construction industry and collecting a 'deposit' from forty men who wished to be put on the list. He was never seen again. ProDESC brought these migrants together with others with whom they had worked since 2011, beginning a process of analysis and debate over ways to address the fraud and other abuses in the recruitment industry. The group reviewed the existing laws regarding recruitment in Mexico, many learning for the first time that recruitment fees were banned. They discussed why these regulations are routinely ignored in practice. Ultimately, the migrants decided that, in order to take on this fraudulent recruiter and other problems in the industry, they would need to build power as a group rather than asserting claims individually.

With ProDESC serving as a source of guidance and information, and after several months of research and further discussion, the workers formed the Coalición de Trabajadoras y Trabajadores Temporales de Sinaloa (Sinaloa Temporary Workers' Coalition) in October 2013. The Coalition's mission is to support its migrant members' direct involvement in improving conditions of recruitment and work abroad, including the demand for a place at the table for migrants themselves in the Mexican government's policy making on issues of recruitment and labour migration.

A total of forty migrants declared themselves founding members of the Coalition. Many more had been participating in the meetings, but declined to join for fear of retaliation from employers and recruiters. Over the course of late 2013 and early 2014, the Coalition introduced itself to local and federal government officials, beginning to make its presence known. The Coalition's first goal was to obtain redress for the fraud victims. In January 2014, the Coalition met with officials from the Mexican Ministry of Labour and Social Welfare ('STPS' for its initials in Spanish), to present itself as an organisation and to ask the government to take administrative action in the case of the Monterrey fraud. As a starting point, its members requested that STPS undertake an inspection of the recruitment agency, using a power STPS possessed under existing law, but had not employed.

This meeting proved critical in several respects. First, STPS recognised the Coalition as an interlocutor, acknowledging that labour migrants were a category of Mexican workers on whose behalf STPS was mandated to act. In the past, STPS had denied that H-2 workers were entitled to its protection, stating that, because migrants' employers were in the United States, the US government was responsible for addressing issues that arose in the migration process, with the support if necessary of the Mexican consular network. Yet the only protection from recruitment abuse for migrants was to be found in Mexican labour law, enforced exclusively by STPS. STPS's recognition of the Coalition as a group of *workers* represented a significant victory for ProDESC's ongoing campaign to have the Mexican government accept its obligation to protect migrants' rights as labour rights from the moment of recruitment.[18]

Second, STPS responded to the Coalition's request by carrying out an inspection of the Monterrey agency, one of the first times it had ever used this power. The inspection revealed 27 violations of the law.[19] ProDESC then filed a collective criminal complaint with the Sinaloa Prosecutor's Office on behalf of fifteen of the defrauded men, seeking what would be the first ever fraud conviction of a Mexican labour recruitment agent.[20] Because Mexican law has no provisions that make a recruiting firm liable for criminal malfeasance, this complaint is a novel effort on ProDESC's part to use the law criminalising individual fraud in order to penalise corporate action against a class of workers.[21] The case is currently under investigation.

As the 2014 season ended and workers returned to Mexico, ProDESC again began meeting with the Coalition. As of spring 2015, it was evident that fear was on the rise among returning workers. Since the Coalition was founded, workers have been blacklisted by employers and recruiters for their activism. Observing this, others have become afraid to step forward. This and other challenges that the Coalition faces are substantial. It is not by chance that the fraud case that the Coalition chose to pursue as its first initiative was against a recruitment agent based in the distant state of Monterrey. Such a target raises far fewer concerns of retaliation than taking on a local recruiter with relationships in the community, which the workers fear would lead directly to blacklisting. In addition, Sinaloa is notorious as a headquarters for narcotics trafficking, which increasingly has expanded to include the movement of human beings as well as drugs over borders.[22] Pursuing

[18] Interviews with Dante López, ProDESC, 1 October 2014; Atzín Gordillo Acevedo, ProDESC, 1 October 2014.

[19] STPS, Acta Final/Resolución, 26 March 2013 [*sic*, date should be 26 March 2014] (copy on file with author). While this amount is low, the imposition of a fine at all is significant, as it is the first time that STPS has penalised a recruiter of H-2 workers.

[20] Interviews with Atzín Gordillo Acevedo, ProDESC, 1 October 2014; Dante López, ProDESC, 1 October 2014; Alejandra Ancheita, ProDESC, 20 November 2014.

[21] The Mexican Ley Penal de Trata (Criminal Trafficking Law) 2012 (Mex) art 10 does include a narrow provision criminalising a firm's recruitment of workers into trafficked situations, but it does not apply to fraud or other recruitment abuses independent of trafficking.

[22] See Richard Marosi, 'The Strands of the Sinaloa Drug Cartel Web', *Los Angeles Times*, 26 July 2011. See also Jeffrey Scott Shapiro and T Michael Andrews, 'Declaring War on the Cartels', *The Washington Times*, 23 July 2014.

cases against recruiters located in Sinaloa increases the risk of retaliation by organised crime.

Despite these obstacles, the Coalition is determined to move forward. Members are eager to explore options beyond legal cases, and anticipate developing their own policy proposals to present to the Mexican government. They are considering founding a workers' centre that may include worker-controlled recruitment as one of its functions. ProDESC and Coalition members are also contemplating the launch of new chapters of the Coalition in Mexican states beyond Sinaloa.

B. FLOC's Collective Bargaining Agreement with the North Carolina Growers' Association[23]

The Farm Labor Organizing Committee (FLOC) is a farm worker union based in Ohio.[24] In the wake of FLOC's success organising Ohio tomato and cucumber pickers in the 1980s, brand-name companies turned to North Carolina in the 1990s seeking cheaper produce harvested by non-union H-2A workers. FLOC followed them south. After a five-year boycott targeting key pickle processor Mount Olive, and a parallel set of lawsuits[25] against the North Carolina Growers' Association (NCGA), Mount Olive's primary source of H-2A labour, FLOC succeeded in negotiating a three-way accord with Mount Olive and NCGA in 2004.[26] The agreement raised workers' wages, created incentives for growers to provide workers compensation coverage, and committed NCGA to recognising the outcome of a card-check vote on union representation by its workers.[27]

[23] This case study is based on multiple interviews with Baldemar Velasquez and Justin Flores of FLOC in 2013 and 2014, in addition to other sources cited here. Parts of this case study are adapted from Gordon, *Global Labor Recruitment* (n 3).

[24] FLOC 2013 LM-2, available by entering query at http://kcerds.dol-esa.gov/query/getOrgQry.do (US Department of Labor) (hereinafter Union Search).

[25] The National Labor Relations Act, which governs union recognition in most US industries, does not cover agricultural workers. See, eg 29 USC § 152(3). There is thus no federal law that requires growers to heed a vote for unionisation by a majority of their employees; any such agreement must be negotiated between the parties. In that context, litigation was a critical factor in bringing NCGA to the table. A key case was *De Luna-Guerrero v North Carolina Grower's Ass'n, Inc* 370 F Supp 2d 386 (EDNC 2005).

[26] For an overview of the FLOC strategy leading up to the Mount Olive campaign, see David Dalton, *Building National Campaigns: Activists, Alliances, and How Change Happens* (Oxford, Oxfam, 2007) 32. For the assertion that NCGA is the largest H-2A employer, see Victoria Bouloubasis, 'Be Our Guest Worker', *The American Prospect*, 7 November 2013.

[27] Interview with Baldemar Velasquez, Founder and President, Farm Labor Organizing Committee (FLOC), 18 July 2014; Julie M McKinnon, 'FLOC Sets its Sights on Future Fights', *The Blade*, 3 October 2004; Teófilo Reyes, '8000 "Guest Workers" Join Farm Union in North Carolina', *Labor Notes*, 30 September 2004. After the first three years, Mount Olive has continued to make a small increase annually to the amount it passes through NCGA for workers' wages: interview with Baldemar Velasquez, FLOC, 18 July 2014.

When the majority of NCGA workers subsequently signed cards supporting unionisation, FLOC and the NCGA bargained the first US guest worker union contract in September 2004.[28] A decade after it was first signed, the FLOC/NCGA agreement remains the largest and the most sustained example of union representation of guest workers in US history. It currently covers about 7,500 H-2A workers labouring for approximately 640 growers through the NCGA.[29]

Recruitment is a primary focus of the FLOC/NCGA contract. As the entity managing recruitment from the United States, NCGA sits at the top of the labour supply chain. It is NCGA that applies to the US government for H-2A visas, and manages the distribution of workers to growers once the migrants arrive. To find and process the workers in Mexico, NCGA contracts with CSI Labor Services, a major Mexican H-2 recruitment firm headquartered in Monterrey. CSI, in turn, contracts with local recruiters and their agents in other parts of Mexico.

In the wake of the NCGA contract, migrants gained a new set of rights during the recruitment process, with FLOC overseeing NCGA's and CSI's compliance. A system that had previously been based solely on grower preferences (including a notorious blacklist for workers who complained of mistreatment) was converted to one based in part on seniority. Within the tiers described below, workers now have priority in order of years worked with the H-2A program. Growers must demonstrate just cause for firing and refusing to rehire workers, and give three warnings before taking disciplinary action. There is a formal grievance procedure for violations.

The current FLOC-NCGA contract creates four tiers of workers. First priority goes to those designated by growers as 'preferred', including experienced workers and—a recent addition—their relatives if the employer wishes.[30] Vacancies are next filled by 'active' workers in order of seniority, independent of employer preferences. This permits migrants to challenge violations of their rights during the season with the assurance that if, as a result, they are not listed as 'preferred' by the employer for the following season, they will be hired elsewhere as an active worker.[31] In the context of H-2A work, this is a unique and deeply meaningful protection.

[28] The accord was amended and renewed in 2008 and again in 2012.

[29] Interview with Baldemar Velasquez, FLOC, 21 March 2014. See also Karin Rives, 'Guest Workers Note Progress: Labor Contract has Brought Changes', *Raleigh News & Observer*, 29 August 2005.

[30] Employers also have the right to designate a worker 'no return' under certain circumstances; such a designation will bar a worker from participation in the programme. NCGA and FLOC Agreement 2012 art 5. FLOC challenges these designations when it believes that they are retaliatory: interview with Baldemar Velasquez, FLOC, 18 July 2014.

[31] Ibid. By the terms of the contract, any worker with at least one year of seniority, who finished the last season in good standing and who submits a bid, must be placed in a job the following season: ibid. It is important to note that this is only possible because the FLOC contract is with the NCGA, an association of multiple H-2A employers. If a union has a

The third tier is for preferred workers who want to take a job with a different employer; those workers get access to the remaining full-season jobs through a bid system the union has created. Finally, as of 2012, any worker with three years or more in the H-2A programme can recommend new workers with no experience. These 'zero seniority' workers are usually hired at the end of the season when relatively little work remains, but then have the advantage of being considered 'active' workers the following year.[32] Active FLOC members can submit these requests through the union, which then follows up with the NCGA to confirm that the recommended workers are indeed hired. FLOC Vice President Justin Flores describes this provision as a 'big plus' in terms of recruiting members.[33]

Over time, FLOC has addressed additional aspects of the recruitment system that continued to breed abuse despite the initial contract. For example, the FLOC-NCGA agreement now forbids cash payments from workers to recruiters, even though the law would otherwise permit recruiters to charge migrants up front for the cost of the visa and ground transportation. (Employers must reimburse workers for both expenses soon after arrival.) After several years of observing the situation, the union concluded that allowing cash to change hands in this context too often opened the door for recruiters to demand additional side payments from workers. The agreement was amended so that workers deposit money for legitimate expenses with a designated bank, and give recruiters the bank receipt. The recruiter can then arrange for bank-to-bank transfers to the US consulate and the bus company.[34]

Recruiters fought back against FLOC's incursion on their territory for years. When FLOC opened its Monterrey, Mexico office in 2005, recruiters subjected its staff to escalating harassment and surveillance, broke into the office, and are believed to be responsible for the 2007 torture and murder of Santiago Rafael Cruz, a FLOC organiser, inside the union's Monterrey headquarters.[35] After failing to defeat FLOC, however, and following the institution of protective measures for FLOC by the Inter-American Court of Appeals in the wake of the murder, recruiters have made an uneasy peace with the union, and there have been no major incidents since 2007.

contract with a single employer, it would be necessary to negotiate a rehire guarantee with that employer to achieve parallel protection.

32 Interviews with Baldemar Velasquez, FLOC, 21 March 2014 and 18 July 2014. See also NCGA and FLOC Agreement 2012 art 5.6.

33 Interview with Justin Flores, Vice President, FLOC, 19 September 2014.

34 Interview with Baldemar Velasquez, FLOC, 21 April 2014.

35 See Dan La Botz, 'Farm Labor Organizer Murdered in Mexico', *Counterpunch*, 14–16 April 2007.

The Monterrey office continues in operation today as the base for FLOC's Mexico operations. It has two full-time staff, both former H-2A workers. Vice President Flores oversees the union's Mexico operations from its base in North Carolina. The Monterrey office is charged with implementation of the contract's recruitment provisions and the management of related grievances, and the co-ordination of the union's organising and leadership training efforts for workers while they are in Mexico.[36]

During the winter, while members are in Mexico, FLOC's Monterrey office co-ordinates and carries out meetings in regions where its membership is concentrated.[37] These gatherings attract between 30 and 100 people each. At them, FLOC leaders discuss the NCGA contract recruitment and bidding process, and highlight the protections offered by union membership. In March, FLOC holds an annual national membership meeting in Monterrey, attended by 60–80 of the union's most active members (for many, a journey of 16 hours or more). The meeting ensures that member-leaders are prepared to educate co-workers on the contract provisions, help file grievances, and defend their rights under the contract.

When the recruitment season begins in January, FLOC staff in Monterrey manage the Mexico end of the bid system, fielding calls from workers seeking information about their recruitment status or wanting to address a problem. When contract procedures have been violated with regard to a particular worker's recruitment, they inform the NCGA, which works with CSI to resolve the problem.[38] If violations remain unaddressed, Monterrey staff investigate and pursue the issue on behalf of the worker.

FLOC staff take advantage of the multiple outreach opportunities the Monterrey location offers as the hub of H-2 migration from Mexico to the United States.[39] FLOC staff discuss the union with non-members headed for North Carolina, emphasising its capacity to intervene to prevent abuses in recruitment or on the job, and encouraging workers to sign a union card before they depart. Since North Carolina is a 'right to work' state, workers do not automatically become union members on being hired by a company that has signed a union contract. Non-member workers must receive the same wages and contract protections as dues-paying members. This puts FLOC in the position of constantly having to explain and demonstrate the advantages of union membership to workers who could easily free-ride on

[36] Interview with Baldemar Velasquez, FLOC, 21 March 2014.

[37] Interview with Justin Flores, FLOC, 19 September 2014.

[38] Ibid.

[39] 94% of all H-2A visa holders come from Mexico, and 50% of all H-2A applications are processed through the Monterrey consulate. See US Government Accountability Office, *H-2A Visa Program: Modernization and Improved Guidance Could Reduce Employer Application Burden* (Washington, DC, GAO, 2012) 15.

the contributions of others.[40] FLOC also reaches out to migrants bound for other states and industries, putting the union in a position to identify new avenues for organising.

FLOC President Baldemar Velasquez and Vice President Flores describe having a base in Mexico as crucial to the union's success in organising H-2A workers. In addition to the practical benefits of managing the recruitment process in the country where it is taking place, organisers spend time with workers where they are much more comfortable and candid than they can be under the 24-hour surveillance that characterises H-2A labour. Flores believes that having migrants see the union as an active presence at both their origin and destination has been critical in building worker trust and confidence in FLOC. This has translated into an effective base for recruitment. It is often in Mexico, not in North Carolina, where H-2A workers sign FLOC union cards, deepen their ties with the union, and begin to take on leadership roles.

Flores notes, however, that much of what FLOC has reaped from having a strong presence in Mexico could not have been achieved without full integration between FLOC's Monterrey and North Carolina offices, or in the absence of a collective bargaining agreement binding key actors in the supply chain. He cautions that, without these factors, a US-based organisation with a Mexico office will be limited to the much slower and less effective mechanisms of legal redress and policy appeals.

C. CIERTO, a UFW-EFI Recruitment and Training Pilot Based in Mexico[41]

United Farm Workers (UFW) is known around the world for its pioneering approach to organising farm workers under the leadership of Cesar Chavez in the 1960s and 70s. At its peak, its membership approached 50,000 workers.[42] In the past few decades, however, the consolidation of the retail

[40] In addition to access to the union's advocacy on behalf of friends and family whom the member nominates for zero seniority positions, FLOC has developed a set of benefits available only to dues-paying members. These include a small amount of financial assistance in case of an emergency need to return to Mexico, a minimal weekly payment if the worker is injured on the job and has not yet received workers compensation (a process for which the union offers legal representation), and a death benefit for family members: interview with Justin Flores, FLOC, 11 November 2014.

[41] This case study is based on multiple interviews with Erik Nicholson, Joe Martinez and Jaime Padilla of United Farm Workers (UFW) in 2013 and 2014, in addition to other sources cited here. Parts of this case study are adapted from Gordon, *Global Labor Recruitment*.

[42] See Marshall Ganz, *Why David Sometimes Wins: Leadership, Organization, and Strategy in the California Farm Worker Movement* (New York, Oxford University Press, 2010) 7.

food industry, among other factors, has posed serious challenges to the union's ability to sustain its organising model.[43] The union's membership in mid-2015 was about 4,500.[44] In response, the union is exploring new ways to improve wages and working conditions for farm workers in a context where supermarkets and other retailers demand prices so low that unionised farmers are unable to stay in business.[45]

The UFW's leading effort in this regard is its participation in the Equitable Food Initiative (EFI), a multi-stakeholder organisation developed in collaboration with FLOC and other migrant and farm worker organisations. EFI has developed a certification system addressing three issues: farm worker wages and working conditions, environmental stewardship and food safety,[46] with an extensive set of standards to cover these three areas. The initiative seeks to have a broad impact on industrial agriculture by adding 'value and quality throughout the food system, benefiting workers, growers, retailers and consumers alike'.[47]

This 'value proposition' grows from the observation that the large sums lost to the industry due to waste, spoilage, contamination and consumer concerns about food safety could be mitigated by improved training, compensation, and retention of farm workers; and in particular by involving workers in the process of solving these problems before they affect a company's bottom line.[48] The EFI programme provides support for growers to create problem-solving structures on each farm, through which they can work collaboratively with workers to eliminate waste and hazards. Workers receive higher wages at firms that are EFI-certified as long as the grower remains in good standing, creating incentives for them to work with the grower to achieve and maintain compliance.[49] EFI encourages growers to share the increased profits created by this process with workers in the form of raises and bonuses.[50] A pillar of the EFI program is the involvement of farm workers at all levels, including in developing the standards themselves.

EFI has invited major retailers to require EFI certification from their growers, with retailers funding the cost of growers' compliance by paying

[43] Interview with Erik Nicholson, National Vice President, United Farm Workers and Chair, Equitable Food Initiative (EFI), 28 May 2014.

[44] UFW 2012 LM2, Line 20, at Union Search.

[45] Interviews with Erik Nicholson, UFW and EFI, 28 May 2014 and 14 July 2014; Joe Martinez, Global Advocate and Mexico Program Director, UFW, 17 April 2014 and 21 July 2014.

[46] See http://www.equitablefood.org/. EFI standards are available at http://www.equitablefood.org/#!certification/c24gy.

[47] EFI, 'Labor-Management Collaboration Makes for Better Produce', http://www.equitablefood.org/#!what_we_do/cjcr.

[48] Interviews with Erik Nicholson, UFW and EFI, 28 May 2014 and 14 July 2014.

[49] See http://www.equitablefood.org/#!certification/c3c.

[50] Author's interview with Erik Nicholson, UFW and EFI, 14 July 2014; EFI, *The Equitable Food Initiative Standard* (Washington, DC, EFI, 2013) 11.

slightly more for certified produce.[51] Two companies are EFI's initial participants: Costco and (on a smaller scale) Bon Appetit, a high-end food service provider.[52] These retailers require EFI certification for some, and eventually all, of the fruits and vegetables that they purchase. In 2013, Costco initiated its participation by asking its produce suppliers to volunteer to become EFI certified, while making clear that all its produce purchasing decisions would soon depend on certification and ongoing compliance.[53] The salad greens brand Earthbound Organics, and Andrews & Williamson, a major strawberry grower with 2,000 acres under production in the US and Mexico, stepped forward. Their first farms were certified in July 2014.[54] Costco and Bon Appetit are covering their suppliers' costs for certification.

The EFI standards address recruitment as well as working conditions. In order to be certified, a grower must ensure that H-2A recruitment is free of cost to the worker, and that the recruiter complies with recruitment laws in workers' origin countries and in the United States and does not discriminate on the basis of gender.[55]

To help EFI-certified businesses demonstrate that their recruitment practices meet these requirements, and to train workers on how to work in compliance with the standards—including, most critically, to identify practices that stand in the way of higher standards on safety, product quality and productivity, and ways to collaborate with growers to resolve them—the UFW is in the pilot phase of a Mexico-based initiative called CIERTO (Centro de Investigación, Entrenamiento, y Reclutamiento del Trabajador Organizado, or Center for Research, Recruitment and Training of the Organised Worker). CIERTO is currently structured as a project of the UFW, but the intent is to transition to an independent not-for-profit operation, and within five years to be supported entirely through employer payments.

CIERTO is both a worker training endeavour and an alternative, union-run recruitment enterprise. Its goals include removing the recruiter as

[51] Interviews with Erik Nicholson, UFW and EFI, 28 May 2014; Joe Martinez, UFW, 17 April 2014. For details about certification see: EFI, 'EFI Supporting Documents', http://www.equitablefood.org/#!certification/c3c7.

[52] Interview with Erik Nicholson, UFW and EFI, 14 July 2014. For an example of Costco's public support for EFI, see Herb Weisbaum, '"Culture-Changing" Initiative to Stop Food Contamination on the Farm', *NBC News*, 19 August 2013.

[53] Interview with Erik Nicholson, UFW and EFI, 28 May 2014. See also Stephanie Strom and Steven Greenhouse, 'On the Front Lines of Food Safety', *The New York Times*, 24 May 2013. Costco has since informed several of its suppliers that they must obtain EFI certification in order for Costco to continue purchasing their products: interview with Erik Nicholson, UFW and EFI, 14 July 2014.

[54] Interview with Erik Nicholson, UFW and EFI, 14 July 2014. A large grower will have scores of farms in varying locations; under EFI each farm must be audited and certified individually.

[55] EFI, *The Equitable Food Initiative Compliance Criteria*, Version 1.0 (Washington, DC, EFI, 2014) 28–30.

a source of debt, fear and retaliation for workers, freeing them to participate in the EFI programme without fear of repercussions; reducing turnover and increasing workers' ability to rely on rehire in successive seasons; and training the workforce in the value they add to the supply chain.[56] CIERTO initiated its first training pilot in January 2015 at an Andrews & Williamson (A&W) farm custom-built for the EFI programme in Baja California, Mexico.[57] During the first half of 2015, these workers will migrate internally to Baja California to pick strawberries and organic tomatoes in A&W fields. The next stage of the pilot will involve H-2A recruitment for EFI-certified Costco suppliers' fields in the United States. CIERTO plans to scale up its recruitment and training rapidly to cover at least 1,000 workers in its second year.[58]

Third party verification of growers' compliance with EFI's recruitment and job treatment standards will be managed by EFI's auditor, while CIERTO's recruitment practices will be monitored by Catholic Relief Services Mexico.[59] Workers will play critical roles in reporting violations of the EFI standards. As one grower seeking EFI certification told *The New York Times*, referring to the monitoring role that farm workers play on certified farms, 'This program means that instead of one auditor coming around once in a while to check on things, we have 400 auditors on the job all the time'.[60]

V. ANALYSIS

Each of the efforts described above involves the creative rethinking of traditional organising models on a substantial scale.

ProDESC has supported the emergence of an organised coalition of migrant workers for the first time ever in Mexico, seeking to represent their own interests before the Mexican government and advocate for improved recruitment and working conditions more broadly. In a context where Mexican law does not allow the formation of a union of those who work abroad, and Mexican unions have shown no interest in organising or representing those who leave the country, the Coalition offers a previously unexplored way of representing the country's large migrant sector.

FLOC is the only US union to organise substantial numbers of H-2 workers, maintain an office for them in their home country, and negotiate

[56] Interview with Erik Nicholson, UFW and EFI, 14 July 2014.

[57] EFI decided that the first pilot should involve internal migration to avoid the extra layer of complication added by United States immigration law. It plans to expand to include H-2A workers by mid-2015: interview with Joe Martinez, UFW, 12 November 2014.

[58] Ibid.

[59] Email to author from Joe Martinez, 15 December 2014.

[60] Strom and Greenhouse, 'On the Front Lines' (n 53).

and service a collective bargaining agreement that addresses their terms of recruitment alongside other protections. And, finally, the UFW has stepped outside the collective bargaining mould entirely with its support for EFI and for CIERTO, which reconceptualises fair recruitment for migrant workers as an essential part of a supply-chain certification scheme emphasising worker–employer collaboration on improvements in the production process, leading to increased firm profitability and higher compensation for migrants.

All three bodies have concrete plans for significant expansion in the short term—and significant uncertainty about exactly how their plans will unfold. ProDESC and the Coalition are contemplating a national network of coalition branches, but face continued challenges to organising posed by migrants' fear of retaliation and the drug crime and impunity rampant throughout much of Mexico. FLOC is in the midst of a campaign targeting major tobacco company RJ Reynolds, which has put up stiff resistance for almost a decade. If successful, the campaign will bring tens of thousands of additional H-2A workers under contract with the union. EFI-CIERTO has barely begun its first training as this is written, but has the strategy and funding in place to be training and recruiting well over a thousand H-2A workers by 2016 and many more thereafter.

Even at this early stage, the initiatives profiled here offer critical insights about what it will take to build a strong presence in Mexico of Mexican and US trade unions, human rights and other advocacy organisations, and migrants to the United States, engaged together in combatting the abuses of recruitment at home and of employment abroad. As a starting point for future work, I will briefly outline some key challenges in the Mexico–US context, and then highlight two issues with which these and other efforts must grapple.

A. Challenges/Obstacles to Active Participation by Migrants

Migrants who depend on recruiters for access to work abroad are in a difficult position when it comes to defending their rights during recruitment and on the job. Willing workers are plentiful around the world; positions legally open to labour migrants, by comparison, are few. Recruiters have a chokehold on access to most of these positions. Employers, too, have great power over guest workers. Immigration laws in the United States and many other countries make low-wage temporary migrants entirely dependent on a single employer to maintain their visas. Most employers subcontract recruitment to agencies that in turn deal with brokers in remote communities, creating a labour supply system that allows each actor plausibly to deny any knowledge or legal responsibility for abuses that take place further down the chain. This system delivers to employers a labour force coerced into silence by debt, need and fear. A migrant who speaks up risks losing the current job on which they and their family depend, the visa that allows them to remain employed in the United States, and the hope of finding future work through their recruiter.

The unique circumstances of each country further complicate this picture. In Mexico, migrants face the additional fear created by the role of organised crime in recruitment.[61] Mexican government officials have offered little by way of protection. Indeed, it has recently come to light that Mexican consular officials in Canada themselves created a blacklist barring the rehiring of several migrants who supported a UFCW-Canada union organising campaign on a farm staffed by guest workers.[62] Until very recently, Mexico had made little effort to address abuses in the recruitment process, and none to strengthen and modernise its law in the field. The United States, for its part, has been an unwilling partner, until recently largely refusing to acknowledge any responsibility for recruitment since it takes place on Mexican soil.[63]

Finally, with ProDESC as an exception, very few Mexican non-profit organisations have made the treatment of Mexican migrant workers by recruiters and foreign employers a focus of their work. Mexican human rights organisations have tended to focus on the abuses of migrants to and through Mexico from Central America, rather than those affecting Mexicans abroad. In addition, little funding is available for Mexican organisations seeking to work on out-migration. No Mexican trade unions have sought to address the recruitment or working conditions of Mexican migrants to the United States. In one sense, this is not surprising: trade unions in Mexico, as elsewhere around the world, are focused on the concerns of their current membership. To shift their focus to migrants would be to advocate for workers who no longer pay dues and no longer work in the country. Mexican workers who migrate seasonally, however, might argue that their work lives *as a whole*, both at home and abroad, should be of concern to Mexico's unions. There are certainly trade unions in other countries of origin that have made the rights of migrants a major issue.[64] In Mexico, the high level of corruption and the predominance of corporatist and company unions, and the fact that the more democratic elements of the Mexican

[61] See generally Carr, 'Search for a Round Peg' (n 8).

[62] See *Certain Employees of Sidhu & Sons Nursery Ltd* BCLRB (20 March 2014).

[63] See, eg Centro de los Derechos del Migrante, *Recruitment Revealed* 24. In 2014, as an outcome of ministerial consultations resulting from a series of NAALC complaints on the treatment of migrant workers, the US government formally committed to working with the Mexican government to provide migrants and employers with information on migrants' rights during recruitment and on the job. 'Ministerial Consultations Joint Declaration', http://www.dol.gov/opa/media/press/ilab/ILAB20140543-US-Mex-Declaration.pdf.

[64] See, eg: Jennifer Gordon, *Towards Transnational Labor Citizenship: Restructuring Labor Migration to Reinforce Workers' Rights* (Berkeley, CA, U Berkeley Law School, 2009) 33–38.

labour movement are preoccupied with a fight for survival in the face of government repression, are among the impediments to such a perspective.[65]

B. Key Areas of Focus for the Future

If migrants are to become involved on a larger scale as actors and agents in the fight against recruitment abuses, they will require systematic support in a number of areas. Here I highlight two factors that appear particularly important at the current stage: (i) effective protection from retaliation by recruiters and employers, and (ii) transnational advocacy and organising structures that workers can access wherever they are in the migration chain.

Protection from Retaliation

In order to be able to fill the roles recommended in this chapter, migrant workers must be protected against retaliation. Such measures are necessary to curtail the ability of recruiters, employers and origin governments to blacklist guest workers who defend their rights; and of employers to fire such workers knowing that the US government will then deport them. Both Mexican and US law have inadequate protections in this regard, and what provisions exist are largely unenforced.

In the absence of effective laws, the US-based case studies reveal two alternative approaches to anti-retaliation measures. FLOC uses a collective bargaining agreement to ban retaliatory firing and make rehire presumptive. Its NCGA contract establishes a baseline of hiring by seniority, with a presumption of annual return. The union has the right to challenge firings or refusals to rehire that the worker believes are retaliatory. EFI/CIERTO also leverages supply chain pressure, and also forbids retaliation, but focuses on making the rehire of trained and experienced workers attractive to growers that want to obtain or retain EFI certification. This is reinforced by penalties against participating growers that retaliate against workers.[66]

Within the United States, the National Guestworkers Alliance has launched a number of innovative initiatives to combat retaliation in guest worker programs. NGA has fought for over 600 guest workers to be granted so-called 'T' or 'U' visas after they were fired for their activism in labour disputes. The visas are available to victims of trafficking and certain labour crimes

[65] For a discussion of corporatism and corruption in Mexican unions, see: Graciela Bensusán and Kevin J Middlebrook, *Organized Labor and Politics in Mexico: Changes, Continuities and Contradictions* (Washington, DC, Brookings Institution Press, 2012). For a brief overview of recent human rights concerns relating to Mexican unions, see US State Department, *Mexico 2013 Human Rights Report* (Washington, DC, State Department, 2014) 41–44.

[66] EFI Standards, http://www.equitablefood.org/#!certification/c24gy.

who are supporting efforts to prosecute the perpetrators. They permit the visa holders to remain and work in the United States with their families, eventually opening the door to permanent residence and citizenship. NGA's legal team has also begun to use fora like the National Labor Relations Board to contest retaliation against and blacklisting of guest workers in the home country by recruiters as well as in the US by employers. It is currently piloting an Anti-Forced Labor Accord for US-based multinational brands. The accord requires signatories to prohibit retaliation in their supply chains, including by recruiters.[67]

It is worth reiterating how many of these strategies rely on the dynamics of the supply chain. FLOC uses supply chain pressure in its organising campaigns to bring end users in the *product supply chain* to the table, with the goal of winning card-check recognition for the union and the right to bargain a contract with growers. Growers are then required to take responsibility for the actions of the recruiters in the *labour supply chain*. EFI is wholly built around the principle of shared responsibility and shared benefit within the supply chain. Its ultimate penalty for a grower whose recruiter violates the EFI standards is removal from access to critically important supply chain buyers. The NGA accord is also a supply chain initiative.

The importance of supply chain mechanisms as components of efforts to regulate recruitment requires repeated emphasis, given the high level of subcontracting in industries that use guest workers and the fact that recruitment itself is almost always a subcontracted function. To be effective, supply chain initiatives must impose swift and substantial economic penalties on non-compliant recruiters and employers. Predictable enforcement of penalties—and, in some contexts, incentives for compliance—are necessary to create meaningful market consequences that will shift the incentives of key actors away from participation in labour supply chains characterised by abusive recruitment practices.[68] This is essential given the weaknesses of the existing legal framework. Finally, end users must fund the improvements that they demand from their suppliers.

[67] Interview with JJ Rosenbaum and Jacob Horwitz, NGA, 25 April 2014; emails to author from JJ Rosenbaum, 19 December 2014, 21 December 2014, 7 January 2015 and 8 January 2015; Forced Labor Prevention Accord (on file with author); Michelle Chen, 'What if Your Ability to Stay in This Country Depended on Your Employer', *The Nation Blog*, 12 June 2014.

[68] The Fair Food Program of the Coalition of Immokalee Workers, and the enforcement of its Fair Food Code of Conduct by the Fair Food Standards Council, is an excellent example of a worker-driven programme that has created market consequences for non-compliance with a code of conduct. See, eg Gordon, *Global Labor Recruitment* (n 3) 57–61; Fair Food Standards Council, *Fair Food Program: 2014 Annual Report* (Sarasota, FL, Fair Food Standards Council, 2014).

Transnational Institutional Support

In order to participate effectively in efforts to change the way they are recruited, migrants also need ongoing institutional support. Because guest workers by definition live part of the year at home and part of the year abroad, this can only truly be effective if it is present in both places.[69] Models for achieving this include a destination country institution with an active presence in the origin country (or an origin country institution with an active presence in the destination country, although this has yet to emerge in the Mexico–US context),[70] or active collaborations between organisations that bridge the two locations.

Given the paucity of potential Mexican partners noted above, it is not surprising that the most common structure for binational support for migrants has been for United States organisations to open an office, sponsor a program or run a campaign in Mexico. At times, all of these organisations have also sought to work directly with Mexican actors.

The models of a US organisation with a Mexican base and of a transnational collaboration between independent Mexican and US organisations each have advantages. The all-in-one approach of a US entity with a base in Mexico, represented here by FLOC and the EFI-CIERTO, facilitates a unified strategy, because the work plan in both places can be centrally coordinated to further one mission. While communication, decision-making and transparency can be challenging within a single organisation when it operates across borders, the obstacles pale by comparison to those faced by independent groups attempting to collaborate transnationally. In addition, supply chain strategies that seek to hold employers responsible for the actions of their recruiters require the capacity and authority to operate at a high level within destination countries' legal and political systems, functions that to date have required US-based lawyers and organisers.

However, Mexican-led initiatives, such as the ProDESC Coalition profiled here, offer strengths often lacking in destination-country-run approaches. These include essential expertise in Mexican law and policy, and the authority to act within those realms; institutional knowledge of and alliances with other Mexican actors; a deep understanding of the country's economy and politics; and the ability to make autonomous decisions about goals and strategy that further their own goals in the Mexican context. Lacking such a perspective, a unilateral effort by a destination country organisation runs the risk of making avoidable errors, marginalising key origin country actors, minimising the origin country government's responsibility for addressing

[69] See generally Gordon, *Towards Transnational Labor Citizenship* (n 64).

[70] It has, however, been piloted elsewhere. See, eg Gordon, *Towards Transnational Labor Citizenship* 41–43 (discussing a Philippines union working in Hong Kong).

recruitment violations, and creating solutions that prioritise destination country interests.

Although democratic collaborations between organisations in both countries are normatively desirable, they face many hurdles. For a Mexico–US collaboration to be genuine, successful, and sustained, actors must go beyond information sharing, signing a joint petition or attending meetings together. Mexican organisations have much less access to funding than those based in the United States, and operate under conditions that raise grave concern for the security of their staff and members. They do not have the option to pull out should conditions become too dangerous. From the perspective of many Mexican activists, past efforts at transnational advocacy have too often replicated North–South power dynamics.[71] To address these imbalances and the difficulties of communication and co-ordination across national borders, it is critical that these transnational relationships grow from a democratic process through which the participants identify shared goals and strategies that advance both organisations' missions, and be undergirded by a commitment to joint problem solving, transparency (including with regard to funding) and the open exchange of information.

VI. CONCLUSION

It is important to acknowledge that there are places where migrants are unlikely to be able to take active roles in the fight for fair recruitment practices. At a minimum, precursors to meaningful migrant engagement include the presence in either (and ideally both) the origin or the destination country of trade unions or civil society organisations that are dedicated to working on recruitment issues in ways that include migrants as key actors, rather than only as the recipients of services; a political environment that allows at least some room for activism; and the possibility of activating existing protections against retaliation or creating new ones. Where these elements are in place, however, as in Mexico and the United States, ProDESc's Coalition, FLOC's NCGA contract, and the UFW's EFI-CIERTO initiative demonstrate that groups of migrants can organise against recruitment abuses in ways once inconceivable, challenging previously entrenched practices of employers, recruiters and governments.

[71] See Jennifer Gordon, *Concept Paper: Funding Transnational Work on Immigration Issues along the United States-Mexico-Central America Corridor* (New York, Unbound Philanthropy, 2012) 11; Alejandra Ancheita, interviews conducted for project on Genuine Transnational Collaboration, 2010, cited here with Ancheita's permission.

16

Decent Labour Standards in Corporate Supply Chains

The Immokalee Workers Model

JAMES J BRUDNEY*

I. INTRODUCTION

TRANSNATIONAL CORPORATE SUPPLY chains have emerged as a dominant approach to global production in the twenty-first century. They are central to the profitable manufacture and distribution of garments, footwear, electronics, toys and other retail goods. They also play a significant part in efficient agricultural production in the United States and elsewhere.

These supply chains are shaped by brand-name retail companies that are in a position to determine what goods are produced, assembled or harvested and in which locations. The brands sit at the top of a network that includes contractors of various sizes, usually in geographically dispersed locations. Tens of millions of individuals work in supply chains, mostly in nations with developing economies. These individuals, predominantly female and often migrants from rural areas or across national borders, labour under harsh and at times abusive working conditions to produce food, clothing or electronic devices for domestic consumption and for export on a global scale. Some labour conditions have improved in recent decades, but progress overall has been limited despite concerted efforts being made through various national and international legal channels and through voluntary private initiatives.

* I thank Natalie Turchi for excellent research assistance, and Jennifer Gordon, Steve Hitov, Greg Asbed and Laura Safer Espinoza for insightful comments on earlier drafts. This chapter is current as of October 2015.

This chapter begins by briefly discussing reasons why current well-intentioned efforts to protect workers in corporate supply chains have been inadequate to the task. Underlying the shortcomings of public law and private voluntary efforts are two core challenges. One is assuring sufficient levels of worker involvement to guarantee an effective voice in identifying abusive practices, formulating labour standards priorities, and designing a system that can achieve compliance. The second is providing a system of monitoring that is sufficiently comprehensive and rigorous so that enacted or approved standards are in fact meaningfully implemented.

The chapter's main focus is to describe in depth an approach developed in the US agricultural setting by the Coalition of Immokalee Workers (CIW), a worker-based human rights organisation in southwest Florida. Over the past decade, CIW campaigns of worker and consumer pressure have led to negotiated bilateral agreements with national and international retail brands (fast food chains, food service companies and supermarkets) that have implemented a prescribed substantial wage increase and dramatically improved other conditions for tens of thousands of workers in Florida's tomato-growing industry. The agreements are monitored and enforced through an unprecedented programme combining worker-driven complaint investigations and comprehensive audits, co-ordinated by the Fair Food Standards Council (FFSC), a third-party monitor launched by CIW in 2011. This framework of private labour standards agreements negotiated with leading food retail brands and imposing severe market consequences on suppliers who fail to comply—based on extensive annual audits and an omnipresent complaint resolution system in which workers play pivotal roles—offers distinctive lessons for labour relations in global corporate supply chains.

Finally, the chapter presents preliminary thoughts on whether the CIW model can be replicated on a larger scale, such as the Asian garment production industry, which traverses national borders. This is a complicated question, with a number of extrinsic factors militating against simple or unitary solutions. Still, given the scope of success achieved by the CIW and FFSC against what seemed insuperable challenges for decades, it is a question fully worth exploring.

II. SHORTCOMINGS OF CURRENT PUBLIC AND PRIVATE LAW APPROACHES

A. Public Norms: National and International

National Regulation

National labour standards norms have force-of-law impact in principle, but serious challenges exist with respect to implementation of these norms—especially though not exclusively in developing countries. Some problems are doctrinal. Labour laws typically address only employer–employee relationships, making it difficult to reach often-remote suppliers that have subcontracted with the lead firm. These laws also tend to provide protections for full-time or regular employees rather than irregular, casual or short-term contract labour. Undocumented migrant workers are especially vulnerable in both developing and developed countries; they often have sharply limited rights and remedies and they justifiably fear being deported if they assert whatever rights they have.[1] Finally, labour laws lack authority beyond national borders.

Apart from the doctrinal issues, national regulation in this area faces major structural challenges. One is lack of resources: developing countries often have vastly inadequate numbers of labour inspectors,[2] and these inspectors tend to operate in restrictive bureaucratic contexts, unable to pursue new or distant worksites as an industry reconfigures its production capacities. A related challenge is a lack of will to enforce: data on implementation suggests systematic problems in many developing countries.[3] Cost competitiveness is an important aspect, in that self-interest encourages weak enforcement to avoid production shifts by multinational brands to other suppliers or even other countries. Lack of will may also evolve into corruption or misuse of the monitoring process—sometimes to punish immigrant workers as an auxiliary to law enforcement.[4]

A final structural obstacle is that the low-wage workers whom public regulation is meant to protect too often have limited input into the regulatory design process. Those with vested financial interests in the status quo tend to exercise disproportionate influence—if not outright control—over

[1] See generally Cathryn Costello and Mark Freedland (eds), *Migrants at Work: Immigration and Vulnerability in Labour Law* (Oxford, Oxford University Press, 2014).

[2] See, eg ILO, *Report of the Committee of Experts on the Application of Conventions and Recommendations* (Geneva, ILO, 2015), addressing Convention No 81 for Bangladesh at 320; for India at 335–36; for Pakistan at 352; for Korea at 338; for Turkey at 361; for Honduras at 334; for Slovenia at 359.

[3] Inspections that regularly are less than thorough or adequate may be due to limited transportation resources, absence of legal staff, and/or lack of power to issue fines. See, eg ILO, *Report of the Committee of Experts* (2015) addressing Convention No 81 for Bangladesh at 320–21; for Colombia at 323–24; for Qatar at 356–57.

[4] See ILO, *Labour Inspection: General Survey of the Committee of Experts on the Application of Conventions and Recommendations on Convention 81* (Geneva, International Labour Conference, 2006) 24–25. Here the ILO criticises inspectors being used to enforce immigration laws in lieu of their primary duty to protect workers. For examples of individual countries using labour inspectors in this way, see ILO, *Report of the Committee of Experts* (2015) addressing Convention No 81 for Luxembourg at 340; for Malaysia at 344; ILO, *Report of the Committee of Experts on the Application of Conventions and Recommendations* (Geneva, ILO, 2014), addressing Convention No 81 for Bulgaria at 358; for Poland at 389–90; for Saudi Arabia at 398; for Spain at 402.

the content and quality of enacted protections. Even in modern democracies such as the US, the constitutional respect accorded to money in the legislative and electoral processes has amplified the role played by wealth in diluting worker-protection outcomes.

For all these reasons, when national laws address minimum wage and working hour standards, or safety and health requirements, implementation is very often lax.[5] To take one example, a recent study of wage practices in the garment supply chain throughout Asia found widespread failure to follow basic legal regulations involving minimum wage, overtime pay, paid holidays and social insurance contributions; the study also reported the presence of dual or triple bookkeeping on a systematic basis.[6] As one respected international labour official observed more than a decade ago, 'labour legislation without inspection is an exercise in ethics, but not a binding social discipline'.[7]

ILO Standards

In its 1998 Declaration of Fundamental Principles and Rights at Work, the International Labour Organization (ILO) identified eight fundamental labour standards conventions that are now widely perceived as benchmarks for human rights in the global workplace.[8] These eight conventions, plus the two governance conventions on the operation of labour inspectorates and on consultation among the ILO's tripartite constituencies,[9] comprise an international foundational structure for assessing government commitment to socially responsible working conditions. Every Asian country

[5] See ILO, *Wages and Working Hours in the Textiles, Clothing, Leather, and Footwear Industries* (Geneva, ILO, 2014) 16–23; SwedWatch, *Play Fair: A Campaign for Decent Sportswear* (Stockholm, SwedWatch, 2013) 9–10.

[6] See Daniel Vaughan-Whitehead, 'How "Fair" Are Wage Practices Along the Supply Chain? A Global Assessment' in Arianna Rossi, Amy Luinstra and John Pickles (eds), *Towards Better Work: Understanding Labour in Apparel Global Value Chains* (Geneva, ILO, 2014) 68, 72–100. See also ILO, *Wages and Working Hours* 22–23.

[7] Francis Blanchard, former Director-General of the ILO, quoted in Wenjia Zhung and Kinglun Ngok, 'Labour Inspection in Contemporary China: Like the Anglo-Saxon Model, but Different' (2015) 153 *International Labor Review* 561, 562.

[8] These eight conventions address freedom of association and collective bargaining (No 87 and 98), non-discrimination (No 100 and 111); forced labour (No 29 and 105); and child labour (No 138 and 182). See generally Janice Bellace, 'The ILO Declaration of Fundamental Principles and Rights at Work' (2009) 17 *International Journal of Comparative Labour & Industrial Relations* 269.

[9] The labour inspection convention (No 81) and the convention mandating consultation among governments, labour organisations and employer organisations (No 144) establish basic norms for monitoring and enforcing labour standards and fostering dialogue among labour, employers and government with respect *inter alia* to ratification and reporting on ILO conventions.

that is heavily involved in garment production has ratified most of these conventions, and some have ratified nine or all ten.[10]

None of these core conventions, however, addresses wage levels and protections. Although the ILO convention concerning minimum wage fixing, which entered into force in 1972, makes special reference to developing countries, only one of the major garment-producing countries in Asia has ratified it.[11]

Moreover, ratification is not the same as effective compliance by national governments. Some countries that have ratified conventions on freedom of association and collective bargaining have banned or restricted trade union activities.[12] Ratifying governments also have in effect accepted regular employer resistance and violations of the right to organise at the factory level.[13] Other governments that have not ratified conventions No 87 or 98 are less than supportive of independent trade unions.[14] This lack of compliance in law and practice is important because union density and access to collective bargaining are generally viewed as integral to developing sustainable labour cost models that can provide for basic wages and hours protection in conjunction with commitments to efficiency and worker effort.[15]

To be clear, ILO norms have played an integral role in the overall effort to promote compliance with transnational labour standards, and many national governments have made progress in implementing and enforcing those norms. In addition, ILO norms now figure prominently in transnational corporations' voluntary efforts to create socially responsible labour

[10] As reported on the ILO website (www.ilo.org), Indonesia and Sri Lanka have ratified all ten; Bangladesh and Cambodia nine of ten; and China, India, Thailand and Vietnam have between five and seven ratifications.

[11] As reported on the ILO website, Sri Lanka ratified Convention No 131 in 1975; more than 20 of the 52 countries that have ratified this Minimum Wage Fixing Convention are in Latin America or Africa.

[12] See European Commission, *Bangladesh Sustainability Compact: Technical Status Report* (Brussels, European Commission, 2015). See also Jim Yardley, 'Fighting for Bangladesh Labor, and Ending up in Pauper's Grave', *New York Times*, 9 September 2012.

[13] See SwedWatch, *Play Fair* (discussing widespread employer abuses in Indonesia) (n 5); Human Rights Watch, *'Whoever Raises their Head Suffers the Most': Workers' Rights in Bangladesh's Garment Factories* (New York, Human Rights Watch, 2015) (discussing abuses by employers in Bangladesh). See also International Trade Union Confederation, *The 2015 ITUC Global Rights Index: The World's Worst Countries for Workers* (Brussels, ITUC, 2015) 59–63 (describing systematic abuses in Colombia, El Salvador, Guatemala and Honduras, all countries that have ratified conventions No 87 and No 98).

[14] See eg Simon Clarke, Chang-Hee Lee and Do Quynh Chi, 'From Rights to Interests: The Challenge of Industrial Relations in Vietnam' (2007) 49 *Journal of Industrial Relations* 545, 551–53; Chris King-Chi Chan and Elaine Sio-Ieng Hui, 'The Dynamics and Dilemma of Workplace Trade Union Reform in China: The Case of the Honda Workers' Strike' (2012) 54 *Journal of Industrial Relations* 653, 654–55.

[15] See generally Doug Miller, 'Regulating the "Wage Effort Bargain" in Outsourced Apparel Production: Towards a Model' in Rossi, Luinstra and Pickles (eds), *Towards Better Work* (n 6) 103, 120–21.

conditions that will appeal to Western consumers and investors, as I will explain in the next section.

Still, the record on the ground in developing nations, where global supply chains are principally located, has been generally disappointing. Apart from the frequent recalcitrance of governments—for reasons noted above—national attempts to encourage or require compliance with ILO standards are no match for transnational firms that already outsource garment, footwear, cell phone or food production to multiple countries. These firms can and do relocate away from efforts at labour standards enforcement that are perceived as threatening to their profit margins. Moreover, without a sufficiently central role for worker organisations, ILO norms are unlikely to be implemented effectively even by dedicated and well-funded government inspectors or courts. Independent worker organisations are better able than bureaucrats to gain the trust of reticent or language-inhibited workers; to gather important testimony and documents away from the workplace and after hours; and to understand and propose adjustments in the operational realities of a particular industry.[16]

B. Private Norms: Corporate Codes of Social Responsibility

Given the complexities of regulating and enforcing labour standards in transnational supply chains, workers' organisations and their allies—consumers, investors, NGOs—as well as corporate management have increasingly pursued private regulatory alternatives. These private systems of labour standards regulation rely primarily on market incentives, generally reinforced by third party certification and monitoring, in an effort to implement decent labour standards protections.[17] Although such private initiatives often invoke public international norms as part of their compliance framework, they face their own set of challenges and limitations.

Since the 1970s, transnational corporations in large numbers have adopted codes of conduct that declare their voluntary commitment to workers' rights, often identifying the fundamental ILO conventions as embodying those rights. Supporters view corporate codes as 'attracting consumers or investors who prefer to engage with a socially responsible company, and [as] mollifying regulators who must allocate their limited resources among

[16] See generally Janice Fine and Jennifer Gordon, 'Strengthening Labour Standards Enforcement Through Partnerships with Workers' Organisations' (2010) 38 *Policy & Society* 552; Janice Fine, 'Strengthening Labor Standards Compliance Through Co-Production of Enforcement' (2014) 23(2) *New Labor Forum* 76, 78.

[17] See generally Martijn Scheltema, 'An Assessment of the Effectiveness of International Private Regulation in the Corporate Social Responsibility Arena' (2014) 21 *Maastricht Journal of European & Comparative Law* 383.

delinquent actors'.[18] Insofar as the codes announce a pledge to promote humane working conditions, and are used to guide or constrain supervisors in their personnel practices, they have contributed to improved labour standards in parts of the global supply chain. For several well-established reasons, however, this form of corporate self-regulation has profound weaknesses.[19]

First, the regulatory landscape in which voluntary compliance programmes typically operate is a far cry from the US or European settings that include independent and active trade unions, a professionalised and essentially reputable labour standards bureaucracy, and a reasonably attentive and unconstrained media community. In the Asian countries that currently form the heart of the global supply chain for apparel, footwear and electronics, inadequate regulatory systems undermine workers' willingness to speak out. Moreover, a thinner knowledge base about levels of pay, working hours and other employment conditions, combined with fearful or uninterested domestic media, contribute to a low level of transparency. In this context, meaningful monitoring and effective sanctions—which are needed if the codes are to avoid being consigned to window dressing—are virtually impossible to achieve.[20]

The primary business response, internal monitoring of code compliance by corporate human rights departments, is simply inadequate when applied to global suppliers.[21] Advance notice of site visits effectively invites suppliers or contractors to engage in deceptive strategies: modifying standard bookkeeping practices, concealing workplace hazards and scripting workers for auditor interviews.[22] Beyond the problems associated with double sets of books and orchestrated worker participation, auditors' interviews are too often conducted exclusively on site at the plant, where workers justifiably anticipate subsequent management questioning or retaliation. These internal factory audits also tend to be patterned after company financial audits; the auditors rely primarily on top-down examination of documentary records rather than time-consuming investigation of shop-floor processes and lengthy worker interviews.[23]

[18] James J Brudney, 'Envisioning Enforcement of Freedom of Association Standards in Corporate Codes: A Journey for Sinbad or Sisyphus?' (2012) 33 *Comparative Labor Law & Policy Journal* 555, 555.

[19] See generally Frederick Mayer and John Pickles, 'Re-embedding the Market: Global Apparel, Value Chains, Governance, and Decent Work' in Rossi, Luinstra and Pickles (eds), *Towards Better Work* 22–29.

[20] See Brudney, 'Envisioning Enforcement' (n 18) 569.

[21] See Mayer and Pickles, 'Re-embedding the Market' (n 19) 28–29.

[22] Brudney, 'Envisioning Enforcement' (n 18) 570 and sources cited.

[23] See Richard Locke, Matthew Amengual and Akshay Mangla, 'Virtue out of Necessity? Compliance, Commitment and the Improvement of Labor Conditions in Global Supply Chains' (2009) 37 *Policy & Society* 319, 332; Axel Marx and Jan Wouters, *Redesigning Enforcement in Private Regulation: The Case of International Labor Governance*, Working Paper No 126 (Leuven, Leuven Centre for Global Governance Studies, 2013) 1, 5–8; Brudney, 'Envisioning Enforcement' (n 18) 571 and sources cited.

Problems of objectivity, depth and transparency may be partially alleviated if monitoring is truly independent. An outside monitoring enterprise is more likely to conduct unannounced site visits, to engage neutral experts for record review, and to interview workers away from the worksite where they should feel less intimidated.[24] Importantly, however, the independent monitor is unlikely to succeed in contacting and communicating with workers away from the plant without the presence of an actively involved trade union or other workers' organisation.[25]

Even for independent monitors and auditors, there remain other obstacles. These monitors are funded by the brands, and thus risk losing clients if they are too assiduous in their criticism of compliance efforts. Moreover, the opaque web of subcontracting relationships often includes short-term agreements and constant shifting between suppliers. Complex arrangements for payroll and benefits distributions may be similarly difficult to penetrate.[26] A clear system of sanctions also must be in place for use against code violators; this requires initiative and leadership from corporate managers rather than outside monitors.[27] Finally, assuming that monitoring identifies problems in a factory or with a subcontractor in several factories, the expense involved in corrective action and subsequent audits to monitor ongoing compliance often results in relocation of production facilities in an effort to maintain acceptable profit margins.[28]

Underlying these obstacles is an inherent tension between corporations' principled espousal of labour standards and their pragmatic insistence on price-driven competition among suppliers. One indicator of this tension is the extent of comparative investment. Corporate personnel and resources dedicated to assuring that the right products arrive at the right locations at the right time and price far outweigh the corporate resources devoted to protecting the human rights of the workers manufacturing, distributing or growing those products.

Not surprisingly, global suppliers in apparel, footwear, electronics and other labour-intensive industries understand that, because corporate management negotiates primarily on price, suppliers must keep costs low in

[24] See generally Social Accountability International (SAI), http://www.sa-intl.org/; Worldwide Responsible Accredited Production (WRAP), http://www.wrapcompliance.org/.

[25] Brudney, 'Envisioning Enforcement' (n 18) 571–72 and sources cited; Dennis Arnold, 'Workers' Agency and Power Relations in Cambodia's Garment Industry' in Rossi, Luinstra and Pickles (eds), *Towards Better Work* (n 6) 212, 215.

[26] See Marx and Wouters, *Redesigning Enforcement* (n 23) 7–8.

[27] Brudney, 'Envisioning Enforcement' (n 18) 572 and sources cited.

[28] See Jill Esbenshade, *Monitoring Sweatshops* (Philadelphia, PA, Temple University Press, 2004) 110–11.

order to compete successfully for business.[29] As a result, suppliers operate to a considerable extent outside the soft regulatory framework, concealing this arrangement from the transnational corporations with which they contract for production. Many if not most of these corporations continue to do business with non-complying suppliers out of choice, ignorance or perceived necessity.[30] And the level of non-compliance is not curable through auditing approaches that are characteristically top-down, highly centralised and lacking in substantial continuous involvement from workers and their organisations.[31]

C. Core Shortcomings

Neither the ILO conventions and accompanying national government enforcement machinery nor the private codes of social responsibility have adequately addressed substandard working conditions in the global supply chain. These approaches represent progress, but they also reveal two core shortcomings: insufficient worker participation on the ground in identifying the problems to be addressed within the existing human rights framework, and the absence of a strong organisational approach to monitoring and remediation.

To be sure, it is difficult to develop effective worker participation when freedom of association and collective bargaining rights are discounted or suppressed under national law and practice. And it is difficult to generate effective monitoring and enforcement mechanisms without clear national commitments that include substantial funding. While these twin challenges can hardly be overstated, the structure of corporate supply chains offers possibilities for responsive engagement based on the special role that lead firms often play in co-ordinating and controlling sourcing decisions.[32]

Empirical studies indicate that private governance mechanisms are most effective when these lead firms exert considerable power in their value chain, when consumers and/or advocacy groups can engage in collective action, and when improved workplace conditions align with commercial concerns.[33] These mechanisms appear to be especially effective when lead

[29] See Miller, 'Regulating the "Wage Effort Bargain"' (n 15) 104. See generally Scott Nova and John M Kline, 'Social Labeling and Supply Chain Reform' in Jennifer Bair, Doug Miller and Marsha Dickson (eds), *Workers Rights and Labor Compliance in Global Supply Chains* (London, Routledge, 2013).

[30] Brudney, 'Envisioning Enforcement' (n 18) 571 and sources cited.

[31] See Marx and Wouters, *Redesigning Enforcement* (n 23) 8.

[32] See generally Arianna Rossi, Amy Luinstra and John Pickles, 'Introduction' in Rossi, Luinstra and Pickles (eds), *Towards Better Work* (n 6) 3.

[33] See Frederick Mayer and Gary Gereffi, 'Regulation and Economic Globalization: Prospects and Limits of Private Governance' (2010) 12(3) *Business & Politics* art 11.

firms permit or encourage opportunities for worker representation and subsequent participation in decision making about workplace conditions and practices,[34] and when auditors act less like inspectors charged with uncovering code of conduct violations and more like consultants engaged in joint problem solving and sharing of best practices among global buyers and their suppliers.[35] One recent and remarkably successful model that has utilised these mechanisms arises not in the garment or electronics industries but in the comparably challenging arena of agricultural labour.

III. THE FAIR FOOD PROGRAM AS A MODEL

A. Background

In the early 1990s a group of migrant farm workers from Mexico, Haiti and Guatemala, labouring in and around the southwest Florida town of Immokalee, formed the Coalition of Immokalee Workers (CIW).[36] In its initial years, the CIW used community-wide strikes and work stoppages in the tomato fields to pressure Florida growers to improve piece rates and eliminate violence by crew leaders. The coalition also worked closely with the US Department of Justice to investigate and prosecute seven separate farm labour slavery cases in Florida, involving over a thousand workers and fifteen different supervisors.[37]

Agriculture in the United States has long been an exploitive and low-wage industry.[38] Growers in the modern era are able to recruit and retain often-desperate workers from a vulnerable immigrant population. The CIW's efforts to pressure the Florida tomato growers yielded some modest successes, but the coalition was unable to generate substantial wage increases or to force the growers into genuine negotiations. By the end of the 1990s, the CIW shifted its strategic approach in a way that is directly relevant to the dilemma confronting workers in global supply chains.

[34] See Richard M Locke, Fei Qin and Alberto Brause, 'Does Monitoring Improve Labor Standards? Lessons from Nike' (2007) 61 *Industrial & Labour Relations Review* 3.

[35] See Richard M Locke, *The Promise and Limits of Private Power: Promoting Labor Standards in a Global Economy* (Cambridge, Cambridge University Press, 2013) 180–81.

[36] See Greg Asbed and Sean Sellers, 'The Fair Food Program: Comprehensive, Verifiable and Sustainable Change for Farm Workers' (2013) 16 *University of Pennsylvania Journal of Law & Social Change* 39, 43. Asbed is one of the coalition's founders. See John Bowe, *Nobodies: Modern American Slave Labor and the Dark Side of the New Global Economy* (New York, Random House, 2007) 27. The CIW is not a traditional trade union and does not engage in collective bargaining—nor do the workers it speaks for have a legal right to do so given their exclusion from the National Labour Relations Act (NLRA) as agricultural employees.

[37] See Sean Sellers and Greg Asbed, 'The History and Evolution of Forced Labor in Florida Agriculture' (2011) 5(1) *Race/Ethnicity: Multidisciplinary Global Contexts* 29, 37–40.

[38] See Asbed and Sellers, 'The Fair Food Program' (n 36) 40–41.

The domestic market for tomato production is highly concentrated. Florida produces virtually all fresh-market field-grown tomatoes harvested between October and May in the United States, and 50 per cent of annual domestic production.[39] The industry estimates that more than 30,000 workers are required to grow and hand harvest this crop.[40]

Based on its own analysis, the coalition determined that major pressure on wages and working conditions came from the corporate food industry and its aggregated purchasing power. As is true in the garment, footwear and electronics industries, fierce competition among corporate brands creates substantial downward price pressures on suppliers or growers, whose response in turn is to impose similar downward pressure on wages and working conditions in their own operations.[41] After determining that the top of the industry would need to be on board, the CIW focused its efforts on brand name retail companies that have consolidated power and market share in several areas: fast food operations (Subway, McDonald's, Burger King and Yum Brands—Taco Bell's parent company); institutional food service providers (Aramark, Compass and Sodexo); and major supermarkets (Whole Foods, Trader Joe's, Kroger, Publix).[42] The CIW strategy was to direct concerted activities by farm workers and consumers at these brands.

B. Better Labour Standards for Farm Workers: Four Major Components

As a workers' organisation, the CIW has approximately 5,100 members out of a total tomato fields–related labour force of over 30,000 at any one time. The great majority of the workforce are undocumented immigrants.[43] Worker's join and participate in a range of regularly scheduled activities including Wednesday evening meetings, Sunday women's meetings, Saturday movie nights and the operation of a local FM radio station.[44] A CIW Central Committee meets monthly to review and plan for activities and new approaches; participation in all activities is open and self-selected. The CIW has been described as 'founded in liberation theology-influenced

[39] Fair Food Standards Council, *Fair Food Program 2014 Annual Report* (Sarasota, FL, FFSC, 2014) 6.

[40] Ibid.

[41] See 'About CIW', http://ciw-online.org/about.

[42] Asbed and Sellers, 'The Fair Food Program' (n 36) 44.

[43] Roughly 80 per cent are undocumented. See Jennifer Gordon, notes from her exchange with Sean Sellers during February 2014 site visit.

[44] Details on the CIW operation are reflected in its various website entries and also in the author's communications with CIW and FFSC personnel since March 2014.

principles of popular education, leadership development, and collective action'.[45] The CIW approach essentially consists of four separate but interrelated components.

Pressuring the Brands for Bilateral Agreements Featuring a Wage Premium

The first component was a sustained national campaign generating pressure on the brands, based on an alliance of farm workers and consumers. The campaign used speaking tours, long-distance marches, protests, hunger strikes, online organising, consumer boycotts and other grassroots activities aimed at publicising the purchasing-power role of the large brand retailers, thereby making these brands accountable for labour conditions in their tomato supply chains.[46]

The first buyer that CIW targeted was Taco Bell. It took four years of comprehensive campaigning by workers and consumers before Taco Bell (through its parent Yum Brands) acceded in 2005 to the demands set forth by CIW's Fair Food Program. The company agreed to pay a penny a pound more for its Florida tomatoes. This fair food premium, designed to reverse the downward pressure on farm worker wages, has evolved into a sophisticated set of payment mechanisms by participating brands that generates millions of dollars annually in additional wage payments.[47] Taco Bell also agreed to shift its purchases of Florida tomatoes to growers that complied with a human rights–related code of conduct developed by the coalition.

Subsequently, CIW initiatives led to similar bilateral agreements with other big-name fast food chains: McDonald's (2007), Burger King (2008), Subway (2008) and Chipotle (2012); with national supermarkets: Whole Foods (2008) and Trader Joe's (2012); with institutional food service providers: Compass (2009), Bon Appetit (2009), Aramark (2010) and Sodexo (2010); and more recently with Walmart (2014), Fresh Market (2015) and Ahold (2015), the parent company of the Stop & Shop and Giant supermarket chains.[48]

It is worth noting that the more recent agreements have been negotiated in the absence of any targeted campaign of public pressure. This development may reflect new participating buyers' felt need to keep up with their competitors who already participate in the Fair Food Program. Alternatively (or additionally), new buyers may independently perceive that participation is valuable for reasons of supply chain risk management, efficiency,

[45] Asbed and Sellers, 'The Fair Food Program' 4 (n 36) 3.

[46] Ibid 44.

[47] FFSC, *FFP Annual Report* (n 39) 29, 39–40. The amount increases with each new corporate participant that enters the programme.

[48] Ibid 6; Steve Hitov, General Counsel to CIW, personal communication, July 2015.

consumer goodwill or basic fairness. Whatever the explanation, it seems that constant campaigning may not be a necessary element of the model, although the potential for public pressure from workers and consumers almost certainly is.

The basic framework for the agreements includes both parties' recognition that avoidance of conflict between them is valuable consideration. The buyer agrees to provide a designated fair food wage premium; to purchase Florida tomatoes from participating growers and cease purchasing from growers that lose their participating status; and to co-operate with CIW and its independent auditors regarding efforts to verify compliance by growers with the Fair Food Code of Conduct. CIW agrees to refrain from engaging in disparaging protests or demonstrations regarding the issues covered by the agreements, and to conduct operations regarding those issues in the manner described under the Fair Food Program.[49]

Starting in 2007, the Florida Tomato Growers Exchange (FTGE) threatened its members with fines if they complied with the agreements being negotiated between CIW and an increasing number of major brands.[50] Although the FTGE invoked antitrust concerns, the individual contracts negotiated between CIW and each major brand would seem to be vertical agreements, lawful under a 'rule of reason' approach, rather than horizontal restraints of trade.[51]

The FTGE resisted vigorously for years, refusing to pass on the penny-a-pound premium that was being accumulated by the buyers. At one point, millions of dollars were being placed in an escrow fund. In 2010, two large growers began co-operating with CIW; shortly thereafter, the FTGE and CIW signed an agreement pursuant to which virtually all growers have participated on a statewide basis, covering well over 90 per cent of Florida's $650 million tomato industry.[52]

Between 2010 and 2015, participating buyers contributed almost 20 million dollars in wage premiums to improve farm worker wages. The Fair Food Standards Council (FFSC)[53] monitors the supply chain records to ensure that these premium funds are flowing from buyers to growers, either as monthly lump-sum payments or as a separate item incorporated into buyers' day-to-day purchases.[54] Workers receive 87 per cent of the premium

49 Steve Hitov, personal communication, March 2014 and June 2015.

50 Steven Greenhouse, 'Tomato Pickers' Wages Fight Faces Obstacles', *New York Times*, 24 December 2007.

51 See US Senate, *Ending Abuses and Improving Working Conditions for Tomato Workers: Hearing of the Committee on Health, Education, Labor, and Pensions*, 110th Cong, 56–60 (2008) (prepared statement of 26 law professors regarding legality of tomato growers' compliance with agreements between farm workers and fast-food companies).

52 FFSC, *FFP Annual Report* (n 39) 6.

53 The FFSC is a third-party monitor launched by CIW in 2011.

54 See FFSC, *FFP Annual Report* (n 39) 39–40.

funds as a line-item bonus on their pay checks. Growers are permitted to retain 13 per cent to offset increased payroll taxes and administrative costs.[55] Notably, brands are thus financially contributing to their suppliers to help them defray costs associated with establishing a suitably transparent wage increase structure.

A Worker-Driven Code of Conduct, Reinforced by Effective Complaint Resolution

In addition to wage premiums, one key element of the Fair Food Agreements negotiated with each participating buyer is a commitment to require its suppliers to abide by the Fair Food Code of Conduct.[56] Apart from requiring compliance with applicable local, state and federal laws, the code sets forth certain prohibitions that carry immediate consequences if violated: prohibitions against forced labour and child labour of any kind, the use or threat of physical violence, and sexual harassment involving physical contact.[57] The code also includes detailed requirements for accurate timekeeping as well as documentation that must appear on all pay slips.[58]

Importantly, the code establishes a ban on subcontracting of employment: all farm workers are hired by growers as employees.[59] For decades prior to 2010, the Florida tomato-growing industry—like agricultural employment in general—was characterised by multiple complex subcontracting arrangements which often shielded growers from legal responsibility for labour abuses.[60] Under the Code of Conduct, however, all farm workers must be employees of the grower—this includes workers supervised by crew leaders who are themselves contractors rather than being employed by the grower. And all these employees are required to participate in the grower's orientation process—including training on their rights under the FFP.

The Fair Food Code is not a static document; it has developed over time through continuous dialogue among workers, growers and buyers.[61] Many code features are based on farm workers' distinctive knowledge of, or familiarity with, problems in the tomato harvesting fields. These include a

[55] Ibid 40, referencing Appendix A of the Fair Food Code of Conduct Guidance Manual.

[56] Ibid 50–55. The wage premium is included in the Code of Conduct.

[57] Ibid 52.

[58] Ibid 51. On timekeeping, the code specifies that all compensable hours must be recorded, with accurate hours kept by growers through a system (such as time clock punch or card swipe) in which employees control their time registration devices. The code requires that payslips display pay period, hours worked, wages, and the fair food premium as a separate line item.

[59] Ibid.

[60] Ibid 16. See generally *Aimable v Long & Scott Farms* 20 F3d 434 (11th Cir 1994); *Alviso-Medrano v Harloff* 868 FSupp 1367 (MD Fla 1994); *Arredondo v Delano Farms Co* 2012 WL 2358594 (ED Cal 2012).

[61] See Fair Food Standards Council, 'Fair Food Code of Conduct & Selected Guidance', http://www.fairfoodstandards.org/code.html.

prohibition against over-filling or 'cupping' buckets, complete with a visual standard for bucket filling; elimination of previously unrecorded and unpaid waiting time in the fields; provision of a safe shaded area in the fields (through durable, mobile shade structures) and the ability to access it during rest breaks; and training on sexual harassment and discrimination prevention provided to all workers and supervisors.[62]

Another key element is worker-to-worker education regarding the code that takes place on the farm during paid working time.[63] Growers provide a booklet and video to all workers at the point of hire; these materials, describing the code and its contents, are written and acted by the CIW and its members.[64] During subsequent CIW education sessions at the job site, workers talk to one another about their experiences and the rights generated from those experiences, including the right to make complaints with no retaliation.[65] Workers also are informed that FFSC will visit growers to ask questions, conduct monitoring and enforce the agreement. Health and safety committees must be established at every farm, providing a structured voice for workers on such issues.

Finally, there is a 24-hour hotline to bilingual FFSC auditors who investigate complaints and resolve them, normally in a collaborative fact-finding and resolution process with participating growers.[66] There are other ways to report code violations, including by informing CIW personnel. Since 2011, over 500 worker complaints about participating growers have been received; almost all have been investigated and processed to resolution.[67] Worker education includes an emphasis on workers' role as monitors of their own rights, both in the workplace and in their interactions with the programme's designated monitoring organisation.

A Comprehensive Auditing Structure

Perhaps the linchpin to the Fair Food Program model is the FFSC auditing process, conducted by its 11-person staff.[68] In order to ensure transparency and co-operation with the code, FFSC auditing must be at once in-depth and

[62] These provisions are set forth in the code (FFSC, *FFP Annual Report* (n 39) 51–53) and explained in other sections of the report: 19–20 (sexual harassment), 26–27 (bucket-filling standards), 31 (shade in the fields).

[63] FFSC, *FFP Annual Report* (n 39) 9–10.

[64] Ibid 22.

[65] Ibid 21.

[66] Ibid 22–23, 34–35.

[67] Ibid 34–35. Almost 50 per cent of complaints received were found to be valid; almost 25 per cent were found not valid and/or not to have alleged a code violation; approximately 20 per cent resulted in some action agreed upon by the participating grower and complaining worker(s) without formal disposition of the complaint; and the remainder were either informational in nature or else workers chose not to proceed.

[68] Ibid 7.

nuanced in its application. The auditing mandate has resulted in the development of tools to determine what information is reviewed and accessible to the auditors. The process of assessing information obtained from the tools leads to an evaluation of each grower that includes prepared findings and a corrective action plan where necessary improvements have been identified.

The first and possibly most important auditing tool is the interview guidelines, customised for each participating grower. Accessibility to all levels of management and workers ensures there is little opportunity for interference with information collection. Intimidation or coaching of workers during the auditing process is grounds for probation or suspension from the programme.[69]

The FFSC audits every grower every season, and audits extend to multiple locations when they exist. It normally interviews over half a grower company's workers, which is well above traditional auditing sample sizes.[70] For a fairly large operation—over 500 workers—the FFSC will send eight auditors who spend three to four days on site.[71] Interview packets for field workers, crew leaders and management each contain a comprehensive and specific set of questions to ask, and issues on which to comment. Because the interview packets for crew leaders and management pose very similar questions tailored somewhat differently, they provide an opportunity to enhance transparency (and minimise manipulation of facts) through obtaining the same information from both sources.[72] The auditors also spend substantial amounts of time interviewing workers in the fields and in a variety of other settings. They ride the buses with workers, visit workers' housing for follow-up conversations and to check on the housing quality, and provide cards that include the hotline phone number.[73] This intensive, hands-on and time-consuming level of involvement assures that the auditors develop a thorough and fine-grained understanding of labour conditions on the ground.

A second tool utilised is document requests that enable the comprehensive collection of relevant written materials. The document request process begins well in advance of the site visit: the lead auditor typically makes contact with the grower and initiates this process one to one-and-a-half months before the audit team arrives on site.[74] FFSC requests eight distinct categories of documents as part of its management and operations audit.[75]

[69] Ibid 15.
[70] Ibid 10.
[71] Notes of Jennifer Gordon from site visit and interviews with FFSC staff, 12 January 2014.
[72] Examples of interview questions and guidelines are on file with the author.
[73] See Gordon, notes from site visit (n 71).
[74] Ibid.
[75] The categories are general; hiring and registration; training and communication of policies; work environment; complaint procedure; wages, hours and pay practices; health and safety; and housing. Document request samples are on file with author.

In addition to records and policy documents on management systems and personnel procedures, which are obtained prior to the audit or at the management interview, there are payroll document reviews from several pay periods that are used to ensure proper compensation (including distribution of the fair food premium) as well as accurate timekeeping mechanisms and minimum wage compliance.[76] These payroll document reviews are conducted after field operations audits so that financial investigators can verify and utilise in their analyses data that has been provided by workers.

As part of the payroll audit, FFSC randomly selects five personnel files for review, in order to verify proper documentation of registration, training, injuries and disciplinary actions.[77] The auditors also prepare charts keyed to various report sections (eg transparency and co-operation; hiring and registration; worker training; crew leader and supervisor training; health and safety; wages, hours and pay practices) that are used as categories for interviews, field notes or document requests. For each report section, the auditor describes the control objective, preparation and inquiry procedures, and testing procedures. This approach fosters greater uniformity in the auditing process and also guides the auditors by enabling them to collect detailed information on the way each grower operates.[78]

Within ten days following the collection of audit data, the FFSC submits a preliminary evaluation of findings to the participating grower, indicating the likelihood of good standing or probation/suspension from the programme. If certain findings appear to be especially troubling, the preliminary evaluation will be accompanied by an expedited preliminary audit report that provides an overview of the most problematic findings and suggests corrective actions to avoid probation or suspension.[79]

After the expedited preliminary findings, and within eight weeks of FFSC's payroll audit, growers receive a full assessment report for the season that includes an overview of the audit process, a summary of major findings, and an in-depth description of the findings according to key programme areas tailored to sections of the audit tools as mentioned above. At the beginning of each assessment report section is a breakdown of issues addressed from a prior year's corrective action plan (CAP), issues unaddressed from the prior year's CAP, new issues revealed during the audit, and any further corrective action required. Following this assessment, FFSC and the grower agree on a

[76] FFSC, *FFP Annual Report* (n 39) 7. The FFSC also monitors participating buyer payments of the fair food premium to participating growers.

[77] Judge Laura Safer Espinoza, Director of the FFSC, personal communication, March 2014 and July 2015. Given the number of individuals employed by growers, having advance knowledge that five files will be pulled at random is unlikely to result in any manipulation of data.

[78] Ibid.

[79] Ibid; sample documents on file with author.

corrective action plan specifying findings and CAP measures. The CAP then forms the basis for the next season's audit, which assesses the grower's performance related to the agreed-upon CAP as well as addressing the grower's performance in the months since the prior audit, using the same detailed format.

The goal of this comprehensive data collection effort is to ensure compliance in practice with the code. Where deficiencies arise, the objective is to provide the grower with an effective roadmap towards full code implementation. The auditing process is designed to monitor the activity of growers over a period of time, and to foster a working relationship between the FFSC and each growers' organisation.[80] But ultimately, compliance with the code is required if the grower wants to remain in the programme.

In the three seasons between 2011 and 2014, the FFSC conducted 81 management interviews and 98 payroll audits, resulting in 86 corrective action plans.[81] FFSC auditors visited over 100 farm locations, interviewed 7,000 workers on and off-site, and conducted almost 300 on-site interviews with crew leaders to assess knowledge of code requirements and compliance at the field level.[82] In a signal of the value attached to these audits by the growers themselves, some participating growers have begun requesting that FFSC audit their out-of-state operations, that is, farm locations that are not covered by the programme.[83]

As comprehensive and effective as the FFSC's audit protocols are in practice, it is worth repeating that the FFP considers workers themselves to be the essential frontline defenders of their own rights. Workers are empowered by the multiple layers of education as to their rights under the Code of Conduct, and by the efficacy of the protected complaint mechanism. For all 54 complaints in which FFSC found that some form of retaliation had been taken against workers, resolutions were successfully achieved, including the rehiring of all terminated workers, disciplinary actions and retraining for the offending supervisors, and public apologies along with reaffirmations of the right to complain without fear of retaliation from management.[84] The FFSC emphasises that it is able to overcome certain inherent limitations of the traditional audit-only monitoring approach by effectively deputising

[80] See FFSC, *FFP Annual Report* (n 39) 10–11.

[81] Ibid 33. There is a higher number of payroll audits because many growers have multiple locations—each farm location within a company is recorded as a separate audit. The higher number of CAPs than management interviews is likely due to the fact that in a few instances the same owner has implemented the same policies and procedures across more than one company—in those cases, there is no need to interview management twice. Laura Safer Espinoza, personal communication, July 2015.

[82] FFSC, *FFP Annual Report* (n 39) 33.

[83] Ibid. See also ibid 15–16 (reporting statements from growers appreciating the audit process and results).

[84] Greg Asbed and Laura Safer Espinoza, personal communication, July 2015.

30,000 workers as monitors; this also provides a further deterrent to supervisors who might consider violating workers' rights.[85]

Enforcement Through Market Consequences

When—as occurs in the great majority of instances—an audit discloses violations warranting a corrective action plan, remediation is a relatively rapid process. Growers must comply with the code or they will lose the ability to sell their tomatoes to buyers in the FFP. This threat of lost business has been a substantial incentive for compliance even though the FFP encompasses a relatively small percentage of all purchases of Florida tomatoes.[86] Importantly, the FFP's market-based effectiveness has not required that participating brands (McDonald's, Sodexo, Walmart et al) collectively exercise control over a majority of sales from one or more Florida tomato growers. Instead, these brands simply must have control over enough of the market so that a majority of individual suppliers will not want to lose so large a proportion of their business. This in turn suggests that a model relying on market consequences can effect significant change in labour conditions by channelling the efforts of a relatively low number of buyers.

If growers violate the code's zero-tolerance provisions (addressing forced labour of any kind; systemic use of child labour; sexual harassment involving physical contact; use or threat of physical violence), they may be suspended from the programme for varying lengths of time.[87] By August 2014, seven growers had been suspended and nine more had been placed on probation.[88] Brands may not purchase tomatoes from suspended growers for a 90- to 180-day period within the Florida growing season.[89] To uphold these market consequences, auditors review brands' monthly supply chain records to be sure that they only source Florida tomatoes from participating growers in good standing.[90] Supervisors who violate the zero-tolerance provisions must be terminated, and they are ineligible for employment at

[85] Supervisors who were persistent bad actors have been weeded out through suspensions and terminations. Because the FFP makes the participating grower responsible for the conduct of its supervisors under the code, many growers have also engaged in proactive self-policing for the first time. Ibid.

[86] Roughly 20 per cent of overall Florida tomato sales fall under the purview of the FFP. Steve Hitov, personal communication, July 2015.

[87] Suspension is automatic for instances of forced labour or systematic child labour. For the other zero tolerance events, the perpetrator must be discharged or the grower is suspended. For all other code violations, growers are prodded to take corrective action, and failure to do so results in probation. A grower placed on probation has 15 days to fix the outstanding problem(s) or it is suspended. See FFSC, *FFP Annual Report* 34; Steve Hitov, personal communication, July 2015.

[88] FFSC, *FFP Annual Report* (n 39) 34.

[89] Laura Safer Espinoza, personal communication, March 2014.

[90] FFSC, *FFP Annual Report* (n 39) 11.

Fair Food Program farms for up to five years, depending on the nature of the offence.[91]

At the same time, the audit and enforcement process includes space for collaboration. Many growers have developed their own systems: this often involves a point person handling complaints from workers about conditions and violations who makes sure that complaints percolate up to management. When FFSC finds a violation for the first time, it tries to provide a remedial roadmap or plan. And while the protections of the code are fixed, there is also a Guidance Manual that provides some assistance on how to interpret and apply various code provisions. The manual is drafted and updated by a working group consisting of CIW plus several growers.[92] Further, some growers now send FFSC their own policies to review and if necessary to make recommendations for achieving compliance. Growers also have invited FFSC on site to train their supervisors.

FFSC monitoring and enforcement are effective because there is a real hammer: loss of market share imposed by the brands through their separate agreements with CIW. The auditing system has now completed its fourth full season (November 2014 to April 2015). Initially, there was a significant amount of angry pushback from growers, and some baseline requirements were not being fulfilled.[93] It also took a certain amount of time for the workers to trust FFSC enough to report complaints.[94] By the middle of the first full season of operations, in winter and spring of 2012, the number of complaints had substantially increased. After three years, there appear to be fewer serious instances of non-compliance, and the complaints with respect to growers that have participated in the FFP for several seasons have become more routine.[95]

The FFP is being extended in 2015 to 10,000 more workers, at Florida bell pepper farms and to tomato suppliers in Georgia, South Carolina and Virginia.[96] Walmart has taken the lead in expanding the FFP to the three new states. As in Florida, the FFSC will monitor for growers' compliance with the Code of Conduct and for payment of the FFP wage premium.[97]

[91] Ibid 19. An offending supervisor must undergo FFSC-approved training before employment eligibility at participating growers can be reinstated. Failure by a participating grower to impose these sanctions on offending supervisors results in suspension from the programme.

[92] Steve Hitov, personal communication, March 2014; see also Guidance Manual.

[93] Laura Safer Espinoza, personal communication, March 2014.

[94] Ibid.

[95] Workers and a growing number of supervisors have expressed relief to FFSC monitors that the industry's worst actors no longer have a place at FFP farms. After three full seasons, FFSC's annual report for 2013–14 confirmed the absence of any cases of forced labour, violence by supervisors against workers or sexual assault. FFSC does continue to receive complaint line calls reporting instances of these abuses from workers on non-FPP farms. Laura Safer Espinoza, personal communication, July 2015.

[96] See Steven Greenhouse, 'Farm Labor Groups Make Progress on Wages and Working Conditions', *New York Times*, 3 July 2015.

[97] Steve Hitov, personal communication, July 2015.

C. Distinctively Effective Aspects

The Fair Food Program is substantially more successful than other corporate compliance programmes in the labour standards area. A central element is that *workers define the issues to be addressed, notably including a focus on wage increases*. The Code of Conduct addresses worker needs and priorities arising in a particular industry and location. This minimises the risk of compliance becoming a public relations issue. The focus is on resolving workers' perceived problems rather than cleaning up a brand's reputation.

A second, related element is that *workers have multiple ways to report violations and are protected in doing so*. It is hard to overstate the value of a structure where, having identified the priorities, workers also can feel secure in identifying when those priorities are not being met. Audits that are extensive and well-staffed, including off-site worker interviews, buttress the importance of workers' effective ability to report violations. Moreover, the worker education programmes and 24-hour complaint hotlines create considerable risk of violations being exposed outside the audit process. This effectively discourages unwanted conduct by field-level supervisors and encourages growers to disclose fully their relevant conduct and activities as part of the audit. Once again, corporate motivation is centred on programme improvement.

A third important element of the Fair Food Program approach is its *attention to management accountability*. There is an immediate meaningful impact for failure to comply. The FFSC code is framed primarily with reference to market-based consequences rather than legal rights or traditional legal remedies. The code bypasses international labour standards that are unavailable to these workers under the US legal system, notably the right to collective bargaining for agricultural employees.[98] Beyond lack of availability, however, market consequences would seem a more effective deterrent than legal remedies such as fines or cease-and-desist orders, because of their timing and certainty as well as their magnitude.

A final distinct element is that *brands are required to work closely with their product suppliers to co-ordinate responsive compliance efforts*. With respect to the wage premium, brands put funds into the supply chain to support the costs associated with changes they demand from those suppliers.[99] The brands also have a direct interest in their suppliers' audit performance. Payroll audits review and assess growers' monthly reporting of premium distributions to individual workers, including lists of field-level supervisors

[98] See 29 USC § 152(3) (excluding agricultural employees from NLRA coverage).

[99] See FFSC, *FFP Annual Report* (n 39) 40, referencing the 87–13 per cent split discussed above.

who are not eligible to receive the premiums.[100] In addition, the brands' monthly supply chain records are audited to assure that they only source tomatoes from participating growers in good standing.[101] Brands are thus directly and continuously engaged with their suppliers on labour standards priorities, analogously to how they *sua sponte* engage those suppliers on pricing and delivery priorities in the course of their regular market-driven decision making.

IV. REPLICATING THE IMMOKALEE WORKERS MODEL: SOME PRELIMINARY THOUGHTS

Success with a universe of 30,000 tomato field workers does not neatly translate to the challenges facing millions of apparel or footwear workers in multiple countries. There are differences in national law and practice across the global supply chain that result in varied approaches to labour standards protection and contract enforcement. These variations, along with differences in national languages and cultures, pose added challenges to brands seeking to negotiate with and monitor performance of multiple suppliers. One obvious example involves implementing the ban on subcontracting of employment given different legal approaches to employee status across different national legal systems.

Further, the relative ease of mobility for suppliers of these other products makes it harder for multinational brands to develop a closed system that captures all or substantially all participants in the supply chain.[102] Growers of tomatoes in the US are essentially constrained by climate from relocating out of south Florida between November and April. Other agricultural products that may become a focus for CIW campaigns, such as bell peppers and strawberries, are similarly limited in geographic terms as a result of climate-driven conditions.

Garment and footwear production do not face the same constraints. They are basically low-capital, labour-intensive operations, allowing factories to relocate to other countries or even to other parts of the same country. The increased use since 2005 of short-term fixed duration employment contracts between garment suppliers and their production workers has facilitated the process of relocating factories by making it easier to terminate workers'

[100] Ibid 29. The wage premium is listed as a separate line item on each worker's pay stub.

[101] Ibid 11.

[102] The Worker Rights Consortium has developed a designated supplier programme (DSP), encouraging major apparel brands to concentrate control over working conditions by sourcing at fewer factories and occupying a larger share of output at those factories. See Worker Rights Consortium, *The Designated Suppliers Program—Revised* (Washington, DC, WRC, 2012). Major brands have not adopted the DSP approach and appear reluctant to do so on their own initiative.

employment while also making it harder for workers to organise and protect their interests. These fixed-duration contracts (FDCs) are probationary and typically valid for three to six months, though they can be extended further if workers and employers agree on specific terms. The FDC problem has become especially acute under Cambodian labour law, although it exists in other countries as well.[103]

Without wanting to minimise such difficulties, I would point to several factors that arguably support prospects for replication of the CIW model.

A. Vulnerability of Worker Populations

Some may assert that workers toiling in the global garment, footwear or electronics supply chains present an immeasurably more intimidating set of obstacles than what CIW has had to overcome. Yet no-one in the early 1990s would have thought that what CIW and FFSC have accomplished was even conceivable, given centuries of oppressed farm labour in the southern US—including over 200 years of slavery, a century of sharecropper exploitation and decades of abusive conditions for the largely migrant labour that today constitutes the agricultural workforce. CIW and its allies have ended farm labour slavery in the industry (with the help of the Justice Department) and secured basic labour standards protections for tens of thousands of tomato pickers. They have not achieved total success, and their campaigns continue in Florida and other parts of the country. Still, any argument that the challenges involving global supply chain workers are inherently more daunting than those faced by agricultural migrant workers in the southern US states is less than persuasive.

B. Precariousness of Legal Rights

Although agricultural workers in the US fall outside the scope of the NLRA for organising a trade union or engaging in collective bargaining, they are accorded basic constitutional protection for freedom of association.[104] It may be argued that this legal protection for collective voice relieves some precariousness for CIW members and supporters in their campaign to secure

[103] See Arnold, 'Workers' Agency' 221–22 (Cambodia) (n 25); SwedWatch, *Play Fair* 9 (Indonesia) (n 5). See generally Stephen Sonnenberg and Benjamin Hensler, *Monitoring in the Dark: An Evaluation of the International Labor Organization's Better Factories Cambodia Monitoring and Reporting Program* (Stanford, CA, Stanford Human Rights Clinic and WRC, 2013).

[104] See generally *McLaughlin v Tilendis* 398 F2d 287, 289 (7th Cir 1968); *Atkins v City of Charlotte* 296 FSupp 1068, 1077 (WD NC 1969).

labour standards improvements and protections. However, it is worth reiterating that the CIW success stems from a contractual rather than legislative approach, featuring a privately generated code of conduct enforced through market-based consequences. In this respect, the CIW approach resembles US unions' recent success in negotiating neutrality agreements with individual employers. Those agreements have increased prospects for union recognition and collective bargaining by contracting around the perceived limitations of labour legislation.[105] And while agricultural migrants will not be arrested or murdered for talking about worker protection strategies—as they might be in other countries—these workers, who lack the protection of the NLRA, can be fired for engaging in concerted activities. For desperately poor individuals, this amounts to a not insignificant penalty. Even federal minimum wage, overtime and occupational safety laws that do cover farm workers are notoriously under-enforced in farm labour settings.[106]

Apart from these weaknesses in US law and practice, migrants face the pervasive fear of deportation when responding to exploitive labour conditions. Guest workers' visas are tied to a job with a particular employer. If these workers quit in search of better wages or conditions, they will likely lose their right to work and stay in the US. Should they dare to file complaints challenging workplace conditions or discrimination, they may be fired and again confront the loss of their lawful status as visitors.[107]

C. Focus on Market Consequences

The precarious legal situation of migrant farm workers presumably influenced the direction of the CIW model away from the judicial system and toward private regulation enforced by major brands through market-based consequences. That such an intrinsically vulnerable population has used worker-driven democratic processes to improve labour standards through negotiation with a powerful corporate chain of command suggests possibilities.

Factory workers in Southeast Asia are comparably vulnerable to migrant farm workers in the US in many respects, given that national laws either do not recognise their basic rights or—more likely—do not protect and enforce those rights. Further, workers in these supply chains are often themselves

[105] See James J Brudney, 'Neutrality Agreements and Card Check Recognition: Prospects for Changing Paradigms' (2005) 90 *Iowa Law Review* 819.

[106] See Maria Ontiveros, 'Migrant Labour in the United States: Working Beneath the Floor for Free Labour?' in Costello and Freedland (eds), *Migrants at Work* (n 1) 180, 184–91; *Frank Diehl Farms v Sec'y of Labor* 696 F2d 1325 (11th Cir 1983).

[107] Ontiveros, 'Migrant Labour in the United States' 185–87.

migrants—they may be far from home, far from their families, and not able to understand the predominant language or local culture.[108] These migrants may be especially vulnerable under local labour laws, both because as temporary or irregular workers they face difficult legal status issues similar to their Florida counterparts, and because labour inspectors may inappropriately enforce immigration laws against them.

Accordingly, one might hypothesise that the most effective entity to insist on change in global supply chains is the multinational corporation rather than the national government, local trade union or worker NGO. To be sure, corporate brands will become change agents only in response to pressure brought against them, including pressure in the US and/or Europe. But major retail brands are familiar with such pressures to improve basic working conditions, brought by trade unions, university students, institutional investors and consumers more generally. Representatives from worker organisations in Asian countries, supported by NGOs in those countries, might make strategic appearances in alliance with US or EU consumer and investor groups and unions in order to impose more targeted public pressure on these brands.

Since the 1990s, efforts by consumers and NGOs, and also traditional and social media, have increasingly linked the reputation of lead retail firms to their suppliers when it comes to abusive or harsh labour practices.[109] Notwithstanding the opacity of global supply chains, multinational brands are coming to understand in business terms the reputational advantages of proactive strategies—including improvements beyond those applied under local law—as well as the attendant risks when refusing to accommodate local activism.[110] Absent a pervasive national government presence as a capable monitor and enforcer, corporate motivation may have to come primarily from privately negotiated arrangements, supplemented or complemented by assistance from the ILO and NGOs. To take two examples, ILO audit data from export-oriented garment factories in Cambodia indicate that reputation-conscious global buyers have been driving improved

[108] See, eg Clean Clothes Campaign, *Migrant Workers in Thailand's Garment Factories* (Amsterdam, Clean Clothes Campaign, 2014) 17; Vicki Crinis, 'Sweat or No Sweat: Foreign Workers in the Garment Industry in Malaysia' (2010) 40 *Journal of Contemporary Asia* 589, 599; Arnold, 'Workers' Agency' (n 25) 214; Richard Record, Stephanie Kuttner and Kabmanivanh Phouxay, 'Voting With Their Feet? Explaining High Turnover and Low Productivity in the Lao Garment Sector' in Rossi, Luinstra and Pickles (eds), *Towards Better Work* 149.

[109] See generally Kevin B Sobel-Read, 'Global Value Chains: A Framework for Analysis' [2014] *Transnational Legal Theory* 364, 388–89; Locke, *The Promise and Limits of Private Power* (n 35) 1–3, 12–13.

[110] See, eg Simon Zadek, 'The Path to Corporate Responsibility' *Harvard Business Review*, December 2004, pp 125–32; Debora L Spar and Lane T La Mure, 'The Power of Activism: Assessing the Impact of NGOs on Global Business' (2003) 45 *California Management Review* 79.

compliance with ILO standards.[111] And the tragic 2013 factory collapse at Rana Plaza, which killed over 1,100 workers, has resulted in a major push by many Western retailers and apparel brands to improve safety at Bangladeshi factories.[112]

What CIW essentially concluded with respect to tomato growers may be seen as applicable to garment, footwear or electronics suppliers. Despite only a modest level of control over most production facilities in their supply chains, Nike, Adidas or Apple regularly insist on certain levels of quality, price and timing from their suppliers, and terminate them for failing to meet those levels. Leading brands arguably can add wage premiums and industry-specific labour protections to their negotiated deals on the same basis.

[111] See Locke, *The Promise and Limits of Private Power* (n 35) 170–71 and sources cited therein. One added incentive for compliance in Cambodia is factories' interest in securing a licence to export from the Cambodian government. See generally ILO, 'Better Factories Cambodia', http://www.ilo.org/asia/whatwedo/projects/WCMS_099340/lang--en/index.htm.

[112] See generally Bangladesh Accord for Fire and Building Safety, http://bangladeshaccord.org/; Alliance for Bangladesh Worker Safety, http://www.bangladeshworkersafety.org/. These two organisations together are responsible for thousands of new factory inspections and corrective plans at hundreds of plants. See generally Steven Greenhouse, 'Two Groups Complete Inspections of 1,700 Garment Factories', *New York Times*, 13 October 2014.

17

Reducing Worker-Paid Migration Costs

PHILIP MARTIN

I. INTRODUCTION: FOUR MIGRATION PHASES

MATCHING WORKERS WITH jobs involves costs that are usually assumed by employers seeking workers and individuals seeking jobs. Employers advertise for workers, request that current employees inform their friends and relatives about vacancies, and notify public and private employment services that they are seeking workers. Workers seeking jobs contact employers directly, ask their social networks about job openings, and turn to public and private agencies that help workers find jobs.

The major cost for both employers and workers in job search is opportunity cost, the cost of not having a job filled for employers and the cost of not working while engaged in job search for workers. Employer financial costs of advertising or paying recruiters, and worker costs of visiting employers and public and private agencies, are usually small relative to these opportunity costs.

There are four major phases in the temporary international labour migration process, and each can generate costs that are paid by workers, especially those going abroad for the first time. Employers set the migration process in motion by developing job descriptions, obtaining government approvals to fill jobs with migrant workers (usually after seeking and failing to find local workers), and contacting workers in another country directly or via a recruiter to fill the job. If the employer utilises a local recruiter, that recruiter may incur costs to contact workers in another country directly or via a recruiter in the workers' country of origin.

Migrant workers appear in the second phase, when they learn about foreign job opportunities, obtain contracts to fill foreign jobs, apply for passports and undergo health, criminal and other checks before receiving visas, and have their documents and contracts approved before travelling abroad to fill the foreign job. Some migrant workers receive weeks or months of language, skills or other training before departure. Even if the training is free, migrants may incur opportunity costs during the time that they study rather than work.

The third phase involves migrant workers employed abroad, typically for two or three years. As the end of her contract approaches, a migrant can seek to have her contract renewed and remain abroad or return to her country of origin to rest before going abroad again. If they return to stay, migrants can use savings from employment abroad to start a small business or to find a wage job. Some migrants are entitled to end-of-service bonuses, reimbursement of some expenses, and refunds of social security contributions upon completion of their contracts.

The fourth phase in the migration process involves re-integration at home or preparations to go abroad again. The re-integration process is not well understood, so there is little reliable data on the share of migrants who work abroad once and return to stay versus those who cycle between work abroad and rest at home. Farm employers report that workers admitted under seasonal programmes that permit eight or ten months of employment abroad often return year after year for one or two decades. However, there are many reports of so-called serial migrants who work two or three years abroad, return for a year or two, and then go abroad again.

Workers incur several types of costs in each of the four phases, including monetary costs and opportunity costs. For example, the opportunity costs of not working may be higher than the travel costs paid by rural workers who must go to capital cities to sign contracts and receive pre-departure training. Migrants may also incur costs if they receive substandard wages and benefits abroad or if they work in jobs that do not utilise their skills. In some migration corridors, maximum migration costs and their division between employers, workers, recruiters and government agencies are specified in bilateral agreements or programme rules. In others, only some or none of worker-paid migration costs are regulated.

The first cost for many workers involves learning about the foreign job. What costs (if any) do workers incur, and can a sensible division be made between monetary, opportunity and other worker-paid costs? Second, exactly how do migrants obtain contracts to fill foreign jobs? Many migrants live in rural areas, while most foreign job offers arrive in cities where licensed recruiters are located. What payments do migrants make to recruiters and sub-agents? Exactly how does recruitment occur? For example, do recruiters or sub-agents rely on networks and ask current migrants to refer friends and relatives, do they periodically visit villages and make job offers, hold job fairs in areas with workers, or recruit in some other way?

Third, once workers have contracts to fill foreign jobs, they must satisfy employer and government requirements before leaving their country and entering another. What are the monetary and other costs involved in obtaining passports and visas, undergoing health and criminal checks, having the contract checked, and perhaps receiving pre-departure training and orientation? Fourth, after all papers are in order, migrants depart for the foreign job. Who pays transport costs: employers or migrants, or are travel costs shared? Do migrants pay first and seek reimbursement from their employers after arrival or after they have completed a certain portion of the work contract, or do employers pay transport costs and deduct them from migrant wages?

ILO conventions recommend that employers pay all migration costs for the migrant workers they hire. Some migrant-receiving countries try to enforce this, as in the US H-2A and H-2B programmes, while others specify the shares of migration costs that employers and migrants must pay, as with Canada's Seasonal Agricultural Worker Programs with Caribbean countries and Mexico, and the Australia-New Zealand Pacific Island seasonal worker programmes. Some migrant-sending countries, including the Philippines, set maximum worker-paid migration costs at one month's foreign earnings or 4.2 per cent of foreign earnings for a two-year contract and 2.8 per cent for a three-year contract, but do not regulate opportunity costs incurred by migrants.

Anecdotal evidence and migration cost studies suggest that many migrants pay far more than 5 per cent of their expected foreign earnings in migration costs. Some, especially South Asians moving to Gulf Co-operation Country (GCC) destinations, pay up to a third of what they expect to earn abroad.[1] Costs are further increased if low-skilled migrants borrow money at high interest rates, making them vulnerable abroad because they are reluctant to return with no easy way to pay migration-related debts. A migration cost database is the first step to develop evidence-based recommendations to reduce migration costs to benefit both workers who can depart with less migration debt and employers whose workers may be more productive because they worry less about migration debts.

This chapter has four sections. The first outlines the recruitment process, explaining the steps that workers typically follow to learn about foreign jobs and get contracts to fill them. The second defines the monetary and opportunity costs that arise in the recruitment process and the third summarises worker-paid migration costs in Korea, Kuwait and Spain. The fourth section outlines options to reduce worker-paid recruitment costs.

[1] Philip Martin, Manolo Abella and Christiane Kuptsch, *Managing Labor Migration in the Twenty-First Century* (New Haven, CT, Yale University Press, 2006).

II. THE THREE R's OF THE LABOUR MARKET: RECRUITMENT, REMUNERATION AND RETENTION

Work is the exchange of effort for reward. Work involves employees giving control over some of their time to employers in exchange for monetary wages and work-related benefits. Unlike many other market transactions, such as a customer buying an item in a store, work is unusual because it requires a continuous relationship between employer and employee. Employers and workers interact continuously in the workplace, as supervisors assess employee performance and workers consider their satisfaction with the job. Employers may terminate the employment of unsatisfactory workers, and dissatisfied workers may quit their jobs.

All labour markets have three major functions, namely, recruitment, remuneration and retention. Recruitment matches workers with jobs, remuneration or the wage and benefit system motivates workers to perform, and retention systems assess workers to identify and retain the best workers.

National borders often complicate these three-R labour market processes. For example, if jobs are in one country and workers in another, language differences, variance in education and training systems, and national definitions of skills and occupations can make it hard to match workers and jobs efficiently. Intermediary recruiters add another layer between workers and jobs that can lead to miscommunication, and government checks in both sending and receiving countries introduce more gatekeepers and potential costs and complications for workers seeking foreign jobs.

The other two R-functions may also be complicated by national borders. ILO conventions and many national laws call for equal pay for equal work, so that all workers with the same job title receive the same wage regardless of their citizenship or work-permit status. However, some industries, occupations and areas may become dominated by migrant workers over time, and wages in these jobs may not rise as fast as overall wages. If governments do not enact policies to push up wages in the absence of market forces, wages can stagnate in migrant-dominated sectors, as occurred under the 1942–64 Mexico-US Bracero programme in commodities in which guest workers were over half of all workers.[2]

The final labour market function, retention, is also complicated by migration. Most studies suggest that more experienced workers have higher productivity, which is why employers develop systems to retain experienced workers. However, guest worker programmes that require workers to depart after two or three years mean the departure of experienced

[2] Philip Martin, *Importing Poverty? Immigration and the Changing Face of Rural America* (New Haven, CT, Yale University Press, 2009).

workers and their replacement with new employees who must be trained. Some governments allow employers to sponsor even low-skilled workers for permanent resident status, which tends to tie migrants to their sponsoring employer until they are free to seek jobs in the host-country labour market, but most require departure when contracts end.

Labour markets are information exchanges marked by asymmetric information.[3] Employers are most knowledgeable about the jobs they offer, and workers know more than employers about their abilities and competencies. Employers have developed a variety of strategies to *screen* applicants to find the best workers, including setting minimum education and experience requirements, asking current workers to refer qualified friends and relatives, and advertising or using recruiters to find qualified workers. Meanwhile, workers may *signal* their abilities to employers by earning credentials and certificates and gaining experience to demonstrate they will be good employees. Employer screening and worker signalling have been core concerns of labour economics for several decades.[4]

When workers and employers do not share a common language or have experience with the same education and training systems, they often rely on intermediaries to facilitate worker–job matches.[5] Recruiters who understand the requirements of the jobs offered by employers can find and screen the best workers to fill them. When workers are low-skilled, recruiters may act as the port of entry into a business. For example, some firms rely on temporary help firms to bring new workers into the workplace. If these workers prove to be satisfactory after a probationary period, they can make the transition to regular employees of the firm.[6]

National borders add more layers between workers and jobs and often complicate the recruitment process. Employers may turn to recruiters in their own countries to find workers in other countries. These local recruiters may recruit foreign workers directly or transmit employer job offers to recruiters in countries with workers, where local recruiters and their subagents recruit and screen workers. In other words, national borders offer opportunities for recruiter investment and specialisation that can make the process of filling vacant jobs more efficient *or* add layers that increase costs and allow rent seeking because low-skilled workers do not understand the process.

[3] George Akerlof, 'The Market for Lemons: Quality Uncertainty and the Market Mechanism' (1970) 84(3) *Quarterly Journal of Economics* 488.

[4] John Riley, 'Silver Signals: Twenty-Five Years of Screening and Signaling' (2001) 34 *Journal of Economic Literature* 432.

[5] David Autor (ed), *Studies of Labor Market Intermediation* (Chicago, University of Chicago Press, 2009).

[6] Some manufacturing firms have a branch of a temp firm such as Manpower on the premises. All newly hired employees are Manpower employees who usually wear distinctive clothing and begin in easy-to-learn jobs. If they prove to be proficient workers, they can become 'regular' employees of the factory where they work.

International borders should *increase* employer investment in recruitment to ensure good worker–job matches, but in practice employers often invest little to recruit low-skilled foreign workers and sometimes charge foreign workers for jobs. If employers can charge workers for jobs and pay them low wages because large wage gaps between origin and destination countries lead to more workers wanting to work abroad than there are jobs (excess supply), employers have incentives to hire too many workers. Overhiring may be in the narrow short-term economic interest of employers, but not in the interest of countries that want to raise productivity, wages and competitiveness over time. Overhiring to collect worker payments can also fuel corruption in other aspects of the labour migration system, including overcharging workers.

III. WORKER-PAID MIGRATION COSTS

This section covers three topics, namely, the difference between recruiters as long-term partners of the employers to whom they provide workers versus recruiters who act as short-term agents for employers; the division of the wage wedge that prompts migration between employers, workers and the other parties involved; and the relative success that co-operation has brought to reducing remittance costs versus the difficulties of reducing recruitment costs.

A. Partner versus Agent Recruiters

Recruiters who match workers and jobs are paid for their services by employers, workers or both. Employers generally pay some or all recruitment costs for highly skilled workers, including managers, health care professionals and engineers, because there are relatively few such workers and the consequences of poor worker–job matches can be costly to the employer. Some recruiters who match college-trained workers with foreign jobs become *partners* of employers, anticipating repeat business that makes it worthwhile to learn employer requirements and spread this investment in understanding the employer's needs over many placements.

Recruiters who place low-skilled workers in foreign jobs are more often *agents* than partners. Agents may bring parties together for a one-time transaction, which gives them less incentive to learn about employer and worker needs. In low-skilled occupations such as domestic service and construction labour, where there are often more workers seeking foreign jobs than there are jobs available, agent-recruiters can charge workers to move up the queue, using worker-paid fees as a way to ration foreign jobs. Even if low-skilled workers know they are paying higher-than-government-set fees for foreign jobs, they may not complain if they get what they want, a foreign job that offers a higher wage.

B. Dividing the Wage Gap

Wage gaps between countries motivate international labour migration. Most workers will not pay this entire wage gap to recruiters, since that would mean that migration away from family and friends would generate the same wages as working at home. However, many workers will pay more than the typical one month's foreign wages or 5 per cent of foreign earnings, which some governments specify as the maximum amount private recruiters should charge.

Dividing the wage wedge between employers, workers, recruiters and governments is a major unresolved issue in migration and development, a subject discussed at a UN High-Level Dialogue (HLD) in October 2013. The ILO recommendation to have employers pay all recruitment costs for migrant workers and the widespread perception that many workers pay too much in migration costs has spurred an effort to reduce worker-paid migration costs. The HLD's concluding statement laid out five priorities, beginning with the need to integrate migration into the global development agenda and making migration a catalyst for development by protecting the rights of migrants and lowering migration costs.[7]

C. Remittance versus Recruitment Costs

International co-operation has reduced remittance costs and called attention to the return and re-integration of migrant workers and the potential of citizens who remain abroad, the diaspora, to send home remittances and ideas that speed development at home. After the 9/11 terrorist acts, governments co-operated to make it easier to send small sums over borders via regulated financial institutions.

Changing policies plus technology have reduced the cost of sending $200 from one country to another from 15 per cent or $30 to less than 10 per cent or $20 over the past decade. The World Bank's 5x5 programme aimed to

[7] The second priority is to improve lives and work for migrants by lowering remittance costs and improving the recognition and transfer of skills over borders. Third is to develop plans to help migrants in crisis and fourth is more data on migrants moving within the various migration corridors, including migrant characteristics and migration and remittance costs. The fifth HLD priority is to develop a strategy to achieve the first four priorities, and to have the strategy endorsed by governments at global forums.

reduce remittance costs by another five percentage points over five years, that is, to lower average remittance costs to 5 per cent by 2014. Average remittance costs were reported to be 7.7 per cent of the amount transferred early in 2015.[8]

With technology and government co-operation continuing to reduce remittance costs, recruitment is the new frontier to lower migration costs and increase the development payoff of labour migration. Low recruitment costs and good worker–job matches result in satisfied workers and employers and good labour migration outcomes for governments in both migrant sending and receiving countries. If migration costs are low, migrant workers capture more of the wage wedge that encourages migration and employers have highly motivated workers.[9] Low worker-migration costs can help governments to manage migration by reducing the need for them to deal with dissatisfied, terminated, runaway and overstaying workers.

High migration costs can have the opposite effects. High costs can prompt migrant workers to seek jobs for which they lack necessary skills in a quest for higher wages to repay migration debts, to take second jobs while abroad to repay migration debts but that make them irregular, or to overstay their visas to achieve savings targets. Employers may be dissatisfied with the performance of workers who are worried about repaying recruitment debts as well as workers sent by recruiters more interested in collecting recruitment fees than in making optimal worker–job matches.

Given the benefits of good rather than poor worker–job matches, why do high migration costs and poor worker–job matches persist? There are many reasons, including perverse incentives. Remittance transactions are frequent, so money-transfer firms have an incentive to offer low-cost services to win repeat business. Recruitment occurs less frequently, and employers may not care who is recruited if their major business is selling job offers that result in the issuance of work visas. Similarly, recruiters may not care whom they send abroad if their major source of revenue is charging workers before departure.

Making money by being merchants of labour rather than sending workers abroad to produce useful goods and services creates perverse incentives for many workers. Consider the example of low-skilled Bangladeshis recruited to be standby workers at airports in GCC countries for $200 a month. These young workers, who will earn $2,400 a year or $7,200 over three

[8] World Bank, 'Remittance Prices Worldwide' (2015), https://remittanceprices.worldbank.org/en.

[9] Wage differences can act as efficiency wages, as when employers pay more than the market wage to workers who are hard to monitor in order to encourage them to work without close supervision. Higher-than-market efficiency wages motivate workers because they know that loss of their job would result in lower wages.

years, often incur $2,000 or more in pre-departure migration costs, perhaps financed by selling or mortgaging the family's farmland. Once abroad, the workers may sit around waiting to be called to work, prompting some to seek second jobs that make them irregular. In this case, the fact that wages are low and migration costs high gives migrants incentives to engage in behaviour that can make them worse off, such as when they are detected working illegally and deported.

IV. KOREA, KUWAIT AND SPAIN

There were three major findings from interviews with legal, low-skilled and recently arrived migrant workers interviewed in Korea, Kuwait and Spain in 2014:

— Migration costs were generally less than one month's foreign earnings except in Kuwait, where migrants paid an average four months' Kuwaiti wages in migration costs.
— There is significant variation in worker-paid migration costs within and across bilateral migration corridors. For example, Bangladeshis paid more than Indians to migrate to Kuwait.
— There was surprisingly large variation in the cost of many standard items such as passports, medical tests and other prepare-to-depart services whose cost should be the same for all workers.

Worker-paid migration costs averaged $1,525 in Korea, or 1 to 1.5 months of typical foreign worker earnings. Most of the workers had 36-month contracts, so they could expect to earn $36,000 at $1,000 a month or $54,000 at $1,500 a month.[10] Since migrant worker contracts can be extended for an additional 22 months at the request of employers and migrants, migration costs of $1,525 can be less than 3 per cent of expected earnings in Korea if migrants stay in Korea for the almost five years they are allowed to stay.

Worker-paid migration costs in Kuwait averaged $1,900, and average monthly earnings were $465, so migration costs averaged four months' earnings. With two-year contracts, migrant workers earn an average of $11,160 in Kuwait and worker-paid migration costs are a sixth of earnings. For Egyptians, many of whom were employed at home at an average wage

[10] An unpublished 2014 ILO survey found that most E-9 or Employment Permit System (EPS) workers were men with nine years of schooling and under the age of 30. Most EPS migrants earned between one million ($965) and 1.7 million ($1,600) won a month. The Korean minimum wage is 5,210 won ($5) an hour in 2014, but most migrants earn more than the minimum wage because they work overtime hours.

of $165 a month, earning over $600 a month in Kuwait was four times more than at home.

Worker-paid migration costs to fill seasonal farm jobs in Spain averaged $530 or half a month's average earnings of $1,000. Most seasonal farm workers were employed in Spain from four to nine months, making worker-paid migration costs 6 to 12 per cent of expected earnings. Migration costs are relatively low despite only seasonal earnings because all of the workers interviewed had previous Spanish work experience and Spanish regulations require employers to pay half of worker transportation costs. When workers arrived from afar (Ecuador), employers usually paid the full cost of inbound transportation and deducted transport costs from worker earnings at the rate of E90 ($100) a month.

A. Migrants in Korea

Migrants vary in several ways that affect worker-paid costs. For example, almost 90 per cent of the workers interviewed in Korea had been in Korea less than three months. Almost 80 per cent were employed in manufacturing, 86 per cent were men and 61 per cent were in Korea for the first time, but many had been employed in foreign jobs in other countries and saw working in Korea as a step up from GCC and other Asian destinations.

Over 95 per cent of the migrants interviewed were in their 20s and 30s, 55 per cent were married, and 85 per cent had completed secondary school or more. They supported on average three dependents at home. Average earnings of migrants at home were $225 a month, versus $765 in Korea, for a wage gap of 3.4. (Many migrants had just arrived in Korea and may not have yet been offered the overtime work that usually pushes migrant earnings to over $1,000 a month.) Median home-country earnings were $190 and median Korean earnings were $1,000, or 5.3 times more.

Average worker-paid costs were $1,525, but median costs were $1,300, meaning that average costs were increased by the relatively few workers who had very high recruitment and other costs. The average cost of the seven migration-related expenses reported by 60 per cent or more of the sample was $830, including an average of $365 for international transportation and $250 to learn Korean. The other four expenses, for passports, medical exams, security checks, welfare funds and visas, cost $15 to $70 each.

The migrants interviewed in Korea were from Thailand, Indonesia and Vietnam. Thais reported migration costs of $1,550, but two-thirds reported paying recruitment fees that averaged $980. Half of the Thais borrowed money to work in Korea. These Thai borrowers had repaid 90 per cent of what they borrowed when interviewed, but still owed significantly more, suggesting high interest rates. Median earnings in Korea were 3.3 times median earnings in Thailand, suggesting a smaller wage gain for Thais than for Indonesians and Vietnamese.

Indonesians had average total migration costs similar to Thais, about $1,500, but reported slightly lower costs for Korean language, medical, security and similar fees. Over half of the Indonesians reported internal migration costs that averaged $420, more than the average of $308 for international travel to Korea. Indonesians earned an average of $174 a month at home. Given their median earnings of $1,050 a month in Korea, they earned seven times more in Korea.

Vietnamese workers reported the lowest migration costs of $1,200, but with a wide variation around this average. The median and mode costs for Vietnamese workers were $630, but the average was $1,200, indicating very high costs for some workers. Most of their migration-related costs were similar to those of Thais and Indonesians, although the Vietnamese reported paying more to learn Korean and more for international travel. Vietnamese earned a median $190 at home and $1,120 or six times more in Korea.

These data suggest that the Employment Permit System (EPS), introduced in 2003 and, since 2007, the only way for most Korean SMEs to hire non-ethnic Koreans, functions reasonably well for most migrants, allowing them to repay their migration costs with less than two months of Korean earnings. Most of the high costs were incurred by relatively few workers for recruitment fees, other payments and job searches. Reducing very high costs for the relatively few workers who incur them would reduce overall worker-paid migration costs for migrants.

The EPS is a government-to-government agreement. Admissions under the EPS begin with an annual quota set by the Korean government and allocated by sector. The 2015 quota of 42,400 includes 32,890 EPS slots for new or first-time migrants and 9,510 for migrants who were previously employed in Korea. Over 85 per cent of the 2015 visas are for workers employed by small Korean manufacturing firms, with the remainder for farmers, fishers and construction firms.

Foreigners who want to work in Korea must pass a Korean language test to be placed on the list from which Korean employers select migrant workers, often after Skype interviews. Selected migrants enter Korea with three-year E-9 visas that can be renewed for another 22 months. After four years and 10 months, E-9 foreigners must leave Korea for at least three months, but those who depart Korea as required can return to their previous Korean workplace without retaking the Korean language test. There are proposals to offer training and support at home to departing E-9 foreign workers so that they are more likely to go home.

Public agencies in 15 Asian countries maintain lists of workers who have passed the Korean language test and are eligible to be selected to work in Korea. These agencies reported that workers who qualified and were selected to work in Korea paid an average of $925 to learn Korean and buy tickets to travel to Korea, much less than estimates of $3,500 to $5,000 in migration costs paid by trainees in the past to go to Korea.[11]

B. Migrants in Kuwait

Over 100 migrant workers from India (30 workers, including five women), Bangladesh (20 workers), Sri Lanka (20 workers, including 15 women), and Egypt (30 workers) were interviewed in March 2014 in Kuwait. Most (excluding Bangladeshis) arrived in Kuwait within the past five years, and half had not completed secondary school.

These migrants reported an average of $1,900 in migration costs and a median of $1,700, but there was a large variance around the mean and mode. Average monthly earnings in Kuwait were $465 and median earnings were $430, suggesting that migrant workers paid an average four months' Kuwaiti wages in migration costs.

There was more variance in migration costs in Kuwait than in Korea and Spain. By nationality, Bangladeshis paid an average of $3,100 in migration costs, Egyptians $2,900, Indians $1,250 and Sri Lankans $320; most of the Sri Lankans were female domestic workers. Bangladeshis reported that visa costs averaged $2,300 and airfares $500, while Egyptians reported paying an average of $2,500 for visas and $200 for airfares. Indians paid an average of $345 for visas and Sri Lankans $85, so high visa costs primarily separate Bangladeshis and Egyptians from Indians and Sri Lankans.

Most migrants borrowed money to work in Kuwait. The share of migration costs that was borrowed ranged from just over 50 per cent for Sri Lankans to over 85 per cent for Egyptians. Egyptians borrowed from friends and relatives, including those who were or had been migrants in Kuwait previously, while Bangladeshis and Indians who borrowed took loans from pawn shops and moneylenders, respectively. The amount borrowed reflected each nationality's migration costs. Egyptians borrowed an average of $3,150, while Sri Lankans borrowed an average of $540.

In Kuwait, Egyptians earned an average of over $600 a month or almost four times their earnings of $165 a month at home. Sri Lankans, most of whom were domestic workers, earned an average of $340 a month in Kuwait, but most were not employed at home. Indians earned an average of $500 a month, which was about 2.5 times their average earnings of $190 a month at home. Migrant workers must have a sponsor (*kafeel*), and at least a fifth of those interviewed were not working for their *kafeel*.

[11] Young-bum Park, 'Temporary Low-skilled Migrant Worker Program in Korea: Employment Permit Scheme' (2013) 189 *Arbor*, http://arbor.revistas.csic.es/index.php/arbor.

Kuwait is an example of a high-cost destination for low-skilled migrant workers. Migration costs average four months' Kuwaiti earnings, but there are distinct differences by nationality, with Bangladeshis and Egyptians paying far more than Indians and Sri Lankans. There is also a wide variance in migration costs even within binational corridors, with some workers paying three or more times more than others from the same country.

The major reasons for these high average costs and the high variance in costs is a migration system that is fairly opaque to workers. With no easy way to enter GCC countries other than with work permits that tie them to a sponsor, migrants pay recruiters who control access to sponsors. Sponsors may charge for visas, and then pass their right to hire migrant workers on to local recruiters who mark up the price, and then on to foreign recruiters who mark up the price again. The GCC system thus illustrates how layers of intermediaries can increase worker-paid costs. It is notable that Sri Lankan domestic workers had the lowest migration costs.

C. Migrants in Spain

Some 171 migrant workers employed in Spanish agriculture were interviewed in January–February 2014, including 42 from Bulgaria, 33 from Ecuador, 44 from Morocco, 19 from Poland and 30 from Romania. Most had low migration costs, primarily because many had zero costs for items that are common in other migration corridors, from visas to medical exams. All had previous Spanish work experience, and workers reported that regulations requiring employers to pay at least half of worker transportation costs were enforced. Worker-paid migration costs were generally less than half of a migrant's monthly earnings of $1,000 a month.[12]

Since the migrant farm workers interviewed had worked in Spain previously, and intra-EU migrants do not need visas or medical checks, fewer than half of the migrants reported any costs for passports and even fewer reported costs for visas and medical checks. Travel costs were also low, an average of less than $30 for internal travel costs in the home country and $300 for international travel costs, but with marked differences: $100 for Moroccans, $350 for East Europeans and $1,100 for Ecuadorians who can stay nine months in Spain.[13]

[12] Earnings data were not collected from migrants in Spain. If workers earned the minimum wage of €39.5 or $54 for a 6.5 hour day, they earn $270 for a 5-day week or $324 for a six-day week and $1,080 to $1,300 a month.

[13] Spanish employers must pay half of the transportation costs of the inbound workers they recruit. Most advance the entire cost of inbound transportation and then deduct the worker's share from earnings over the duration of their contract, typically at the rate of €90 a month. With employers advancing transportation costs, there is less need for workers to borrow money to travel to Spain.

Focusing on worker-paid costs incurred by at least 40 migrants finds that transportation costs were two-thirds of average costs of $530, with a wide variance reflecting the cost of getting to Spain. Three fourths of the migrants interviewed in Spain did not take out loans to cover migration costs. The quarter that took out loans reported relatively small loans averaging $350 but debts of over $500, suggesting high interest rates.

Most of the migrants employed to fill seasonal jobs in Spanish agriculture are from rural areas in Morocco, Eastern Europe and Ecuador. Migrating to Spain to do farm work is, for some, an alternative to rural–urban migration within their countries of origin. Most of the migrants had less than secondary-school education,[14] and the Moroccan women often had less than nine years' schooling, suggesting that migrating to Spain to do farm work was one way to remain within agriculture while working in a higher-wage country. Many of the Moroccans wanted to settle in Spain, while most of the Eastern Europeans wanted to return to their countries of origin.

The migrants, who harvested fruits and vegetables in Spain, were mostly unemployed or self-employed in agriculture at home, making it hard to calculate the average wage wedge. Less than a seventh of all migrants had wage-paying jobs before migrating to Spain. Of the 40 per cent who reported *any* income before migrating to Spain, from wage work or self-employment, mean and mode monthly earnings at home were $160 a month, suggesting that work in Spain increased earnings by six times.

V. CONCLUSIONS

Migration costs for low-skilled workers who cross national borders can be high, which lowers remittances and the positive impacts of migration on development, while leaving migrant workers more vulnerable abroad. There are four major phases in the migration process that can lead to high worker-paid costs, including destination country employers obtaining permission to hire migrant workers, workers learning about foreign jobs, obtaining contracts from foreign employers, acquiring passports and other documents, and undergoing pre-departure training and orientation. The third phase involves employment abroad, where migrants may not receive all of the wages and benefits promised or do different work than was specified in their contracts, and the fourth phase of return and reintegration or

[14] The East Europeans were best educated, but most did not complete secondary school. Many of the Moroccans had less than five years' schooling, and the Ecuadorians averaged less than seven years' schooling.

preparing to go abroad again may involve workers not receiving appropriate end-of-service and other benefits before departure.

Migrant workers incur monetary costs when they make payments to recruiters and others for foreign jobs, pay for documents and checks, and pay for training. They may also incur opportunity costs as they travel to recruiters, government agencies and training centres, and once abroad they may pay for recruitment indirectly in the form of lower wages and benefits. Learning more about worker-paid migration costs, and especially how they vary by migration corridor and worker level of skill, could suggest policies to reduce such costs and increase the benefits of migration for the development of migrant-sending countries as well as worker protections.

Interviews with workers in Korea, Kuwait and Spain found that most earned at least five times more abroad than they were earning at home. Most paid less than a month's foreign earnings in migration costs, which made migration costs a lower share of earnings in high-wage Korea, where migrants can stay almost five years, than in lower-wage Spain, where migrants were employed less than a year in agriculture. Migrants in Kuwait paid the highest migration costs and had the lowest average earnings, paying an average of four months' Kuwaiti earnings in migration costs. Bangladeshis and Egyptians paid far more than Indians and Sri Lankans.

Worker-paid migration costs are the new frontier in making the international labour migration system more efficient and protective of migrant workers. The interviews with legal and low-skilled migrants in Korea, Kuwait and Spain lead to three major lessons. First, policy matters, as highlighted by the low migration costs to migrate to Spain because of EU free-movement rules covering Eastern Europeans and Spanish policies that make employers pay at least half of worker transportation costs. Reducing transportation costs, which are often the largest single expense of migrant workers, lowers costs and the need to borrow money to work abroad. The highest average costs in Kuwait are explained largely by worker-paid visa costs.

Second, most migrants earned four to six times more abroad than they did at home. Migrants moving to Spain had the largest average earnings gap of over six to one, largely because so many had very little education and were unemployed or self-employed at home. Competition to migrate to Korea for up to five years meant that migrants who were selected had more education and higher home-country earnings, making the average earnings gap about four to one. Migrants to Kuwait earned three to four times more than they would at home for those with earnings before departure.

Third, migrants report paying very different fees for standard items such as passports and medical checks. It is not clear why costs for such standard items varied so widely, but the variance likely reflects the fact that many migrants rely on others to help them to navigate the process of going abroad. Streamlining the pre-departure process so that migrants can navigate it with less assistance, and ensuring that government and other agencies that provide services to migrants are operated honestly and efficiently, could help to reduce migration costs.

Migration is a journey of hope and fear, hope for economic mobility with higher foreign wages and fear of complex and costly migration processes at home and unknown jobs abroad. Making the migration process more transparent and efficient can reap dividends for employers, migrants, and both sending and receiving societies.

18

Temporary Labour Migration and Workplace Rights in Australia

Is Effective Enforcement Possible?

ROSEMARY OWENS

I. INTRODUCTION

AUSTRALIA'S HISTORIC RESISTANCE to temporary labour migration has dissipated in the wake of its increasing integration into the global economy and its commitments and obligations under international trade agreements.[1] Nonetheless critics of the migration regulations establishing Australia's main skilled temporary labour migration programme suggest, at least implicitly, that there is an ongoing need for more public debate about its desirability and further reform.[2] Likewise, the lack of any specific migration regulation governing much of Australia's low-skilled temporary labour migration has also been identified as problematic.[3]

At the heart of these discussions is concern about the exploitation of temporary migrant workers and the potential for that to undermine labour standards for all workers. In recent times, it has become more commonplace to argue that the only really successful way of eradicating the exploitation of migrant workers is to tackle the structure of the temporary migration labour market, because that is the most significant cause of their precariousness and consequent vulnerability to exploitation. The dependence on a sponsoring employer and restricted rights to residence both feature strongly as recognised

[1] See Mary Crock, Sean Howe and Ron McCallum, 'Conflicted Priorities? Enforcing Fairness for Temporary Migrant Workers in Australia' in Cathryn Costello and Mark Freedland (eds), *Migrants at Work: Immigration and Vulnerability in Labour Law* (Oxford, Oxford University Press, 2014) 430.

[2] See, eg Joanna Howe, 'The Migration Legislation Amendment (Worker Protection) Act 2008: Long Overdue Reform, But Have Migrant Workers Been Sold Short?' (2010) 23 *Australian Journal of Labour Law* 251.

[3] See Joanna Howe and Alexander Reilly, 'Meeting Australia's Labour Market Needs: The Case for a New Low-Skill Work Visa' (2015) 43 *Federal Law Review* 259.

elements of this precariousness.[4] Thus, it is the migration laws that are often the main focus of scholarly attention. Some scholars have argued for urgent radical reform. Others have said that more specific regulation of low-skilled temporary labour migration through conditions attached to the visas of these migrants (both loosening and tightening constraints on employers and labour market restrictions on visa holders) will produce more targeted, and therefore superior, outcomes, rather than a simple reliance on ordinary workplace regulation.[5] Laurie Berg recognises the intersection of migration and labour law as an important element in the regulatory production of precariousness, and analyses the way in which visa conditions and penalty regimes operate to produce precariousness.[6] In the work of Joo-Cheong Tham, the focus shifts more to regulation of the workplace and he argues that the intersection of the temporary labour migrant's precarious status and poorly regulated sectors of the labour market is a structural problem.[7]

While, at various times in the recent past, the possibilities for exempting some temporary migrant workers from the application of Australia's workplace laws have been considered, in fact laws implementing standards in Australian workplaces are equally applicable to all migrant and local workers. Indeed, as Mary Crock et al suggest, there can be little doubt that a necessary prerequisite of ongoing community acceptance of temporary labour migration is the confidence that all workers will be treated in such a way that Australia's labour standards are not undermined by exploitative behaviour:

> Australians are increasingly tolerant of temporary workers. Significant cases of underpayment continue to occur, and while the system is now arguably structurally fairer, this tolerance is likely to be dependent on the consistent ability of Australian agencies to ensure these workers' rights can be appropriately enforced and that Australian terms and conditions are not undercut.[8]

Crock et al express a guarded optimism about the capacity of Australia's workplace regulatory system to maintain standards and eliminate exploitation. Tham too has concluded that

> there is a structural risk of non-compliance with labour laws in relation to temporary migrant work with two interacting sources, precarious migrant status

[4] See, eg Visa Subclass 457 Integrity Review, *Final Report* (Canberra, Commonwealth of Australia, 2008) (*Deegan Review*) 69.

[5] See, eg Alexander Reilly, 'Low-Cost Labour or Cultural Exchange? Reforming the Working Holiday Visa Programme' (2015) 26 *Economic and Labour Relations Review* 474; Howe and Reilly, 'Meeting Australia's Labour Market Needs' (n 3).

[6] See Laurie Berg, *Migrant Rights at Work: Law's Precariousness at the Intersection of Migration and Labour* (London, Routledge, 2015).

[7] Joo-Cheong Tham, submission to the Senate Education and Employment References Committee Inquiry into 'The Impact of Australia's temporary work visa program on the Australian labour market and on temporary work visa holders', Submission No 3, 29 April 2015.

[8] Crock, Howe and McCallum, 'Conflicted Priorities?' (n 1) 446.

> and poorly regulated industries. The risk does not necessarily translate into the reality of non-compliance—it can be mitigated through effective and robust laws.[9]

The robustness of any system of workplace regulation depends not only on its purposes and capacity for responsiveness to the structure of the labour market, including recognition of its role in constructing the labour market, but also on the effectiveness of its system of enforcement. Effective enforcement remains a vital element in ensuring all workers, including temporary migrant workers, are protected from exploitation and, consequently, the integrity of labour standards is upheld.

The Australian system of workplace laws is now focused more on individual rights than it was in the pre-global era. In many other developed economies, workplace rights have also become more individualised and collective labour rights less prevalent. In almost all jurisdictions this development has meant that the main thrust of enforcement has come to depend on individuals asserting their rights. This presents the greatest risk for the most vulnerable workers. It also places greater strain on the resources of enforcement agencies.[10] In countries such as Britain it has been said that the enforcement approach

> is flawed in that too much reliance is placed on individuals having to assert and pursue their statutory rights, which generally require only passive compliance from employers, and too little weight is placed on State agency inspection, monitoring and enforcement, and on other levels of enforcement which would require or encourage proactive employer action to deliver fairer workplaces by addressing structural, systemic and organisational issues, beyond individual cases of rights infringement.[11]

The indications are that in the United Kingdom the impact of such a system on migrant workers has been particularly problematic.[12]

The effectiveness of Australia's enforcement agency responsible for workplace matters, the Fair Work Ombudsman (FWO), was under the spotlight in 2015 following media revelations of the pervasiveness of gross exploitation of 'low-skilled' temporary migrant workers in Australia.[13]

[9] Tham, submission to the Senate Education and Employment References Committee 22.

[10] See, eg Linda Dickens, 'Introduction—Making Employment Rights Effective: Issues of Enforcement and Compliance' in Linda Dickens (ed), *Making Employment Rights Effective: Issues of Enforcement and Compliance* (Oxford, Hart Publishing, 2012).

[11] Linda Dickens, 'Fairer Workplaces: Making Employment Rights Effective' in Dickens (ed), *Making Employment Rights Effective* 207.

[12] See, eg Catherine Barnard, 'Enforcement of Employment Rights by Migrant Workers in the UK: The Case of EU-8 Nationals' in Costello and Freedland (eds), *Migrants at Work*. While admitting the need for more empirical research, Barnard shows that available material seems to demonstrate that in the UK only about 2 appeals out of 2,000 per year involve migrant workers.

[13] Two investigative television programmes were particularly powerful: 'Slaving Away: The Dirty Secrets behind Australia's Fresh Food', *Four Corners*, Australian Broadcasting

There was evidence that migrants in the horticulture and food processing industries are frequently paid wages well below the minimum required by law, work long hours with no overtime payments, are subjected to sexual and other forms of harassment, and are often housed in substandard conditions.[14] These workers were mostly young people on working holiday visas (visa 417, which enables its holder to extend their stay for 12 months if they have worked for three months in a regional area), who had been recruited through labour hire agencies. They perform work for some of the major suppliers to some of the biggest national and/or international businesses, retailers and restaurants/cafes. When confronted with the evidence of exploitation, the businesses frequently resorted to platitudes defending the values of their organisation and restating their commitment to ethical behaviour by all in the supply line, although some quickly announced they had terminated their contracts with the labour supply companies identified as engaging in exploitative practices.[15] In the retail sector there was evidence that, even though there had been previous interventions by the FWO,[16] there was ongoing collusion between some franchisee supermarket operators who were engaging in the systematic exploitation of young international students through underpayment of wages and long hours. The vulnerability of these students and their reluctance to report infringements of their workplace rights were increased by being effectively forced to breach the restrictions on working hours in their visas.

This chapter examines the Australian system of enforcement of workplace rights particularly as it applies to temporary migrant workers. The first section sets out briefly the role and operation of the main compliance

Commission, 4 May 2015; '7-Eleven: The Price of Convenience', *Four Corners*, Australian Broadcasting Commission and Fairfax Media, 31 August 2015. Amongst other things, the issues raised in these programmes were drawn to the attention of the Inquiry into the Impact of Australia's Temporary Work Visa Programs on the Australian Labour Market and on the Temporary Work Visa Holders by the Senate Standing Committee on Education and Employment of the Australian Parliament established in March 2015. See http://www.aph.gov.au/Parliamentary_Business/Committees/Senate/Education_and_Employment/temporary_work_visa. A Ministerial Working Group to help protect vulnerable foreign workers was also established, see Senator the Hon Michaelia Cash, 'Ministerial Working Group to Help Protect Vulnerable Foreign Workers', media release, 15 October 2015.

[14] On exploitation of migrant workers in agriculture elsewhere, see, eg Jennifer Gordon, 'Roles for Workers and Unions in Regulating Labour Recruitment in Mexico', ch 15 in this volume; Charles Wolfson, Petra Herzfeld Olsson and Christopher Thörnqvist, 'Forced Labour and Migrant Berry Pickers in Sweden' (2012) 28 *International Journal of Comparative Labour Law and Industrial Relations* 147.

[15] Some commitments were revealed to be hollow due to the practice of 'phoenixing': see Mark DeBono, 'Crackdown Continues on Exploitation of Migrant Workers on Victorian Farms', *ABC News Just In*, 22 May 2015.

[16] See, eg *Fair Work Ombudsman v Bosen Pty Ltd* [2011] VMC 81; *Fair Work Ombudsman v Haider Pty Ltd* [2015] FCCA 2113.

and enforcement agency, the FWO. Previous research by John Howe, Tess Hardy and Sean Cooney has evaluated the operations of the FWO up until the end of 2012.[17] The second section of this chapter goes on to examine the operations of the FWO from mid-2012 to mid-2015, by focusing on its activities, and especially enforceable undertakings (EUs), that concern temporary labour migrants in order to consider the FWO's effectiveness in eradicating exploitation. The conclusion of the chapter is that, considering the resources available to it, the FWO has been remarkably effective (although by no means perfect) in tackling the problems of exploitation of temporary labour migrants. However, its performance in this area has been effected largely through an approach that can be labelled 'responsive' regulation, and the indications are that its systemic impacts remain much more limited. While a 'strategic' approach to regulation has been a part of the FWO's approach to the implementation of its duties, more is required in this arena before the agency could be considered to be truly effective.

II. THE FAIR WORK OMBUDSMAN

A. The Role of the FWO Generally and in Relation to Migrants

The FWO is established under the Fair Work Act 2009 (Cth), and is the successor to the investigative agencies and inspectorate which was revamped in 2006 when the WorkChoices legislation transformed Australia's workplace regulatory system including by introducing a new set of national statutory minimum standards and individual protections.[18] Its role is to promote, monitor, investigate and enforce compliance with the Fair Work legislation and other regulatory instruments made under it.[19] The FWO can utilise a broad range of enforcement strategies. They include own-initiative investigations and conducting audits and campaigns. As well as litigation and court proceedings, the FWO can issue compliance notices and, since 2009, it has had the power to enter into enforceable undertakings.[20]

In a general assessment of the activities of the FWO (and its predecessor agencies) between 2006 and 2012, John Howe, Tess Hardy and Sean Cooney

[17] See Tess Hardy and John Howe, 'Too Soft or Too Severe? Enforceable Undertakings and the Regulatory Dilemma Facing the Fair Work Ombudsman' (2013) 41 *Federal Law Review* 1.

[18] See Rosemary Owens, Joellen Riley and Jill Murray, *The Law of Work*, 2nd edn (Melbourne, Oxford University Press, 2011) ch 3; Tess Hardy, 'A Changing of the Guard: Enforcement of Workplace Relations Laws Since Work Choices and Beyond' in Anthony Forsyth and Andrew Stewart (eds), *Fair Work: The New Workplace Laws and the Work Choices Legacy* (Sydney, Federation Press, 2009).

[19] Fair Work Act 2009 s 682(1)(d).

[20] Fair Work Act 2009 s 715.

concluded that achieving compliance with minimum employment standards remains 'a major and ongoing challenge in Australia'.[21] Noting that the enforcement problems in Australia are exacerbated by, amongst other things, the structure of modern labour markets and increased labour migration, Howe et al observed that the FWO's approach to enforcement embodies principles of both 'responsive regulation'[22] and 'strategic enforcement'.[23] While the size of the FWO was increased in line with its enhanced role in 2006, the increase in resources, which initially accompanied those changes, declined after 2010 due to budgetary restrictions. Howe et al found that the response of the FWO was to become 'more strategic and sophisticated in its enforcement activities'.[24] In particular, and in light of the principles of 'responsive' and 'strategic' regulation, the FWO transformed itself from an 'aggressive enforcer' into an agency which had a greater focus as an 'educator': it implemented more targeted campaigns, as well as restructuring itself internally to maximise the impact of its inspectorate through specialisation, and focused on dispute resolution and compliance rather than investigation and enforcement. Where litigation was adopted, it was usually in relation to small and medium sized operators in sectors such as restaurants, and proved to be highly successful, especially as it was backed by a significant increase in penalties for breaches of the legislation.[25] Howe and Hardy also concluded that the FWO had made 'limited but promising use' of its newer powers to use enforceable undertakings but that more work was required to evaluate their effectiveness.[26]

This chapter takes up that invitation and examines the role of the FWO specifically in relation to temporary migrant workers, focusing in particular on low-skilled workers and enforceable undertakings in the period 2012–2015. As a preliminary point, it can be noted that, since 2012, the role of the FWO has also been extended to monitor employer obligations in relation to skilled (457 visa) temporary migrant workers under the Migration Amendment (Temporary Sponsored Visas) Act 2013 (Cth), which conferred on the FWO the powers exercised by inspectors under the

[21] John Howe, Tessa Hardy and Sean Cooney, *The Transformation of Enforcement of Minimum Employment Standards in Australia: A Review of the FWO's Activities from 2006–2012* (Melbourne, Centre for Employment and Labour Relations Law, University of Melbourne, 2014) 10.

[22] Ian Ayres and John Braithwaite, *Responsive Regulation: Transcending the Deregulation Debate* (Oxford, Oxford University Press, 1992).

[23] David Weil, *Improving Through Strategic Enforcement Workplace Conditions: A Report to the Wage and Hour Division* (Washington, DC, US Department of Labour, 2010). See also David Weil, 'Enforcing Labor Standards in Fissured Workplaces: The US Experience' (2011) 22(2) *Economic and Labor Relations Review* 33.

[24] Howe et al, *The Transformation of Enforcement* (n 21) 9.

[25] Tess Hardy, John Howe and Sean Cooney, 'Less Energetic but More Enlightened? Exploring the Fair Work Ombudsman's Use of Litigation in Regulatory Enforcement' (2013) 35 *Sydney Law Review* 565.

[26] Hardy and Howe, 'Too Soft or Too Severe?' (n 17).

Migration Act 1958 (Cth).[27] Any breaches discovered by the FWO must be reported to the Department of Immigration. The vesting of these powers in the FWO immediately raises some concerns in terms of the enforcement of labour standards. A basic principle of international law and its standards on labour inspection is that labour inspection and effective enforcement must not be compromised by the fact that there is anything irregular about the status of the migrant worker: 'the primary duty of labour inspectors is to protect workers and not to enforce immigration law'.[28] Furthermore, reposing migration inspectorate roles on labour inspectors may amount to a diminution in resources available to the primary purpose of enforcing labour standards.[29]

B. The FWO and the Problem of Compliance with Labour Standards for Temporary Migrant Workers

There is no doubt that the Australian media has increasingly focused the spotlight on enforcement and the role of the FWO in relation to temporary migrant labour. In a public statement in response to the allegations in the Four Corners programme 'Slaving Away: The Dirty Secrets behind Australia's Fresh Food', the agency pointed out that many of the matters raised by the media were not unknown to it and it went on to provide a summary of the extensive range of recent activities that it had instigated in pursuit of issues relating to temporary migrant workers.[30]

Recognising the particularly vulnerable position of migrant workers, and in order to deal with the challenge to enforcement posed by this, the FWO established an Overseas Workers Team (OWT) in mid-2012. The OWT is not only focused on matters of enforcement as it relates to the rights of individual migrant workers, but also is involved centrally in all aspects of the agency's compliance work as it relates to migrant workers, including undertaking inquiries and audits, and conducting campaigns. In mid-2013,

[27] For comment see John Howe, Tess Hardy and Sean Cooney, 'Mandate, Discretion and Professionalism at an Employment Standards Enforcement Agency: An Antipodean Experience' (2013) 35 *Law and Society* 1.

[28] See ILO, *Labour Inspection*, Report of the Committee of Experts on the Application of Conventions and Recommendations, General Survey of the Reports Concerning the Labour Inspection Convention 1947 (No 81), and the Protocol of 1995 to the Labour Inspection Convention, 1947, and the Labour Inspection Recommendation, 1947 (No 81), the Labour Inspection (Mining and Transport) Recommendation, 1947 (No 82), The Labour Inspection (Agriculture) Convention, 1969 (No 129), and the Labour Inspection (Agriculture) Recommendation, 1969 (No 133), International Labour Conference, 95th session, 2006, [77]–[78].

[29] Ibid.

[30] See FWO, 'Statement in Response to 4-Corners Report', 7 May 2015, http://www.fairwork.gov.au/about-us/news-and-media-releases/2015-media-releases/may-2015/20150507-fwo-statement-in-response-to-4-corners.

the FWO initiated a three-year 'Harvest Trail' programme, following the FWO's own observations of the low levels of compliance in the horticultural sector.[31] The 'Harvest Trail' programme aimed specifically to assist growers and labour hire companies in that sector who were 'confused' about their workplace obligations. In November 2013, when further matters concerning the poultry industry were brought to the attention of the FWO by the media and the Australian Meat Industries Employees' Union, a second inquiry in that area was established. Almost two years later, the FWO produced its report, detailing non-compliance with a wide range of workplace laws, lack of good governance arrangements in labour supply chains, and significant exploitation of migrant overseas workers.[32] The follow-up announced in the report is to focus on the role of accessories, sham arrangements and the production of false or misleading records (including the role of accounting and legal professionals in the latter).

This sector-specific approach, aimed broadly at educating both workers and employers about their obligations in relation to workplace rights, has also been applied in other areas in which migrant workers are frequently to be found, such as hospitality, convenience stores and trolley collecting. In February 2015, the FWO also initiated a two-year investigation into the exploitation of migrant workers in the clothing industry.[33] However, since 2012, some of the projects of the FWO have also focused much more specifically on seeking to understand the way in which the 'migration' rules are influencing 'labour' issues relating to temporary labour migration. Thus, in August 2014, prompted by allegations that the condition regarding 88-day specified work in various designated regional areas and industries was being exploited, the FWO announced it would undertake a review of the entitlements of migrants on working holiday visas. The FWO's approach to the review has been not only to engage with the community, and to work with employer organisations, key trade unions and other stakeholders, in order to gain an insight into any anomalies in the system, but also to analyse the data held by the Department of Immigration and Border Protection.[34]

[31] Specific campaigns initiated by the FWO in relation to migrant workers were not new. See, eg FWO, *Far North West Compliance & Audit Education Campaign 2010: Final Report* (Melbourne, FWO, 2010); FWO, 'Watchdog Helps to Educate International Students on Workplace Rights', media release, 27 July 2009; FWO, 'SA Fast Food Industry Campaign Results', media release, 7 April 2011; FWO, 'Pooraka Produce Markets Campaign Results', media release, 7 June 2011. Arguably these campaigns became better targeted when led by the OWT.

[32] Commonwealth of Australia, *A Report on the Fair Work Ombudsman's Inquiry into the Labour Procurement Arrangements of the Baiada Group in New South Wales (Baiada Report)* (Canberra, Commonwealth of Australia, 2015).

[33] Bridget Brennan, 'Fair Work Ombudsman Investigating Exploitation of Migrant Clothing Workers Union Claims are Being Paid as Little as $3 an Hour', *ABC News PM*, 24 March 2015.

[34] See FWO, 'Fair Work Ombudsman to Review Entitlement of Overseas Visa-Holders on Working Holidays', media release, 4 August 2014.

Nonetheless, it remains true that responsiveness to complaints regarding individuals is also a major thrust of the FWO's operations. In terms of individual assistance, there is no doubt that a substantial allocation of the FWO's resources is devoted to temporary migrant workers. As the FWO outlined in its May 2015 statement, in recent years the agency had responded to 6,000 requests for assistance from individual visa holders, and recovered more than $4 million in outstanding wages and entitlements. Advice and assistance had been provided to more than 5,000 overseas workers through its Infoline.[35] As part of its services, the FWO offers an interpreter service, and information provided on its website intended to inform workers of their rights is also provided in 27 languages. Both the annual reports and statistics of the FWO reveal the significance of the challenge to enforcement of workplace standards posed by temporary migrant labour. One in ten requests to the FWO for assistance comes from migrant workers. In the 2013–2014 financial year, the FWO recovered $1.103 million in underpaid wages and entitlements for almost 700 workers who were visa holders. In the nine months to April 2015, it had recovered $1.281 million for 345 visa holders. In terms of litigation, between 2009 and mid-2015, the FWO had commenced 60 litigations regarding migrant workers, representing 20 per cent of all such activity in the period. In some of these cases, the penalties have been significant.[36] However, given the scale of enforcement issues facing the FWO generally and the limited nature of its resources, there has been increased utilisation of EUs to deal with problems of the enforcement of temporary migrant workers' individual rights.

III. ENFORCING WORKPLACE RIGHTS FOR TEMPORARY MIGRANT WORKERS USING ENFORCEABLE UNDERTAKINGS (EUs)

One of the key elements of the FWO's enhanced regulatory armoury is its power to enter into EUs, which was established by the Fair Work Act 2009. Enforceable undertakings are statutory agreements between the FWO and an alleged wrongdoer in relation to alleged breaches of the legislation. The power of the FWO to enter an EU is conditional upon it having a 'reasonable belief' that there has been a breach of the legislation, and the EU is given by 'the person in relation to the contravention'.[37] In addition, the FWO's

[35] However, this is a small proportion of the estimated total number of migrant workers in Australia. See Joo-Cheong Tham, Iain Campbell and Martina Boese, 'Why is Labour Protection for Temporary Migrant Workers so Fraught? An Australian Perspective', ch 8 in this volume.

[36] See, eg *Fair Work Ombudsman v ACN 146 435 118 Pty Ltd (no 2)* [2013] FCCA 803 imposing a penalty of $343,860 against the company and its manager for deliberately underpaying six cleaners, including five migrant workers.

[37] Fair Work Act 2009 ss 715, 550.

internal policy guidance requires that there be an element of 'public interest' and that it is appropriate 'in all the circumstances' to adopt this process.[38] EUs may include admissions, and promises or commitments in relation to future compliance. Characterised as 'co-operative compliance', they were introduced as an alternative to court proceedings.[39] While the contravention of an EU does not itself attract a civil penalty, a failure to adhere to commitments made in an EU may be enforced through the courts. EUs are publicised on the FWO's website, and to date most such cases have also attracted significant coverage from mainstream media. This is part of the FWO's strategy for ensuring that, in addition to the undoubted unwanted publicity for the relevant employing person/business, the EU also operates as a general deterrent. Ultimately EUs are 'responsive regulatory' instruments which rely on trust and self-regulation. However, while for this reason they are often argued to be superior at engendering long-term compliance, they also risk being exposed as a too-soft option where the 'stick' of stronger mechanisms are not effectively enforced.

As part of their larger study on the FWO as an enforcement agency, Hardy and Howe also studied all 26 EUs accepted by the FWO between 1 July 2008 and 30 June 2012,[40] and concluded that they demonstrated a range of benefits over formal litigation.[41] While they noticed that sometimes there were extensive delays of up to 18 months in formalising an EU, nonetheless they concluded that the process was generally speedier than court litigation.[42] They also acknowledged that EUs may advantage offenders who are more sophisticated and resourced well enough to engage in negotiations with the FWO and able to make recompense. In addition, Hardy and Howe also criticised them for being less than transparent, and not involving third parties (such as trade unions). However, they argued that, all things considered, EUs are better deterrence mechanisms and more effective than court proceedings especially in being able to include provisions that could not be made as part of a court order.[43] With few restrictions on their content, EUs generally include not only admissions, recompensatory promises, and undertakings in relation to future training and compliance, but also more creative and proactive clauses, such as those which serve a community function by requiring sums of money to be paid to external community organisations (while admitting that such payments might be more symbolic than effective, and perhaps could be better targeted to

[38] See FWO, 'Enforceable Undertakings Policy', www.fairwork.gov.au/fwoguidancenotes/GN-4-FWO-Enforceable-Undertakings-Policy.pdf.

[39] Explanatory Memorandum, Fair Work Bill 2008 (Cth) 400.

[40] Hardy and Howe, 'Too Soft or Too Severe?' (n 17).

[41] Ibid 31–33.

[42] Ibid 19–20.

[43] Ibid 15.

compliance improvements), as well as apologies, and publicity in the wider workplace as well as in the community more generally through the media. In conclusion, Hardy and Howe considered that EUs are 'generally quicker, less costly and more certain' and that these benefits do not compromise 'deterrent, rehabilitative or restorative outcomes'.[44]

Since the study undertaken by Howe and Hardy, the FWO has made significantly greater use of EUs. Between 1 July 2012 and 30 June 2015, 59 EUs were entered into by the FWO, 21 of which were cases revealing exploitation of temporary migrant workers.[45] With a few exceptions, all concerned migrants who were undertaking low-skilled work predominantly as working holiday makers or international students.

In each of these cases, serious levels of underpayment of the migrant workers were revealed.[46] In all cases, the underpayments were the result of multiple contraventions of the minimum wage rates set by awards—not only a failure to pay the basic minimum standard wage, but also failures to pay the casual loading (generally 25 per cent) and penalty rates applicable to overtime work, work on weekends or public holidays. In several instances, migrant workers had been subjected to 'unpaid trials' or 'unpaid training' for which they were not, but should have been, paid.[47] In others, payment of wages was withheld in the early weeks or months of work, ostensibly to ensure that the worker stayed in employment for a longer period or for other spurious reasons.[48] The most egregious example revealed by the EUs during this period under study concerned 30 Filipino and 13 Chinese skilled labourers brought to Australia by the Chia Tung Development Corp Ltd.[49] Accommodating their workers in cramped and substandard conditions, the practice of this Taiwanese-based corporation was not to pay its workers at all for the first three months when they received instead only a $15 per day food allowance. Thereafter, while the workers were paid $27 per hour they had 'fees' unlawfully deducted for visa processing, flights, insurance, food and transport, leaving them with approximately only $9 per hour. In all but one instance (where the worker had already returned to their home country), rectification of the full outstanding amounts of wages had been made to the workers by the time the EU was signed.

[44] Ibid 7.

[45] All EUs are available on the FWO website, www.fairwork.gov.au.

[46] See, eg *85 Degrees Coffee Australia Pty Ltd Enforceable Undertaking*, 5 June 2015.

[47] See, eg *Abella Travel Pty Ltd Enforceable Undertaking*, 17 December 2014; *KYB Pty Ltd Enforceable Undertaking*, 7 March 2014.

[48] See, eg *UB Partners Pty Ltd and Mr Ujjwal Singh Enforceable Undertaking*; FWO, 'Nando's Restaurant Withheld Wages and Short Changed Korean Worker Thousands of Dollars', media release, 17 April 2015.

[49] See *Chia Tung Development Corp Ltd Enforceable Undertaking*, 30 February 2015; FWO, 'Chinese, Filipino Workers Short-Changed $873,000 and Housed in Overcrowded Accommodation', media release, 20 April 2015.

In one other instance, an EU relating to a migrant worker also dealt with a contravention of the 'adverse action' provisions of the legislation. In July 2014, the shifts of a foreign worker on a skilled graduate visa were cancelled and she was dismissed after querying her wage rate with her employer. Her complaint to the FWO prompted it to inquire further into the business of the employer, revealing that six members of staff, including three foreign workers, had also been underpaid. The EU provided that the employer pay compensation of $2,000 for the adverse action taken.[50] In such cases, it is evident that there may be significant monetary 'rewards' to an employer who co-operates with the FWO. From the employer's perspective, the recompense paid to the employee was a trivial amount in comparison to the penalty (up to $10,200 for individuals and $51,000 for companies) which could have been imposed by a court had a breach been proved under the 'adverse action' provisions.

Given the significance to migrant workers of the amounts generally found owing to them, and the fact that they are in Australia for a limited period of time, the speed of the EU process is an important consideration in whether it delivers some justice to them. While Hardy and Howe noted that the speed of the process was a distinct advantage, they indicated that it often took over 18 months for the FWO to conclude an EU, a matter about which some within the agency expressed concern. In the group of EUs concluded between 2012 and 2015, generally a significantly shorter period of time has been taken to bring the process to a conclusion. Indeed, the vast majority of EUs since March 2014 were finalised within 12 months of the alleged contraventions and, in some cases, within as little as two or three months.[51]

In most EUs, there are provisions which also require notices to be provided for specified periods of time to other employees at the workplace regarding the admissions of the employing business, and notifying workers as to the undertakings made in relation to future compliance, including the requirement for speedy rectification for any other underpayments.[52]

Because the EU is seen as a tool to ensure greater compliance in the future, another feature to be found in all of the relevant EUs put in place for small or medium businesses is that the employer will take proactive steps to demonstrate their awareness of their duties under the legislation (including knowledge of how to calculate the correct rates of pay). Recognising that many small businesses are not well resourced, these commitments are invariably implemented through registration of their business on the FWO's 'My Account' portal and a requirement to demonstrate their capability to

[50] See *Senan Pty Ltd Enforceable Undertaking*, 1 May 2014.

[51] See, eg *Chia Tung Development Corp Ltd EU*, 30 February 2015, addressing alleged contraventions between September 2014 and February 2015.

[52] See, eg *UB Partners Pty Ltd Enforceable Undertaking*.

access and use it. This is just one feature of the agency's assistance targeted at small to medium enterprises, which includes a small business help line and a range of self-help tools on the web. In addition, not uncommonly, there are commitments to arrange for an external audit of the business (often for a period of several years) with a requirement to submit those audited books to the FWO. In some instances where the business is large enough, there are also commitments to ensure that staff undertake additional training with an eye to future compliance. Because failure to comply with statutory requirements for record keeping is a common feature of the contraventions, the undertakings regarding future compliance extend to the provision of payslips to employees and the keeping of appropriate records.

As Tham et al have noted, the sectors in which temporary migrant workers are typically to be found are notorious for non-compliance with labour standards.[53] The cases involving EUs concerning temporary labour migration between 2012 and 2015 confirm this. The restaurant and retail sector are the subject of a number of these EUs. Interestingly, the first line of defence by several of the employers was that they were in fact paying 'the market rate' to their workers and/or that the visa worker agreed to work for a rate below the minimum set in the award because it was higher than that paid by their previous employer.[54] The EUs made in the context of low-skilled migrant workers who are working in low-paid sectors of the economy reveal the way in which community conversations regarding compliance become distorted and inverted, or may disingenuously be presented as such. The importance of a 'market rate of pay' for migrant workers has been widely discussed in relation to 457 skilled worker temporary visas. The current legal requirement that employers pay the 'market rate' of pay to 457 visa workers originated in the context of skilled migrants working in the mining sector and is intended to ensure that those workers are not simply paid the minimum award wage, but a higher amount equivalent to that set in enterprise agreements in the sector. However, in low-skilled sectors (such as the restaurant and retail sector), enterprise agreements are rare, and the award minimum prevails. In this context, a 'market rate' set according to prevailing exploitative practices is being deployed as an excuse for contravention of minimum wage standards.[55]

In the period under examination, two of the EUs arose in the context of the food processing industry. Atypically for this sector, one of these EUs concerned skilled workers (electricians, welders, etc) on 457 visas who had been employed to install animal feed mills in rural New South Wales.[56]

[53] See Tham et al, 'Why is Labour Protection for Temporary Migrant Workers so Fraught?: A Perspective from Australia', ch 8 in this volume.

[54] See *MK Train Pty Ltd Enforceable Undertaking*, 12 August 2014; *Fine Food Gallery Pty Ltd Enforceable Undertaking*, 1 October 2014.

[55] See, eg FWO, 'Sushi Bar Reimburses Korean Backpacker, Revamps Workplace Practices after $5000 Underpayment', media release, 11 February 2015.

[56] See *Chia Tung Development Corp Ltd EU*.

In the other case from this sector, B&E Poultry Holdings signed an EU in late October 2014, part of which returned to two Taiwanese backpackers the $25,000 in wages that was owing to them.[57] Both of these EUs raise important questions about their appropriate use in tackling the exploitation of temporary migrant workers.

In many instances, the FWO in entering an EU makes it clear that the relevant employing business had not previously come to its attention for alleged breaches of the legislation. This was the case, for instance, with the Chia Tung Development Corp Ltd EU. Given FWO's stated guidance of only using EUs in appropriate circumstances, surprisingly the B&E Poultry Holdings EU involved a company which had previously been required to pay back tens of thousands of dollars in underpaid wages: since 2012, it had been required to pay back $140,000 to 15 other employees.[58] B&E Poultry Holdings not only owned and operated food processing plants, but it also operated a labour hire agency. B&E Poultry Holdings Pty Ltd is one of the six principal contractors for the Baiada Group, which in NSW was the subject of a then concurrent inquiry by the FWO, the report of which made serious adverse findings regarding the group and its subcontracting chain.[59] In addition, one of the Baiada Group of companies had itself previously entered into an EU in 2011.[60] In such circumstances, when the agency already knew so much about the problematic workplace issues in the supply chain in the poultry industry, it is very difficult to understand why an EU would have been considered appropriate, although clearly the fact that the company had voluntarily paid back the money, and issued apologies, worked in its favour. Indeed, in a not-insignificant number of the other EUs in the period under examination, the business in alleged contravention of the legislation had either previously come to the attention of the FWO (MK Train), had previously experienced problems that were revealed on follow-up investigation to be continuing (Sing Ky) or, like B&E Poultry, had previously voluntarily resolved problems (Abella). To the extent that the issues all involved particularly vulnerable temporary labour migrants, the 'multiple chances' given for correction and self-regulation seems to indicate a 'too soft' approach which is inappropriate even in the face of other pressures (such as limits on resourcing).

Given the sectors involved, a 'too soft' approach is also particularly concerning when the factual circumstances behind several of the cases revealed that a number of the employers entering the EUs had particularly targeted migrant workers. The evidence gathered by the FWO showed,

[57] *B&E Poultry Holdings Pty Ltd Enforceable Undertaking*, 1 August 2014.
[58] See FWO, '$25,000 Returned to Taiwanese Backpackers', media release, 9 October 2014.
[59] See Commonwealth of Australia, *Baiada Report* (n 32).
[60] *BPL Adelaide Pty Ltd Enforceable Undertaking*, 15 December 2011.

for example, that Mr Singh specifically recruited Korean nationals by placing job advertisements for vacancies in the Korean language.[61] Likewise, the employer of the Fine Food Gallery specifically recruited through the Korean community website.[62] However, while the EU signed by Mr Singh required him, appropriately it would seem, to place dual language notices advising of the contraventions and the commitments in the EU, there was no such requirement incorporated in some of the other EUs.

While the restaurant and retail industries are much more likely to recruit on an individual basis from within Australia, including as indicated above by targeting migrant workers, skilled 457 visa workers are much more likely to be recruited though an offshore company. Such was the case with the Taiwanese-based Chia Tung Development Corp Ltd, which was reported to have brought dozens of migrant workers to Australia (in particular Filipino workers on 457 visas and Chinese workers on s 400 temporary short-stay work visas). For this reason, it can be seen that one of the undertakings incorporated in its EU—that as well as the restitution of pay to individual workers, the corporation also committed to making a donation of $10,000 to the Philippine-Australian Community Services Support organisation—was intended to have wider systemic impact. While the effectiveness of such clauses is difficult (perhaps impossible) to evaluate, when such community organisations are often the ones to provide first-level practical support to temporary migrant workers, such payments can make a real difference to their capacity to assist (and in reality it is often such groups, rather than trade unions, that provide the only readily available means of practical support to newly arrived migrant workers). However, given the scale on which corporations such as Chia Tung Development Corp Ltd operate, the impact of such payments on it is not likely to be great.

During the period under examination, the FWO entered EUs with a range of businesses from global corporations to small businesses who operate as sole director companies. The latter tend not to be well resourced, although in a number of instances some individuals were operating several businesses, sometimes as part of franchise arrangements.[63] An important element in the EUs with such businesses is that the individual person who is operating as the sole director is also made a party to the EU as well as their corporation, thus ensuring greater accountability in any subsequent cases of activities using a different corporate entity.

[61] See *UB Partners Pty Ltd Enforceable Undertaking*; FWO, 'Nando's Restaurant Withheld Wages'.

[62] See *Fine Food Gallery Pty Ltd Enforceable Undertaking*; FWO, 'Sushi Bar Reimburses Korean Backpacker' (n 55).

[63] See, eg *Ausnutrie Pty Ltd and Austrirocks Pty Ltd Enforceable Undertaking*, 10 October 2014; *UB Partners Pty Ltd EU*; *Fine Food Gallery Pty Ltd EU*.

In relation to larger entities, the problem of 'phoenixing' is also likely to be more problematic. In several of the EUs, the commitments evidenced an attempt by the FWO to counter any adverse consequences of such behaviour. B&E Poultry Holdings, for instance, was part of a group of companies with quite elaborate arrangements that operated several businesses across two Australian states (Queensland and New South Wales). Part of the undertakings in the EU it entered into was an agreement that, in relation to any subsidiary companies and transferees, it would 'take all reasonable steps' to ensure that its associated entities (as defined under Corporations Act 2001 (Cth) s 50AAA) complied with workplace laws. It also agreed to monitor the compliance of those entities and ensure rectification of any contraventions; to report to the FWO every six months for the next two years on steps undertaken to achieve this; and, in the event that there was a transfer of business in the next two years, to provide a copy of the EU to the transferee and details of the transfer to the FWO. Similar clauses were also incorporated into the EU with Chia Tung Development Corp Ltd in addition to obligations to take all reasonable steps to ensure that its Australian companies (Chiatung Australia Pty Ltd; Innovation Hi Tech Australia Pty Ltd; and all associated companies as defined under Corporations Act 2001 (Cth) s 50AAA) complied with the laws establishing work standards.

Whether a business is large or small, in very many of the sectors in which temporary migrant workers are working, one of the pervasive enforcement challenges comes from the structure of the industry through outsourcing and supply chains, as well as the use of labour hire agencies. In dealing with these problems, the FWO considers that one of its most significant achievements is the approach it has adopted with some of the large corporate players in Australia, who are amenable to mitigating the damage that can be done to their corporate reputation through the exploitation of workers upon whom their operations (sometimes directly) depend.

One of the EUs concluded in the period under consideration concerned the Fine Food Gallery Pty Ltd, which conducted its business from a small counter/premises inside one of the two major supermarket chains operating in Australia. Fine Food Gallery Pty Ltd prepared, packed and displayed 'Sushi Izu' branded sushi both for their own display fridges and for Woolworths fridges and, regardless of the fridge from which customers selected the sushi, they paid for the product at the Woolworths check-out. As part of its investigation in this case, the FWO also conducted an audit of all other sushi providers which had a similar relationship with Woolworths—however, in none of them were problems detected.

Nonetheless, this approach pointed to the resolve of the FWO to try to tackle systemic issues, rather than simply focus on the individual case at hand. In 2014, The Fair Work Ombudsman, Natalie James, indicated in a speech, 'Risk, Reputation and Responsibility', the preparedness of her agency to scrutinise contracts in the supply chain and to use the accessorial liability provisions of the legislation. In particular, in that speech, she highlighted the Coles trolley collectors' litigation, which also concerned migrant workers amongst others, to argue that the large players in the market must use due diligence when outsourcing to low-cost providers.[64] She summarised the trolley collectors' case thus:

> In the past six years, the Fair Work Ombudsman and its predecessor have recouped more than $433,000 for 528 trolley collectors at supermarket sites across Australia.
>
> And yet 2011 census data tells us that there are only around 1,500 trolley collectors in the entire industry ... We have also placed 11 matters before the courts alleging underpayment of trolley collectors.
>
> Of the 7 matters that have been decided, penalties totalling $288,000 have been handed down in cases alleging the underpayment of dozens of trolley collectors by more than $426,000 ...
>
> The ASX guidelines on corporate governance observe that a listed entity's reputation is one of its most valuable assets and, if damaged, can be one of the most difficult to restore.[65]

The Coles trolley collectors' case followed court proceedings initiated in 2012 against two men, Mr Al Hilfi and Mr Al Basry, who had been subcontracted by the Starlink International Group Pty Ltd/Starlink Operations Group Pty Ltd, which in turn had a contract for trolley collection from Coles but which by the time of the court proceedings was in liquidation. In *FWO v Al Hilfi*, the judge described Mr Al Hilfi as 'not a sophisticated businessman', who was effectively subject to the direction of the parties with whom he had contracted to perform the work.[66] In the circumstances, the second and third respondents had the capacity to control, direct or influence (or all of these) the conduct of Mr Al Hilfi in relation to the wages and conditions that he paid and accorded to his employees, and the practices that Mr Al Hilfi applied in the conduct of his business, including with respect to issuing payslips and keeping employee records.

This case involved four young Indian men in their 20s who spoke little English. At the top of the subcontracting chain stood the supermarket giant, Coles, whose contracts for trolley collection had a total value of more than $30 million. Aiming to get a more systemic result, the FWO entered into an EU with Coles rather than pursuing its prosecution of the supermarket

[64] Natalie James, 'Risk, Reputation and Responsibility', speech to the ALERA Conference, Gold Coast, Qld, 29 August 2014. See also *FWO v Al Hilfi* [2012] FCA 116; *FWO v Al Hilfi* [2015] FCA 313; *FWO v Al Hilfi* [2016] FCA 193; *FWO v South Jin Pty Ltd* [2015] FCA 1456.

[65] Ibid, citing ASX Corporate Governance Council, *Corporate Governance Principles and Recommendations*, 3rd edn (2014) 19.

[66] *FWO v Al Hilfi* [2015] FCA 313 [27].

giant.[67] As part of the EU, Coles acknowledged that 'it is responsible for compliance with all aspects of the law across its business operations'. It also accepted that it has an 'ethical and moral responsibility to require standards of conduct from all entities and individuals directly involved in the conduct of its enterprise' (clause R of the EU) and 'that the traditional contracting model it formerly utilised to obtain trolley collection services from trolley contractors was highly vulnerable to exploitation and the perpetuation of poor employment practices by its trolley contractors including underpayment in the industry' (clause S of the EU).

Coles was thus acknowledging that in the conduct of its business it needed not only to comply with the law but also to meet community and social expectations to provide equal, fair and safe work opportunities and to stamp out exploitation. As a consequence of the court proceedings, Coles revamped its trolley collection system: it changed from using 30 lead contractors to having a single national trolley provider administered under a single payroll, conducted and operated by an independent third party; in many stores, it brought trolley collection 'in house'; and it established a hotline for complaints relating to trolley collection at head office with a dedicated investigator. At the same time, Coles' new trolley contractor was party to a Deed of Proactive Compliance with FWO, and Coles committed to ongoing support in ensuring compliance.[68] Finally, Coles made ex gratia payments under the EU totalling $220,174.69 to FWO to be forwarded as payments to the trolley collectors.

The extent to which the Coles trolley case EU becomes a model or precedent adopted by others is yet to be seen, although some of the early indications are positive.[69] The admission of 'ethical and moral responsibility' stops short of admitting 'legal responsibility'. In her 2014 speech,

[67] See *Enforceable Undertaking between the Commonwealth of Australia (as represented by the Office of the Fair Work Ombudsman) and Coles Supermarkets Australia Pty Ltd*, 6 October 2014. This followed a Federal Court decision in which Coles had failed in its attempt to get the Court to rule that it had no case to answer in relation to the FWO's allegations against it: *FWO v Al Hilfi* [2012] FCA 116.

[68] See Coles, *Annual Report pursuant to the enforceable undertaking between the Commonwealth of Australia as represented by the Office of the Fair Work Ombudsman and Coles Supermarkets Pty Ltd*, 3 November 2015. This 'proactive compliance' approach has also been recommended to combat the problems in the 7-Eleven franchise group: see FWO, *A Report of the Fair Work Ombudsman's Inquiry into 7-Eleven: Identifying and Addressing the Drivers of Non-Compliance in the 7-Eleven Network* (Commonwealth of Australia 2016). On common law 'proactive compliance deeds' see Hardy and Howe, 'Too Soft or Too Severe?' (n 17) 11.

[69] In the follow-up to the *Baiada Report*, Baiada has likewise accepted its 'moral and ethical responsibility' for the working conditions of those in its supply chain and entered into a three-year *Proactive Compliance Deed between the Commonwealth of Australia (as represented by the FWO) and Baiada Poultry Pty Ltd (ACN 002925948) and Bartter Enterprises Pty Ltd (ACN 000451374)* in October 2015, in which it agreed to make good past underpayments by contractors and to work in partnership with the FWO to ensure future compliance with workplace laws by all its suppliers.

Ms James referred to the accessorial liability provisions in the legislation and indicated that:

> We are using accessorial liability more and more, so that we can hold individuals involved in contraventions to account.
>
> Last financial year, 38 penalty decisions were handed down in matters that the Fair Work Ombudsman has put before the courts.
>
> Thirty of those involved penalty orders against an accessory, amounting to a total of $753,809.
>
> In 9 of these matters, the employing company was in liquidation and the Court ordered that compensation owed to employees be paid from the accessory's penalty.[70]

The accessorial liability provisions in the legislation are to be found in s 550(1) of the Fair Work Act 2009 which states that 'a person who is involved in a contravention of a civil remedy provision will also be taken to have contravened that provision'. However, the section goes on to define 'involved in' as satisfied only where a person:

> (2) (a) has aided, abetted, counselled or procured the contravention; or
> (b) has induced the contravention, whether by threats or promises or otherwise; or
> (c) has been in any way, by act or omission, directly or indirectly, knowingly concerned in or party to the contravention; or
> (d) has conspired with others to effect the contravention.

To date, the interpretation of this provision has been quite strict, with the courts indicating that it requires actual, rather than constructive, knowledge of the essential matters making up the contravention.[71] In some cases, the accessorial liability provisions have been applied with some success,[72] but in many cases, the requirements for proof can be insurmountable.[73]

IV. CONCLUSION

The effectiveness of any system of enforcement of workplace laws may be assessed in at least two different ways. If it is to be measured by how seriously an enforcement agency treats an area that is problematic in terms of compliance, the FWO, with its strategic allocation of a considerable portion

[70] James, 'Risk, Reputation and Responsibility' (n 64).

[71] See, eg *FWO v Devine Marine Group Pty Ltd* [2013] FCA 1135 [44]–[46]; *FWO v South Jin Pty Ltd* [2015] FCA 1456 [227]–[236].

[72] See, eg *Fair Work Ombudsman v Hongyun Chinese Restaurant Pty Ltd (In Liquidation) & Ors* [2013] FCCA 52; *FWO v South Jin Pty Ltd* [2015] FCA 1456.

[73] See, eg *FWO v Devine Marine Group Pty Ltd* [2013] FCA 1135.

of its resources to issues such as temporary migrant labour, may be judged to be quite effective. On the other hand, if effectiveness is judged in terms of the results achieved in light of the size of the problem of compliance, then clearly the FWO's operations barely scratch the surface in terms of achieving compliance with labour standards for all migrant workers.

However, rather than seeing these two approaches as distinct, a more realistic assessment must take into account both of the above aspects in measuring success. Australia's enforcement agency is far more effective than that of many comparable jurisdictions, and some of the recent developments, whereby the FWO has used EUs to engage the co-operation of larger business to take responsibility for respect for workplace rights in their supply chains, are particularly promising. However, it is also apparent that there remains a large and ongoing challenge in ensuring compliance with labour standards in Australia. And this is clearly the case in relation to temporary migrant workers, especially in small and medium sized enterprises. While much has been achieved, the system is not perfect. The analysis in this chapter of the EUs entered into between 2012 and 2015 which concern issues of temporary migrant labour indicates that, in the FWO's practice, the tension between principles of 'responsive regulation' and 'strategic regulation' may have swung too far towards 'responsive regulation'. As others have noted, in the context of other jurisdictions, responsive regulation assumes the co-operation of stakeholders and their commitment to the set of principles embodied in the legislation.[74] In relation to temporary migrant workers, a too soft approach has no real impact on those who profit greatly from the exploitation of these workers and the general deterrence effect of EUs is obviously weak. Responsive regulation also requires strong resourcing and, in the end, adequate back-up from litigation.[75] To be truly effective, and given the size of the problems concerning employment of temporary migrant labour in Australia, there can also be no doubt that the resourcing of the FWO needs to be increased.[76] In addition, while the record of the FWO in litigating in relation to breaches of the law involving migrant workers is quite strong, provisions making easier the successful prosecution of those who are accessories and at the top of supply chains and higher penalties need to be put in place for litigation to have a deeper regulatory impact. Only with such changes does the strategic approach to regulation that the FWO has also adopted have a chance of becoming truly effective.

[74] See, eg Bob Hepple, 'Agency Enforcement of Workplace Equality' in Dickens (ed), *Making Employment Rights Effective* (n 10) esp 64–65.

[75] Ibid.

[76] Indeed the Productivity Commission has now recommended this. See Productivity Commission, *Workplace Relations Framework, Final Report* (Canberra, Productivity Commission, 2015) especially ch 29, recommendation 29.2.

Index

Page numbers in **bold** refer to information in tables.

agencies, *see* recruitment agencies
agency workers, 56
  Temporary Agency Work Directive, 75
  Intra-Corporate Transferees Directive, 57
Australia, 131–32, 173–75
  457 visa scheme:
    background, 132–37
    benefits, 134–37
    criticisms of programme, 137
      interests of employers, 137–39
      labour law and, 139–42
    Deegan Report, 140–41, 189–90
    demand-driven nature, 132–34
    non-compliance, 184–86
    rationales:
      meeting domestic skills shortages, 134–35
      stronger labour market outcomes, 135
    reform, 142
      need for cohesion between labour and migration law, 145–47
      regulatory design, 142–43
      structural design, 143–44
  cohesion between labour and migration law:
    exercise of rights under Fair Work Act 2009, 145–46
    prevention of information passed to immigration authorities, 146–47
    protection of employees, 145
  enforcement of workplace rights, 393–97, 411–12
    enforceable undertakings, 401–11
    role of Fair Work Ombudsman, 397–401
  Fair Work Ombudsman, 144, 395–97
    enforceable undertakings, 401–11
  labour protection, 180–82
    enforcement of workplace rights, 393–97, 411–12
      enforceable undertakings, 401–11
      role of Fair Work Ombudsman, 397–401
  non-compliance, 182–84, **199**, 199–200
    457 visa scheme, 184–86
    causes, 187–88
      vulnerability of 457 visa workers, 188–91
      vulnerability of international student workers, 191–94
    international student workers, 186–87
    poorly regulated industries, 194–99
  Productivity Commission, 135–36
  recruitment agencies:
    regulation of, 397–99, 406, 408–09
  relationship between employer demand and investment in training, 136
  'temporary migrant worker' defined, 175–76
    implications of definitions, 176–77
  see also Fair Work Ombudsman; Temporary Work (Skilled) Visa (subclass 457)
Australian Human Rights Commission, 182

Austria, 103–04
guest worker programmes, 91
policy reform, 91
posted workers, 91–92
free services mobility and, 105–06
labour market, impact on, 103–04
prospects for posted work in the EU/EEA, 106–07
temporary workers distinguished, 103–04
workers from EU members states with transitional regulations, 104–05
workers from third countries, 104–05
seasonal workers:
agriculture and forestry, 92, 94–95
construction, 92, 93–94
international comparisons, 93–95
labour market, impact on, 96–99
agriculture and forestry, 99–101
tourism, 102
unemployment, 99
wages, 99, **100–01**
legal framework, 95–96
posted workers distinguished, 103–04
prospects for, 102–03
tourism, 92–93, 95

bilateral investment treaties, 6, 48
controversial features, 48–49
bilateral migration/labour agreements, 25, 47, 55, 67, 89
Australia, 178
Immokalee, 38, 352
wage premiums and, 362–64
worker-paid migration costs and, 378
bilateral service agreements, 14
bilateral trade agreements, 13–14
Blue Card Directive (2009/50/EC), 52–54, 59

Canada:
criminal and immigration law, 160
domestic servitude, 170–71
vulnerability of workers, 159
forced labour, 168–70
immigration and labour law, 158–60
Immigration and Refugee Protection Act 2001, 160
International Centre for Criminal Law Reform and Criminal Justice Policy (ICCLR), 166
Live-In Caregiver Program, 158–59
recruitment agencies:
regulation of, 152, 159–60, 166–67
servitude, 161, 164–65
jurisdictional issues, 165–67
Temporary Foreign Workers Program, 158
trafficking, 161
jurisdictional issues, 163
R v Ladha, 163
R v Orr, 161–63
West Coast Domestic Workers Association (WCDWA), 166–67
see also domestic labour; domestic workers
Charter of Fundamental Rights (Charter), 52, 55–56, 249
nationals of third countries, 261
seasonal workers, 257
China-Australia Free Trade Agreement (ChAFTA), 13, 84–85
citizenship, 277–80
concept, 280–81
evolution of, 281–84
state sovereignty and, 282–84
permanent residency distinguished, 283–84, 293–94
restrictions and:
access to alternative employment, 293
family rights, 293
rethinking the relationship between citizenship and work, 284–85
bargaining power, 291
communitarian perspective, 290
contribution and membership, 286–87
democratic legitimacy, 289–90
equality and membership, 289–92

freedom to choose a path in life, 288–89
human dignity and membership, 288–89
identity, 287
integration and membership, 287–88
invitation to work, 287
jus soli and *jus sanguinis* compared, 285
language barriers, 287–88
sense of worth, 288
social networks and, 287–88
territorial presence and membership, 285–86
theory of private property, 286
toil and entitlement, 286–87
trade-offs, 290–91
unequal employment relations, 291–92
vulnerability, 290
workers' relationship with receiving states, 292–93
see also status and vulnerability
Commonwealth Racial Discrimination Act 1975 (Cth), 182
Comprehensive Economic and Trade Agreement (CETA), 48–49, 82–83, 88
contribution and membership, 286–87
invitation to work, 287
theory of private property, 286
toil and entitlement, 286–87
corporate social responsibility:
transnational corporate supply chains, 356–59
costs, *see* migration costs

'decent work' agenda, 4, 12, 40, 256–58
challenges, 27–29
Austria, 94
domestic workers, 204, 243
pursuit of, 25–27
seasonal workers, 94
see also International Labour Organization
Deegan Report (Aus), 140–41, 189–90
defining 'temporary labour migration', 7–8
Australia, 175–76
implications of definitions, 176–77
Italy, 265–66
third-country nationals, 262–63
'seasonality' and, 265–66
demand-driven programmes:
Australia's 457 visa, 131–37, 147
challenges to approach, 137–42
seasonal migration and, 268–69
Sweden, 219
see also Temporary Work (Skilled) Visa (subclass 457)
demand for skilled workers, 113–14
caps and quotas, 118–19
demand-side restrictions, 119–26
meeting the skills shortage, 127–30
points-based scheme, 117–18
supply-side restrictions, 126–27
Tier 2 (General) Visa scheme (UK), 115–18
Work Permit scheme, 115–16
domestic labour:
Canada, 155
Europe, 155
UK, 154
USA, 154–55
see also domestic workers
domestic workers, 24, 151–52, 382
Canada, 151–52, 170–71
construction, 154–56, 158–60
exploitation, 152
forced labour and, 168–70
servitude, 161–65
combatting, 165–67
trafficking, 160
'unfreedom', 153–54
construction, 154–56
jurisdiction, 156–58
mechanisms of legal redress, 155–56
social difference, 154
temporal and spatial variations, 154
workplace and residence, 154

ILO Convention on Decent Work for Domestic Workers, 166–67, 170, 204, 239
Kuwait, 388–89
Sweden, 204–05, 222
UK, 27–28, 236–37
Overseas Domestic Worker visa, 223, 229–34
vulnerability of, 238–39

economic efficiency and temporary labour migration, 20–22
competition for work/jobs, 21–22
demand for skilled workers, 113–14
caps and quotas, 118–19
demand-side restrictions, 119–26
meeting the skills shortage, 127–30
points-based scheme, 117–18
supply-side restrictions, 126–27
Tier 2 (General) Visa scheme (UK), 115–18
Work Permit scheme, 115–16
economic integration:
regulatory challenges:
changing nature of migration, 10–12
economic rationale, 8–9
global economic integration and, 8–19
labour and trade boundaries, 12–19
trade in services, 65–67, 71
commercial presence, 72
presence of natural persons, 72–75
human rights issues, 16–17
liberalisation, 14–15
redistributive benefits, 16
regulation of processes:
CETA, 82–83
ChAFTA, 84–85
exemptions from GATS principles, 80–81
market access, 81
'most-favoured nation', 80–81
no general guarantee of national treatment, 81
positive posting, 81
TiSA, 85–87
TPP, 83–84
TTIP, 85–87
employer demand for skilled workers, 113–14
employer sponsorship programmes, 224
Australia, 85, 135–36
457 visa scheme, 133, 136, 137, 139–40, 143–47, 177
non-compliance, 197–98
sponsorship obligations, 182, 184–86, 189, 393
termination of employment, 190
working conditions, 191
kafala system, 229, 388
Kuwait, 388–89
permanent residency and, 381
UK, 113–14, 118
Certificates of Sponsorship, 118
job offers as a precondition for entry, 119–20
labour market testing, 120–21
language standards, 127
self-sufficiency, 127
Tier 2 (General) Visa Scheme (UK), 114–30
wages requirements, 125
enforceable undertakings (Aus), 401–05
case studies, 405–07, 408–11
establishment of, 401
Fair Work Act 2009, 401
larger businesses, 408
small businesses and, 407
enforcement of workplace rights:
Australia, 393–97, 411–12
enforceable undertakings, 401–11
role of Fair Work Ombudsman, 397–401
enforcement through market consequences, 369–70
Fair Work Ombudsman (Aus), 397–401
feasibility of enforcement, 316
recruitment regulation, 350
migrant participation and, 333

EU law:
  Blue Card Directive (2009/50/EC), 52–54, 59
  flexisecurity model, 248–49
  freedom of movement, 18–19, 245
  Green Paper on an EU approach to managing economic migration, 247
  Green Paper on modernising labour law, 247–48
  intra-corporate transferees, 43
    regulation, 77–78
    transnational networks, 49–50
  migration law:
    asylum policy, 50–51
    Blue Card Directive, 52–54, 59
    Charter of Fundamental Rights, 55–56
    harmonisation attempts, 51–52
    illegal immigration, 51
    labour market efficiency, 51
    migration status, 53–54
    Single Permit Directive, 51–53
    third-party nationals, 50
  regulation, 241–44, 248–49
    Blue Card Directive, 52–54, 59
    Charter of Fundamental Rights, 55–56
    freedom of movement, 245
    intra-corporate transferees, 77–78
    prohibition of chains of temporary contracts, 248
    prohibition of discrimination, 248
    reunification of families, 246
    seasonal workers, 249–56
    Single Permit Directive, 51–53
    subsidiarity and proportionality, 244, 251–52
    third-country nationals, 245–46
  seasonal workers, 28, 43
    labour rights and relations, 59–61
    personal scope, 56–57
    prevention of 'overstaying', 51
    sanctions against employers, 219–21
    Seasonal Workers Directive (Art.17), 219–21
    Sweden, 219–21
    temporal and transnational dimensions, 58–59
  Single Permit Directive, 51–53
  see also Intra-Corporate Transferees Directive; Seasonal Workers Directive; Single Permit Directive
equality and membership, 289–92
  bargaining power, 291
  communitarian perspective, 290
  democratic legitimacy, 289–90
  trade-offs, 290–91
  unequal employment relations, 291–92
  vulnerability, 290
European Convention on Human Rights (ECHR), 27–28
  criminalisation of exploitative employment, 238–39
  criticism of, 237–38
  Overseas Domestic Workers visa and, 235–36, 237–38
  prohibition of slavery, servitude, and forced and compulsory labour, 223–24, 230–31, 235
European Court of Human Rights (ECtHR):
  criticisms of UK's Overseas Domestic Workers regime, 230–34
  modern slavery case law, 230–32

fair food program, Immokalee (USA), 360–61
  labour standards, 361–62
    comprehensive auditing, 365–69
    enforcement through market consequences, 369–70
    pressuring brands for bilateral agreements, 362–64
    worker-driven code of conduct regarding complaint resolution, 364–65
  replication in other industry sectors, 372–73
    focusing on market consequences, 374–76
    improving precarious nature of legal rights, 373–74

improving vulnerability status of workers, 373
success of, 371–72
Fair Work Act 2009 (Cth), 145, 180–81, 191
accessorial liability, 411
breaches, 146, 183
establishing of Fair Work Ombudsman, 144, 397
establishing of enforceable undertakings, 401
Fair Work Ombudsman (Aus), 144, 180–81
assessment of activities, 397–99
compliance with labour standards and, 399
clothing sector, 400
food industry, 399–400
response of FWO to complaints, 399–401
effectiveness, 395–97, 411–12
enforceable undertakings (EUs), 401–05
case studies, 405–07, 408–11
larger businesses, 408
small businesses and, 407
enforcement role, 397–401
establishment, 397
forced labour:
Canada, 168–70
domestic workers, 168–70
ECHR:
prohibition of slavery, servitude, and forced and compulsory labour, 223–24, 230–31, 235
ILO standards and, 166–67
foreign direct investment, 48
bilateral investment treaties, 48
controversial features, 48–49
GATS and, 72, 74

General Agreement on Trade in Services (GATS), 13, 14–15
foreign direct investment, 72, 74
regulation of trade-related processes:
exemptions from GATS principles, 80–81
global challenges to temporary labour migration:
labour approach, 34–36
law and policy, 36–37
regulatory responses, 32–40
responsive regulation, 37–38
rights-based approach, 32–34
globalisation and temporary labour migration, 47–50
changing nature of migration, 10–12
foreign direct investment, 48
intensification of transnational activity, 48–49
investment across borders, 47
trade in goods and services, 47–48

Highly Skilled Migrants Programme (HSMP) (UK), 116
human dignity and membership, 288–89
freedom to choose a path in life, 288–89
sense of worth, 288
human rights, 16, 224–26
consent, 228–29
labour rights as, 226–28
non-discrimination principle, 26
pursuit of 'decent work', 25–27
see also European Convention on Human Rights; European Court of Human Rights
human rights law, *see* European Convention on Human Rights

Immigration and Refugee Protection Act 2001 (IRPA) (Can):
labour trafficking, 152, 160–65, 171
integration and membership, 287–88
identity, 287
language barriers, 287–88
social networks and, 287–88
International Centre for Criminal Law Reform and Criminal Justice Policy (ICCLR) (Can), 166
International Convention on the Protection of the Rights of All

Migrant Workers and Members of the Families 1990, 283
International Labour Organization, 6, 11–12, 227, 251
  Convention on Domestic Work, 166–67, 170, 204, 239
  criminalisation of illegal entry and residence, 273
  'decent work' agenda, 40, 94, 204, 243, 256–58
    challenges, 27–29
    pursuit of, 25–27
  Declaration on Fundamental Principles and Rights at Work 1998, 243
  equal pay for equal work, 380
  fair migration agenda, 25–27, 32, 174, 243–44
  forced labour, 166–67
  labour standards, 30–31, 35, 37, 243, 354–56, 375–76
    inadequacies, 359
  migration costs and, 379, 383
  migration status, 68–69
  Multilateral Framework on Labour Migration, 30–31, 174–75
  non-compliance with worker protection, 174–75
  posted workers, 103–04
  regulatory role, 243–44
  rights-based agenda, 12–13, 60
  'temporary migrant workers' definitions, 176
  transnational corporate supply chains, 354–56
  'triple win', 20
intra-corporate transferees (ICTs), 43
  EU law:
    labour market efficiency, 51
    labour rights and relations, 59–61
    personal scope, 57–58
    posted workers, 62–63
    temporal and transnational dimensions, 58–59
  regulation, 77–78
  transnational networks, 49–50
Intra-Corporate Transferees Directive (2014/66/EU), 43
  labour market efficiency, 51
  labour rights and relations, 59–61
  personal scope, 57–58
  posted workers, 62–63
  temporal and transnational dimensions, 58–59
Italy, 259–60
  employment contract, 261
  equal treatment and rights, 261–62
  residency and 263–65
  seasonal workers:
    protection from exploitation, 268–71
    residence permits, 267–68
    seasonal work permits, 265–88
    'seasonality' defined, 265–66
    securitisation policies, 273–74
  third-country nationals:
    access to labour market, 262
    'temporary labour migration' defined, 262–63

labour intensification, 17–18
labour law:
  Australia:
    discrimination law, 181–82
    Fair Work Act, 180–81
    non-compliance, 182–87, **199**, 199 200
      457 visa workers, 184–86
      causes, 187–94
      international student workers, 186–87
      poorly regulated industries, 194–99
  commodification, 256–57
  de-commodification, 257–58
  migration law, impact of, 44–47
  non-compliance, 174–75, 182–87, **199**, 199–200
    457 visa workers, 184–86
    causes in Australia, 187–88
      vulnerability of 457 visa workers, 188–91

vulnerability of international student workers, 191–94
international student workers, 186–87
poorly regulated industries, 194–99
trade law distinguished, 12, 67
see also seasonal workers

membership, *see* citizenship
migrant personal work and services providers, 87–89
see also recruitment agencies
Migration Act 1958 (Cth), 182, 191, 398–99
migration costs:
case studies, 391
Korea, 385, 386–88
Kuwait, 385–86, 388–89
Spain, 386, 389–90
four phases of migration, 377–78
ILO conventions, 379
monetary costs, 378–79, 391
opportunity costs, 378–79, 391
recruitment processes, 380–82
remuneration, 380
retention, 380–81
worker-paid recruitment costs, 382
agent recruiters, 382
options to reduce, 391–92
partner recruiters, 382
remittance and recruitment costs, 383–85
wage gaps, 383
migration law:
EU law:
asylum policy, 50–51
Blue Card Directive, 52–54
Charter of Fundamental Rights and, 55–56
harmonisation attempts, 51–52
illegal immigration, 51
labour market efficiency, 51
migration status and, 53–54
Single Permit Directive, 51–52
third-party nationals, 50
impact on work relations, 45–46
labour law, impact on, 44–47
migration status, 44, 46–47
seasonal work, 46
supply and demand of migrant workers, 45
Migration Regulations 1994 (Cth), 182, 191
migration status, 44, 46–47, 53–54
see also status and vulnerability
Migration Advisory Committee (MAC) (UK), 23, 117
mobility:
basic model:
applicable regulation, 76–77, **79**
intra-corporate transfers 77–78
recruitment from abroad, 77
self-employed, 78
type of labour, 75–76, **76, 77**
entrepreneurial migration, 70–71
labour migration of employees/ workers, 68–69
trade in services, 71
commercial presence, 71, 72
consumption abroad, 71
cross-border supply, 71
presence of natural persons, 71, 72–75
types, 67–68
modern slavery, 223–24, 239–40
consent, 228–29
criminalisation of exploitative employment, 238–39
kafala system, 229–30
labour rights as human rights, 226–28
Overseas Domestic Worker visa scheme, 230
criticisms by ECtHR, 230–34
ECtHR case law, 230–32
see also domestic labour; domestic workers; Modern Slavery Act 2015; Overseas Domestic Worker Visa
Modern Slavery Act 2015 (UK), 223–24, 232, 234–37, 238, 240
most-favoured nation, 80–81

Overseas Domestic Worker Visa (UK), 223–24
criticisms by ECtHR, 230–34

ECtHR case law, 230–32
modern slavery and, 230

permanent residency, 9, 29–30, 68, 173–74, 278, 292, 296–97, 301, 302–03, 308, 316
457 visa scheme, 140, 182, 187–88, 190, 193
Australia, 140, 176–77, 182, 187–88, 190, 193
citizenship distinguished, 153, 281, 283–84, 293–94
employer sponsorship and, 140
ethics, 316, 317
implications of recognising residence, 295–97
live-in carer program, 158–59, 161–62, 166, 168–70
R v Orr, 161–62
Singapore, 224
Sweden, 207, 257
points-based system (UK):
Certificates of Sponsorship, 118
goal, 117
implementation, 117–18
Overseas Domestic Workers visa scheme and, 229–30
Tier 2 (General) Visa Scheme, 117–18
posted workers, 19, 61–62
Austria, 91–92, 109–10
free services mobility and, 105–06
labour market, impact on, 103–04
prospects for posted work in the EU/EEA, 106–07
temporary workers distinguished, 103–04, 107–09
workers from EU members states with transitional regulations, 104–05
workers from third countries, 104–05
Intra-Corporate Transferees Directive, 62–63
Posted Workers Enforcement Directive (2014/67/EU), 19, 92
Posted Workers Enforcement Directive (2014/67/EU), 19, 92
precariousness, 23–24
457 visa workers, 177–82
employer non-compliance, 182–84, 184–86, 188–91
'decent work', 25–27
international student visa schemes, 177–82
employer non-compliance, 182–84, 186–87, 191–93
migrant domestic workers, 151–53, 170–71
construction through immigration and labour laws, 158–60
forced labour, 168–70
jurisdiction, 156–58, 165–67
legal characterisation, 153–56
servitude, 161–67
trafficking, 160–65
'unfreedom', 153–56
see also status and vulnerability
Price of Rights: Regulating International Labor Migration, 299–309
case for a global migrant rights database, 321–33
focus and methods:
case for mixed method approach, 314
interaction with other immigration policies, 313
limits of quantitative methods, 313–14
gaps and exceptional cases:
free movement in the EU, 310–12
irregular migration, 310
Sweden, 312–13
methodology, 323–25
see also protection of rights
protection of rights, 299–300
'core rights' approach, 309
ethics and, 308, 317–19
feasibility of enforcement, 316
global governance:
human rights, 319–20
strategies for migrant rights activists, 320–21
migrant rights and labour immigration policy, 300–01

national interest and, 305–07
openness versus rights, 301–02
skilled workers, 303–04
temporary migration programmes, 302
trade-off between access and rights, 304–05
policy-making process, 314–16
trade-off between access and rights, 304–05, 307–08

recruitment agencies, 75–79, 269
regulation of agencies:
Australia, 397–99, 406, 408–09
Canada, 152, 166–67
Mexico, 331, 335–36, 345
Sweden, 210
transnational agencies, 282
worker-paid migration costs, 377–78, 382, 391–92
Canada, 159–60
Korea, 387–88
recruitment regulation, 350
Mexico, 331
case study, 334–37, 341–44
migrant participation and:
challenges, 345–47
importance of, 332
democracy and self-representation, 332
effective monitoring and enforcement, 333
quality of initiatives, 332–333
rights and representation, 333
protection from retaliation, 347–48
transnational institutional support, 349–50
role for workers and unions, 329–30
protection from retaliation, 347–48
transnational institutional support, 349–50
USA, 331
case study, 337–41
see also recruitment agencies
regulation, 241–44
agency workers, 56–57, 75
EU, 241–44, 248–49
freedom of movement, 245
prohibition of chains of temporary contracts, 248
prohibition of discrimination, 248
reunification of families, 246
seasonal workers, 249–56
subsidiarity and proportionality, 244, 251–52
third-country nationals, 245–46
global challenges to temporary labour migration, 37–40
ILO:
'decent work' agenda, 243
challenges, 27–29
pursuit of, 25–27
Declaration on Fundamental Principles and Rights at Work 1998, 243
fair migration agenda, 25–27, 174, 243–44
labour standards, 243
Multilateral Framework on Labour Migration, 174
intra-corporate transferees, 43, 51, 57–63
migrants as part of the supply chain, 241–42
policy, 22–23
posted workers, 19, 91–92, 109–10
free services mobility and, 105–06
Intra-Corporate Transferees Directive, 62–63
labour market, impact on, 103–04
Posted Workers Enforcement Directive (2014/67/EU), 19, 92
prospects for posted work in the EU/EEA, 106–07
temporary workers distinguished, 103–04, 107–09
workers from EU members states with transitional regulations, 104–05
workers from third countries, 104–05
recruitment regulation, 350
Mexico, 331

case study, 334–37, 341–44
migrant participation and, 332–33
challenges, 345–47
protection from retaliation, 347–48
transnational institutional support, 349–50
protection from retaliation, 347–48
transnational institutional support, 349–50
USA, 331
case study, 337–41
responsive regulation, 37–38
role for workers and unions, 329–30
seasonal workers (Italy):
protection from exploitation, 268–71
residence permits, 267–68
seasonal work permits, 265–88
'seasonality' defined, 265–66
securitisation policies, 273–74
seasonal workers (Spain):
case law, 255–56
collective bargaining, 254–56
current labour law, 254–55
flexisecurity model and, 253
hiring process, 253–54
lack of unemployment protection 254
legal treatment, 252–53
maximum length of stay, 252, 253
pressure from EU, 249
recognition of human rights and, 251
subsidiarity and proportionality, 244, 251–52
temporary contracts, 253
social effect on migrants, 29–32
Sweden, 206–07
trade in services, 13–14
CETA, 82–83
ChAFTA, 84–85
exemptions from GATS principles, 80–81
market access, 81
'most-favoured nation', 80–81
no general guarantee of national treatment, 81
positive posting, 81
TiSA, 85–87
TPP, 83–84
TTIP, 85–87
USA, 242
regulatory challenges, 3–5
bilateral agreements and, 38
'decent work' and, 27–29
defining temporary labour migration, 7–8
economic efficiency, 20–23
economic integration:
changing nature of migration, 10–12
economic rationale, 8–9
global economic integration and, 8–19
labour and trade boundaries, 12–19
labour inspectorates and, 39
precarious nature of temporary migrant work, 23–27
responses to, 5–6, 34–40
corporate social responsibility, 351–76
effective enforcement, 393–412
human rights approach, 34
labour law approach, 34
reducing worker-paid costs, 377–92
rights-based approach, 32–34
roles for workers and trade unions, 329–50
social effect of regulation, 29–31
trade unions and, 38, 329–50
residency:
citizenship distinguished, 283–84, 293–94
implications of recognising residence, 295–97
see also permanent residency
rule of law, 174–75

seasonal agricultural workers scheme (UK), 116

seasonal workers:
Austria, 109–10
agriculture and forestry, 92, 94–95
construction, 92, 93–94
international comparisons, 93–95
labour market, impact on, 96–99
agriculture and forestry, 99–101
tourism, 102
unemployment, 99
wages, 99, **100–01**
legal framework, 95–96
posted workers distinguished, 103–04, 107–09
prospects for, 102–03
tourism, 92–93, 95
Italy:
protection from exploitation, 268—71
residence permits, 267–68
seasonal work permits, 265–88
'seasonality' defined, 265–66
securitisation policies, 273–74
Spain:
case law, 255–56
collective bargaining, 254–56
current labour law, 254–55
flexisecurity model and, 253
hiring process, 253–54
lack of unemployment protection 254
legal treatment, 252–53
maximum length of stay, 252, 253
pressure from EU, 249
recognition of human rights and, 251
subsidiarity and proportionality, 244, 251–52
temporary contracts, 253
Seasonal Workers Directive (2014/36/EU), 28, 43
Art.17, 219–21
labour rights and relations, 59–61
personal scope, 56–57
prevention of 'overstaying', 51
sanctions against employers, 219–21
Sweden, 219–21
temporal and transnational dimensions, 58–59
sector-based scheme (UK), 116
Single Permit Directive (2011/98/EU), 51–52, 53
Spain:
labour market reform, 254–56
regulation of seasonal workers:
case law, 255–56
collective bargaining, 254–56
current labour law, 254–55
flexisecurity model and, 253
hiring process, 253–54
lack of unemployment protection 254
legal treatment, 252–53
maximum length of stay, 252, 253
pressure from EU, 249
recognition of human rights and, 251
subsidiarity and proportionality, 244, 251–52
temporary contracts, 253
statistics and trends, 249–50
unemployment, 250–51
sponsors, *see* employer sponsorship programmes
status and vulnerability, 44, 46–47, 278–79
457 visa workers, 188–91
citizenship rights, 279–80, 292–94
contribution and membership, 286–87
equality and membership, 289–92
human dignity and membership, 288–89
integration and membership, 287–88
territorial presence and membership, 285–86
domestic servitude, 159
EU law and, 53–54
ILO, 68–69
improving vulnerability status of workers:
fair food program, Immokalee (USA), 373

international student workers, 191–94
see also citizenship
subsidiarity and proportionality:
EU law, 244, 251–52, 254, 257
Sweden, 203–05, 221–22
abuse of labour market regime, 211–13
employment contracts, 213–16
fixed-term contracts, 216
permanent contracts, 216–18
legalistic approach, 205–06
regulation, 206–07
Offer of Employment, 213–16
sanctions against employers, 219–21
Seasonal Workers Directive, 219–21
social assistance, 218–19
Special Employment Contracts, 221
statistics and trends, 208–11

Temporary Work (Skilled) Visa (subclass 457) (Aus):
background, 132–37, 177–78
benefits, 134–37
criticisms of programme, 137
interests of employers, 137–39
labour law and, 139–42
Deegan Report, 140–41, 189–90
demand-driven nature, 132–34
non-compliance, 184–86
causes, 188–91
poorly regulated industries, 194–99
rationales:
meeting domestic skills shortages, 134–35
stronger labour market outcomes, 135
reform, 142
need for cohesion between labour and migration law, 145–47
regulatory design, 142–43
structural design, 143–44
Special Category Visa (subclass 444), 178
'temporary migrant worker' defined, 175–76
implications of definitions, 176–77
Temporary Skilled Migration Income Threshold, 182
working holiday programme, 178–80
territorial presence and membership, 285–86
jus soli and *jus sanguinis* compared, 285
third-country nationals:
EU and, 50–54, 245–46, 260–61
conditions of access to work, 262–65
posted workers, 104–05
seasonal workers, 56–57, 60, 99, 206, 251–52, 267–68, 272
Tier 2 (General) Visa Scheme (UK), 114, 130
background:
points-based system, 117–18
work permit system, 115–16
caps and quotas, 118–19
demand-side restrictions:
job offers as preconditions for entry, 119–20
labour market testing, 120–21
malleability of skills, 123–25
shortage occupations and sectors, 121–23
wages requirement, 125–26
supply-side restrictions:
language skills requirement, 126–27
personal attributes and grounds, 126
self-sufficiency, 127
trade in services, 13–14
background, 65–67
human rights issues, 16–17
liberalisation, 14–15
redistributive benefits, 16
regulation of processes:
CETA, 82–83
ChAFTA, 84–85
exemptions from GATS principles, 80–81
market access, 81
'most-favoured nation', 80–81

no general guarantee of national treatment, 81
positive posting, 81
TiSA, 85–87
TPP, 83–84
TTIP, 85–87
Trade in Services Agreement (TiSA), 13–14, 48, 85–87
trade law:
labour law distinguished, 12, 67
see also posted workers
trade unions:
recruitment regulation and, 329–30, 350
Mexico, 331, 334–37, 341–44
migrant participation and:
challenges, 345–47
importance of, 332–33
protection from retaliation, 347–48
transnational institutional support, 349–50
USA, 331, 337–41
Trans-Pacific Partnership (TPP), 13, 48, 83–84
Transatlantic Trade and Investment Partnership (TTIP), 13, 85–87
transnational corporate supply chains, 351–52
fair food program, 360–72
private norms:
core shortcomings, 359–60
corporate social responsibility, 356–59
public norms:
ILO standards, 354–56
national regulation, 352–54
see also fair food program, Immokalee

United Kingdom:
admission regime:
caps and quotas, 118–19
demand-side restrictions:
job offers as preconditions for entry, 119–20
labour market testing, 120–21
malleability of skills, 123–25
shortage occupations and sectors, 121–23
wages requirement, 125–26
supply-side restrictions:
language skills requirement, 126–27
personal attributes and grounds, 126
self-sufficiency, 127
domestic labour and workers, 27–28, 154, 236–37
Overseas Domestic Worker visa, 223, 229–34
vulnerability of, 238–39
European Court of Human Rights (ECtHR):
criticisms of UK's Overseas Domestic Workers regime, 230–34
employer sponsorship programmes, 113–14, 118
Certificates of Sponsorship, 118
job offers as a precondition for entry, 119–20
labour market testing, 120–21
language standards, 127
self-sufficiency, 127
Tier 2 (General) Visa Scheme (UK), 114–30
wages requirements, 125
Highly Skilled Migrants Programme, 116
Migratory Advisory Committee, 23, 117
Modern Slavery Act 2015, 223–24, 232, 234–37, 238, 240
Overseas Domestic Worker visa scheme, 223–24
criticisms by ECtHR, 230–34
ECtHR case law, 230–32
modern slavery and, 230
points-based system:
Certificates of Sponsorship, 118
goal, 117
implementation, 117–18

Overseas Domestic Workers visa scheme and, 229–30
Tier 2 (General) Visa Scheme, 117–18
seasonal agricultural workers scheme, 116
sector-based scheme (UK), 116
skills shortages, 127–28
declining training of resident workforce, 128–29
long-term shortages, 128
short-term cyclical shortages, 128
system effects and, 129
work permit system (UK):
Highly Skilled Migrants Programme and, 116
liberalisation, 115–16
Tier 2 (General) Visa Scheme, 115–16
see also Tier 2 (General) Visa Scheme (UK)
Universal Declaration of Human Rights (UDHR), 227–28, 282–83, 292

vulnerability, *see* status and vulnerability

work permit system (UK):
Highly Skilled Migrants Programme and, 116
liberalisation, 115–16
Tier 2 (General) Visa Scheme, 115–16
World Trade Organization (WTO), 12
liberalisation of world trade in services, 14
see also General Agreement on Trade in Services